DEVELOPING MATERIALS FOR LANGUAGE TEACHING

Brian Tomlinson

continuum
LONDON • NEW YORK

Continuum

The Tower Building
11 York Road
London SE1 7 NX

15 East 26th Street
New York
NY 10010

First published 2003

British Library Cataloguing-in-Publication Data
A catalogue record for this book is available from the British Library.

ISBN: 0-8264-5917-X (paperback) 0-8264-5918-8 (hardback)

Typeset by YHT Ltd., London
Printed and bound in Great Britain by Cromwell Press, Trowbridge, Wiltshire

Contents

PART E – TRAINING IN MATERIALS DEVELOPMENT

List of Contributors

Roger Barnard, Tara Art University, Tokyo
Rod Bolitho, University College of St Mark and St John
Christophe Canniveng, UNITEC, School of Languages, University of Auckland
Rosa-Maria Cives-Enriquez, Motiva Language and Training Specialists Limited
Vivian Cook, University of Essex
Bao Dat, National University of Singapore
Beverly Derewianka, Hong Kong University
Irma K. Ghosn, Lebanese American University, Byblos
David A. Hill, Freelance, Budapest
Carlos Islam, University of Maine
Patrick Lyons, Bilkent University, Ankara
Alan Maley, Assumption University, Bangkok
Chris Mares, University of Maine
Mertxe Martinez, University of Auckland
Hitomi Masuhara, Leeds Metropolitan University
Claudia Ferradas Moi, T. S. Eliot Institute, Buenos Aires
Paul Nation, Victoria University of Wellington
Ruxandra Popovici, British Council, Bucharest
Alan Pulverness, NILE (Norwich Institute of Language Education)
Rani Rubdy, Assumption University, Bangkok
Claudia Saraceni, University of Luton
Duriya Aziz Singapore Wala, Times/Media Publishers, Singapore
Jeff Stranks, Cultura Inglese, Rio de Janeiro
Brian Tomlinson, Leeds Metropolitan University
Dorothy Zemach, University of Oregon

Preface

Brian Tomlinson

This book has developed from a realization that the recent explosion in interest in materials development for language teaching, both as 'a field of study and as a practical undertaking' (Tomlinson, 2001), has not yet been adequately catered for by the literature on materials development. A number of books have dealt with important aspects of materials development and have raised issues of great significance to the developers and users of language learning materials (for example, Sheldon, 1987; McDonough and Shaw, 1993; Byrd, 1995; Hidalgo *et al.*, 1995; Cunningsworth, 1996; Tomlinson, 1998; Richards, 2001). But no book has provided a comprehensive coverage of the main aspects and issues in materials development for language learning. And no book has attempted to view current developments in materials development through the eyes of developers and users of materials throughout the world. This is what *Developing Materials for Language Teaching* aims to do. It has been designed and written (by native and non-native speakers of English from eleven different countries) so that it can provide both an overview of what is happening in the world of materials development for language teaching and a stimulus for development and innovation in the field. It includes reference to the teaching of languages other than English (for example, Italian, Spanish, Japanese) and offers both objective and critical overviews of current issues in the field and proposals for principled developments for the future. It has been written so that it can be used as a coursebook on teachers' courses and on postgraduate courses in applied linguistics, and also to provide stimulus and refreshment for teachers, publishers and applied linguists in the field.

Ultimately, 'It is the language teacher who must validate or refute specific proposals' for applying linguistic and psycholinguistic theory to language teaching (Chomsky, 1996: 46) and it is the language teacher who must validate or refute the materials which are developed for the language classroom. Widdowson (2000: 31) offers the 'applied linguist' as a 'mediating agent' who must make 'insights intelligible in ways in which their usefulness can be demonstrated'. In this book we offer the informed and reflective practitioner as the ideal agent for mediating between theory and practice. Some of the contributors to this book might be labelled teachers, some materials developers, some applied linguists, some teacher trainers and some publishers. But all of them share four things in common. They have all had experience as teachers of a second or foreign language (L2), they have all contributed to the development of L2 materials, they have all kept in touch with developments in linguistic, sociolinguistic and psycholinguistic theory and they all have respect for the teacher as the person with the power to decide what actually happens in the language classroom.

This book is dedicated to classroom teachers and teachers in training. It aims to help them to make decisions about materials for themselves and to help them and others to contribute to the development of materials which can facilitate the acquisition of an L2. It does so by applying insights gained from applied linguistics, from materials development and from classroom practice.

This volume is being used as the core textbook for the Distance Version of the MA in Materials Development for Language Teaching in the Centre for Language Study at Leeds Metropolitan University. For information about this course, please contact Brian Tomlinson at B.Tomlinson@lmu.ac.uk

References

Byrd, P. (1995) *Material Writer's Guide.* New York: Heinle and Heinle.

Chomsky, N. (1996) *Powers and Prospects: Reflections on Human Nature and the Social Order.* London: Pluto.

Cunningsworth, A. (1995) *Choosing Your Coursebook.* Oxford: Heinemann.

Hidalgo, A. C., Hall, D. and Jacobs, G. M. (eds) (1995) *Getting Started: Materials Writers on Materials Writing.* Singapore: RELC.

McDonough, J. and Shaw, C. (1993) *Materials and Methods in ELT: A Teacher's Guide.* London: Blackwell.

Richards, J. (2001) *Curriculum Development in Language Education.* Cambridge: Cambridge University Press.

Sheldon, L. E. (ed.) (1987) *ELT Textbooks and Materials: Problems in Evaluation and Development.* ELT Documents 126. London: Modern English Publications/The British Council.

Tomlinson, B. (ed.) (1998) *Materials Development in Language Teaching.* Cambridge: Cambridge University Press.

Tomlinson, B. (2001) 'Materials development', in R. Carter and D. Nunan (eds) *The Cambridge Guide to Teaching English to Speakers of Other Languages.* Cambridge: Cambridge University Press, pp. 66–71.

Widdowson, H. G. (2000) 'On the limitations of linguistics applied'. *Applied Linguistics,* **21** (1), 3–25.

Introduction: Are Materials Developing?

Brian Tomlinson

What is Materials Development?

Materials development is both a field of study and a practical undertaking. As a field it studies the principles and procedures of the design, implementation and evaluation of language teaching materials. As an undertaking it involves the production, evaluation and adaptation of language teaching materials, by teachers for their own classrooms and by materials writers for sale or distribution. Ideally these two aspects of materials development are interactive in that the theoretical studies inform and are informed by the development and use of classroom materials. (Tomlinson, 2001: 66)

This book deals with both the aspects of materials development outlined above. For example, Chapter 6 (Tomlinson) and Chapter 23 (Nation) deal with the principles and procedures of aspects of the development of materials and Chapter 1 (Tomlinson) and Chapter 2 (Rubdy) deal with the principles and procedures of the evaluation of materials. On the other hand, for example, Chapters 7 (Mares), 8 (Singapore Wala) and 30 (Lyons) focus on the actual writing of materials.

There is also a third aspect of materials development which is dealt with in this book, that is the use of materials development as a means of facilitating and deepening the personal and professional development of teachers (e.g., Chapters 27 (Tomlinson), 29 (Canniveng and Martinez) and 31 (Popovici and Bolitho)). There is a growing inclusion of materials development on courses for teachers: for example Leeds Metropolitan University runs an MA in Materials Development for Language Teaching, and MA TESOL/Applied Linguistics courses throughout the world now include modules on materials development. This is mainly because of the realization that, 'Every teacher is a materials developer' (English Language Centre, 1997) who needs to be able to evaluate, adapt and produce materials so as to ensure a match between the learners and the materials they use. It is also because of the realization that one of the most effective ways of 'helping teachers to understand and apply theories of language learning – and to achieve personal and professional development – is to provide monitored experience of the process of developing materials' (Tomlinson, 2001: 67). This concrete experience of developing materials as a basis for reflective observation and conceptualization enables teachers to theorize their practice (Schon, 1987).

Although a number of chapters in this book focus primarily on one of the three aspects of materials development described above, many of them deal with two or even three of these aspects. For example, Chapter 19 (Stranks) looks at both the theories and the practicalities of developing grammar teaching materials, Chapter 20 (Masuhara) looks at the application of reading research and theory to the development of coursebook materials for teaching reading, and Chapter 28 (Tomlinson and Masuhara) considers the theoretical principles of using simulations for learning, outlines procedures for developing and using simulations and reflects on actual examples of simulations used on materials development courses for teachers. In addition, a number of chapters (for example Chapter 25 (Bolitho) and Chapter 26 (Pulverness)) focus on issues related to the content of materials, as well as concerning themselves with the application of theory to practice.

What are Materials?

In this book 'materials' 'include anything which can be used to facilitate the learning of a language. They can be linguistic, visual, auditory or kinaesthetic, and they can be presented in print, through live performance or display, or on cassette, CD-ROM, DVD or the internet' (Tomlinson, 2001: 66). They can be instructional, experiential, elicitative or exploratory, in that they can inform learners about the language, they can provide experience of the language in use, they can stimulate language use or they can help learners to make discoveries about the language for themselves. See also Richards (2001: 251) for a definition of materials.

Most language learning materials are in print and most of the chapters in this book focus on print materials. However, Chapter 10 (Hill), for example, focuses on visuals, Chapter 21 (Hill and Tomlinson) and Chapter 24 (Ferradas Moi) focus on auditory materials, Chapter 12 (Derewianka) and Chapter 13 (Ferradas Moi) focus on the computer and the Internet, Chapter 14 (Cives-Enriquez) focuses on live materials and Chapter 20 (Masuhara) focuses on a multi-dimensional approach. Most materials are instructional ('instructional materials generally serve as the basis for much of the language input learners receive and the language practice that occurs in the classroom' (Richards, 2001: 251)) and many of the chapters in this book focus on materials for instruction. However, many other chapters advocate more attention being paid to experiential materials (e.g., Chapters 4 (Saraceni), 15 (Islam) and 21 (Hill and Tomlinson)) and to elicitative materials (e.g., Chapters 16 (Cook) and 25 (Bolitho) focus on materials stimulating learner discovery).

What are the Issues in Materials Development?

What should Drive the Materials?

The obvious answer to this question is that the needs and wants of the learners should drive the materials. But teachers have needs and wants to be satisfied too (Masuhara, 1998) and so do administrators, with their concerns for standardization and conformity with, for example, a syllabus, a theory of language learning, the requirements of examinations and the language policies of a government (see Chapter 3 (Singapore Wala) and Chapter 30 (Lyons) in this volume for discussions of the multiple requirements of a national and of institutional textbooks). These needs and wants are not irreconcilable and, in my experience, they can best be satisfied by localized projects which consult learners, teachers and administrators before, during and after the materials writing process. This is what happened in the process of developing the most satisfactory textbook I have ever been involved in, *On Target*, a coursebook for secondary school students in Namibia. Prior to the writing of the book, students and teachers were consulted all over Namibia about what they wanted and needed from the book. During the writing of the book, Ministry of Education officials were present throughout each day in which 30 teachers wrote the materials, and the syllabus, the curriculum and the examination documents were frequently referred to. After the writing of the book, it was trialled extensively and revised in relation to the feedback which was provided by students, teachers and officials. A similar approach is currently being followed by Bilkent University in Turkey in the production of new textbooks for their English courses. See Tomlinson, 1995, 2001, for descriptions of these projects and Chapter 31 (Popovici and Bolitho) in this book for descriptions of similar projects.

Both the projects described above decided to adopt a text-driven approach rather than a syllabus-driven, grammar-driven, functions-driven, skills-driven, topic-driven or theme-driven approach. That is, they decided to start by finding written and spoken texts with a potential for affective and cognitive engagement, and then to use a flexible framework to develop activities connected to these texts. Later on they would cross-check with the syllabus and the examination requirements to ensure satisfactory coverage. For a description and justification of such an approach, see Chapter 6 (Tomlinson) in this book.

The situation is complicated in the case of materials produced by publishers for commercial distribution. 'The author is generally concerned to produce a text that teachers will find innovative, creative, relevant to their learners' needs, and that they will enjoy teaching from ... The publisher is primarily motivated by financial success.' (Richards, 2001: 257). Publishers obviously aim to produce excellent books which will satisfy the wants and needs of their users but their need to maximize profits makes them cautious and conservative and any compromise with the authors tends still to be biased towards perceived market needs rather than towards the actual needs and wants of the learners. For discussions of the compromises necessitated by the commercial production of materials (and especially of global coursebooks) see Ariew (1982), Bell and Gower (1998) and

Richards (2001), as well as Chapters 7 (Mares), 8 (Singapore Wala), 15 (Islam) and 19 (Stranks) in this volume.

Who should Develop the Materials?

These days most commercial materials are written by professional materials writers writing to a brief determined by the publishers from an analysis of market needs. These writers are usually very experienced and competent, they are familiar with the realities of publishing and the potential of the new technologies and they write full-time for a living. The books they write are usually systematic, well designed, teacher-friendly and thorough. But they often lack energy and imagination (how can the writers be imaginative all day and every day?) and are sometimes insufficiently relevant and appealing to the actual learners who use them (see Tomlinson *et al.*, 2001).

Dudley Evans and St John (1998: 173) state that 'only a small proportion of good teachers are also good designers of course materials'. This observation is contrary to my experience, as I have found that teachers throughout the world only need a little training, experience and support to become materials writers who can produce imaginative materials of relevance and appeal to their learners. This has certainly been the case with teachers on materials development courses I have run in Brazil, Botswana, Indonesia, Japan, Malaysia, Mauritius, the Seychelles, Vanuatu and Vietnam, and on textbook projects I have been a consultant for in Bulgaria, China, Turkey and Namibia (Tomlinson, 2001).

This issue is addressed in a number of chapters in this book, for example Chapters 6 and 27 (Tomlinson), Chapter 30 (Lyons) and Chapter 31 (Popovici and Bolitho).

How should Materials be Developed?

Typically, commercial materials are written over a long period of time by a pair or small group of writers (e.g., in the year 2000 *Inside Out* (Kay and Jones), *Landmark* (Haines and Stewart), *Wavelength* (Burke and Brooks) and *Clockwise* (McGowen, Richardson, Forsyth and Naunton) were published). The materials usually take a long time to produce because these days most of the materials produced are courses (supplementary books are generally not considered profitable enough), since most courses have multiple components (for example Greenall (1995) has seven components per level) and because the important review and trialling process takes time. The result very often is a drop in creative energy as the process drags on and the eventual publication of competent but rather uninspiring materials.

My own preference is for a large team approach to writing materials, which aims at fast first draft production by many people followed by refinement by a smaller group of experts. This is the procedure that the Namibian and Bilkent projects referred to above decided to follow. In the writing of the Namibian coursebook, *On Target* (1996), 30 teachers were selected to provide a team of varying age, experience and expertise and were then brought from all over the country to Windhoek. On the first day, I demonstrated some innovative approaches to extend the teachers' repertoires of activity types and to stimulate thought and discussion about the principles of language learning. On the second day, we worked out a flexible framework to use in producing the materials and made some decisions together about the use of illustrations, music, cassettes, etc. Then, for four days the teachers wrote and monitored materials in small teams while a small group of facilitators supported them and cross-checked with the syllabus. That way we managed to complete the first draft of the whole book in one week, and then this was trialled, revised, edited and published within the year. In Bilkent University we followed a similar procedure and 20 teachers in small teams produced and monitored 60 units within a week for a group of four 'writers' to select from, revise and trial.

In both cases described above, the teachers managed to inspire each other with ideas, to maintain creative energy, to relate their materials to the actual learners who were going to use them and to suggest useful improvements to each other's materials. All this was achieved to a far greater degree than I have ever managed when writing a coursebook by myself, with a partner or in a small team working at a distance from each other. And all this was achieved because a large group of enthusiastic teachers were working together for a short time.

How should Materials be Evaluated?

Materials are often evaluated in an ad hoc, impressionistic way, which tends to favour materials which have face validity (i.e., which conform to people's expectations of what materials should look like) and which are visually appealing. In order to ensure that materials are devised, revised, selected and adapted in reliable and valid ways, we need to ensure that materials evaluation establishes procedures which are thorough, rigorous, systematic and principled. This often takes time and effort but it could prevent many of the mistakes which are made by writers, publishers, teachers, institutions and ministries and which can have negative effects on learners' potential to benefit from their courses. For ways of achieving this, see Chapters 1 (Tomlinson), 2 (Rubdy), 4 (Saraceni) and 5 (Islam and Mares) in this volume.

Should Texts be Authentic?

Materials aiming at explicit learning usually contrive examples of the language which focus on the feature being taught. Usually these examples are presented in short, easy, specially written or simplified texts or dialogues, and it is argued that they help the learners by focusing their attention on the target feature. The counter-argument is that such texts overprotect learners, deprive them of the opportunities for acquisition provided by rich texts and do not prepare them for the reality of language use, whereas authentic texts (i.e., texts not written especially for language teaching) can provide exposure to language as it is typically used. A similar debate continues in relation to materials for the teaching of reading and listening skills and materials for extensive reading and listening. One side argues that simplification and contrivance can facilitate learning; the other side argues that they can lead to faulty learning and that they deny the learners opportunities for informal learning and the development of self-esteem.

> Most researchers argue for authenticity and stress its motivating effect on learners (e.g., Bacon and Finneman, 1990; Kuo, 1993; Little *et al.*, 1994). However, Widdowson (1984: 218) says that 'pedagogic presentation of language ... necessarily involves methodological contrivance which isolates features from their natural surroundings'; Day and Bamford (1998: 54–62) attack the 'cult of authenticity' and advocate simplified reading texts which have the 'natural properties of authenticity' and R. Ellis (1999: 68) argues for 'enriched input' which provides learners with input which has been flooded with exemplars of the target structure in the context of meaning focused activities. See also Widdowson (2000). (Tomlinson, 2001: 68)

My own view is that meaningful engagement with authentic texts is a pre-requisite for the development of communicative and strategic competence but that authentic texts can be created by interactive negotiation between learners as well as presented to them (see Breen and Littlejohn, 2000, as well as Chapters 4 (Saraceni), 6 (Tomlinson) and 14 (Cives-Enriquez) in this volume). I also believe, though, that for particularly problematic features of language use it is sometimes useful to focus learners on characteristics of these features through specially contrived examples (providing that the examples are based on observation of typical authentic use). For further discussion of the issue of authenticity see, for example, Chapters 4 (Saraceni), 18 (Barnard and Zemach), 19 (Stranks) and 20 (Masuhara) in this volume.

Other Issues
Other issues which have received attention in the literature and which feature in this book include:

- Do learners need a coursebook? (See Hutchinson and Torres, 1994; Tomlinson, 2001; and Chapters 4 (Saraceni) and 14 (Cives-Enriquez) in this volume.)
- Should materials be learning or acquisition focused? (See Tomlinson, 1998c; Tomlinson, 2001; and Chapters 6 (Tomlinson), 20 (Masuhara), 22 (Dat) and 23 (Nation) in this volume.)
- Should materials be censored? (See Tomlinson, 2001; Wajnryb, 1996; and Chapter 4 (Saraceni) in this book.)
- Should materials be driven by theory or practice? (See Bell and Gower, 1998; Prowse, 1998; and Chapters 6 (Tomlinson) and 11 (Maley) in this volume.)
- Should materials be driven by syllabus needs, learner needs or market needs? (See Masuhara, 1998; and Chapters 6 (Tomlinson), 8 (Singapore Wala), 18 (Barnard and Zemach) and 31 (Popovici and Bolitho) in this volume.)
- Should materials cater for learner expectations or try to change them? (See Chapters 9 (Tomlinson), 14 (Cives-Enriquez), 16 (Cook) and 31 (Popovici and Bolitho) in this volume.)

- Should materials aim for language development only or should they also aim for personal and educational development? (See Chapters 4 (Saraceni), 9 (Tomlinson) and 31 (Popovici and Bolitho) in this volume.)
- Should materials aim to contribute to teacher development as well as language learning? (See Tomlinson, 1995; and Chapters 1 (Tomlinson), 29 (Canniveng and Martinez), 30 (Lyons) and 31 (Popovici and Bolitho) in this volume.)

What are the Current Trends in Materials Development?

It is arguable that there is nothing much new going on in materials development and that in the area of commercially produced materials there is even a sort of principled going back. This is justified by publishers by reference to their confidential research into what learners and teachers want (e.g., the return to the centrality of grammar highlighted in Tomlinson *et al.*, 2001: 84). But in my view it is almost certainly driven by economic constraints and the ever-increasing cost of producing the sort of multicoloured, multicomponent coursebook which seems to attract the biggest sales these days. As a result, publishers dare not risk losing vast sums of money on a radically different type of textbook, they opt for safe, middle-of-the-road, global coursebooks which clone the features of such best-selling coursebooks as *Headway* and they cut down on non-profit-making supplementary materials. Unfortunately this then has a washback effect on non-commercial materials, as teachers and curriculum developers tend to imitate the approaches of best-selling coursebooks on the assumption that this must be what learners and teachers want (though the reality is more likely that the models are the books which have been promoted most expensively and successfully by their publishers).

There is some hope of progress, though, and in my list of current trends below I have noted a number of positive ones:

Positive Trends
- There are more materials requiring investment by the learners in order for them to make discoveries for themselves from analysis of samples of language in use (e.g., Bolitho and Tomlinson, 1995; Joseph and Travers, 1996; Carter and McCarthy, 1997; Haines and Stewart, 2000).
- There are more materials making use of corpus data reflecting actual language use (e.g., Carter and McCarthy, 1997; Fox, 1998; Willis, 1998).
- There are more interactive learning packages which make use of different media to provide a richer experience of language learning and to offer the learner choice of approach and route (Parish, 1995).
- There are more extensive reader series being produced with fewer linguistic constraints and more provocative content (e.g., Prowse, 1999; Tomlinson and Maley (in progress)).
- There is an increase in attempts to personalize the learning process by getting learners to relate topics and texts to their own lives, views and feelings (e.g., Kay and Jones, 2000).
- There is an increase in attempts to gain the affective engagement of learners

(Tomlinson, 1998a) by involving them in texts and tasks which encourage the expression of feelings (e.g., Burke and Brooks, 2000).

- There is an increasing use of the Internet as a source of current, relevant and appealing texts (Tomlinson, 2001: 71; Chapters 6 (Tomlinson), 12 (Derewianka) and 18 (Barnard and Zemach) in this volume).
- There is some evidence of a movement away from spoken practice of written grammar and towards experience of spoken grammar in use (e.g., Carter and McCarthy, 1997).
- There is an increase in the number of ministries (e.g., in Bulgaria, Iran, Morocco, Namibia, Romania and Russia) and institutions (e.g., Bilgi University in Istanbul; Bilkent University in Ankara) which have decided to produce their own locally relevant materials (see Tomlinson, 1995, 2001; and Chapter 31 (Popovici and Bolitho) in this book).

Negative Trends
- There is a return to the 'central place of grammar in the language curriculum' (Soars and Soars, 1996), which contradicts what my own confidential research for a British publisher revealed about the needs and wants of learners and teachers and which goes against many of the findings of Second Language Acquisition Research (Tomlinson, 1998d: 5–22; Ellis, 1999; Tomlinson *et al.*, 2001).
- There is a far greater prominence given in coursebooks to listening and speaking than to reading and writing (Tomlinson *et al.*, 2001).
- There is an assumption that most learners have short attention spans, can only cope with very short reading and writing texts and will only engage in activities for a short time.
- There is an assumption that learners do not want and would not gain from intellectually demanding activities while engaged in language learning.
- There is a neglect (or sometimes an abuse) of literature in coursebooks, despite its potential as a source of stimulating and engaging texts and despite the many claims of methodologists for the potential value and appeal of literature (e.g., Duff and Maley, 1990; Lazar, 1993; Tomlinson, 1994, 1998b; Maley, 2001; and Chapters 4 (Saraceni), 6 (Tomlinson), 9 (Tomlinson), 11 (Maley), 13 (Ferradas Moi) and 24 (Ferradas Moi) in this volume.
- There is a continuing predominance of analytical activities and a neglect of activities which could cater for learners with other preferred learning styles (Tomlinson, 1999: 10; Tomlinson *et al.*, 2001; Chapter 5 (Islam and Mares) in this volume).
- There is an 'absence of controversial issues to stimulate thought, to provide opportunities for exchanges of views, and to make topic content meaningful' (Tomlinson *et al.*, 2001) and there is a resultant trivialization of content (see, for example, Chapters 4 (Saraceni) and 20 (Masuhara) in this volume.
- There is a tendency to underestimate learners linguistically, intellectually and emotionally.

Obviously my evaluation of the trends above is subjective and is related to my principles and beliefs. Another materials developer might come to very different conclusions as a result of holding different principles and beliefs.

What is the Future of Materials Development?

The authors of the chapters in this book each give their version of what they would like to see as the future of materials development. The reality is that publishers will probably still play safe and stick to what they know they can sell; but the hope is that a decrease in customer satisfaction and an increase in local materials development projects will help some of the following to develop:

- greater personalization and localization of materials;
- greater flexibility and creativity of use;
- more respect for the learners;
- more affectively engaging content;
- a greater emphasis on multicultural perspectives and awareness;
- more opportunities for learners with experiential (and especially kinaesthetic) learning style preferences;
- more attempts made to engage the learner in the language learning process as an experienced, intelligent and interesting individual;
- more attempts made to use multidimensional approaches to language learning.

MATSDA

MATSDA (the Materials Development Association) is an association founded in 1993 by Brian Tomlinson, which is dedicated to improving the future for materials development. It runs conferences and workshops on materials development and produces a journal, *Folio*, twice a year, which provides a forum for the discussion of materials development issues and a channel for the dissemination of new ideas and materials. Recently, for example, MATSDA has held conferences at Leeds Metropolitan University on 'Materials for Cultural Awareness' and 'Alternatives in Language Teaching', has held conferences in Singapore and South Africa, has held pre-course events at the JALT Conference in Japan and the FAAPI Conference in Argentina and has held workshops on developing extensive readers (in Ilkley) and on developing materials for assessment and evaluation (in Ingleton).

Anybody who is interested in joining MATSDA should contact the secretary, Hitomi Masuhara (*H.Masuhara@lmu.ac.uk*) and anybody who would like more information about MATSDA activities should contact the president, Brian Tomlinson (*B.Tomlinson@lmu.ac.uk*).

References

Ariew, R. (1982) 'The textbook as curriculum', in T. Higgs (ed.) *Curriculum Competence and the Foreign Language Teacher*. Lincolnwood, IL: National Textbook Company, pp. 11–34.

Bacon, S. M. and Finneman, M. D. (1990) 'A study of the attitudes, motives and strategies of university foreign language students and their disposition to authentic oral and written input'. *Modern Language Journal*, **74** (4), 459–73.

Bell, J. and Gower, R. (1998) 'Writing course materials for the world: a great compromise', in B. Tomlinson (ed.) *Materials Development in Language Teaching*. Cambridge: Cambridge University Press, pp. 116–29.

Breen, M. P. and Littlejohn, A. (eds) (2000) *Classroom Decision-making: Negotiation and Process Syllabuses in Practice*. Cambridge: Cambridge University Press.

Bolitho, R. and Tomlinson, B. (1995) *Discover English* (2nd edn.). Oxford: Heinemann.

Burke, K. and Brooks, J. (2000) *Wavelength*. Harlow: Pearson Longman.

Carter, R. A. and McCarthy, M. J. (1997) *Exploring Spoken English*. Cambridge: Cambridge University Press.

Day, R. and Bamford, J. (1998) *Extensive Reading in the Second Language Classroom*. Cambridge: Cambridge University Press.

Dudley-Evans, T. and St John, M. (1998). *Developments in English for Specific Purposes*. New York: Cambridge University Press.

Duff, A. and Maley, A. (1990) *Literature*. Oxford: Oxford University Press.

Ellis, R. (1999) 'Input-based approaches to teaching grammar: a review of classroom oriented research'. *Annual Review of Applied Linguistics*, **19**, 64–80.

English Language Centre (1997) Unpublished handout from the English Language Centre, Durban, South Africa.

Fox, G. (1998) 'Using corpus data in the classroom', in B. Tomlinson (ed.) *Materials Development in Language Teaching*. Cambridge: Cambridge University Press, pp. 25–43.

Greenall, S. (1995) *Reward*. Oxford: Heinemann.

Haines, S. and Stewart, B. (2000) *Landmark*. Oxford: Oxford University Press.

Hutchinson, T. and Torres, E. (1994) 'The textbook as an agent of change'. *ELT Journal*, **48** (4), 315–28.

Joseph, F. and Travers, T. (1996) *Candidate for CAE*. London: Phoenix ELT.

Kay, S. and Jones, V. (2000) *Inside Out*. Oxford: Macmillan/Heinemann.

Kuo, C. H. (1993) 'Problematic issues in EST materials development'. *English for Specific Purposes*, **12**, 171–81.

Lazar, G. (1993) *Literature and Language Teaching: A Guide for Teachers and Trainers*. Cambridge: Cambridge University Press.

Little, B. L., Devitt, S. and Singleton, S. (1994) 'Authentic texts, pedagogical grammar and language awareness in foreign language learning', in C. James and P. Garrett (eds) *Language Awareness in the Classroom*. London: Longman, pp. 123–32.

McGowen, B., Richardson, V., Forsyth, W. and Naunton, J. (2000) *Clockwise*. Oxford: Oxford University Press.

Maley, A. (2001) 'Literature in the language classroom', in R. Carter and D. Nunan (eds) *The Cambridge Guide to Teaching English to Speakers of Other Languages*. Cambridge: Cambridge University Press, pp. 180–5.

Masuhara, H. (1998) 'What do teachers really want from coursebooks?', in B. Tomlinson (ed.) *Materials Development in Language Teaching*. Cambridge: Cambridge University Press, pp. 239–60.

On Target (1996) Windhoek: Gamsberg Macmillan.

Parish, J. (1995) 'Multi-media and language learning'. *Folio*, **2** (1), 4–6.

Prowse, P. (1998) 'How writers write: testimony from authors', in B. Tomlinson (ed.) *Materials Development in Language Teaching*. Cambridge: Cambridge University Press, pp. 130–45.

Richards, R. (2001). *Curriculum Development in Language Teaching*. Cambridge: Cambridge University Press.

Schon, D. (1987) *Educating the Reflective Practitioner*. San Francisco, CA: Jossey-Bass.

Soars, L. and Soars, J. (1996) *Headway*. Oxford: Oxford University Press.

Tomlinson, B. (1994) *Openings. Language through Literature: An Activities Book* (new edn.). London: Penguin.

Tomlinson, B. (1995) 'Work in progress: textbook projects'. *Folio*, **2**, (2), 26–31.

Tomlinson, B. (1998a) 'Affect and the coursebook'. *IATEFL Issues*, **145**, 2021.

Tomlinson, B. (1998b) 'And now for something not completely different'. *Reading in a Foreign Language*, **11** (2), 177–89.

Tomlinson, B. (1998c) 'Introduction', in B. Tomlinson (ed.) *Materials Development in Language Teaching*. Cambridge: Cambridge University Press, pp. 1–24.

Tomlinson, B. (ed.) (1998d) *Materials Development in Language Teaching*. Cambridge: Cambridge University Press.

Tomlinson, B. (1999) 'Developing criteria for materials evaluation'. *IATEFL Issues*, **147**, 10–13.

Tomlinson, B. (2001) 'Materials development', in R. Carter and D. Nunan (eds) *The Cambridge Guide to Teaching English to Speakers of Other Languages*. Cambridge: Cambridge University Press, pp. 66–71.

Tomlinson, B., Dat, B., Masuhara, H. and Rubdy, R. (2001) 'EFL courses for adults'. *ELT Journal*, **55** (1), 80–101.

Tomlinson, B. and Maley, A. (eds) (in progress) *World Wide Readers*.

Wajnryb, R. (1996) 'Death, taxes and jeopardy: systematic omissions in EFL texts, or life was never meant to be an adjacency pair'. Paper presented at the Ninth Educational Conference, Sydney.

Widdowson, H. G. (1984) *Explorations in Applied Linguistics 2*. Oxford: Oxford University Press.

Widdowson, H. G. (2000) 'On the limitations of linguistics applied'. *Applied Linguistics*, **21** (1), 3–25.

Willis, J. (1998) 'Concordances in the classroom without a computer', in B. Tomlinson (ed.) *Materials Development in Language Teaching*. Cambridge: Cambridge University Press, pp. 44–66.

Evaluation and Adaptation
of Materials

CHAPTER

1

Materials Evaluation

Brian Tomlinson

What is Materials Evaluation?

Materials evaluation is a procedure that involves measuring the value (or potential value) of a set of learning materials. It involves making judgements about the effect of the materials on the people using them and it tries to measure some or all of the following:

- the appeal of the materials to the learners;
- the credibility of the materials to learners, teachers and administrators;
- the validity of the materials (i.e., is what they teach worth teaching?);
- the reliability of the materials (i.e., would they have the same effect with different groups of target learners?);
- the ability of the materials to interest the learners and the teachers;
- the ability of the materials to motivate the learners;
- the value of the materials in terms of short-term learning (important, for example, for performance on tests and examinations);
- the value of the materials in terms of long-term learning (of both language and of communication skills);
- the learners' perceptions of the value of the materials;
- the teachers' perceptions of the value of the materials;
- the assistance given to the teachers in terms of preparation, delivery and assessment;
- the flexibility of the materials (e.g., the extent to which it is easy for a teacher to adapt the materials to suit a particular context);
- the contribution made by the materials to teacher development;
- the match with administrative requirements (e.g., standardization across classes, coverage of a syllabus, preparation for an examination).

It is obvious from a consideration of the effects above that no two evaluations can be the same, as the needs, objectives, backgrounds and preferred styles of the participants will differ from context to context. This is obviously true of an evaluation of the value of a coursebook for use with sixteen-year-olds preparing for a Ministry of Education Examination in South Africa compared to an evaluation of the same coursebook for use with teenagers and young adults being prepared for the Cambridge First Certificate at a language school in Oxford. It is also true for the evaluation of a set of materials prepared for Foundation Level learners in a university in January compared with a set of materials for the same type of learners prepared in the same university in July. The main point is that it is not the materials which are being evaluated but their effect on the people who come into contact with them (including, of course, the evaluators).

An evaluation is not the same as an analysis. It can include an analysis or follow from one, but the objectives and procedures are different. An evaluation focuses on the users of the materials and makes judgements about their effects. No matter how structured, criterion referenced and rigorous an evaluation is, it will be essentially subjective. On the other hand, an analysis focuses on the materials and it aims to provide an objective analysis of them. It 'asks questions about what the materials contain, what they aim to achieve and what they ask learners to do' (Tomlinson, 1999: 10). So, for example, 'Does it provide a transcript of the listening texts?' is an analysis question which can be answered by either 'Yes' or 'No'. 'What does it ask the learners to do immediately after reading a text?' is also an analysis question and can be answered factually. As a result of answering many such questions, a description of the materials can be made which specifies what the materials do and do not contain. On the other hand, 'Are the listening texts likely to engage the learner?' is an evaluation question and can be answered on a cline between 'Very unlikely' and 'Very likely'. It can also be given a numerical value (e.g., 2 for 'Unlikely') and after many such questions have been asked about the materials, subtotal scores and total scores can be calculated and indications can be derived of the potential value of the materials and of subsections of them. For example, a coursebook which scores a total of 75 per cent or more is likely to be generally effective but, if it scores a subtotal of only 55 per cent for listening, it is unlikely to be effective for a group of learners whose priority is to develop their listening skills.

A detailed analysis of a set of materials can be very useful for deciding, for example, if anything important has been missed out of a draft manuscript, for deciding how closely it matches the requirements of a particular course and as a database for a subsequent evaluation of the materials. Ideally analysis is objective, but analysts are often influenced by their own ideology and their questions are biased accordingly. For example, in the question 'Does it provide a lot of guided practice?', the phrase 'a lot of' implies it should do and could interfere with an objective analysis of the materials. Analysts also often have a hidden agenda when designing their instruments of analysis. For example, an analyst might ask the question 'Are the dialogues authentic?' in order to provide data to support an argument that intermediate coursebooks do not help to prepare learners for the realities of conversation. This is legitimate if the analysis questions are descriptive and the subsequent data provided is open to evaluative interpretation. For example, I conducted an analysis of ten lower-level coursebooks (Tomlinson, 1999: 10) to provide data to support my argument that such books were too restricted in their emphasis on language form, on language practice rather than use and on low-level decoding skills. My data revealed that nine out of the ten books were form and practice focused and that in these books there were five times more activities involving the use of low-level skills (e.g., pronouncing a word) than there were involving the use of high-level skills (e.g., making inferences). I was then able to use my data to argue the need for lower-level coursebooks to be more holistic and meaning focused and to be more help to the learners in their development of high-level skills. But a different analysis could have used the same instruments and the same data to argue that lower-level coursebooks were helping learners to develop from a confident base of low-level skills.

Many publications on materials evaluation mix analysis and evaluation and make it very difficult to use their suggested criteria because, for example, in a numerical evaluation most analysis questions would result in 1 or 5 on a five-point scale and would thus be weighted disproportionately when combined with evaluation questions, which tend to yield 2, 3 or 4. For example Mariani (1983: 28–9) includes in a section on 'Evaluate your coursebook' such analysis questions as, 'Are there any teacher's notes ...' and 'Are there any tape recordings?' alongside such evaluation questions as, 'Are the various stages in a teaching unit adequately developed'. And Cunningsworth (1984: 74–9) includes both analysis and evaluation questions in his 'Checklist of Evaluation Criteria'. Cunningsworth does recognize the problem of mixing these different types of questions by saying that, 'Some of the points can be checked off either in polar terms (i.e., yes or no) or, where we are talking about more or less of something, on a gradation from 1 to 5' (1984: 74). My preference for separating analysis from evaluation is shared by Littlejohn (1998) who presents a general framework for analysing materials (pp. 192–202), which he suggests could be used prior to evaluation and action in a model which is sequenced as follows:

- Analysis of the target situation of use.
- Materials analysis.
- Match and evaluation (determining the appropriacy of the materials to the target situation of use).
- Action.

Principles in Materials Evaluation

Many evaluations are impressionistic, or at best are aided by an ad hoc and very subjective list of criteria. In my view it is very important that evaluations (even the most informal ones) are driven by a set of principles and that these principles are articulated by the evaluator(s) prior to the evaluation. In this way greater validity and reliability can be achieved and fewer mistakes are likely to be made.

In developing a set of principles it is useful to consider the following:

The Evaluator's Theory of Learning and Teaching

All teachers develop theories of learning and teaching which they apply in their classrooms (even though they are often unaware of doing so). Many researchers (e.g., Schon, 1983) argue that it is useful for teachers to try to achieve an articulation of their theories by reflecting on their practice. For example Edge and Wharton (1998: 297) argue that reflective practice can not only lead to 'perceived improvements in practice but, more importantly, to deeper understandings of the area investigated'. In a similar way I am going to argue that the starting point of any evaluation should be reflection on the evaluator's practice leading to articulation of the evaluator's theories of learning and teaching. In this way evaluators can make overt their predispositions and can then both make use of them in constructing criteria for evaluation and be careful not to let them weight the evaluation too much towards their own bias. At the same time evaluators can learn a lot about themselves and about the learning and teaching process.

Here are some of my theories, which I have articulated as a result of reflection on my own and other teachers' practice:

- Language learners succeed best if learning is a positive, relaxed and enjoyable experience.
- Language teachers tend to teach most successfully if they enjoy their role and if they can gain some enjoyment themselves from the materials they are using.
- Learning materials lose credibility for learners if they suspect that the teacher does not value them.
- Each learner is different from all the others in a class in terms of his or her personality, motivation, attitude, aptitude, prior experience, interests, needs, wants and preferred learning style.
- Each learner varies from day to day in terms of motivation, attitude, mood, perceived needs and wants, enthusiasm and energy.
- There are superficial cultural differences between learners from different countries (and these differences need to be respected and catered for) but there are also strong universal determinants of successful language teaching and learning.
- Successful language learning in a classroom (especially in large classes) depends on the generation and maintenance of high levels of energy.
- The teacher is responsible for the initial generation of energy in a lesson; good materials can then maintain and even increase that energy.
- Learners only learn what they really need or want to learn.
- Learners often say that what they want is focused language practice but they often seem to gain more enjoyment and learning from activities which stimulate them to use the target language to say something they really want to say.
- Learners think, say and learn more if they are given an experience or text to respond to than if they are just asked for their views, opinions and interests.
- The most important thing that learning materials have to do is to help the learner to connect the learning experience in the classroom to their own life outside the course.
- The most important result that learning materials can achieve is to engage the emotions of learners. Laughter, joy, excitement, sorrow and anger can promote learning. Neutrality, numbness and nullity cannot.

I could go on for pages more articulating theories which I did not really know I believed in so strongly. These theories are valid for me in that they have come from seven years of classroom language learning and 36 years of teaching a language in seven different countries. They will be of considerable help when it comes to me constructing my own criteria for materials evaluation. However, what is valid for me from my own experience will not be valid for other evaluators and users of materials from their experience and I must be careful not to assume that my criteria will be the correct criteria. For example, from a quick glance at the extracts from my theories above it is obvious that I favour a holistic rather than a discrete approach to language learning, that I think flexibility and choice is very important and that I value materials which offer affective engagement to both the learner and the teacher. I must be careful not to insist that all learning materials match my requirements.

Learning Theory

Research into learning is controversial as there are so many variables involved and local circumstances often make generalization precarious. However, it is important that the materials evaluator considers the findings of learning research and decides which of its findings are convincing and applicable. The conclusions which convince me are that:

- Deep processing of intake is required if effective and durable learning is to take place (Craik and Lockhart, 1972). Such processing is semantic in that the focus of the learner is on the meaning of the intake and in particular on its relevance to the learner.
- Affective engagement is also essential for effective and durable learning. Having positive attitudes towards the learning experience and developing self-esteem while learning are important determiners of successful learning. And so is emotional involvement. Emotions must be 'considered an essential part of learning' (Williams and Burden, 1997: 28) as they 'are the very centre of human mental life ... [they] link what is important for us to the world of people, things and happenings' (Oatley and Jenkins, 1996: 122).
- Making mental connections is a crucial aspect of the learning process. In order for learning to be successful, connections need to be made between the new and the familiar, between what is being learned and the learner's life and between the learning experience and its potential value in the future.
- Experiential learning is essential (though not necessarily sufficient) and, in particular, apprehension should come to the learner before comprehension (Kolb, 1984; Tomlinson and Masuhara, 2000).
- Learners will only learn if they need and want to learn and if they are willing to invest time and energy in the process. In other words, both instrumental and integrative motivation are vital contributors to learning success (Dörnyei and Otto, 1998).
- Materials which address the learner in an informal, personal voice are more

likely to facilitate learning than those which use a distant, formal voice (Beck *et al.*, 1995; Tomlinson, 2001b). Features which seem to contribute to a successful personal voice include such aspects of orality as:

Informal discourse features (e.g. contracted forms, ellipsis, informal lexis)

The active rather than the passive voice

Concreteness (e.g., examples, anecdotes)

Inclusiveness (e.g., not signalling intellectual, linguistic or cultural superiority over the learners)

Sharing experiences and opinions

Sometimes including casual redundancies rather than always being concise. (Tomlinson, 2001b)

- Multidimensional processing of intake is essential for successful learning and involves the learner creating a mental representation of the intake through such mental processes as sensory imaging (especially visualization), affective association and the use of the inner voice (Kaufman, 1996; Masuhara, 1998a; Tomlinson, 2000b, 2000c, 2001a). As Berman (1999: 2) says, 'we learn best when we see things as part of a recognised pattern, when our imaginations are aroused, when we make natural associations between one idea and another, and when the information appeals to our senses.' One of the best ways of achieving multidimensional representation in learning seems to be a whole person approach which helps the learner to respond to the learning experience with emotions, attitudes, opinions and ideas (Jacobs and Schumann, 1992; Schumann, 1997, 1999).

As a materials evaluator I would convert the conclusions above into criteria for the assessment of learning material. For example, I would construct such criteria as:

- To what extent are the materials related to the wants of the learners?
- To what extent do the materials help the learners to achieve connections with their own lives?
- To what extent are the materials likely to stimulate emotional engagement?
- To what extent are the materials likely to promote visualization?

Second Language Acquisition Research (SLA)

SLA research is so far inconclusive and has stimulated many disagreements and debates (e.g., about the value of the explicit teaching of discrete language points). However, there is now a sufficient consensus of opinion on certain facilitating features of language learning for them to be useful in helping to articulate the principles to be used as a basis of materials evaluation. In Tomlinson (1998b: 5–22) I discussed the principles of second language acquisition which I think SLA researchers would agree are relevant to the development of materials for the teaching of languages. Some of these principles are summarized below:

- 'Materials should achieve impact' (through novelty, variety, attractive presentation and appealing content).
- 'Materials should help learners to feel at ease' (e.g., through the use of white space to prevent clutter and the use of texts and illustrations which they can relate to their own culture, through a supportive approach which is not always testing them and through the use of a personal voice).
- 'Materials should help the learners to develop confidence' (e.g., through 'pushing' learners slightly beyond their existing proficiency by involving them in tasks which are challenging but achievable).
- 'What is being taught should be perceived by learners as relevant and useful' (Krashen, 1982; Wenden, 1987; Stevick, 1976).
- 'Materials should require and facilitate learner self-investment' (e.g., through giving learners responsibility for making decisions and through encouraging them to make discoveries about the language for themselves (Rutherford and Sharwood-Smith, 1988; Tomlinson, 1994)).
- 'Learners must be ready to acquire the points being taught' (both in terms of linguistic, developmental readiness and of psychological readiness too (Meisel *et al.*, 1981; Pienemann, 1985)).
- 'Materials should expose the learners to language in authentic use' (ideally to a rich and varied input which includes unplanned, semi-planned and planned discourse and which stimulates mental response).
- 'The learners' attention should be drawn to linguistic features of the input' (so that they are alerted to subsequent instances of the same feature in future input (Schmidt, 1992; Seliger, 1979; White 1990)).
- 'Materials should provide the learners with opportunities to use the target language to achieve communicative purposes' (in order to automatize existing procedural knowledge, to check the effectiveness of their existing hypotheses (Swain, 1985) and to develop strategic competence (Canale and Swain, 1980)).
- 'Materials should take into account that the positive effects of instruction are usually delayed' (and therefore should not expect effective production immediately to follow initial presentation but should rather ensure recycling and frequent and ample exposure to the instructed features in communicative use).
- 'Materials should take into account that learners differ in learning styles' (Oxford and Anderson, 1995) (and should therefore ensure that they cater for learners who are predominantly visual, auditory, kinaesthetic, studial, experiential, analytic, global, dependent or independent).
- 'Materials should take into account that learners differ in affective attitudes' (Wenden and Rubin, 1987) (and therefore materials should offer variety and choice).
- 'Materials should maximize learning potential by encouraging intellectual, aesthetic and emotional involvement which stimulates both right and left brain

activities' (through a variety of non-trivial activities requiring a range of different types of processing).

- 'Materials should provide opportunities for outcome feedback' (i.e., feedback
  on the effectiveness of the learner in achieving communication objectives
  rather than just feedback on the accuracy of the output).

Richards (2001: 264) considers this 'list' to be 'somewhat cumbersome ... to
apply' (even though in Tomlinson, 1998b, it is not presented as a list and is not
intended as an instrument for practical application) and he suggests the following list of the 'qualities each unit in the materials should reflect':

- Gives learners something they can take away from the lesson.
- Teaches something learners feel they can use.
- Gives learners a sense of achievement.
- Practises learning items in an interesting and novel way.
- Provides a pleasurable learning experience.
- Provides opportunities for individual practice.
- Provides opportunities for personalization.
- Provides opportunities for self-assessment of learning.

At the risk of becoming even more cumbersome, I would now add the following
to my list:

- Materials should help the learner to develop cultural awareness and sensitivity
  (Byram and Fleming, 1998; Tomlinson, 2000b).
- Materials should reflect the reality of language use.
- Materials should help learners to learn in ways similar to the circumstances in
  which they will have to use the language.
- Materials should help to create readiness to learn (e.g., by helping learners to
  draw their attention to the gap between their use of a feature of communication and the use of that feature by proficient users of the language, or by
  involving the learners in a task in which they need to learn something new in
  order to be successful).
- Materials should achieve affective engagement (Tomlinson, 1998a).

The important thing is for materials evaluators to decide for themselves which
findings of SLA research they will use to develop principles for their evaluation.
Ultimately what matters is that an evaluation is principled, that the evaluator's
principles are made overt and that they are referred to when determining and
carrying out the procedures of the evaluation. Otherwise the evaluation is likely to
be ad hoc and mistakes will be made. A textbook selected mainly because of its
attractive appearance could turn out to be very boring for the learners to use; a
review which overemphasizes an irritating aspect of the materials (e.g., a particular character in a video course) can give a distorted impression of the value of the
materials; a course selected for national use by a ministry of education because it

is the cheapest or because it is written by famous writers and published by a prestigious publisher could turn out to be a very expensive disaster.

Types of Materials Evaluation

There are many different types of materials evaluation. It is possible to apply the basic principles of materials evaluation to all types of evaluation but it is not possible to make generalizations about procedures which apply to all types. Evaluations differ, for example, in purpose, in personnel, in formality and in timing. You might do an evaluation in order to help a publisher to make decisions about publication, to help yourself in developing materials for publication, to select a textbook, to write a review for a journal or as part of a research project. As an evaluator you might be a learner, a teacher, an editor, a researcher, a Director of Studies or an Inspector of English. You might be doing a mental evaluation in a bookshop, filling in a short questionnaire in class or doing a rigorous, empirical analysis of data elicited from a large sample of users of the materials. You might be doing your evaluation before the materials are used, while they are being used or after they have been used. In order to conduct an effective evaluation you need to apply your principles of evaluation to the contextual circumstances of your evaluation in order to determine the most reliable and effective procedures.

Pre-use Evaluation

Pre-use evaluation involves making predictions about the potential value of materials for their users. It can be context-free, as in a review of materials for a journal, context-influenced as in a review of draft materials for a publisher with target users in mind or context-dependent, as when a teacher selects a coursebook for use with her particular class. Often pre-use evaluation is impressionistic and consists of a teacher flicking through a book to gain a quick impression of its potential value (publishers are well aware of this procedure and sometimes place attractive illustrations in the top right-hand corner of the right-hand page in order to influence the flicker in a positive way). Even a review for a publisher or journal, and an evaluation for a ministry of education is often 'fundamentally a subjective, rule of thumb activity' (Sheldon, 1988: 245) and often mistakes are made. Making an evaluation criterion-referenced can reduce (but not remove) subjectivity and can certainly help to make an evaluation more principled, rigorous, systematic and reliable. This is especially true if more than two evaluators conduct the evaluation independently and then average their conclusions. For example, in the review of eight adult EFL courses conducted by Tomlinson *et al.* (2001), the four evaluators devised 133 criteria together and then used them independently and in isolation to evaluate the eight courses before pooling their data and averaging their scores. Even then, though, the reviewers admitted that, 'the same review, conducted by a different team of reviewers, would almost certainly have produced a different set of results' (p. 82).

Whilst-use Evaluation

This involves measuring the value of materials whilst using them or whilst observing them being used. It can be more objective and reliable than pre-use evaluation as it makes use of measurement rather than prediction. However, it is limited to measuring what is observable (e.g., 'Are the instructions clear to the learners?') and cannot claim to measure what is happening in the learners' brains. It can measure short-term memory through observing learner performance on exercises but it cannot measure durable and effective learning because of the delayed effect of instruction. It is therefore very useful but dangerous too, as teachers and observers can be misled by whether the activities seem to work or not.

Exactly what can be measured in a whilst-use evaluation is controversial but I would include the following:

- Clarity of instructions
- Clarity of layout
- Comprehensibility of texts
- Credibility of tasks
- Achievability of tasks
- Achievement of performance objectives
- Potential for localization
- Practicality of the materials
- Teachability of the materials
- Flexibility of the materials
- Appeal of the materials
- Motivating power of the materials
- Impact of the materials
- Effectiveness in facilitating short-term learning

Most of the above can be estimated during an open-ended, impressionistic observation of materials in use but greater reliability can be achieved by focusing on one criterion at a time and by using pre-prepared instruments of measurement. For example, oral participation in an activity can be measured by recording the incidence and duration of each student's oral contribution, potential for localization can be estimated by noting the times the teacher or a student refers to the location of learning while using the materials and even motivation can be estimated by noting such features as student eye focus, proximity to the materials, time on task and facial animation.

Whilst-use evaluation receives very little attention in the literature, but Jolly and Bolitho (1998) describe interesting case studies of how student comment and feedback during lessons provided useful evaluation of materials, which led to improvements being made in the materials during and after the lessons.

Post-use Evaluation

Post-use evaluation is probably the most valuable (but least administered) type of evaluation as it can measure the actual effects of the materials on the users. It can measure the short-term effect as regards motivation, impact, achievability, instant learning, etc., and it can measure the long-term effect as regards durable learning and application. It can answer such important questions as:

- What do the learners know which they did not know before starting to use the materials?
- What do the learners still not know despite using the materials?
- What can the learners do which they could not do before starting to use the materials?
- What can the learners still not do despite using the materials?
- To what extent have the materials prepared the learners for their examinations?
- To what extent have the materials prepared the learners for their post-course use of the target language?
- What effect have the materials had on the confidence of the learners?
- What effect have the materials had on the motivation of the learners?
- To what extent have the materials helped the learners to become independent learners?
- Did the teachers find the materials easy to use?
- Did the materials help the teachers to cover the syllabus?
- Did the administrators find the materials helped them to standardize the teaching in their institution?

In other words, it can measure the actual outcomes of the use of the materials and thus provide the data on which reliable decisions about the use, adaptation or replacement of the materials can be made.

Ways of measuring the post-use effects of materials include:

- tests of what has been 'taught' by the materials;
- tests of what the students can do;
- examinations;
- interviews;
- questionnaires;
- criterion-referenced evaluations by the users;
- post-course diaries;
- post-course 'shadowing' of the learners;
- post-course reports on the learners by employers, subject tutors, etc.

The main problem, of course, is that it takes time and expertise to measure post-use effects reliably (especially as, to be really revealing, there should be measurement of pre-use attitudes and abilities in order to provide data for post-use comparison). But publishers and ministries do have the time and can engage the expertise, and teachers can be helped to design, administer and analyse post-use instruments of measurement. Then we will have much more useful information, not only about the effects of particular courses of materials but about the relative effectiveness of different types of materials. Even then, though, we will need to be cautious, as it will be very difficult to separate such variables as teacher effectiveness, parental support, language exposure outside the classroom, intrinsic motivation, etc.

For a description of the process of post-use evaluation of piloted materials see Donovan (1998), and for suggestions of how teachers could do post-use micro-evaluations of materials, see Ellis (1998).

Standard Approaches to Materials Evaluation

My experience of materials evaluation in many countries has been rather worrying. I have sat on National Curriculum committees which have decided which books should be used in schools purely on the basis of the collective impressions of their members. I have written reviews of manuscripts for publishers without any criteria being specified or asked for. I have had my own books considered by Ministry of Education officials for adoption without any reference to a coherent set of criteria. I have read countless published reviews (and even written a few myself) which consist of the reviewers' ad hoc responses to the materials as they read them. I have conducted major materials evaluations for publishers and software companies without being given or asked for any criteria. I wonder how many mistakes I have contributed to. On the other hand, I was encouraged by a major British publisher to develop a comprehensive set of principled criteria prior to conducting an evaluation for them and I recently led a team of evaluators in developing a set of 133 criteria prior to evaluating eight adult EFL courses for *ELT Journal* (Tomlinson *et al.*, 2001).

Most of the literature on materials development has so far focused on materials evaluation, and useful advice on conducting evaluations can be found in Brown, 1997; Byrd, 1995; Candlin and Breen, 1980; Cunningsworth, 1984, 1995; Donovan, 1998; Daoud and Celce-Murcia, 1979; Ellis, 1995, 1998; Grant, 1987; Hidalgo *et al.*, 1995; Jolly and Bolitho, 1998; Littlejohn, 1998; McDonough, 1998; McDonough and Shaw, 1993; Mariani, 1983; Richards, 2001; Roxburgh, 1997; Sheldon, 1987, 1988; Skierso, 1991; Tomlinson, 1999; Tomlinson *et al.*, 2001; and Williams, 1983. Many of the checklists and lists of criteria suggested in these publications provide a useful starting point for anybody conducting an evaluation but some of them are impressionistic and biased (e.g., Brown (1997) awards points for the inclusion of tests in a coursebook and Daoud and Celce-Murcia (1979: 305) include such dogmatic criteria as, 'Are the vocabulary items controlled to ensure systematic gradation from simple to complex items?'). Some of the lists lack coverage, systematicity and/or a principled base, and some give the impression that they could be used in any materials evaluation ('there can be no one model framework for the evaluation of materials; the framework used must be determined by the reasons, objectives and circumstances of the evaluation' (Tomlinson, 1999: 11)). Most of the lists in the publications above are to some extent subjective as they are lists for pre-use evaluation and this involves selection and prediction. For example, Tomlinson *et al.* (2001: 81) say, 'We have been very thorough and systematic in our evaluation procedures, and have attempted to be as fair, rigorous, and objective as possible. However, we must start this report on our evaluation by acknowledging that, to some extent, our results are still inevitably subjective. This is because any pre-use evaluation is subjective, both in its selection of criteria and in the judgements made by the evaluators.'

A useful exercise for anybody writing or evaluating language teaching materials would be to evaluate the checklists and criteria lists from a sample of the publications above against the following criteria:

- Is the list based on a coherent set of principles of language learning?
- Are all the criteria actually evaluation criteria?
- Are the criteria sufficient to help the evaluator to reach useful conclusions?
- Are the criteria organized systematically (for example, into categories and subcategories which facilitate discrete as well as global verdicts and decisions)?
- Are the criteria sufficiently neutral to allow evaluators with different ideologies to make use of them?
- Is the list sufficiently flexible to allow it be made use of by different evaluators in different circumstances?

More useful to a materials evaluator than models of criteria lists (which might not fit the contextual factors of a particular evaluation) would be a suggested procedure for developing criteria to match the specific circumstances of a particular evaluation. I would like to conclude this chapter by suggesting such a procedure below.

Developing Criteria for Materials Evaluation

My experience, both personally and of students and teachers, is that it is extremely useful to develop a set of formal criteria for use on a particular evaluation and then to use that set as a basis for developing subsequent context-specific sets. Initially this is demanding and time-consuming, but it not only helps the evaluators to clarify their principles of language learning and teaching but it also ensures that future evaluations (both formal and informal) are systematic, rigorous and, above all, principled.

One way of developing a set of criteria is as follows:

Brainstorm a List of Universal Criteria

Universal criteria are those which would apply to any language learning materials anywhere for any learners. So, for example, they would apply equally to a video course for ten-year-olds in Argentina and an English for academic purposes textbook for undergraduates in Thailand. They derive from principles of language learning and provide the fundamental basis for any materials evaluation. Brainstorming a random list of such criteria (ideally with other colleagues) is a very useful way of beginning an evaluation, and the most useful way I have found of doing it is to phrase the criteria as specific questions rather than to list them as general headings.

Examples of universal criteria would be:

Do the materials provide useful opportunities for the learners to think for themselves?
Are the instructions clear?
Do the materials cater for different preferred learning styles?
Are the materials likely to achieve affective engagement?

Subdivide Some of the Criteria

If the evaluation is going to be used as a basis for revision or adaptation of the materials, or if it is going to be a formal evaluation and is going to inform important decisions, it is useful to subdivide some of the criteria into more specific questions.

For example:

Are the instructions:
   succinct?
   sufficient?
   self-standing?
   standardized?
   separated?
   sequenced?
   staged?

Such a subdivision can help to pinpoint specific aspects of the materials which could gain from revision or adaptation.

Monitor and Revise the List of Universal Criteria

Monitor the list and rewrite it according to the following criteria:

Is Each Question an Evaluation Question?
If a question is an analysis question (e.g., 'Does each unit include a test?') then you can only give the answer a 1 or a 5 on the five-point scale which is recommended later in this suggested procedure. However, if it is an evaluation question (e.g., 'To what extent do the tests provide useful learning experiences?') then it can be graded at any point on the scale.

Does Each Question Only Ask One Question?
Many criteria in published lists ask two or more questions and therefore cannot be used in any numerical grading of the materials. For example, Grant (1987) includes the following question which could be answered 'Yes; No' or 'No; Yes': '1 Is it attractive? Given the average age of your students, would they enjoy using it?' (p. 122). This question could be usefully rewritten as:

1. Is the book likely to be attractive to your students?
2. Is it suitable for the age of your students?
3. Are your students likely to enjoy using it?

Other examples of multiple questions are:
Do illustrations create a favourable atmosphere for practice in reading and spelling by depicting realism and action? (Daoud and Celce-Murcia, 1979: 304) Does the book provide attractive, interesting (and perhaps exciting) language work, as well as a steady and systematic development of the language system? (Mariani, 1983: 29)

Is Each Question Answerable?
This might seem an obvious question but in many published lists of criteria some questions are so large and so vague that they cannot usefully be answered. Or sometimes they cannot be answered without reference to other criteria, or they require expert knowledge of the evaluator.
For example:

Is it culturally acceptable? (Grant, 1987: 122)
Does it achieve an acceptable balance between knowledge about the language, and practice in using the language? (Grant, 1987: 122)
Does the writer use current everyday language, and sentence structures that follow normal word order? (Daoud and Celce-Murcia, 1979: 304)

Is Each Question Free of Dogma?
The questions should reflect the evaluators' principles of language learning but should not impose a rigid methodology as a requirement of the materials. If they do, the materials could be dismissed without a proper appreciation of their potential value.
For example, the following examples make assumptions about the pedagogical procedures of coursebooks which not all coursebooks actually follow:

Are the various stages in a teaching unit (what you would probably call presentation, practice and production) adequately developed? (Mariani, 1983: 29)
Do the sentences gradually increase in complexity to suit the growing reading ability of the students? (Daoud and Celce-Murcia, 1979: 304)

Is Each Question Reliable in the Sense that Other Evaluators would Interpret it in the Same Way?
Some terms and concepts which are commonly used in applied linguistics are amenable to differing interpretations and are best avoided or glossed when attempting to measure the effects of materials. For example, each of the following questions could be interpreted in a number of ways:

> Are the materials sufficiently authentic?
> Is there an acceptable balance of skills?
> Do the activities work?
> Is each unit coherent?

There are a number of ways in which each question could be rewritten to make it more reliable and useful. For example:

> Do the materials help the learners to use the language in situations they are likely to find themselves in after the course?
> Is the proportion of the materials devoted to the development of reading skills suitable for your learners?
> Are the communicative tasks useful in providing learning opportunities for the learners?
> Are the activities in each unit linked to each other in ways which help the learners?

Categorize the List

It is very useful to rearrange the random list of universal criteria into categories which facilitate focus and enable generalizations to be made. An extra advantage of doing this is that you often think of other criteria related to the category as you are doing the categorization exercise.
Possible categories for universal criteria would be:

Learning Principles
Cultural Perspective
Topic Content
Teaching Points
Texts
Activities
Methodology
Instructions
Design

Develop Media-specific Criteria

These are criteria which ask questions of particular relevance to the medium used by the materials being evaluated (e.g., criteria for books, for audio cassettes, for videos, etc.). Examples of such criteria would be:

Is it clear which sections the visuals refer to?
Is the sequence of activities clearly signalled?
Are the different voices easily distinguished?
Do the gestures of the actors help to make the language meaningful in realistic ways?

Obviously these criteria can also be usefully categorized (e.g., under Illustrations, Layout, Audibility, Movement).

Develop Content-specific Criteria

These are criteria which relate to the topics and/or teaching points of the materials being evaluated. 'Thus there would be a set of topic related criteria which would be relevant to the evaluation of a business English textbook but not to a general English coursebook; and there would be a set of criteria relevant to a reading skills book which would not be relevant to the evaluation of a grammar practice book and vice versa.' (Tomlinson, 1999: 11).
    Examples of content-specific criteria would be:

Do the examples of business texts (e.g., letters, invoices, etc.) replicate features of real-life business practice?
Do the reading texts represent a wide and typical sample of genres?

Develop Age-specific Criteria

These are criteria which relate to the age of the target learners. Thus there would be criteria which are only suitable for five-year-olds, for ten-year-olds, for teenagers, for young adults and for mature adults. These criteria would relate to cognitive and affective development, to previous experience, to interests and to wants and needs.
    Examples of age-specific criteria would be:

Are there short, varied activities which are likely to match the attention span of the learners?
Is the content likely to be cognitively challenging?

Develop Local Criteria

These are criteria which relate to the actual or potential environment of use. They are questions which are not concerned with establishing the value of the materials per se but rather with measuring the value of the materials for particular learners in particular circumstances. It is this set of criteria which is unique to the specific evaluation being undertaken and which is ultimately responsible for most of the decisions made in relation to the adoption, revision or adaptation of the materials. Typical features of the environment which would determine this set of materials are:

- the type(s) of institution(s);
- the resources of the institution(s);
- class size;
- the background, needs and wants of the learners;
- the background, needs and wants of the teachers;
- the language policy in operation;
- the syllabus;
- the objectives of the courses;
- the intensity and extent of the teaching time available;
- the target examinations;
- the amount of exposure to the target language outside the classroom.

Develop Other Criteria

Other criteria which it might be appropriate to develop could include teacher-specific, administrator-specific, gender-specific, culture-specific or L1-specific criteria and, especially in the case of a review for a journal, criteria assessing the match between the materials and the claims made by the publishers for them.

Trial the Criteria

It is important to trial the criteria (even prior to a small, fairly informal evaluation) to ensure that the criteria are sufficient, answerable, reliable and useful. Revisions can then be made before the actual evaluation begins.

Conducting the Evaluation

From experience I have found the most effective way of conducting an evaluation is to:

- make sure that there is more than one evaluator;
- discuss the criteria to make sure there is equivalence of interpretation;
- answer the criteria independently and in isolation from the other evaluator(s);
- focus in a large evaluation on a typical unit for each level (and then check its typicality by reference to other units);
- give a score for each criterion (with some sets of criteria weighted more heavily than others);
- write comments at the end of each category;
- at the end of the evaluation aggregate each evaluator's scores for each criterion, category of criteria and set of criteria and then average the scores;

- record the comments shared by the evaluators;
- write a joint report.

See Tomlinson *et al.* (2001) for a report of a large-scale evaluation in which four evaluators from different cultures independently evaluated eight adult EFL courses using the same 133 criteria (weighted 0–20 for Publisher's Claims, 0–10 for Flexibility and 0–5 for the other categories of criteria).

Conclusion

Materials evaluation is initially a time-consuming and difficult undertaking. Approaching it in the principled, systematic and rigorous ways suggested above can not only help to make and record vital discoveries about the materials being evaluated but can also help the evaluators to learn a lot about materials, about learning and teaching and about themselves. In addition, doing evaluations formally and rigorously can eventually contribute to the development of an ability to conduct principled informal evaluations quickly and effectively when the occasion demands (e.g., when asked for an opinion of a new book; when deciding which materials to buy in a bookshop; when editing other people's materials). I have found evaluation demanding but rewarding. Certainly, I have learned a lot every time I have evaluated materials, whether it be the worldwide evaluation of a coursebook I once undertook for a British publisher, the evaluation of computer software I once undertook for an American company, the evaluation of materials I have done for reviews in *ELT Journal* or just looking through new materials in a bookshop every time I visit my family in Cambridge. I hope, above all else, that I have learned to be more open-minded and that I have learned what criteria I need to satisfy when I write the best-selling coursebook I still plan one day to write.

References

Beck, I. L., McKeown, M. G. and Worthy, J. (1995) 'Giving a text voice can improve students' understanding'. *Research Reading Quarterly*, **30** (2).

Berman, M. (1999) 'The teacher and the wounded healer'. *IATEFL Issues*, **152**, 2–5.

Brown, J. B. (1997) 'Textbook evaluation form'. *The Language Teacher*, **21** (10).

Byram, M. and Fleming, M. (1998) *Language Learning in Intercultural Perspective.* Cambridge: Cambridge University Press.

Byrd, P. (1995) *Material Writer's Guide.* New York: Heinle and Heinle.

Canale, M. and Swain, M. (1980) 'Theoretical bases of communicative approaches to second language teaching and testing'. *Applied Linguistics*, **1** (1), 11–47.

Candlin, C. N. and Breen, M. (1980) 'Evaluating and designing language teaching materials'. *Practical Papers in English Language Education* Vol. 2. Lancaster: Institute for English Language Education, University of Lancaster.

Craik, F. I. M. and Lockhart, R. S. (1972) 'Levels of processing: a framework for memory research'. *Journal of Verbal Learning and Verbal Behaviour*, **11**, 671–84.

Cunningsworth, A. (1984) *Evaluating and Selecting EFL Teaching Material*. London: Heinemann.

Cunningsworth, A. (1995) *Choosing Your Coursebook*. Oxford: Heinemann.

Daoud, A. and Celce-Murcia, M. (1979) 'Selecting and evaluating textbooks', in M. Celce-Murcia and L. McIntosh (eds) *Teaching English as a Second or Foreign Language*. New York: Newbury House.

Donovan, P. (1998) 'Piloting – a publisher's view', in B. Tomlinson (ed.) *Materials Development for Language Teaching*. Cambridge: Cambridge University Press, pp. 149–89.

Dörnyei, Z. and Otto, I. (1998) 'Motivation in action: a process model of L2 motivation'. *Working Papers in Applied Linguistics*, **4**, 43–69.

Edge, J. and Wharton, S. (1998) 'Autonomy and development: living in the material world', in B. Tomlinson (ed.) *Materials Development for Language Teaching*. Cambridge: Cambridge University Press, pp. 295–310.

Ellis, R. (1995) 'Does it "work"?' *Folio*, **2** (1), 19–21.

Ellis, R. (1998) 'The evaluation of communicative tasks', in B. Tomlinson (ed.) *Materials Development for Language Teaching*. Cambridge: Cambridge University Press, pp. 217–38.

Grant, N. (1987) *Making the Most of Your Textbook*. Harlow: Longman.

Hidalgo, A. C., Hall, D. and Jacobs, G. M. (1995) *Getting Started: Materials Writers on Materials Writing*. Singapore: RELC.

Jacobs, B. and Schumann, J. A. (1992) 'Language acquisition and the neurosciences: towards a more integrative perspective'. *Applied Linguistics*, **13** (3), 282–301.

Jolly, D. and Bolitho, R. (1998) 'A framework for materials development', in B. Tomlinson (ed.) *Materials Development in Language Teaching*. Cambridge: Cambridge University Press.

Kaufman, G. (1996) 'The many faces of mental imagery', in C. Cornoldi *et al. Stretching the Imagination: Representation and Transformation in Mental Imagery*. Oxford: Oxford University Press.

Kolb, D. (1984) *Experiential Learning: Experience as the Source of Learning and Development*. Englewood Cliffs, NJ: Prentice Hall.

Krashen, S. (1982) *Principles and Practice in Second Language Acquisition*. Oxford: Pergamon.

Littlejohn, A. P. (1998) 'The analysis of language teaching materials: inside the Trojan Horse', in B. Tomlinson (ed.) *Materials Development for Language Teaching*. Cambridge: Cambridge University Press, pp. 190–216.

McDonough, J. (1998) 'Survey review: recent materials for the teaching of ESP'. *ELT Journal*, **52** (2).

McDonough, J. and Shaw, C. (1993) *Materials and Methods in ELT*. Oxford: Blackwell.

Mariani, L. (1983) 'Evaluating and supplementing coursebooks', in S. Holden (ed.) *Second Selections from Modern English Teacher*. Harlow: Longman.

Masuhara, H. (1998a) 'Factors influencing the reading difficulties of advanced learners of English as a foreign Language when reading authentic texts'. Unpublished PhD thesis, University of Luton.

Masuhara, H. (1998b) 'What do teachers really want from coursebooks?', in B. Tomlinson (ed.) *Materials Development for Language Teaching.* Cambridge: Cambridge University Press, pp. 239–60.

Meisel, J., Clahsen, H. and Pienemann, M. (1981) 'On determining developmental stages in natural second language acquisition'. *Studies in Second Language Acquisition,* **3**, 109–35.

Oatley, K. and Jenkins, J. (1996) *Understanding Emotions.* Cambridge, MA: Blackwell.

Oxford, R. L. and Anderson, N. J. (1995) 'A crosscultural view of learning styles'. *Language Teaching,* **28**, 201–15.

Pienemann, M. (1985) 'Learnability and syllabus construction', in K. Hyltenstam and M. Pienemann (eds) *Modelling and Assessing Second Language Acquisition.* Clevedon, Avon: Multilingual Matters.

Richards, J. (2001) *Curriculum Development in Language Education.* Cambridge: Cambridge University Press.

Roxburgh, J. (1997) 'Procedures for the evaluation of in-house EAP textbooks'. *Folio,* **4** (1), 15–18.

Rutherford, W. and Sharwood-Smith, M. (1988) (eds) *Grammar and Second Language Teaching.* Rowley, MA: Newbury House.

Schmidt, R. (1992) 'Psychological mechanisms underlying second language fluency'. *Studies in Second Language Acquisition,* **14**, 357–85.

Schon, D. (1983) *The Reflective Practitioner.* London: Temple Smith.

Schumann, J. A. (1997) *The Neurobiology of Affect in Language.* Boston: Blackwell.

Schumann, J. A. (1999) 'A neurobiological perspective on affect', in J. Arnold (ed.) *Affect in Language Learning.* Cambridge: Cambridge University Press.

Seliger, H. (1979) 'On the nature and function of language rules in language teaching'. *TESOL Quarterly,* **13**, 359–69.

Sheldon, L. E. (ed.) (1987) *ELT Textbooks and Materials: Problems in Evaluation and Development.* ELT Documents 126. London: Modern English Publications/The British Council.

Sheldon, L. E. (1988) 'Evaluating ELT textbooks and materials'. *ELT Journal,* **42** (4).

Skierso, A. (1991) 'Textbook selection and evaluation', in M. Celce-Murcia and L. McIntosh (eds) *Teaching English as a Second or Foreign Language.* Boston: Heinle and Heinle.

Stevick, E. (1976) *Memory, Meaning and Method.* Rowley, MA: Newbury House.

Swain, M. (1985) 'Communicative competence: some roles of comprehensible input and comprehensible output in its development', in S. Gass and C. Madden (eds) *Input in Second Language Acquisition.* Rowley, MA: Newbury House.

Tomlinson, B. (1994) 'Pragmatic awareness activities'. *Language Awareness,* **3** (3), 119–29.

Tomlinson, B. (1998a) 'Affect and the coursebook'. *IATEFL Issues*, **145**, 20–1.

Tomlinson, B. (ed.) (1998b) *Materials Development in Language Teaching.* Cambridge: Cambridge University Press.

Tomlinson, B. (1999) 'Developing criteria for materials evaluation'. *IATEFL Issues*, **147**, 10–13.

Tomlinson, B. (2000a) 'A multi-dimensional approach'. *The Language Teacher Online*, 24/07.

Tomlinson, B. (2000b) 'Materials for cultural awareness: combining language, literature and culture in the mind'. *The Language Teacher*, **24** (2), 19–21.

Tomlinson, B. (2000c) 'Talking to yourself: the role of the inner voice in language learning'. *Applied Language Learning*, **11** (1), 123–54.

Tomlinson, B. (2001a) 'Connecting the mind: a multi-dimensional approach to teaching language through literature'. *The English Teacher*, **4** (2), 104–15.

Tomlinson, B. (2001b) 'Humanising the coursebook'. *Humanising Language Teaching*, **5** (3). Canterbury: Pilgrims.

Tomlinson, B. (2001c) 'Materials development', in R. Carter and D. Nunan (eds) *The Cambridge Guide to Teaching English to Speakers of Other Languages.* Cambridge: Cambridge University Press.

Tomlinson, B., Dat, B., Masuhara, H. and Rubdy, R. (2001) 'EFL courses for adults'. *ELT Journal*, **55** (1), 80–101.

Tomlinson, B. and Masuhara, H. (2000) 'Using simulations on materials development courses'. *Simulation & Gaming: An Interdisciplinary Journal of Theory, Practice and Research*, **31** (2), 152–68.

Wenden, A. (1987) 'Conceptual background and utility', in A. Wenden and J. Rubin *Learner Strategies in Language Learning*. Hemel Hempstead: Prentice Hall.

Wenden, A. and Rubin, J. (1987) *Learner Strategies in Language Learning*. Hemel Hempstead: Prentice Hall.

White, L. (1990) 'Implications of learnability theories for second language learning and teaching', in M. Halliday, J. Gibbons and H. Nicholas (eds) *Learning, Keeping and Using Language, 1*. Amsterdam: John Benjamins.

Williams, D. (1983) 'Developing criteria for textbook evaluation'. *ELT Journal*, **37** (3).

Williams, M. and Burden, R. L. (1997) *Psychology for Language Teachers.* Cambridge: Cambridge University Press.

CHAPTER

2

Selection of Materials

Rani Rubdy

Introduction

The coursebook has become an almost universal element of ELT, playing as it does a vital and positive part in the everyday job of teaching and learning of English (Hutchinson and Torres, 1994). The plethora of material that continues to be produced unabated bears ample testimony to its perceived importance not simply as one of the main 'tools of the trade' in the language classroom but as 'the visible heart' of any ELT programme (Sheldon, 1988: 237). As Cunningsworth has noted, the wealth of published material that is available on the market today makes the selection of the right coursebook a challenging task, requiring teachers to make informed and appropriate choices when selecting coursebooks and supporting materials (Cunningsworth, 1995: 1).

What makes it vital to develop even more accurate and revealing ways of evaluating and selecting coursebooks is that materials themselves have evolved into more complex objects. While in the early days ELT coursebooks contained mainly reading texts accompanied by a set of comprehension questions and a few grammar and vocabulary exercises, materials today frequently offer 'packages' for language teaching and learning which include workbooks, teachers' guides, audio and video support and even CALL programmes with precise indications of the work that teachers and learners are to do together in a way that effectively structures classroom lessons (Littlejohn, 1998: 190). Indeed, materials have more and more come to be viewed as 'an embodiment of the aims, values and methods of the particular teaching learning situation' (Hutchinson, 1987: 37) to the extent that, as Hutchinson observes, the selection of materials probably represents the single most important decision that the language teacher has to make.

The selection of materials involves matching the given materials against the context in which they are going to be used and the needs and interests of the teachers and learners who work within it, to find the best possible fit between them. This calls for major strategic decisions based on informed judgement and professional experience, forcing teachers to identify their priorities: As Littlejohn rightly observes, 'We need to be able to examine the implications that use of a set of materials may have for classroom work and thus come to grounded opinions about whether or not the methodology and content of the materials is appropriate for a particular language teaching context' (Littlejohn, 1998: 190–1).

The number of variables that affect the success or failure of coursebooks in particular contexts have made it necessary to identify appropriate criteria on which to base these decisions. The range and multiplicity of criteria that reflect these variables in the literature typically relate to learner goals and needs, learning styles, proficiency levels, language teaching methods, classroom contexts and processes, as well as the potential of materials for generating motivation, variety and interest. Approaches that evaluate and select materials only on the basis of such overtly observable properties that reside in the texts, tasks and activities, however, represent to some extent a static view of materials. Since materials are a powerful stimuli for generating learning, a more dynamic approach would be one which selects materials for their potential not only to engage the learners' and teacher's attention and effort, but also to draw substantial contributions from the teacher, the learners and the collective group as a whole that can be transformed into worthwhile learning experiences in the course of classroom interaction.

This chapter will review the approaches and criteria that have been employed in the selection of instructional materials in ELT and assess the theoretical and pedagogical assumptions underlying them. In view of the fact that the requirements of particular learning/teaching situations are often varied, and hence cannot be met by any one ideal coursebook, however impressive or eminent, it will propose a framework for selecting materials which, while incorporating criteria that form part of conventional wisdom, prioritizes the potential that all good materials have for flexibility, adaptability and relevance to the changing needs, goals and interests of the modern-day language learner.

The Roles and Functions of Coursebooks

It might be helpful to begin by examining current thinking regarding the role and functions of coursebooks. This should help bring clarity to the act of judging the worth of coursebooks, particularly in the face of the broad variation found among teachers of English across the world who use them, and the diversity in the objectives for learning English that exists among their students.

Recent years have seen a renewed debate about the desirability of ELT coursebooks in facilitating the teaching and learning of English. Some scholars object to them in principle on grounds that published materials do not always provide the types of texts and activities that a teacher is seeking for a given class (Block, 1991). Others argue that they tend to have a constraining effect on the freedom of action of the teacher, predetermining the content and procedures for learners and pre-empting creativity and exploration on the part of teachers (Prabhu, 1988). Because coursebooks are typically produced centrally by a group of 'specialists' for another group to use locally in a top-down fashion (Maley, 1998: 279) they can act as instruments of institutional control or serve a range of commercial interests (Bell and Gower, 1998: 117) that could be disempowering for teachers. In this view, 'The teacher becomes little more than a cipher for a prepared text' (Hutchinson and Torres, 1994).

To combat this trend of over-reliance on the textbook, a strong case has been made for the promotion of teacher-generated materials (Block, 1991; Dubin, 1988) and for greater learner involvement in materials adaptation (Clarke, 1989; Riggenbach, 1988), more in tune with a learner-centred philosophy that characterizes contemporary classrooms. Block (1991), for instance, contends that the way core language is contextualized in many commercial materials often renders it irrelevant and outdated. He maintains that the personal touch that the teacher can bring to his/her materials is unparalleled by the stereotypical activities that characterize many of them. Clark (1989) pleads for creative learner involvement in materials adaptation and shows how giving learners a more contributory role can serve not only to make existing materials more relevant but also more motivating for the learner.

Notwithstanding these developments, there are those who argue that 'coursebooks provide teachers and learners with a range of professionally developed materials within tried and tested syllabus structures', allowing teachers to spend their valuable time more on facilitating learning than materials production (Bell and Gower, 1998: 116). Advocacy of coursebooks has come from scholars who strongly believe that coursebooks should be seen as a means of 're-skilling' rather than 'de-skilling' teachers (O'Neil, 1982; Hutchinson and Torres, 1994; Edge and Wharton, 1998) and that, provided they are used flexibly, they *can* be adapted and supplemented to meet the needs of specific classes (Bell and Gower, 1998: 117). They state the following advantages for the use of coursebooks:

1. Coursebooks fulfil a wide range of practical needs, particularly in contexts where English is being taught in a non-English-speaking environment and where teachers either lack training or sufficient time to analyse each group's needs.
2. The coursebook helps provide a route map for both teachers and learners, making it possible for them to look ahead to what will be done in a lesson as well as to look back on what has been done.
3. Coursebooks provide structure and predictability, which help give participants in social interactions like lessons a safe base, a platform for negotiation and exploration.
4. By dealing with a certain amount of routine work for teachers, the coursebook frees them to attend to more important aspects of lesson planning (including materials adaptation and supplementation), and to concentrate on using their creative skills.
5. Coursebooks provide teachers, particularly those lacking in training and experience, with a sense of self-confidence and security.
6. Most coursebooks are designed and developed by experts in the field, conversant with current theoretical approaches and methodological practices. The quality of sophistication in their design, content and organization would be difficult to match with home-grown materials.
7. Coursebooks can act as agents of change, allowing innovative ideas to be introduced within their structured framework in a way that enables teachers and learners to develop in harmony with these new ideas. Indeed, Edge and

Wharton (1998) see the ELT coursbook functioning as a genre of mass communication, where its authors can enter into positive dialogue with teachers and students on a number of issues of current significance to ELT professionals.

Not surprising, then, to see why the selection of materials has come to involve 'considerable professional, financial and even political investment' – not just by teachers and learners – but other stakeholders as well, such as administrators, educational advisors, education ministries and state governments, making the task a high profile one (Sheldon, 1988: 237). Conflict of interests can arise between commercial agencies who view ELT books as big business and use aggressive marketing strategies to exploit the situation and those committed to the choice of a coursebook simply for its value for effective classroom use. This explains the current polarization of views, fluctuating between the perception that coursebooks are valid, labour-saving tools, on the one hand, and the belief that they are just 'skilfully marketed' 'masses of rubbish' (Brumfit, 1980: 30), on the other.

We are reminded of Allwright's considered view about the limited usefulness of ELT materials, expressed some two decades ago: 'The whole business of the management of language learning is far too complex to be satisfactorily catered for by a pre-packaged set of decisions embodied in teaching materials' (Allwright, 1981). Hence the feeling that published materials can at best only represent 'poor compromises between what is educationally desirable on the one hand and financially viable on the other' (Sheldon, 1988: 237), thus justifying Cunningsworth's (1984) cautionary note about coursebooks being good servants but bad masters.

The debate has raised many important questions regarding the relationship between ready-made ELT materials and the teaching and learning process that warrant serious consideration. Some of these have been identified by Bell and Gower (1998: 117), as summarized below:

1. Given that creativity is to be preserved as an important pedagogical principle, how can we ensure that coursebooks do not take away investment and responsibility from teachers and learners?
2. How can one ensure that coursebooks reflect the dynamic and interactive nature of the learning process while at the same time maintaining the consistency of the syllabus?
3. Although it is true that no coursebook can cater for all the individual needs of all learners all of the time, how can sufficient material be provided so as to meet most needs most of the time and provide enough flexibility to enable teachers to individualize it?
4. If the language provided in many coursebooks is conventional rather than real life, how can samples of use that are as natural as possible be provided?
5. If coursebooks are frequently predictable in format and content, how can the material be made more lively?

These questions help refocus attention on precisely the kinds of issues that are problematic about ready-made ELT materials for which those arguing in favour of teacher and student-generated materials see them as providing solutions in being able to address more effectively such aspects of classroom lessons as teacher responsibility, creativity and investment as well as learner initiative and receptivity – indeed, just the kind of intangible attributes that inhere in good materials, or to be more precise, in materials that provide a 'good fit'. Because such materials are likely to be directly responsive and relevant to the specific needs of a particular group of teachers and learners and the circumstances of their learning, they are likely to optimize teacher and learner contributions to the learning process and thereby enhance learning itself. At the same time, reduced reliance on pre-determined content and greater control over the teaching–learning process entails greater teacher and learner freedom, creativity and choice, thus contributing to the desirable educational goals of independence and autonomy for both.

Materials Evaluation and Selection

Ellis speaks of the strong surge of interest in the goals, roles and methods of evaluation in recent years (Alderson and Beretta, 1992; Rea-Dickins and Germaine, 1992; Weir and Roberts, 1994), and attributes this trend primarily to the increase in the influence of mainstream educational theory and in part to the need to carry out large-scale programme evaluations for external funding agencies like the ODA, the British Council and USAID (Ellis, 1998: 217). He goes on to make a distinction between *macroevaluations* of such large-scale projects, typically carried out for accountability and/or developmental purposes and *microevaluations*. The latter are carried out by teachers on a day-by-day and lesson-by-lesson basis and focus less on the programme as a whole and more on what specific activities and techniques appear to 'work' in the context of a particular lesson. By this definition, materials evaluation, selection and adaptation fall under the purview of microevaluation, as does the evaluation of teachers' and learners' classroom behaviours. Ellis argues that since it is microevaluation which is compatible with many teachers' perspective about what evaluation involves, encouraging teachers to adopt a micro- rather than a macroperspective to evaluation will help them undertake evaluation that accords with their own perspective.

At this point, another distinction that will be useful to make is that between the evaluation of materials (see Chapter 1 (Tomlinson) in this volume) and their selection. Evaluation, like selection, is a matter of judging the fitness of something for a particular purpose. However, while it is true that the selection of materials inevitably involves, or subsumes, a process of evaluation, evaluation can be undertaken for a variety of purposes and carried out in a variety of ways. In the selection of materials, on the other hand, what assumes primary importance is the analysis of learner needs and interests and how these are addressed. Consequently, in the selection of materials usually it is the most *appropriate* rather than the best that wins.

Additionally, since the selection of materials necessarily takes place *before* classroom use, typically its concern is with what Breen and Candlin (1987) and Breen (1989) describe as '*tasks-as-workplans*', i.e., the analysis of materials 'as they are' in a state of pre-use. This is distinct from the evaluation of 'materials in action', i.e., with what actually happens in the classroom when materials are in-use or in what in Breen's terminology would be '*tasks-in-process*', the point when teachers and learners bring their own personal contributions, and from '*tasks-as-outcomes*', the learning that may accrue post-use. Thus while the evaluation of materials would involve assessing how effective and useful the materials are found to be in actual use by a specific group of teacher and students or how effective they may have been in promoting learning, selection of materials is concerned with the *potential* that a set of materials may have in effectively and efficiently supporting learning, as a 'frame' for learning and teaching opportunities.

The framework I intend to propose in this chapter will therefore be oriented towards analysing materials 'as they are' – pre-use, more in line with Littlejohn's (1998) proposal, than concerning itself with materials in-use or post-use and will essentially focus on criteria for measuring the *potential* of what teachers and students can *do* with them in the classroom. Such an evaluation is motivated by the need to choose materials that will be relevant and appropriate for a particular group of learners and also by the need to identify specific aspects of the materials that require adaptation. I would, however, hasten to maintain, with McDonough and Shaw (1993: 79), that evaluation of materials in this manner is just one part of a complex process and that materials once selected 'can only be judged successful after classroom implementation and feedback'.

Existing Proposals for Evaluating Materials

Numerous evaluation checklists have been designed down the years to help teachers make a systematic selection of textbooks (Tucker, 1975; van Lier, 1979; Williams, 1983; Breen and Candlin, 1987; Hutchinson and Waters, 1987; Sheldon, 1988; McDonough and Shaw, 1993; Cunningsworth, 1984, 1995; Littlejohn, 1998). These vary in the extent to which they reflect the priorities and constraints that might characterize specific contexts of ELT teaching. Tomlinson (in this volume) has referred in greater detail to previous approaches to evaluating materials. Hence only a brief sketch will be attempted here.

Some of the earliest attempts at developing teacher-friendly systems for rigorous assessments include the elaborate questionnaires designed by Tucker (1975), van Lier (1979) and Williams (1983). However, these checklists have not had the currency they deserve, partly due to their lack of ready access and also because of the ad hoc manner in which coursebook selection is most often made (Sheldon, 1988). Furthermore, priorities in language teaching have themselves undergone considerable change accompanying the growth of research and academic enquiry in the last two decades.

Frequently the evaluation instruments and checklists are organized into two or more levels or stages to reflect the decision process the teachers need to go through (Ellis, 1998: 220). For instance, Breen and Candlin's (1987) interactive, step-by-step guide to coursebook evaluation envisages two phases, one addressing the 'overall usefulness' of the materials and another aiming at 'a more searching analysis' with a particular group of learners and classroom situation in mind. Arguing for the need to look below surface features to discover the value system and assumptions underlying materials design, Hutchinson (1987) likewise views evaluation as an interactive process involving a subjective and objective analysis of materials and the extent to which they match teacher and student needs in a given context. More recently, McDonough and Shaw (1993) have also proposed two complementary stages, beginning with an 'external evaluation' and moving on to an in-depth 'internal evaluation' of two or more units in terms of presentation of skills, grading and sequencing of tasks, kinds of texts used and the relationship between exercises and tests.

Sheldon's very useful framework (1988) covers a range of criteria from those relating to purely practical factors like availability and physical characteristics such as layout and graphics to more psychological and psycholinguistic aspects such as learner needs and learning objectives, their assumed background, target age range, culture, conceptual and schematic development, expectations and learning preferences. Organizational factors such as provision of linkage, sequencing/grading, stimulus/practice/revision, recycling and internal and external coherence as well as criteria that address appropriacy, authenticity, cultural bias and flexibility are also given considerable importance.

To date, the most comprehensive and thorough is Cunningsworth's (1984, 1995) proposal for materials evaluation, taking as it does the learner's context and learning principles as its starting point. The general guidelines identified (1995) and the criteria they inform are presented alongside useful case studies, illustrated with clear examples from current published materials relating to areas of grammar, phonology and discourse as well as the language skills.

Focusing on materials as a *pedagogic* device, Littlejohn's (1998) analysis contains two main dimensions: *publication*, which refers to the 'tangible' or physical aspects of the materials, and *design*, which relates to the thinking underlying its production and use – including its aims, how the tasks, language and content in the materials are selected and sequenced and the nature and focus of the content. Utilizing Breen and Candlin's (1987) notion of process competence, Littlejohn is interested in what learners are precisely asked to *do* by drawing upon their *knowledge, abilities* and *skills* and the modes of classroom participation the activities foster. An extremely useful aspect is his ability to show how it works in practice as one moves through the different 'levels' of analysis, from a consideration of the more easily identifiable aspects to the more abstract and complex.

Finally, Tomlinson's (1998) 'Introduction' to *Materials Development in Language Teaching* provides an overview of many of the tenets and basic principles of second language acquisition that are currently relevant to an understanding of what good materials, as well as principled judgements about them, should contain. The value of materials for Tomlinson lies in their effectiveness in encouraging learners to make discoveries for themselves through self-investment, through intellectual, aesthetic and emotional engagement with authentic input, through a sensitivity to learners' readiness to learn, supported by opportunities for genuine interaction and purposeful communication. Although there is no general consensus on how languages are learned, most teachers would agree that many of these principles are precisely those which are widely believed to contribute to successful learning.

A principal problem with checklists and questionnaires of the kind discussed above is that they frequently involve making general, impressionistic judgements about materials rather than providing an in-depth and systematic investigation of what they contain. Secondly, as Sheldon argues, the discursive format in which they are presented often makes it difficult to separate description, guidance and criticism (Sheldon, 1988: 241). A useful suggestion put forward by him is to build a compendium of reviews culled from various sources, including 'student-generated' and 'teacher-consensus' reviews, so that teachers can access what has been thought and said about various books over a period of time instead of having to reinvent the wheel anew.

Then again, as coursebook criteria are emphatically local, no one is really certain what criteria and constraints are actually operative in ELT contexts worldwide. Any culturally restricted global list of criteria produced cannot therefore hope to be definitive. Nor is it possible for all the criteria identified to be deployed simultaneously. Obviously, factors that relate specifically to each consumer's unique situation will get selected and even these might not be applicable in most local environments without considerable modifications. This is true as much for any framework of evaluative criteria proposed as it is in expecting a perfect fit for any set of materials produced for a wide market.

Sheldon says it correctly, 'It is clear that coursebook assessment is fundamentally a subjective, rule-of-thumb activity and that no neat formula, grid or system will ever provide a definitive yardstick' (Sheldon, 1988: 245). The survey guides that have been proposed, although of practical use to teachers, raise many questions relating to how the materials should be considered and, crucially, how one aspect should be weighted in relation to another. Ellis (1998: 221) observes, for instance, how many of the guides specifically ask whether the materials contain authentic texts, ignoring the complexity of the whole question of authenticity in language teaching as pointed out by Widdowson (1979). He also points out how a positive rating on a criterion of authenticity (i.e., the materials contain authentic texts) may be matched with a negative rating on the criterion of vocabulary load (i.e., the number of new words introduced is excessive). It is not clear how the materials evaluator is to reconcile these conflicting ratings.

Therefore, rather than impose a system of analysis in the form of a linear, static checklist that elicits a response of plus/minus marks, the framework I intend to propose presents evaluative parameters as a configuration containing a cluster or complex of criteria reflecting variables which need to be examined as interacting with each other rather than in isolation, while simultaneously bearing a relationship with the whole. Such a composite of variables, it is hoped, will help teachers plot out a more coherent and complete picture of the potential that a set of materials holds for language learning and assess their suitability to the particular circumstances of a given context, without losing a sense of their complexity.

A Framework for the Selection of Coursebooks

What aspects of materials we focus on in evaluating them will largely depend upon the purposes one has in looking at the materials. It is possible to describe materials in terms of the quality of the paper and binding, pricing, layout, size, typeface and so on, but a more pedagogic focus, rather than simply a pragmatic one, would lead one to examine those aspects of materials that more directly aid the teaching–learning process (Littlejohn, 1998), and this is what will be aimed at here. If we consider the selection of materials as involving two stages of analysis, as conventional wisdom suggests, the first stage would consist of assessing the content of the book in relation to its professed aims. Thus, for example, if a coursebook states as an underlying principle of its materials that students need to engage in authentic communication in order to develop 'real-life' communication skills, in the light of the current refocusing of the question of authenticity, where it is not primarily the materials themselves that have to be authentic, but rather the response to the materials, teachers will need to ask what the learners are required to *do* with these materials and whether this response is motivated by an authentic *need* to communicate, involving, say, the addressing of content rather than form, at the very least, in assessing the validity of the claims made (Hall, 2001). This stage would also include considering whether the target age range, culture, assumed background and entry/exit levels of students have been clearly specified in the blurb and the extent to which they are valid and appropriate to the intended learners.

The second stage of analysis would involve assessing the effectiveness of materials in terms of the specific needs and context of the intended learners as well as how well they serve the teaching–learning process. The framework I propose basically addresses this stage of evaluation and consists of three broad categories, each assessing the potential validity of the materials in relation to:

1. the learners' needs, goals and pedagogical requirements;
2. the teacher's skills, abilities, theories and beliefs; and
3. the thinking underlying the materials writer's presentation of the content and approach to teaching and learning respectively.

These I will term Psychological Validity, Pedagogical Validity, and Process and Content Validity.

A diagrammatic representation of these in Figure 2.1 places at the very centre of the evaluation process the three main elements of the classroom: the learners, the teacher and the materials to represent the interaction that takes place between them. Note that the sample of criteria representing the inner concentric circle has to do with those features that are found to reside overtly in the texts, tasks and activities and is therefore viewed as elements that are 'tangible' or

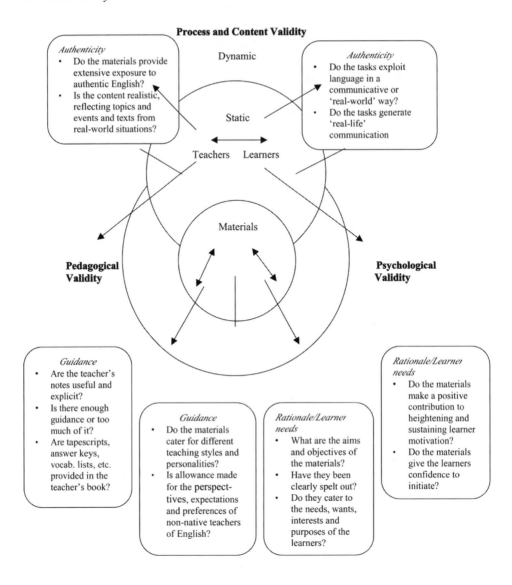

Figure 2.1 A static versus dynamic model of materials evaluation

amenable to a straightforward surface level mode of analysis. If we choose to stop with an analysis of these criteria alone such an evaluation would constitute what I call a *static* mode of evaluation. The criteria indicated as part of the outer concentric circle, however, involve a more in-depth analysis, requiring that we 'look beneath the surface' (Hutchison, 1987) to discover through a series of subjective judgements and inferences the more dynamic features of materials design. These are features that have to do with the more abstract qualities of flexibility, creativity and exploration, all of which are viewed as activating the learning process through teacher and learner-initiated contributions and hence call for a *dynamic* model of evaluation.

Psychological Validity

The need for student-centredness in recent years has made it necessary to conduct some sort of needs analysis, whether in the construction of a syllabus or a set of materials. It follows that a key question in choosing a coursebook would be, 'How does the book relate to the needs of the learners?' We know of course that the need to communicate lies at the heart of all language learning. Since this involves not just communicating within the classroom but, ultimately, in the real world outside, the materials must also take into account students' longer-term goals. This in turn would entail not merely teaching them 'how to learn' within classroom settings by raising awareness of different styles and strategies but also enabling them to take advantage of any opportunity to learn outside the classroom. In terms of materials, this means that the experience of working with the activities contained in them should provide students with confidence in their ability to communicate despite difficulties (Hall, 2001: 230–1).

Taking this aspect of student-centredness a step further, one might wish to find out to what extent the materials have the potential to foster self-directed, independent learning. As Tomlinson (1998) notes, the most significant role of materials is to involve students in decision-making about their own learning. One way of doing this is to channel their energies towards making existing materials more relevant and motivating; another would be to involve them in generating their own materials out of the reading and listening texts provided, as well as other source materials, to suit their own level and interest. Integral to the plan of a coursebook can be made this movement from teacher-defined tasks to tasks identified by students themselves; and from there on to a stage where student groups define areas of interest to work on and select materials from different sources on their own to generate task outcomes. The point is, do the materials have built into them such opportunities for student-initiated resource generation or is everything specified in advance?

Even where claims are made about fostering learner autonomy, the question to ask is whether learners are involved in making decisions about their own learning or do the materials encourage learner autonomy in a conservative sense only, which means learners do some study without teacher intervention but have no self-directed goals and have not developed effective learning strategies. Do the learners have sufficient control over the meanings and interactions that are generated in the classroom using the materials? As Edge and Wharton (1998: 296) point out, 'if learners in classrooms can initiate interaction patterns and create the meanings they want to personally express, then there is more chance that they will be able to make use of such learning to exploit outside sources for learning when they find them.' The following criteria mirror these issues:

Rationale/Learner Needs

What are the aims and objectives of the materials?

Have they been clearly spelt out?

Do they cater to the needs, wants, interests and purposes of the learners?

Are the materials appropriate and are they likely to be effective in helping learners to acquire English?

Do the materials make a positive contribution to heightening and sustaining learner motivation?

Do the materials give the learners confidence to initiate communicative events and persist with the attempted communication despite difficulties?

Do the materials cater for the development of language skills that would enable them to operate effectively in their future academic or professional life?

Independence and Autonomy

Is the learner a decision-maker or just a receiver of information?

Do the materials encourage independent language learning?

Do the materials encourage learners to guess, predict, discover, take risks, try-out several alternatives?

Do they give learners plenty of opportunities to make choices which suit their linguistic level, their preferred learning styles, their level of involvement in the text and the time available to them?

Do the materials involve the learner in thinking about the learning process and in experiencing a variety of different types of learning activities?

Do they allow sufficient time to think and reflect on their learning?

Do the materials help individual learners discover their learning styles and preferences, study habits and learning strategies?

Do the materials provide explicit instruction on various language learning strategies and suggest ways of using and developing them?

Is a sufficient range of strategies provided?

Do they encourage learners to evaluate their strategies or the learning activities or its content?

Do the materials allow self-monitoring and feedback?

Self-development

Do the materials/texts engage the learners both cognitively and affectively?

Do the materials credit learners with a capacity for rational thought and problem-solving?

Do they also involve the learner's emotions in the learning process?

Do the materials allow for the development of creative and critical thinking skills?

Do the materials allow scope for the development of a desirable set of attitudes?

Do the materials allow the individual to develop his or her talents as fully as possible?

Do the materials involve the learners as human beings rather than just as language learners?
Do the materials help build personality and learner voice and give learners an understanding about themselves?

Creativity
Do the materials exploit the learners' prior knowledge and experience and provide opportunities for further development?
Do the materials allow sufficient opportunities for student inventiveness and energy and encourage their participation in resource generation?
Do the materials provide additional challenging activities for highly motivated learners?
Have opportunities been built into the materials for learners to contribute?

Cooperation
Do the materials offer opportunities for cooperative learning, through pair and group work activities and information exchange tasks?
Are students encouraged to learn from and help one another and, more importantly, able to work in a less stressful atmosphere in the classroom?
Do they encourage positive interdependence by giving each individual a specific role to play in the activity allowing him/her to contribute actively to the group interaction?

Pedagogical Validity

Current trends in education, technological advances, information explosion and the communications revolution have all come together to cause new and diversified demands to be made on the teacher. So that, while tending to their learner's linguistic growth and development, teachers are themselves impelled continually to improve and develop their own skills and abilities and acquire new ones. This requires teachers not only to reflect on their practice (Schon, 1983; Richards, 1993) but also calls for a certain attitude of openness to new possibilites and a desire to continue to learn. A commercial coursebook can play an important role in teacher development if it offers teachers the opportunity to learn more about the language and about approaches to teaching in a way that allows them to integrate new ideas into their experiences of reflective practice to achieve a synthesis of a wide variety of teaching-related schemata (Edge and Wharton, 1998).

In one sense, a coursebook by itself has little operational value until the teacher populates it with his/her own ideas and experiences and brings it to life. Yet the potential for materials to influence the way teachers operate is considerable. This is because coursebooks embody a whole lot of theoretical positions and principles. By providing practical guidance on how to deal with particular texts and activities, suggesting innovative methods and approaches and offering alternative plans and procedures to enable teachers to maintain student motivation in class, or generate productive interaction, coursebooks can act as powerful catalysts for consciousness-raising, particularly in the case of untrained or novice teachers. Even for experienced teachers, seeking to excel their practice with new ideas, course materials can hold the seeds for effecting such transformations. Not in the conventional sense of overt preaching or prescription, but through the incorporation of current thinking in teacher self-development which increasingly recognizes that teachers cannot be developed by an outside agent and that this can best be brought about most effectively through self-initiated effort, course materials can motivate teachers to explore possibilities for self-actualization, restricted only if the teacher is reluctant to grow professionally. As Edge and Wharton rightly observe, then, 'a coursebook designed to encourage teacher development, if it is successful, will itself be the subject of evaluation, adaptation and critical use' (1998: 297). An important criterion for evaluating materials would then relate to the extent to which they engage the teacher's constantly evolving critical standpoint and facilitate the expanding and refining of the teacher's schemata in the process.

In addition, on a more mundane level, we would want to know whether the materials show a sufficient measure of compatibility with the teacher's existing skills and abilities and his/her own personal theory of teaching or beliefs about how language is learned. Given that teachers are expected to be capable of generating a supportive psychological climate and sustain learner motivation and interest in class, to what extent do the texts and topics incorporated in the coursebook help the teacher evoke learner interest and investment? To what extent do they allow teacher (or learner) choice, including the option to select, adapt and supplement these when required by the classroom group?

Edge and Wharton point out that the most obvious prerequisite for teachers to take responsibility for their professional development is choice. Experienced teachers are known not to follow the script of a coursebook inflexibly: 'They add, delete and change tasks at the planning stage, and they reshape their plans during the lesson in response to the interactions that take place' (Edge and Wharton, 1998: 300). This prompts us to ask, to what extent the materials facilitate this kind of flexible use of the coursebook and foster the teacher's capacity for creativity and flexibility, in addition to providing practical guidance for classroom use? Questions under this category would include:

Guidance
Are the teacher's notes useful and explicit?
Is there enough guidance or too much of it?
Are the tapescripts, answer keys, vocabulary lists, structural/functional inventories and lesson summaries provided in the teacher's book?
Do the materials cater for different teaching styles and personalities?
Is allowance made for the perspectives, expectations, and preferences of non-native teachers of English?

Choice

Are teachers encouraged to present the lessons in different ways?

Do the materials offer the teacher scope for adaptation and localization?

Do they encourage the teacher to add, delete, change and improvise?

Do they foster in teachers a sense of choice and control in exploiting the content?

Reflection/Exploration/Innovation

Do they foster teacher receptivity to innovation and experimentation?

Do they encourage teacher creativity, imagination and exploration?

Do they help to raise the teacher's critical consciousness by facilitating reflection about the materials themselves and the methods implicated in them?

Is the teacher encouraged to evaluate each lesson?

Process and Content Validity

The design of a coursebook and the way in which its authors intend it to be used is an essential part of its theoretical position. This set of criteria, therefore, relates to the overall view the coursebook writer holds, or wishes to project, about the nature of language, the nature of language learning and his educational philosophy in general. It also relates to the way in which these views are carried over into the tasks and activities that learners are required to perform and the nature of these activities in terms of their clarity and coherence of presentation, their sufficiency, accessibility and appropriacy. The information gathered under this category thus relates to the methodology, content, format, layout and design features of the materials as well as the theoretical assumptions about language and language learning that underpin them.

Methodology

Does the coursebook reflect the insights and findings from current theory and research on second language acquisition?

Do learners need to know what the sentences/texts mean or simply to manipulate forms?

Do the materials make use of what we know about the value of permitting a silent period at the beginning stages or in the learning of a new feature?

Do the materials help develop both the declarative knowledge and procedural knowledge of the learners as well as contribute to broader educational goals?

Is there a sufficient balance between analytical and experiential modes of learning?

Is there an explicit and conscious focus on rules and explanations or are there opportunities for the learners to discover the patterns in the first place?

What existing knowledge are learners expected to bring to the materials? Is their knowledge of communication exploited?

Content

Do the materials provide a rich, varied and comprehensible input in order to facilitate informal acquisition as well as conscious attention to linguistic and pragmatic features of the texts?

Are the topics/texts current and cognitively challenging and do they help enrich the learners' personal knowledge and experience and foster a positive personality?

Are there varied activities at different levels of task difficulty?

Are the materials well contextualized?

Do the materials call for a sufficiently good mix of closed and open-ended responses?

Are the grammatical explanations adequate?

Do the materials use complex metalanguage?

Do they suffer from terminological looseness?

Appropriacy

Is the level and the intended audience clearly spelt out?

Is it pitched at the right level of maturity and language and at the right conceptual level?

Is the material interesting, varied and topical enough to hold the attention of learners?

Is the author's sense of humour or philosophy obvious or appropriate?

Is the authorial voice friendly and supportive or patronizing?

Authenticity

Do the materials provide extensive exposure to authentic English through purposeful reading and/or listening activities?

Is the content realistic, reflecting topics and events and texts from real-world situations?

Do the activities relate to pupils' interests and 'real-life' tasks?

Do the tasks exploit language in a communicative or 'real-world' way?

If not, are the texts unacceptably simplified or artificial?

Do the texts generate 'real-life' communication processes?

Cultural sensitivity

What aspects of culture are in focus?

Are the materials relevant/suitable/appropriate to the learners' cultural context and sensitive to their values and beliefs?

Do the materials reflect awareness of and sensitivity to sociocultural variation?

Does the book show parallels and contrasts between the learners' culture and others?

Is this done in a non-patronizing way?

Does the coursebook enshrine stereotyped, inaccurate, condescending or offensive images of gender, race, social class or nationality?

Are accurate or 'sanitized' views of the USA or Britain presented; e.g., are uncomfortable social realities (for instance, unemployment, poverty, family breakdowns, racism) left out?

Layout/Graphics
Is there a clarity of design and layout?
Is there an optimum density and mix of text and graphical material on each page, or is the impression one of clutter?
Are the artwork and typefaces functional? Colourful? Appealing?
Is there enough white space on each page?

Accessibility
Is the material clearly organized and easy to access?
Are there indexes, vocabulary lists, section headings and other methods of signposting the content that allow the student to use the material easily, especially for revision or self-study purposes?
Is the learner given clear advice about how the book and its contents could be most effectively exploited?
Are the instructions for carrying out activities clearly and concisely but adequately articulated?
Can learners navigate with ease their way through the material in order to have a clear view of the progress made?

Linkage
Are the units and exercises well linked in terms of theme, situation, topic, pattern of skill development or grammatical/lexical 'progression'?
Does the textbook cohere both internally and externally (e.g., with other books in a series)?

Selection/Grading
Is the linguistic inventory presented appropriate for the students' purposes, bearing in mind their L1 background?
Is the selection and grading of tasks and activities based on a clearly discernible system (e.g., frequency counts for vocabulary, cognitive load for tasks)?
Does the introduction, practice and recycling of new linguistic items seem to be shallow/steep enough for the intended students?

Sufficiency
Is the book complete enough to stand on its own, or must the teacher produce a lot of ancillary bridging material to make it workable?
Can the course be taught using only the student's books, or must all the attendant teaching aids be deployed?

Balance/Integration/Challenge
Do the activities allow the learner to go beyond a merely superficial under-

standing of the text/discourse and require interpretive and inferential skills that call for higher-order critical thinking?
Is there a good balance between receptive and productive knowledge, skills and abilities?
Is the focus on the product or the process of learning or both?

Stimulus/Practice/Revision

Are there sufficient opportunities for students to use and practise their conversational strategies and skills?
Is there sufficiently rich exposure to language data through opportunities for extensive reading?
Do the materials provide for recycling of content, of vocabulary and structures?
Is allowance made for revision, testing and ongoing evaluation? Are self-checks provided?

Flexibility

Do the materials allow for flexible use of tasks/texts/activities, permitting them to be exploited or modified as required by local circumstances? Or is it too rigid in format, structure and approach?
Do they allow for alternative sequencing/routes/paths? Or is the order of activities in the curriculum and the pace at which they must be done quite fixed?
Do the materials make too many demands on teachers' preparation time?
Do the materials expect students to spend too much time on their homework?
Is there a wide range of supplementary materials and teaching aids available?

Educational Validity

Does the textbook accord with broader educational concerns (e.g., the nature and role of learning skills, concept development in younger learners, the function of 'knowledge of the world', etc.)?

For each of these criteria it is possible to grade a coursebook on a scale of 0–5, or 0–10 or even 0–20, depending on the relative weight the teacher evaluator would like to assign to it. It is possible to assign some of the categories relatively more weight than others. Further, evaluative comments under each subcategory, which may be treated as forming a complex of interacting criteria, should help provide a basis for a qualitative assessment to supplement the quantitative analysis.

Conclusion

There has been recent awareness that coursebook evaluation is not a straightforward exercise and that depending on its purpose and the context of use it can embrace different perspectives (prospective, ongoing and/or retrospective) and can be multidimensional (external and/or internal; static and/or dynamic).

Increasingly, there has also emerged the view that obtaining the perceptions of users (teachers and learners) as well as the analyst (whether the researcher or external evaluator, as the case may be) in the evaluation process is essential, that situational and syllabus requirements have to be considered and that claims made by materials writers have to be verified. There is also a recognition that there could be a thin line between attempts to provide teachers with a sense of confidence, security and guidance on the one hand and killing off the teachers' instinctive search for imaginative and intelligent solutions and creativity, on the other. These different perspectives inform the conceptualization of the multidimensional evaluation model presented above.

References

Alderson, J. C. and Beretta, A. (eds) (1992) *Evaluating Second Language Education.* Cambridge: Cambridge University Press.

Allwright, D. (1981) 'What do we want teaching materials for?' *ELT Journal,* **36** (1), 5–18.

Allwright, D. (1984) 'The importance of interaction in classroom language learning'. *Applied Linguistics,* **5**, 156–71.

Bell, J. and Gower, R. (1998) 'Writing course materials for the world: a great compromise', in B. Tomlinson (ed.) *Materials Development in Language Teaching.* Cambridge: Cambridge University Press, pp. 116–29.

Block, D. (1991) 'Some thoughts on DIY materials design'. *ELT Journal,* **45** (3), 211–17.

Breen, M. P. (1987) 'Learner contributions to task design', in C. N. Candlin and D. F. Murphy (eds) *Language Learning Tasks.* London: Prentice Hall.

Breen, M. P. (1989) 'The evaluation cycle for language learning tasks', in R. Johnson (ed.) *The Second Language Curriculum.* Cambridge: Cambridge University Press, pp. 187–206.

Breen, M. P. and Candlin, C. N. (1987) 'Which materials?: a consumer's and designer's guide', in L. E. Sheldon *ELT Textbooks and Materials: Problems in Evaluation and Development.* ELT Documents 126. London: Modern English Publications/The British Council, pp. 13–27.

Brumfit, C. J. (1980) 'Seven last slogans'. *Modern English Teacher,* **7** (1), 30–1.

Clarke, D. F. (1989) 'Materials adaptation: why leave it all to the teacher?' *ELT Journal,* **43** (2), 133–41.

Cunningsworth, A. (1984) *Evaluating and Selecting ELT Materials.* London: Heinemann.

Cunningsworth, A. (1995) *Choosing Your Coursebook.* Oxford: Heinemann.

Dubin, F. (1988) 'The roles of L2 teachers, learners, and materials developers in the context of new technologies', in B. K. Das *Materials for Language Learning and Teaching.* Singapore: RELC Anthology Series 22, pp. 129–36.

Edge, J. and Wharton, S. (1998) 'Autonomy and development: living in the materials world', in B. Tomlinson, (ed.) *Materials Development in Language Teaching.* Cambridge: Cambridge University Press, pp. 295–310.

Ellis, R. (1998) 'The evaluation of communicative tasks', in B. Tomlinson (ed.) *Materials Development in Language Teaching*. Cambridge: Cambridge University Press, pp. 217–38.

Greenall, S. (1992) 'Development and change in course design and textbooks – 10 years on', in D. A. Hill (ed.) *The State of the Art*. Basingstoke: Modern English Publications/The British Council.

Hall, D. R. (2001) 'Materials production: theory and practice', in D. R. Hall, and A. Hewings (eds) *Innovations in Language Teaching*. London: Routledge, pp. 229–39.

Hutchinson, T. (1987) 'What's underneath?: an interactive view of materials evaluation', in L. E. Sheldon (ed.) *ELT Textbooks and Materials: Problems in Evaluation and Development*. ELT Documents 126. London: Modern English Publications/The British Council.

Hutchinson, T. (1988) 'Making materials work in the ESP classroom', in D. Chamberlain and R. Baumgardner (eds) *ESP in the Classroom: Practice and Evaluation*. ELT Documents 128. London: Modern English Publications/The British Council.

Hutchinson, T. and Torres, E. (1994) 'The textbook as agent of change'. *ELT Journal*, **48** (4), 315–28.

Hutchinson, T. and Waters, A. (1987) *English for Specific Purposes: A Learning-Centred Approach*. Cambridge: Cambridge University Press.

Littlejohn, A. (1998) 'The analysis of language teaching materials: inside the Trojan Horse', in B. Tomlinson (ed.) *Materials Development in Language Teaching*. Cambridge: Cambridge University Press, pp. 190–216.

McDonough, J. and Shaw, C. (1993) *Materials and Methods in ELT*. Oxford: Blackwell.

Maley, A. (1998) 'Squaring the circle – reconciling materials as constraint with materials as empowerment', in B. Tomlinson, (ed.) *Materials Development in Language Teaching*. Cambridge: Cambridge University Press, pp. 279–94.

O'Neil, R. (1982) 'Why use textbooks?' *ELT Journal*, **36** (2), 104–11.

Prabhu, N. S. (1988) 'Materials as support, materials as constraint'. Paper presented at the Annual SEAMEO RELC Seminar on Materials for Language Learning and Teaching, April 1988.

Rea-Dickins, P. and Germaine, K. (1992) *Evaluation*. Oxford: Oxford University Press.

Richards, J. C. (1993) 'Beyond the textbook: the role of commercial materials in language teaching'. *RELC Journal*, Singapore, **24** (1), 1–14.

Riggenbach, H. (1988) 'Tapping a vital resource: student-generated materials', in B. K. Das, *Materials for Language Learning and Teaching*. Singapore: RELC Anthology Series 22, pp. 117–24.

Schon, D. (1983) *The Reflective Practitioner*. London: Temple Smith.

Sheldon, L. E. (1987) *ELT Textbooks and Materials: Problems in Evaluation and Development*. ELT Documents 126. London: Modern English Publications/The British Council.

Sheldon, L. E. (1988) 'Evaluation of ELT textbooks and materials'. *ELT Journal*, **42** (4), 237–46.

Tomlinson, B. (ed.) (1998) *Materials Development in Language Teaching*. Cambridge: Cambridge University Press.

Tucker, C. A. (1975) 'Evaluating beginning coursebooks'. *English Teaching Forum*, **12** (3–4), 355–61.

van Lier, L. (1979) 'Choosing a new EFL course'. *Mextesol Journal*, **3** (3), 2–140.

Weir, C. and Roberts, J. (1994) *Evaluation in ELT*. Oxford: Blackwell.

Widdowson, H. (1979) *Explorations in Applied Linguistics*. Oxford: Oxford University Press.

Williams, D. (1983) 'Developing criteria for textbook evaluation'. *ELT Journal*, **37** (30).

CHAPTER

3

A Coursebook is What It is because of What It has to Do: An Editor's Perspective

Duriya Aziz Singapore Wala

Introduction

Located precariously in the materials development cycle between publisher and writer(s), the development/design team and the writer(s) and the publisher and curriculum developers and teachers, the editor operates as the fulcrum of a materials development project, maintaining balance and ensuring that the project continues to progress towards publication. The editor functions as a filter and a crucial point of contact between content originated by the writers and its expression through layout, design, illustration, marketing and promotion. To function effectively, an editor needs to get under the skin of the project, to go beyond the surface of the text, to go past what the coursebook says to discover what it means. The editor needs to understand the kinds of functions a coursebook must perform in the context within which it will operate and he or she must also understand the kind of resources that can be employed meaningfully in order for these functions to be performed.

There are certain skills that are common and basic to all editors no matter which genre of publishing they operate in – these are basic copy and linguistic editing and people and project management skills. It is not my intention to focus on these in this chapter. In fact, the twelve-point guide 'How to Be the Ideal Editor' (O'Dell) (reproduced in Appendix 1 with permission from *Folio*) explains this more graphically and humorously. Instead, in this chapter I will attempt to relate some basic concepts of systemic functional linguistic theory (most often associated with the work of Michael Halliday and his colleagues) to ELT coursebooks in order to show how these concepts can help to understand better the roles and functions of a coursebook and the resources it can call upon to operate effectively within an accepted system and structure. Having introduced some of these concepts and related them to ELT coursebooks, the second part of the chapter will present an application of these concepts to the first level of four coursebooks that were produced as part of the materials development initiative in Singapore described in detail in Chapter 8 of this book.

While this chapter is largely retrospective, resulting from my experience of editing and developing coursebooks, as well as my exposure to functional linguistics, its applications are intended to be proactive.

The ELT Coursebook as a Communicative Act

A typical way of looking at a coursebook would be to see in what way and to what extent it addresses:

- Teachers' needs
- Learners' needs
- Syllabus outcomes/guidelines
- Publisher's needs
- Writer's needs

The needs that one prioritizes would of course depend on who one is and one's location on the materials development process.

One would ask questions such as: What approach and methodology does the book adopt? Who is the intended user? What is the scope and sequence of the course? Are the texts and tasks interesting? Appropriate? Effective? How are the learning outcomes achieved? How can they be assessed? Is the difficulty level of the texts and tasks appropriate to the target learners? And so on. One would take into consideration aspects such as the specifications – number of pages, size, quality of paper, design and layout, price – and availability of other components of the packages such as CDs, workbooks, teacher guides and other resources.

However, there is a need to go beyond a mere listing of the presence or absence of these features and attributes to consider what their presence or absence means. How are these various features and attributes organized and structured to create meaning? What kind of meaning does it create? What language does the coursebook speak? Essentially, a coursebook is a collection of choices made from a variety of options available. The choices made are meaningful. An important aspect of meaning being communicated by the coursebook is to consider what the coursebook is saying about:

- the teacher;
- the learner;
- itself;
- English and learning English.

What means does the coursebook employ, wittingly and unwittingly, to convey these meanings?

Why should we bother to think about the coursebook in this way? The coursebook can be considered a communicative act of itself but it is also a dynamic artefact that contributes to and creates meaning together with other participants in the context of language teaching. Just as language does not exist of and by itself

– we do not talk just for the sake of talking, but rather to communicate meaning –
so too the coursebook – it does not exist for its own sake. The coursebook fulfils a
need, a purpose, it performs a function, conveys meaning. It is important for the
developers of the materials to be aware of the need, purpose, function and
meaning so that appropriate and adequate resources may be employed to address
and convey them. If we look at a coursebook as a semiotic system, we begin to see
that it is structured along various levels to create meaning through the selection of
resources from various options available to perform specific functions in specific
contexts. This section explores, albeit at a very elementary level:

1. the notion of the ELT coursebook as a communicative act,
2. the potential for functions to be performed and meanings to be communicated by an ELT coursebook.

In order to do this, some functional questions are asked of the ELT coursebook
using terminology and concepts originally coined for use by systemic functional
linguists looking to draw semantic and functional maps upon language use. In
Halliday's words, 'Language is as it is because of what it has to do' (1978: 19).
Following this view, the choice of linguistic sign, the word and the ways in which
words are combined in the clause, are related to the function(s) to which the
language is being put. The explanation can be extended to understand coursebooks. If we take the perspective that a coursebook (or any other materials, for
that matter) is the way it is because of what it has to do, it opens up a new vantage
point from which to explore the materials development exercise – a coursebook is
as it is because of what it has to do. So whether a coursebook is one colour or two
colours, whether it adopts a thematic or structural approach, whether it 'is' at all
is a reflection of what it has to do. And, just as language becomes dysfunctional
and communication breaks down when inadequate or inappropriate resources
(linguistic and otherwise) are employed to convey meaning, so, too, a coursebook
fails to convey its meaning and perform its function when adequate or appropriate resources fail to be employed. Such a perspective provides a more functionally focused way of reviewing or evaluating coursebooks where the questions
the reviewer asks of the book are twofold – How 'is' the book? What does the book
have to do? And what is the correlation between the two?

Functional linguistics further qualifies that the meanings we ascribe to language are socially constructed and negotiated, or, in Halliday's words, 'The
particular form taken by the grammatical system of language is closely related to
the social and personal needs that language is required to serve' (Halliday, 1970:
142). This means that language and, by extension to our case, coursebooks, do
not exist in a vacuum – they exist for and are shaped by a purpose within a
particular context of use, culture and ideology.

When asking functional questions about coursebooks, we must not focus just
upon coursebooks but upon their contexts as well. Functional grammarians
identify three contexts of use within which language operates – those of situation,
culture and ideology. The same can be applied to coursebooks as well. The

coursebook forms a response to a complex social need that is constructed by the pedagogical situation in which it is produced. The principal constituent of this pedagogical situation is the students' need, or perceived need, for a simplified compendium of knowledge (whether knowledge of 'facts' or of generalized advice on matters such as writing processes). The social knowledge that constitutes this need is shared by teachers and students, who participate together in the social conditions of its construction: the classroom environment.

Register theory describes the impact of dimensions of the immediate context of situation of a language event on the way language is used. These dimensions exist in the context of situation for coursebooks as well. Three key dimensions of the situations are identified as having significant and identifiable impacts on language use. These three dimensions, the register variables of mode (amount of feedback and role of language/coursebook), tenor (role relations of power and solidarity between speaker/listener and, in our case between coursebook and teacher/learner) and field (topic or focus of activity), can be used to explain why language is, or, in our case, the coursebook is, the way it is.

The concept of genre can be used to describe the context of culture for coursebooks, by exploring the staged, step-by-step structure cultures institutionalize as ways of achieving goals. Genre is more than a set of recognizable formal features. As defined by Pare and Smart, it is 'a distinctive profile of regularities across four dimensions: a set of texts, the composing processes involved in creating these texts, the reading practices used to interpret them, and the social roles performed by readers and writers'. It is these roles and composing and reading processes, not the surface features, that really tell us what a coursebook is. The genre arises from the situation, not vice versa. If we wish to change the genre of the coursebook, we must do so by changing the elements of the situation that reproduces it. Editors and other materials developers must be knowledgeable, therefore, about the situation within which the coursebook will operate and the situation that gave rise to the particular genre of coursebook in the first place. Whether the dominant model of the classroom is that of a knowledge-reception or a knowledge-making model will have implications for the final manifestation of the coursebook. And, looking at a coursebook, one can predict the model on which the language teaching context will operate. The implications for this for editors are that they must be well aware of the context of use as well as the correlation of this to materials design.

The role and function of materials in a language curriculum system is defined with respect to content (the syllabus) and with respect to learner and teacher roles (Richards and Rodgers, 1997). While the syllabus defines the linguistic content in terms of language elements, specifies the selection and ordering of particular language items to be taught that represent the elements and defines the goals for language learning, 'the instructional materials ... specify subject matter content ... define or suggest the intensity of coverage for particular syllabus items ... and define (or imply) the day-to-day learning objectives that (should) collectively constitute the goals of the syllabus' (Richards and Rodgers, 1997: 25).

The role of a coursebook reflects or must reflect decisions concerning its primary goal and form, the relation the coursebook holds to other sources of input and the abilities of the teacher. A particular design for an instructional system may imply a particular set of roles for instructional materials in support of the syllabus and the teachers and learners (Richards and Rodgers, 1997: 25). Thus, a coursebook must take into consideration not just the learning outcomes and aims and objectives defined by the syllabus, it must also be informed by teacher needs and abilities and the context of teaching in the classroom. This context will shape its form or genre.

Editors must recognize (and advise their teams accordingly) that, if coursebooks try to be the medium for forcing top-down change, they are likely to fail both commercially and educationally – 'It is a basic principle of all writing that writers should take their readers into account ... coursebook authors must: take teacher's current views and skills seriously; recognise the practical opportunities and drawbacks of any innovation, not only on learners but on teachers and educational institutions; anticipate change by a gradual movement towards new ways of looking at language' (Hopkins, 1994: 14).

A higher level of context is the level of ideology. Whatever genre we are involved in, and whatever the register of the situation, our use of language will also be influenced by our ideological positions: the values we hold (consciously and unconsciously), the biases and perspectives we adopt. The 'hidden curriculum' (Cunningsworth, 1995) that forms part of any educational programme is unstated and undisclosed. Coursebooks will, directly or indirectly, communicate sets of social and cultural values that are inherent in their make-up. A curriculum (and teaching materials form part of this) cannot be neutral because it has to reflect a view of social order and express a value system implicitly or explicitly (Cunningsworth, 1995: 90).

On account of this ideological aspect which is not immediately evident, the editor and other materials developers need to read critically their coursebook to unearth what some of its unstated values are. While this aspect of materials development and evaluation takes a different perspective from that of language content or methodology, it is at least as important because the value system encoded in a coursebook can influence the perceptions and attitudes of learners, generally, and towards learning English, in particular. These concerns about the hidden curriculum and the ideological implications of materials design have significance for materials developers, as materials for language teaching must take into account not only content and methodology but, equally significantly, cultural and ideological factors and their representations. Ideology is implicit and complicit in the texts chosen as well as the choice of texts, in the tasks prescribed and the positioning of the teacher and learner.

Following the discussion above, in the process of planning and development, editors and other materials developers must ask the following questions of coursebooks:

- How do learners (and teachers) use coursebooks?
- How is the coursebook structured for use?

- What is the context in which the coursebook will be used?
- What dimensions of context have an impact on coursebook use?
- Which aspects of the coursebook and its use will be affected by particular dimensions of the context?
- What view of the world, of English, of learning English, of the teacher and of the learner is presented explicitly and implicitly by the coursebook?

Just as in language, a functional perspective would say that meanings are realized through words and structures that are in turn realized through sounds and letters, in coursebooks, syllabus objectives are realized through a scope and sequence which are in turn realized through a methodology for language teaching that underlies unit and task design and text selection.

Just as in language, the three levels of operation presented in Figure 3.1 relate to each other systematically and systemically and yet within each level, they also operate on a structured system governed by rules based on their function, so, too, each level of the coursebook must relate to the other systematically and systemically and, within the level itself, be governed by its own rules for structure and function.

Let us now venture further into the exploration of the ELT coursebook using a functional perspective to explore the kinds of meaning a coursebook communicates in the contexts within which it operates and the levels along which it is structured. Any semiotic mode develops resources for fulfilling three kinds of broad communicative functions (metafunctions in Halliday's terminology) or for making three main kinds of meaning simultaneously – ideational, interpersonal and textual.

	LANGUAGE	COURSEBOOKS
CONTENT	Semantics (meanings)	Syllabus objectives/ outcomes
	Lexicogrammar (words and structures)	Scope and sequence
EXPRESSION	Phonology/graphology Sounds/letters	Methodology for language teaching

Figure 3.1 Three levels of operation

The Ideational Metafunction

The first of these functions, the 'ideational', is based on the informative properties inherent in language by representing the values and knowledge shared by
the communicators. This is the realization of the 'field' of discourse circum-
scribing what the speakers are 'engaged in doing' (Halliday, 1978: 222). By
predominantly influencing the actual content of the speech event, it will manifest
itself mainly in the lexicogrammatical options chosen.

In the context of the coursebook, the ideational metafunction would be the
actual content that the coursebook has to convey – topics, themes, grammar rules
and conventions of usage, etc. Curriculum developers want the content to cover
all the items listed in the syllabus. Teachers want the content to be sufficient to
teach language effectively and adequately and prepare the learners for the exams.
Publishers want the range of topics, themes, items and others features covered to
be one that will meet approval from both curriculum developers/reviewing
authorities as well as teachers. Writers want, in addition to the content prescribed
by the syllabus, to be able to include their own favourite topics, themes or items or
at least those that they are convinced will be useful to the teacher and learner.

The Interpersonal Metafunction

The 'interpersonal' metafunction comprises uses of language representative of
'social and personal relations' (Halliday, 1973: 40), and is connected with the
'tenor' of discourse as determined by the roles assumed by, or assigned to, the
interlocutors. Thus, statements may be expressed as affirmations in the indicative
(mode) or assumptions may be expressed tentatively in the conditional (mode)
or by being put as questions, i.e., the choice of 'mood' and 'of modality' is
affected (Halliday, 1978: 223).

In the context of the coursebook, the interpersonal function is performed by
the narratorial voice and the positioning of the teachers and learners vis-à-vis the
the coursebook narratorial voice. Does the coursebook 'tell' the teacher and
learner what to learn or do or does it allow discovery and exercising of options
and making choices? Does the coursebook engage the learner as an equal,
allowing him or her to participate in the creation of knowledge or is it a passive
knowledge-reception model along which the coursebook operates? Do the tasks
and activities address the learner directly using the imperative form or is the third
person used? What does the use or absence of illustrations say about how the
coursebook positions the learner? How does the coursebook design and layout
position the learner?

The Textual Metafunction

The 'textual' function, finally, ensures the effectiveness of a communicative act by
providing a texture incorporating the 'remaining strands of meaning potential'
'into the fabric of linguistic structure' (Halliday, 1973: 42). On the corresponding

level of the 'context as a semiotic construct' (Halliday, 1978: 189), the 'mode' of discourse represents 'a particular rhetorical channel', which is chosen in relation to the function a speech act has to fulfil, and is thus responsible for achieving coherence in a text (cf. Halliday, 1978: 223). Without the cohesion thus achieved, Halliday claims that 'the remainder of the semantic system cannot be effectively activated at all' (Halliday, 1976: 27).

In relation to the coursebook we can ask how the ideational and interpersonal aspects of meaning come together to form a coherent whole in the materials. The structure and organization of the book as a whole as well as its component units, the relation between the various tasks and texts, the design of the book, the use of icons and other signifiers all help the coursebook to cohere, or come together.

When we look at the coursebook as a semantic system, we begin to understand it as a system organized as sets of choices. Each choice in the system acquires its meanings against the backdrop of other choices which could have been made. This semiotic interpretation of the 'system' of a coursebook allows us to consider the appropriacy or inappropriacy of different choices of resources within the coursebook at various levels, in relation to their contexts of use. While none of these decisions will be made by the editor (or anyone else, for that matter) in isolation, the other stakeholders in these decisions will have other emphases. Publishers will be interested in minimizing costs and maximizing profits. Writers will be complicit with the ideology of their approach and method and will want to the pursue it. It is the editor, therefore, who must be able to visualize how the three metafunctions can come together coherently in a manner in which the agendas of the various stakeholders are satisfactorily addressed.

Following the discussion above, an editor can ask the following questions of the coursebook planned or being developed:

- What are the resources available for making meaning? How are they being used?
- What are the different meanings that are being conveyed simultaneously through the various choices that have been made?
- Is there congruence between the meanings conveyed by the resources chosen and the objectives or intentions of the materials developers?
- How can resources be chosen more effectively to convey meaning?

Each of these rather abstract points will now be illustrated with examples from five ELT coursebooks developed as part of the materials development exercise described in Chapter 8 of this book.

From Theory to Analysis

Let us first identify the contexts of use of ELT coursebooks using examples from *English For Life 1, The Odyssey 1, Eureka! 1, Step Ahead 1* and *English Expressions 1.*

These coursebooks were published in Singapore in 2001 as part of a new initiative by the Ministry of Education.

If we take the view that the coursebooks form a response to a complex social need that is constructed by the pedagogical situation in which they are produced, and bear in mind the process that leads to their being adopted by teachers for use in schools – approval by the Ministry of Education and selection by teachers – we begin to understand why each of these coursebooks is the way it 'is'. In order to gain the coveted approval from the Ministry, different ways of meeting the criteria listed in the syllabus are evident in these coursebooks. For example, developing creative and critical thinking skills in pupils is an important initiative and this is addressed by having sections that focus on thinking in each unit of the various books – Think Tank (*The Odyssey 1*), Thinking Skills (*Step Ahead 1*), Smart Starts (*Eureka! 1*), Thinking (*English Expressions 1*).

The immediate context of situation of use also affects the way a coursebook is. English language teachers in Singapore have to use these coursebooks in order to achieve the outcomes defined by a new syllabus. Among these outcomes is an understanding of the structure and function of text types and critical literacy in terms of sensitivity to purpose, audience and context. There is also an increased emphasis on the use of information technology in ELT. These concerns have shaped the mode of the coursebook in that the coursebooks are more task based and geared towards independent learning with the teacher acting more as a facilitator. The coursebook is no longer a repository of knowledge but more of a manual on how to acquire the linguistic knowledge outlined in the scope and sequence. However, teachers still need a certain 'comfort level', hence course-books such as *Step Ahead 1* still include some measure of 'teaching' or 'telling' of linguistic knowledge – explanations of the structure and function of various grammatical and discourse features rather than a more discovery-based approach.

The impact of the dimension of tenor within the context of situation – role relations of power and solidarity between coursebook and teacher/learner and between teacher and reader is evident in the coursebooks in different ways and to different extents. An example to illustrate this would be the introduction to the reading texts in different coursebooks. *Step Ahead 1* (p. 37) introduces a reading text thus:

> The following passage is from *Penny Pollard's Letters,* a fictional collection of letters written by a young girl named Penny Pollard ...
> Penny uses many casual words in her letter, and she writes as if she were simply recording her thoughts. This style reflects her open and cheerful personality. In the following passage, Penny tells her friend Mrs Bettany about what happened when she had to take care of baby Lisa for a day. (Jones and Mann, 2001)

English Expressions 1 introduces a reading task thus:

> Have you ever thought that being crazy could benefit the world?

A group of comedians in England had this idea and they started Comic Relief, a charity to help the poor all over the world...
Read their appeal on the Internet in preparation for Red Nose Day 1999. Red Nose Day is a 'crazy' event organized by Comic Relief every two years. Look for ways in which they try to persuade people to take part. (Davis and Tup, 2001)

Comparing the two introductions, it is easy to see that the writers of the first wish to remain in control, since they tell the readers exactly what to expect ('In the following passage, Penny tells her friend Mrs Bettany about what happened when she had to take care of baby Lisa for a day ...') and what to find ('many casual words in her letter, and she writes as if she were simply recording her thoughts ...'). The teacher and learner are positioned as being relatively powerless. On the other hand, in the second introduction, the learner is invited to interact with the text by seeking their personal response and past experience('Have you ever thought that being crazy could benefit the world?') and by allowing them to engage with the text to make their own discoveries and learn independently ('Look for ways in which they try to persuade people to take part.'). The coursebook engages the learner and the teacher in a more equal relationship, though of course it still identifies the parameters of the reading task ('ways in which they try to persuade people ...').

The third dimension of context of situation, field – topic or focus of activity – sheds further light on why the coursebook is the way it is. A quick and easy way to analyse field would be to look at the unit headings of each book. Unit 1 in each book is headed thus: 'Me and my friends' (*English Expressions 1*), 'The Attractions of Singapore' (*English for Life 1*), 'Links' (*Eureka! 1*), 'Instructions' (*Step Ahead 1*) and 'This is a true story ...' (*The Odyssey 1*). The first three coursebooks emphasize the thematic content of the unit, the last two highlight the text type the unit focuses on. And these reflect the major preoccupation of the unit, its organizing principle and that of its tasks and activities.

Identifying the features of the coursebook that relate them as belonging to a particular genre enables us to describe the context of culture for coursebooks. Again, exploring the five coursebooks used, certain features are apparent – the organization of the books into units, declaration of objectives and outcomes at the outset of each unit, the use of icons and division of the units into neat sections. However, genre is more than a set of recognizable formal features. The regularities across dimensions imply and reflect the assumptions made of and during the composing processes involved in creating these texts, the reading practices used to interpret them and the social roles performed by teachers and learners. It is these roles and processes and not the surface features that really tell us what a coursebook is. The genre arises from the situation, not vice versa. It is because of the emphasis on preparation for examination, for example, that almost all the coursebooks have O-level-exam-style comprehension activities in the related workbooks. If such a focus on examinations in the coursebook is not considered desirable, then it needs to be addressed at the systemic level – the curriculum should not emphasize the exams too much. In the end, the genre of the coursebook is made by and is a reflection of the culture within which it exists and not vice versa.

Applying the three levels at which a coursebook operates functionally to a unit in *The Odyssey 1* we find the following, as set out in figure 3.2. This operational framework can (and should) be applied to any and all units of the coursebooks to ensure that there is a neat fit.

An analysis of the five coursebooks shows that the contents of the books are fairly similar. This is because they primarily perform the same ideational function – to address the outcomes outlined in the syllabus. The interpersonal function performed can be seen from the tenor of the coursebooks – their positioning vis-à-vis the teacher and learner. This is often evidenced in the grammatical struc-turing in the narratorial voice of the coursebook. *English for Life 1*, for example, often uses the phrases 'as you read' and 'decide …' to frame its activities and tasks. This not only addresses and engages the reader directly, it also puts him or her in a position of power by allowing him or her to make the choice. Such

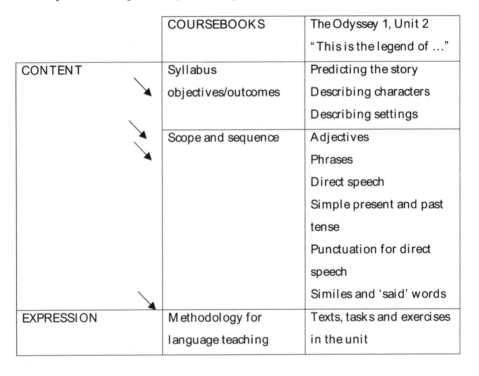

Figure 3.2 The three functional levels of a coursebook

activities which require the reader to make a choice as to what to do or how to proceed imply a more equal relationship as opposed to a more unequal rela-tionship implied by rubrics such as 'Answer these questions to learn more about *Stone Soup: A Russian Folktale.*' *(Step Ahead 1*, p. 69) and 'In this exercise you will evaluate the truth of the proverbs by following these steps …' (*ibid.*, p. 75).

The textual function operates in the form of discourse markers and cohesive devices within the coursebook and within each unit to ensure fluidity between the interpersonal and ideational functions so that the teacher and learner essentially knows what to do and when. Using boxes and borders to highlight examples and structure as *Step Ahead 1* does clearly indicate to the learner how to access that information in respect to the rest of the text. Use of different colours, fonts and typefaces, icons and subheadings and other such headings also perform the textual metafunction to indicate a development or stage in a sequence and its relation to the rest of the text.

Conclusion

This chapter has been an attempt to apply some basic concepts of functional linguistics to the ELT coursebook with a view to seeing how a coursebook is more than just a collection of linguistic items – it is a reflection of a particular world-view based on the selection of resources. An understanding of the system of choices and resources available will enable the editor (and any other materials developer) not just to select resources more effectively but also to understand better what a particular selection or choice reflects or implies.

References

Beaugrande, R. (1991) *Linguistic Theory: The Discourse of Fundamental Works*. Harlow: Longman.

Bell, J. and Gower, R. (1998) 'Writing course materials for the world: a great compromise', in B. Tomlinson (ed.) *Materials Development in Language Teaching*. Cambridge: Cambridge University Press, pp. 116–29.

Blake, M. E. (2001) *Eureka! Interactive English for Secondary Levels*. Coursebook 1A. Singapore: SNP Education Pte Ltd.

Brent, D. (1994) 'Writing classes, writing genres, and writing textbooks'. *Textual Studies in Canada*, **4**.

Chan, P., Kwa, N. and Khoo-Wang, S. (2001) *English for Secondary 1 – The Odyssey*. Longman: Singapore.

Chandler, D. (1994) *Semiotics for Beginners*. URL: *http://www.aber.ac.uk/gc/semiotic.html*

Cobley, P. (ed.) (1996) *The Communication Theory Reader*. London: Routledge.

Cunningsworth, A. (1995) *Choosing Your Coursebook*. Oxford: Heinemann.

Curriculum Planning and Development Division, Ministry of Education (2001). *English Language Syllabus 2001 – For Primary and Secondary Schools*.

Davis, C. W. and Tup, F. (2001) *English Expressions for Secondary 1*. Singapore: Oxford University Press.

Eggins, S. (1999) *An Introduction to Systemic Functional Linguistics*. London: Pinter.

Fiske, J. (1982) *Introduction to Communication Studies* (2nd edn.). London: Routledge.

Goodman, S. (1996) *Visual English*, in S. Goodman and D. Graddol (eds) *Redesigning English: New Texts, New Identities*. London: Routledge.

Hall, S. (ed.) (1997) *Representation: Cultural Representations and Signifying Practices*. London: Sage.

Halliday, M. (1973) *Explorations in the Function of Language*. London: Edward Arnold.

Halliday, M. (1978) *Language as Social Semiotic*. London: Edward Arnold.

Halliday, M. (1985) *An Introduction to Functional Grammar*. London: Edward Arnold.

Halliday, M. and Hassan, R. (1976) *Cohesion in English*. London: Longman.

Harmer, J. (1997) 'Classrooms in my mind'. *Folio*, July 1997, **4** (1), 33–5.

Hopkins, A. (1995) *Modern English Teacher*, **4** (3).

Hughes, P. (1973) *The Teacher's Role in Curriculum Design*. Sydney: Angus and Robertson Publishers.

Jolly, D. and Bolitho, R. (1998) 'A framework for materials writing', in B. Tomlinson (ed.) *Materials Development in Language Teaching*. Cambridge: Cambridge University Press, pp. 90–115.

Jones, H. and Mann, R. (2001) *Step Ahead. Textbook for Secondary 1*. Singapore: Pan Pacific Publications.

Kress, G. and Van Leeuwen, T. (1990) *Reading Images: The Grammar of Visual Design*. London: Routledge.

Ministry of Education (Singapore). *Approved Textbook List. http://nsinte1. moe.edu.sg/project/db/atl/db_puatl.nsf/*

Ministry of Education (Singapore) Curriculum Planning & Development Division. *http://www1.moe.edu.sg/cpdd.htm*

Ministry of Education (Singapore) *Education in Singapore. http://www1.moe. edu.sg/educatio.htm*

Ministry of Education (Singapore), External Review Team (1997) 'Learning, creating, communicating: a curriculum review'. *http://www1.moe.edu.sg/Speeches/Curry%20Revue%20Report.htm*

Ministry of Education (1998a) 'Educational publishers to play bigger role in producing instructional materials for schools'. Press release dated 4 February 1998. Reference No: Edun 25–02–008. *http://www1.moe.edu.sg/Press/980204.htm*

Ministry of Education (1998b) 'Ministry of Education's response to the External Curriculum Review Report'. Press release dated 21 March 1998. Reference No: Edun N25–02–004. *http://www1.moe.edu.sg/Press/980321.htm*

Ministry of Education (1998c) 'Educational publishers to play bigger role in producing instructional materials for schools'. Press release dated 16 July 1998. Reference No: Edun N25–02–004. *http://www1.moe.edu.sg/Press/980716.htm*

Ministry of Education. *Publishing School Textbooks – Frequently Asked Questions. http://www1.moe.edu.sg/cpdd/faq.htm*

Pare, A. and Smart, G. (forthcoming) 'Written genre: A profile of regularities across texts, composing processes, reading practices, and social roles'. Forthcoming in the proceedings of the 'Rethinking Genres' colloquium, Carlton University, April 1992.

Richards, J. C. (1995a) *The Context of Language Teaching.* Cambridge: Cambridge University Press.

Richards, J. C. (1995b) 'Easier said than done: an insider's account of a textbook project', in A. C. Hidalgo, D. Hall, and G. M. Jacobs, (eds) *Getting Started: Materials writers on materials writing.* Singapore: SEAMEO Regional Language Centre, pp. 95–135.

Richards, J. C. (1995c) *The Language Teaching Matrix.* Cambridge: Cambridge University Press.

Richards, J. C. and Rodgers, T. S. (1997) *Approaches and Methods in Language Teaching.* Cambridge: Cambridge University Press.

Saussure, Ferdinand de (1974) *Course in General Linguistics.* Glasgow: Fontana.

Singapore Wala, D. A. (2001) 'The role of teacher feedback in developing instructional materials for teaching english for secondary one'. Unpublished MA Thesis, National University of Singapore.

Thompson, G. (1996) *Introducing Functional Grammar.* London: Arnold.

Tomlinson, B. (ed.) (1998) *Materials Development in Language Teaching.* Cambridge: Cambridge University Press.

Tomlinson, B., Hill, D. A. and Masuhara, H. (2001) *English for Life Coursebook for Secondary 1.* Singapore: Times Media Publishers.

4

Adapting Courses: A Critical View

Claudia Saraceni

Is there a discrepancy between what the students are asked to do in published materials and what happens in real-life language use?
Why is it so difficult to find an adequate and effective coursebook/set of materials for language learning and teaching?
What makes so many coursebooks so repetitive in content and different only in superficial visual impact?
Why is learning a foreign language so stressful for so many people?

Introduction: A Personal View

The conventional approach to materials adaptation can involve many changes to the materials, such as, for example, deleting, reordering, adding, etc. This currently seems to be a widely accepted practice; however, this chapter attempts to put such a process into question, and subsequently to propose a different and somewhat more *radical* view on adapting courses. Research in L2 (foreign and/or second language) learning and acquisition processes has been carried out for decades; innovative ideas in L2 teaching methodology and approaches have been put forward and developed for a long time. However, there seems to be a wide mismatch between such research findings and hypotheses and actual practice in many coursebooks and published materials. 'Many think that there is ... a mismatch between some of the pedagogic procedures of current textbooks and what second language acquisition researchers have discovered about the process of learning a second or foreign language' (Tomlinson, 1998). Perhaps one of the most commonly found activities in coursebooks/published materials is represented by those aiming at practising new grammatical features and testing comprehension. Filling the gaps exercises and reading comprehension tests are only a few examples. It is this type of practice which is extensively present in published materials but, due to its very nature, is based on early production of the target language and so it does not reflect the findings of research in this field. Foreign language teachers are then faced with the problem of either using the published materials as they are, or producing their own set of teaching materials. Both of these choices, in my opinion, have certain drawbacks: the first is in contrast with the very objective of this chapter and with the main objective of the majority of materials developers (the attempt to reduce the distance between research and classroom practice); the second presents various problems, the main one being the fact that it is very time-consuming. It is in this context that I am considering the role and importance of materials adaptation which, in my opinion, appears to be the only realistically feasible option for the practicality and limitations of the classroom reality. This chapter attempts, in fact, to bridge the gap between the theories of L2 research and the practice of language teaching and learning, proposing the adaptation of courses as the key to achieving this aim.

At the moment, the process of materials adaptation is, in the great majority of cases, left in the teachers' hands, and it is largely based simply on their intuition and experience. However, having assessed the importance of materials adaptation as probably the most relevant and useful link between the reality of the language classroom and the research findings, there is obviously a great need to develop further such a process and put into practice those theories and ideas in a more systematic manner, particularly as far as published materials are concerned. Despite the fact that adapting materials seems to be a relatively underresearched process, it is always carried out in the classroom, to different extents, by the teachers. The simple fact of using a piece of teaching/learning material in the classroom inevitably means adapting it to the particular needs of the whole classroom environment by the very process of using it: 'the good teacher is constantly adapting' (Madsen and Bowen, 1978).

Given all the above issues, on the one hand it becomes evident that adaptation is a vital step towards the production of innovative, effective and, most of all, learner-centred/classroom-centred materials. On the other hand, the very process of adaptation itself needs to be put into question since, in my opinion, it apparently presents various contradictions and contrasting points and practices.

Adaptation as Awareness Development

The Role of the Learner in the Adaptation Process

Research has for decades stressed the importance of the learner's role in the learning process; many areas of research since the 1970s have explored and described extensively the advantages of learner involvement in programme design, methodology, materials selection and adaptation (Clarke, 1989). However, learners are traditionally left with a rather passive role in the classroom particularly as far as adapting courses is concerned – 'learner-underinvolvement' (Allwright, 1978). On the other hand, in my opinion, such discrepancy is only apparent because many researchers have actually stressed such a role but at the same time many of them either have not proposed a clear way of putting it into practice or they have provided rather superficial and somewhat contradictory ideas on how to give the learners an active role in the adaptation process. Moreover, such ideas for adapting materials are very often based on language practice and manipulation which, although very extensively used in published materials, do not have any base in research and, in my opinion, are rather ineffective and add to the undue stress of the language learning process. Clarke (1989) provides a typical example of this argument: he acknowledges the importance of the learner's involvement in the adaptation process but proposes such tasks as substitution tables as a way of adapting classroom materials. However, he writes about what he calls a *Negotiated Syllabus* which is *internally generated*, the product of the negotiation between teacher and students, and an *Externally Imposed Syllabus*, which is the syllabus imposed by an external body such as the teacher, an institution or any other administrative authority. There is, however, a fine line between the *Negotiated Syllabus* and the *Externally Imposed Syllabus* in the sense that the former turns out very often to also be an imposed syllabus, *imposed* on the learners by the teacher as the main figure who carries out the adaptation of courses.

If we write about the learner's more *active* role in the adaptation process and his/her *negotiation* with the teacher, we are assuming that the syllabus is the product of the cooperation between the teacher and the learners. In this case, the teacher's input very often tends to become the dominant one, accepted by the learners as the 'right one' and the one to follow. The teacher's adaptation is inevitably the one that receives more space over the learners' one, which is very often perceived to be 'wrong'. To a large extent, the learners are given imposed materials from the teacher, hence their role in the learning process is still rather limited and not truly learner-centred. This idea still comes from the traditional image of teachers feeding knowledge to the class from a higher standpoint. However, this chapter advocates a somewhat different role of the learners and of the teachers. The teaching and learning context should be considered as a whole, whereby we talk about *learner's empowerment* rather than *learner's involvement* (Maley in Tomlinson, 1998: 279–94), and both the teachers and the learners are in a process of developing awareness of learning and teaching through adapting and evaluating courses. The learners become, eventually, the main input providers whereas the teacher's role is simply that of facilitator. These exercises are useful for the teacher and the learners to gain an insight into the principles of language learning and materials design, hence the learners can become aware of their own learning process and learning style. Gradually, such development aims, therefore, at achieving learner independence in a situation where the teachers become totally redundant which, in my opinion, should be the ultimate aim of language teaching as well as of education as a whole.

A Model for Adapting Courses

The process of adaptation of courses is based on an initial evaluation, which should be carried out by the learners, as this chapter advocates. Moreover, if, on the one hand, adapting becomes a responsibility of the learners, on the other hand, this chapter also promotes an alternative approach to the adaptation process, as explained later. Published materials present a kind of paradox: in the majority of cases, in an attempt to cater for all the learning styles and needs, they become rather superficial, non-participatory and based on rather trivial topics. This makes learners feel diminished and reduces their motivation. In a few other cases, the materials tend to focus on such specific needs, styles and interests that they become restricted and can only be effective and useful for a limited group of learners without much flexibility and choice. In my opinion, such contrasting points can be overcome partly by making the materials universally appealing. This can be achieved by leaving part of the responsibility of adapting courses to the materials developers themselves by writing materials with the specific aim of facilitating the inevitable adaptation process: materials purposely designed to be adapted later by their users. In the traditional approach to materials writing, where the whole structure is designed in a very prescriptive way, learners have to follow activities in a specifically ordered manner for the unit to achieve its aims and objectives. Such order and approach should be broken and replaced by a set of materials much more flexible and open to different interpretations and *adaptations* by the learners. Such an alternative approach can be considered a way to make materials more relevant to a wider group of learners without the risk of making them superficial and trivial.

List of Key Features in Materials Adaptation

Rather than a list of criteria for evaluating and adapting, which would be too general and superficial, and in contradiction with the very argument of this chapter, the following is a list of basic key points to take into account when evaluating and adapting courses. These can be used as a proposal to be developed further and adapted to different classroom situations.

Learner-centred
There is a large amount of literature on learner-centred approaches and principles. However, there are very few language teaching and learning materials which, in my opinion, are truly *learner-centred* in the sense that their aims are the development of the learner's awareness (Carter, 1993) of the learning process, linguistic empowerment and therefore learning independence. The materials should put learners at the centre of the learning process and make them the main input providers (hence the ones who adapt the materials), whereas teachers and/ or materials should represent the facilitators of language learning and should provide a mere stimulus, a starting point, for language exposure as well as for different approaches. Materials should, therefore, be written to facilitate adaptation, which should be left mainly in the hands of learners.

Flexibility and Choice
Materials should be flexible in the sense that they should provide learners with the possibility of choosing different activities, tasks, projects and approaches, and therefore of adapting the materials to their own preferred learning needs. At the same time, however, given the fact that the majority of learners, sadly, are not used to this type of approach, they should also be exposed to a variety of different activities and approaches so that they themselves become more flexible, having experienced different ways of learning. Materials, then, should, on the one hand, provide choice but, on the other hand, should also enable learners to develop a variety of skills and learning styles by encouraging them to be exposed to and

choose to experience a wide range of tasks and approaches so that they may become more independent learners. The materials can, for example, include a choice of tasks ranging from analytical ones (such as those based on grammatical awareness) to more creative ones (such as those based on creative writing). The learners can be encouraged to experience them all at one point and then also to make their choice at a later stage.

Open-ended

Aesthetic Experience is an idea which originated from the theory of Aesthetic Response as put forward by Rosenblatt (1968). It refers to the process of reacting spontaneously when reading literature, hence it involves interaction with language and texts. Some of the major elements of such types of experiential response, such as the voice of the narrator and the voice of the reader, as well as the role of the receiver and the one of the producer of the literary input, become overlapping and interchangeable. Aesthetic Experience, therefore, typically represents the immediate response to language and literature *experienced* by the receiver and the producer, as well as their later interpretations and reactions. Literature and Aesthetic Experience are inevitably part of a subjective process which is created every time the text is read or written. The literary process is always different: we have different reactions every time we *aesthetically experience* a poem, a novel, etc. (Saraceni, 2000).

One of the most significant points of *Aesthetic Experience* (Rosenblatt, 1968; Saraceni, 2000) refers to the fact that such experience promotes the subjectivity of materials and their various interpretations. The materials are not based on right/wrong testing and practice but, rather, they are open to many different ideas and points of view; they actually encourage a variety of interpretations and are written with the main purpose of promoting subjectivity of response, whether this be to a reading text or a listening one. If materials present *open spaces* or *gaps* (Eco, 1994), they allow learners to form their own interpretations and ideas and therefore to take control of the adaptation process. In this context, the aim of materials moves from comprehension testing, which allows only a rather superficial intake of the input, towards a deeper understanding and awareness of the language exposure, with the emphasis on individual differences. If materials allow only one right answer, they do not leave space for adaptation, whereas if they are open-ended they can become more relevant to learners thanks to their adaptations (see activity No. 5 of the example of materials provided later on in this chapter).

Relevant

In an attempt to draw a link between the adaptation process and the reading process, materials left open-ended, as explained above, become relevant to learners when they fill those gaps and open spaces with their ideas, interpretations and discussions. It is only at this level that materials acquire significance and become potentially beneficial for the learners. It is, in fact, by virtue of such contributions that materials are produced and adapted. The adaptation process is therefore the very process that can make materials relevant and thus potentially effective for learning development.

Universal

Materials should be based on universally appealing topics which are culturally provoking in the sense that they are culturally specific but, at the same time, they are present in all cultures. A rich source of this type of topics comes from literature, which typically involves themes based on life experiences, feelings, relationships. These are present in all cultures but they can be looked at from different angles. This provides the stimulus for discussion and it enables learners to focus on and become more aware of cultural differences as well as cultural similarities and commonalities. This point is taken into further consideration later in this chapter.

Authentic

Materials should be based on authentic texts, that is texts which have been written for any purpose other than language teaching. At the same time, the activities used with such texts should also be authentic since using tasks such as filling the gaps or answering comprehension-testing questions would make the texts not authentic either. The tasks, therefore, should be based on realistic situations in order to expose the learners to realistic input.

On the other hand, although many researchers and materials developers seem to agree with the above principle of using tasks based on authentic use of language, in my view a significant role is also played by non-authentic tasks with authentic texts, for example, tasks which aim at drawing the learners' attention to certain linguistic features of the input through language awareness activities based on texts taken from authentic sources.

Provocative Topics, Aesthetic Experience and Adapting Courses

A Link between Materials for EFL and Materials for Italian as a Foreign Language

If, on the one hand, the above points can or cannot be considered as the basis for the development of a model for adapting courses based on research rather than on intuition, on the other hand they certainly represent a different and innovative approach to adapting courses, and hence of developing materials for language teaching/learning. In such a model, the adaptation process is considered at two levels:

- adapting materials with the purpose of making them relevant and effective in a specific classroom;
- adapting materials with the purpose of changing their very objectives, in order to reduce the distance between research and practice in the classroom and in the published materials.

The former refers to the more traditional way of looking at the adaptation process where the teacher, in cooperation with the learners, decides what to change (adding, deleting, reordering, etc.) in the materials when adapting them.

The latter represents one of the most significant points of this chapter, for it is probably taking the adaptation process a step further towards raising awareness of materials development and learners' empowerment. It is at this level that the adaptation process becomes relevant to most published materials for language teaching, not only the large amount of materials for English as a Foreign Language (EFL), but also, in my experience, textbooks and materials designed for teaching and learning other languages. A typical example comes from two very commonly used and widely accepted textbooks, the *Headway* Series published by OUP for EFL and the *Italianissimo* series published by the BBC for teaching and learning Italian as a foreign language. Both these sets of materials contain books for different levels of learners, including the teacher's books, and a set of tapes, and *Italianissimo* also includes videos and CD-ROMs. These represent a typical example of so many published materials, which only differ in shape and visual impact but are all based on similar topics and activities, hence similar objectives.

> *The activities*: they are based on language manipulation, such as drills, comprehension testing, substitution tables and so on.
> *The topics*: they are very trivial and very often not relevant to the learners' needs and interests.
> *The objectives:* they are based on the main principle of the Presentation, Practice and Production Approach (PPP), which seems to be overwhelmingly present in so many textbooks for language teaching and yet does not have any basis in research. It is not innovative and, in my opinion, it contributes to the general apparent 'failure' of so many language courses, especially at a beginner's level.

It is in this context that adapting such courses becomes vital and it means changing their activities, their topics and therefore their objectives, moving towards activities based on developing awareness, including *provocative* topics aiming at promoting an *Aesthetic Experience*.

In this framework, culturally provocative topics become significant, in the sense that they provoke a reaction, an aesthetic experience (whether it be positive or negative) which is always personal and subjective for the learners. Therefore such topics can be more involving and motivating and, as they can develop opinions, points of view and various interpretations, they are potentially more beneficial for learners.

However, it seems that the paradoxical element of such a situation is that, in the two textbooks mentioned above, as well as in most teaching/learning published materials, the lower the level, the less controversial and provocative the topics seem to be, particularly for materials published for beginners. In a recent case study I conducted, I found the following topics in common from *Headway, Pre-Intermediate* by John and Liz Soars (OUP, 1991) and from *Italianissimo 1*, BBC series; they seem to reoccur in many lower-level books and are typical of materials for those levels of learners:

- Introductions
- Numbers
- Food and Drink
- Time Expressions
- Expressions of Quantity/Shopping
- The Future
- Transport

Based on my experience as a language teacher and a language learner, I can identify several problems with this type of language teaching materials:

they undermine the learners;
they do not motivate them;
they are very trivial;
they are not new or innovative;
they give a very stereotypical image of the country where the language is spoken;
they do not take into consideration the different cultures in Britain/Italy and of those who are studying English/Italian.

Provocative Topic: A Case Study

In the same case study, I used a short questionnaire with three of my classes at the University of Luton (Writing Materials for Language Teaching, MA in TEFL and Italian for post-beginners) in an attempt to find out what type of topics students found controversial and provocative, and if there were any of these which they found offensive (the questionnaire and the detailed results can be found in Appendix 4.1 and 4.2). It was interesting to find that, when asked explicitly, the students found the following topics provocative: the Death Penalty, Abortion, Animal Testing, Genetic Engineering, Cannabis Legalization, the Euro, Freedom of Belief, Asylum, Politics, Homosexuality, War, Racism, Violence, Drugs, Television. Somehow, this confirmed my expectations. However, when I tried out in class different activities using various topics of discussion, the topics they found most controversial and provocative were not included in the above list but were to do with personal life and covered Family, Parents, Relationships, Emotions, Inner Self. These are universally appealing but, at the same time, culturally different and very subjective, and therefore they provoke different reactions.

However, although the students I used those topics with certainly felt provoked and carried out a discussion, at first a few of them showed some resistance to such personal depths. Students in general are used to traditional ways of being taught; they are not always ready to face provocative topics and to go beyond the usual type of lessons based on the usual *safe* topics. They are so used to traditional, reassuring lessons that they believe in that way of learning. They need to be exposed to a different type of input and of discussion to be able to express their opinions and to develop interpretations and points of view.

An Example of Materials Designed to be Adapted by the Learners

The following is an example of activities which provide the stimulus for discussion and are purposely designed to be adapted and taken further by the learners.

CULTURAL ASPECTS OF LANGUAGE LEARNING

Using Culturally Provocative Texts

1. You are going to read a poem called 'The Enemies', by Elizabeth Jennings. Before you read it discuss briefly the following in pairs/small groups of three or four:

   • Who and what do you think the poem is about?

2. Considering only the title, what kind of information do you expect to find in this poem? Think about and write down the following:

   • A list of questions you are asking yourself before you read the poem.
   • The answers to the questions you expect to find in this poem.

3. While reading the poem, now, see if you can find the answers to the questions you set before or not:

   Make a note when you find them;
   Make a note when you find points you did not expect before;
   Stop reading the poem if you are not interested anymore by it and make a note.

The following can be used by the teacher as a stimulus and/or a starting point for the above activity to be used if necessary:

   • Who do you think the enemies are?
   • Do they remind you of anybody you know?
   • What do you think the people in the poem are feeling?
   • What do you think they are thinking/talking about?

Now you can choose one of the following tasks, 4a, 4b or 4c, or try them all.

4a. In your pairs/small groups decide the following by going back to the poem and underlining the parts that help you answer these questions:

- How does the poem make you feel?
- Which line, word or verse provoked such reactions?
- Which line, word or verse do you think best represents the whole poem?

Discuss with your partner/s and try to explain, in your own words, your answers to the above points. Try to find a linguistic feature from the poem to justify your answers (the vocabulary, the tense system, the structure).

4b. Working with your partner/s, decide how to respond to the poem by relating it to your country and your culture (adapt it to an audience from your own country); you can choose one of the following possibilities or decide your own:

a drawing;
a painting;
a piece of music;
a play;
a film;
a dialogue.

4c. Within your groups you can now choose one of the following projects:

a. Write a different poem for your own country.
b. Find newspaper articles about people considered 'The Enemies' today.
c. Find other poems with a similar theme.

5. You are going to teach the next lesson. With your groups first, and with the rest of the class later, decide how to adapt and develop these activities with your own supplementary materials using the texts you produced in 4b and 4c. [the teacher could give suggestions here, if necessary, on how to adapt this unit rather than what to include.]

The poem

The Enemies

Elizabeth Jennings

Last night they came across the river and
Entered the city. Women were awake
With lights and food. They entertained the band,
Not asking what the men had come to take
Or what strange tongue they spoke
Or why they came so suddenly through the land.

Now in the morning all the town is filled
With stories of the swift and dark invasion;
The women say that not one stranger told
A reason for his coming. The intrusion
Was not for devastation:
Peace is apparent still on hearth and field.

Yet all the city is a haunted place.
Man meeting man speaks cautiously. Old friends
Close up the candid looks upon their face.
There is no warmth in hands accepting hands;
Each ponders, 'Better hide myself in case
Those strangers have set up their homes in minds
I used to walk in. Better draw the blinds
Even if the strangers haunt in my own house.'

The above materials represent only a short example of the type of teaching/ learning materials decribed in this chapter: it has been designed with the purpose of adapting it in mind. The process of adaptation is left to the learners who are first exposed and stimulated by the poem and then are gradually left more and more to choose their own path and the types of activities they want to follow. Towards the end they are the providers of the input and of the activities themselves and they are going to adapt the materials according to their own choices (see activity No. 5.). The materials also include examples of different activities for the students to choose from; however, as a way to get them started at first, since they may not be used to these kind of tasks, they may be encouraged to try more than one activity.

It can be argued that these activities are so open-ended that they may leave the learners lost and confused about what to do and how to carry out the tasks. However, this process of awareness development can only be achieved rather slowly with a gradual process of getting the learners used to taking control of the lesson. Moreover, the activities are simply a few examples; they need to be supplemented and completed by other tasks which could be provided by the learners: they choose the further input they want to bring to the class (newspaper articles, poems, songs) to look at the topic from different angles.

The poem itself is quite open to different interpretations; it offers various points of discussion and the language used is rather simple and accessible. The learners are also encouraged to consider their own reading process and their reader's response (activities 1, 2, 3) in order to become more aware of their own learning process. To emphasize such awareness further, the teacher/the materials could also choose to ask the learners, at the end of the activities, to compare such activities with more traditional activities found in a typical example of published materials.

It is in this context that the adaptation process reaches a different level from the more traditional way of considering it. Within the framework of L2 materials development, materials should be designed to be adapted so that adapting would start at the point of writing the materials. Therefore I am advocating not only adapting existing materials but, more particularly, a change in the process of materials development itself.

Conclusions

'No second language acquisition research can provide a definite answer to the real problem of second language teaching at this point ... There is no pre-determined correct theory of language teaching originating from second language acquisition research' (Cook, 1996). Probably, within the framework of language teaching and learning and of L2 acquisition research, there is nothing closer to the truth than the above statement. At the same time, there are so many theories and hypotheses that classroom practice is also determined by different trends which swing from one extreme to the other. However, the value of certain alternative and innovative approaches and ideas, such as the ones proposed by this chapter, is not based so much on whether they have their origins in empirical evidence or not. It is rather coming from their very innovative nature which provokes discussion and points of view and hopefully constitutes a break from the traditional widely accepted approaches.

Rather than provide answers, the final purpose of this chapter is to open up possibilities and discussions, to promote research that would take the process of adaptation beyond the superficial level it is at at the moment. Rather than a conclusion, this is, therefore, a further starting point to be considered and developed and the ideas presented in this chapter represent hypotheses rather than empirical facts. The main point of this chapter is to question the process of adaptation, the way it has been done until today, and to attempt to start a debate on how to develop it and to consider it from different angles.

Moreover, this chapter ultimately attempts to put forward the idea that there is a great need for materials which promote learners' empowerment, materials which enable learners to *express themselves* in a foreign language rather than simply *communicate. Expressing themselves* here means to enable learners to use the target language in the same way as they would use their native language. This also involves achieving the same aims and reaching a deeper understanding of the differences between the two languages. *Communicating*, on the other hand, refers to a more superficial idea of using the language in order to transfer new information between two people or two groups of people. Furthermore, this chapter aims at allowing learners to use the foreign language in order to become aware and appreciate the culture of that language rather than simply understand its lexical meaning. Language learning should mean achieving a deeper understanding of different cultures, including the learners' own culture, rather than focusing on stereotypes.

Appendix 4.1

Semester 1   *Academic year 2000/01*

Questionnaire

Please answer the following questions as part of an experiment I am conducting on culture and materials for language teaching.

1. What is your native language?

2. What do you consider to be your nationality?

3. What are the topics you are interested in?

4. Try to describe here your experience of different cultures.

5. Are there any topics/subjects that might offend you? If yes, can you list them here?

6. Are there any topics/subjects you might find controversial/provocative? If yes, can you list them here?

7. Can you explain in your own words, the reasons for your answers in 5 and 6?

Appendix 4.2

Using Culturally Provocative Texts

Results of the questionnaire

1. *Nationalities*: 12 Greeks, 8 English/British, 7 Germans, 4 Spanish, 1 Korean, 1 Slovakian, 1 Nigerian, 1 Gabon.
2. *Native languages*: 12 Greek, 9 English, 7 German, 4 Spanish, 1 Korean, 1 Slovakian, 1 French.
3. *Topics found interesting*: Dialects/Pronunciation, Music, Travelling, Art, Languages, Sports, Nature, Pollution, Fashion, Animals, Theatre, Cinema, Computers, Internet, Formula One, the Bible, Literature, Business, Basic Grammar, Drawing, History, Psychology, Traditions, Human Rights, Relationships, Drugs, Food, Habits and Hobbies.
4. *Topics considered offensive*: None (26), Nationalistic topics, Disrespectful topics, Topics which hide the truth, Cruelty, Injustice, Poverty, Too personal and intimate topics, English/German relations after the Second War World, UK as a special island, USA as the police of the world.
5. *Topics considered controversial*: Death Penalty, Abortion, Animal Testing,

Genetic Engineering, Cannabis Legalization, the Euro, Freedom of Belief, Asylum Politics, Homosexuality, War, Racism, Violence, Drugs, Television.

References

Allwright, D. R. (1978) 'Abdication and responsibility in language teaching'. *Studies in Second Language Acquisition*, **2** (1).

Allwright, D. R. (1981) 'What do we want teaching materials for?'. *ELT Journal*, **36** (1), 5–18.

Carter, R. (1993) 'Language awareness and language learning', in M. Hoey (ed.) *Data, Description and Discourse*. London: Harper Collins.

Clarke, D. F. (1989) 'Materials adaptation: why leave it all to the teacher?'. *ELT Journal*, **43** (2).

Cook, V. (1996) *Second Language Learning and Second Language Teaching*. London: Edward Arnold.

Eco, U. (1979) *Lector in Fabula*. Milano: Bompiani.

Eco, U. (1994) *Sei Passeggiate Nei Boschi Narrativi*. Milano: Bompiani.

Hirvela, A. (1996) 'Reader-response theory and ELT'. *ELT Journal*, **50** (2).

Iser, W. (1978) *The Act of Reading, A Theory of Aesthetic Response*. Baltimore: Johns Hopkins University Press.

Jiang, W. (2000) 'The relationship between culture and language'. *ELT Journal*, **54** (4).

Madsen, K. S. and Bowen, J. D. (1978) *Adaptation in Language Teaching*. Boston: Newbury House.

Rosenblatt, M. L. (1968) *Literature as Exploration*. Oxford: Heinemann.

Rosenblatt, M. L. (1978) *The Reader, the Text, the Poem*. Carbondale, IL: Southern Illinois University Press.

Saraceni, C. (2000) 'Aesthetic experience and the learner'. *Proceedings of the First Teaching and Learning Conference*. University of Luton.

Tomlinson, B. (ed.) (1998) *Materials Development in Language Teaching*. Cambridge: Cambridge University Press.

CHAPTER

5

Adapting Classroom Materials

Carlos Islam and Chris Mares

Introduction

In many cases, the teacher using published materials in any given classroom is not involved with creating the materials and may have little to do with adopting the materials for her institution. However, even when the classroom teacher selects the book, knows every student in the class well and is using materials designed specifically for the context they are in, she will still have to adapt the materials either consciously or subconsciously.

Materials adaptation can span a range of procedures from adding carefully contextualized role plays with the objective of providing more opportunities to communicate to not finishing a pronunciation drill because of time constraints. Whether pre-planned or spontaneous, materials adaptation is an integral part of the success of any class. An awareness of the various reasons for adapting materials (as well as of current approaches and procedures) can be beneficial when considering how best to use the materials adopted for the classroom.

One reason for adaptation is that published materials are necessarily constrained by the syllabus, unit template and other space concerns. Not all material, therefore, is fully developed. A good teacher's guide will supplement materials with useful alternatives and adaptations, but where this does not happen or a teacher does not have the teacher's guide, adaptation will become part of the creative dialogue between teachers and published materials.

After reviewing the current state of the field, this chapter will make suggestions for and give examples of innovative and principled approaches to materials adaptation. Example adaptations of current commercial coursebooks will include materials for beginner and intermediate learners studying in their home country, as well as high-intermediate to advanced learners studying in a country where the target language is predominant.

Reasons for Adaptation

There are always sound practical reasons for adapting materials in order to make them as accessible and useful to learners as possible. However, reasons for adaptation have varied and changed as the field has developed and views on language acquisition and teaching practice have become better informed by research and experience.

Within this historical context, it is easy to understand why some teachers will wish to adapt materials. For example, before the advent of the communicative approach, many coursebooks focused largely on structure and were heavily influenced by the legacy of grammar translation methods of teaching. Language was viewed primarily in structural terms and was not treated as a tool for communication, while learning was seen in terms of forming correct behavioural patterns. Despite an increased awareness and sensitivity to language as communication and learning as a developmental process, many teachers were finding themselves faced with materials that did not reflect these teaching and learning principles.

In their book *Materials and Methods in ELT* (1993), McDonough and Shaw devote a chapter to the issue of adapting materials. They quote Madsen and Bowen (1978) to set a context for materials adaptation: 'Effective adaptation is a matter of achieving "congruence" ... The good teacher is ... constantly striving for congruence among several related variables: teaching materials, methodology, students, course objectives, the target language and its context, and the teacher's own personality and teaching style.'

McDonough and Shaw's list of reasons for adaptation clearly reflects a concern that communicative language teaching implies an unsystematic approach to grammar presentation and a belief that a systematic approach to grammar presentation is necessary.

Not enough grammar coverage in general
Not enough practice of grammar points of particular difficulty to these learners
The communicative focus means that grammar is presented unsystematically
Reading passages contain too much unknown vocabulary
Comprehension questions are too easy, because the answers can be lifted directly from the text with no real understanding
Listening passages are inauthentic, because they sound too much like written material being read out
Not enough guidance on pronunciation
Subject matter inappropriate for learners of this age and intellectual level
Photographs and other illustrative material not culturally acceptable
Amount of material too great/too little to cover in the time allocated to lessons
No guidance for teachers on handling group work and role-play activities with a large class
Dialogues too formal, and not really representative of everyday speech
Audio material difficult to use because of problems to do with room size and technical equipment
Too much or too little variety in the activities
Vocabulary list and a key to the exercises would be helpful
Accompanying tests needed

In *Choosing Your Coursebook* (1995), Cunningsworth also includes a chapter that deals with the challenge of materials adaptation and provides a list of possible reasons for adapting materials. There is quite a bit of overlap between the two lists, but Cunningsworth draws on a knowledge of learner styles and the learner as a whole, considerations which are absent from McDonough and Shaw's list. According to Cunningsworth, adaptation depends on factors such as:

The dynamics of the classroom
The personalities involved
The constraints imposed by syllabuses
The availability of resources
The expectations and motivations of the learners

Adaptation is also appropriate when materials are not ideal, as presented in the following:

Methods (e.g., an exercise may be too mechanical, lacking in meaning, too complicated).
Language content (e.g., there may be too much emphasis on grammar your students learn quickly or not enough emphasis on what they find difficult).
Subject matter (e.g., topics may not be interesting to students or they may be outdated or not authentic enough).
Balance of skills (e.g., there may be too much emphasis on skills in the written language or skills in the spoken language, or there may not be enough on integrating skills).
Progression and grading (order of language items may need to be changed to fit an outside syllabus or the staging may need to be made steeper or more shallow).
Cultural content (cultural references may need to be omitted or changed).
Image (a coursebook may project an unfriendly image through poor layout, low quality visuals, etc.).

Candlin and Breen (1980) focus on adaptation issues that relate to materials specifically designed for communicative language learning. Their list implies that published materials are limited in that they do not provide many opportunities for real communication; instead they simply provide oral practice of linguistic structures:

Communicative materials do not provide enough opportunities for negotiation (personal or psychological) between the learner and the text.
Communicative materials do not provide enough opportunities for interpersonal or social negotiation between all participants in the learning process, between learners and teachers, and learners and learners.
Activities and tasks do not promote enough communicative performance.
Activities and tasks do not promote enough metacommunicating opportunities.
Activities and tasks do not promote co-participation. Teachers and learners are not involved as co-participants in the teaching–learning process.

A brief look at these lists quickly demonstrates the numerous classroom situations when materials adaptation is advisable. Recognizing that your classroom materials need some kind of adaptation may be an intuitive feeling or an articulated thought. The challenge is finding ways to make the materials work for your class.

Objectives and Techniques for Adaptation

Having clear objectives is a necessary starting point for adopting any materials. Clear adaptation objective(s) for the materials or knowing what 'works' for your class will help guide your choice of adaptation technique(s) as well as help decide the appropriate content or language choice.

McDonough and Shaw start a list of objectives that a teacher may hope to achieve by adapting classroom materials. They state that, in order to attain greater appropriacy from materials, you can adapt to:

Personalize
Individualize
Localize
Modernize

We, Islam and Mares, would expand this list to include:

Add real choice
Cater for all sensory learner styles
Provide for more learner autonomy
Encourage higher-level cognitive skills
Make the language input more accessible
Make the language input more engaging

Add Real Choice

In recent years, many language teaching professionals have supported the principle of giving language learners choice in their learning decision-making. This often means that learners get the option to study Unit 3 before Unit 2, or learners get to choose the passage they read.

In choosing the term 'real choice' we are referring to learners deciding how they want to learn rather than what they want to learn. That is to say, learners can decide whether they would like to follow a route that caters to their preferred cognitive learning style (style matching) or to try a cognitive style that is less comfortable (style stretching). Learners could choose between the styles of field dependent or independent, global or analytical, impulsive or reflective, intuitive-random or concrete-sequential, perceiving or judging, and feeling or thinking, among others (for definitions of these learning styles, see Reid, 1995).

Cater for All Sensory Learning Styles

In her survey of 1388 students, aimed at identifying preferred sensory learning styles, Reid (1987) found that all ESL learners have strong kinaesthetic learning style preferences. However, an analysis of any major coursebook series will show that although the auditory and visual sides of learners are catered for, there is rarely any opportunity for learners to receive kinaesthetic input.

Provide for More Learner Autonomy

Adapting material to provide for learner autonomy may mean including learner training with the objective of helping learners acquire language outside the classroom or without the guidance of the teacher. An example may be setting time in class for reading and listening for pleasure and discussing material that students liked or did not like, rather than using the material to exemplify discrete language points or as text for comprehension questions. Activities that encourage learners to discover independently rules and conventions about the target language could also have the potential to create autonomous learners.

Encourage Higher-level Cognitive Skills

Encouraging higher-level cognitive skills means adapting materials in such a way as to require students to hypothesize, predict, infer, make connections and associations and visualize. This type of higher-level cognitive activity engages and motivates students as well as assists in transferring language skills already developed in their first language to the target language.

Make the Language Input More Engaging

There are different ways to make input more engaging. One way is to rewrite or re-record text, to give it more authenticity or interest. Another way is to change the form of input. For example, a reading text as input might be presented as a game or interactive activity, rather than simply as a reading passage. Another way to make input more engaging is to change the nature of the tasks. For example, rather than have a reading task which focuses on comprehension, switch the task to prediction, or allow students to finish creatively a story with their own ending. By participating in this type of activity, learners still demonstrate comprehension or a lack of comprehension but without direct testing and the risk of failure.

Techniques for Adaptation

After recognizing a gap (mismatch or non-congruence) between published teaching materials and the needs and objectives of the classroom, the teacher has to address the practicalities of adapting the material to meet her class objectives more closely. McDonough and Shaw (1993) and Cunningsworth (1995) offer lists of techniques that may be used when adapting materials better to 'fit' a specific class.

These techniques are:

Adding; extending and expanding
Deleting; subtracting and abridging
Simplifying
Reordering
Replacing material

Adding

When adding to published materials the teacher is supplementing the existing materials and providing more material. The teacher can do this by either extending or expanding.

Extending

When extending an activity the teacher supplies more of the same type of material, thus making a quantitative change in the material. For example, an activity may practise a particular grammar point by asking the learner to complete a sentence with the missing verb in the correct form, such as the simple past. The coursebook may have provided ten sentences for this treatment, but the teacher may value this type of activity for her particular class and adapt the coursebook by adding five more sentences with missing verbs.

Expanding

Expanding classroom material is different from extending in that it adds something different to the materials; the change is qualitative. For instance, the teacher may feel her students need to be made aware of the different sounds of verb endings when used in the simple past but the coursebook does not address this phonetic issue. Consequently, she may add an activity or series of activities that deal with the phonetics of the past simple. The teacher may want to draw students' attention to the fact that, when pronouncing the verbs visited, played and worked, the endings (-ed) are pronounced /id/, /id/ and /t/ respectively. Other expansions could involve including a discussion to contextualize and personalize the topic of a particular unit of study, or including a TPR phase to make difficult language items in a reading or listening text more comprehensible.

It is important to note that additions to materials can come at the beginning, at the end or in the middle of the materials being adapted.

Deleting; Subtracting and Abridging

As with the technique of adding, material can be deleted both quantitatively (subtracting) or qualitatively (abridging). When subtracting, for example, a teacher can decide to do five of the questions practising the simple past tense instead of the ten in the coursebook. When abridging, however, the teacher may decide that focusing attention on pronunciation may inhibit the learner's fluency and decide not to do any of the pronunciation exercises in a coursebook.

Simplifying

When simplifying, the teacher could be rewording instructions or text in order to make them more accessible to learners, or simplifying a complete activity to make it more manageable for learners and teachers. It is worth pointing out here that there is a distinct danger of distorting language when attempting to simplify a text and thus making the text inauthentic.

Reordering

When reordering, the teacher has decided that it makes more pedagogic sense to sequence activities differently. An example is beginning with a general discussion before looking at a reading passage rather than using the reading as a basis for discussion.

Replacing Material

When replacing material a teacher may decide that a more appropriate visual or text might serve an activity better than the ones presented in the published material. This is often the case with culturally specific or time-specific activities. A teacher may decide to replace an illustration for one that students could identify with more closely or use information concerning a popular figure with whom the students are familiar rather than the one presented in the published materials.

Teachers may also decide to replace a whole activity depending on the goals of a particular class or lesson. For example, a reading activity might be replaced with a listening activity.

Three Examples of Materials Adaptation

In order to exemplify some of the adaptation principles and techniques mentioned in this chapter, we will describe three real teaching scenarios and select published coursebooks that could be realistically used in each of the scenarios. We will then suggest specific adaptations for each coursebook in order to tailor the materials better to each teaching scenario.

Scenario One

A class of 34 junior high school students in a Japanese public (not private) school. The students are 12 to 13 years old, and there are 17 boys and 17 girls in the class. The students have all had between one and two years of English instruction at elementary school but have difficulty in understanding simple oral communication. The students currently spend five hours a week in English class.

This group of students needs more exposure to a wide and rich range of language input in a variety of contexts. The coursebook used for this class is *New Horizon 1* (Tokyo Shoseki, 2002).

Rationale for Adaptation

Page 50 of *New Horizon 1* (see Figure 5.1) presents everyday verbs in the present simple. Four verbs are presented in a single context and only in writing. The activity lacks kinaesthetic and auditory sensory input. The input is also limited and impoverished. Students are not given a choice about how they learn nor are they given an opportunity to personalize the input.

The materials could be expanded by adding a TPR phase at the beginning of this unit of study to provide kinaesthetic and auditory input as well as richer, more contextualized text. Learners also have an opportunity to attend to the input globally and interpret meaning before analysing the input to understand its form.

1. Teacher mimes Becky's daily routine. Asks students to guess what Becky does each day.
2. Teacher acts out Becky's daily routine while reading the script.
3. Students act Becky's routine while teacher reads the script.

Becky's Daily Routine (script)

Every day Becky wakes up at 6:30 in the morning.
She stretches her arms and rubs her eyes and she yawns.
Then she brushes her teeth and takes a shower.
Sometimes she likes to sing in the shower.
She puts on her clothes and eats her breakfast, usually toast and coffee.
After breakfast, she speaks to her dog.
At 7:30 she leaves her apartment and takes the subway to school.

On Saturday and Sunday she usually wakes up at 9:30 in the morning.
She stretches her arms and rubs her eyes and she yawns.
Then she brushes her teeth and takes a shower.

On Saturday she usually plays tennis or runs in the park.

The activity on page 50 provides limited opportunities for analysing the input. By extending the activity through adding more information about Becky's routine the opportunities for analysing linguistic forms are increased.

For example, the procedure below could be followed:

Extend the exercise on page 50 by adding sentences about Becky.
Students write sentences that they remember about Becky's routine.

Figure 5.1 Scenario 1, *New Horizon 1*, p. 50

Students underline the verbs in the sentences about Becky.
Students put verbs in two columns, regular and irregular verbs.

> She plays tennis well.
> She goes to the gym.
> She works hard.
> She likes to sing.

> *Regular*   *Irregular*
> plays   goes
> works
> likes

The following expansion activity provides students with a choice about how they would like to continue processing the input analytically or globally. It also provides a choice between visual, auditory or kinaesthetic processing as well as an opportunity to personalize the input.

> Teacher gives students written version of script. Students change script to make it true for themselves. For example, 'Every day I wake up at 7:20 in the morning.'
> *Or*
> Student tells a partner his/her daily routine.
> *Or*
> In small groups, students mime their daily routine. The other students guess what's happening.

Scenario Two

A class of sixteen private language school students in Spain. The students range from 18 to 46 years old. Ten of the students are women and six are men. The majority of the students are professional business people but five are undergraduates at the local university. The students attend the private language school for three hours a week in the evening and they are in the middle of their third year of study at the school. They have been classified at a lower-intermediate level of proficiency and have difficulty in communicating more than simple personal information.

This group of students needs more opportunities to use English and activities which engage their interest. The coursebook used for this class is *New Headway Pre-Intermediate* (OUP, 2001).

Rationale for Adaptation
The topic, 'rooms', has the potential for vocabulary development but would be more effective with an initial personalized context in order better to engage

5 Think of questions to ask about free time and holiday activities.

- What do you do in your free time?
- What do . . . at the weekend?
- . . . any sports?
- Do you like . . . ?
- Where . . . holiday?
- Do . . . winter holiday?

Stand up! Ask two or three students your questions. Use short answers when necessary. Find out who has the most hobbies and holidays.

Do you like skiing?   *No, I don't.*

Check it

6 Tick (✓) the correct sentence.

1 ☐ Where you go on holiday?
   ☐ Where do you go on holiday?

2 ☐ Do you have any children?
   ☐ Do you have got any children?

3 ☐ I'm Hans. I'm coming from Germany.
   ☐ I'm Hans. I come from Germany.

4 ☐ This is a great party! Everyone is dancing.
   ☐ This is a great party! Everyone dances.

5 ☐ I don't have a mobile phone.
   ☐ I no have a mobile phone.

6 ☐ Jack's a policeman, but he doesn't wear a uniform.
   ☐ Jack's a policeman, but he no wear a uniform.

7 ☐ 'Where is José?' 'He's sitting by the window.'
   ☐ 'Where is José?' 'He sits by the window.'

8 ☐ I'm liking black coffee.
   ☐ I like black coffee.

VOCABULARY
Daily life

1 Match the verbs and nouns.

have	a film on TV
wash	to my friends
watch	my hair
talk	breakfast

make	to music
listen	my homework
relax	a cup of tea
do	on the sofa

have	posters on the wall
clear up	the mess
do	a shower
have/put	the washing-up

cook	magazines
go	a meal
put on	make-up
read	to the toilet

T 2.4 Listen and check.

2 Match the activities from exercise 1 with the correct room.

Kitchen
_____
_____
_____

Bathroom
_____
_____
_____

Living room
_____
_____
_____

Bedroom
_____
_____
_____

3 Do you like where you live? Choose your favourite room. What do you do in that room?

I like my bedroom a lot because I've got lots of posters on the walls. I listen to music and do my homework . . .
I like my living room. The walls are white, and I love the big, comfortable sofa . . .

4 Describe your favourite room to a partner. Don't say which room it is. Can your partner guess?

Figure 5.2 Scenario 2, from *New Headway Pre-Intermediate*

students, activate topic schema, create as well as activate linguistic schema and create a need for the target vocabulary.

The vocabulary activities, *Daily Life*, could be expanded by starting with the following pair of work questions before matching the verbs and nouns in activity 1.

1. Ask a partner:
    How many rooms do you have in your house or apartment?
    Which room do you use most?
    Which room do you use least?
    Which is your favourite room?

Replace question 3 in *Daily Life* with the following:

2. Draw a floor plan of your favourite room and label the furniture and other features, including wall colours, windows, etc. Describe the room to your partner, then tell him/her what you do in that room.

Example:
My favourite room is my bedroom. The bed is next to the window. The window looks out onto the backyard. My computer is on a desk next to my bed ... The walls are blue and the curtains are ... I study in my room, listen to music and ... I spend a lot of time in my bedroom.

Scenario Three

A multilingual oral communication class of twelve full-time language students at a university ESL programme in the USA. The students range in age from 18 to 24. There are seven women and five men in the class and their nationalities are Saudi Arabian, Japanese, Korean, Costa Rican, Pakistani, Russian and Venezuelan. They are all trying to matriculate as undergraduate students in different academic departments of the university. They are currently attending 20 hours of ESL classes a week. They are classified as having upper-intermediate and advanced level proficiency.

This group of students needs interesting and thought-provoking content that naturally encourages the use of higher-level cognitive skills. The coursebook they are using is *Interchange 3* (CUP, 1991).

Rationale for Adaptation
The topic, 'dreams', for the conversation activity (*Interchange 3*, p. 25, activity 8; See Figure 5.3) is interesting but has no schema-raising activity to help students get engaged in the topic. A series of brief questions about dreams would prepare students for the listening as well as offer further opportunity for spoken inter-action. This type of schema-raising activity has the potential to activate language as well as topic schemata with the potential of facilitating student's comprehension of the listening text.

8 CONVERSATION

1 Listen.

A: You know, I had a really strange dream last night.
B: Oh, yeah? What was it about?
A: Well, I dreamed that I was driving in the country late at night when I saw a UFO land on the road in front of me.
B: And then what happened?
A: Well, first, I got out of my car. While I was standing there, this strange green creature came out of the UFO. I tried to run away, but I couldn't move. Then, as it was coming nearer, it put out its hand and touched my face. It felt wet and horrible!
B: Ugh! And . . .?
A: And then I woke up and found my cat on my pillow. It was licking my face!

2 *Pair work* Now close the book. How much of the dream can you remember?

3 *Group work* Take turns talking about a dream you once had.

Figure 5.3 Scenario 3, from *Interchange 3*, p. 25, activity 8

The listening section of this unit could be expanded by adding a discussion activity before the listening on page 25.

1. Ask a partner about his or her dreams:

    Do you remember your dreams?
    Do you have any recurring dreams (the same dream again and again)?
    Have you ever had a nightmare (a bad, scary dream)?
    Have you ever kept a dream journal (written down your dreams)?
    Can you remember the dreams you had last night?

The post-listening group work (activity 3) does not become redundant, rather the activity offers a further chance for students to review or develop their ideas. However, as it stands the activity does not offer any language support and might leave students unsure how to start or finish their explanations.

The following prompts could be added to activity 3, Group work, on page 25.

2. Start like this:

    I remember a dream I had last night/yesterday/a week ago, etc.

It was a great/scary/funny/strange dream.

Finish like this:

That's it. It really was a great/scary/funny/strange dream.

The listening activity could be replaced with a reading activity that encourages higher-order cognitive skills, or a choice could be offered between the listening activity or the reading activity below.

Begin with the schema-raising questions in activity 1 above but add the following questions:

1. Do you think dreams have any special meaning?

After students have asked the schema-raising questions, poll the class to see if anyone believes dreams have a special meaning. Elicit answers. If someone says yes, try and write a model on the board, such as, 'Dreams about falling probably mean you are worried about something.'

2. Read the following paragraph about dreams. Tell a partner if you have had any dreams like these.

Dreams and their Meanings
We all have dreams and they all mean something, even though we may not remember them. At least that is what many psychologists believe.

   Here is a list of dream topics and the possible interpretations: dreams about flying mean you want to escape from something; dreams about finding money mean you need money; dreams about getting gifts also mean you want something; dreams about being in a strange place mean you are worried about something; dreams about falling or being chased also mean you are worried about something. Many of these dreams are anxiety dreams but, as you know, we dream about different things and the meanings may not always be clear.

3. Can you think of any other dream topics and what they mean? Tell a partner.

4. Read the dream below and decide what it means. Check your interpretation with a partner.

A Dream
When I was at high school, I often had the same dream. I was in class, sitting at my desk listening to the teacher when suddenly I realized that I wasn't wearing any trousers! In my dream I felt very hot and uncomfortable and I didn't know what to do. At that moment I always woke up sweating and breathing hard.

An Interpretation
I guess it means the person was ... What do you think?

5. After students have talked about their dreams and their possible meaning, ask some students to retell their dream to the class.

Provide further opportunities for using higher-order cognitive skills by expanding this activity. Ask students to visit the following websites to read more about dreams and their meanings.

http://www.dreammoods.com/
http://www.djmcadam.com/dreams.htm

Conclusion

Classroom materials need to be adapted in a principled manner to reflect needs within particular teaching contexts, current understanding of second language acquisition and good teaching practices. The three scenarios above exemplify a wide range of possible teacher choices for adapting published materials and demonstrate the flexibility and creativity of adaptation.

References

Candlin, C. N. and Breen, M. (1980) 'Evaluating and designing language teaching materials'. *Practical Papers in English Language Education.* Vol. 2. Lancaster: Institute for English Language Education, University of Lancaster.

Cunningsworth, A. (1995) *Choosing Your Coursebook.* Oxford: Heinemann.

Madsen, K. S. and Bowen, J. D. (1978) *Adaptation in Language Teaching.* Boston: Newbury House.

McDonough, J. and Shaw, C. (1993) *Materials and Methods in ELT: A Teacher's Guide.* London: Blackwell.

Reid, J. (1987) 'The learning style preferences of ESL students'. *TESOL Quarterly,* **21**(1), 87–111.

Reid, J. (ed.) (1995) *Learning Styles in the ESL/EFL Classroom.* Massachusetts: Heinle and Heinle.

Richards, R. with Hull, J. and Proctor, C. (1991) *Interchange 3.* Cambridge: Cambridge University Press.

Soars, L. and Soars, J. (2001) *Headway Pre-Intermediate.* Oxford: Oxford University Press.

Tokyo Shoseki (2002) *New Horizon 1.* Tokyo: Tokyo Shoseki.

Comments on Part A

Brian Tomlinson

There are a number of divergent views expressed in Part A (for example, the contrasting views on materials adaptation expressed by Chapters 4 (Saraceni) and 5 (Islam and Mares)), and Chapter 3 (Singapore Wala) is an important reminder that it is not only the views of the writers and teachers that count in the development of materials for language teaching. However, there are a surprising number of commonalities of opinion given the very different backgrounds and localities of the contributors. There seems to be quite a strong agreement that:

- Evaluation and adaptation of materials are of vital importance in relation to the learning process and they should not be left to the impromptu intuitions of teachers under pressure of time and institutional constraints. Instead they should be processes which are built into the development of any materials, and time and training should be given to the users of materials to enable them to make principled and effective decisions.
- We should acknowledge that the users of materials include learners, teachers, administrators and publishers, and that their needs should be reconciled in principled ways in the development, evaluation and adaptation of materials.
- We should recognize that the wants of the potential users of materials should be cared for as well as their needs. This is especially true of learners and teachers, who will not make effective use of the materials if they do not relate to their interests and lives at the time of using them. But it is also true of administrators and publishers, who are not going to promote materials effectively that they do not believe in.
- We need flexibility not only in the design of learning materials but also in the ways in which materials are evaluated and adapted. Most importantly, this flexibility should be one of the main aims when developing frameworks for evaluation and adaptation and its achievement should ensure principled connections between materials, target learners and specific environments of learning. One way to achieve this is to ensure that frameworks always leave space for local criteria and another is to involve the users of materials in the process of evaluation and adaptation. I am about to embark on materials development/adaptation projects in Brazil, China, Iran and Turkey and I will

be strongly advising that both universal and local evaluation criteria are developed and applied, and that typical users of the materials are involved in the development, evaluation and adaptation of the materials.

My own view is that the most important point to make about materials evaluation and adaptation is that we need to do a lot more research into the effect of materials on durable learning and on the learners' ability to make use of what they have learned from materials in their post-course lives. At the moment, there is too much talk about whether materials 'work' or not, without clear definition of what 'work' means. For the publisher, 'work' means sells well; for the administrator, it often means ease of standardization, and examination success for the institution; for the teacher, it often means ease of preparation, and fit with the syllabus and the timetable; for the learner, it can mean interesting and achievable or matching expectations. But surely for all these users it should also mean that the materials achieve their short and long-term learning objectives. To measure this aspect of materials working is very difficult. It has to be longitudinal, it can be expensive and it is very difficult to control such variables as teaching skill, class rapport, intrinsic motivation and exposure to the language unrelated to the materials. It is amazing how rarely such post-use evaluation is attempted by publishers, by writers, by teachers or by researchers. Perhaps now that so many MA courses encourage dissertations on materials development and some people are actually doing PhDs on materials development (e.g., at Leeds Metropolitan University), there is more chance of such important research being done.

One way of carrying out post-use evaluation of a set of materials (or adaptations of a set of materials) would be:

1. Specify the short-term and long-term learning objectives of a set of materials.
2. Control the use of these materials with comparable classes in perhaps four different institutions, with different teachers teaching two different but equivalent classes in each institution. The control would include specifications of time to be spent on each component of the materials, which components would be set for homework, which components would be localized, etc.
3. At the beginning of the course administer tests assessing the learners' pre-course ability in relation to both short and long-term learning objectives.
4. Ask the teachers to keep a diary in which they note any divergence from the agreed procedures and any comments they have on the value of the materials.
5. Administer questionnaires to the learners during the course asking about their attitude towards the materials they are using.
6. Administer whilst-use tests assessing the learners' progress in relation to short-term learning objectives (e.g., such facilitating skills as circumlocution in vocabulary use, deduction of meaning in reading, the use of visualization in extensive listening).
7. Administer end-of-course tests assessing the learners' progress in relation to both short and long-term learning objectives.

8. Administer end-of-course questionnaires to the learners asking questions about any extra exposure the learners have had to the language and any factors which they think have influenced their progress other than the materials.
9. Administer end-of-course questionnaires to the learners asking them to evaluate the materials they have used.
10. Administer end-of-course questionnaires to the teachers asking them to evaluate the materials they have used.
11. After maybe three months, bring the learners back together in each institution and (a) administer tests assessing the learners' progress in relation to long-term learning objectives and application; and (b)administer questionnaires to the learners asking questions about any extra exposure the learners have had to the language since the course ended and any factors which they think have influenced their progress other than the materials.
12. Collate and analyse the data.
13. Make decisions about the value of components of the materials and of the materials overall.
14. Recommend adaptations to the materials.

Obviously such a research project would be demanding in terms of expertise, time and resources but it would certainly not be impossible for a major commercial publisher to carry out such research, and it is the sort of project which the Materials Evaluation and Development Unit in the Centre for Language Study at Leeds Metropolitan University intends to carry out. Such research could not claim to prove anything about the effectiveness of materials but it would provide indications which we are not currently gaining from pre-use and whilst-use evaluations.

PART B

Principles and Procedures
of Materials Development

6

Developing Principled Frameworks for Materials Development

Brian Tomlinson

Introduction

Creative Intuition in Materials Development

There have been a number of accounts in the literature by materials developers of the process they follow when developing materials. Rather surprisingly, many of them describe processes which are ad hoc and spontaneous and which rely on an intuitive feel for activities which are likely to 'work'. Prowse (1998) reports the responses of 'ELT materials writers from all over the world' who 'met in Oxford in April 1994 for a British Council Specialist Course with UK-based writers and publishers' (p. 130). When asked to say how they wrote their materials, many of them focused on the creative process of writing (e.g., 'writing is fun, because it's creative'; 'writing can be frustrating, when ideas don't come'; 'writing is absorbing – the best materials are written in "trances"' (p. 136)) and Prowse concludes that 'most of the writers quoted here appear to rely heavily on their own intuitions, viewing textbook writing in the same way as writing fiction, while at the same time emphasizing the constraints of the syllabus. The unstated assumption is that the syllabus precedes the creation' (p. 137). Most of the writers focus on what starts and keeps them writing and they say such things as, 'writing brings joy, when inspiration comes, when your hand cannot keep up with the speed of your thoughts' (p. 136) and 'In materials writing mood – engendered by peace, light, etc. – is particularly important' (p. 137). However, they say very little about any principles of learning and teaching which guide their writing or about any frameworks which they use to facilitate coherence and consistency. This is largely true also of some of the writers talking about writing in Hidalgo *et al.* (1995), of some of the writers describing their writing processes in Tomlinson (1998c) and of some of the writing processes reported in Richards (2001). For example, Cochingo-Ballesteros (1995: 54) says, 'some of them (drills) are deeply expressive of my own beliefs and give me aesthetic fulfilment' and Maley (1995: 221) says that writing instructional materials 'is best seen as a form of operationalised tacit knowledge' which involves 'trusting our intuitions and beliefs. If a unit of material does not "feel" right, no amount of rational persuasion will usually change my mind about it.' Richards (1995: 105), however, whilst referring to his need to listen to the local classical music station when writing, concludes that the process of materials writing is '10 per cent inspiration and 90 per cent perspiration'.

Frameworks for Materials Development

There are exceptions to the focus on creativity reported above. A number of writers in the books mentioned above focus on the need to establish and be driven by unit outlines or frameworks. For example, Rozul (1995: 213) reports a lesson format (based on Hutchinson and Waters, 1984) which includes the following key components:

- Starter
- Input
- General Information
- Language Focus
- Tasks

Fortez (1995: 74) describes a framework (also based on Hutchinson and Waters, 1994) which has eight sequential 'features', Richards (1995: 102–3) describes the process of designing a 'design or frame for a unit in a textbook' which can 'serve as a formulae which the author can use in writing the book' and Flores (1995: 60–2) outlines a lesson format with the following basic stages:

- Listening with Understanding
- Using Grammar in Oral Interaction
- Reading for Understanding
- Writing
- Literature

   Whilst I agree with the value of establishing a unit framework prior to writing, I would prefer my frameworks to be more principled, coherent and flexible than many of the frameworks in the literature on materials development, many of which provide no theoretical justification for their staging or sequencing (one notable exception being Ribe (2000: 66–77) who outlines and justifies a principled task sequence for a negotiated project framework).

   Jolly and Bolitho (1998: 97–8) have an interestingly different approach to frameworks and focus not on a unit framework but on a framework for developing materials which involves the following procedures:

- Identification of need for materials
- Exploration of need
- Contextual realization of materials
- Pedagogical realization of materials
- Production of materials
- Student use of materials

- Evaluation of materials against agreed objectives

Principles in Materials Development

Most writers on the process of materials development focus on needs analysis as their starting point (e.g., Rozul, 1995: 210; Luzares, 1995: 26–7; Fortez, 1995: 69–70). However, some writers report starting by articulating their principles. For example Bell and Gower (1998: 122–5) started by articulating the following principles which they wanted to guide their writing:

- Flexibility
- From text to language
- Engaging content
- Natural language
- Analytic approaches
- Emphasis on review
- Personalized practice
- Integrated skills
- Balance of approaches
- Learner development
- Professional respect

Flores (1995: 58–9) lists five assumptions and principles which were articulated after initial brainstorm sessions prior to the writing of a textbook in the Philippines, Tomlinson (1998c: 5–22) proposes fifteen principles for materials development which derive from second language acquisition research and theory, Tomlinson (1999b) describes a principled and flexible framework designed to help teachers to develop materials efficiently and effectively and Penaflorida (1995: 172–9) reports her use of the six principles of materials design identified by Nunan (1988):

- Materials should be clearly linked to the curriculum they serve
- Materials should be authentic in terms of text and task
- Materials should stimulate interaction
- Materials should allow learners to focus on formal aspects of the language
- Materials should encourage learners to develop learning skills, and skills in learning
- Materials should encourage learners to apply their developing skills to the world beyond the classroom

And, most emphatically, Hall (in Hidalgo *et al.*, 1995: 8) insists that:

Before planning or writing materials for language teaching, there is one crucial question we need to ask ourselves. The question should be the first item on the agenda at the first planning meeting. The question is this: How do we think people learn language?

Hall then goes on to discuss the following theoretical principles which he thinks should 'underpin everything else which we do in planning and writing our materials' (p. 8):

- The Need to Communicate
- The Need for Long-Term Goals
- The Need for Authenticity
- The Need for Student-Centredness

What I am going to do in this chapter is to outline two frameworks for materials development which aim to be principled, flexible and coherent, and which have developed from my answers to the question about how we think people learn language. One is text-driven and ideal for developing coursebooks and supplementary classroom materials. The other is task-driven and ideal for localizing and personalizing classroom materials, and for autonomous learning.

A Text-driven Approach to Materials Development

The Framework

This is a framework which I have used on materials writing workshops in Argentina, Botswana, Brazil, Japan, Malaysia, Mauritius, the Seychelles, Singapore and Vietnam and on textbook projects in Namibia and Turkey (Tomlinson, 2001b). In all those countries I found it helped writers (mainly teachers with little previous experience of materials development) not only to write principled and coherent materials quickly, effectively and consistently but also to articulate and develop their own theories of language learning and language teaching at the same time.

Text Collection
You come across and/or create texts (written or spoken) with the potential for engagement. By engagement, I mean a willing investment of energy and attention in experiencing the text in such a way as to achieve interaction between the text and the senses, feelings, views and intuitions of the reader/listener. Such texts can help the reader/listener to achieve a personal multidimensional representation in which inner speech, sensory images and affective stimuli combine to make the text meaningful (Tomlinson, 1998d, 2000c). And sometimes they can help the reader/listener to achieve the sort of aesthetic response described by Rosenblatt (1968, 1978) in which ultimately the reader enters the text and lives in it.

Such a representation can achieve the affective impact and the deep processing which can facilitate language acquisition. It can also help the learners to develop the confidence and skills which can give them access to valuable input outside and after their course. (Tomlinson, 1999c: 62)

Such texts are those which first of all engage ourselves in the ways described above and they can come, for example, from literature, from songs (see Chapter 24 (Ferradas Moi)), from newspapers and magazines, from non-fiction books, from radio and television programmes and from films. Obviously, such texts cannot be easily found and certainly cannot be found quickly in order to illustrate teaching points (as Bell and Gower (1998) found out when they tried to find engaging, authentic texts to illustrate predetermined teaching points in their intermediate level coursebook). It is much easier and much more useful to build up a library of potentially engaging texts and then to let the texts eventually selected for target levels determine the teaching points. And it is obviously much more effective to teach language features which have first been experienced by the learners in engaging texts than to impose 'unengaging' texts on learners just because they illustrate predetermined teaching points.

This library development stage is ongoing and context free. Its purpose is to create a resource with the potential for subsequent matching to particular contexts of learning.

Text Selection
In this stage you select from your library of potentially engaging texts (either one text for a particular lesson or a number of texts for a set of materials or a textbook). As the materials are going to be driven by the text(s) this stage is very important and should be criterion-referenced. Initially, it is a good idea to apply the criteria explicitly; but eventually this can be done intuitively.

The criteria which I have found help to achieve effective selection are:

- Does the text engage me cognitively and affectively?
- Is the text likely to engage most of the target learners cognitively and effectively?
- Are the target learners likely to be able to connect the text to their lives?
- Are the target learners likely to be able to connect the text to their knowledge of the world?
- Are most of the target learners likely to be able to achieve multidimensional mental representation of the text?
- Is the text likely to stimulate divergent personal responses from the target learners?
- Is the linguistic level of the text likely to present an achievable challenge to the target learners?
- Is the cognitive level of the text likely to present an achievable challenge to the target learners?

- Is the emotional level of the text suitable for the age and maturity of the target learners?
- Is the text likely to contribute to the personal development of the learners?
- Does the text contribute to the ultimate exposure of the learners to a range of genres (e.g., short stories, poems, novels, songs, newspaper articles, brochures, advertisements, etc.)?
- Does the text contribute to the ultimate exposure of the learners to a range of text types (e.g., narrative, description, persuasion, information, justification, etc.)?

I would rate each text on a five-point scale and would not select any text which did not achieve at least 4 on each of the criteria above.

Note
1. Usefulness for teaching a particular language feature is a dangerous criterion as this can tempt writers into the selection of texts which do not engage the learners and which, therefore, do not help them to achieve durable learning of the teaching point.
2. Obviously many of the texts on an ESP (English for Specific Purposes) or EAP (English for Academic Purposes) course should relate to the target learners' purposes for doing the course but if all the texts do this explicitly there is a danger of tedium and, therefore, of lack of engagement. This is a lesson I learned when a group of Saudi Arabian pilots complained that they were bored with reading about aircraft and airports and, almost simultaneously, a group of Iraqi diplomats complained that they were fed up with reading about politics and diplomacy. Both groups then responded very enthusiastic-ally to the inclusion of poetry on their courses. The important point is that affect is vital for learning, even on courses with very specific purposes (Tomlinson, 1999a). Without it there is a danger that language learning 'can reduce the learner from an individual human being with views, attitudes and emotions to a language learner whose brain is focused narrowly on the low-level linguistic de-coding which ... prevents the learner from achieving multidimensional representation of the L2 world' (Tomlinson, 1998a: 20). This means that the learners are not using their whole minds, that a multi-plicity of neural connections are not being fired and that meaningful and durable learning is not taking place.
3. While it is important to expose learners to a range of genres they are likely to encounter outside and after their course, I have found that the best way to achieve affective engagement is to include literature. By this I do not mean the classics of the literary canon but rather well-written texts which narrate, describe, argue or evoke in ways which encourage the reader to respond in personal and multidimensional ways, and which leave gaps for the reader to fill in (Tomlinson, 1994a, 1998b, 2000a, 2001a). Ideally these texts (especially for lower levels) are linguistically simple but cognitively and emotively com-plex (see the example below).

4. It is very rare that a text engages all the learners in a class. What we are aiming at is engaging most of them in a given class and all of them over a course. The best way I have found of achieving this is to make sure that many (but not all) of the texts relate to the basic universal themes of birth, growing up, going to school, starting a career, falling in love, getting married and dying (though this is a taboo topic in some countries).

Text Experience

In this stage you experience the selected text again. That is, you read or listen to it again experientially in order to re-engage with the text. This re-engagement is essential so that you can design activities which help the target learners to achieve similar engagement. Without this stage there is a danger that you study the text as a sample of language and end up designing activities which focus the learners on linguistic features of the text.

   Of course, if you fail to re-engage with the text you should reconsider your decision to select it to drive your materials.

Readiness Activities

As soon as you have re-engaged with the text, you start to devise activities which could help the learners to experience the text in similar multidimensional ways. First of all, you devise readiness activities which get the learners ready for the reading experience. You are aiming at helping the learners to achieve the mental readiness which readers take to L1 texts and to inhibit the word fixation and apprehension which L2 readers typically take to texts (Tomlinson, 2000b). 'The activities aim to stimulate mental activity relevant to the content of the text by activating connections, by arousing attention, by generating relevant visual images and by getting the learner to use inner speech to discuss relevant topics with themselves. What is important is that all the learners open and activate their minds not that they answer questions correctly' (Tomlinson, 1999c: 63). These activities are different from 'warmers' in that they are not necessarily getting the learners to talk but are aiming primarily to get the learners to think. They could ask the learners to visualize, to draw, to think of connections, to mime, to articulate their views, to recount episodes from their lives, to share their knowledge, to make predictions: anything which gets them to activate connections in their minds which will help them when they start to experience the text. For example, if the text is about an embarrassing moment, they can be asked to visualize embarrassing moments in their own lives to help them to empathize with the sufferer in the text. If the text is about tourists, they can be asked to think about and then act out in groups typical tourist scenarios in their region. If the text is about a child's first day at school they can be asked to think about and then share with a partner their first day at school. And, because the activities aim at mental readiness rather than language practice, any activity involving talking to others can be done in the L1 in monolingual lower-level groups.

   The important point is that the lesson starts in the learners' minds and not in the text and that the activities help the learners to gain a personal experience of the text which connects it to their lives.

Experiential Activities

These are activities which are designed to help the learners to represent the text in their minds as they read it or listen to it and to do so in multidimensional ways which facilitate personal engagement. They are things they are encouraged to do while reading or listening and should therefore be mental activities which contribute to the representation of the text and which do not interrupt the processing of it nor add difficulty or complexity to the task. They could include, for example, trying to visualize a politician as they read about him, using inner speech to give their responses to provocative points in a text, trying to follow a description of a journey on a mental map or thinking of examples from their own lives to illustrate or contradict points made in a text. The activities should not involve writing answers to questions nor discussing things in pairs or groups, as this can interrupt the experience and make representation more difficult.

These activities need to be given to the learners just before they start to read or listen to the text and should be given through concise and simple instructions which are easy to remember and apply. For example:

> You're going to listen to a poem about a child's first day at school. Imagine that you are that child and that you are standing alone in the playground at the beginning of your first day at school. As you listen to the poem, try to see in your mind what the child could see in the playground.

Experiential activities can be either related to a given text, as in the example above, or they can be part of a process approach which involves the learners in participating in the creation of the text, as in the examples below:

- The teacher reads aloud a text and pauses at salient points while learners shout out predictions of the next word or phrase.
- The teacher dictates a text and then pauses at salient points while learners compare what they have written with their partners and then write the next line (an approach which can be particularly effective with poetry).
- The teacher reads aloud a text while the learners act it out (an approach which can be particularly effective if each group of learners plays a different character in a story together).
- The teacher reads aloud most of a text and then gets groups of learners to write their own endings.
- The teacher gives the learners draft texts on which an 'editor' has written suggested changes in the wording and then gets them to write out a final version of their own.

Intake Response Activities

These are activities which help the learners to develop and articulate what they have taken in from the text. They focus on the mental representation which the learners have achieved from their initial reading of the text and they invite the learners to reflect on this representation rather than return to the text. Unlike conventional comprehension questions, these activities do not test learners on their comprehension of the text. Instead they give the learners a positive start to their post-reading/listening responses by inviting them to share with others what the text means to them. They cannot be wrong because they are not being asked about the text but about their personal representation of it. However, it is possible that their representation is only partial (or even superficial) and the process of sharing of it with others can help to extend and deepen it.

Intake response activities could ask the learners to think about and then articulate their feelings and opinions about what was said or done in the text. They could ask them to visualize, to draw or to mime what they can remember from the text. Or they could ask them to summarize the text to someone who has not read it or to ask clarification questions of the teacher or of someone else who knows the text well.

These activities should not be graded or criticized but the teacher can help the learners to deepen their initial responses by asking questions, by guiding them to think back to particular sections of the text or by 'feeding' them extracts from the text to stimulate further thought and discussion.

Development Activities
'These are activities which provide opportunities for meaningful language production based on the learners' representations of the text' (Tomlinson, 1999c: 63). They involve the learners (usually in pairs or small groups) going back to the text before going forward to produce something new. So, for example, after experiencing a story called 'Sentence of Death' about a man in Liverpool being told that he has four hours to live, the learners in groups rewrite the story so that it is based in their own town. Or, after experiencing a story called, 'They Came from the Sea: Part 1', they sit in a circle and take it in turns to suggest the next sentence of 'They Came from the Sea: Part 2'. Or, after working out from an advertisement the good and bad points of a vehicle called the C5, they design an improved C6 and then write an advertisement. The point is that they can base their language production both on what they have already understood from the text and on connections with their own lives. While talking or writing they will gain opportunities to learn new language and develop new skills and, if they are affectively engaged in an achievable challenge, they will learn a lot from each other and from the teacher (if she/he moves around the room helping learners when they ask for assistance).

Input Response Activities
These are activities which take the learners back to the text and which involve them in studial reading or listening tasks aimed at helping them to make discoveries about the purposes and language of the text.

Interpretation Tasks

These are input response tasks which involve the learners thinking more deeply about the text in order to make discoveries about the author's intentions in creating it. They are aimed at helping learners to develop critical and creative thinking skills in the target language and they make use of such task types as:

- Deep questions (e.g., What points about society do you think the writer is making in his modern version of *Little Red Riding Hood?*)
- Debates about issues in the text
- Critical reviews of the text for a journal
- Interviews with the characters
- Interviews with the author

Awareness Tasks

These are input response activities which provide opportunities for the learners to gain awareness from a focused study of the text (by awareness I mean a gradually developing apprehension which is different from knowledge in that it is internal, personal, dynamic and variable). The awareness could be of language use (Bolitho and Tomlinson, 1995), of communication strategies (Tomlinson, 1994b), of discourse features, of genre characteristics or of text type features. The awareness tasks usually involve investigation of a particular feature of a text plus 'research' involving checking the typicality of the investigated feature by analysing the same feature in use in other, equivalent texts. So, for example, you could ask the learners to work out generalizations about the form and function of 'in case of' from the poem by Roger McGough called 'In Case of Fire', and then get the learners to find and compare examples of 'in case of' in notices and instruction manuals. Or you could ask learners to make generalizations about a character's use of the imperative when talking to his father in a scene from a novel; or ask them to work out typical features of the genre of advertisement from examining a number of advertisements in a magazine. The important point is that evidence is provided in a text which the learners have already experienced holistically and then they are helped to make focused discoveries through discrete attention to a specified feature of the text. That way they invest cognitive and affective energy and attention in the learning process and they are likely to increase their readiness for acquisition (Pienemann, 1985; Tomlinson, 1994b).

Using the Framework

The above framework is best used flexibly. Obviously some stages must precede others (e.g., readiness activities before experiential activities) and there are strong arguments for some stages preceding others (e.g., intake response before input response so that the learners progress positively from what they already understand to what they need to think more carefully about). However, there is no need to follow all the stages in the framework (it depends on the engagement and the needs and wants of each particular class), the sequence of some of the stages can vary (e.g., the development activities can come before or after the input response activities) and sometimes the teacher might decide to focus on a particular type of activity because of the needs of the learners (e.g., after a brief intake response activity the teacher might spend the rest of the lesson on a genre awareness activity because the particular genre exemplified by the text (e.g., scientific report) is a new and important one for the particular class). It is useful, though, for the materials developer to include all the stages in the actual course materials so that the teachers (and possibly the learners) can make decisions for themselves about which stages to use and what sequence to use them in. The important point is that apprehension should come before comprehension (Kolb, 1984) and that the learners are encouraged to respond holistically, affectively and multidimensionally to a text before being helped to think more deeply about it in order to learn something from it.

By using the framework as a guide you can very quickly develop principled and engaging materials either for a particular class or for a course of materials. I have used it myself to prepare cover lessons at five minutes' notice and I have used it in Japan, Singapore and Turkey to help teachers to produce an effective unit of material in just fifteen minutes.

An Example of the Framework in Use Here is an example of a text-driven framework used to produce the materials for a ninety-minute lesson:

'I'm an old, old lady'

1. Tell the learners to think of an old woman they know. Tell them to try to see pictures of their old woman in their minds, to see where she is, to see what she is doing, to see what she is wearing. Tell them to talk to themselves about their feelings towards the old woman.
2. Tell the learners to form pairs and to tell each other about their old woman. Tell them to describe the pictures of their old woman in their mind and to express their feelings towards her.
3. Tell the learners you are going to read them a poem about an old woman and that, as they listen, they should try to see pictures of her in their minds and to talk to themselves about their feelings towards her.
4. Read the poem below to the learners:

> I'm an old, old lady
> And I don't have long to live.
> I am only strong enough to take
> Not to give. No time left to give.
> I want to drink, I want to eat,
> I want my shoes taken off my feet
> I want to talk but not to walk
> Because if I walk, I have to know
> Where it is I want to go.

I want to sleep but not to dream
I want to play and win every game
To live with love but not to love
The world to move but me not move
I want I want for ever and ever
The world to work, the world to be clever.
Leave me be, but don't leave me alone.
That's what I want. I'm a big round stone
Sitting in the middle of a thunderstorm.
There you are: that's true.
That's me. Now: you.
(John Arden, 'Phineus', from the *The Happy Haven*)

5. Tell the learners to think back over the poem, to see pictures of the old lady in their minds and decide what they think about her.
6. Tell the learners to get into groups and discuss their responses to the following statement about the old lady in the poem:

'I don't like this lady. She's very selfish.'

7. Give the learners the poem and three pictures of very different old ladies. Then tell them to decide in their groups which of the old ladies wrote the poem.
8. Get each group to join with another group and discuss their answers to 6 and 7 above.
9. Tell the learners to do one of the following, either individually, in pairs or in small groups:

   • You are the old lady. Write a letter to your son in Australia.
   • You are the old lady. Write your diary for today.
   • The old lady goes to the park and meets an old man on a park bench. Write the dialogue between them.
   • You are the old lady's family. Hold a meeting to decide how you can help her.

10. Get the students in groups to discuss the following questions:

   • What do you think the old lady means when she says, 'I'm a big round stone Sitting in the middle of a thunderstorm'?
   • How do you think old ladies that you know are similar to or different from the lady in the poem?
   • What similarities and differences do you think the poem illustrates between your own culture and British culture?

11. Get the learners to do the following:

    i.   What tense does the old lady use throughout her poem. Why do you think she uses this tense?

Find examples from other texts of this tense being used with this function.

    ii.   The old lady uses a number of imperatives.

- List all the imperatives in the poem.
- Write a generalization about the form of the imperative as illustrated by the examples in the poem.
- Write a generalization about the function of the imperatives which the old lady uses in the poem.
- Find examples from other texts of the imperative being used with the same function as it is in the poem.

Table 6.1 A summary of the text-driven framework

Stage	Procedure	Principles	Objectives
Text Collection	Find or create potentially engaging texts (written or spoken)	Affective engagement is a prerequisite for durable learning	To build a library of texts with the potential for engaging learners
Text Selection	Select a text suitable in level and theme for your target learners	Texts need to be matched with learners	To find a text with the potential for useful engagement for the target learners
Text Experience	Read or listen to the text experientially	Apprehension should come before comprehension	To start from an experience which you can try to help the learners to approximate
Readiness Activities	Devise activities which could help the learners achieve mental readiness for	Experiencing a text is a multidimensional process involving sensory imaging,	To help the learners to experience a target language text in the

	experiencing the text	inner speech and the establishment of affective and cognitive connections	multidimensional way they would automatically use when experiencing an L1 text
Experiential Activities	Devise whilst-reading or listening activities which will help the learners to process the text in an experiential way	L2 learners tend to process a text in a studial way in an insecure attempt to achieve total comprehension	To help the learners to move away from their tendency to study texts so that they can engage with the text instead experientially
Intake Response Activities	Devise activities which help learners to articulate and develop their mental representations of the text	Learning is facilitated by starting positively from what the learners do know and understand	To encourage learners to process their representation of a text rather than the text itself and to encourage them to be relaxed and confident in their response to texts
Development Activities	Devise activities which help the learners to use their representation of the text as a basis for language production activities	Mental connections facilitate learning	To help learners express themselves in the target language intelligently and creatively
Input Response Activities	Devise activities which help the learners to go back to the text and to discover patterns and regularities of language use in the text	A good time to analyse a text is just after an enjoyable multidimensional experience of it. Helping learners to make discoveries for	To get the learners to develop their analytical skills and their ability to make discoveries about the use of the target language for

		themselves can be an effective way of promoting long-term learning	themselves
Trialling	Try out the materials with a typical target class	Matching materials to learner needs and wants is an ongoing, dynamic process	To find out how usable and motivating the materials are
Evaluation	Use questionnaires, interviews and analysis of the learners' work to find out what effect the materials had on the learners	Giving learners a chance to evaluate their learning process can not only provide useful information but can also motivate and stimulate learners	To show learners they are respected and to find out what effect the materials had on them
Revision	Produce an improved version of the materials	Materials developers and teachers need constantly to improve their materials to achieve a closer match with learner needs and wants	To match the needs and wants of the learners

A Web-based Adaptation of the Framework

Although the framework above is primarily text-driven it can be adapted to become an activity-driven framework with the text to base the activities on being chosen by the learners from a library of texts either provided for them or built up over a period of time by themselves. Or the materials can be based on units of text genres (e.g., advertisements, reports, jokes, announcements, stories, etc.) and the learners can be asked to find an appropriate and engaging text from the Internet, as in the following example from a textbook I am writing called, *English from the Web*.

NEWSPAPER REPORTS 1

(Artwork 1 – A collage of extracts from world newspapers in English to include: headlines; photos and captions; editorial comment; letters to the Editor; cartoons.)

1. **Get Ready**
   Think about stories which have been in the news recently. Select two of these stories and then for each one:

   - create pictures in your mind of what happened;
   - see what happened in your mind as a series of headlines in English;
   - predict in your mind a picture of what will happen next in the story;
   - see in your mind a caption in English underneath the picture;
   - see in your mind future newspaper headlines in English for the story.

   If you are working with other learners, share your creations with them.

2. **Reading the News**

   Select one of your stories from 1 above and then try to find articles, editorials, letters and photographs relating to it from some of the following newspaper websites:

   Σ   *http://news.excite.com/news*
   Σ   *http://news.excite.com/news/reuters (Reuters)*
   Σ   *http://www.iht.com (The Internation Herald Tribune)*
   Σ   *http://www.guardian.co.uk (The Guardian)*
   Σ   *http://www. sunday-times.co.uk (The Sunday Times)*
   Σ   *http://www.the-times.co.uk (The Times)*
   Σ   *http://www.telegraph.co.uk (The Telegraph)*
   Σ   *http://www.ireland.com (The Irish Times)*
   Σ   *http://www.latimes.com (The Los Angeles Times)*
   Σ   *http://www.nytimes.com (The New York Times)*
   Σ   *http://www.news.com.au (The Australian)*
   Σ   *http://www.smhcom.au (The Sydney Morning Herald)*
   Σ   *http://www.japantimes.co.jp (The Japan Times)*
   Σ   *http://www.straitstimes.asial.com.sg (The Straits Times – Singapore)*
   Σ   *http://mg.co.za/mg (The Daily Mail and Guardian – South Africa)*

3. **Making Notes**

   Make notes on the report you have just been reading under the following headings:

My Feelings
The Facts
Opinions
The Issues
My Predictions

If you are working with other people compare notes and then revise your own notes if you wish.

4. **Article Writing**

Use your notes above to write a summary article on the story for an English language newspaper or magazine in your own country (you can make one up if you like). In your article focus:

- either on your views about what has happened;
- or on the issues which this story raises.

Try to lay your article out using the conventions of the news genre. For example, use headlines, headings, bold type, photographs, captions, etc.

5. **Comparing Reports**

Go back to the web pages which you read in 2 and focus on three of them. Read each one carefully and then make notes on the differences between them under the following headings:

Prominence Given to the Story
The Facts
Main Emphasis
Attitudes
Style

Compare your notes with those of other people if you can.

6. **Language Work**

   i.   *Direct and Reported Speech*

   a.   Read the following report from *The Guardian* (Thursday 11 May 2000) on the intervention of British troops in Sierra Leone.

MPs press for debate on Sierra Leone

By Mark Tran

ROBIN COOK is facing demands for a full parliamentary debate as British troops stand alongside UN peacekeeping troops defending the capital, Freetown. Pressure was building today in Parliament for a full debate on Britain's role in Sierra Leone as British paratroopers dug in alongside UN peacekeeping forces in the Aberdeen peninsula to the west of the capital, Freetown.

Although the area is not in the path of rebels, whose advance on Freetown was blocked by forces loyal to President Ahmad Tejan Kabbah, British army officials delivered a blunt message. 'We hope we won't be having to get into a fight with anyone – but we are well prepared if we have to do so,' said an army official when asked whether British troops were on standby to help UN troops. The tough warning will do little to ease the concern among MPs, who are clamouring for answers from the government. MPs from all sides are pressing for a debate on Sierra Leone and the Commons leader, Margaret Beckett,

promised to convey their demands to Robin Cook, the Foreign secretary.

But she reprimanded Tories who said there was an urgent need to discuss it, saying British soldiers would be no safer if MPs deliberated on their fate. To Tory protests, she said: 'I accept these are very important matters but I very much doubt whether the welfare and safety of a single British soldier will be affected by whether or not we discuss these matters next week.'

Mrs Beckett was responding to Tory MP Ian Bruce, who asked why HMS *Ocean* had been diverted from a Nato exercise to take part in the Sierra Leone mission while Britain's allies were not helping out. She dismissed Tory MP John Wilkinson's argument that Britain should now pull out because its national interest was not affected.

Her comments came after Downing Street said the Prime Minister had emphasized to ministers at their weekly Cabinet meeting that British troops 'were there for evacuation and not for combat'. The government has repeatedly stressed that was the limit of their mission.

Read the article again and as you read it pay particular attention to the direct speech and the reported speech in the report, e.g.:

'... "were there for evacuation and not for combat" ...' = direct speech.
'... who asked why HMS *Ocean* had been diverted ...' = reported speech.

Using examples from the text, complete the following statements:

In this report:

- direct speech is used when the actual words ... (e.g. ...)
- reported speech is used when it is the content rather than ... (e.g. ...) or when the reporter wants to save ... (e.g. ...)

b. Read again each of the web pages which you analysed above and consider how each article reports what people said. For each article do the following:

- Does the article use mainly reported speech or direct speech? Why do you think this is so?
- For each instance of reported speech say why you think the writer used reported speech instead of direct speech.
- For each instance of direct speech say why you think the writer used direct speech instead of reported speech.
- Is there anything distinctive you notice about the use of reported speech in news reports/articles?
- Is there anything distinctive you notice about the use of direct speech in news reports/articles?

c. Compare your discoveries above with other people's discoveries. Then together look at other news stories on the web to confirm or develop your discoveries.

d. Write notes on Direct and Reported Speech in your *Use of English* file.

ii. *The Passive*

a. There are many instances of the passive voice in the report from the *Guardian* above (e.g., 'Mrs Beckett was responding to Tory MP Ian Bruce, who asked why HMS *Ocean* had been diverted from a Nato exercise'). Without looking back at the report, say why you think the passive is likely to be used in such a report.

   Find all the examples of the passive in the report and for each one say what you think its function is.

b. Look at the headlines on a newspaper web page and predict one report which is likely to make frequent use of the passive and another report which is unlikely to use the passive.

Read the two reports to check if your predictions are correct.

For each passive used in the two reports say what you think its function is.

c. Complete the following generalizations about the typical use of the passive in newspaper reports and write them in your *Use of English* file:
The passive is typically used in newspaper reports to:

- avoid direct ... (e.g. ...)
- indicate that the doer of an action is ... (e.g. ...)
- indicate that it is not ... who is the doer of an action ... (e.g. ...)

7. **Writing an Article**

Find a news story which interests you by surfing some of the newspaper web sites listed above.
Predict what is going to happen tomorrow in the story you have chosen.
Imagine that it is now 'tomorrow' and that you are a news reporter. Write the report of what has happened. Try to keep to the genre conventions and style of the original report but also try to make the report as appealing and interesting as you can.
Wait until the next day and then read the new real report and compare it with your report for:

- content
- style
- use of language

8. **Follow-Up**

Read a news story on the web every day for a week. For each story:

- Read it first of all for content and then talk to yourself about it after you have read it.
- Read it again and think about the use of language (especially direct and indirect speech and the passive).

Conclusion

The examples of the use of principled frameworks outlined above are intended as illustrations of the value of developing frameworks prior to developing materials. My main argument is that the activities in a course should match with learner needs and wants and with principles of language learning, and that they should be developed in ways which provide flexibility of use to learners and teachers as well as coherence of connection. The best way to achieve this is to consider both the target context of use for the materials and the principles and experience of the writers, and then to develop a flexible framework to guide the development of the units. Later on, compromises might have to be made in relation to the realities of administrative and publisher needs but at least the writing process will start with the learner as the focus and with principles in mind.

References

Arden, J. (1962) 'The happy haven'. *New English Dramatists* 4. London: Penguin.

Bell, J. and Gower, R. (1998) 'Writing course materials for the world: a great compromise', in B. Tomlinson (ed.) *Materials Development in Language Teaching.* Cambridge: Cambridge University Press, pp. 116–29.

Bolitho, R. and Tomlinson, B. (1995) *Discover English* (new edn.). Oxford: Heinemann.

Cochingo-Ballesteros, C. A. (1995) 'Spoken English handbooks and audio tapes for the elementary grades', in A. C. Hidalgo, D. Hall and G. M. Jacobs (eds) *Getting Started: Materials Writers on Materials Writing.* Singapore: SEAMEO Regional Language Centre, pp. 46–56.

Flores, M. M. (1995) 'Materials development: a creative process', in A. C. Hidalgo, D. Hall and G. M. Jacobs (eds) *Getting Started: Materials Writers on Materials Writing.* Singapore: SEAMEO Regional Language Centre, pp. 57–66.

Fortez, G. E. (1995) 'Developing materials for tertiary level expository writing', in A. C. Hidalgo, D. Hall and G. M. Jacobs (eds) *Getting Started: Materials Writers on Materials Writing.* Singapore: SEAMEO Regional Language Centre, pp. 67–81.

Hidalgo, A. C., Hall, D. and Jacobs, G. M. (eds) (1995) *Getting Started: Materials Writers on Materials Writing.* Singapore: SEAMEO Regional Language Centre.

Hutchinson, T. and Waters, A. (1984) *Interface: English for Technical Communication.* London: Longman.

Jolly, D. and Bolitho, R. (1998) 'A framework for materials writing', in B. Tomlinson (ed.) *Materials Development in Language Teaching.* Cambridge: Cambridge University Press, pp. 90–115.

Kolb, D. (1984) *Experiential Learning: Experience as the Source of Learning and Development.* Englewood Cliffs, NJ: Prentice Hall.

Luzares, C. E. (1995) 'Scientific writing: developing materials without reinventing the wheel', in A. C. Hidalgo, D. Hall and G. M. Jacobs (eds) *Getting Started: Materials Writers on Materials Writing.* Singapore: SEAMEO Regional Language Centre, pp. 25–30.

Maley, A. (1995) 'Materials writing and tacit knowledge', in A. C. Hidalgo, D. Hall and G. M. Jacobs (eds) *Getting Started: Materials Writers on Materials Writing.* Singapore: SEAMEO Regional Language Centre, pp. 220–39.

Nunan, D. (1988) 'Principles for designing language teaching materials'. *Guidelines,* **10**, 1–24.

Peinemann, M. (1985) 'Learnability and syllabus construction', in K. Hyltenstam and M. Peinemann (eds) *Modelling and Assessing Second Language Acquisition.* Clevedon, Avon: Multilingual Matters.

Penaflorida, A. H. (1995) 'The process of materials development: a personal experience', in A. C. Hidalgo, D. Hall and G. M. Jacobs (eds) *Getting Started:*

Materials Writers on Materials Writing. Singapore: SEAMEO Regional Language Centre, pp. 172–86.

Prowse, P. (1998) 'How writers write: testimony from authors', in B. Tomlinson (ed.) *Materials Development in Language Teaching.* Cambridge: Cambridge University Press, pp. 130–45.

Ribe, R. (2000) 'Introducing negotiation processes: an experiment with creative project work', in M. P. Breen and A. Littlejohn (eds) *Classroom Decision Making: Negotiation and Process Syllabuses in Practice.* Cambridge: Cambridge University Press.

Richards, J. C. (1995) 'Easier said than done: an insider's account of a textbook project', in A. C. Hidalgo, D. Hall and G. M. Jacobs (eds) *Getting Started: Materials Writers on Materials Writing.* Singapore: SEAMEO Regional Language Centre, pp. 95–135.

Richards, J. C. (2001) *Curriculum Development in Language Education.* Cambridge: Cambridge University Press.

Rosenblatt, M. L. (1968) *Literature as Exploration.* Oxford: Heinemann.

Rosenblatt, M. L. (1978) *The Reader, the Text, the Poem.* Carbondale, IL: Southern Illinois University Press.

Rozul, R. H. (1995) 'ESP Materials Development: the writing process', in A. C. Hidalgo, D. Hall and G. M. Jacobs (eds) *Getting Started: Materials Writers on Materials Writing.* Singapore: SEAMEO Regional Language Centre, pp. 209–18.

Tomlinson, B. (1994a) *Openings.* London: Penguin.

Tomlinson, B. (1994b) 'Pragmatic awareness activities'. *Language Awareness,* **3** (3), 119–29.

Tomlinson, B. (1998a) 'Affect and the coursebook'. *IATEFL Issues,* **145**, 20–1.

Tomlinson, B. (1998b) 'And now for something not completely different; an approach to language through literature'. *Reading in a Foreign Language,* **11** (2), 177–89.

Tomlinson, B. (ed.) (1998c) *Materials Development in Language Teaching.* Cambridge: Cambridge University Press.

Tomlinson, B. (1998d) 'Seeing what they mean: helping L2 readers to visualise', in B. Tomlinson (ed.) *Materials Development in Language Teaching.* Cambridge: Cambridge University Press, pp. 265–78.

Tomlinson, B. (1999a) 'Adding Affect to ESP (English for Special People)'. *ESP SIG Newsletter,* **15**, 26–34.

Tomlinson, B. (1999b) 'Developing materials for materials evaluation'. *IATEFL Issues,* **147**, 10–13.

Tomlinson, B. (1999c) 'Materials development for language teachers'. *Modern English Teacher,* **8** (1), 62–4.

Tomlinson, B. (2000a) 'A multidimensional approach'. *The Language Teacher Online,* 24/07.

Tomlinson, B. (2000b) 'Beginning to read forever'. *Reading in a Foreign Language,* **13** (1), 523–38.

Tomlinson, B. (2000c) 'Talking to yourself: the role of the inner voice in language learning'. *Applied Language Learning,* **11** (1), 123–54.

Tomlinson, B. (2001a) 'Connecting the mind: a multi-dimensional approach to teaching language through literature'. *The English Teacher*, **4** (2), 104–15.

Tomlinson, B. (2001b) 'Humanising the coursebook'. *Humanising Language Teaching*, **5** (3). Canterbury: Pilgrims.

CHAPTER
7

Writing a Coursebook

Chris Mares

Introduction

Coursebooks are designed to give cohesion to the language teaching and learning process by providing direction, support and specific language-based activities aimed at offering classroom practice for students. Furthermore, many coursebooks claim to provide learners with exposure to language in use. With these points in mind, coursebooks have often provided the syllabus for language programmes and multi-level series have taken learners from beginners to advanced level. From the global perspective, coursebooks have also provided non-native-speaker teachers with the support and security necessary for many of them to tackle more 'communicative'-type classes, rather than the more traditional grammar translation classes of the past. Clearly, therefore, coursebooks have had a significant impact on many students and teachers, as well as shaping the English language curricula in many institutions. In this chapter, I will consider the nature of current mainstream coursebooks, examine the process of writing a coursebook, consider the realities of writing for the commercial market and then move on to consider the need to break from the current coursebook paradigm, before giving an account of my own experience as a coursebook writer.

The Nature of Coursebooks

Most coursebooks are based on a linear model of language learning, leading from the simple to the more complex as reflected in the graded grammar syllabuses uses that underpin many of the coursebooks on the market today, including the *Interchange*, *Headway*, *Atlas* and *Online* series. In terms of language practice, much of the communicative practice tends to come from contextualized functional drills which are often highly controlled, thus bringing into question the claim to being 'communicative' as in this example from *Interchange 2*:

  A: Complete these conversations. Then practise with a partner.
  1. A: Could you tell me a little about yourself?
        Where were you born?
     B: I ... born in South Korea.
     A: ... did you grow up there?
     B: No, I ..., I ... up in Canada.

Other drills follow a similar 'listen and practise' format which, it will be argued, belongs more to the language learning paradigm, rather than the acquisition paradigm. It should be said, though, that an increased focus on personalization has led to a degree of genuine communication, as in this example from *Online 2*:

Ask three people:
What would you do if you had more time/money?

I would...

3. In a group. Tell each other what you found out.

Many coursebooks are production rather than comprehension-based, reflecting the desire to have students use language as soon as possible – this satisfies the popular belief concerning the so-called 'communicative classroom' – that students should be using language as soon as possible. The belief, however, does not reflect what we know about language acquisition and the need for a silent period (Krashen, 1981). In fact, in many cases students are forced to produce language before they are ready, which only creates an illlusion of production or communication as learners are only mimicking the text or teacher (see Part C, Chapter 15, 'Materials for Beginners', in this volume).

The Process of Writing

A main reason for writing a coursebook is the desire to produce more effective materials that truly engage learners, are pedagogically sound and have a general appeal beyond the tastes of one individual in his/her own teaching environment. This urge to write could be due to a dislike of current materials or to a simple mismatch between student needs and the materials available. It could also occur when a teacher feels that the materials available do not reflect the pedagogic principles concerning language learning and teaching held by that teacher. Or the urge to write could simply spring from a teacher's innate creativity.

The creative act of writing when unfettered is a wonderfully liberating experience. To transpose one's best kept secrets onto the page for others when it springs from true conviction and informed principles is a very satisfying experience. However, commercial publishing is often in the challenging situation of catering to a global market that may not always be ready for the innovation that some writers propose. At the same time, some writers may not pitch their materials at non-native-speaker teachers who may feel uncomfortable teaching in a less structured environment where partial learning is viewed as a stage rather than a deficiency. When I first began to write commercial materials I was subconsciously writing for clones of myself, teachers who had chosen to take a further degree in order to better their understanding of language teaching and learning, teachers who were familiar with the principles of language acquisition. I was not writing for non-native teachers with low confidence in their command of the English language, but in the world of 'the market' these teachers make up a sizeable slice.

Writing takes a great deal of time, and prospective writers must decide whether they have or can make the time needed, given the usual constraints of full-time jobs and the need for a life. Furthermore, the financial returns from writing a coursebook may not be realized for a year after the material appears on the market and when they are realized they may not be substantial. In short, the desire to write a coursebook and get it published requires serious commitment, sacrifice and, most significantly, compromise.

Writing Commercial Material for a Conservative Market

Mainstream publishers are reluctant to present non-native-speaker teachers, untrained or very busy teachers with materials that are radically different from existing materials as there is a serious risk of rejection in an essentially conservative and very competitive market. Ideally, publishers would invest money in ambitious pilot texts used at leading high schools and colleges, teachers at all levels would be involved, teacher training would be offered and ongoing support given to users. The tendency however, is for publishers to look for materials that fall under a general umbrella of acceptability yet have a twist or pizzazz that make them marketable. Generally this spark involves current buzzwords or phrases such as 'communicative', 'multiple intelligences', 'authentic dialogues', 'learner strategies' or 'learner styles', which are used in the promotional material but are not necessarily addressed meaningfully in the materials, as in this extract from *True Colors:*

Pair Practice
Practice the conversation and vocabulary with a partner. Use your own words.
B: I need to see Dr...
A: How about ... this afternoon?
B: This afternoon? Gosh, I'm going to be ... until ... Is tomorrow a possibility?
A: Let's See. How about...?

Writing a coursebook, then, is only a part of the process of bringing material into the classroom. Most writing occurs under contract with a publishing house which means that other forces than sound current pedagogy are at work. These forces essentially reflect market constraints. In short, a new approach may not be enough to convince editors or sales managers of the viability of an expensive project which has no guarantee of success.

Approaching a Publisher

The most sensible strategy for a prospective writer is to write a proposal for a coursebook consisting of a rationale, a provisional scope and sequence for the book and three pilot units. The rationale needs to include a description of the principles underlying the book as well as a description of how the book meets the needs of the market. The provisional scope and sequence need to show clearly how the book is organized as a whole and to have enough detail to illustrate the basic organization of each unit. The three pilot units should be carefully chosen to illustrate the original features of the book. At the pilot stage, it is worth taking some risks in terms of testing the market to see if the new features are going to be acceptable. Another part of the proposal should be a review of the competition with a clear explanation of how the proposed text both parallels and differs from the competition. Having put together a proposal, it is then necessary to contact an acquisitions editor in a publishing house that has a foothold in the target market of the coursebook.

In the experience of this writer, acquisitions editors are always 'interested' in prospective materials, partly because they have nothing to lose from unsolicited manuscripts. Showing interest in a writer's work is also usually enough to seduce a writer into writing more units or perhaps reworking units already submitted. During this time, an acquisitions editor will attempt to determine the viability of a project from in-house colleagues in editing and marketing and sales as well as commissioned readers. This process is part of the pre-contract dance and can go on for months and have both happy and tragic endings. A happy ending would involve the signing of a contract and the chance to work with an editor and publishing house who share the writer's vision. A less happy ending could involve the signing of the contract under the condition of product revision, which could involve serious compromise on behalf of the writer. A tragic ending could involve the rejection of a proposal that a writer felt to be innovative, pedagogically sound and in keeping with current research.

Defining a New Paradigm

It is clear that the global coursebook market is essentially conservative, rooted in an essentially structural approach which focuses on linguistically graded material; this is certainly true of the *Atlas*, *Interchange* and *Online* series. Nevertheless, publishers are eager for incremental novelty and fresh ideas. This, I feel allows for the possibility of a shift to a new paradigm, that is less focused on learning, and more focused on acquisition. This move would involve:

Moving away from the linear grammar-based syllabus towards non-linguistically graded material that is intuitively pitched at the target level of the learner and shifting the focus from production to comprehension, with more listening at the lower levels.

Treating speaking in a delicate manner, an option rather than a requirement, particularly at the lower levels.

Using authentic and modified texts of a wide variety, from poems, short narratives, dialogues, monologues, to short stories and extracts from novels.

Activities involving a great deal of visualization and personalization with students being trained to reflect and respond affectively.

Looking at language in a more lexical way, in terms of word grouping, powerful verbs and collocations. A move towards consciousness-raising activities would reflect this new focus.

Tasks in which the outcome is communication-based rather than accuracy-based.

Systematic recycling of language in different contexts to facilitate acquisition.

From New Paradigm to New Product – The Quest for Innovation

Moving away from a linear grammar sequence means moving away from a view of language that believes that learners need to learn 'simple' structures first and then move systematically on to more 'complex' structures. This move can be exciting for writers yet disturbing for publishers and prospective users, whether teachers or learners. If we move away from the grammar-based syllabus then how do we organize the syllabus? One question that needs to be asked is whether we need a linear-graded syllabus at all? Part of the appeal of a graded syllabus is the apparent sense of progression and progress that can be created. However, is this how we should evaluate progress? The goal of a coursebook should be to provide the learner with comprehensible input and to expose the learner to as much language as possible in an engaging way, over time, rather than prescribe what should be learned. In this regard a new paradigm for coursebook writing would involve a focus on natural acquisition and not on proscribed learning.

A new approach would be to pitch coursebook material at level 'bands' where the tasks are graded rather than the language. Another alternative would be to have tasks graded within units, each unit consisting of a bank of texts and task types, not all of which would necessarily be used by a teacher. This approach would allow not only for flexibility within the framework of a coursebook, but also for flexibility within the framework of a unit. Teachers would be able to shape the book more to their own needs, by virtue of non-linear structure. In a case such as this, each unit would need to contain a variety of task types of varying length and complexity, serving different purpose, yet each unit would be designed around the intent to provide comprehensible input and to engage learners.

Respecting the beginner learner's need for a silent period in the language acquisition process has at least two consequences for materials writers. The first is that beginner learners would not be forced to speak by activities in the coursebook. Secondly, for all learners at all levels there would be acknowledgement of the need for a silent period or lag time between input and output for processing and consciousness-raising. One suggestion would be to provide tasks that focus specifically on comprehension, both of context and text. Tasks therefore would include schema-raising activities – drawing, imagining, moving, making connections, miming, etc. Finally, activities would also need to reflect different learner styles and intelligence types.

Motivation and investment are keys to language learning. One text type that can quickly engage a learner and lead to schema-raising and visualization is poetry. The very spareness of form, the power of imagery and the opportunities for exemplifying stress and intonation make poetry a rich resource. Poems do not necessarily need to be complete, as stanzas, single lines or simply collocations are all powerful as input. Poetry can be used for dictation, pronunciation work, review, topic introduction or simply for pleasure. For writers, poems can appear on the page in their complete forms, in partial form or on tape or in teachers' guides. Folk tales and urban myths are another underused resource, particularly folk tales from around the world. Again, the imagery, the power of universal themes and the appeal of narrative make this text form ideal for engaging learners of all ages. Stories can easily be adapted to a specific level or for the purpose of recycling language. It is not necessary to work with complete stories as it is possible to focus on beginnings or endings or particular scenes within a story. Activity types can involve drawing, matching and miming, at the lower levels, and more sophisticated analysis at higher levels. Extracts from stories are also a powerful tool. These can be presented through teacher reading, tape or reading, or simply visually. Again, universal human themes work best, anything that can be related to experientially – living, learning, working, loving, helping, caring, etc. Any text working with human traits, whether noble or ignoble, will work.

A comprehension-based approach to materials writing naturally leads to a break from the traditional Present, Practise, Produce (PPP) paradigm which has still held so much sway in recent so-called 'communicative' material. A more relevant paradigm is the Observe–Hypothesize–Experiment cycle noted by Lewis (1993) and others and this is complemented by Nunan's comment (1999), on our tendency to learn partially many different things rather than systematically gain control over building blocks that lead to an organized fluency.

One Writer's List of Truths

All writers develop a view of the publishing world based on their own experience. Here is a list of truths I feel I have learnt:

- Writers need to know, understand and feel a certain amount of empathy for the constraints under which publishers, editors and marketing departments operate.
- Publishers generally feel more comfortable with material that is the same but different.
- Publishers may not feel able to run the risk of publishing material that is too far from that currently available.
- A good editor is invaluable.
- The work of an editor is highly demanding and some editors are much better than others.
- Different editors have different philosophies, work styles and expectations.
- Editors have to answer to the marketing department, the publisher and the writers.
- Editors move from publisher to publisher so do not be surprised if you work with more than one over the space of a single project.

- Editors are always interested in new material but interest is no guarantee that material will be published.
- Editors need to be judged on an individual basis.
- Editors are not always fully informed in terms of current research findings.
- Submitting a proposal and getting positive feedback is not the same as getting a contract.
- Getting a contract may involve great changes to the initial proposal.
- The final contract may involve writers producing material that they view as good but compromised.
- Most people in publishing have worked for more than one publisher.
- Coursebooks are far easier to criticize than they are to write.

One Writer's Experience

My personal journey as a coursebook writer has led to frustration, disappointment, satisfaction, opportunity and a degree of qualified success. It is a journey worth reporting to those thinking of embarking on a similar adventure. Fortunately, it was not a journey I undertook alone and I thoroughly recommend co-authoring with a well-chosen partner.

I began writing with the enthusiasm and unfettered idealism of youth armed with an MA in Applied Linguistics, an RSA TEFLA Diploma and about five years of teaching experience. On reflection, the acquisitions editors and sales representatives we met must have been intrigued and encouraged by our freshness and bubbly naivety. They must also have held back on their concerns which would emerge later in the writing process. Our material, originally written in the late 1980s, was free of graded grammatical syllabuses. In fact, it was free of virtually any conventional constraints with respect to unit length or template. We believed in providing rich language input and engaging tasks. Our units were not fettered by templates but steered by our feelings about what would be interesting material for students to work with. We felt that different topcis might require different amounts of time to cover in an interesting way. They did not all merit the same treatment in terms of number of pages per unit, number of activities, etc. Unfortunately, we were writing for ourselves, or for teachers with a similar educational, cultural and philosophical background. What we had failed to grasp was the fact that we were entering a market which operated according to well-established principles, the most important being that publishing is a business and businesses are run for profit. For a number of years we struggled with the tension that existed between writing materials we believed in and materials someone else believed would sell. We, like the publishing houses, were interested in innovation and principled pedagogy; however, our perspectives were different. The principled pedagogy that we believed in required teachers to belong to a particular teaching generation whose education and training had been fuelled by SLA research findings. We were, in fact, addressing a very limited market. We heard this information before we fully internalized it. Our convictions were stronger than our pragmatic sense and it took a while to understand that the art of compromise is a vital one to learn for any writer. Compromise comes in different forms, from complete cop out involving the surrender of most beliefs to principled choice made for the greater good within a sound pedagogic framework. We feared the former before understanding that the latter was an acceptable alternative. One obvious compromise we made was to drop the notion of level bands for language and to impose a graded grammar syllabus.

At this point, it is worth clarifying that what I was learning was a lot about the process of writing. We had submitted a proposal, sent in sample units, revised the proposal and sample units before parting with our first publisher, a process which lasted over a year. With more know-how, we moved onto our second publisher. At this stage we understood that there was a generalizable model that the publisher used to operate. It appeared to be that what was needed in the coursebook market was something new and different, but not too new and definitely not too different. This translated in reality as a desire for so-called communicative material, underpinned by a graded grammar syllabus. Neither of these requirements truly reflected current research positions in that they demanded output rather than being comprehension-based and they also assumed learning was a predictable and incremental process rather than an unpredictable and non-incremental process, at least not according to a linear model.

Our refined material was initially topic-based. We accepted the need for a template though we compromised by having a varying template within a consistent page limit. We accepted that listening scripts should be limited to a certain number of lines and we grudgingly tried to work with the notion of 'white space'. 'White space' essentially means a lack of business on the page, a user-friendly page where all stages in any given activity are transparent and doable. White space means that rubrics and instructions have to be clear and brief. In order to get all our material to fit into the agreed template, we simply used a smaller font, went to single spacing and failed to leave any room for the necessary visuals. As we moved along in our learning curve, we would periodically receive feedback from readers, editors or marketing people. One comment was that we needed to describe the grammar being presented. We tried to argue that we were not presenting grammar, but language, of which grammar was only an aspect, and possibly the least important. At this stage, we were told that the grammar syllabus needed to be graded according, apparently to precedent, which as far as we could tell meant that the simple past could not be addressed until around Unit 7. This seemed odd to us, but apparently it was a market constraint. Market constraints are crucial in the world of publishing. It is the marketing people who are in contact with the users and the ones who get most feedback concerning what people want and need.

Strategizing

If you are considering writing a coursebook, there are a number of questions that deserve serious thought.

1. Why do I want to write a coursebook?

Your motivation should stem from a desire to produce materials that you feel would be better for you, your students and other teachers working in a similar environment.

2. How will my coursebook contribute to the market?

   Your coursebook needs to offer something new and different to the market. This could be from the point of view of syllabus, language presentation, format or activity type. Your book is a product that will be competing with other products; other people need to sell it and to have a clear idea what they are selling.

3. Who will/will not be able to use my coursebook?

   Your coursebook needs to be pitched at a market niche where its projected sales will fall into line with marketing expectations for a product. To do this there needs to be a clear sense of the target teacher group in terms of their language ability, education, teacher-training experience, willingness to try new things and time available for preparation. If teachers need extra training in order to use your coursebook, it is unlikely that it will appeal to the sales and marketing people involved in the project. This information will filter back to you through your editor.

4. What will teachers and learners get from my coursebook that they cannot get elsewhere?

   If your coursebook provides material that is more authentic, activities that work better, practice that is perceived as more useful or some 'extra' feature not available in other coursebooks, this will give your book an edge in the market.

5. How will my coursebook be structured?

   Your coursebook should be user-friendly in that teachers should be able to use it within the system they work, i.e., if they teach 14-week sessions then fourteen units, or seven taught over two sessions, would be attractive. Too much or too little material will be seen as a problem.

6. Will my coursebook be part of a series?

   Coursebooks do better if they are part of a series. The number of books required in a series depends on the market you are writing for. Market research can quickly establish these parameters.

7. Do I envisage my coursebook requiring teacher guides, workbooks, resources packs, a website?

   A coursebook seldom exists alone. A teacher's guide is a standard requirement. These guides can come in many forms but they need to provide tapescripts, if not in the coursebook, answers, a description of the unit template and a rationale. Some guides may include mini-lesson plans, and possible extension activities. Some, too, may include photocopiable materials. Workbooks can be seen as useful homework tools. If the coursebook itself downplays grammar, the workbook could be seen as place for supplementary activities focusing more on grammar. Workbooks do not tend to offer more text recycling language in different contexts. Other aspects of the package might include a CD-ROM, a website or an integrated video.

8. What parts of the writing would I be prepared to delegate to others?
    The writing of a coursebook takes an enormous commitment of time and energy. If the coursebook itself is merely one part of a more complex equation then it would be worth considering giving some of the writing of other material to others. Care should be taken that it is someone who understands the nature of your coursebook and is sympathetic to your pedagogical approach.

9. What look do I envisage my coursebook having?
    A coursebook has an image or feel depending on whether it is full colour, four colour, glossy paper or matt. The presence of photos only or illustrations only or a combination of both will also influence the look. The look a book has will influence the way teachers react to the material. It is important that a book has the right look for the market niche. A coursebook aimed at a young adult market should not look as if it is aimed at young teens.

10. What unique features will my coursebook have?
    Marketers need a selling point, something to point at or show to potential users that will immediately be identified as something they need. With regard to this point, transparency is important. Will your material have a distinct feature that a sales representative could point to and easily explain to a potential adoptee? Unique features could involve the way in which language has been presented, the activity type, supplementary resources and the unit template.

11. What type of promotional activity am I prepared to become engaged in?
    Being willing to appear at conferences, workshops and seminars is a plus. Authors need visibility. Offering training sessions and demonstrations is also a good thing.

Conclusion

Successful coursebooks are big business and the nature of the market means that there is a continual search for new material. New, however, needs to be qualified, in the sense that it cannot be too different from what is currently available. What is currently available is greatly influenced by the best-sellers which have an appealing simplicity and an inherent teachabilty but tend to adhere to a linear-graded structural syllabus which lends itself to a learning paradigm, rather than an acquisition paradigm. A coursebook focus on acquisition would provide lin-guistically ungraded, yet accessible language and a variety of engaging tasks which would involve students through prediction, visualization, mime and other affect-ively oriented activities.

When writing, do not write just for yourself. Remember you are writing for a market. You need to know the market, which means getting as much information as you can about the market and writing for that market. Take into consideration the typical teacher in that market in terms of their language competence and level of training. Secondly, do not simply rewrite what has already been written. Teachers choose new books because they want something new, not simply a repackaged version of something with which they are already familiar.

Given the above, a prospective writer needs to juggle the constraints of the market with the quest for something new and different yet accessible, and teachable. In the recent past, this has resulted in coursebooks that have a generic quality to them but that may claim to appeal to a marketable aspect of current research findings in areas such as learner strategies, learner training and multiple intelligences. As an optimist, I would say that the market will not be able to carry more of the same for much longer, which means that writers looking to break patterns and move towards an acquisition paradigm will be well placed for the coming years.

References

Ellis, R. (1994) *The Study of Second Language Acquisition.* Oxford: Oxford University Press.

Gershon, S. and Mares, C. (1995) *Online.* Oxford: Heinemann.

Krashen, S. (1981) *Second Language Acquisition and Second Language Learning.* Oxford: Pergamon Press.

Larson-Freeman, D. (1986) *Techniques and Principles in Language Teaching.* Oxford: Oxford University Press.

Lewis, M. (1993) *The Lexical Approach.* Hove: Language Teaching Press.

McLaughlin, B. (1987) *Theories of Second Language Learning.* London: Edward Arnold.

Maurer, J. and Schoenberg, I. E. (1998) *True Colors.* New York: Addison Wesley Longman.

Nunan, D. (1993) *Designing Tasks for the Communicative Classroom.* Cambridge: Cambridge University Press.

Nunan, D. (1995) *Atlas.* Boston: Heinle and Heinle.

Nunan, D. (1999) *Plenary Address.* TESOL 1999, Vancouver, BC.

Richards, J. C., Hull, J. and Proctor, S. (1999) *New Interchange.* Cambridge: Cambridge University Press.

Soars, L. and Soars, J. (1996) *Headway.* Oxford: Oxford University Press.

Tomlinson, B. (ed.) (1998) *Materials Development in Language Teaching.* Cambridge: Cambridge University Press.

Publishing a Coursebook: Completing the Materials Development Circle

Duriya Aziz Singapore Wala

Introduction

Materials development for language teaching is a highly complex process involving many different stakeholders located at different points within the curriculum development framework. In order for an approach to language teaching to be translated into principled methodology, it is necessary to develop a design for an instructional system that takes into account (a) the syllabus, (b) learner roles in the system, (c) teacher roles in the system and (d) instructional materials types and functions (Richards and Rodgers, 1995). Thus, syllabus designers or curriculum specialists, teachers and learners are three important sources of feedback for the materials developer. Recognizing that 'the human mind does not work in [a] linear fashion', Jolly and Bolitho propose that the materials development process, in addition to evaluation as an essential component, must also include a variety of 'optional pathways and feedback loops' which make the whole process 'dynamic and self-regulating' (Jolly and Bolitho, 1998).

Nature of Pathways and Loops in Materials Development

This chapter takes off from Jolly and Bolitho's proposal of incorporating optional pathways and feedback loops to suggest that these loops and pathways must be carefully built into the materials development process so that it remains 'dynamic and self regulating'. While Jolly and Bolitho's proposal seeks to incorporate feedback from end-users to gauge the effectiveness of the materials in the classroom, this chapter takes a wider, macroview of materials development for language teaching to consider how feedback loops must be created along the materials development process to facilitate the incorporation of feedback not just from teachers and pupils but also from curriculum developers and other central bodies that may have an interest in the materials. These stakeholders in the materials for language teaching must have a channel to provide feedback at significant milestones in the development process so that their feedback can be considered and incorporated into the materials meaningfully and in time (Ibe, 1976; Yalden, 1987). Abu Samah (1988) notes, 'There seems to be a persistent problem about open discussions between curriculum planners and textbook writers'. Open dialogue between curriculum developers, materials developers and teachers would yield feedback that might help to address the differing and different ability levels and needs in the classroom.

Most materials developers recognize the importance of writing materials that are designed to serve the needs of particular teachers and learners (Bell and Gower, 1998; Hopkins, 1995; Harmer, 1997; Donovan, 1998). In order to do this effectively, they must be aware of classroom realities and also test any assumptions that they make about the teachers and learners. At the same time, the materials developers must be prepared to put the materials constantly to the test in classroom situations (Yalden, 1987; Halim, 1976; Gonzales, 1995) and the materials development process must be designed to allow flexibility to make revisions.

It is inevitable that review, feedback and the uses that they are put to are often a compromise on account of constraints of time, resources and other factors (Ibe, 1976; Bell and Gower, 1998). Donovan (1998) points out that the decisions to pilot, what to pilot and for how long to pilot have repercussions on schedules and costs, as piloting a complete year's material clearly impacts on to the development schedule. Time has to be allowed for writing a whole level and preparing this for the pilot, which together might take a year or more in themselves. Added to this is the piloting year, followed by a period of revision, making a total of at least two and possibly three years. However, understanding the significance, nature and extent of feedback desirable at each stage from the various stakeholders will perhaps offer some measure of control over what must be compromised and to what extent.

Existence of Feedback Loops in Materials Development

Looking retrospectively at his 31 years of experience of materials production for language teaching in the Philippines, Gonzales (1995) remarks that there is increasing recognition that 'the Filipino teacher and Filipino language specialist know best what is needed for the Philippines ... The emerging criterion for good language materials is that they are interesting to the students and useable in class; the ultimate test is then usability for teaching with the end-users (teachers and students) as the best judges' (Gonzales, 1995:4). Recognizing the important role that feedback from end-users plays in making materials more effective, Gonzales reports that the process and schedule for materials development now involves a greater amount of planning as 'each book has to be field tested by try-out with a sample of students and teachers who provide feedback before the materials are actually printed and distributed' (Gonzales, 1995: 5).

Describing the provision for trialling and feedback in a materials development project in the Philippines that resulted from a new government policy on education, Pascasio (1995) writes that her team sought to ensure the validity of the scope and sequencing of the lessons, the correctness of illustrations, accuracy of instructions and relevance of the content to the age group by putting the materials through five triallings before the final edition was published.

Villamin (1988) outlined four phases in the preparation of three sets of materials for Philippine learners: design, development, evaluation and dissemination. Feedback and validation of the effort was sought by Villamin's team at every stage of the development process. Villamin reports that the conceptual framework which was developed during the design phase and the experimental materials developed during the development phase were reviewed and validated by experts. The evaluation phase comprised a pilot try-out with the target population and a revision of the sample materials based on the feedback. During the dissemination phase, a final version of the materials was produced for field-testing.

Reflecting on almost four decades of materials production in India, Tickoo (1995) recounts the role of piloting, review, evaluation and feedback in the shaping of the English instructional materials produced. He outlines the following evaluation/feedback measures undertaken by his team while developing materials for a state-level system in Hyderabad, India:

- Critiquing by a group of colleagues.
- Teaching of the materials of the first book in a school by the writer, observation and critique by the class teacher.
- Evaluation of materials by teachers in a school some distance away from the city. The feedback received from teachers at this stage 'forced a basic rethink' of the draft lessons.
- Major revision and retrial of the materials based on feedback.

Tickoo writes that the review, evaluation and incorporating of feedback on drafts resulted in a rethinking of the materials in terms of both structural as well as cultural and ideological representations within the materials,

> in writing textual materials for a state-level system in a multilingual and multicultural developing society it becomes necessary to satisfy different sets of criteria which, in some cases, do make contradictory demands. Some of them arise from such a society's needs to teach the values it wants to foster. Some arise in the desire to make education a handmaiden of economic progress and social reconstruction. (Tickoo, 1995: 39)

Evidently, Tickoo recognizes that there are different and differing stakeholders in the materials being developed and they operate with different agendas and priorities and all these must be taken into account. Tickoo adds that the textbook writer must accept the fact that 'a perfect textbook is an ideal' and the best means towards that ideal is to keep the textbook always 'standing in print', which means that good textbooks have to be revised regularly and at defined intervals, incorporating feedback received from end-users.

In his account of the evolution of a somewhat global textbook series commissioned by a commercial publisher, Richards (1995) outlines the steps taken to determine the suitability of the materials.

- Before embarking on the actual writing, Richards, together with his publishers, did some research on what potential users of the course might be looking for. The project editor interviewed classroom teachers. The publisher's marketing representatives, who are in daily contact with schools and teachers, were also an important source of feedback.
- A group of consultants, who were experienced teachers in the kinds of institutions where the course could be used, were identified to provide input to the project. Through the consultants, information was also sought from students.
- A sample unit of material to be piloted in a private university in Tokyo was developed. Richards and the project editor explained the project to the programme director and observed two teachers teaching the materials.
- Following the piloting of the unit, Richards and the editor met with the teachers to discuss the unit, spoke with students about the materials and also met with a focus group of teachers from the same institution to get their reactions to the unit.
- Richards used the feedback to do a first draft of the first book.
- The first draft was sent to reviewers identified by the publisher.
- The reviewers' and editor's feedback was then considered before a second draft was written.
- The second draft will also be field-tested and further revisions will be made based on feedback from teachers and students.

Roxburgh (1997), a member of the Bilkent University School of English Language Textbook group, observes that 'We found piloting essential for improving the materials. Changes were made to the topics, to texts, to activities and to teachers' notes. Piloting gave us a greater awareness of our target users, both students and teachers' (Roxburgh, 1997: 17). Reflecting on the role of evaluation in textbook design, Roxburgh comments that evaluation forced her team of writers to consider the age and the cultural and educational background of the students. They had to make compromises in their materials so that the materials were more appropriate for the expectations, existing learning strategies and learning styles of the students and also adaptable to the teaching styles and methods of the teaching body.

Reporting on the progress of three textbook projects that he had been involved in, in Namibia, Morocco and Bulgaria, Tomlinson (1995) remarks on the trend in materials development in recent years for the Ministries of Education in several countries to develop their own new English textbooks to meet the changed and distinctive needs of students in their secondary schools. A common element in these three projects, Tomlinson has noted, is that the need for these materials arose out of the Ministries' desire to produce materials customized to their needs and agenda. It has also resulted in the greater involvement of teachers in these projects – in writing, reviewing and piloting the materials and providing feedback.

Tomlinson describes a textbook project in Namibia as having the following stages:

1. Consultation of teachers and students during which feedback and wish lists were sought from teachers and students from all over the country via questionnaires.
2. Analysis of feedback during which the responses received to the questionnaires were considered.
3. Thirty teachers came together and then worked together to design and write the book. The first draft was written by the teachers at an eight-day workshop.
4. The first draft was trialled in schools all over Namibia.
5. Based on feedback from the schools, the first drafts were revised by an editorial panel for publication.
6. Finally, there was the copy-editing, final design and publishing by publishers in Namibia.

The Case of Singapore

The following section presents a case study of a materials development project in Singapore.

Background Information

The latter half of the last decade has seen the Ministry of Education in Singapore put in place several new initiatives to ensure that the education system remain effective, relevant and contemporary. Following up on the recommendations of an External Review Team appointed by Parliament, the ministry announced in February 1998 that the publication of textbooks and other instructional packages would be devolved to the private sector from 2000. The rationale behind this move was to 'harness the expertise and creativity of the educational publishers, leading to a greater variety of interesting and stimulating instructional materials for selection'. The Ministry would continue to develop syllabuses for all the subjects but would no longer be involved in writing and producing instructional materials for most subjects in the curriculum.

In order to ensure the quality of the materials, the ministry announced that it would put in place a new 'Textbook Authorization Process'. Commercial educational publishers would develop instructional materials based on the new syllabuses to be issued by the Ministry of Education and they would be guided in the materials development process by the Ministry. The materials would be subject to a review commissioned by the Ministry of Education and only upon approval would the materials be sanctioned as suitable for use in schools and included in the Approved Textbook List.[1] The publishers would then promote the materials in schools and teachers would decide which of the materials best suited their needs and the needs of their pupils.

The Textbook Authorization Process includes a schedule of development and of submission of the materials to the Ministry for approval. According to the schedule of development put in place by the Textbook Authorization Process, the core instructional materials for teaching English for Secondary 1 were to be submitted to the Ministry of Education for review and approval by 30 November 1999, barely one year after the draft syllabus had been issued to publishers. Approval would be granted by May the following year and the materials would then be listed in the Approved Textbook List of the Ministry of Education, indicating that these materials were suitable for adoption by schools.

While commercial publishers have been developing materials for secondary schools in Singapore based on the syllabuses issued by the Ministry, this was the first time so many publishers would be developing materials concurrently based on the schedule implemented by the Ministry. The extremely challenging schedule meant that the time available to publishers for seeking feedback and making changes was limited. This in turn restricted the extent, scope and nature of feedback sought and the stages at which it was sought. Also, the fact that as many as eight publishers were developing materials at the same time meant that the materials would be promoted to schools for adoption at the same time as they all had to be available for use in schools by January 2001. This made the materials development exercise a highly competitive one and publishers' teams were eager to safeguard their 'secrets'. This then meant that fearing their 'secrets' would be made known to other publishers, publishers would not be keen on, or at least would be very cautious about, circulating draft copies of their materials for feedback from teachers or to pilot their materials in schools.

The following is a brief account of the development of one level of materials under the Textbook Authorization Process.

Planning

Following the announcement by the Ministry of Education of the new textbook initiative, the Textbook Authorization Process, in February 1998, the publishers made the decision to develop an instructional package for secondary English, as the cohort was large enough to require a sizeable print run if adoptions were healthy. The search for the team began.

Assembling a team was no easy task – getting together people who could work closely and comfortably together on a creative task given severe time and budgetary constraints required considerable networking. Having considered various options – of having full-time writers, of having contracted writers, of having only one full-time writer, we settled on having one writer who would work on writing the materials during his free time, as he already held a full-time teaching job. An ideal situation would have been, of course, to have more writers on the team working closely together, but this proved to be difficult to realize – writing styles needed to jell, there needed to be a consistent and principled approach and methodology and there needed to be an obvious and evident progression and continuum of development as the units progressed. All this would have been better achieved with a larger team of writers, however, ironically enough, with the very tight time-frame and schedule, this was not possible. There simply would not be enough time to cross-reference across units, so it seemed that it would work better with only one writer working simultaneously at different units that were in different stages of development.

Market Research

In late 1998, a Market Survey Questionnaire was distributed to teachers at a Teacher's Network event to gather feedback from teachers about the existing materials, as well as to gather data about the needs of teachers. The data from the responses to the questionnaire was analysed and discussed informally by the team. The data gathered through the questionnaire was very useful as the team realized that teachers should be involved in the planning and decision-making since they know the exact problems they face. If they are involved in the innovation, they are able to give 'real' solutions to 'real' problems (Nisbet, 1975, cited in Suvarnis, 1991). The data collected led to some perceptions and intuitions being formed about what teachers needed and wanted.

Based on the responses to this questionnaire, the team made the following decisions:

1. To have an IT component that would be customized to the package. Teachers could use it to teach the textbook.
2. The role and contents of the workbook had to be considered seriously as teachers were quite dissatisfied with the workbooks currently available.
3. The texts used in the materials needed to be interesting, current and appealing to the target learners.
4. A wide range of activities needed to be provided to motivate the learners.
5. The coursebook would be modular and would provide opportunities for project and group work.
6. Thinking skills would feature prominently in the materials.
7. There should be lots of opportunities for practice of grammar items.
8. The teacher's guide must include an answer key.

Developing the Conceptual Framework and Sample Units

In November 1998, the first syllabus briefing was held in which a brief document, 'Notes to Publishers', was distributed. The contract documents were also made available to publishers wishing to develop the materials. Shortly afterwards, a draft syllabus was distributed to the publishers. The immediate tasks at hand for publishers were to complete the contract document providing the detailed information sought as well as submitting a conceptual framework to the English team at Curriculum Planning and Development Division (CPDD) of the Ministry of Education.

The next couple of months involved intense planning and discussion about the methodology of the materials, the physical components of the package, the size of the team it entailed, as well as the implications of these on budgetary and man-power resources and their availability. It was decided at this point to hold some focus group sessions with teachers as participants. The teachers would provide detailed and focused feedback on their needs and wants. Getting teachers to agree to attend these sessions was no easy task, given their workload, as well as the fact that even Saturdays are taken up in schools.

Focus Group Session 1 was attended by the editorial and development team and staff from the marketing and IT departments. The feedback from Focus Group Session 1 was discussed and taken into consideration when developing the framework of the materials as well as deciding the components of the package. It helped the team confirm the ideas they had been developing since taking into consideration feedback to the questionnaire. More importantly, it helped clarify for the developers the role the instructional materials would play in the curriculum. Teachers expect the materials to occupy a particular place and to function in a particular way within the instructional system. Successful materials, therefore, would have to address and satisfy these expectations. Innovative materials would, by the same token, have to be introduced in such a way that teachers were able to participate alongside them and together with them in the instructional system. Teachers, too, would have to be ready to accept this innovation and to modify their own roles as teachers.

Given a new syllabus, teachers' feedback and involvement in materials development would help teachers ease into a new or modified system or role by having materials developed in such a way that they feel they are customized to them. Following the feedback from the first focus group session, the team made the following decisions:

1. One O-level-style comprehension exercise would be provided for every coursebook unit.
2. Teaching of grammar would feature prominently in the materials with plenty of opportunities for contextualized learning and practice.
3. Texts by local and regional writers would be used to a greater extent, also texts located in Singapore and the region.
4. More authentic texts would be used.
5. Graphic organizers would be customized for the various tasks the students were required to carry out.
6. The units would be organized around text types and be driven by specific texts.
7. Some activities in the units would be devoted to raising the critical awareness of students about the text.
8. Instead of a single coursebook, the coursebook would be divided into two parts – A and B.
9. The workbook would take the form of tear-out worksheets.
10. The coursebook would be in full colour and would have a 'fun' look, appealing to teenagers.
11. The publisher would plan on conducting training workshops and seminars for teachers.

Following feedback received from Focus Group Session 1, the team developed the conceptual framework for the materials and submitted it to the English Unit in CPDD for review and approval in February 1999. At the same time, the team began to develop a sample unit.

The team had a meeting with CPDD officers who had reviewed the conceptual framework. Based on this feedback and feedback received from teachers in the questionnaire and the first focus group session, the team continued to develop the sample unit. Once a fairly stable draft of the first unit was ready, the team decided to present it to the teachers together with the conceptual framework in another focus group session.

The participants in Focus Group Session 2 were the same as those in Session 1. They were presented with the conceptual framework first. The principles, approach and methodology underlying the package were explained to them. Next, the participants were each given a copy of the sample unit of the coursebook and of the corresponding workbook unit. The participants were asked to consider these and provide feedback on them, using the feedback forms provided. It must be borne in mind that, at this point, the teachers who attended the focus group sessions had not seen drafts of the new syllabus. Their feedback was based, therefore, on their understanding of the existing syllabus and their beliefs and experiences of what worked and what did not in the context of the classroom environment and the current curricular aims and objectives.

The feedback from Focus Group Session 2 helped the team confirm and further develop the ideas they had been considering since the earlier feedback exercises. It helped them understand better what teachers were looking for in textbooks in a more concrete way, that is, with reference to the conceptual framework and the sample unit. Using the sample unit, the teachers who participated in the focus group session were able to give specific examples and details about what they felt worked and did not work for their learners.

The feedback from teachers led to focused discussion on and modification of the sample unit. The team reviewed the sample unit in the light of feedback received in Focus Group Session 2 and made substantial changes to it before submitting it to the English Unit of the CPDD for review and comment. Some of the more significant changes made following feedback from teachers were:

1. A change in the texts used in the unit to include an extract from a novel by a Singaporean writer in which the protagonist was female. This change and the one mentioned in (2) below were motivated by concerns over the 'hidden curriculum' (Cunningsworth, 1995: 90) and the ideological, social and cultural representations made in and through texts.
2. Some of the texts that were too British and too dated were to be removed.
3. Summary writing activities were to be included.
4. The original Text B was moved to the Worksheets and an O level type of comprehension exercise as well as summary writing activity were added.
5. The activities in the coursebook were contextualized to an even greater extent.

6. The language of the instructions was made simpler and friendlier.
7. A Study Skills section was added.
8. The number of worksheets and grammar items and exercises was increased.

A revised form of the sample unit was submitted to the English Unit of the CPDD for review and comment. Members of the development team met with the curriculum specialists from CPDD in early June 1999 to receive their feedback on the sample unit. Verbal feedback on the sample unit was given.

Following the meeting with the curriculum specialists, the development team met to discuss their comments and to consider the changes that needed to be made.

Writing the Materials

Meanwhile, the writing of the coursebook and workbook was in full swing. The team would meet every fortnight to provide feedback on drafts of units already circulated and suggest modifications or changes and to plan for upcoming units.

As laser proofs of the materials had to be submitted by 30 November 1999, this meant that the team had six months in all to write and rewrite the coursebook and workbook units, source for materials and photographs, clear permissions, decide on layout and design and get artwork and illustrations done for a whole year's teaching materials. As there was a significant audio and video segment in the materials, recordings and filming had to be arranged and photography sessions had to be arranged. These could not be done at a later date, as being text-driven, the activities and tasks designed would depend on the texts themselves, many of which were to be authentic, undoctored texts.

In addition to this, the writer also had to make copious notes to include in the teacher's edition at the time of writing the units, lest the objectives and outcomes be forgotten as time passed.

Given the enormous amount of work that needed to be completed in such a short time, many of the tasks that normally would have been done consecutively had to be done simultaneously. Similarly, as several units were in different stages of progress at any one time, the units were destabilized. This means that it was not possible to say any one unit was really final, till all the units were final because changes made to one unit resulted or required changes to be made to later or earlier units. So the units were in a constant state of flux.

Given this situation of extremely tight deadlines and a huge task to complete, it was not possible to carry out any more teacher feedback exercises on the materials in the way that had been done earlier. As a result, the team relied on feedback they had received during the earlier feedback exercises and on informal feedback from teachers. This informal feedback consisted of showing the proofs of the units in their various stages of development to different teachers and soliciting feedback from them in terms of their immediate reactions etc. These teachers tended to be friends, colleagues or associates of members of the development team, generally what Bell and Gower (1997) refer to as 'inner sanctum' readers.

Submission of Coursebook for Review

The coursebooks and two sets of worksheets were submitted to the English Unit of the CPDD in mid-December 1999 along with a recording of the video and audio segments that accompanied each unit. Under the Textbook Authorization Process, 'the textbooks developed by commercial publishers [would] be reviewed by a panel of independent professional reviewers from schools and tertiary institutions, etc.' (*http://www1.moe.edu.sg/cpdd/faq.htm*).

Developing the Support Materials

Following submission of the coursebook and workbook materials to CPDD for review and approval, the development team commenced in January to plan the teacher's support materials as well as the IT resources for the package. Bearing in mind feedback received from teachers by means of the questionnaire, as well as the focus group sessions, the team decided that:

1. There would be a teacher's edition of the coursebooks as well as a teacher's copy of the worksheets.
2. The teacher's editions of the coursebooks would be in wraparound format – this meant that there would be slightly reduced versions of the coursebook pages accompanied by teacher's notes 'wrapped around' the reduced coursebook pages. In addition to the objectives and intended outcomes, the teacher's edition would contain suggestions for modifying the activities to suit mixed ability or different ability levels. The teacher's editions of the coursebooks would also have detailed schemes of work for the teachers.
3. The teacher's copy of the worksheets would have the answers, suggested answers or criteria for marking for appropriacy in answers, written into the worksheets for easy reference for the teachers.
4. As teachers constantly felt the need for additional materials that would supplement and augment specific areas of language teaching addressed in the coursebook, it was decided to develop a series of supplementary materials that would be linked to the core textbook package but would still be stand-alone and focus on particular areas such as reading skills, or summary writing and so on.
5. As approval was expected sometime in April–May 2000, it was time also to decide the format and contents and design of the CD-ROMs that would accompany the materials as at least one unit would need to be ready to market the materials.

While the team was aware that the above-listed things needed to be done, there were several uncertainties. First of all, the team would have to assume that approval would definitely be given by the CPDD. Secondly, it was not certain, even if provisional approval were given, what kind of changes CPDD would require the team to make to the materials before final approval was given. Given these uncertainties, it was difficult to finalize anything in the teacher's resource materials. Developing IT materials also requires considerable investment of time, money and manpower and given the uncertainties, it was unclear how and when to proceed. Extensive changes to the materials would mean that work done on the teacher's guides (coursebook and worksheets) would need to be undone and redone and the same would be the case for the CD-ROMs. At the same time, however, it was important to have some of the resource materials ready for promotion to schools.

In addition to this was the fact that the team also had to plan the next level of materials for Secondary 2. They were not able to do this effectively either as they wanted to wait and see the reaction from CPDD to the materials already submitted.

Piloting

As there was a period of almost four to five months before there would be any word from CPDD regarding the materials, the team decided it would be a good time to pilot the materials in a few schools. However, the team felt that the pilot would be meaningful only if the CD-ROM component was also ready for the piloting. Also, this would allow the team to get some feedback from teachers on the design and contents of the CD-ROM as well. Moreover, in addition to the coursebook and worksheets, the teacher's notes for these units would also need to be ready. In order to teach the materials effectively, teachers would need time to make lesson plans for the new materials. In addition, as the teachers were still teaching based on the old syllabus, and these pilot materials were based on the new syllabus, teachers would have to reconcile the objectives and outcomes of the new materials with those that were already specified in their work plans.

Considering all these contingencies, it was decided that the most practical thing to do would be to pilot just one unit of the coursebook together with the related worksheets. The team set about developing the teacher's notes and the CD-ROM component for Unit 6, the unit chosen.

Meanwhile, an effort was under way to get schools to agree to participate in the piloting. This was no mean feat. Heads of departments and teachers themselves were reluctant, thinking of the disruption and extra work piloting would cause; principals and vice-principals were hesitant, not wanting to disrupt the routine of the classes. Some felt that, as this was a commercial enterprise, they were not obliged to participate and, indeed, the vice-principal of one school commented that he/she saw no reason to participate in something that would benefit a commercial publisher.

In the end, five schools agreed to pilot the materials. By the time the teacher's notes and the CD-ROM component of Unit 6 were ready, it was already the end of March 2000. At this time, the number of classes that would pilot the materials in each school was confirmed. Briefing sessions were held for the teachers who would be teaching the pilot. The CD-ROMs were installed into the laptops of the participating teachers. The teachers were also given Pilot Feedback Forms. The teachers would convey their feedback to the publishers through these forms. Photocopied units of coursebooks and worksheets were provided to the schools for the students to use. Schools did not allow the publishers to sit in and observe the materials being taught in the class as they felt this would be compromising the security of the school.

It was envisaged that the schools would begin piloting the materials by mid-April and end perhaps by mid-May 2000. The team expected to get feedback from the schools by the end of May to early June. While the team recognized that the schedule of the pilot meant that no real changes could be made to the course-book and worksheets, nonetheless the exercise would be valuable as the feedback would be useful for the development of:

1. the teacher's support materials;
2. the CD-ROMs;
3. the next level of the materials.

Approval and Publication

In May 2000, the publishers were notified by CPDD that the materials had been given provisional approval for use in schools. The team met with the curriculum specialists from the English Unit who explained that provisional approval had been granted and specified the changes that would need to be made before final approval would be given to the materials for printing and inclusion in the Approved Textbook List.

The changes to the coursebooks and workbooks recommended by CPDD had to be carried out in order for final approval and inclusion in the Approved Textbook List. This also meant further changes to the CD-ROMs and to the teacher's support materials. The coursebook pages had to be finalized before work could begin on the teacher's edition of the coursebooks as the coursebook pages were replicated therein.

Feedback from the Piloting Exercise

Meanwhile, the team was in touch with the piloting schools. Of the five schools that piloted the materials, teachers from only three schools filled in and returned the Pilot Feedback Forms by late June–early July. One of the other schools provided verbal feedback while the fifth school provided no feedback at all.

Data from the feedback forms was considered carefully by the team and the following decisions were made:

1. While a lot of very useful feedback was given pertaining to the coursebook and worksheets in terms of the texts, tasks, design and layout, etc., this feedback could not be incorporated into the level of materials on which it was based but would have to be taken into consideration when developing the other levels of material.

2. Some of the feedback from the teachers unwittingly revealed that the piloting teachers themselves were not very clear about the principles and terms incorporated into the new syllabus.
3. Feedback given on the teacher's notes for Unit 6 would be useful in developing the rest of the teacher's editions.
4. Feedback on the CD-ROM was that the design and opening screens were not very user-friendly and would have to be redesigned. The size of the text was also too small when projected in the classroom – this would be increased.

Role and Effectiveness of Feedback in the Case Study

Recounting his experience of receiving and incorporating feedback on a different coursebook subjected to the same Textbook Authorization Process, Tomlinson (1999) comments on the role of feedback:

> As the books develop, feedback tries to change them … This feedback comes from inspectors in ministries, from reviewers commissioned by the publishers, from editors who are understandably more conservative than the publisher who commissioned the book in the first place, and from newcomers to the editorial team who were not involved in the original concept development for the book (this always happens). The big questions are: How far can you trust the experience of these feedbackers? How representative are their views? How aware are they of the preferences of the end-users of the book? How far should the writers go in making compromises along the cline towards a profitable but unprincipled book? (Tomlinson, 1999: 3)

Tomlinson's concerns bring to the fore a tension that exists in materials development. As writer, he obviously feels ownership of the materials and wants them to be developed according to his or his team's beliefs and principles about language teaching. However, his publishers are the ones investing resources and capital in developing and marketing the product. They want to be assured of market share and profitable returns. There is also the fact that the writers are always complicit with their own ideologies and beliefs – albeit unwittingly – and will resist any effort to tamper with them. So, how does the publisher ensure that what the writer proposes is really what the teachers and learners want?

This raises questions such as whose feedback should be sought, by whom, at which stage and through what process. Tomlinson and Gower and Bell (1997) question the credibility and the ability of the feedbackers to provide meaningful feedback. And the questions they raise spawn further questions – what is the process of review and feedback? What is the methodology? Where are the feedbackers located in the language teaching and education scene? At what stage is the feedback provided? On what aspects of the materials should feedback be sought and provided? How much of the feedback should be heeded? And who decides all these questions?

Countering these concerns, Donovan (1998), Publishing Director ELT, Cambridge University Press, explains that the benefits of piloting for publishers, authors and their materials derive from the opportunity to validate materials before publication. This encourages innovation in that the results can give the publisher the confidence to commit the necessary investment to complete the development. Being able to report the results of successful piloting when launching new material can also add to the credibility of the publication.

The Textbook Authorization Process does not recommend any procedures for review or revision despite the fact that teachers and learners will be seeing and using the materials for the first time from January 2001. The 'usability' of materials in the classroom (Gonzales, 1995) will be put to the test only then in the absence of any concerted or large-scale trialling or evaluation of the instructional materials in their entirety. While recognizing that there will always be constraints and limits in any instance of materials development, and that the method of development will often be a 'compromise between the ideal and the feasible' (Ibe, 1976), the materials development process must require, allow and provide for the materials to be 'standing in print' (Tickoo, 1995) so that they can be revised regularly, and at defined intervals, incorporating feedback from end-users.

In the case study presented above, the schedule of development and submission of materials for approval to the Ministry of Education is an important aspect of the Textbook Authorization Process as this has implications on the process of materials development itself. The schedule of development imposes deadlines and limitations to the number and kind of stages the materials go through as well as the rigour and quality-control checks that can be applied and the number and kind of reviews and revisions that can be made. This in turn restricts the extent, scope and nature of feedback sought and the stages at which it is sought. While there is scope for some procedures of feedback in the initial stages of the process to analyse needs, once the development of the materials itself commences, the deadlines leave very little scope for feedback to be sought, considered and incorporated into the materials. There is no scope at all for trialling or piloting the materials in schools with actual users and for revising materials based on feedback received.

In addition to this, there was no requirement or recommendation by the Ministry of Education in the Textbook Authorization Process to include stages and procedures in the materials development process that would require publishers to seek and incorporate teacher feedback into the materials being developed. As the onus was on commercial publishers to seek feedback from teachers independently, schools and teachers were reluctant to participate in what they saw as a commercial project. This was also a limiting factor on the scope of teacher feedback as it limited the number of teachers and schools who participated in the feedback exercises as well as the extent and duration of the feedback exercises.

Instructional materials do not just address curriculum needs and syllabus objectives, they must also address teacher and learner needs. While curriculum needs and syllabus needs have ostensibly been addressed through the review procedures put in place, teacher and learner needs could have been better addressed through more dedicated and rigorous procedures of seeking, documenting and incorporating teacher feedback át various stages of the development of materials.

Incorporating Feedback Loops in the Materials Development Process

The decision to seek feedback, the measures through which this feedback is sought and how long the feedback exercises last have repercussions on schedules and costs as it clearly impacts on to the development schedule. Time has to be allowed for writing and preparing the materials for evaluation and feedback, revision based on the feedback and then feedback on the changes. Planners of any materials development process have to be prepared to accommodate this in the development and implementation plan, with implications for finance, return on investment and the timing of publication being given due consideration.

Piloting and other such feedback exercises obviously require willing institutions, teachers and students to carry out the exercise and, as Donovan (1998) points out, and the development team discovered, they may not be so easy to come by. Efforts need to be made to develop 'goodwill, trust and a constructive relationship between [feedbackers] and publishers' (Donovan, 1998). Involvement of the Ministry of Education in materials development projects (Tomlinson, 1995; Tickoo, 1995; Gonzales, 1995; Pascasio, 1995; Villamin, 1988) greatly facilitates review, feedback, piloting and evaluation procedures. It makes it easier to procure the participation of schools and teachers. Projects with governmental backing have extensive support and access to information and can assume infrastructural support as well. While government agencies may relinquish their role as developer of materials, they could and should continue to fund the research and development aspects of materials development by offsetting the costs or part of the cost of piloting the materials in the interests of serving learners' needs.

Teachers themselves need to recognize the significant role they can play and contributions they can make in the development of useful and effective materials to teach English. Teachers can take a proactive, indeed a creative, stance by suggesting ways and means through which their feedback can be sought with minimum disruption to their teaching routine. The role played by teacher feedback in materials development and the kind of changes it can bring about in the materials will also depend upon the credibility and the ability of the feedbackers to provide valid, considered and worthwhile feedback.

In order to participate meaningfully in materials development, teachers need to be aware of the syllabus, changes in assessment, any new initiatives and changes or developments in language teaching methodology and pedagogy. They must, of course, be well aware of their learners' abilities and disabilities, interests and motivations. Teachers must also be willing to spend time and effort to provide detailed feedback as well as to deal with some disruption to their classes when piloting materials. Ministry officials and publishers need to work together to see how they can motivate teachers to bear with these inconveniences.

Materials developers – both writers and editors need to understand the role that materials play in the instructional system and they need to take feedback from teachers into account when developing materials. Materials developers must develop materials with the teacher and learner in mind. They must be conscious of the assumptions they make about teachers and learners and constantly question these assumptions and put them to the test by trying out the materials. This can be done if means and opportunities for reviewing and piloting the materials before they are actually published, adopted and used are provided to the developers by allocating sufficient time in the schedule and resources in the budget to research and development, particularly feedback from teachers.

Even prior to this, publishers need to factor into their budgets the cost and resources and implications on schedule that mechanisms and procedures for review and feedback from teachers will have. Commercial publishers need to recognize that profits in publishing educational materials come from credibility. This requires a tradition of research and development and sincerity, which in turn require long-term investment. This, of course, is not an easy task, but as Yaw (1999) points out, 'The challenge and the problem will be the business justification of such a course of action. This will depend on the business goals and commitments of individual publishers.'

Curriculum planners need to consider the time taken for meaningful review and feedback and will need to work these as well as processes of feedback, review and revision and their documentation into any materials development process.

Conclusion

There is a need to recognize and identify the integrated or interdependent sets of processes that comprise materials development in language teaching and a need to identify the interstitial spaces where the different aspects of curriculum development and the participants involved in these processes interact or depend on one another (Singapore Wala, 2001). Syllabus designers and curriculum planners are located in the future – their work is to construct a framework to create a future. They work with ideals and abstracts in mind. They work with objectives and outcomes in mind. They will also measure and evaluate materials based on these criteria. Teachers, on the other hand, are mired in the present. They must teach today's learner, in today's classroom, within today's curriculum, system and school environment. For the teacher, the syllabus is the theory and the textbook is the manual that will enable the practice. Teachers work with a textbook developed a few years ago in hand and the practical realities of the situation staring them in the face. Such is the location from which teachers will evaluate materials. Materials developers occupy a kind of twilight zone – materials must answer present-day teacher needs for tomorrow's class with a view to meeting the goals of education for the future. Given these different and distinct locations, it is important that the materials development process allows for dialogue between these participants through several 'meeting points' (Gower and Bell, 1997) between their 'worlds'.

Moreover, materials development is a process that perhaps comes at the end of a whole change of curricular innovation and reform – syllabus redesign, new methodologies, etc. – and so it is important when planning the process that a cause-and-effect chain of events be visualized, bearing in mind the implications of all these and the extent to which they can be carried out simultaneously and also which of them must be done consecutively and in what sequence. Having developed a policy and a plan for a process, language education policy planners must ask and answer the following questions: What are the assumptions that are being made about the different participants in the process vis-à-vis the objectives of the exercise? Are they reasonable and realistic? Do the procedures put in place make it possible for the process to accomplish the objectives?

Given the complex nature of curriculum development when viewed thus, there needs to be sufficient space, resources, motivation and obligation for careful data gathering and documentation, planning, experimentation, monitoring, consultation, evaluation and incorporation of feedback, otherwise 'simplistic solutions ... that address only one dimension of the process' (Richards, 1990) will be advocated.

References

Abu Samah, A. (1988) 'Materials for language learning and teaching: new trends and developments – the Malaysian scene', in B. K. Das (ed.) *Materials for Language Learning and Teaching.* Singapore: SEAMEO Regional Language Centre.

Bell, J. and Gower, R. (1998) 'Writing course materials for the world: a great compromise', in B. Tomlinson (ed.) *Materials Development in Language Teaching.* Cambridge: Cambridge University Press, pp. 116–29.

Chan, P. (1987) 'Curriculum innovation: A study of the CLUE programme with reference to teachers' attitudes and concerns'. MA dissertation, National University of Singapore.

Cunningsworth, A. (1995) *Choosing your Coursebook.* Oxford: Heinemann.

Donovan, P. (1997) 'Piloting course materials for publication'. *Folio,* 4 (1), 13–15.

Donovan, P. (1998) 'Piloting – a publisher's view', in B. Tomlinson (ed.) *Materials Development in Language Teaching.* Cambridge: Cambridge University Press, pp. 149–89

Dubin, F. (1988) 'The roles of L2 teachers, learners and materials developers in the context of new technologies', in B. K. Das (ed.) *Materials for Language Learning and Teaching.* Singapore: SEAMEO Regional Language Centre.

Dubin, F. and Olshtain, E. (1986) *Course Design.* Cambridge: Cambridge University Press.

Gonzales, A. B. (1995) 'ESL materials for Philippine use in primary and secondary schools: across three paradigmatic generations', in A. C. Hidalgo,

D. Hall and G. M. Jacobs *Getting Started: Materials Writers on Materials Writing.* Singapore: SEAMEO Regional Language Centre, pp. 1–7.

Gower, R. and Bell, J. (1997) 'From teaching to writing – principles and process'. *Folio,* **4** (1), 10–13.

Halim, A. (1976) 'Decision-making in language course design', in G. H. Wilson (ed.) *Curriculum Development and Syllabus Design for English Teaching.* Singapore: SEAMEO English Language Teaching Centre.

Harmer, J. (1997) 'Classrooms in my mind'. *Folio,* 4(1), 33–5.

Hopkins, A. (1995) 'Revolutions in ELT Materials?' *Modern English Teacher,* **4** (3).

Hughes, P. (1973) *The Teacher's Role in Curriculum Design.* Sydney: Angus and Robertson Publishers.

Ibe, M. D. (1976) 'Evaluation: ideals and realities', in G. H. Wilson (ed.) *Curriculum Development and Syllabus Design for English Teaching.* Singapore: SEAMEO English Language Teaching Centre.

Jolly, D. and Bolitho, R. (1998) 'A framework for materials writing', in B. Tomlinson (ed.) *Materials Development in Language Teaching.* Cambridge: Cambridge University Press, pp. 90–115.

Lacey, C. (1976) 'Problems of sociological fieldwork: a review of the methodology of "Hightown Grammar" ', in M. Shipman (ed.) *The Organization and Impact of Social Research.* London: Routledge & Kegan Paul.

Nair, S. (1995a) 'Monitoring the implementation of the English language syllabus (1991) secondary level'. Paper presented at symposium, *The Implementation of the English Language Curriculum in Singapore,* 16–18 February 1995. SEAMEO RELC – Australia Institutional Links Project.

Nair, S. (1995b) 'Monitoring the implementation of the EL syllabuses (1991)'. Day 1, Group Discussion 1 at symposium, *The Implementation of the English Language Curriculum in Singapore,* 16–18 February 1995. SEAMEO RELC – Australia Institutional Links Project. Report, pp. 32–6.

Nisbet, J. D. (1975) 'Innovation: bandwagon or hearse', in A. Harris *et al.* (eds) *Curriculum Innovations.* Buckingham: The Open University Press.

Nisbet, J. D. and Watt, J. (1980) 'Case study'. *Rediguide 26.* Nottingham: University of Nottingham School of Education.

Nunan, D. (1988) *Syllabus Design.* Oxford: Oxford University Press.

Pascasio, E. M. (1995) 'The English series – experiencing language: a response to the Philippine Bilingual Policy', in A. C. Hidalgo, D. Hall and G. M. Jacobs *Getting Started: Materials Writers on Materials Writing.* Singapore: SEAMEO Regional Language Centre, pp. 82–94.

Penaflorida, A. H. (1995) 'The process of materials development: a personal experience', in A. C. Hidalgo, D. Hall and G. M. Jacobs *Getting Started: Materials Writers on Materials Writing.* Singapore: SEAMEO Regional Language Centre pp. 172–86.

Richards, J. C. (1985) *The Context of Language Teaching.* Cambridge: Cambridge University Press.

Richards, J. C. (1990) *The Language Teaching Matrix.* Cambridge: Cambridge University Press.

Richards, J. C. (1995) 'Easier said than done: an insider's account of a textbook project', in A. C. Hidalgo, D. Hall and G. M. Jacobs *Getting Started: Materials Writers on Materials Writing.* Singapore SEAMEO Regional Language Centre, pp. 95–135.

Richards, J. C. and Rodgers, T. S. (1986) *Approaches and Methods in Language Teaching.* Cambridge: Cambridge University Press.

Roxburgh, J. (1997) 'Procedures for evaluation of in-house EAP textbooks'. *Folio,* **4** (1), 15–18.

Singapore Wala, D. A. (2001) 'The role of teacher feedback in developing instructional materials for teaching English for Secondary One'. Unpublished MA thesis, National University of Singapore.

Suvarnis, S. (1991) 'A study of the new English Language syllabus for lower secondary classes'. Project for Dip in Applied Linguistics. Singapore SEAMEO Regional Language Centre.

Tickoo, M. L. (1995) 'Materials for a state-level system: a retrospective record', in A. C. Hidalgo, D. Hall and G. M. Jacobs *Getting Started: Materials Writers on Materials Writing.* Singapore SEAMEO Regional Language Centre, pp. 31–45.

Toh, K. A. (1994) 'Teacher-centred learning is alive and well'. *Teaching and Learning,* **15** (1), 12–17.

Toh, K. A., Yap, K.-C., Springham, S. V., Pee, S. and China, P. (1997) 'Developing curriculum in Singapore: teacher-academic partnerships', in J. Tan, S. Gopinathan and H. W. Kam (eds) *Education in Singapore: A Book of Readings.* Singapore: Simon & Schuster.

Tomlinson, B. (1995) 'Work in progress: textbook projects'. *Folio,* **2**, (2), 26–30.

Tomlinson, B. (ed.) (1998) *Materials Development in Language Teaching.* Cambridge: Cambridge University Press

Tomlinson, B. (1999) 'What do you think? Issues in materials development'. *Folio,* **5** (1), 3–4.

Villamin, A. M. (1988) 'Multi-level skills and values-oriented reading materials for K–10'. Paper presented at regional seminar on *Materials for Language Learning and Teaching: New Trends and Developments,* 11–15 April 1988.

Yalden, J. (1987) *Principles of Course Design for Language Teaching.* Cambridge: Cambridge University Press.

Yaw, C. (1999) 'Educational challenges in the new millennium: a publisher's perspective'. Paper presented at MERA-ERA Conference 1999.

Yeoh, O. C. (1984) *Curriculum Innovations and the Curriculum.* Singapore: Institute of Education.

Official Documents Cited

Curriculum Development Institute of Singapore (1991). *English Language Syllabus 1991 (Secondary)*

Curriculum Planning and Development Division, Ministry of Education (2001) *English Language Syllabus 2001 – For Primary and Secondary Schools.*

EL2 Unit, Ministry of Education, Singapore (1976) *The Teaching and Learning of EL2: Guidelines (Draft)*.

Ministry of Education (Singapore) Approved Textbook List. *http://nsinte1.moe.edu.sg/project/db/atl/db_puatl.nsf/*

Ministry of Education (Singapore) Curriculum Planning and Development Division. *http://www1.moe.edu.sg/cpdd.htm*

Ministry of Education (Singapore) Desired Outcomes of Education. *http://www1.moe.edu.sg/desired.htm*

Ministry of Education (Sinagpore) Education in Singapore. *http://www1.moe.edu.sg/educatio.htm*

Ministry of Education (Singapore) Posting of Contract Proposal Received. *http://www1.moe.edu.sg/cpdd/posting_of_contract_proposal_received%20 (new).htm#Sec%20EL*

Ministry of Education (Singapore) External Review Team (1997) 'Learning, creating, communicating: a curriculum review'. *http://www1.moe.edu.sg/Speeches/Curry%20Revue%20Report.htm*

Ministry of Education (1998a) 'Educational publishers to play bigger role in producing instructional materials for schools'. Press release, 4 February 1998. Reference No: Edun 25–02–008. *http://www1.moe.edu.sg/Press/980204.htm*

Ministry of Education (1998b) 'Ministry of Education's response to the External Curriculum Review Report'. Press release, 21 March 1998. Reference No: Edun N25–02–004. *http://www1.moe.edu.sg/Press/980321.htm*

Ministry of Education (1998c). 'Educational publishers to play bigger role in producing instructional materials for schools'. Press release, 16 July 1998. Reference No: Edun N25–02–004. *http://www1.moe.edu.sg/Press/980716.htm*

Ministry of Education 'Publishing school textbooks – frequently asked questions'. *http://www1.moe.edu.sg/cpdd/faq.htm*

Humanizing the Coursebook

Brian Tomlinson

Introduction

My first and most dramatic attempt to humanize a coursebook took place one wintry night in Liverpool 35 years ago. As a very young teacher of a night school class of underpriviledged underachievers I could take the tedium no more. I ordered the class to line up along the window with their middle-class, middle-of-the road coursebooks in their right hands. We opened the windows and, on the command 'throw', they threw their coursebooks away. Now we had no irrelevant materials for the English class and, in fact, now we had no materials at all. So, instead the students brought their own. Soon we had a lot of comics and magazines and even one or two books as well. Then we had a lot of fun devising activities together that involved the students in doing things that connected to themselves.

In my 35 years of teaching English since that dramatic act of defiance in Liverpool I've suffered countless other coursebooks (including some I've written myself) which have needed humanizing because they didn't engage the learners I was using them with and because they didn't manage to connect with the learners' lives. Sometimes it wasn't the coursebook's fault; the books were potentially humanistic (including, I hope, those written by myself) but they didn't match the psychological and sociological realities of my particular groups of learners. Often, though, it was the fault of the coursebooks because they didn't sufficiently take into account the resources of the learner as a human being. Many of these coursebooks concentrated on the linguistic and analytical aspects of language learning and failed to tap the human being's potential for multidimensional processing. That is, they made insufficient use of the learners' ability to learn through doing things physically, to learn through feeling emotion, to learn through experiencing things in the mind. They didn't acknowledge that, for human beings, the most important factor in learning is affect (Arnold, 1999; Schumann, 1999). In order to achieve effective and durable learning, language learners need to relax, feel at ease, develop self-confidence and self-esteem, develop positive attitudes towards the learning experience and be involved intellectually, aesthetically and emotionally (Tomlinson, 1998c). They also need to make use of their experience of life, their interests and enthusiasms, their views, attitudes and feelings and, above all, their capacity to make meaningful connections in their minds. Not many coursebooks encourage them to do this.

Instead, many of them use an interrogative approach which continually under-estimates and questions the ability of the learners, and which often results in diminishment and loss of self-esteem for the learner and a minimalizing of opportunities for effective learning.

I hope from reading this Introduction it's becoming clear that what I mean by a humanistic coursebook is one which respects its users as human beings and helps them to exploit their capacity for learning through meaningful experience. I hope it's also becoming clear that by humanizing the coursebook I mean adding activities which help to make the language learning process a more affective experience and finding ways of helping the learners to connect what is in the book to what is in their minds.

Humanizing without the Coursebook

One way of humanizing a coursebook is for the teacher to replace sections of it with more humanistic materials which involve the learners in gaining and reflecting on experience. Or, as with my Liverpool example, for the teacher to take the drastic step of replacing the coursebook altogether. This was a step which I also took with a class of domestic science and handicraft teachers at a primary teacher-training college in Vanuatu. They were a class of women with at least ten years' experience of apparently failing to learn English formally and with no confidence at all in their ability to use English for communication. No course-book ever written could have helped them (unless it had been written for that class alone) and I soon decided to replace the book we'd been allocated. Instead I told them that they were each going to write a novel. They were asked to think of an environment they knew well and to develop a story situated in it. When they'd recovered from their shock, they set about the task and then spent every English lesson for the term writing their novels, while I made myself available as an informant and supporter. In true Melanesian style, they read each other's work in progress and made helpful suggestions. They quickly gained confidence and self-esteem and soon they were illustrating their books with the beautiful drawings which they all seemed capable of and 'publishing' them in elaborate and attractive ways. I'm not claiming that by the end of term their English had mi-raculously improved, but they'd all written, revised and 'published' books which were at least 60 pages long. Even if they hadn't acquired much English (though I'm sure they did), they'd done something in English which they were proud of and they'd gained far more confidence and self-esteem than all their coursebooks put together had ever given them.

Perhaps the best example of partial replacement I've experienced was a teacher in a high school in Jakarta who asked her class if they liked their coursebook. Of course, in typical Indonesian fashion, they told her what they thought she wanted to hear and were unanimous in their praise of the book. However, she persisted and eventually persuaded them to tell her what they really thought of the book. It seems that they found it very boring and, in particular, disliked the dull reading texts which seemed to have no connection with their lives. The teacher's response was to divide the class into twelve groups (the same number as weeks in the semester) and to give Group 1 responsibility for finding something interesting for the class to read in English. Group 1 spent the week searching Jakarta for a text which could engage their peers and on the Friday they delivered it to the teacher. On the Monday she used the text for the reading class and then challenged Group 2 to find an equally interesting text for the following week. This procedure continued for the whole of the semester with the students finding the texts and the teacher supplying a variety of potentially engaging activities. The next semester the teacher asked the class if they wanted to continue to find their own texts and was rewarded with a resounding, 'Yes!' This time, however, she told Group 1 that, not only were they responsible for finding an interesting text but that they were also responsible for developing the activities and for 'teaching' the reading lesson on the Monday. On the Friday, Group 1 showed their text and activities to the teacher and she gave them some advice for their lesson on the Monday. This procedure continued for the whole semester, with the teacher sitting in the back of the students' class while they gained confidence and enjoyment connected to their lives (an experience similar to that of Jensen and Hermer (1998: 191) who found that 'the pupils are the best collaborators in a performance-based learning environment. They even find and devise exercises and games themselves, research situations and texts').

Other examples of partial replacement from my experience include:

- Getting a class of Italian university students to script and record a radio soap opera set in the college they were visiting in England (by giving each small group responsibility for producing an episode).
- Helping a multilingual class of intermediate-level learners to video their versions of poems, short stories and extracts from novels.
- Getting classes of high school students in Indonesia to participate in TPR Plus activities (e.g., collective miming of stories, making of sculptures, painting of murals, cooking of meals, etc.) which start off with the students following instructions spoken by the teacher but then develop into activities initiated by the students themselves.
- Encouraging teachers in Indonesia and Japan to get students to develop their own class libraries by staggering into class with a huge cardboard box and inviting the students to come and look at their new class library. Of course, the box was empty and the students were challenged to fill it with reading material which would interest their friends. In many cases, the students quickly filled their box as a result of visits to travel agents, embassies, newspaper offices, publishers and supermarkets. And one enterprising class in Jakarta even looked for English-sounding names in the telephone book and then visited houses asking for unwanted books, magazines and newspapers for their libraries.
- Encouraging teachers in Japan to give each student in their class a blank cassette and then prompting them to record something interesting in English for their class Listening Library (one teacher told me a year later that her class now had over a thousand cassettes in their Listening Library).

For other ideas for supplementing the coursebook with student-centred, student-initiated activities providing sensory experience of language learning, see Jensen and Hermer (1998), who quote a father in Bateson (1972) telling his daughter, 'All that syntax and grammar, that's rubbish. Everything rests on the notion that there is such a thing as "just" words – but there isn't.' They advocate a performance approach which promotes 'a full sensory, physical and emotional appreciation of the language' (p. 179) and provide many practical examples of how to achieve their humanistic aims.

Humanizing with the Coursebook

Often teachers are obliged to use a coursebook in all their lessons. In such cases they can humanize it by reducing the non-humanistic elements of the book and by expanding and adding to those sections which invite the learners to think, feel and do in order to learn.

Here's an example of such an approach:

1. getting the whole class to act out a variation of a coursebook reading text from the teacher's spoken instructions;
2. giving them the coursebook text and asking them in groups to find as many differences as they can between the two similar texts within a demanding time limit;
3. organizing a competition in which the groups take it in turns to articulate a difference without referring back to the text;
4. stimulating the groups to develop an extended version of the text in a local context;
5. giving the students some of the coursebook activities for homework.

Other coursebook-based humanistic activities I've used include:

- Getting students individually and then in groups to draw a version of a reading or listening text before doing the coursebook comprehension activities (e.g., how they think the boy sees the school in Roger McGough's poem 'First Day at School' (1979); how they think the young whale sees the people on the beach in 'The Great Whale's Mistake' (Bell and Gower, 1991: 141)).
- Getting students in groups to work out what happens in my mime of a text prior to reading the text in the coursebook.
- Getting students to dramatize texts they are going to read in the coursebook from my spoken narrative of the text.
- Getting one group of students to mime their version of a text from the coursebook which another group are going to read and then inviting that group to tell the story of the text before they read it.
- Giving the students part of a coursebook text and then asking them to complete it themselves before reading the text in the coursebook and doing the associated activities.

- Getting the whole class to write a local version of a coursebook text by inviting them to shout out sentences and later to revise and connect them into a coherent story.
- Giving the students the comprehension questions from the coursebook and getting them to write the text they are based on.
- Getting students to bring photographs to class to represent their local application of a coursebook text or task they've used in a previous lesson.
- Getting students to act out coursebook dialogues in voices appropriate to a given context (e.g., the shop assistant is the customer's ex-boyfriend).
- Getting students to suggest different contexts for a coursebook dialogue which would change its meaning.
- Getting students in pairs to continue and develop a coursebook dialogue into a dramatic event with each student playing one of the characters.
- Getting students to write the inner speech monologues of characters in a coursebook dialogue (e.g., the outwardly polite shopkeeper who is getting inwardly incensed by the customer who can't make his mind up).

Developing Humanistic Coursebooks

Of course, the ideal scenario for most hard-pressed teachers would be to be able to use a coursebook which is already humanistic. Is it possible to develop coursebooks which are humanistic and which at the same time satisfy the conservative caution of the publishers, as well as the requirements of conventional institutions, curricula and administrators? It is. But it's not easy; and no coursebook can be completely humanistic for all its users because it can't possibly relate directly to each user's life.

There are a number of ways of developing coursebooks which are more humanistic.

Writing in Large and Varied Teams

Writing a coursebook (and especially a series of coursebooks) can be a long and laborious process. Often the writer(s) start out energized with enthusiasm and ideas but, after making the almost inevitable compromises with the understandably conservative editor, and after churning out innumerable units with the same format, they start to lose their creative energy. Long before the end of the book/series, the writers have changed their main objective to completing the book so that it can start to repay them for the tedious time they've devoted to it and so it can give them back their life. One way of stimulating and maintaining creative energy is to write coursebooks quickly in large and varied teams. The team might consist of new and experienced teachers, new and experienced materials writers, a poet, an artist, an applied linguist, a musician, a Chief Examiner and a cartoonist, all pooling their resources and stimulating each other. That's how we wrote a secondary school English coursebook for Namibia (Tomlinson, 1995) and how we're writing a series of coursebooks at Bilkent

University in Ankara. We wrote the Namibian coursebook with a team of 30 writers in six days. On the first day, I demonstrated novel humanistic approaches and activities to stimulate thought and ideas. On the second day, we worked out a flexible unit framework and divided into ten writing teams of three. Each team wrote a Unit 1 designed to engage the learners and interest them in the book. The units were displayed on the wall and voted for by everybody in a competition to decide on the unit most likely to appeal to the learners. The winners revised their unit and developed another one while all the other teams wrote a new unit each. Throughout each working day representatives were present from the Ministry of Education and from the publisher (Gamsberg Macmillan) and they were kept busy giving permission and advice. Also, specialist members of teams (e.g., the artist, the poet, the Chief Examiner) were visited for feedback and suggestions. The units were displayed, monitored and revised, and a small team of advisors checked the units against the syllabus and against lists of student and teacher needs. They also sequenced and connected the units and were eventually responsible for a final editing and revision of the book. The result was the most imaginative and humanistic coursebook I've ever been involved in, mainly because the short intensive writing period helped generate and maintain energy and the varied interaction with other human beings helped put the focus on the people involved in the learning process rather than on the language being learned.

Using a Text-driven Approach

The teams in the Namibian project described above started not by selecting a language point but by selecting a potentially engaging text from the books, magazines, newspapers and cassettes made available to them. They devised pre-reading or listening activities to help to activate the learners' minds in readiness for connecting the texts to their own lives and they developed post-reading activities aimed at helping the learners to articulate and develop their mental representations of the text. In other words, the initial emphasis was on the people experiencing the texts and not on the language in them. Later, the writers developed activities focusing on the content of the text and helping the learners to connect it to their own lives. Then they developed language activities focusing on language features which were salient in the text. Because we'd checked that the texts chosen constituted a representative sample of the main genres and text types, it was not too surprising that the language features chosen for the activities corresponded very closely with the language features listed in the syllabus.

In my experience as a writer and facilitator of coursebooks, the text-driven approach described above can be a very effective way of ensuring that a course-book is humanistic. If the initial focus is on a potentially engaging text it's much more likely that the writer will keep the learners in mind than if the initial focus is on a language item or skill. And it's much easier to develop learning activities to match a text than it is to find an engaging text to match teaching points.

Using a Multidimensional Approach

A multi-dimensional approach aims to help learners to develop the ability to produce and process an L2 by using their mental resources in ways similar to those they use when communicating in their L1. Doing so not only helps learners to maximise their brain's potential for communicating in an L2 but it also maximises their brain's potential for learning. (Tomlinson, 2000a)

A multidimensional approach is based on the principle that using affect, mental imagery and inner speech is what we do during effective language use and what we do during effective and durable learning, too. As Berman (1999: 2) says, 'we learn best when we see things as part of a recognised pattern, when our imaginations are aroused, when we make natural associations between one idea and another, and when the information appeals to our senses.' The procedures which can be used in a coursebook to apply the principles of a multidimensional approach (and thus to create a humanistic coursebook) include:

- engaging affect (i.e., emotional involvement, positive attitudes towards the learning experience and self-esteem) through activities which involve learners recalling and recounting personal experiences, thinking about and articulating their own attitudes and views and creating their own personal mental representations of what they listen to and read;
- imaging activities (Tomlinson, 1998c) which encourage learners to create mental images while processing or producing language (an 'overwhelming amount of empirical evidence seems to show that imagery is a remarkably effective mediator of cognitive performance, ranging from short-term memory to creativity' (Kaufman 1996: 77));
- inner voice activities which encourage learners to talk to themselves in an L2 inner voice while processing and producing language in the L2 (Tomlinson, 2000a, 2000b);
- kinaesthetic activities which involve learners in momentary mental activity before following instructions in the L2 in order to perform physical activities such as playing games, miming stories, making models and cooking meals (Asher, 1994; Tomlinson, 1994a);
- process activities which help learners to create a version of a text themselves before reading or listening to the complete text (Tomlinson, 2000a).

Using Literature

In my experience, one of the best ways to achieve the objectives mentioned so far in this chapter is to use literature as a means of stimulating multidimensional mental activity during language learning (Tomlinson, 2001). This only works if the learners are helped and encouraged to experience the literature rather than study it, if the texts are accessible without glossaries and introductions and if the literature relates to the learners' lives (Tomlinson, 1998b). I've found that the best way to do this is to build up a library of texts which are linguistically simple but cognitively and emotionally complex, and then to use them as the basis of humanistic activities which encourage personal engagement and response (Tomlinson, 1994a). Unfortunately most coursebooks rarely use literature (Tomlinson *et al.*, 2001) and when they do, they usually ask learners to read the text carefully and then answer comprehension questions on it. They thus ensure that the learners study the text. The text remains a text and the learners fail to create literature from it. As a result, the text has little impact on their minds, their lives or their language acquisition.

Varying the Unit Focus

One of the reasons why many coursebooks are considered to be superficial and dull is that most of them try in each unit to cover the four skills, plus grammar, vocabulary and pronunciation points. This inevitably leads to a bits-and-pieces approach which often provides only very brief, trivial and disconnected encounters with the language being learned. If most of the units had only one main focus there would be a better chance of providing more sustained and meaningful encounters with the language in use and, therefore, of developing a more humanistic coursebook. For example, Unit 1 could focus on a reading project (involving a number of texts), Unit 2 could focus on an extensive listening task, Unit 3 could focus on an extensive writing task, which includes reading, listening and speaking in preparation and follow-up activities, and Unit 4 could provide grammar, vocabulary and pronunciation activities focusing on salient features in Units 1 to 3. That way the emphasis is more likely to be put on communication between people and less on unconnected bits of language. And the language work will be related to what the learners have already experienced.

Talking to the Learners

The voice of most coursebooks is semi-formal and distant, and matches the stereo-type of the knowledge-transmitting teacher talking at his learners. The writers reveal very little about their personalities, interests, beliefs and experiences and spend most of the time either telling the learners what to learn, do and say or interrogating them about what they know. It's a very unequal and anti-humanistic relationship which does little to encourage or engage the learner. For example, a recent survey of eight adult EFL coursebooks concluded that the 'the voices of the authors are neutral and semi-formal' (Tomlinson *et al.*, 2001: 88); though it did find that two of the courses 'managed to be neutral, yet at the same time friendly and supportive' (*ibid*).

What I'd 'like to see materials writers do is to chat to the learners casually in the same way that good teachers do' (in all cultures) 'and to try to achieve personal contact with them by revealing their own preferences, interests and opinions' (Tomlinson, 1998c: 8–9). There is research evidence that using a personal voice in a textbook can foster deeper and more durable learning (Beck *et al.*, 1995) and that the best way to achieve this is to include features of orality. The features I would recommend to the coursebook writer are:

- Informal discourse features (e.g., contracted forms, ellipsis, informal lexis).
- The active rather than the passive voice.
- Concreteness (e.g., examples, anecdotes).
- Inclusiveness (e.g., not signalling intellectual, linguistic or cultural superiority over the learners).
- Sharing experiences and opinions.
- Sometimes including casual redundancies rather than always being concise.

Connecting to the Learners' Views and Opinions

The easiest way to make a coursebook humanistic is to ensure that in most activities the learners are asked about their own views, attitudes, feelings and opinions, that they are helped to think of their own examples and connections and that they are made to feel as though they are equal interactants with the coursebook writers and with the authors of texts which the coursebook includes. Not many coursebooks achieve this, but in the survey of courses mentioned above it was considered that *Language in Use* (Doff and Jones, 1991) and *Landmark* (Haines and Stewart, 2000) 'respect the learners as individuals, and seek to engage them personally in many of their activities' (Tomlinson *et al.*, 2001: 87).

Providing Text-free Generalizable Activities

It's possible to develop a set of generalizable activities (Maley, 1998) which can be used with texts selected by the learner from a resource pack of materials, from a library, from the Internet or from his/her own resources. This ensures that the text relates to learners and is likely to engage them, and this is the way I'm writing a coursebook called *English from the Web*. In this book each unit provides the learners with a set of generalizable pre-reading, whilst-reading and post-reading activities for a particular genre (e.g., sports reports, cartoons, advertisements) and then suggests websites from which the learners can select texts which appeal to them for use with the activities.

Even more humanistic and productive would be an approach which provides generalizable activities in a coursebook plus guidance and stimulus to help the learners write their own texts for use with the activities (either for themselves or for a bank for other learners to select from).

Including Awareness Activities

Once learners have engaged with a text, achieved a multidimensional representation of it and developed and articulated their personal responses to it, I've found it can be very useful to help them to make discoveries for themselves from a more intensive reading of the text. Language awareness activities (Bolitho and Tomlinson, 1995), pragmatic awareness activities (Tomlinson, 1994b) and cultural awareness activities (Tomlinson, 2001), in which learners eventually work things out for themselves, can not only facilitate language acquisition and mental development, but they can also considerably increase self-esteem and independence.

Providing Alternatives

Providing a choice of route (e.g., analytical v. experiential), of texts (e.g., on different topics or at different levels) and of tasks (e.g., in relation to different learning styles) is a fairly easy way to personalize coursebooks and, therefore, to make them more humanistic.

Localizing Coursebooks

One of the main reasons why global coursebooks are not normally humanistic is that in trying to cater for everybody they end up engaging nobody. They have to make sure that their content and approach is not unsuitable for any type of learner, that their choice of topics and texts doesn't disadvantage any learners and, above all, that they don't offend or disturb any learners. The result, very often, is a book which presents 'a sanitised world which is bland and dull and in which there is very little excitement or disturbance to stimulate the emotions of the learner' (Tomlinson, 1998a: 20), a world which is characterized by Wajnryb (1996: 291) in her analysis of two best-selling coursebooks as 'safe, clean, harmonious, benevolent, undisturbed and PG-rated. What is absent is significant – jeopardy, face threat, negotiation, implicature ... and context.' Learning a language in such a world can reduce the learner from an individual human being with views, attitudes and emotions to a language learner whose brain is focused narrowly on low-level linguistic decoding.

One way of connecting a coursebook to the real world which the learner lives in is obviously to localize coursebooks. It's no accident that the two most humanistic coursebooks I know are published for local markets, *On Target* (1995) for Namibia and *Search 8* (1997) for Norway. Unfortunately, local coursebooks don't generate as much profit as global coursebooks and, despite a recent trend of producing localized versions of coursebooks, the global coursebook is going to remain the resource used by the majority of learners of English in the world. However, it wouldn't be too difficult to:

- provide a bank of texts, tasks and illustrations for the teacher to select from in order to replace or supplement sections of a global coursebook not relevant to their learners;
- produce global coursebooks with generalizable activities which are supplemented by local photocopiable packs of texts and illustrations;
- include in the teacher's book suggestions for localizing the texts and activities in a global coursebook;

- include activities in a global coursebook in which the learners localize some of the texts and the tasks by modifying them in relation to the world they know.

Conclusion

Humanistic approaches to language learning can facilitate both language acquisition and personal development. Unfortunately, most language learners learn from coursebooks and most coursebooks are not humanistic. However, it's not that difficult to make a coursebook more humanistic and it is possible to develop coursebooks which are both humanistic and profitable. We owe it to our learners to try.

Note

This chapter was first published as: Tomlinson, B. (2001) 'Humanising the coursebook'. *Humanising Language Teaching*, **5**(3). Canterbury: Pilgrims.

References

Arnold, J. (ed.) (1999) *Affect in Language Learning.* Cambridge: Cambridge University Press.

Asher, J. (1994) 'The total physical response: a stress-free, brain compatible approach to learning'. *SEAL*, Autumn, 22–5.

Bateson, G. (1972) *Steps to an Ecology of Mind. Collected Essays in Anthropology, Psychiatry, Evolution, and Epistemology.* San Francisco: Chandler Publishing Company.

Beck, I. L., McKeown, M. G. and Worthy, J. (1995) 'Giving a text voice can improve students' understanding'. *Research Reading Quarterly*, **30** (2).

Bell, J. and Gower, R. (1991) *Intermediate Matters.* Harlow: Longman.

Berman, M. (1999) 'The teacher and the wounded healer'. *IATEFL Issues*, **152**, 2–5.

Bolitho, R. and Tomlinson, B. (1995) *Discover English* (new edn.). Oxford: Heinemann.

Doff, A. and Jones, C. (1991) *Language in Use.* Cambridge: Cambridge University Press.

Haines, S. and Stewart, B. (2000) *Landmark.* Oxford: Oxford University Press.

Jensen, M. and Hermer, A. (1998) 'Learning by playing: learning foreign languages through the senses', in M. Byram and M. Fleming (eds) *Language Learning in Intercultural Perspective.* Cambridge: Cambridge University Press.

Kaufman, G. (1996) 'The many faces of mental imagery', in C. Cornoldi *et al. Stretching the Imagination: Representation and Transformation in Mental Imagery.* Oxford: Oxford University Press.

McGough, R. (1979) 'First day at school', in R. McGough and M. Rosen *You Tell Me.* London: Kestrel.

Maley, A. (1998) 'Squaring the circle – reconciling materials as constraint with materials as empowerment', in B. Tomlinson (ed.) *Materials Development in Language Teaching*. Cambridge: Cambridge University Press, pp. 279–94.

Schumann, J. A. (1999) 'A neurobiological perspective on affect', in J. Arnold (ed.) *Affect in Language Learning*. Cambridge: Cambridge University Press.

Tomlinson, B. (1994a) *Openings*. London: Penguin.

Tomlinson, B. (1994b) 'Pragmatic awareness activities'. *Language Awareness*, **3**(3), 119–29.

Tomlinson, B. (1994c) 'TPR materials'. *Folio*, **1**(2), 8–10.

Tomlinson, B. (1995) 'Work in progress: textbook projects'. *Folio*, **2**(2), 14–17.

Tomlinson, B. (1998a) 'Affect and the coursebook'. *IATEFL Issues*, **145**, 20–1.

Tomlinson, B. (1998b) 'And now for something not completely different; an approach to language through literature'. *Reading in a Foreign Language*, **11**(2), 177–89.

Tomlinson, B. (ed.) (1998c) *Materials Development in Language Teaching*. Cambridge: Cambridge University Press.

Tomlinson, B. (2000a) 'A multi-dimensional approach'. *The Language Teacher Online*, 24 July.

Tomlinson, B. (2000b) 'Talking to yourself: the role of the inner voice in language learning'. *Applied Language Learning*, **11**(1), 123–54.

Tomlinson, B. (2001) 'Connecting the mind: a multi-dimensional approach to teaching language through literature'. *The English Teacher*, **4**(2), 104–15.

Tomlinson, B., Dat, B., Masuhara, H. and Rubdy, R. (2001) 'EFL courses for adults'. *ELT Journal*, **55**(1), 80–101.

Wajnryb, R. (1996) 'Death, taxes and jeopardy: systematic omissions in EFL texts, or life was never meant to be an adjacency pair'. Ninth Educational Conference, Sydney.

The Visual Element in EFL Coursebooks

David A. Hill

Introduction

Since Pit Corder's (1966) ground-breaking *The Visual Element in Language Teaching*, a number of methodologists have written books showing the importance of various kinds of pictures in English language teaching (ELT): Wright (1976), McAlpin (1980), Bowen (1982), Wright (1989), Hill (1990) and Wright and Haleem (1991). A section called 'Pictures and Images' leads off the chapter on 'Educational Technology and Other Teaching Equipment' in the third edition of the ELT industry's standard teacher's textbook (Harmer, 2001). Articles on using visuals of one kind or another still appear regularly in the various journals for ELT professionals (e.g., Brand, 1997; Cundale, 1999; Porcaro, 2001). And, of course, British ELT coursebooks have moved on from the picture-free times of E. Frank Candlin in the 1960s, through the early black-and-white line drawings of Broughton and O'Neill in the 1970s, to the current range of materials which are full of stylish colour drawings and state-of-the-art photographs.

Given this plethora of words about using visuals, and the vast quantity of pictures available in current British coursebooks aimed at the international market for young adults and adults, this chapter seeks to examine what use is actually being made of pictorial material there, and to suggest what use might be made of it.

Visuals in Recent British Coursebooks

What do We Get?

In order to see what the current situation is with regard to British coursebook visuals, I examined four publications spanning the previous decade:

Headway Pre-Intermediate (J. Soars and L. Soars, (1991) Oxford: Oxford University Press)
Upper Intermediate Matters (J. Bell and R. Gower (1992) Harlow: Longman)
Cutting Edge Intermediate (S. Cunningham and P. Moor (1998) Harlow: Longman)

Inside Out Intermediate (S. Kay and V. Jones (1998) London: Macmillan Heinemann)

Initially I was interested to find out the balance between black-and-white and colour illustration, and between drawings and photographs within the main text pages of the coursebook units (see Table 10.1) These figures only show the existence of a separate, individual illustration, regardless of size. All four books are roughly A4 format (*c.* 21 cm × 30 cm), and the pictures typically vary in size from 20.5 cm × 16 cm down to 3 cm × 4 cm.

Table 10.1 The balance of illustrations, drawings and photos in four coursebooks

	Headway	*Matters*	*Cutting Edge*	*Inside Out*
Pages of text	111	145	125	134
Colour drawings	59	87	114	50
B&W drawings	77	1	9	23
Total drawings	136	88	123	73
Colour photos	92	111	77	111
B&W photos	30	16	16	11
Total photos	122	127	93	122
Total pictures	258	215	216	195

I was then interested in analysing what the pictures were actually illustrating. I decided to examine only the colour photos (CP) and colour drawings (CD) for each of the four books under consideration, as these generally constituted the largest percentage of illustrations. I categorized them according to subject (see Table 10.2).

These figures indicate, then, that 204/701 pictures (=29.1 per cent) showed actions, people doing things, while 171/701 pictures (=24.4 per cent) showed portraits, and interactions between people. Places 84/701 (=12 per cent) and objects 71/701 (=10.1 per cent) were much less frequent. It is interesting to note

Table 10.2 Analysis of colour photos and colour drawings in four coursebooks

Book	*Headway*		*Matters*		*Cutting Edge*		*Inside Out*		*Totals*
Picture	CD	CP	CD	CP	CD	CP	CD	CP	
Portrait	3	35	4	32	1	34	3	59	171
Place	11	18	3	3	23	2	5	6	71
Object	7	10	5	21	14	11	2	14	84
Interaction	19	3	42	28	40	8	14	17	171
Action	19	26	33	27	36	22	26	15	204
Totals	59	92	87	111	114	77	50	111	701

that the vast majority of the portraits are photographs (160) as opposed to drawings (10) – presumably because of the ease with which publishers can obtain them from picture agencies – while the majority of interactions were drawings (115) rather than photos (56) – presumably because many of the interaction situations required by authors are not available as photographs.

While this analysis of *what* pictures are to be found in coursebooks is intrinsically interesting, it may be more revealing about the process of textbook production than it is about *how* the pictures are expected to be used.

How are They Used?

Use versus Decoration

The first analysis conducted was to find out how many of the pictures were specifically used in the text, and how many were merely there for decorative purposes. This analysis was only carried out on the two most recent books, *Cutting Edge Intermediate* and *Inside Out Intermediate*, in an attempt to gauge current publishing trends (Table 10.3).

Table 10.3 Use versus decoration in two coursebooks

	Cutting Edge	*Inside Out*	*Totals*	*Percentages (%)*
Photos: Decoration	57	83	140	34.1
Photos: Use	36	39	75	18.2
Drawings: Decoration	44	42	86	20.9
Drawings: Use	79	31	110	26.8
Totals	216	195	411	100

The Table shows that over the two books, 34.1 per cent + 20.9 per cent = 55 per cent of all illustrations were purely decorative, with students not asked to use them in any way. Whilst not claiming that statistics about two current coursebooks are in any way representative of all coursebooks, my intuition is that similar figures could be derived from a fuller analysis. What do these figures seem to imply? That ELT publishers, editors and authors think that it is more important to provide attractive space-filling accompanying illustrations in their coursebooks than it is to provide pictures with related activities.

Of course, this situation merely highlights what I see as one of the major problems in the production of coursebooks: the authors, unless they specifically say they want a particular picture, and demand to see it before it is included, leave the selection of the illustrations up to the editors, providing a written artwork brief where necessary. It is the editors who decide what there is room for, what fits in terms of design, colour and layout and how many pictures they can afford to buy from picture agencies to have enough illustrations per unit without going over budget. And in many ways they do a very good job – most contemporary British coursebooks are very attractive products which students and teachers enjoy using.

Harmer (2001: 135) puts forward the view that pictures used for what he terms 'ornamentation' are important because:

> if the pictures are interesting they will appeal to at least some members of the class strongly. They have the power (at least for the more visually oriented) to engage students.

Whilst it is probably true that students today prefer the colourfully decorated pages of current textbooks as opposed to the picture-free pages of the 1960s and early 1970s, that may well be because they are used to being surrounded by visual images in all areas of everyday life. Some students may also respond to such ornamentation 'strongly', although whether that strong appeal translates directly into any language learning benefits is a moot point. Harmer is equally vague about what kind of engagement the more visually oriented students might display. I suspect it would require a lengthy and subtle longitudinal study to prove that illustration-as-mere-decoration has any direct effect on student attitudes to English or to language learning, or indeed helps the learner to learn English better.

What Kind of Use?

Given that 45 per cent of the illustrations in the two coursebooks considered do have activities attached to them, it would be instructive to analyse exactly what kind of use is being made of them. To discuss this aspect of the issue, I will again refer only to *Cutting Edge Intermediate* and *Inside Out Intermediate*. The following activity types were found in the two books:

a. Activities dealing with precise elements of the unit language focus (syntax/ vocabulary):

- Finding objects from a written list in the picture.
- Matching written texts with pictures.
- Using situations in pictures to work out what people are saying.
- Using the pictures as cues for written grammar drills.
- Giving physical descriptions of people in the pictures.

b. Activities working on listening comprehension:

- Recognizing and labelling people/objects on the basis of a listening passage.
- Spotting differences between details in the picture and information given on tape.
- Deciding what people are saying in the pictures based on taped dialogues.

c.   Finding or giving information:

- Illustrations which clarify details in a reading text.
- Looking for information in the picture.

d.   Deduction and creativity

- Making judgements and inventing information about people and situations in the pictures.

Such an analysis might lead one to make a distinction between purely functional illustrations which have the aim of making comprehension of the language easier (e.g., a photograph of an object or a drawing of an event in the text) and those whose object is to stimulate a mental and linguistic response (e.g., an illustration positioned to allow reader speculation at the end of one and before the beginning of another piece of text). One might also distinguish between those illustrations which aim to facilitate explicit teaching (e.g., defining the meaning of words by having a picture of their referents) and those which facilitate tasks (e.g., by illustrating an interactive situation which students are using the language for).

It can be seen that the illustrations are largely being used for fairly low-level language practice, with few activities aimed at stimulating students to use the language creatively starting from the pictures. Such an activity would be *Roads* (Hill, 1990: 34), in which students are given pictures of different types of country roads (e.g., lanes through fields, mountain roads, forest roads) on which there are no people or vehicles. When they have examined their pictures they are asked to imagine that they are standing on that road and to write down responses to the following:

a.   something they can see outside the picture to their left;
b.   something they can hear;
c.   something they can see outside the picture to the right;
d.   something they can smell;
e.   something they find on the road and pick up to take with them;
f.   something they see which they do not like when they walk down the road and out of the picture.

The students then discuss their responses with partners – I usually make them talk to someone who has a similar picture to theirs, and someone who has a very different picture. The result is always a lengthy conversation initially about their immediate responses to the questions, followed by discussion of reasons for those responses and then, frequently, by talk about the places, what they remind them of, etc., etc.

What Might We Do with Visuals in Coursebooks?

It seems to me that having 55 per cent of the pictures in a given coursebook used purely for decorative purposes is a great waste of effort on the part of the publisher and a great waste of opportunity for the language learner and teacher. I do not doubt that many teachers use the decorative pictures accompanying, say, reading passages, for arousing interest and/or awareness of topic by discussing what the learners can see in the pictures. However, let us see what we find in a coursebook.

Look at the exercise from *Cutting Edge Intermediate*, which is fairly typical of the use of decorative pictures (see Figure 10.1). Firstly, there is a sense in which the use of the picture feels deceitful, in that, because of its positioning, it seems to be fully integrated with the surrounding texts and the activity's instructions, but actually it plays no real part in them at all.

The activity is a basic grammar practice exercise involving a choice between a series of paired items. The picture provides a context of a kind: in the rubric we are told it shows 'a group of friends who have just graduated from university', and the texts the students have to work on are connected to the future work plans of some students after university. However, the picture is not used for any linguistic purpose. The activity would work just as well with no picture, and the instruction: 'Read the notes about a group of friends who have just finished university and choose the correct alternative', and then the texts underneath. For item 4 in the exercise, for example, I do not choose 'to work' rather than 'working' because I can see a picture of Eliza.

Supposing the author, editor and designer wanted to keep the picture and texts more or less as they are, it would have been very easy to lead into the language task through some picture-related discussion, using rubrics such as:

— How do students usually celebrate when they have got their university results in your country?

— Look at the picture below. How is this group of British students celebrating? Try to decide where they are and what they're eating. What are they actually doing at the moment? Why? What do you think they are saying to each other?

It would also have been possible to include a matching element, whereby there was a short description of each person (e.g., 'Richard's the one with the striped shirt') and the instruction: 'Draw an arrow from the information box to the picture of the person it talks about'.

In this way, for very little extra effort on the part of the materials writer, editor and designer, there would have been a lot more language production on the part of the learners. What is more, the new language suggested would actually be related to what is seen in the picture, rather than the external facts which the original deals with.

3 a) The picture below shows a group of friends who have just graduated from university. Read the notes and choose the correct alternative.

'Dan's parents, who are both lawyers, really want (1) *him to become* / *that he becomes* a lawyer too, but he isn't so sure. He's about (2) *going* / *to go* on a long holiday to think things over. Who knows what'll (3) *happen* / *happening* when he gets back.'

'This is Eliza. She's hoping (4) *to work* / *working* in fashion. Ideally, she'd like (5) *being* / *to be* a fashion editor for a glossy magazine. A bit strange considering she studied Ancient History!'

'Amanda's just finished a Business Studies course and intends (6) *to work* / *work* in Personnel Management eventually, but first she's decided (7) *to go* / *going* travelling for a while.'

'Heather did Drama Studies, and is hoping (8) *become* / *to become* an actress. She's working at the moment as a waitress, but she's also doing lots of auditions, and she's determined (9) *being* / *to be* a star one day.'

'This is me, Richard. I have no real plans at the moment. I'm thinking (10) *of going* / *to go* abroad for a while, but basically I just seem to enjoy being with all my friends! I'm really going (11) *missing* / *to miss* them.

Figure 10.1 An exercise from *Cutting Edge Intermediate*, p. 50

And it is this issue of dealing only with what is seen, or dealing with what the learner knows, thinks or deduces which I would like to touch on now. Pit Corder was, to my knowledge, the first to make the distinction between 'talking *about*' a picture and 'talking *with*' a picture (1966: 35). If you talk *about* a picture you are limited and constrained by what you see in the picture – 'there are five people, three young women and two young men, sitting around a table in a restaurant. On the table are … They are raising their glasses' and so on. It is factual and visible. It is also useful to revise certain bits of the language system. However, it need not always be an end in itself, but the way into talking *with* the picture: 'I think Eliza looks nice – she seems to know how to enjoy herself. She's really laughing. She looks fun to be with. She reminds me of my friend Linda.' Here, with a suitable task, the picture allows learners to bring their own reality to the lesson. Coursebooks seem to offer very few opportunities for students to use pictures to stimulate their own inner meanings.

In this author's coursebook for the Italian Biennio, *Corpus*, a series of good colour photographs are used on a large scale with relation to some pages on Art Nouveau (1994: 220–1). Firstly, they are used to consolidate vocabulary encountered in a listening passage about collecting Art Nouveau objects. There is a relatively simple labelling activity ('talking *about*') first, and then there follows a series of three questions which broaden the topic out to a discussion of the learners' feelings related to the Art Nouveau objects illustrated ('talking *with*').

Conclusion

This chapter has sought to show the nature of typical illustration used in British ELT coursebooks aimed at young adults and adults. It has shown that a majority of pictures included are used only for decorative purposes and that those used for language purposes tend to concentrate on low-level language skills related to basic language manipulation. It has suggested how such materials might be improved, and has gone on to exemplify the type of materials which is deemed necessary for a more meaningful and involved kind of language learning experience.

References

Bowen, B. M. (1982) *Look Here! Visual Aids in Language Teaching*. London: Macmillan.

Brand, Q. (1997) 'Art and art galleries: resources for teachers'. *English Teaching Professional*, **5**, 34–5.

Broughton, G. *et al.* (1970) *Success with English*. Harmondsworth: Penguin.

Candlin, E. F. (1975) *New Present Day English*. London: Hodder and Stoughton.

Cundale, N. 'Picture this'. *Modern English Teacher*, **8**(2), 37–40.

Harmer, J. (2001) *The Practice of English Language Teaching*. Harlow: Longman.

Hill, D. A. (1990) *Visual Impact*. Harlow: Longman.

Hill, D. A. and Rizzo, R. A. (1994) *Corpus: An English Language Course for the Biennio.* Milano: Ghisetti & Corvi.

McAlpin, J. (1980) *The Magazine Picture Library.* London: George Allen & Unwin.

O'Neill, R., Kingsbury, R. and Yeadon, T. (1971) *Kernel Lessons Intermediate.* Harlow: Longman.

Pit Corder, S. (1966) *The Visual Element in Language Teaching.* London: Longman.

Porcaro, J. W. (2001) 'Newspaper cartoons'. *Modern English Teacher,* **10**(2), 29–33.

Wright, A. (1976) *Visual Materials for the Language Teacher.* Harlow: Longman

Wright, A. (1989) *Pictures for Language Learning.* Cambridge: Cambridge University Press.

Wright, A. and Haleem, S. (1991) *Visuals for the Language Classroom.* Harlow: Longman.

CHAPTER

11

Creative Approaches to Writing Materials

Alan Maley

Introduction

Creativity is widely regarded as a desirable quality in many domains: music, the visual arts, literature, science – and even in finance and business. It is equally a quality which inspires distrust and even hostility. The history of art and scientific discovery is replete with examples of innovative practitioners ostracized and persecuted by their contemporaries for their 'insane' or dangerous ideas.

The foreign language teaching field, on the whole, rates rather low on creativity, however. Teaching is, by its very nature, a conservative profession. The institutionalization of teaching into regular classroom hours encourages the development of relatively comfortable routines. Examinations further encourage conformity. And, in the present global economy, market forces tend to discourage publishers from taking creative risks. This is not to deny that ELT in particular saw some significant instances of creativity and innovation in the last quarter of the twentieth century, including the paradigm shift from structural-situational to communicative approaches. It is tempting to wonder whether the current creative lull presages another burst of innovation in the near future, and to speculate about what direction this might take (see Conclusion).

In any event, the concept of creativity and its relevance to language teaching seems to warrant exploration. In the first part of this chapter, I shall therefore attempt to clarify *what* creativity is, *why* we should take it seriously, *who* the stakeholders in creativity are and *how* it has been implemented. In the second part, I shall offer a framework for generating creative materials and suggest some avenues for further exploration.

Part I: What is Creativity?

Key Components

It is the nature of buzzwords such as 'creativity' (cf. 'communicative') that they acquire a large number of different meanings through widespread and often indiscriminate use. I have therefore attempted to winnow out some core components of the notion of creativity. A cursory analysis of writings on creativity theory yielded the following semantic clusters, which are suggestive for a clearer definition of this polyvalent term.

a. *'Newness': original, innovative, novelty, unusual, surprising* To be qualified as creative, we have to recognize that something new has been brought into being. Yet all creative ideas owe a debt to what has gone before. It is their ability to use the past to frame the present in a new light which characterizes creativity.

b. *'Immediacy': sudden, flash, illumination, spontaneous* This aspect is best characterized by the 'Eureka' supposedly uttered by Archimedes as he leapt from his bathtub. Many creative geniuses report that their insights came to them in a flash of sudden clarity.

c. *'Respect': awe, wonder, admiration, delight, aaah!* The truly creative act gives rise to feelings of pleasurable recognition on the part of others. A typical reaction would be, 'Why didn't I think of that?'

d. *'Experiment': exploration, curiosity, preparedness, tacit knowledge, puzzle, problem-solving, play, heuristic* Most kinds of creativity seem to involve some kind of 'playing around' with things, with asking the question 'What if . . .?', the ability to think the unthinkable. But curiosity alone is rarely enough. Being prepared, in the sense of well-informed, about an area is an essential prerequisite. ('Fortune favours only the prepared mind', Louis Pasteur, 1854.) This preparedness is often based on 'tacit knowledge' (Polanyi, 1967; Schon, 1983), or 'mastery', which expert practitioners seem able to call upon effortlessly. Often heuristics are used to save time, heuristics being general procedures or rules of thumb such as 'consider the negative', 'do the opposite', 'make it bigger/smaller'.

   'Heuristics are used to prune the search tree. That is, they save the problem-solver from visiting every choice point on the tree, by selectively ignoring parts of it' (Boden, 1990: 98). Such playing around is done within a given conceptual space. 'In short, nothing is more natural than "playing around" to gauge the potential – and the limits – of a given way of thinking. This is not a matter of abandoning all rules, but of changing the existing rules to create a new conceptual space' (Boden, 1990: 46).

e. *'Divine': intuition, insight, imagination, inspiration, illumination, divine spark, gift, hunch, mysterious, unconscious* The idea that creativity is a mysterious, unknowable gift from God is widespread and ancient. Most contemporary writers on creativity do not, however, subscribe to this idea, preferring instead to investigate how creative acts come about. There is, however, agreement that much creative activity is unconscious.

   The belief in creativity as a God-given quality fosters the notion that only some, chosen, people are capable of creativity. A more reasonable and humane view is that everyone is capable of creativity in varying degrees. H(istorical)-creativity, which involves producing something no one in history has ever created before, is the stuff of genius – Mozart, Picasso, Einstein, Shakespeare.

But this does not preclude P(ersonal)-creativity, which involves individuals making creative discoveries which are new to them, if not to history.

f. *'Seeing relationships': connections, associations, combinations, analogies, metaphors, seeing in a new way, peripheral attention, incubation, reconfiguring* There is general agreement that an important component of creativity is the ability to make new connections, often between apparently unrelated data. Koestler (1989) called this bisociation, and the surrealists used it as a principle for generating new artistic creations. It has also been used by some writers on teaching, such as Gianni Rodari (1973) and Jacqueline Held (1979). However, in order to see new relationships, it may be necessary to suspend conscious attention, so that material which is on the periphery of our attention may gain access to the unconscious layers of mind. The notion that these ideas are stimulated by a period of incubation, while the conscious mind occupies itself with other things, is a constant theme of writers on creativity.

g. *'Unpredictable': randomness, chance, serendipity, coincidence, chaos* It is a paradox of creativity that it cannot be predicted, nor consciously invoked. It apparently comes about partly through chance happenings. Fleming's discovery of penicillin, Newton's apple and Archimedes' bath are all instances. Yet chance discoveries are usually only made by those able to recognize what chance has put in their way. An apple falling on the head of a farmer would more likely have triggered an expletive than a theory of gravity. There is a sense in which we can only discover or create when the time is ripe. And perhaps readiness can lead us to a measure of probabilistic predictability (see Conclusion).

h. *'Acceptability': recognition, relevance, significance, value* However innovative a creation may be, it is unlikely to be taken up unless it is recognized as relevant to the field in which it occurs. The idea of using crystals to facilitate language learning recently mooted in the IATEFL Newsletter, *Issues* (Power, 2000) had all the hallmarks of novelty and surprise we associate with creativity. But it was not perceived as relevant by fellow professionals (Swan, 2001). Creative ideas must therefore be historically apt and relevant, as well as merely novel. 'Even P-creativity requires that systematic rule-breaking and rule-bending be done in domain-relevant ways' (Boden, 1990: 254).

Approaches to Creativity

Creativity has long attracted the attention of theorists. Gardner (1993), picking up on Francis Galton's nineteenth-century work on geniuses, has investigated biographical aspects of creativity in a number of H-creative people, hoping to find common factors among them. Significantly, he has chosen geniuses from all seven of his types of intelligence (Gardner, 1985). His concentration on H-creativity does not help us very much, however.

Storr (1972), by contrast, has approached creativity through psychoanalysis, arguing that, although highly creative people often behave oddly, it is precisely their creative urge which keeps them sane. In this sense, creativity clearly has a therapeutic function.

Csikszentimihaly (1988) takes a multidimensional view of creativity as an interaction between individual talent, operating in a particular domain or discipline, and judged by experts in that field. This helps to explain why some ideas, though creative, do not emerge until the time is ripe. For example, Leonardo da Vinci designed flying machines, but the technological prerequisites for building and flying them had to await the development of the internal combustion engine and the discovery of petroleum in economically large quantities. Csikzentimihaly also has interesting observations about the role of 'flow' (Csikszentimihaly, 1990) in creativity: the state of 'effortless effort' in which everything seems to come together in a flow of seamless energy.

Both Koestler (1989) and Boden (1990) have sought a cognitive psychological explanation for creativity. Koestler, in his monumental *The Act of Creation* (Koestler, 1989) takes up Helmholtz' and Wallas' idea of creativity as a four-stage process. Given a 'problem', 'puzzle' or 'conceptual space', the creative mind first prepares itself by soaking up all the information available. Following this first Preparation stage, there is a stage of Incubation, in which the conscious mind stops thinking about the problem, leaving the unconscious to take over. In the third stage, Illumination, a solution suddenly presents itself (if you're lucky!). In the final Verification stage, the conscious mind needs to check and elaborate on the insights gained. Koestler cites many examples, especially from science, to support his theory. He goes on to suggest that the process operates through the bisociation of two conceptual matrices, not normally found together. The juxtaposition of hitherto unrelated areas is held to facilitate a sudden new insight.

By contrast, Boden (1990) takes an AI (Artificial Intelligence) approach to investigating creativity. She asks what a computer would need to do to replicate human thought processes. This leads to a consideration of the self-organizing properties of complex, generative systems through processes such as parallel distributed processing. For her, creativity arises from the systematic exploration of a conceptual space or domain (mathematical, musical, linguistic). She draws attention to the importance of constraints in this process. 'Far from being the antithesis of creativity, constraints on thinking are what make it possible' (p. 82). 'It is the partial continuity of constraints which enables a new idea to be recognised, by author and audience alike, as a creative contribution. The new conceptual space may provide a fresh way of viewing the task domain and signposting interesting pathways that were invisible – indeed impossible – before' (p. 83). Boden's approach is richly suggestive for language acquisition and materials writing, in that both are rooted in complex, self-organizing systems.

Why do We Need Creativity?

1. It is psychologically inevitable, given the nature of the human mind, which, as a complex system, is predisposed to generate new ideas.
2. It is also inevitable historically. As Kuhn (1970) has shown, any given domain tends to follow a cyclical pattern of development. After a period of dominance by one paradigm, accepted by all, with knowledge and procedures

routinized, there comes a period of questioning, the discovery of new insights and ideas which supplant the old paradigm. The cycle then continues. In language teaching, we can consider the nineteenth-century Reform Movement as one such paradigm shift, and the Communicative Approach perhaps another.

3. It is necessary for survival. The context in which language teaching and learning takes place is constantly evolving under the pressure of other forces: changing demands, changing technology, changing economic needs, etc.. We are obliged to respond to this by changing ourselves, and at an ever-accelerating rate (Gleick, 1999). Creativity tends to accompany change, as we seek adaptive solutions to new opportunities and constraints.
4. Creativity stimulates and motivates. Teachers who actively explore creative solutions tend to be more alive and vibrant than those content to follow a routine. Students given the opportunity to exercise their own creativity tend to respond positively. The materials writer who approaches the job creatively is likely to produce more interesting materials.
5. Language use, and language learning, are inherently creative processes. Two recent books (Lecercle, 1990; Cook, 2000) have drawn attention to the fact that much natural language use is not merely utilitarian and transactional, nor merely interactional. People indulge in vast amounts of creative language play, through punning, riddles, jokes, spoonerisms, insults, deliberate ambiguity, unusual collocations, mixed metaphors, mimicry, games with names and irreverence (e.g., 'Jane Mansfield's reputation was vastly inflated'). Likewise, children learning their first language play around with it a great deal, constantly testing its limits creatively. I would argue that these features should at least be given some space in teaching materials. Literature, as the supreme example of linguistic playfulness, clearly has a key revitalizing role to play here.

Who are the Stakeholders?

Clearly, as this is a book focusing on materials writing, I believe materials writers themselves should exercise creativity. This may be manifested in the content they choose to include (texts, visuals, etc.), or the procedures they offer or through the outcomes they aim to achieve. (For more on Content, Process and Outcomes see below.) They may also show creativity in the ways they manage to work within the constraints imposed by the publisher, the syllabus or the examination. Publishers, too, have a key role to play as promoters of creative ideas. Unhappily, the cut-throat competition and high investment costs in current publishing tend to discourage the taking of risks – and creative ideas will always represent a degree of risk. There are some signs that this situation may be changing, however.[1]

A major aspect of the materials writer's creativity is the extent to which creativity is stimulated in the teachers and students using the materials. Materials which offer the teacher choice and flexibility to develop in ways they judge to be appropriate are likely to produce more creative behaviours. This view corresponds with Prabhu's (1990) notion of a 'sense of plausibility', whereby teachers function best when they operate within a framework of their own evolving set of beliefs and practices.

The question of perceived value and relevance by users of creative materials again arises. There is little point in the materials writer exhibiting great personal creativity in the design of materials, if they are rejected as too 'way out' or 'impractical' by those they are intended for. The truly creative materials writer may use quite simple and minimal inputs to stimulate methodological creativity on the part of teachers, or linguistic creativity on the part of learners.

How has Creativity been Applied?

Before moving to the second part, it will be worth reviewing some of the more creative ideas from the recent past.

'Do the Opposite'

In his book *Breaking Rules,* John Fanselow (1987) recommends applying the heuristic 'Do the opposite', as a way of generating new possibilities in language teaching. This injunction can be applied at any level: content, process, roles. For instance, regarding content, if you habitually use written texts, try using listening instead. If you use long texts, try short ones. If you use simplified texts, use authentic ones. Or maybe try doing without texts altogether. Regarding processes, if you use a lot of group and pair work, try some individual and whole class work. If you normally expect immediate answers to your questions, try asking students to delay their replies. Regarding roles, if you do all the teaching, let the students do some of it. If you set tests let students write their own tests (Maley, 1999).

These are no more than examples of quite radical changes which can be brought about by applying this simple yet powerful heuristic.

Designer Methods

The so-called designer methodologies which came to prominence in the 1970s and 1980s (Stevick, 1980) are all interesting applications of the 'do the opposite' heuristic (though I do not suggest that their ideas derive from Fanselow).

The Silent Way (Gattegno, 1976) reverses the idea that the teacher does all the talking, and that it is the teacher's duty to instruct. Instead, learners are thrown back on their own resources to construct painfully their own 'inner criteria' from minimal clues.

In Community Language Learning (CLL) (Curran, 1976), there is no pedagogical text: it is the learners who determine their own dialogic text, and take their own preferred learning pathways into the new language as they proceed from an 'infantile' to a 'mature' state in that language. The teacher is essentially a sympathetic informant.

The principles and practice of Suggestopoedia (Lozanov, 1979; Saferis, 1978), go directly counter to received wisdom in foreign language pedagogy. Learners are required to make no conscious effort to learn. They are exposed to texts of unprecedented length. The relaxed atmosphere created through Baroque music, comfortable chairs and low lighting is decidedly unlike a 'normal' classroom.

Total Physical Response (TPR) (Asher, 1977) confines the early stages of learning to listening alone. Only the teacher speaks, requiring only non-verbal responses as confirmation of comprehension.

Although it is nowadays relatively rare to find any of these methodologies being used in their pure form, they have undeniably had significant effects on current methodologies and materials.

N. S. Prabhu

Prabhu undoubtedly ranks as one of the most original and iconoclastic twentieth-century thinkers on language teaching. Two of his major contributions were the development of procedural, task-based syllabuses (Prabhu, 1987), and of a radically different approach to materials writing (Prabhu, 1989).

Procedural syllabuses have been widely discussed elsewhere (Nunan, 1988; White, 1988), so I shall do no more than draw attention to the fact that they too are an instance of 'doing the opposite'. Rather than designing a tightly controlled, 'a priori' linguistic progression, Prabhu advocates setting a series of tasks with no formal attention to the order of language items. He argues that, while the conscious attention of learners is focused on solving the problem/task, they are unconsciously acquiring language competence.

In his article, 'Materials as Support: Materials as Constraint' (1989), Prabhu criticizes published materials on the grounds that they pre-empt choices which might more properly be made by the teacher. Such materials predetermine the content, the order of presentation and the methodology to be deployed. His radical proposal is to restore to teachers as much control as possible over these areas. He suggests the use of 'semi-materials', where single-type activities such as listening comprehension or collections of raw input would be used, or meta-materials, which would simply offer 'empty' procedures, such as dictation, to be utilized by the teacher according to local need.

Maley (1994) subsequently developed these ideas as 'flexi-materials', by offering an open-ended set of texts, any of which could be chosen by the teacher to use with a limited set of activity types. (For a full description, see Maley in Tomlinson, 1998: 279–94.)

Humanistic Contributions

The 1980s, in particular, saw the emergence of ideas revalorizing the individual/personal aspects of learners. Moskovitz' *Caring and Sharing in the Language Class* (1978) was a landmark volume. Such personalized and values-oriented materials tended to draw on fields outside the narrow confines of linguistics, and to explore new ways of doing familiar things. One of the best examples of this creative re-exploration of a time-honoured practice is Davis and Rinvolucri's Dictation (1988).

In it, the authors submit the 'conceptual space' of dictation to a series of creative variations, reminiscent of the variations explored by Bach and other composers. The field of theatre training was drawn upon by Maley and Duff (1982), and literature was reinterpreted by a number of authors (Maley, 2000: 180–5) as a resource for language learning, rather than as a field of academic study.

More recently, Thornbury and Meddings (2001) have advocated a heuristic strategy which recommends increasing the constraints on teachers. 'Dogme' requires that no artificial aids to teaching be used; instead, total reliance is placed on facilitating learning through the quality of the dialogue between teacher and learners, and among learners. While such a self-denying ordinance has met with a mixed reception (Gill, 2000), it is undeniably creative.

Part II

Having reviewed ways in which creativity theory may illuminate thinking about materials writing, and having given some practical examples of creativity in language pedagogy, it is time to look towards possible future developments.

Chart for Organizing Language Teaching Materials

The following chart (see Table 11.1) is an attempt to systematize the writing of materials. It is not comprehensive, though I have tried to include most items I regard as important.

The *Inputs* comprise all the raw material the writer might wish to consider for inclusion. *Processes* are what is done with that Input. *Outcomes* are the objectives the writer hopes to achieve through the Inputs and Processes. Having made choices of Input-type, the writer then selects the processes learners will engage in to achieve the Outcomes set. Of course, it is perfectly possible to use the chart to generate routine, run-of-the-mill materials. But if the full range of options is considered, this is less likely. In any case, it is equally possible for the materials writer to take a creative angle on any given item. In doing so, it may be useful to draw upon some of what we have learned from creativity theory (see above). This will include:

- Playing around – both as materials writers, and in fostering the playing around element in learners.
- Leaving room for 'chaos' to operate by throwing up new and unexpected regularities in the complex system we are working in.
- Testing the constraints of our conceptual spaces.
- Using heuristics and analogy to stimulate new thinking.
- Allowing time and silence for ideas to incubate (both for materials writers and for the users of the materials).
- Making unusual juxtapositions (perhaps by drawing on other domains, outside language pedagogy).

Table 11.1 A chart for organizing language teaching materials

INPUTS	PROCESSES	OUTCOMES
• People (experiences, feelings, memories, opinions, appearance, etc.)	Generic: • Time (long/short) • Intensity (high/low) • Type (active/ reflective, interactive)	Material outcomes (student texts, visual displays, performance, etc.)
• Topics/Themes	• Mode (individual work, pairs, groups, whole class; public/ private)	Pedagogical outcomes (evidence of learning, test results, fluency, becoming a reader, confidence, learning to learn, handling feedback, meta-competence, etc.)
• Texts (literary/non-literary; published/ student-generated, etc., extensive readers)	• Medium (spoken/ written; processing/ producing)	
• Reference materials (dictionaries, thesauruses, encyclopaedias, reference grammars, etc.)	Management: • routines • instructions • questions	Educational outcomes (increased social/ intercultural awareness, critical thinking, creative problem-solving, independence, etc.)
	Techniques: • questioning • info. gap, opinion gap, etc.	
• Realia (objects, texts, pictures, etc.)	• jigsaw reading/ listening	Psycho-social outcomes (increased self-esteem, self-awareness, confidence, cooperation, group solidarity, responsibility, attitudinal change, etc.)
• Visuals (photographs, videos, 'art', film, etc.)	• process writing • reading skills	
• Audio (words, texts, music, sounds)	• visualizing • inner speech/ rehearsing	
• Internet, CD-ROMs, etc.	Task-types: • brainstorming	
• Games, simulations, role-play, language play	• predicting • classifying • evaluating • problem-solving	
• Oral accounts (stories, jokes, anecdotes, presentations, etc.)	• performing • constructing objects • researching	

- Problems (puzzles, moral dilemmas, logical problems, etc.)

- Projects

- Techniques (improvization, drama, dictation, translation, etc.)

Generative procedures:
- expansion
- matching
- media transfer
- comparison/contrast
- selection/ranking, etc.

- Remembering that novelty is not enough, and that the system we operate in has to be 'ready' and to perceive the relevance of our ideas.
- Capitalizing on the fact that everyone has the capacity for creativity.
- Ensuring that we give due attention to the Preparation and Verification stages of the creative process. Not everything is fun and games.
- Keeping in mind that delight and pleasure are an integral part of the process.

In the following section I shall suggest a number of ways in which the chart might be used.

Some Applications

Inputs

a. People: I have placed this first because we are in danger of overlooking the resource nearest to us, namely the human resource in our own class. Every class has within it a fabulous reserve of personalities, physical types, memories, associations, opinions, skills and knowledge (Campbell and Kryszewska, 1992). Materials should draw upon this human bank account. Most activities can be enriched by the personal perspectives of students.

b. In choosing themes or topics we can also go well beyond the conventional and familiar. There is nothing wrong with such uncontentious themes as sport, hobbies, shopping, cultural festivals and the like. But if our objectives include increasing social and intercultural awareness, and critical thinking skills, we need to cast the net more widely. Wajnryb (1996) has incisively critiqued the bland irrelevance of many teaching materials. Practical examples of more challenging themes include Jacobs *et al.* (1998), who offer a wide range of environmental and global themes. Day and Yamanaka (1998) also explore themes well beyond the conventional boundaries of textbooks.

c. Texts still form the basis of most published materials. Can we exercise greater creativity by widening the choice of text types, particularly by including more literary texts, which expose students to more creative uses of the language? Literary texts also often touch upon precisely those social, cultural and human issues which would broaden our objectives from purely instrumental language teaching to more general educational purposes.

Students themselves can provide textual input in the form of poems, wall newspapers, stories. With the development of word-processing facilities, it is now possible to publish texts with high quality finish. Texts produced by students in one year can become part of the input for the next. Compilations of texts chosen by the students can also be used in a similar way.

Extensive reading is now recognized as the single most effective way of acquiring a foreign language (Day and Bamford, 1998). There exist many excellent series of graded readers, both adaptations and originals, so that we can now speak of a new genre of English writing – literature written for foreign learners. Yet there are at least two ways of creatively changing what is on offer. The first would involve abandoning tight linguistic control through word and structure lists. Instead, writers would concentrate on telling a good story, gauging the language level intuitively by writing for a particular audience.[2] The second would involve abandoning all questions and activity materials, leaving the learner to interact naturally with the text in the manner of a 'real' reader, without these unreaderly distractions.

d. It is now possible to exploit the creative possibilities of the new range of reference materials available, in particular learners' dictionaries (Wright, 1998), and production dictionaries such as the *Activator* (1997). We can encourage students to construct their own reference materials: grammars, phrase books, vocabulary references, cultural references. This can also be linked with the use of *Project Work* (Fried-Booth, 2001).

e. One creative way of approaching realia, visuals and audio input is to pass responsibility for providing input to the learners themselves. They may prepare their own photographic displays, videos, sound collages, perhaps as part of a project. The sense of ownership conferred by personal involvement often gives rise to increased motivation and surprisingly creative outcomes (Stempleski and Tomalin, 2001).

f. The Internet is clearly a massively important resource. But only recently has serious thought been given to ways of using it in an integrated manner, and in ways which creatively exploit its potential (Windeatt *et al.*, 2000; Harmer, 2001). The danger of the Internet, as with all technologies, is that materials writers, along with everyone else, become mesmerized by its technological potential rather than thinking carefully about how it can best be deployed.

g. Inputs from oral accounts offer wide opportunities for creativity in content selection. Brunvand's (1999) collection of Urban Legends is but one example. Oral presentations may also serve as an alternative, more creative, way of teaching pronunciation. The student making an oral presentation is forced to take account of the totality of the communicative event, not just the phonetic accuracy of delivery.

Processes

Processes can also enhance the creative quality of the materials. I shall simply give brief suggestions from each of the five categories in the chart.

a.   Generic: The use of time can be handled creatively, for instance, by setting tight time constraints on some activities. Another example is by giving dictations at normal speed rather than slowly with pauses (Davis and Rinvolucri, 1988). Or by allowing students as much time as they need for tests. Or by helping students to plan their own time. Similar possibilities emerge from the other generic features.

b.   Management: One creative way to manage routines and instructions is to replace verbal with non-verbal cues. Students can quickly learn to use a set of gestures to cover most exigencies: a raised hand for silence, a circular motion for group work, index fingers pointing inward for pair work. Alternatively, all instructions can be given in writing on large flashcards which the teacher holds up when necessary. Both ideas would serve to reduce wear and tear on teachers' voices – a major source of problems (Maley, 2000). For further ideas on the use of gesture in pronunciation work, see Underhill (1994).

c.   The list of techniques given is far from exhaustive but any technique can be applied creatively. Stevick (1986) drew attention to the power of visualization and Tomlinson (2000, 2001) has developed techniques to promote visualization and inner speech in the processing of texts. All too often, we seem to require an explicit verbal or factual 'answer', rather than an internal representation. Underhill (1994) recommends allowing students time to hear and hold utterances in their inner ear before repeating them.

d.   The set of task types is likewise incomplete, but all those listed can be creatively applied. For example, if the task involves evaluating a something (a text, a film, a piece of peer writing), students can devise their own criteria. They can also learn how to offer and receive negative criticism, which has important educational and social outcomes.

e.   The generalizable procedures (Maley, 1998) are in fact a set of heuristics which can be applied to any piece of material. Even so simple a type of media transfer as copying out a prose text in the format of a poem compels a different quality of attention from straightforward copying. Likewise, requiring students to rank a set of texts in terms of their suitability for a given purpose invites careful reading and provokes often heated discussion.

Outcomes

Inputs and Processes interact to produce outcomes but in complex ways not reducible to a formula. I believe, however, that we can greatly extend the range and relevance of Outcomes by thinking creatively about them.

Traditionally, we have been mainly concerned with Material and Pedagogical outcomes: the direct product of learning. Yet even here we can extend the range. As I have suggested earlier, student-generated texts can be much more varied; the availability of word processing makes possible a greater variety and higher quality of products; access to video and sound recording facilities can likewise add to the range of material outcomes. Pedagogical outcomes can also go beyond the traditional reliance on test results and assignments, to encompass enabling skills such as learning to learn (Ellis and Sinclair, 1989), dealing with feedback to and from peers and meta-competence in talking about language and language learning in informed ways.

More broadly educational outcomes emerging from the creative interaction of inputs and processes might include increased awareness and understanding of others, including other cultures, the ability to question received wisdom or information, the ability to solve problems through brainstorming and lateral thinking, and self-reliance. In the psycho-social domain, the creative dimension can give rise to enhanced confidence, self-esteem, and self-awareness leading to responsibility and cooperation to create a positive learning atmosphere (Hadfield, 1990).

Conclusion

I suggested earlier that major creative breakthroughs or paradigm shifts take place when a number of pieces fall into place to make a new pattern. In the case of the shift to a Communicative Approach, a number of developments and ideas crystallized quite rapidly, though many of them had been around for some time. Austin and Searle's work on speech acts; Chomsky's ideas on the deep structure of language, offset by Hymes' ideas on the importance of context of use; the dawning realization that English had genuinely achieved the status of the global language, with all that entailed in language learning needs; the politics of a new European community of states; the development of the tape recorder, video and the photocopier;[3] the coming to maturity of Applied Linguistics, spawning a generation of trained practitioners; the emergence of a smallish group of charismatic applied linguists promoting the new ideas; the support of an (at the time) flourishing group of professionals within the British Council, dedicated to propagating these ideas: all conspired to produce the heady ambrosia of the new approach.

The communicative paradigm has now commanded near-universal acceptance (if only in the form of lip-service) for almost 20 years. Yet it seems to be losing momentum, and voices are increasingly being raised as to its universal suitability. There is also a sense that it has not delivered on the no doubt hyperbolic promise of its earlier years. Are we then on the brink of another creative paradigm shift? Only a fortune-teller would hazard a guess. It is interesting, however, to note the emergence of a constellation of factors which just might gel into a new configuration. Among external factors, I would list:

- The developments in IT, giving access to real information and to virtual, simulated worlds.
- The emergence of small niche publishers, exploiting new publishing technologies which enable them to publish fast, at relatively low cost and to control their print runs on a daily basis. Hence a greater potential for risk-taking.
- The influence of critical theory on English as a global language (Phillipson, 1992; Pennycook, 1994; Holliday, 1994). This might herald a more context-

sensitive approach to teaching English, after a period of almost unbridled metropolitan triumphalism.

- The increase in awareness of global issues, and the importance of educating a new generation in respect for limited global resources.
- The growing understanding of the role of extensive reading in language acquisition.
- The vastly expanded networks of teachers and teachers' associations world-wide, ensuring a more rapid and efficient interchange of information and ideas.

Among internal, personal factors, the following will clearly be influential:

- Developments in the understanding of multiple intelligences (Gardner, 1985).
- Greater understanding of how NLP (Neuro-linguistic Programming) might be applied (O'Connor and Seymour, 1990).
- The emergence of 'play' and 'playfulness' as a major factor in language acquisition and use.
- Advances in cognitive science and in AI, gradually shedding more light on mental processing (Jacobs and Schumann, 1992).
- Work on visualization and inner speech, already touched on above.

This may seem like a rattlebag of loosely (or un-)connected factors – but no more so than those which hatched the Communicative Approach. I remain convinced, however, that, with or without a tectonic paradigm shift, the creative spirit, both in materials writers and among teachers and learners, will survive – and thrive.

References

Asher, J. J. (1977) *Learning Another Language through Actions: The Complete Teacher's Guidebook.* Los Gatos, CA: Sky Oak Productions.

Boden, M. (1990) *The Creative Mind.* London: Abacus.

Brunvand, J. Harold. (1999) *Too Good to Be True: The Colossal Book of Urban Legends.* New York/London: W. W. Norton Co. Inc.

Campbell, C. and Kryszewska, H. (1992) *Learner-based Teaching.* Oxford: Oxford University Press.

Cook, G. (2000) *Language Play, Language Learning.* Oxford: Oxford University Press.

Csikszentimihaly, M. (1988) 'Society, culture and person: a systems view of creativity', in L. J. Sternberg (ed.) *The Nature of Creativity.* New York: Cambridge University Press, pp. 320–39.

Csikszentimihaly, M. (1990) *Flow: The Psychology of Optional Experience.* New York: Harper and Row.

Curran, C. (1976) *Counselling Learning in Second Languages.* Apple River, IL: Apple River Press.

Davis, P. and Rinvolucri, R. (1988) *Dictation.* Cambridge: Cambridge University Press.

Day, R. and Bamford, J. (1998) *Extensive Reading in the Second Language Classroom.* Cambridge: Cambridge University Press.

Day, R. and Yamanaka, J. (1998) *Impact Issues.* Hong Kong: Longman Asia ELT.

Ellis, G. and Sinclair, B. (1989). *Learning to Learn English: A Course in Learner Training.* Cambridge: Cambridge University Press.

Fanselow, J. (1987) *Breaking Rules.* London/New York: Longman.

Fried-Booth, D. (2001) *Project Work* (2nd edn.). Oxford: Oxford University Press.

Gardner, H. (1985) *Frames of Mind: The Theory of Multiple Intelligences.* London: Paladin/Granada Publishers.

Gardner, H. (1993) *Creating Minds.* New York: Basic Books/HarperCollins.

Gattegno, C. (1976) *The Common Sense of Teaching Foreign Languages.* New York: Educational Solutions Inc.

Gill, S. (2000) 'Against dogma: a plea for moderation'. *IATEFL Issues,* **154**.

Gleick, J. (1987) *Chaos.* London: Sphere Books.

Gleick, J. (1999) *Faster: The Acceleration of Just About Everything.* New York: Vintage/Random House.

Hadfield, J. (1990) *Classroom Dynamics.* Oxford: Oxford University Press.

Harmer, J. (2001) *TD Website. ELT Forum. www.eltforum.com.*

Held, J. (1979) *L'imaginaire au Pouvoir.* Paris: Les Editions Ouvrières.

Holliday, A. (1994) *Appropriate Methodology.* Cambridge: Cambridge University Press.

Jacobs, G., Kumarasamy, P., Nopparat, P. and Amy, S. (1998) *Linking Language and the Environment.* Toronto: Pippin.

Jacobs, B. and Schumann, J. A. (1992) 'Language acquisition and the neurosciences: towards a more integrated perspective'. *Applied Linguistics,* **13** (3), 282–301.

Koestler, A. (1989) *The Act of Creation.* London: Arkana/Penguin.

Kuhn, Thomas (1970) *The Structure of Scientific Revolutions* (2nd edn.). Chicago: University of Chicago Press.

Lecercle, J. (1990) *The Violence of Language.* London: Routledge.

Longman Essential Activator (1997) London: Pearson-Longman.

Lozanov, G. (1979) *Suggestology and Outlines of Suggestopedy.* New York: Gordon and Breach.

Maley, A. (1994) *Short and Sweet.* London: Penguin.

Maley, A. (1998) 'Squaring the circle: reconciling materials as constraint with materials as empowerment', in B. Tomlinson (ed.) (1998) *Materials Development for Language Teaching.* Cambridge: Cambridge University Press, pp. 279–94.

Maley, A. (1999) 'The dividends from diversity'. Paper given at Congrès de l'APLIUT, Angers, France.

Maley, A. (2000) *The Language Teacher's Voice.* Oxford: Macmillan Heinemann.

Maley, A. and Duff, A. (1982) *Drama Techniques in Language Learning.* Cambridge: Cambridge University Press.

198   *Alan Maley*

Moskovitz, G. (1978) *Caring and Sharing in the Language Class*. Rowley, MA: Newbury House.

Nunan, D. (1988) *Syllabus Design*. Oxford: Oxford University Press.

O'Connor, J. and Seymour, J. (1990) *Introducing Neuro-linguistic Programming*. London: Mandala/HarperCollins.

Pennycook, A. (1994) *The Cultural Politics of English as an International Language*. London: Longman.

Phillipson, R. (1992) *Linguistic Imperialism*. Oxford. Oxford University Press.

Polanyi, M. (1967) *The Tacit Dimension*. New York: Doubleday and Co.

Power, P. (2000) 'Crystals in the classroom'. *IATEFL Issues*, **156** (4).

Prabhu, N. S. (1987) *Second Language Pedagogy*. Oxford: Oxford University Press.

Prabhu, N. S. (1989) 'Materials as support: materials as constraint'. *Guidelines*, **11** (1). Singapore: RELC.

Prabhu, N. S. (1990) 'There is no best method – why?' *TESOL Quarterly*, **24** (2).

Rodari, G. (1973) *Una Grammatica della Fantasia*. Torino: Einaudi.

Saferis, F. (1978) *Une révolution dans l'Art d'Apprendre*. Paris: Robert Laffont.

Schon, D. (1983) *The Reflective Practitioner*. Avebury: Academic Publishing Group.

Stempleski, S. and Tomalin, B. (2001) *Film*. Oxford: Oxford University Press.

Stevick, E. (1980) *A Way and Ways*. Rowley, MA: Newbury House.

Stevick, E. (1986) *Images and Options in the Language Classroom*. Cambridge: Cambridge University Press.

Storr, A. (1972) *The Dynamics of Creation*. London: Penguin.

Swan, M. (2001) 'Crystal balls: art, science and the onus of proof'. *IATEFL Issues*, **158** (2).

Thornbury, S. and Meddings, L. (2001) 'Dogme out in the open'. *IATEFL Issues*, **161** (6).

Tomlinson, B. (ed.) (1998) *Materials Development for Language Teaching*. Cambridge: Cambridge University Press.

Tomlinson, B. (2000) 'Talking to yourself: the role of the inner voice in language learning'. *Applied Language Learning*, **11** (1), 123–54.

Tomlinson, B. (2001). 'The inner voice: a critical factor in L2 learning'. *The Journal of the Imagination in Language Learning and Teaching*, **6**, 26–33.

Underhill, A. (1994) *Sound Foundations*. Oxford: Macmillan Heinemann.

Wajnryb, R. (1996) 'Death, taxes and jeopardy: systematic omissions in EFL texts, or why life was never meant to be an adjacency pair'. ELICOS Conference Proceedings, Sydney, Australia.

White, R. (1988) *The ELT Curriculum: Design, Innovation and Management*. Oxford: Basil Blackwell.

Windeatt, S., Hardishy, D. and Eastment, D. (2000) *The Internet*. Oxford: Oxford University Press.

Wright, J. (1998) *Dictionaries*. Oxford: Oxford University Press.

CHAPTER

12

Developing Electronic Materials for Language Teaching

Beverly Derewianka

Introduction

The term 'electronic materials' refers to material that has been digitally processed so that the user is able to access it through a single source, usually a computer. In this chapter we will be referring to three major, interrelated dimensions of electronic materials that have proven beneficial to L2 learning: hypermedia, multimedia and communication media.

Hypermedia

Hypermedia (originally 'hypertext') refers to the capacity to make links between 'bits' of information. A link may be

- internal to the current page (e.g., a 'rollover' which causes more information to appear when the cursor is rolled over a hot word or icon; a 'pop-up' which is activated by clicking on a hot word or icon);
- between elements of a particular website or CD-ROM (e.g., by clicking on a link in the text that takes the reader to another page; by clicking on the sidebar menu or navigation bar to go to another area of the site);
- between one site and another site on the web (e.g., by clicking on an icon that takes you to a related website).

The links describe associations between nodes, which are chunks or fragments of information. The pathways between the nodes can vary between tightly controlled or open-ended.

Multimedia

While the nodes were originally restricted to pieces of text, now they can include a variety of media:

- static text
- animated text

- sound
- voice
- still graphics (photos, illustrations, diagrams, icons, maps, etc.)
- animated graphics
- video

These multimedia elements can be combined in various ways and can appear automatically or be accessed by the reader making a deliberate selection.

Communication Media

With the advent of widespread use of local area networking and the World Wide Web, interpersonal communication has become a powerful factor in the development of electronic materials. The acronym IT (information technology) has now been extended to ICT (information and communication technology). Communications can take several forms:

- e-mail
- bulletin boards
- discussion lists
- chat rooms, icq, MUDs and MOOs
- video conferencing

The interactions can be on a one-to-one basis, one-to-many or many-to-many. They can take place in real time (synchronous) or with a delay (asynchronous).

Contributions to Language Learning

In this chapter it will be argued that all of the above resources are currently making a contribution to the language learning enterprise in various ways, but that a fourth phase is now developing where such options are incorporated into an integrated electronic learning environment, posing significant challenges for the materials developer.

This chapter will address the following broad questions:

- What do current theories of language learning tell us about learning to read and write in a second language?[1]
- What contribution can electronic materials make to the learning process?
- What insights does this provide for materials developers?

We will look first at how electronic materials can enhance the experience of learning to read in a second language. We will then consider how such materials can support the learning of L2 writing. Finally we will look at how developers can create learning environments that integrate all the previously discussed attributes of electronic materials. To conclude, various issues will be raised regarding future directions in the development of electronic materials. Throughout the chapter, reference will be made to relevant theory and research. Readers will be able to find out more about programs and projects mentioned by referring to the website addresses included in Appendix 12.1.

Enhancing Reading through Electronic Media

Reading is a highly complex activity that plays a critical role in the process of learning another language. The reader operates at many levels at once, integrating a variety of skills and strategies while seeking to construct meaning.

Practising Lower-level Skills

In the early phases of CALL, and even today, computerized reading activities have tended to focus on the microskills, with the computer playing the role of drill-master.

While poorly designed materials can be unproductive and boring, there is nevertheless a role for electronic materials in developing these lower-level skills. One thing that computers can do well is to help develop automaticity. Fluent readers automatically recognize the majority of frequently used words without resorting to phonic analysis or contextual information, thus freeing up their ability to give attention to higher-level skills such as inferencing and evaluating (Stanovich, 1993; Adams, 1990). L2 readers tend to give more attention to lower-level skills such as sounding out words, thereby decreasing their capacity to focus on meaning. The L2 learner needs to develop automatic recognition of a certain number of high frequency lexical items. By using computers to develop these skills, teachers are freed up to assist learners with those aspects of reading that benefit more from human interaction, such as interpretation and critique.

While many computer programs for teaching these 'bottom-up' skills consist of fairly uninteresting, repetitive, decontextualized drilling, there are some that attempt to engage students interactively in activities that involve constant re-visiting of connected text which contains several instances of the targeted item/s. One approach to teaching these skills is based on the notion of 'noticing'. This is where students' attention is constantly drawn to the form (letters, combinations of letters, patterns, words, grammatical structures) within the context of a specifically constructed reading passage. Chapelle (1998) suggests that an important principle for electronic materials developers derived from second language acquisition (SLA) theory is 'input enhancement' through the highlighting of salient language features.

Even a simple word-processing program can be used to advantage by focusing students' attention on significant, recurring patterns by highlighting, animating, deleting, changing font and type size, and so on. More powerful programs (e.g., Flash, Director) can be used to help the reader notice syntactic units by highlighting these (appropriately 'chunked') as the student listens to the text being read aloud. Text animation (e.g., flashing, movement of letters) can also help to focus the reader's attention on certain features.

Computers can also be used to provide the more intentional, intensive vocabulary practice needed by L2 learners. CAVOCA (a computer-assisted vocabulary acquisition program), for example, uses the computer to encourage the learner to:

    i.   Notice the various properties of the new word: morphological and phonological, syntactic, semantic, stylistic, collocational and so forth;

    ii.   Store the word in the internal lexicon in networks of relationships that correspond to the properties described in (i);

    iii.   Consolidate the storage described in (ii) by means of further exposure to the word in a variety of contexts which illustrate its various properties.

The CAVOCA program takes the learners systematically through the various stages by exposing them to carefully selected L2 material which illustrates the salient features of the new L2 word and/or the differences between the L2 word and its nearest L1 equivalent or counterpart. Because learner involvement is important in the learning process, the program is interactive: at certain points the learner has to make choices ('What do you think the word means?' 'Is the word correct/appropriate in this context?' 'What is the word that is missing in this context?') and is given feedback by the computer. Feedback goes beyond the minimal 'yes' or 'no' response to explain why the answer was right or wrong, to give further examples or to stimulate the student to reflect further on the problem.

A major contribution made by well-designed software in teaching these lower-level skills includes

1.   the provision of a large number of interactive exercises which vary in terms of level of difficulty and area of interest;

2.   the potential for students to work independently and at their own pace;

3.   the customization of exercise programs by tracking the performance of individual learners as they work their way through a bank of exercises and adapting the difficulty level and rate of progress according to how they are performing;

4.   the provision of rich feedback encouraging readers to reflect on their learning;

5.   the ability to supply extensive relevant examples by interrogating corpora such as COBUILD's Bank of England.

Making Reading Easier

Hypermedia makes it possible to build into a single page a number of clickable options to support the L2 reader. These devices, such as pop-ups, rollovers, links to other pages, menus and so on, are unobtrusive and only activated when a reader decides to access the information. With a printed page in a book, what you see is what you get. With a hypermedia page, however, there can be much more information hidden 'behind' than what is immediately visible on the screen.

Multimedia provides the reader with information in a variety of modalities. The interaction of these is of particular interest in understanding and supporting the process of reading in a second language.

In the following section we will look at these features of electronic materials in terms of how they can:

- facilitate L2 reading by providing support to the reader at the point at which it is needed;
- assist L2 readers as they seek to construct meaning from a text.

On-the-spot Help

Computers can make life much easier for the second language reader. The materials developer can insert a variety of tools that make the process of reading much smoother. In particular, when a reader comes across an unknown word, the computer can provide quick, on-the-spot assistance.

Using hypermedia links, for example, the developer is able to provide immediate access to a dictionary. At some sites, a small dictionary window automatically opens when a reading text is selected. The reader can simply type in any unknown word and be provided with the dictionary definition in either L1 or L2.

Dictionaries, however, cannot give context-specific meanings. More efficient are glosses that have been written specifically to explain key words in a particular text. Glossaries are sometimes provided at the end of traditional books, but, with electronic reading materials, glosses can be accessed simply by clicking on a word or icon. The provision of L1 glosses leads to better comprehension and retention than when such support is not available (Hulstijn *et al.*, 1996; Watanabe, 1997) – though even greater retention is achieved through the mental effort of inferring rather than relying on glosses (Hulstijn, 1997).

To address the problem of 'using words to explain words', multimedia offers the possibility of using other modalities as glosses. The reader might be provided with a photo, a diagram, an illustration or an animation to give a clue to the meaning of the word. This may or may not be accompanied by written or spoken text. Lomicka (1998) reports on a number of research studies into students' use of multimedia annotations which suggest that, compared to no glosses or to traditional glosses, these have a positive effect on comprehension.

The GALT (Glossing Authentic Language Texts) program, for example, enables instructors to create glosses using text, picture, digital video, digital audio and a relationship tree. It also provides an audio option so that the entire passage may be read aloud to students. This type of unobtrusive teaching tool expands the amount of information available to students, individualizes the learning experience by hiding the glossing until the student feels the need to access it and permits instructors and students to have more class time to devote to the content of literary texts.

Supporting Comprehension

While the above pop-ups and rollovers can help the L2 reader by providing 'on-demand' support through glosses and definitions, it involves very low-level interactivity – simply clicking and being provided with minimal information at the local level. The contribution of the technology is limited to convenience and speed. Of greater significance, however, is the contribution that electronic materials can make to the construction of meanings beyond the level of the word.

Certain SLA theorists (e.g., Larsen-Freeman and Long, 1991; Sharwood Smith, 1993), for example, propose that input be modified so that it is comprehensible to the learner. Chapelle (1998) suggests that the designer of electronic materials could include modifications in the form of repetition, simplification, restatement, decreased speed and change of input mode. Such modifications could be available by clicking on buttons, thus adapting the input to the needs of individual learners.

Schema theory (e.g., Carrell, 1987) argues that comprehension is enhanced when the reader brings to the text an awareness of the rhetorical structure of the text (i.e., the reader's formal schema). In a well-designed electronic text, the reader should have constant reminders of how the text is structured, both in terms of the current 'page' on the screen and the larger 'text' (e.g., the entire website). When the page is lengthy, for example, the reader is often provided with an advanced organizer at the beginning, summarizing the main points to be covered. Beyond the immediate page, the sidebar menu provides a reminder of the topics available which are related to the current page, and the top or bottom menu lists the main areas covered on the site. The sitemap acts as the contents page of a traditional book and the search function can do the job of an index. The design of the various interfaces and navigation devices are critical in preventing reader disorientation. L2 readers in particular need the support of very user-friendly architecture (Plass, 1998) in order to see how the text is constructed and how the various parts relate to each other.

Practice in recognizing text organization can be provided through electronic text reconstruction tools such as Text Tangler and NewReader, where the teacher can enter a reading passage being used in the class and the program processes it in such a way that the students need to manipulate it to create meaning (e.g., by sequencing a jumbled text).

Schema theory also proposes that the reader's background knowledge is critical to developing an understanding of the text. The more the reader knows about the topic and sociocultural assumptions, the more readily the reader can construct meaning from the text. With a hypermedia text, the developer is able to build in pop-up references that flesh out the text being read. These might take the form of an example or an elaboration, or information about the historical background, or an explanation of a procedure, or a note about theory or a discussion of cultural values. In a traditional text, such digressions would become clumsy and distracting. In hypertext, however, they are backgrounded and only become available if and when the reader decides to access them.

In addition to text, these supports might take the form of graphics (still and animated), video and sound. This encourages multimodal processing, where the reader actively engages with a range of diverse inputs which all contribute to the construction of meaning (Meskill, 1996; Chun and Plass, 1997). Unlike vocabulary glosses which draw attention to a single element of the text, well-designed multimedia force the reader to deal with comprehension of a whole message at the discourse level – filling in gaps, reinforcing hypotheses, identifying relationships, integrating information.

While multichannel communication theory (e.g., Mayer and Sims, 1994) argues that multiple sensory input stimulates learning and retention if the forms of media are relevant to each other, poorly designed multimedia materials can interfere with learning. The designer of electronic materials therefore needs to have a good understanding of the nature of the various multimedia elements, how they make different contributions to the comprehension process and how they can be productively combined. The use of multimedia should be motivated by considerations such as:

1. Is the information provided by the text and graphics mutually supportive? This is particularly important for L2 learners who look to the graphic for confirmation of their meaning-making efforts. Astorga (1999), for example, analyses a number of graphics accompanying a narrative and demonstrates how the participants in the story, the activities that they engage in and the circumstances surrounding those activities are congruent in both text and illustrations.
2. When might it be productive to create incongruence between text and graphics? The creation of dissonance through unlikely juxtapositions, for example, might lead to critical reflection.
3. Are the graphics too much of a distraction? Younger learners in particular suffer from split attention, continually clicking on animated graphics at the expense of concentrating on the text.
4. Do the graphics make the text redundant? If the reader can gain all the necessary information by viewing the graphic, no effort will be made to engage with the verbal text.
5. Might the use of multimedia in fact lead to poorer learning if it supplants key cognitive skills which could otherwise be exercised (e.g., by showing an animation and thereby relieving the student of the mental effort involved in coming to an understanding of the concept)?
6. Does the combination of media result in excessive cognitive load? If the reader has to grapple simultaneously with text, graphics and voice, the information input might be too high.
7. Which medium is best suited to a particular job? It has been suggested, for example, that still graphics are more suitable than video for vocabulary acquisition because more mental effort is required, resulting in superior retention (Chun and Plass, 1996). Video, on the other hand, could be more effective in generating background and cultural understandings. Animated graphics are useful for explaining how something works. Illustrations are

better than photos when you want to make certain features salient for the reader. And so on.

8. Which combinations of media are optimal for comprehension? Kalyuga (2000), for example, reports that a visually presented geometry diagram combined with auditory statements enhanced learning compared to conventional, visual only presentations. And an audio text accompanying a visual diagram was superior to purely visually based instructions.

9. When presenting information in more than one medium, is it best for them to be available simultaneously or sequentially? Delayed presentation of a source of information may reduce working memory load and act as a form of revision or confirmation.

Developing Comprehension Strategies
While the above uses of hypertext and multimedia can facilitate comprehension of text by providing timely support, they do not necessarily assist the learner in the longer term. Proficient readers have a wide range of strategies that they deploy strategically depending on their reading purpose, the type of text, the time available and so on. These include

1. predicting
2. skimming, scanning and searching
3. guessing unknown words from context
4. monitoring their comprehension (backtracking, reading forward)
5. paraphrasing
6. tracking the cohesive links in texts

Strategy training can enhance reading comprehension (Carrell *et al.*, 1989; Jiminez and Gamez, 1996), especially in the case of novice and L2 readers. When a learner comes across an unfamiliar word, for example, the preferred strategy is generally to guess its meaning from the surrounding context. To teach this strategy explicitly, it is possible for the materials developer to identify those words in a reading passage (a) that are key to the meaning of the passage and (b) whose meaning can be retrieved from the context. Clicking on one of these words can highlight those portions of the preceding text that give a clue to the meaning of the word. Alternatively, the reader can be encouraged to read ahead to find the meaning by the highlighting of clues in the ensuing text. By clicking on an icon accompanying the word, the reader can listen to an explanation of the strategy in L1 or L2.

A number of computer programs have been developed to teach the above strategies explicitly to L2 students. Reading and Listening Strategies (REAL), produced by the University of Hull (1999), for example, provides a series of English materials for special purposes. The goal of the REAL Text Units is to enable the learners of English as a foreign language to develop a range of reading strategies (prediction, skimming, scanning, searching and linking) in a systematic way, and to apply these skills to a range of text types.

Carrasquillo and Nunez (1988) investigated the effects of computer-assisted metacognitive strategies on the reading skills and comprehension of a group of primary ESL students. A program that provided reminders to the students about monitoring comprehension strategies (summarizing, clarifying, questioning, comprehension exercises) during the reading process was shown to be effective in enhancing reading comprehension.

The Center for Applied Special Technology (CAST) uses the Reciprocal Teaching Method (RTM) in conjunction with the text-to-speech capacity of the CAST eReader™ software tool, and voice recognition technology to teach four key strategies to primary learners:

- generating questions from the text;
- periodically summarizing;
- predicting upcoming content on the basis of what has been read; and
- clarifying understanding when necessary.

Student–teacher collaboration is underpinned by the computer's unique capacity to provide timely student prompts and scaffold weaknesses.

R-WISE is another program that helps students develop a repertoire of problem-solving heuristics by promoting three different types of activities and modelling each of these for the student:

- identifying concepts and units of meaning in a text;
- formulating interpretations and making inferences; and
- metacognitive control over performative skills.

It develops the students' metacognitive ability to anticipate and detect abstract problem-types and then to deploy, adapt, combine or abandon strategic competence solutions, including attention to decoding, inferencing, text structures and text conventions, language, reading purpose, higher-order strategies and self-monitoring. Adaptive advice is offered at different points in the reading process (Carlson and Larralde, 1995).

While instructional designers might well benefit from examining such programs as the above, Singhal (1999: 8) warns that

> few studies have been longitudinal and have failed to implement programs that teach students a range of reading strategies/skills to become more aware of their own reading processes, and to use strategies effectively in different reading contexts in order to make sense of what they read. Based on such an analysis, it is clear that current theoretical views about what reading is, and what the reading process entails, need to be considered when both designing and implementing computer programs for reading instruction.

Singhal suggests that designers of electronic reading programs should take into account such factors as:

- identifying an authentic reading goal
- providing a meaningful context
- introducing different genres and registers
- catering for individualization (e.g., through a diagnostic component and feedback)
- incorporating interactivity (e.g., request more information or reviews, solicit an exercise, get background info, get additional texts or examples, get contextual information, access a dictionary)
- ensuring that the rhetorical architecture facilitates comprehension
- building in systematic vocabulary expansion
- teaching strategy awareness
- making predictions
- identifying text structure
- defining words based on context
- paraphrasing
- answering comprehension questions
- scanning for information
- identifying rhetorical patterns

Enhancing Writing through Electronic Media

Contemporary writing theory continues to recognize the value of thinking of writing as a process of constructing meaning. There are a number of recursive phases in this process:

- modelling the genre
- demonstrating the process
- brainstorming and researching
- drafting
- conferencing and revising
- editing and publishing

A well-designed writing program will lead the writer through all phases of the writing process, providing as much support as needed along the way.

Modelling the Genre
When writing a text, the writer needs to consider the purpose. Depending on the purpose for writing, the text will be structured in a particular way and will have characteristic language features. Electronic media can be used to introduce L2 writers to the genres of the target culture and language.

The *TeleNex* project, for example, provides a bank of texts covering a range of genres (stories, procedures, recounts, explanations and so on) for teachers of primary L2 learners, each analysed in terms of generic structure and grammatical features. The purpose of recounts, for example, is 'to tell what happened'. The organization of the text, therefore, will be based on a chronological sequence, with an orientation stage and then a recounting of a series of events, with a possible reorientation at the end. This is illustrated by the use of rollovers – when the cursor rolls over each stage of the text it is highlighted in colour and a window appears providing information about the function of that stage. Subsequent files deal systematically with the grammatical features of the genre. One file, for example, might demonstrate how pronouns are used in a recount. By rolling over a list of pronoun types, these features are highlighted in the text. In this way the learners are receiving input on the nature of the type of text they are being asked to write before they have a go at writing one themselves. They can see how such a text is structured and they can be reminded of key grammatical resources in context. If they want to know more about any particular grammatical feature, they can follow a link to another area of the database that provides them with information on that feature, examples of its use and interactive exercises to practise it.

Demonstrating the Process
Before writing a text, it is useful for students to see how such a text is created. This could be done on the computer through an animated tutorial. However, it is preferable that the students participate in the writing experience in collaboration with co-learners and a teacher. In this case, the teacher can profitably use a computer with a projection facility to construct a text jointly with the students. As the students contribute ideas, these can be jotted down using the computer. Drawing on the students' input, the teacher can then demonstrate how these ideas can be shaped into a written text, drawing students' attention to the structure of the text, its grammatical features and the strategies used by proficient writers such as drafting, revising and consulting.

Brainstorming and Researching
Before writing, the writer needs to have something to write about. These ideas can come from brainstorming, drawing on previous experience or from researching. The process of researching is made much simpler by the accessibility of information on the Internet. Finding websites appropriate to the language level and age of the students is not straightforward, however. Electronic materials designed to teach writing should include information on how to find, select and evaluate information sites. For novice learners, the developer should already have identified a number of sites relevant to a particular task and provided activities for the students to do before they enter the site, while they are there and after they leave. These activities might include the development of research strategies and critical thinking skills. Once the students are taking notes, for example, they can use a 'mind-map' program such as IdeaFisher or Inspiration to start organizing their ideas coherently. Carlson and Larralde (1995), for example, advocate the use of 'visual thinking tools' to facilitate the active visual construction of ideas. Some of these programs encourage students to organize their notes according to the demands of the genre (e.g., compare/contrast; problem/solution; whole/part; class/subclass; point/elaboration).

If done in pairs or a group, brainstorming and researching around the computer has been shown to foster purposeful oral interaction, though with L2 students the value of this interaction will depend on their level of proficiency in the target language (Meskill, 1996).

Drafting

Once the student starts to draft a text, the computer becomes a powerful resource. The advent of word processing has revolutionized the writing of text. And yet it is still surprisingly underexploited in the L2 classroom. The ability to jot down embryonic ideas, to change your mind, to make mistakes, to take risks, to cut and paste contributes greatly to the learning of the target language. It is in the process of developing, manipulating, refining and synthesizing information in a written text that learners deepen their knowledge of the language. Using a word processor, students are more motivated to write and tend to produce longer texts. The availability of aids such as an on-line thesaurus and dictionary also contribute to the success of the draft and extend the language of the student. The *Longman Multimedia Dictionary*, for example, provides graphics, sound and video clips to help learners hear a word and see it used in context.

For novice learners, the materials developer can include greater guidance in the drafting process by, for example, providing templates or sample texts that they can use as models or to innovate on. Students writing a recipe for making pizza, for example, might draw on a similar recipe for making toasted cheese.

Conferencing and Revising

An important element of the writing process is receiving feedback from others during the drafting stage. It is difficult, however, for a teacher, especially with a large class, to have on-the-spot, individual consultations with students. This is where the computer comes into its own as a medium for communication. Writers are able to seek help from their teacher, their classroom peers, from students in other classes and in other locations and from unknown others. By using the 'comment' facility in the word-processing program, students can be provided with feedback at specific points in their text from any number of people, each identified by a code letter. In some programs it is possible for the student then to click on a comment, e.g., 'use present perfect here', which links to an interactive, multimedia lesson on the present perfect tense and when to use it. Connected to this might be a grammar chat room with students and tutors who discuss and answer questions about grammar (Tanguay, 1997).

Some sites build in interpersonal feedback facilities as a major feature. *The Journal of Interactive Media in Education*, for example, is an electronic journal where contributors can post their draft articles. Alongside the draft, in another frame, reviewers and other readers give feedback about particular sections of the article. There is often interaction between reviewers and between the author and the reviewers. The articles are available on the site in various stages of publication, with visitors to the site able to observe the process involved in the drafting, reviewing and revision of journal articles.

It is not only in the receiving of feedback that the learner benefits from such interaction, it is also the participation in the interaction itself. The type of communicative writing that surrounds the completion of a task is highly conducive to learning. It is generally spontaneous, fluent and unselfconscious, with the learner more concerned about the task itself than about the accuracy of the language.

Lamy and Goodfellow (1999) argue that there is a place for conscious reflection on language during asynchronous computer-mediated exchanges. Such interaction and reflection is an important factor in second language acquisition, providing opportunities for students to produce 'comprehensible output', to be helped to notice their errors and to take steps to correct their linguistic output (Chapelle, 1998).

Editing

Tools such as spell-checkers, syntax alerts and autoformatting assist at the editing stage. Feedback from grammar checkers is usually in the form of an underlining of an error. More helpful, however, are the programs that give rich feedback on the nature of the error (e.g., Correct Grammar, Right Writer, Grammatik, CorrecText, Reader, Power Edit). The Grammatik parsing engine, for example, was designed to detect and provide feedback on 45 error types in the writing of EFL writing students. The teacher is able to track class or individual student progress.

Even more helpful is the ability to modify such programs to respond to the common errors of a particular group (e.g., Cantonese speakers) (Brock, 1990). Using QBL TOOLS, Chen (1997) found that supplying students with detailed, customized computer-generated error feedback resulted in lower error rates for the test groups, more editing activity, time savings for the teachers and detailed data on the types of errors made by students.

For more advanced learners a concordancing tool can be useful at this stage. A concordancer can be requested to supply examples of specified vocabulary items, phrases or grammatical structures from a corpus of native speaker texts. The concordancer provides data showing how a particular vocabulary item is used in context, or the linguistic environment in which the item generally occurs or regular collocations of that item with other items. In this way, students can check their language usage with that of native speakers.

Building an Electronic Learning Environment

We have seen above how hypermedia, multimedia and communication media are being used to develop specific aspects of L2 learning. Recently, however, increasing emphasis is being placed on using the computer to support an integrated coherent, comprehensive curriculum.

There are a number of commercial multimedia packages that allow students to work through units of work at their own pace, with the program offering feedback, tracking their progress, diagnosing their needs, providing focused, intensive practice in weak skills, adjusting the level and difficulty of the exercises, assessing achievement and keeping records.

Other packages are organized around simulations, where skills are developed incidentally in the course of using the language in the context of problem-solving games and tasks, such as finding missing persons, solving mysteries, finding a suitable apartment to rent and setting up a business.

Most of these packages, however, are relatively self-contained with little scope for teachers to integrate them into the broader curriculum or to modify them (though some do include limited authoring tools). They also tend to focus on the sort of exercises that can be handled by the computer rather than the more open-ended language activities that involve human judgement and interaction.

At the other end of the spectrum are electronic learning environments that rely very little on pre-packaged content but use computer-mediated communication (CMC) as the basis for language learning. These are usually project-based, with groups of students using computers to work together on such tasks as:

• designing their project brief (questions to be pursued, goals, methodology, outcomes, resources)
• accessing information from local databases or the web
• posting their developing understandings in public spaces and receiving feedback from peers, teachers and others with expertise in the area
• interacting around the task with others in chat rooms or by e-mail
• publishing their findings

Such task-based, goal-oriented learning means that students have reasons to talk to each other, to make decisions, negotiate meaning and develop understandings together.

The CSILE (Computer Supported Intentional Learning Environments) project, for example, uses computer-mediated interaction as the basis for their knowledge-building communities. Based on the belief that knowledge is socially constructed, the site is designed so that students' attempts at meaning-making are publicly available for others to contribute to using 'architecture for computer-supported collaborative knowledge-building'.

In another study, Jacobson *et al.* (1996), drawing on Situated Cognition Theory, designed an electronic learning environment that engaged students in real-life, problem-based situations but which also involved the development of more general concepts. The program used hyperlinks which allowed for 'three-dimensional criss-crossing of the conceptual landscape'. The environment included provision for:

• modelling the knowledge in an authentic activity;
• supporting the students doing the task through *scaffolding* or *coaching*;
• allowing students to *articulate* their knowledge and to confront ineffective strategies or misconceptions;
• empowering the students by gradually *fading* or withdrawing support.

The study looked at two groups of students: one which had a higher degree of learner freedom and one which was more guided, with modelling and scaffolding provided. They found that the modelling and scaffolding support helped the students to acquire and flexibly use complex knowledge. They concluded that one of the tasks for the materials developer is to structure the environment in ways that promote 'cognitive apprenticeship'.

Software to support such projects includes tools like WebGuide, which has been designed to mediate and structure collaborative learning and shared cognition. In the developer's own words, WebGuide 'uses an innovative mechanism to define a flexible system of perspectives on a shared knowledge construction space. WebGuide provides an electronic and persistent workspace for individuals and teams to develop and share distinctive points of view on a topic.'

While the former predefined packages of materials provide the teacher and learners with a fully developed curriculum, the latter provides a framework for interactive learning. A challenge for the designer of electronic materials is to create an electronic learning environment that combines the best of all worlds (Berberich, 1995; Kimball, 1998).

If teachers of L2 learners were to create a wish-list to guide developers of such sites, it might include the following:

Learning Materials

- A comprehensive database of multimedia materials packages for various target groups of learners would be available that could be continuously added to.
- Such packages would conform to a predetermined standard in terms of technical requirements and quality of the materials. Materials might be produced by different developers (private and commercial – or combinations) but would only be accepted into the database after being reviewed and approved.
- The packages would include teachers' notes and lesson plans where necessary and guidance as to the theoretical rationale for each activity.
- The materials would be easily accessible and organized so that they could be retrievable according to various criteria (e.g., topic, grammar point, macroskill, genre, task type).
- The materials could be used as a coherent, self-contained curriculum (e.g., by novice teachers or for self-access learning) or teachers could select relevant activities to integrate into a broader classroom program.
- Packages might range from task-based units of work (such as a project) through to one-off activities.
- A unit of work would foster authentic language use but would provide scaffolding (e.g., demonstrations, modelling, animated tutorials, feedback) as students work their way to greater independence. Opportunities for practice of lower-level skills would be built in at appropriate points.
- There would be a balanced coverage of all the macroskills – listening, speaking, reading, writing – as well as opportunities for integrated skills development. Student reflection on their own learning would be integrated into the materials.
- Multimedia would be used judiciously in ways that enhance the learning pro-

cess (e.g., appropriate use of animated glosses, voice recognition, text to speech, voice-over, animated text and graphics, still graphics, video clips).

- An activity would be offered at different levels of difficulty and could be modified to suit individual learners or groups of learners. Authoring tools, 'shells' and templates would be readily available for both teachers and students so that activities could be customized.
- Other tools would be available for use at the point of need (e.g., dictionary, thesaurus, concordancer, student notepads, personalized vocabulary lists, assessment checklists and student records, desktop publishing and multimedia software such as Toolbook).

Pathways for Learning

Using hypermedia links, students would be guided through the materials with varying degrees of freedom.

- Within each package, there would be pop-ups and rollovers to provide 'just in time' assistance, tracking of individual students' responses and achievements and adjustment of support and level of difficulty, and flexible progression through the materials allowing for student decision-making and ownership (e.g., in terms of pace of learning, sequence, content or feedback, level of difficulty, amount of practice).
- Well-designed menus and buttons would enable students to navigate around the site, accessing information, materials and tools needed to complete a given task. There would be multiple entry points and different levels of accessibility. The design of the architecture would encourage students to perceive relationships, hierarchies and engage in pattern-seeking activity. Material would be filtered and distributed in ways that fostered recursive exploration and re-visiting from different angles.
- Spaces would be provided where students could engage in knowledge construction, reflection and purposeful language use.
- Links to other relevant sites would be identified, preferably with guidance provided. Apart from providing information, such sites would increase students' exposure to the target language and make use of authentic contexts.

Interpersonal Communication

Facilities would be built in to the site for both synchronous and asynchronous interaction between:

- teacher and individual students (e.g., for personalized guidance and feedback);
- teacher and whole class (e.g., giving information about course outline, general procedures and guidelines, notices and so on);

- groups of students engaged collaboratively on a specific task and working together in a public space;
- individual students (e.g., students wanting to interact on a one-to-one basis with a fellow student);
- students in other classes/countries engaged in similar tasks (e.g., e-pals, icq, video conferencing);
- students and knowledgeable others (e.g., experts who have been identified from discussion lists who might be able to provide input);
- teachers (e.g., sharing experiences of using the materials, asking for assistance, exchanging teaching suggestions, arranging collaborative activities).

Certainly there are such programs becoming available. WebCT, for example, is a course management system which provides a flexible, integrated environment using the latest technology to foster inquiry, encourage discourse and inspire collaboration. Instructors can construct their own course or purchase e-Learning Resource Packs. And the MALTED Project offers a combination of a sophisticated but easy-to-use database of adaptable resources (the Asset Base) for on-line and off-line use, adjustable feedback, a wide range of templates, a selection of strategic learning situations and a user-friendly authoring tool. But much more work needs to be done in terms of catering for various groups of students of different ages and different levels of proficiency learning different languages.

Conclusion

The issues surrounding the development of electronic materials are manifold: the technical (e.g., download time, changes in hardware); the technological (e.g., rapid developments in the nature of the medium); the practical (e.g., cost/efficiency ratios, availability of computer labs, teachers' computer literacy); the ideological (e.g., power, authority, identity, access); and so on. Here, however, we will restrict discussion to a few issues facing the profession as a whole.

New Literacies

Most of the programs and materials discussed above have used electronic technology to develop traditional literacy. But a new generation of students already in the education system has grown up with computers. Their immersion in electronic worlds has involved different ways of constructing meaning, different ways of interacting, different expectations, different ways of being in the world. Kramsch *et al.* (2000) remind us that the computer is not a neutral medium. Differences in terms of scale, time, readership, rhetorical norms, gatekeeping conventions and ease of use result in a qualitatively different literacy experience.

Reading is no longer a matter of decoding and comprehending a linear, print text. Reading on-line involves finding, selecting, evaluating and critically interpreting net-based information (Warschauer and Healey, 1998). Texts are often fragmented, polyvocal, multimodal and hyperlinked. The hypertext navigational frames mediate how we read, both opening up and constraining the ways in which we construe meaning. The integrity and permanence of texts are no longer assured (Kramsch *et al.*, 2000).

Similarly, writing is no longer a matter of creating a linear, print text. On the one hand, much of the on-line writing done by today's students (e.g., in chat rooms) more closely resembles interactive conversation, but with its own conventions and constraints. It is fluent, rapid, dynamic and elliptical, making assumptions about prior and shared knowledge. On the other hand, the creation of multimedia hypertext documents is a relatively ponderous and time-consuming task, requiring reflection in the selection, combination, organization, cross-referencing, linking and processing of a number of elements. The composing process is increasingly collaborative, with different participants contributing to the 'text' (writer, graphic designer, editor, voice artist, illustrator, technician). There is no longer a clear sense of sole authorship and individual ownership of texts.[2]

Few designers of electronic materials appear to be taking seriously the need to prepare students to deal with the demands of the new literacies, whether in L1 or L2.

Learning Theory and Electronic Materials Design

The new literacies bring into question current theories of language learning and their concomitant pedagogies. Theories of reading traditional print texts have emphasized decoding skills and comprehension strategies. Theories of learning to write have emphasized the lower-level skills of orthography, punctuation and syntax and the higher-order skills involved in the composing process. While these are obviously still important, on-line literacy demands new ways of thinking about how we learn to read and write in both L1 and L2.

Theories relating to traditional print literacy cannot adequately deal with a reading process where critical decisions need to be made at every step of the way, virtual realities need to be negotiated and information from multiple sources needs to be evaluated and synthesized (Warschauer, 2000). Nor with a composing process that involves working with different semiotic tools, new genres, new discourses, changed identities and an enhanced sense of agency (Kramsch *et al.*, 2000).

In order to provide a coherent theoretical rationale to inform the development of electronic materials and learning spaces, there is an obvious need to test current literacy theory in the light of the new demands and possibilities of electronic media.

Insufficient Research

Research into electronic materials is more often about student attitudes towards using computers, their motivation, their self-confidence and interaction around the computer than related to the design of materials.

The literature is replete with pleas for a greater research effort (Turner, 1993; Basena and Jamieson, 1996; Kern and Warschauer, 2000) and there continues to be little rigorous empirical documentation of the educational efficacy of hypertext learning environments (Jacobson *et al.*, 1996; Warschauer and Healey, 1998).

Chun and Plass (1997) outline a research agenda, recommending that studies be designed to determine the effectiveness of specific features of multimedia materials for specific types of learners, for specific learning tasks and for specific cognitive processes. The questions they pose include:

- How should the multimedia information be designed in order to aid in the process of vocabulary acquisition? What types of verbal information are helpful? What types of visual information are helpful?
- What is the effect of presenting both verbal and visual information (e.g., dual coding effect)? What effect will a contiguous presentation of two different types of information have? What effect will a simultaneous presentation of two types of information have (e.g., audio plus textual, audio plus visual)?
- How can an environment be designed to support the highest possible number of learner differences (i.e., how can adaptive environments be designed)? For whom are visuals helpful (e.g., visualizers vs. verbalizers, high vs. low spatial ability learners)? For whom are both verbal and visual information helpful (e.g., high vs. low verbal ability learners, good vs. poor L1 readers, stronger vs. weaker L2 learners)?
- How should multimedia information be designed to help each process of text comprehension (focusing attention, building internal connections, building external connections)? For example, for what types of propositions is visual information, as opposed to, or in addition to, verbal information, helpful (e.g., setting the scene, depicting actions or events)?

Until such questions (and many more) are addressed by researchers, developers of electronic materials are not in a position to confidently design resources that will significantly enhance the learning of second languages.

Appendix 12.1: Websites and programs cited in chapter

CAST (Center for Applied Special Technology): *http://www.cast.org/udl/*
CAVOCA Computer-assisted second language vocabulary acquisition (cited in P. Groot (2000) *Language Learning & Technology,* **4**(1), 60–81)
COBUILD: *http://titania.cobuild.collins.co.uk/*
CSILE (Computer Supported Intentional Learning Environments) OISE, Toronto: *http://csile.oise.utoronto.ca/*
GALT (Glossing Authentic Language Texts), Mary Ann Lyman-Hager, Education Technology Services, The Pennsylvania State University: *http://www.psu.edu/ dept/cac/ets/catalog/completed/GALT/GALT.html*
IdeaFisher (IdeaFisher Systems): *http://www.ideafisher.com/*
Inspiration (Inspiration Software): *http://www.inspiration.com/*

Longman Multimedia Dictionary: *http://www.longman-elt.com/dictionaries/html*
The MALTED Project: *http://www.malted.com*
NewReader (Hyperbole): see demo on *http://www.orst.edu/Dept/eli/celia/macdemos. html*
QBL TOOLS: *http://www.qbl.com.au/products.htm*
REAL (Reading and Listening Strategies), produced by the University of Hull (1999): *http://www.hull.ac.uk/cti/real/*
R-WISE: cited in Carlson and Larralde (1995)
TeleNex – Teachers of English Language Education Centre, Department of Curriculum Studies, Hong Kong University: *http://www.telenex.hku.hk/telec/pmain/primain.htm*
Text Tangler (Research Design Associates)
Toolbook: *http://www.webecon.bris.ac.uk/toolbook/*
WebCT: *http://www.webct.com/*
WebGuide: cited in G. Stahl (2001) 'WebGuide: guiding collaborative learning on the Web with perspectives'. *Journal of Interactive Media in Education*, 2001 (1)

References

Adams, M. J. (1990) *Beginning to Read: Thinking and Learning about Print*. Cambridge, MA: MIT Press.

Astorga, C. (1999) 'The text-image interaction and second language learning'. *Australian Journal of Language and Literacy*, **22** (3), 212–33.

Basena, D. and Jamieson, J. (1996) 'CALL research in second language learning: 1990–1994'. *CAELL Journal*, **7** (1/2), 14–18.

Berberich, F. (1995) 'Computer Adaptive Testing and its extension to a teaching model in CALL'. *CAELL Journal*, **6** (2), 11–18.

Brock, M. N. (1990) 'Customizing a computerized text analyzer for ESL writers: cost versus gain'. *CALICO Journal*, **8**, 51–60.

Carlson, P. and Larralde, V. (1995) 'Combining concept mapping and adaptive advice to teach reading comprehension'. *Journal of Universal Computer Science*, **1** (3).

Carrasquillo, A. and Nunez, D. (1988) 'Computer-assisted metacognitive strategies and the reading comprehension skills of ESL elementary school students'. ERIC Document Reproduction Service No. ED 301838.

Carrell, P. (1987) 'Content and formal schemata in ESL reading'. *TESOL Quarterly*, **21**, 461–81.

Carrell, P., Pharis, B. and Liberto, J. (1989) 'Metacognitive strategy training for ESL reading'. *TESOL Quarterly*, **23** (4), 647–78.

Chapelle, C. (1998) 'Multimedia CALL: lessons to be learned from research on instructed SLA'. *Language Learning and Technology*, **2** (1), 22–34.

Chen, J. (1997) 'Computer generated error feedback and writing process: a link'. *TESL-EJ*, **2** (3 A-1).

Chun, D. and Plass, J. (1996) 'Effects of multimedia annotations on vocabulary acquisition'. *The Modern Language Journal*, **80** (2), 183–98.

Chun, D. and Plass, J. (1997) 'Research on text comprehension in multimedia environments'. *Language Learning & Technology*, **1** (1), 60–81.

Hulstijn, J. (1997) 'Mnemonic methods in foreign language vocabulary learning: theoretical considerations and pedagogical implications', in J. Coady and T. Huckin (eds) *Second Language Vocabulary Acquisition*. Cambridge: Cambridge University Press.

Hulstijn, J., Hollander, M. and Greidanus, T. (1996) 'Incidental vocabulary learning by advanced foreign language students: the influence of marginal glosses, dictionary use, and reoccurrence of unknown words'. *The Modern Language Journal*, **80**, 327–39.

Jacobson, M., Maouri, C., Mishra, P. and Kolar, C. (1996) 'Learning with hypertext learning environments: theory, design and research'. *Journal of Educational Multimedia and Hypermedia*, **5** (3/4), 239–81.

Jiminez, R. and Gamez, A. (1996) 'Literature-based cognitive strategy instruction for middle school Latino students'. *Journal of Adolescent and Adult Literacy*, **40** (2), 84–91.

Kalyuga, S. (2000) 'When using sound with a text or picture is not beneficial for learning'. *Australian Journal of Educational Technology*, **16** (2), 161–72. *http://cleo.murdoch.edu.au/ajet/ajet16/kalyuga.html*.

Kern, R. and Warschauer, M. (2000) 'Theory and practice of network-based language teaching', in M. Warschauer and R. Kern (2000) *Network-based Language Teaching: Concepts and Practice*. New York: Cambridge University Press.

Kimball, J. (1998) 'Thriving on screen: web-authoring for L2 instruction'. *The Internet TESL Journal*, **4** (2) (*http://www.aitech.ac.jp/~iteslj/*).

Kramsch, C., A'Ness, F. and Wan Shun Eva Lam (2000) 'Authenticity and authorship in the computer-mediated acquisition of L2 literacy'. *Language Learning & Technology*, **4** (2), 78–104.

Lamy, M. and Goodfellow, R. (1999) '"Reflective conversation" in the virtual language classroom'. *Language Learning & Technology*, **2** (2), 43–61.

Larsen-Freeman, D. and Long, M. (1991) *An Introduction to Second Language Acquisition Research*. London: Longman.

Lomicka, L. (1998) 'To gloss or not to gloss: an investigation of reading comprehension online'. *Language Learning & Technology*, **1**, (2), 41–50.

Mayer, R. E. and Sims, V. K. (1994) 'For whom is a picture worth a thousand words? Extensions of a dual-coding theory of multimedia learning'. *Journal of Educational Psychology*, **86**, 389–401.

Meskill, C. (1996) 'Listening skills development through multimedia'. *Journal of Educational Multimedia and Hypermedia*, **5** (2), 179–201.

Plass, J. (1998) 'Design and evaluation of the user interface of foreign language multimedia software: a cognitive approach'. *Language Learning & Technology*, **2** (1), 35–45.

Sharwood Smith, M. (1993) 'Input enhancement in instructed SLA: theoretical bases'. *Studies in Second Language Acquisition*, **15**, 165–79.

Singhal, M. (1999) 'Reading and computer-assisted instruction: applications and implications'. *CALL-EJ*, **3** (2).

Stanovich, K. E. (1993) 'Romance and reality'. *The Reading Teacher*, **47**, 280–90.

Tanguay, E. (1997) 'English teachers, prepare yourselves for the digital age'. *Teaching English in the Network Age*, Article No. 1, *http://userpage.fu-berlin.de/ ~tanguay/english-teachers.htm*.

Turner, T. C. (1993). 'Literacy and machines: an overview of the use of technology in adult literacy programs'. (Technical Report TR93–3.) Philadelphia: University of Pennsylvania, National Center on Adult Literacy.

Warschauer, M. (2000) 'The death of cyberspace and the rebirth of CALL'. Plenary paper, *CALL for the 21st Century*, IATEFL and ESADE Conference, July 2000, Barcelona, Spain.

Warschauer, M. and Healey, D. (1998) 'Computers and language learning: an overview'. *Language Teaching*, **31**, 57–71.

Watanabe, Y. (1997) 'Input, intake and retention: effects of increased processing on incidental learning of foreign language vocabulary'. *Studies in Second Language Acquisition*, **19**, 287–307.

13

Hyperfiction: Explorations in Texture

Claudia Ferradas Moi

> I leave to the various futures (not to all) my garden of forking paths.
> (Jorge Luis Borges, 'The Garden of Forking Paths')

Time and technology have a funny way of changing our attitudes. McLuhan's take on print media is that it created our sequential way of thinking. Who's to say we won't simply evolve along with our media and shed our linear bias like an old skin? Once a new, computer-bred generation becomes comfortable living in a systems-oriented world, the idea of reading non-sequential fiction might seem as logical as 1–2–33.

(George Melrod, 'Digital Unbound')

Hypertext and Hyperfiction: Reading Down Forking Paths

In the 1960s, Ted Nelson conceived of a huge electronic network to connect all the information in the world by means of cross-referenced documents. He called this a 'docuverse' and coined the word 'hypertext' to name a tool which would create a non-sequential linking of texts. In the same effervescent decade, both literary theory and computer science were taking steps towards the systematization of textual forms that cited other texts – what Gérard Genette (1962) referred to as 'palimpsests'. For Genette, hypertextuality is the relationship that links text B (the hypertext) to a previous text A (the hypotext) in a way which is not a mere commentary. In this sense, all texts can be said to be potentially hypertextual.

The increasing access to personal computers, the development of interactive technology and the advent of the Internet and the World Wide Web have made Nelson's docuverse a concrete possibility – and his notion of hypertext a reality. In *Literary Machines* (1981), Nelson was then able to write: 'By hypertext I mean non-sequential writing – text that branches and allows choices to the reader, best read at an interactive screen. As popularly conceived, this is a series of text chunks connected by links which offer the reader different pathways.'

In 1992, George P. Landow, a pioneer in the use of hypertext in higher education, wrote a book whose title reveals the impact of hypertext within a cultural context informed by new technologies: *Hypertext: The Convergence of Contemporary Critical Theory and Technology*. In it, hypertext is a digital reality rather than abstract theoretical construct: computer hypertext is defined as 'text composed of blocks of words (or images) linked electronically by multiple paths, chains or trails in an open-ended, perpetually unfinished textuality described by the terms link, node, network, web and path' (Landow, 1992: 3).

Fascinated by the challenge offered by electronic hyperlinks, the American writer Michael Joyce came up with the idea of applying hypertext to the writing of original fiction. He then conceived of a virtual story that would never be read the same way twice: the result was *afternoon, a story*. Hypertext fiction (or *hyperfiction*) had been born.

As George Melrod (1994: 162) defines it, hyperfiction is 'non-linear interactive electronic literature. Potentially, the next stage of evolution for storytelling, where text is made of light instead of ink, where you help the author shape the story, and where you never read the same novel the same way twice.' Hyperfiction can only be read on a computer screen. Readers decide where to go next by consulting the titles of linked passages or let the links between windows or panels (which may be called 'lexias' using Roland Barthes' terminology, as applied in Landow, 1992) take them to an unknown place in the textual geography. They can choose whether to click on a word, on an arrow that takes them backwards or forwards, on YES and NO buttons ... or simply press 'ENTER', which is just like 'turning the page'.

> The result is a kind of narrative collage, a textual kaleidoscope in which the story is cut into fragments and is constantly changing. If it's a bit disorienting, that's part of the idea. Instead of laying out a straight path, hyperfictions set you down in a maze, give you a compass, then let you decide where to go next.
> (Melrod, 1994: 163)

By definition, hyperfiction is strikingly open-ended. This empowers the reader, as s/he is not only able to make decisions such as where to go next or when to 'put an end to the story' but is in control of the process of appropriation (the interaction with the text that leads the reader to 'own' a certain reading of the text) in ways which are hard to achieve within print technology.

Michael Joyce reflects on this in an introductory lexia in his *afternoon, a story*, appropriately called 'Work in Progress':

WORK IN PROGRESS

Closure is, as in any fiction, a suspect quality, although here it is made manifest. When a story no longer progresses, or when it cycles, or when you tire of the paths, the experience of reading it ends. Even so, there are likely to be more opportunities than you think there are at first. A word which doesn't yield the first time you read a section may take you elsewhere if you choose it when you encounter the section again; and sometimes what seems a loop, like memory, heads off again in another direction.

There is no simple way to say this.

Where and how to put an end to a story must always have been one of the main preoccupations of a writer, and it is certainly the focus of the metaliterary concern which pervades the self-referential novel of the last few decades. Hypertext unveils the artificiality of closure, revealing not only the writer's but the reader's role in the creation of that artifice, as well as the arbitrary nature of the paths that may lead to it, for hypertext fiction is a question of texture, or, as Mary-Kim Arnold (1993) has expressed it, 'Words that yield to the touch' – the mediating touch of a mouse.

Now, what words will 'yield' if the reader clicks on them? Joyce's explanation in *afternoon, a story* seems to have established the metaphor:

READ AT DEPTH
I haven't indicated what words yield, but they are usually ones which have texture

So, once again, it is the reader who decides which words 'have texture', which bear a tempting quality, a multi-layered promise that invites exploration … and wherever s/he decides to click, s/he is unlikely to be disappointed.

The nomadic movement of ideas is made effortless by the electronic medium that makes it easy to cross borders (or erase them) with the swipe of a mouse, carrying as much of the world as you will on the etched arrow of light that makes up a cursor … Each iteration 'breathes life into a narrative of possibilities', as Jane Yellowlees Douglas says of hypertext fiction, so that, in the 'third or fourth encounter with the same place, the immediate encounter remains the same as the first, [but] what changes is [our] understanding'. The text becomes a present tense palimpsest where what shines through are not past versions but potential, alternate views. (Joyce, 1995: 3)

Reconfiguring Reading

Like Tennyson's Lady of Shalott, the reader weaves the magic web of narrative possibilities, aware of the chilling power of choice. S/he advances, down the labyrinth of forking paths that Borges (1941) once imagined, sometimes at a loss, sometimes helped by Ariadne's thread (if s/he chooses to consult the map, chart, treemap or outline of links between lexias). But no matter how s/he chooses to do it, the encounter with the Minotaur is a challenge to the stability of the traditional concepts of text, author and reader.

Delany and Landow (1991: 3) point out that:

so long as text was married to a physical media (SIC), readers and writers took for granted three crucial attributes: that the text was *linear, bounded and fixed*. Generations of scholars and authors internalized these qualities as the rules of thought, and they had pervasive social consequences. We can define *Hypertext* as the use of the computer to transcend the linear, bounded and fixed qualities of the traditional written text.

Devoid of paper, tablet, scroll, book ... the text becomes virtual, transient. There is no stable object holding the entire text: all the reader can see is one block of text at a time and explore the electronic links that connect that lexia to others: a variable textual structure that lies behind the blocks and can be represented on screen as a tree diagram, a web, a network ... Ariadne's thread is there, but there is no fixed way out of the labyrinth: you build it as you choose your way down the forking paths.

If hypertext has changed the nature of text, it has also disclosed the nature of underlying reading operations. True, the reader may apply perfectly conventional reading habits in each lexia, but, as Delany and Landow (1991: 4) believe:

> [hypertext] can also provide a revelation, by making visible and explicit mental processes that have always been part of the total experience of reading. For the text as the reader *imagined* it – as opposed to the physical text objectified in the book – never had to be linear, bounded or fixed. A reader could jump to the last page to see how a story ended; could think of relevant passages in other works; could re-order texts by cutting and pasting. Still, the stubborn materiality of the text constrained such operations.

Hypertext, then, is the virtual space where modern literary criticism and pedagogy meet, as the active reader in the learner-centred classroom becomes a reality rather than a desideratum. The reader as 'producer of the text' advocated by Barthes (1970), the active reader of Umberto Eco's open work (1962), the Derridean emphasis upon discontinuity and decentring (Derrida, 1967), all find concrete realization in hyperfiction. So does Bakhtin's conception of dialogism and multivocality (1984), for 'hypertext does not permit a tyrannical, univocal voice. Rather, the voice is always that distilled from the combined experience of the momentary focus, the lexia one presently reads, and the continually forming narrative of one's reading path' (Landow, 1992: 11).

Reconfiguring Education

All this has far-reaching implications for education in general and for literary education in particular. Pulverness (1996: 73), advocating a dialogical approach to the teaching of literature, remarks:

> When the reader adds his or her voice to the host of voices present in the text, s/he experiences the peculiar intimacy of reading and each reader constructs the meaning of the text afresh. Just as words do not mean without context, the literary text does not *contain* meaning, determined by the writer, which it is the reader's task to extract.

This conception has been (and frequently still is) veiled by layers of respect for the mythical authority of writers, critics and literature teachers. Even in classrooms where the existence of multiple readings is acknowledged, there is often an underlying belief in the superiority of the teacher's learned reading, derived from the critics' monopoly of interpretation. Hyperfiction is an empowering tool, for it removes the veil: not only does it offer multiple readings, but multiple texts (or architectural realizations of text). This simply means that no reading (not even the teacher's!) can be considered the 'correct' one, as the text itself is not fixed and it literally grows with every reading. There is no stable entity to be analysed in search of the 'correct' interpretation.

Hyperfiction readers are aware of the fact that they are opening the textual track as they advance, putting together textual chunks whose combination is virtual rather than actual. As they sit in front of the computer, readers are encouraged to fill in 'indeterminacy gaps' (Iser, 1971) in the information as they read (or, rather, navigate) the text. Though they cannot change the author's work, they can discover multiple combinations and can actually type notes on a smaller window as they read, responding to the information gaps in the text. The boundaries between reader and writer are then blurred and the authority of the authorial voice is partially transferred to the reader: the dialogue with the text becomes an intertext that merges with the reading lexias. The reader activates procedural skills to make sense not only of discourse but of the constructive web behind it (which involves awareness of deconstruction).

Hyperfiction in the EFL Class

What contributions can this kind of literature make to a learner-centred classroom where literature is integrated with the teaching of English as a foreign language within a dialogical approach to reading? How can the reading experience be integrated with writing and oral activities that are meaningful? What materials can teachers and students develop using hypertext writing programs and applications?

Experimentally, as the initial stage in a research project, ten advanced EFL students met in Buenos Aires, Argentina, to discuss their reading of two hypertext stories: *Lust* by Mary-Kim Arnold (1993) and *I Have Said Nothing* by J. Yellowlees Douglas (1993). The workshop covered three sessions of three hours each. In the first session, students were introduced to hyperfiction and helped to become familiar with the mechanics and conventions involved. In the second session, they discussed the experience of reading *Lust*. It was not surprising to see that several of them had printed their version to 'bring the text to be analysed' (although you can only print one 'screen' per page, so that the jigsaw puzzle format still remains). The results of the session can be summarized into two main (apparently contradictory) areas:

a. when participants were asked to reflect on their reading experience in writing, the word 'frustrating' was the most recurrent adjective in their comments. The reason for this feeling was ascribed to their incapacity to come to terms with the technology involved:

- they would have preferred to 'turn the page';
- they wanted 'to know where they were going';
- they could not 'get to the end', even though they arbitrarily put an end to the reading process at some point;
- they found 'dead ends' when they did want to go on.

b. when asked to comment on the characters they had 'met' and their relationships, as well as on the events those characters were involved in, they were, on the other hand, evidently enthusiastic, as they were delighted to find that:

- they all had a different story to tell;
- they had read the same 'names' but 'met different people';
- though the events were usually the same, their different position in the sequence resemanticized them: used to the Aristotelian notion of plot understood as a causally related sequence, readers tend to interpret events in the light of what precedes or follows them.

In short: there was a lot to talk about and no one could be said to 'own' the 'right' interpretation.

Lust can hardly be defined as a narrative, even when sequentially printed: it is poetic prose. Students found that the 'common ground' in their readings was connected with certain recurrent motifs (nakedness, a child, a knife, the night, touching) and the images associated with them. They were particularly interested in the polyphonic use of the word 'fabric' and the lexical chain '*texture – blanket – carpet – cotton – wool*', which they found to be metatextually related to the textual fabric, the story they were invited to weave.

For the third session, participants were asked to read *I Have Said Nothing* and to record their reading hypotheses, expectations and comments in writing as they advanced. They returned two weeks later, eager to meet the rest of the group.

I Have Said Nothing is an apparently conventional report of a fatal car accident (or two?), retold from different points of view, sometimes in morbid detail. Though car crashes can be said to have become recurrent in hyperfiction, this story explores the blank screen, silence as a resource, the power of what is left unsaid . . . it is a huge information gap that the reader fills in passionately. Take, for example, the following lexia:

ANATOMY

Do you know what happens when a Chevy Nova with a 280 engine hits you going 75 miles an hour?

Depending on what word you click on, or on whether you decide to take the 'easy' or 'lazy' option and press 'ENTER', you can get the morbid details referred to above

ANATOMIZED

— It fractures your collarbone; your scapula; your pelvis; your sacral, lumbar, thoracic and cervical vertebrae.

— It splinters your ribcage, compressing your liver, kidneys, spleen, stomach, intestines, lungs and heart.

— It fractures your skull and bruises your brain.

— It causes massive haemorrhaging, throws the heart into cardiac arrest and hurls your central nervous system into profound shock.

or a sequence of succinct statements.

EVERY ONE

It breaks every bone in your body.
Including your head.
Then you pass on to the central question

AND THEN...

And then...
Nothing.

At this point, no matter how many times you press ENTER you cannot advance: you have reached a 'dead end'. A meaningful joke, which reminds you of the title of the story: 'I Have Said Nothing'! You then click on *nothing* and manage to get another narrative sequence, only to find that you soon come across this cryptic lexia:

I

Literally, the narrator says nothing, and that is probably why, once the computer is turned off, there is a lot to talk about!

When discussing their reading of this story, participants agreed that the sense of frustration had diminished or disappeared altogether, which they ascribed to the following:

• they were now better acquainted with the reading habits involved in hyperfiction;
• the author had provided schematic maps for those who wanted that sort of help;
• they could reconstruct a narrative line in a way that *Lust* did not allow them to

(they did not need to face the difficulties posed by poetic prose and hyper-fiction at the same time).

The second and third points seem to suggest some kind of nostalgia for the reading habits print technology and traditional linear stories require.

As a pilot experience in the use of hyperfiction with EFL students, the work-shop suggests a few preliminary conclusions:

- carefully planned *pre-computer activity* is needed to acquaint the reader with the necessary information and skills required to approach the new textual form (especially with groups who are not yet comfortable with the use of computers)
- the *computer-based activity* can be frustrating: this is perhaps unavoidable when a new format is encountered, but it also means the teacher may want to select a hypertext which resembles traditional stories to some extent (as *I Have Said Nothing* does) rather than a more radically 'avant-garde' one (such as *Lust*)
- the *post-computer activity* can become a true negotiation between different readers as to what 'the text' means: the teacher or workshop coordinator can count on *information and opinion gaps* that will encourage involvement and give rise to a number of meaningful language activities
- this also encourages *learner autonomy*: hyperfiction reading involves commit-ment on the part of the students. They are responsible for their own reading, as they will have to retell their version and support their views with constant references to the reading they have 'saved'
- the lack of a 'correct' version is particularly encouraging for the more insecure students, who feel free to express their views
- above all, reading hyperfiction and writing comments as the reader advances contributes to the development of *metacognitive strategies*: the learner is encouraged to think about the way in which the textual resources contribute to the building of hypotheses as s/he moves down the textual links; thus, s/he reflects upon his/her own interpretive procedures, and the process raises awareness of the reader's expectations, reading style, the affective factors at play in the building of the textual web and the way this compares to the procedures used by others
- the participants insisted that, as they read hyperfiction at home, the experience became even more exciting as they thought of the next meeting with the other members of the group: it seems that coming to terms with the text involved discussing it with other readers (which ensures *motivation* and encourages *col-laborative learning*)

All this seems to suggest that hyperfiction can make important contributions to the learner-centred EFL class. Apart from its value concerning awareness-raising, hyperfiction can lead to

- the meaningful retelling of a student's reading (asking the others to provide 'closure' and then comparing their suggestions to the ending s/he 'reached')

- highly motivating written tasks, such as descriptions of one character as seen by different readers, or a series of letters (or e-mails) from one character to another, where a number of misunderstandings will be produced by the fact that characters have different information in each case
- meaningful role-play activities (dialogues between characters in the different 'versions')

and many other creative activities for language practice. However, further research needs to be done to corroborate the preliminary conclusions listed above and explore their implications. In particular, it is necessary to investigate whether these statements apply to the needs of EFL students at lower levels of proficiency.

At present, however, no hyperfiction materials seem to be available to suit the needs of EFL students whose standard of English is not considerably advanced. This is an inviting challenge for those teachers who are encouraged by the possibilities of electronic materials design. Can hypertext writing programs be used for students to develop their own stories in class? Again experimentally, I observed a class of 5 upper intermediate EFL students in Buenos Aires give that kind of program a try.

> Just what it is to be literate in social terms is becoming increasingly complex and elusive. While multimedia and digital technologies are redefining literacy, issues of equity also become more pressing ... The new literacies need to include the capacity to 'read' and 'write' the new technologies, and to understand what is entailed in the operation, reception and production of their texts. (Beavis, 1998: 244)

If 'Read[ing] and writ[ing] the new technologies' involves dealing with hypertext, I thought that producing simple hypertexts in class could begin to throw light on different aspects of the hyperreading and hyperwriting process in a foreign language and contribute to the development of the new literacies identified by Beavis.

The project involved the following skills and steps; as seen in Table 13.1. Initially, we were worried by the fact that the task of writing a short hyperfiction piece involved the use of a hypertext writing program. However, students took no time at all to learn how to use the basic functions of the program. They showed an exploratory learning mode (not once did they ask to be given a set of previous instructions) and those with better PC skills collaborated with the others, who, in turn, paid more attention to editing. Yet, in spite of being an upper intermediate group, they still needed a lot of help from the teacher when editing (they did not notice they had failed to conjugate most verbs!), probably because the creation of a story with multiple paths required all their attention. Even punctuation and spelling were overlooked in early drafts, which seems to suggest that content rather than accuracy was the focus of students' attention. This was our main aim, and editing could wait.

Table 13.1 Skills and steps in hyperreading and hyperwriting

Hyperreading	Familiarization with web search	
	Skimming	
	Scanning	
	Reflecting on links	Authorship, reader independence, etc.
	Familiarization with hyperfiction	
Hyperwriting	*Producing hyperfiction*	Using a hypertext program
	Revision	Drafting
		Editing
		Peer correction
	Linking	
Hyperreading	Browsing for revision	
Hyperwriting	Revision	Drafting
		Editing
		Peer correction
Hyperreading	Peer feedback	

When they evaluated the experience, students found it motivating and did not think the program was an obstacle. According to the assessment interview at the end of the project, they thought it had been positive in terms of language learning because they had edited their texts again and again, had discussed the different options they would offer to the reader (though they used the L1 quite often), had 'learnt new vocabulary' and had found the activity 'original' and 'challenging'. However, they had also found it time-consuming: they devoted two ninety-minute classes to the story-writing process and the results were disappointingly simple, with very few links except for those that led the reader down parallel lines in a forking structure. Besides, there were obvious mistakes they discovered when reading their peers' work: 'How can he say "I died immediately" if he is already dead?'

This showed an interesting metacognitive leap. They reflected on

- the value of an activity for language learning
- the way a story is built and their strong dependence as readers on traditional linear narrative: *This is too simple: we know what the end will be*
  X: *'He gave him the money. No, no, he punched him'*
  Y: *'Well, here he can do both!'*
  X: *'Ah, yes!'*

- the clues they should not give the reader in order to keep suspense
- the way narrative paths could intersect to create a more interesting story

The students took the whole idea as a game and seemed to enjoy it. They even wanted to go on working outside class, which means that if we could find ways of training students to use the hypertext program and give them enough time, we could begin to throw light on some of their hyperreading and hyperwriting operations.

In fact, we may even do without a hypertext writing program. Word processors can be used today to establish links from one word to another or from one text to another. This can help students write their own creative hypertextual pieces or even develop critical insights into other texts they have read by establishing intertextual relationships between texts or with their own comments. These can then be uploaded on to a class web page for other readers to share.

I have seen a teacher (who was training students to sit for the IGCSE Literature exam) achieve amazing results by inviting students to hyperlink stories they had written to the texts they had read using a word processor. They not only established links to quotations from the different texts which were thematically linked to their stories or which had influenced them in some way: they also built hypertextual webs that connected their texts to web pages, to quotations from songs or to other texts which they thought were in some way related to their own. Justifying such links was not only good training for the exam essays, in that students were providing relevant evidence to support the points they were making, it also trained them to think critically about the nature of the links we follow whenever we click on the hyperlinks established by others.

In any case, these are just early attempts to develop the literacies demanded by new technologies. As teachers and materials designers, we should bear in mind that, even though we may hail the advent of forms of technology that contribute to the achievement of a more democratic, learner-centred classroom, we must be aware of the implications this may have in the particular context in which we teach and learn. So, for all my enthusiasm, I expect further studies to consider some of the fears and open questions expressed by the participants in the first experimental workshop:

- How satisfying is the reading of a permanently inconclusive work? Can the frustration of visiting the same textual place again and again be overcome with considerations on how the lexia can be reinterpreted in each new occurrence?
- Up to what extent is the reader free to choose where he is going? How much veiled manipulation on the part of the author is there when pre-programmed paths determine where links lead?
- Does hyperfiction really challenge our concept of narrative? Can we do away with the narrative line, subscribing to fragmentary 'video clip aesthetics' or are we putting the chunks together, jigsaw puzzle style, only to reconstruct some form of narrative line?

- How democratic is a form that depends not only on the access to computer hardware and software but on the necessary 'know-how', especially in developing countries, where access and 'know-how' are still the privilege of a few? Does this contribute to McLuhan's global village or to a world whose distribution of power (and empowering knowledge) is becoming more and more unfair?
- Will screens ever replace books? How will a 'reading artefact' look, feel, smell ... in years to come? And how is that likely to change our perception of the world in general?

It will certainly involve much more than the swipe and click of a mouse to understand how, in education in general, and in the EFL class in particular, the elusive attraction of the virtual can contribute to the improvement of the actual.

References

Arnold, M. (1993) *Lust.* Computer disc. *The Eastgate Quarterly Review of Hypertext,* **1** (2), Winter 1994.

Bakhtin, M. (1984) *Problems of Dostoevsky's Poetics.* Edited and translated by Caryl Emerson. Minneapolis: University of Minnesota Press.

Barthes, R. (1970) *S / Z.* Paris: Editions du Seuil. *S / Z* (1976). Translated by Richard Miller, NY: Hill and Wang.

Beavis, C. (1998) 'Computer games, culture and curriculum', in I. Snyder (ed.) *Page to Screen – Taking Literacy into the Electronic Era.* London and New York: Routledge, pp. 234–55.

Borges, J. L. (1941) 'The garden of forking paths' (trans. Donald A. Yates), in *Labyrinths.* New York: New Directions (1964); London: Penguin (1970).

Culler, J. (1983) *On Deconstruction. Theory and Criticism after Structuralism.* London: Routledge.

Delany, P. and Landow, G. (1991) 'Hypertext, hypermedia and literary studies: the state of the art', in P. Delany and G. Landow (eds). *Hypermedia and Literary Studies.* Cambridge, MA: MIT Press.

Derrida, J. (1967) *De la Grammatologie.* Paris: Les Editions de Minuir. *Of Grammatology* (1976). Translated by Gayatri Chakravorty Spivak. Baltimore: Johns Hopkins University Press.

Eco, U. (1962) *L'Opera Aperta.* Milan: Bompiani.

Genette, G. (1962) *Palimpsestos: la literatura en segundo grado.* Madrid: Taurus (1989).

Iser, W. (1971) 'Indeterminacy and the reader's response'. Quoted in K. M. Newton (ed.) (1988) *Twentieth Century Literary Theory: A Reader.* London: Macmillan Education.

Joyce, M. (1990) *afternoon, a story.* Computer disc. Cambridge, MA: Eastgate Press.

Joyce, M. (1995) *Of Two Minds: Hypertext Pedagogy and Poetics.* Ann Arbor: University of Michigan Press.

Landow, G. (1992) Hypertext: The Convergence of Contemporary Critical Theory and Technology. Baltimore and London: Johns Hopkins University Press.

Melrod, G. (1994) 'Digital Unbound'. *Details*, October, 162–5 and 199.

Nelson, T. H. (1981) *Literary Machines*. Swarthmore, PA: Self-published.

Pulverness, A. (1996) 'Outside looking in: teaching literature as dialogue'. *The Hermetic Garage*, Last Number but Three, pp. 69–85.

Yellowlees Douglas, J. (1993) *I Have Said Nothing*. Computer disc. *The Eastgate Quarterly Review of Hypertext*, **1** (2), Winter 1994.

Yellowlees Douglas, J. (1994) 'The quick and the dirty – reading *I Have Said Nothing*'. *The Eastgate Quarterly Review of Hypertext*, **1** (2), Winter 1994.

Comments on Part B

Brian Tomlinson

One of the main points which contributors to Part B seem to be making is that current materials are not fully exploiting the potential for facilitating learning of the resources available to them. They are not fully exploiting:

- the capacity of the brain to learn from experience and, in particular, the role that affect can play in this process
- the knowledge, awareness and experience which learners bring to the process of language learning
- the interests, skills and personality of the learners
- the knowledge, awareness and experience which teachers bring to the process of language learning
- the interests, skills and personality of the learners
- the visual, auditory and kinaesthetic aids available to materials developers
- the potential of literature and, in particular, of storytelling for engaging the learner

Another of the points which contributors to Part B seem to be making is that we are not matching what we know about language acquisition to what we are doing in materials development. For example, we know that repeating the same thing over and over again at the same time does little to help the learner, whereas varied repetition over a period of time is extremely valuable for language acquisition. Yet we still organize coursebooks into units, with each unit focusing on a specific language teaching point. And we know that affective engagement is vital for long-term learning but we continue to provide bland, neutral and trivial texts for learners to read and to listen to.

The third main point made frequently in Part B seems to me to be that we need to be more systematic, rigorous and principled in our approach to materials development. It is understandable that publishers push their writers to develop the type of materials they know they can sell and even that they clone the successful parts of best-selling materials. But the danger is that soon there will be a fixed model of what language materials contain and do, and any deviations from it will break the expectations of the users of the materials and will risk scepticism and rejection because of their divergence from an accepted norm. It is up to the writers, teachers, researchers and learners to show the publishers that it is possible to produce materials which fully exploit the resources of the learners, which match what we know about language acquisition, which connect to learners' lives and which can be commercially successful too.

My view is that we need funded experiments in which universities and publishers combine their expertise and resources to produce and trial innovative language learning materials. Such cooperation between companies and universities is commonplace in engineering and technology but extremely rare in education.

PART C

Developing Materials for Target Groups

14

Materials for Adults: 'I am No Good at Languages!' – Inspiring and Motivating L2 Adult Learners of Beginner's Spanish

Rosa-Maria Cives-Enriquez

Introduction

Experience has taught me that teaching a language to adult students whose main discipline (and perhaps primary interest/work) lies in a field other than languages can prove to be a difficult task. Examples of this occur widely throughout higher education and occasionally in industry. While studying a required 'service' language module, the adult students' level of motivation/enthusiasm is generally lower than is the case when working with subjects/areas deemed to be central to their programme of study, achievement of the desired award or area of specialism at work. To add to the problem, the materials available to adults are very often written for them on the assumption that they are linguists or have linguistic knowledge, and the objectives of the students do not necessarily meet with the coursebook's aims and objectives.

In order to produce and/or enhance materials that would arouse motivation in adult L2 learners, I make use of a combination of theories and models. For example, I use Dörnyei and Csizér's (1998b) '10+1 Commandments for Motivating L2 Learners', which proposes ways to integrate *intrinsic* and *extrinsic* motivation in the classroom. Intrinsic motivation is related to internal needs such as self-satisfaction at performing a task, whereas extrinsic motivation is related to obtaining extrinsic rewards such as marks and prizes. Intrinsic motivation is aimed at arousing natural curiosity and interest by setting optimal challenges in class, providing rich sources of stimulation and developing students autonomy. I also try to create/enhance materials that are thought-provoking, using certain aspects of EBL (Enquiry-Based Learning) (sometimes known as Problem-Based Learning, PBL) which concentrates on the analysis of problem situations as a basis for acquiring knowledge, skills and attitudes (Little and Ryan, 1998). In an EBL curriculum, students work in small groups, with the tutor facilitating, while they explore a practice-based scenario. Learning issues are identified and investigated by students using a range of resources. The potential benefits of an EBL curriculum are that students should develop an integrated body of knowledge, which is clearly relevant to their profession/discipline, while also developing a number of transferable skills. These include skills in information retrieval, problem-solving, team-working and negotiating. In addition, I make use of David Freemantle's (2001) 'Seven Steps to Stimulate Your Imagination', which is concerned with investing in a person's fundamental human needs in order to nurture and create productivity. He encourages us to create and concentrate on fantastic images of the future in order to achieve our desired dream.

In this chapter, I examine practices and activities that I employ in the classroom, allowing the adult student to develop a number of transferable skills, and the tutor to develop/enhance materials that suit the student needs and enthuse both the lecturer and the adult L2 learner. This, to my mind, is a crucial area of materials writing that is rarely spoken of or dealt with; but it is of utmost importance, because the facilitator has to be motivated by the materials that they are using in order to create an appropriate learning environment for the student.

My conclusion does not introduce any new theories in the field of *creating motivational materials for L2 students*, but it reinforces a point that has been made time and time again, that is, if students of any discipline enjoy what they are doing, they will at least make the effort to learn. Secondly, and perhaps a rather poignant remark, is that the facilitator also has to be motivated by the materials and activities in question.

The Emotional Conduit

For any learner of a foreign language, hearing and liking the rhythm of a foreign language, wanting to speak and make themselves understood and wanting to understand the language and culture in question are some of the stimuli that spark the motivational drive to incite or improve their performance in the FL (Spanish in this case). However, if we speak of language/vocabulary/words, it is not only these that create the stimulus but also the way in which they are used; left alone with its words (vocabulary) and structure (grammar), language is merely a string of two-dimensional expressions in the form of phrases, sentences, paragraphs, etc.

I truly believe that, to be effective in eliciting a response from students, the language stimulus has to be right and therefore has to be amplified by the third dimension of emotion:

- Words alone achieve nothing unless they are channelled along the right emotional conduit that connects with another person. In language teaching (or any teaching, for that matter), the learner not only has to feel at ease with the materials and tutor in order to reap the optimum educational benefits, but the language employed by the tutor/facilitator is just as important a motivational factor.
- In addition, from personal experience I feel that 'demotivated' learners feel uncomfortable with materials that are constantly probing them for that 'one' right answer.

- What I always try to do in my Spanish classes is *humanize* the classes, so that by the end of the course the students have an overall personal profile of myself, the tutor, and likewise, they, if they so wish, may impart information about themselves and their family, etc. The fact that I take an interest in them adds to their enthusiasm and, of course, almost everybody enjoys talking about themselves.
- I always ask beginners of Spanish to forget trying to express complex ideas and thoughts in the FL because they will get into a real muddle; instead, I often tell them to enjoy Spanish and pretend that they are a three-year-old acquiring language: I encourage them to explore, ask questions and invent new ones, to be bold and, most importantly, not to be afraid of making mistakes.
- Before we start anything I give them the following *Survival Tools* so that they are able to conduct the flow of information as and how they want. (After all, it is *their* Spanish Class.)

SURVIVAL TOOLS: BEGINNER'S SPANISH
- No entiendo = (I don't understand)
- Repite por favor = (Repeat please)
- ¿Como se dice *book* en español? = (How do you say *book* in Spanish?)
- ¿Como se dice *mesa* en inglés? = (How do you say *table* in English?)
- ¡Mas despacio por favor! = (Slow down please!)

- So, ultimately all communications act as stimuli competing to elicit a desired response. By delicately loading our language with feeling and spirit we can open up an emotional conduit, which connects with others and maximizes the likelihood of the desired response to be obtained; in this case, learning to communicate in Spanish at beginner's level.

How do I Approach This?

In order to enthuse and stimulate my students to become motivated I decided to adopt language teaching approaches, and strategies that differed from those employed in their other modules (i.e., their main discipline), and approached the Spanish curriculum topics in a different way.

I wanted to concentrate on the '10+1 Commandments', (Dörnyei and Csizér, 1998b), for motivating this particular group of L2 Spanish beginners (see list below):

The 10+1 Commandments for Motivating L2 Learners
1. Set a personal example with your own behaviour.
2. Create a pleasant, relaxed atmosphere in the classroom.
3. Present the tasks properly.
4. Develop a good relationship with the learners.

5.   Increase the learners' linguistic self-confidence.
6.   Make the language classes interesting.
7.   Promote learner autonomy.
8.   Personalize the learning process (increase learner involvement).
9.   Increase the learners' goal-orientedness.
10. Familiarize learners with the target culture.
+1: Create a cohesive learner group.
Source: Dörnye and Csizér, 1998b

This I combined with David Freemantle's (2001, Ch. 9) 'Seven Steps to Stimulate your Imagination' (see list below):

1.   Create the conditions for imagination
        Create a relaxing environment
        Refrain from judgement
        Use irrelevant stimuli
        Ensure irregularity and informality
        Be prepared to take risks
        Create a stimulating environment
        Be free of interruption
        Develop skills in imagination and application
        Work hard and practise
2.   Declare your aspiration
3.   Stimulate your imagination
4.   Select the image
5.   Validate the image
6.   Plan the practice
7.   Undertake an 'imaginative review'

I also introduced techniques from EBL (Enquiry Based Learning) – sometimes known as problem-based learning (PBL).

Ultimately I wanted to cater for students who very clearly had different learner needs. Despite them all attending, some *needed* to pass the module, some *wanted* to pass, but my aim/objective was for all of them to reap as much benefit and enjoyment as possible out of the sessions, irrespective of their needs.

I chose the above 'Model of Foreign Language Motivation' because it proposes ways to integrate *intrinsic* and *extrinsic* motivation in the classroom. As mentioned before, intrinsic motivation is related to internal needs such as self-satisfaction at performing a task, whereas extrinsic motivation is related to obtaining extrinsic rewards such as marks and prizes.

David Freemantle's 'Seven Steps to Stimulate the Imagination' (2001, Ch 9) are closely linked to Dörnyei and Csizér's 1998 model (in particular, 1.1–1.9) in that they are both concerned with investing in a person's fundamental human needs in order to nurture and create productivity. They differ in that the former refers to stimulating management in industry and the latter to adult students in the learning environment. Nevertheless, despite their apparent differences, the two are concerned with inspiring, stimulating and motivating people and are therefore inextricably linked.

Enquiry-Based Learning (EBL) was developed to overcome the drawbacks of a subject-based curriculum. The central focus of the approach is the analysis of problem situations as a basis for acquiring knowledge, skills and attitudes (Little and Ryan, 1988). It has been argued that this approach is in fact the natural way in which humans learn, that is by encountering problems which they have to solve in order to survive (Burrows, 1979). Successful implementation of the above does, however, require lecturers with sound facilitation skills, who believe that learning is more than acquiring knowledge, and that students are motivated to learn, and are able to retrieve and interpret information accordingly.

So, in order to apply the above, my first task was to find out how I was going to motivate the students, and the only way of finding out this information was to *ask* them the questions in Table 14.1 and *listen* to their response(s). By opening the channels of communication, we could then work as a team.

Table 14.1 Student Questionnaire
As well as asking the students the questions in 14.1, I made them aware of materials available to them in the language centre. I also introduced the different techniques that I would be using for language learning, be it classroom-based or

Table 14.1 Student Questionnaire

Questions	Responses
1. What are your reasons for learning Spanish?	Love Spanish, beautiful, sexy language
	Have a beautiful sister-in-law and would like to be able to speak to her and maybe find myself a nice Cuban lady
	Would be useful for my future career
	Open lots of opportunities
	Feel ignorant when I can't speak any other language other than English
	No other module that interested me and I hate French
	I was told that it was any easy module
	My friend did it last year with you and said that I had to come to your group because you're good

2. What you would, realistically, like to achieve by the end of the module?	To be able to make myself understood when I go on holiday
	To talk about myself, family, likes, dislikes
	To be fluent eventually but, for now, be able to understand the language
	To pass the module
	To speak to Spanish friends in Spanish
	To find a Spanish girlfriend

ICT (Information and Communication Technology) techniques which would be used as a reinforcement to classroom-based learning.

I announced at this point that we would *not* be using a specific textbook from start to finish, but that I would be sourcing materials from different textbooks and authentic databanks. I also stressed the fact that, although they sometimes might not have a hard copy or anything in print to work from, this did not mean that I had not prepared the lesson; in fact I would be using either authentic, adapted or my own materials to maximize their learning experience. The above methods would, in fact, add to the range/variety of materials being used with the aim of motivating and stimulating them to learn Spanish and thus maximize their learning experience.

Finally I asked them voluntarily to provide me with feedback about the course (questions posed, exercises covered, problems encountered, what they enjoyed and why), at regular intervals. I was determined to *listen* to them and work with them collaboratively to maximize their learning potential.

Adaptation of Models

The following are examples of how I have adapted Dörnyei and Csizér's (1998b) model and D. Freemantle's 'Seven Steps' to create the conditions for imagination in my classroom and thereby apply the *stimulus factor* to the language learning environment:

Encourage an Atmosphere whereby People are Relaxed and do not Feel Intimidated, Pressurized or Threatened

This allows learners to unleash their creativity. I introduce games at regular intervals in my teaching, making the language classes fun, interesting and seemingly effortless. I also give the students the opportunity to personalize an already existing game if they so wish, so that it can be adapted to their needs, giving them a real sense of achievement, and satisfaction.

So what exactly can a student learn/achieve through playing games? Well, let me take the example of *Scrabble* here, which is one that they, at beginner's level, seem to love. First and foremost, it is a hugely successful game worldwide, with over 100 million sets being sold in 121 countries. Secondly, it serves the purpose in mind, allowing the tutor to exploit language for entertainment:

- Unlike any other game, Scrabble draws heavily on morphological knowledge; in fact it is purely morphological, making it one of the most, if not *the* most word-based game in the market.
- Its multiplying premium squares provides an excellent opportunity for students to revise numbers, and I always encourage them to count out loud (though they seem to do it instinctively); when faced with difficulties I found them to be extremely helpful and encouraging towards each other.

For example:

Student A: [38] 'treinta y ... I've given you the "*thirty*" bit so you do the "*eight*" in Spanish.'
Student B: '¡ocho!'
Student A: 'Si ... yes ... I knew you knew it!'

This encourages team-support/spirit.

Scrabble is a fundamentally graphical affair, and finding words/verbs in the infinitive or conjugated forms in the dictionary allows the student(s) the autonomy to explore new words and their meanings; but from this wordsearch arise the following dilemmas:

- Do we accept abbreviations?
- When do we start accepting Anglicisms that are now so clearly part of the Spanish language/culture; for example 'e-mail', 'weekend', etc.?

One of the students suggested taking the above game to another level, that is, trying to construct a sentence/question with a given word, for an extra team point. If it were a question, it had to be answered by the opposite team. The above was agreed by the Spanish group and it was applied. It was amazing to see their collaborative use of:

¿Quién? Who?
¿Qué? What/Which?
¿Cuándo? When?
¿Dónde? Where?
¿Cómo? How?
¿Cuánto? How (much/many)?

I would agree that:

The pleasure of scrabble is in part born of a reversal of perceived linguistic constants. Using language for something other than communicating is in itself a joyous escapism. Scrabble simply converts such value into precise scores – made up of values attributed to each letter of the alphabet within a rigorously economic framework of scarcity. (Pires, 2001: 7)

The beautiful thing here is that the Spanish group in question actually turned the above into a communicative/interactive exercise, encouraging an exchange of ideas and information.

Finally, I agree with Guy Cook (2000: 204) when he says that language play 'involves simulation, competition, the creation of social networks and creative thinking' and that 'play – albeit with varying degrees of complexity – can take place at all levels of proficiency'.

Never Judge Students on their Initial Performance/Contribution However Minimal it may Appear

Allow students to explore their creativity and linguistic potential and assess them after they have been allowed to 'grow' and flourish. After all, 'Certain structures are acquired when learners are mentally ready for them' (Dulay *et al.*, 1982). The quiet ones have a way of pleasantly surprising me. In fact, in this particular group I had a particular student who had a stutter in English and felt very self-conscious of that fact in Spanish. I was able to work with her on vocalization techniques and eventually her stutter in English and Spanish almost disappeared as her confidence grew.

In the whole of their thirteen-week course I did not formally assess the students, but provided constant feedback and support and monitored their progress in the exercises that they did in class and individually at home. They compiled a dossier of all this work and eventually they were allowed to choose their six best pieces of work, making sure that at least four were concerning the basic skills (i.e., reading, writing, oral, aural). Finally I told them that they would have to sit an exam testing these four skills (reinforcing what they had been told at the beginning). By doing it this way, they had to produce the work in a non-threatening fashion and they felt that they had some control over their final mark by choosing six best pieces of work.

On the one hand, I sometimes feel that, in their efforts to monitor progress, tutors can sometimes become *obsessional overassessors*, who are in fact interfering with the learners' motivation and adding to their stress levels, and ultimately creating a negative learning environment. On the other, we are faced with institutionalized goals/aims/objectives that we have to comply with. *So what do we do?*

Be Irrational Now and Again

By doing something that does not comply with the norm, it will stimulate and surprise the group.

I took my brother's *Scalextric* into another class (London Business School) one day and asked a group of young executives to help me make up the kit; by the time we had finished, they had all sat on the floor, taken their jackets and ties off and got into two teams without me having to instruct them.

I then told them to take their respective cars round the track, making as many car noises as possible. At first I got the 'silent treatment', so I just told them to excuse me while I went to the ladies. I took my time and in fact observed them from a TV screen outside the classroom (out of sight), which allowed any passerby to tune into the respective training rooms. The executives tentatively began to 'play' and, when I returned fifteen minutes later, all I could hear was 'BRRR . . .', 'Phahh', 'ARGHH'; my exercise had served its purpose.

They were all able to vocalize and even roll their Rs in a relaxed, non-threatening environment! In fact, when it came to rolling their Rs in future lessons, many of them inadvertently reverted back to using the imaginary remote control in order to produce the sound.

In addition to the above example, offering a sweet or chocolate as a reward can stimulate learners to produce more, especially if they like the sweets! Or it simply serves the function of adding to the desired informality and fun element.

Be Informal and Personalize the Learner Experience

In another session we were discussing likes and dislikes and food was very much on the agenda, so I decided to ask them '*¿Quién tiene hambre/sed?*' ('Who's hungry/thirsty?'). They all said that they wanted tea/coffee/sandwiches/crisps etc. and spontaneously started to order things in Spanish; they appointed a class representative to go and fetch the items in questions and, when the person returned, they all ate and drank, and even shared some of their food.

This was my 'imagination' session, if you like, since I had gauged that the students were having an off day and I thus reacted to their mood. This then led the students to talk about their native cuisine, as the group was a multiethnic group. They were from Pakistan, Jamaica, Germany, Ghana, Turkey, Italy and Sheffield! It led to a wealth of information being exchanged and I, too, told them about Spanish food and how each region had its special dish and I compared it to Latin American food. At the next session we all bought one sample of a typical native dish and explained the ingredients and how it was cooked to the group.

Be Prepared to Take Risks

We delude ourselves that repetition will produce the same old successes. Repetition and routine are risky. Similarly, stepping out of routine by introducing imaginative ideas is also risky. (Freemantle, 2001: 178)

I decided to introduce an authentic (very short) Latin American poem to the beginner's class. The following text(s) was a combination of *adapted* authentic texts: an untouched poem and questions that I invented myself and used with my students to entice them to be creative and add to their repertoire of adjectives (adapted from Jarvis *et al.*, 1999: 76).

Ejercicio A: (Exercise A)
Lee el siguiente texto (Read the following text):

Alfonsina Storni (Argentina: 1892–1938)

Alfonsina Storni fue lo que hoy llamamos una feminista, una mujer de ideas liberales que luchó contra los prejuicios y las convenciones sociales de su época por conseguir una mayor libertad para la mujer. Su poesía es a veces torturada e intelectual. En su poesía se reflejan la inquietud de su vida. Pensaba que la mujer, a pesar de ser igual que el hombre, vive en una especie de esclavitud con respecto a éste. El final de la vida de Alfonsina Storni fue trágico; al saber que tenía cáncer escribió una breve composición poética que tituló 'Voy a morir' y se suicidó tirándose al mar.

Ejercicio B: (Exercise B)
Utiliza 5 adjetivos para describir la personalidad de Alfonsina. Puedes inventar los adjetivos o extirparlos del texto.
(Use five adjectives to describe Alfonsina's personality. You may invent five adjectives or lift them from the text.)

Ejercicio C: Preparación (Exercise C: Preparation)
* *Lee* **Cuadrados y angulos** *en voz alta*
* (Read *Squares and Angles* out loud [this was suggested by the students])
* *¿Qué te sugiere a ti las palabras* **Cuadrados y angulos**?
(What do the above words *Squares and Angles* suggest to you?)

Casas enfiladas°, casas enfiladas,	*in a line*
casas enfiladas,	
cuadrados° cuadrados, cuadrados,	*squares*
casas enfiladas,	*soul*
Las gentes ya tienen el alma° cuadrada,	
ideas en fila°	*en . . . in a row*
y ángulo en la espalda;	
yo misma he vertido° ayer una lágrima°,	*he . . . has shed/a tear*
Dios mío, cuadrada.	

(*De El dulce daño*)

Ejercicio D: Dime (Exercise D: Tell me)
1. *Según Alfonsina Storni, ¿cómo es el alma de la gente?*
   (According to Alfonsina, 'what are the peoples' souls like?)
2. *¿Cómo ve el mundo Alfonsina Storni?*
   (How does Alfonsina see the world?)

3. *¿Qué crítica hace Alfonsina Storni en su poema?*
   (What criticism does Alfonsina make in her poem?)
4. *¿Qúe nos trata decir la autora de su mundo?*
   (What is the author trying to tell us about her world?)

Ejercicio E: Idea Final (Exercise E: Final Thought)
¿Te gustaría producir tu propia poesía en español? Inténtalo solo/a o en group.
(Would you like to create your own poetry in Spanish? Try individually or in a group.)

Admittedly, two out of the class of nine students decided not to accept the offer and asked whether they could work collaboratively on other exercises.

Create a Stimulating Environment

An imaginative environment will stimulate the imagination. (Freemantle, 2001: 179)

One of the German students was a Harry Potter fanatic and asked whether she could give a brief presentation on the above, using visuals. She wanted to read to the class, so I suggested she distributed the typed script to the class. She had approached me beforehand to make sure that what she was writing made sense. She did not come to see me personally but sent me an e-mail saying,

Rosa, mando mi historia de Harry Potter en el 'attachment'. Puedes mirar y comentar y mandar. Gracias, Asita.

[Translation: 'Rosa, I'm sending my Harry Potter story in the attachment. Could you look and comment and send. Thanks, Asita.']

Although the above message is not one hundred per cent grammatically correct (nouns and pronouns missing and overuse of 'y', i.e., 'and'), she was able to make herself understood. I did not send the message back 'corrected', but she asked me in the session how she could have improved upon her writing and we, as a group, gave her some suggestions.

Another Sports Science student suggested that we all take part in a circuit class that he had to present to his fellow students. He suggested that we go one step further and he would give us instructions in Spanish. So here we were reinforcing the numbers, (reflexive) verbs and giving instructions using set phrases in Spanish ('*Tenemos que*' + infinitive = 'we have to' + infinitive) as well as remembering the parts of the body; expressing likes and dislikes ('*me gusta/no me gusta*' + infinitive) and 'my *** hurts' ('*me duele*' + part of the body), etc. Luckily, all of the group bar one member decided to participate; the one who did not participate watched from afar, but I saw her out of the corner of my eye lifting her arm and counting on her fingers.

Be Free of Interruption

Allow students to 'take time out' to think about things. Continuous prompting is unnecessary and I feel that it interrupts their thought process. Allow them to ask each other questions and talk amongst themselves. Give them the freedom to think and the opportunity to ask questions. For example, in listening comprehension, I always allow them to listen first to the text and to respond to questions once they have familiarized themselves with it.

What I always aim to do in preparing listening comprehension materials is to keep students' interests and experience firmly in mind, so that the language encountered clearly reinforces the language that has been learnt in the past. This also raises their confidence levels at being able to identify language and allows them to do well.

Develop Skills in Imagination and Application

Imagination requires two skills. First, the skill to create the fantasy and drag the pertinent image from it. Second, the skill to bring the image to life. (Freemantle, 2001: 180)

All the students in the Spanish class had a fantasy in mind when they walked into the classroom: whether it be the thought of hearing themselves speak Spanish fluently; getting a Spanish/Latin American girlfriend; being able to appreciate poetry and literature; or, just to feel empowered and take away the 'ignorant' factor by understanding some Spanish when they are abroad with family and friends, is enough stimulus to get one started.

I therefore think that it is up to the tutor somehow to bring the image to life; for example, at the end of their semester and exams, the whole group suggested we celebrate, so I recommended a *tapas* bar in London and gave them directions as to how to get there in Spanish:

*'El Sábado 30 de julio, vamos a cenar a **la finca** en londres. Quedaremos a las 7.30 en la finca. La estación de metro mas próxima es Angel.*
Hasta el Sábado!
P.D. Si hay algun problema:
***Mi Móbil: 07957**_____, **Mi número de Casa:**_____, **Mi Email:**_____*

They all arrived on time at the bar. There were two who arrived at 8.00 pm without an apology in sight, but I just put it down to cultural differences, because I knew enough about their respective cultures to know that it had not been rude or intentional.

We all had a great evening. They ordered their drinks and food in Spanish; asked me for help in Spanish; and later we went to the salsa bar upstairs, and one of our students even exchanged telephone numbers with a Colombian girl. So, in a way, all their individual dreams and aspirations were being fulfilled by allowing them to absorb themselves totally in the Spanish language, culture and environment.

On another occasion (in the classroom), the students asked me to watch a Spanish film, which I was a bit nervous and hesitant to introduce at this stage. Instead of denying them the pleasure, I decided to take the risk and allowed them to watch a film that is very beautiful but could also be very fast in parts; the film is entitled '*Como agua para chocolate*' ('Like Water for Chocolate'). Rather than allowing them to listen to the dialogue, I asked them to write the script based on the body language. (I chose a scene that was very emotive, in which a young chap was declaring his undying love to a young lady. In the next scene, you see the mother and daughters in the kitchen preparing food and finally a tense moment when the mother denies the daughter's hand in marriage, because she is the youngest of them all, and offers her eldest sister as an alternative.)

I asked them to consider the following:

A: *Imagínate que eres español/a o latinoamericano/a. ¿como escribirías el guión para esta película, tomando en cuenta lo que hemos estudiado sobre los españoles/lation-americanos y sus costumbres?*

(Imagine that you are Spanish/Latin American. How would you write the script for this film, bearing in mind what you have studied about Spanish / Latin American customs?)

B: *¿Cómo reaccionaría una persona(s) de tu cultura?*

(How would someone from your culture react?)

The exercise provided a very fruitful session in which not only did we explore the Spanish language and culture, but it also gave me an insight into how they, being from different cultures, thought and reacted.

The fact that *I wanted* to learn about them made them feel good.

Finally, as a trainer and tutor I am constantly trying to explore different ways in which to enthuse my students and encourage them to use technology-enhanced language learning programmes. Unfortunately, to date I am disappointed with what I have encountered and am reluctant to recommend them unless I am happy that they do achieve a learning objective. With the huge advance in memory capabilities and access to the Internet and World Wide Web, the language tutor and learner has at his/her disposal a vast array of resources.

Data mining and extraction, dictionaries, encyclopaedias, realia and other items are so freely available that the problem has actually shifted from how to find the resources available to how to sift through the enormous quantity of sometimes useless information on offer, and how to use it within the confines of the curriculum/course outlines and restrictions of the copyright and intellectual property laws. (Bangs, 2000: 38)

We, as a group, found a particular site (*www.ilovelanguages.com*) which has a clear and lively layout (capturing our attention!), with links to a wealth of information and facts for dozens of languages. I found that both I and my students were absorbed for a considerable time. However, I would only recommend this website as reinforcement and enhancement to already studied grammar points or vocabulary; this can by no means replace the tutor. Although it offered the student the opportunity to take a stroll through a virtual community, for example, it failed to produce the stimulus that we, as a group, were looking for and there was not really an appropriate level of interactivity or feedback. Often when feedback is provided it is exclusively of the *extrinsic* variety (*Muy Bien* (very good), *Bien* (good), *¡Inténtalo de Nuevo!* (Try again!)), rather than the *intrinsic* form where the feedback is part of the activity and is in the hands of the learner.

My opinion is that feedback must be rich, readily available and useful to the learner, so we decided to turn the above exercise into a structured learning exercise, where I took on the role of guide and praised them for doing well and/or explained questions/queries; the above exercise thereby provided the students with the level of intrinsic and extrinsic motivation that they were originally seeking.

Thus, from the perspective of the tutor, I have concluded that very few materials produced offer the necessary level of interactivity, feedback and adaptability.

On the plus side, it is often said that using ICT can:

- Improve outreach to student bodies
- Improve productivity in learning
- Offer appropriate levels of feedback
- Offer individual learning experiences
- Save on some costs

On the negative side, it is also suggested that it can:

- Engender remoteness
- Be difficult to control/access/follow
- More often than not offer poor feedback or none at all
- Be difficult to individualize
- Be costly to create and once created, buy certain packages. (Bangs, 2000: 38–41)

While the above site was interesting from a visual/representational point of view, I feel that all too often what is seen are learning materials that can allow a learner to get 'lost in cyberspace'. Too many programmes offer language learning courses which make little, if any, attempt at structuring the language to offer a meaningful progression for the learner. Context is obviously of vital importance for the language learner and his/her learning process, and perhaps the main challenge is to enable the learner to obtain the appropriate degree of 'authentic' language alongside the opportunity to navigate within and interact in the foreign language environment.

So I believe that, although many programmes are being piloted and some more sophisticated programmes will undoubtedly be created in the future, this situation is unlikely to improve greatly in the immediate or near future.

Work Hard and Practise

The above, I guess, applies to both tutors and their students, the saying, 'Achievement is one per cent inspiration and ninety-nine per cent perspiration', applies to any profession. The difference between one tutor and another is not just the power of the imagination, thought and planning process, but the drive with which the above is realized to achieve a standard of teaching which is far superior to any other. The image of perfection that we have in our minds and endeavour to achieve can only be attained by sheer hard work.

Conclusion

As you can see from the chapter, I do not introduce any new theories in the field of 'Creating motivational materials for L2 adults'. I simply wanted to reinforce the following points that a student, irrespective of age, sex, nationality, etc., (no matter how motivated/demotivated) will depend on the tutor to stimulate him/her to learn.

I believe that this can only be done if:

1. The tutor concerned is enjoying what he/she is doing (and therefore motivated at potentially creating a group of linguists, be it beginners or advanced), and employing techniques and stimuli that will enhance and inspire a motivational learning environment.
2. I believe that, in the classroom situation, we are all vulnerable, and if we relay that message to students they will respect us and feel more at ease in our company. I truly believe that the classroom situation is and should be an explorational forum for the tutor and students alike. (After all, no two sessions are alike and it is a constant learning process for all of us involved, whether we are instructing or being instructed). We should be ourselves and feel free to inspire and feel inspired by our students. If you feel passionately about what you do, and I do about the Spanish language, it will show, and that energy is almost contagious; I constantly gain my motivation, inspiration and spontaneity from my students as it really is a team effort. Having said this, examining the motivational process is a complex issue/subject.

A point that I hope has been reinforced in this chapter is that language learning does not occur as a result of the transmission of facts about a language or from a succession of rote memorization drills. It is the result of opportunities for meaningful interactions with others in the target language.

All I can say is that I am in complete agreement with Graham's concluding words:

If there is a message I wish to convey with what has been presented in this chapter, that message is that classroom motivational life is complex. No single word or principle such as reinforcement or intrinsic motivation can possibly capture this complexity. (Graham, 1994: 31–48)

I feel that, ultimately, the stimulus of language (i.e., mother tongue and/or Foreign Language) is a very powerful one and it should be used to motivate and be motivated, and aid us in producing our desired end result.

References

Alison, J. (1993) *Not Bothered? Motivating Reluctant Language Learners in Key Stage 4*. London: CILT.

Bangs, P. (2000) 'Technology enhanced language learning'. *The Linguist*, **39** (2), 38–41.

Brophy, J. (1998) *Motivating Students to Learn*. Boston, MA: McGraw-Hill.

Burrows, H. S. (1979) 'The rationale and structure of problem-based learning'. *The Learner*, **7**, 39–41.

Cook, G. (2000) *Language Play, Language Learning*. Oxford: Oxford University Press.

Dörnyei, Z. (1994) 'Motivation and motivating in the foreign language classroom'. *Modern Language Journal*, **78**, 273–84.

Dörnyei, Z. (1998) 'Motivation in second and foreign language learning'. *Language Teaching*, **31** (3), 117–35.

Dörnyei, Z and Otto, I. (1998a) 'Motivation in action: a process model of L2 motivation'. *Working Papers in Applied Linguistics*. London: Thames Valley University, **4**, 43–69.

Dörnyei, Z. and Csizér, K. (1998b) 'Ten commandments for motivating language learners: results of an empirical study'. *Language Teaching Research*, **2**, 203–29.

Dulay, H., Burt, M. and Krashen, S. (1982) *Language Two*. New York: Oxford University Press.

Fallows, S. and Ahmet, K. (1999) *Inspiring Students: Case Studies in Motivating the Learner*. London: Kogan Page.

Freemantle, D. (2001) *The Stimulus Factor – The New Dimension in Motivation*. Harlow: Pearson.

Graham, S. (1994) 'Classroom motivation from an attributed perspective', in H. F. O'Neil, J. R. and M. Drillings (eds) *Motivation: Theory and Research*. Hillsdale, NJ: Lawrence Erlbaum, pp. 31–48.

Jarvis, A., Lebredo, R. and Mena Ayllón, F. (1999) *Aventuras Literarias* (5th edn.). Boston, MA: Houghton Mifflin Company.

Little, P. and Ryan, G. (1991) 'Educational changes through problem-based learning'. *Australian Journal of Advanced Nursing*, **5** (4), 31–5.

O'Malley, M., Chamot, A. and Kupper, L. (1989) 'Listening comprehension strategies in second language acquisition'. *Applied Linguistics*, **4**.

Pires, M. (2001) 'Scrabble: a linguistic perspective'. *The Linguist*, **40** (1), 4–7.

Tomlinson, B. (1998) *Materials Development in Language Teaching*. Cambridge: Cambridge University Press.

Websites

www.3.enciclonet.com
www.ilovelanguages.com
www.linguanet.org.uk
www.maseducativa.com

15

Materials for Beginners

Carlos Islam

Introduction

Jill Johnson (1995) in her article, 'Who Needs Another Coursebook?' criticized second language learning beginner coursebooks for being all the same in terms of thematic topics and their approach to language learning and teaching. She suggested that commercial materials are overly influenced by factors connected to classroom management and class dynamics rather than what we know about language acquisition. She was especially concerned with the emphasis on talking in the target language from day one of learning a language.

My intuition, gained from a number of years of teaching EFL/ESL in various countries, tells me Jill Johnson has a point. So, on a recent trip to the bookstore, I picked up three beginner coursebooks: *New Interchange* (CUP), *Atlas* (Heinle and Heinle) and *Headstart* (OUP), and took them back to my office for an analysis of their content and pedagogy. All three coursebooks are written by successful ELT authors and professionals. *Headstart* is written by Liz and John Soars, the *Headway* authors, in collaboration with Briony Beaven; *New Interchange* is by Jack Richards along with Jonathan Hull and Susan Proctor; and *Atlas* by David Nunan. All the coursebooks are aimed at young adult and adult beginner learners. *New Interchange* and *Atlas* are marketed in East and South-East Asia whereas *Headstart* is targeted at a European audience.

A book at a time, I listed topics, read the descriptions explaining the approaches taken to learning and categorized activities to get a sense of methodology and the authors' beliefs about language learning.

Current Convention

Content

I expected that there would be some topic overlap between these books but I was surprised at how many of the same topics appeared in the books. *New Interchange* and *Atlas* even shared the same unit title, 'Do You Like Jazz?' for their units on music, movies and entertainment. Not counting the review units, *Atlas* has twelve units and all except one of its topics are replicated in *New Interchange*'s sixteen units. Because of *Headstart*'s explicitly grammatical focus, it has a couple of unit topics that *New Interchange* does not include (likes and dislikes, and objects and adjectives) and it also features a unit on seasons and months, but its nine other themes are covered in *New Interchange*. *New Interchange*, by the way, is the most recent edition of *Interchange*, which was first published in 1990, and its only topic change is the addition of Unit 16. Table 15.1 is a list of *Atlas*'s, *New Interchange*'s and *Headstart*'s topics.

Table 15.1 Topics included in *Atlas, New Interchange* and *Headstart*

Atlas	New Interchange	Headstart
1. introductions, greetings, names, nationalities, friends	introductions, greetings, names, countries, nationalities	introductions, greetings
2. families, addresses, descriptions	occupations, school, daily schedules	countries, nationalities
3. occupations, routines	clothing, shopping, spending habits, prices	jobs, occupations
4. people, descriptions, clothing	music, movies, TV, entertainers, dates	family
5. review	families, family life	food and drink
6. movies, entertainment, leisure, sport	sports, exercise, routine	objects and adjectives
7. food, drink, eating habits, parties	weekend, free time, vacations	leisure activities
8. ability, hobbies	neighbourhood, stores, housing	likes and dislikes
9. vacations, dates, plans, necessity	people descriptions, clothing	daily routines
10. review	past experiences, unusual events	houses, rooms and furniture
11. hotels, travel, restaurants, food and drink	cities, home towns, countries	prices in shops and cafés
12. the weekend, advice, suggestions	health problems, medications, remedies	seasons and months
13. horoscopes, predictions, plans	food and restaurants	

14. reasons, instructions, work	world geography, countries, the environment
15.	invitations, leisure time activities, telephone messages
16.	life changes, hopes and plans for the future

The topics used in these coursebooks include vocabulary and functions that are potentially useful to language learners from any culture. They can be especially useful to those learners who need quick exposure to survival language skills. However, a large part of the problem with these established beginner coursebooks, and EFL/ESL textbooks in general, is that there is no real choice between them.

What happens to the learner who repeats a course at this level or is returning to the level after an absence from language learning? Add to this the fact that coursebooks at higher levels mostly repeat the same topics. In these situations, teachers do not have much choice but to design another lesson around 'your family' or 'your leisure activities'. When I set out to look for materials that could provide my learners with exposure to alternative more engaging topics, I am forced to turn to supplementary materials, or spend time I do not have creating my own material.

No publisher, teacher, researcher or materials writer would deny that the potential for language acquisition is enhanced when language input is relevant, significant, salient, engaging and of interest to the learner. The topics presented in *Headstart*, *New Interchange* and *Atlas* may fulfil these criteria the first time round for some learners but the second and third presentation of the same topics must significantly diminish any potential for acquisition to take place.

Publishers research their target markets and say, 'this is what the teachers want', and they are right. I also believe, however, that teachers and learners want this and more. They want topics that allow for imagination, creation and affective engagement as well as topics that cover everyday survival language.

There is a place and need for at least one coursebook that offers completely different topics and themes. A beginner coursebook manuscript my colleague, Chris Mares, and I are currently developing for a US publisher includes unit topics such as *Strange Days*, *The Way We See Things* and *The Unexpected*. The feedback we had from the six reviewers the publisher surveyed was encouraging:

> The topics seem very interesting. The topics sounds interesting ... This unit is entitled Strange Days. I found the unit itself quite strange. I do not fully understand some of the titles. I would be interested in learning more about ... The topics used in the text are a bit unusual. The topics listed in the prospectus

seem interesting ... I think it is difficult to say what will be interesting to students, but as long as the topics are interesting to the teacher, she will be more likely to make them interesting for the students.

A publisher's concern with making coursebook content and activities transparent and easy to use is understandable, but teachers know better than anyone that the language and activities need to be consistently engaging in order for the learner to pay attention and to create the conditions for acquisition to take place.

Approach and Methodology

Like most people searching for clues to a book's design, I read the promotional blurb on the back covers before looking at each unit's exercises in detail. The authors of *Headstart* write, '*Headstart* breaks new ground by confronting realistically and honestly the problems that beginners face, whilst at the same time drawing judiciously on current methodologies and approaches.'

In Unit 1 of *Headstart* nearly half the exercises only require the learner to listen and repeat and the remaining exercises are mostly controlled practice. The presentation cycle of the unit almost exclusively involves listen and repeat exercises as would an audiolingual course, and the function to be practised is *greetings* which, as we have seen, is very conventional for EFL beginner coursebooks. The listen and repeat pattern is followed throughout the book with very little variation, so where is the 'newly broken ground' and 'current methodology and approach'? In their introduction, the Soars make reference to 'manageable communicative activities' which is an allusion to the controlled pair work exercises in the book designed to practise structures presented earlier in the unit. I would argue that *Headstart* is very teachable, and that many novice teachers would find its methodology transparent and well structured, but it is not communicative (see Thompson, 1996, for a discussion of communicative language teaching), ground-breaking or new.

Like *Headstart*, more than half of the exercises in Unit 1 of *New Interchange* are listen and repeat or read and practise activities and the rest are tightly controlled comprehension questions or discussions with predetermined questions and answers. In its blurb, *New Interchange* says it 'features high interest topics, [has a] focus on both accuracy and fluency and a multi-skills syllabus ... The underlying philosophy is that language is best learned when used for meaningful communication.'

I had already heard David Nunan, author of *Atlas* and ex-president of TESOL, articulate some of his thoughts about teaching and learning in a skilful presentation given at the TESOL 2000 convention in Vancouver, Canada. He told the audience seven stories about six language learners and one grammatical morpheme he had taught. His stories echoed and supported much of what has been written about in SLA research papers over the past 30 years as well as the long-sustained views held by many about language learning and teaching.

The stories of ... dramatize the asymmetrical relationship between teaching and learning. They also illustrate the idea that language development is not linear but organic. Learners do not learn one thing perfectly one at a time; they learn numerous things imperfectly all at once, and their understanding and usage evolve through complex, interrelated sets of stages (Nunan, 1999). The stories begin to provide possible answers to Allwright's (1984) question: 'Why don't learners learn what teacher's teach?' ... In short learners do not learn what teachers teach in a linear, additive fashion ... learning will be enhanced if learners are given opportunities to contribute their own ideas, experiences and feelings to the learning process and if the curriculum reflects the fact that language acquisition is complex, organic and inherently unstable. As Stevick (1989) reminded us, we should beware of building a system of teaching around one type of learner.

Given Nunan's views on language learning and teaching, I expected *Atlas* to be radically different in approach from *Headstart*. Where *Headstart*'s activities mostly practise short pieces of simplified dialogue and text, the language presented in *Atlas* would be more complex and longer. Inferring from Nunan's speech, it would be reasonable to expect that the activities in *Atlas* would be less controlled and allow for learner creativity instead of the listen and repeat exercises found in *Headstart*. Rather than a behavioural approach to learning, where learners mimic the teacher focusing on form and accuracy, *Atlas* would emphasize a wide, varied and engaging input focusing on meaning, fluency and exposure.

Again, almost half (16 out of 35) of the first unit's activities are either listen and repeat, read and repeat or write and practise exercises. The rest test comprehension, test to see if the learner can distinguish between different sounds and all exercises have right and wrong answers. The language is predictable in content, simplistic and is used explicitly to present and practise linguistic forms.

Although each book differs in degree, they all follow a behavioural approach to language learning, borrow extensively from audiolingual pedagogy and focus on form and accuracy with very little attention given to meaning and fluency.

Oral Production

A problem with all beginner material, not just the three books reviewed above, lies with the idea that students want to learn the language to speak it, so from day one that is what we try to do, teach learners to speak. However, as beginner learners do not actually know much about the language or anything of the language, they have to mimic the teacher or the tape and slowly build up competence in the target language by rote learning. This approach may create the illusion of satisfying a false learner expectation of being able to say something meaningful in the target language from the first day, but in fact probably damages the learner's prospects of becoming fluent in the target language within a reasonable period of time.

If materials writers and publishers can learn anything from second language acquisition research, it is that language acquisition takes time and that during the initial period of acquiring a language the learner is silent. That is, the language learner is unable to produce any real meaningful language (see Krashen, 1981, 1982; Ellis, 1994). If we decide to go against this principle of acquisition and encourage learners to speak in the target language immediately, we run the risk of triggering off a series of disruptive consequences to learning.

When learners are forced to speak in the target language before they are ready, or, in other words, before they have acquired enough language to do so, they will suffer from cognitive overloading (see Colvin-Clark and Taylor, 1994; Johnson, 1995). As Johnson (1995) points out, the beginner learner is so 'busy trying to identify sounds, word boundaries, decode and recall word or phrase meanings and hold it all in working memory' that there is very little or no processing energy left for language production. I am arguing that these processes have to become automatized (see McLaughlin *et al.*, 1983; McLaughlin, 1987) before learners are able to devote enough spare processing energy to meaningful production. If these processes are not automatized, learners cannot access what has been acquired and if production is forced before enough language has been acquired, there is nothing to access. Thus, learners are again asked to overload their cognitive circuits.

An insistence on premature production can cause considerable affective problems for the learner too. Confident, competent and interesting people outside of the language learning class 'can easily despair at being confronted by failure in handling such seemingly trivial tasks. Where the course material is reduced to even simpler transactions to avoid such overload, I feel bored, if not insulted; alternatively, if I go along with this step-by-step approach, I'm constantly feeling it will take forever to function as myself' (Johnson, 1995). These sentiments, I feel, are echoed all over the world in classrooms where conventional beginners EFL/ESL textbooks are used. Learners start off with a negative experience to learning the target language, which in turn distances them from the language and acts as a barrier to effective learning. A resistance to acquiring the language can develop either consciously or unconsciously (see Dulay *et al.*, 1982, for an explanation of the Affective Filter Hypothesis) as a result of this initial and often continued negative experience of language learning.

Learner Styles

It seems to me that conventional beginners textbooks are strongly biased towards the learning preferences of analytic, studial, left brain learners at the expense of global, experiential, right brain learners (see Ellis, 1989; Oxford and Anderson, 1995, for a discussion of these learning styles). This approach that beginners' textbooks take of emphasizing an analytic, step-by-step linear method to the learning of linguistic structures is detrimental for two reasons. Firstly, there is a strong body of research which suggests that the majority of EFL/ESL learners are positioned towards the global, experiential, right brain end of the learning style cline (see Reid, 1987, for a discussion of learner style research findings). Thus we can infer that the majority of learners are being marginalized by the current set of beginners' books. Moreover, perceptual learning style research overwhelmingly suggests that most learners prefer kinaesthetic input over auditory and visual forms of language input. None of the beginners' coursebooks I have seen accommodate this type of learner, however. All the input is mostly auditory, with few clues to meaning, or visual with very short snippets of written text. Catering for kinaesthetic learners would involve learners experiencing and interacting with the language through physical action rather than memorizing and analysing the language. Secondly, research evidence also suggests that the ability of students to employ multiple learning styles results in greater classroom success (Reid, 1987), concluding that emphasizing a particular style of learning is not the most effective approach.

Coursebook Sales

It is not surprising that the conventional EFL beginner's textbook sells when there is nothing else to challenge it. Moreover, most teachers need a textbook to base their courses around because they are either too busy or lack the experience to produce their own material for every lesson of a whole course.

The commercial coursebooks I have reviewed in this chapter are very good at clearly presenting essential vocabulary and simple linguistic structures, as well as providing user-friendly lessons and progression. These books are valuable teaching tools and are successful but clearly cater for one style of learning and teaching.

By providing an alternative style of coursebook, publishers would not only capture a market made up of teachers who are willing to experiment and who are tired of the conventional, but teachers, students and institutions will also be encouraged to buy more materials. I believe the established coursebooks will continue to be purchased alongside books that provide different content matter and an alternative pedagogy and that these books would be used to supplement each other as needed.

Alternative Beginner Materials and Coursebooks

A Change of Approach

The primary problem of EFL beginners' coursebooks is their obsession with immediate language production and its associated cognitive and affective issues for language learners. Common sense would dictate that the immediate objectives of any beginner's language course should be the development of learners' language competence via a comprehension approach to learning.

Comprehension approaches to language learning are based on the premiss that conversational fluency will develop as the result of learning to understand a language (Swaffar and Woodruff, 1978; Winitz, 1981). Nobody would argue against the fact that native speakers of a language do not explicitly learn the grammatical rules of the utterances they produce but they rely on their tacit knowledge of the language. So why do so many EFL/ESL courses concentrate on learning and memorizing rules, patterns and structures? Moreover, why do those courses take the stance that the development of language competence is a linear process where learners are presented with one rule, demonstrate that it has been learned by producing it and are then presented with the next rule.

Winitz (1981) persuasively argues for a non-linear approach to language learning. He takes the position that the interrelationships among components of a grammatical system are complex and great in number. Acquisition of a particular grammatical element requires an understanding of many, often distantly related structures. Thus, he reasons that correct usage of a particular grammatical element cannot be acquired until a large part of the grammar of a language is understood. This truth, seemingly evident to most language teachers and successful learners, is in contrast to the linear system adopted by conventional EFL textbooks, which emphasize the mastery in production for each unit of language presented.

Language instruction grounded in a comprehension approach, if done thoughtfully, can avoid the problems of overloading and stress often involved in conventional beginner level textbooks. Furthermore, a comprehension approach to learning is inherently non-linear and, depending on how it is practised, would cater for a majority of learners, in that it provides a global experiential emphasis to learning.

I do not think this kind of approach would be considered controversial or particularly innovative outside ELT coursebook publishing. Since the mid-1980s a number of US university ESL programmes have adopted an approach called Focal Skills (see Hastings, 1995, for an explanation and assessment of the focal skills approach). The basic principle of this approach is that learners are exposed to comprehensible input with no production requirement until they are ready to go onto a reading programme and then writing. Oral production is brought in gradually and is not forced. Typically in these programmes, a learner who is tested as a beginner spends at least three months just being exposed to language mostly produced by their teacher before they see any written text or are required to speak. The language is made accessible through actions, pictures, films and video where the teacher explains what is happening (learners are not expected to understand dialogue) and realia.

An Ageing Methodology for New Materials

Total Physical Response, which has been around for over thirty years now (see Asher, 1977, and Larsen-Freeman, 1986, for a detailed explanation of TPR methods and techniques), is a learning method grounded in a comprehension approach. There have been many reported successful learning outcomes with the use of TPR (Asher, 1969, 1972, 1977, 1994; Sano, 1986; Tomlinson, 1994), but it has failed to make it into mainstream coursebooks or classrooms. Reasons for this could be that it is seen as difficult to reproduce TPR classes in a textbook format and that TPR does not resemble traditional ideas of academic pursuit, that is, there is little studial work done in the way of writing or analysis. A typical TPR class following Asher's model consists of the teacher giving instructions (initially only using the imperative form of verbs) for the learners to carry out. TPR courses start with simple commands such as 'stand up', 'sit down' and 'walk', then gradually move on to commands such as 'stand up, point at the door and then walk to the door' and then go on to more complicated commands such as 'if the person to your right is wearing something blue, give your pen to the person on your left. However, if the person on your right isn't wearing anything blue, then give your pen to the person on your right.'

As Asher (1977) points out, this method is successful because it caters for the majority of learners who seem to be kinaesthetic in their preferred perceptual learning styles as well as global and experiential in their general styles. These are what are known as right brain learning processes, that is, kinaesthetic, global and experiential learning are processed in the brain's right hemisphere. TPR, then, might seem to be the answer for my complaints about conventional beginners' textbooks. However, it is only part of the answer. Although TPR does address the problems of cognitive overloading, linear progression and only catering for analytic learners and its associated affective issues, it does not cater for learners who do have a preferred analytical learning style nor for the analytical side of global learners. After all, none of these style categories is absolute, rather, they are extremes of different clines on which all learners fall somewhere between the extremes. It is also worth remembering that learners undoubtedly benefit from 'style stretching' (Reid, 1987): learning through styles that are not necessarily their own preferred dominant styles. This, I think, is an important failing of Asher's TPR method and a significant factor as to why its popularity has not spread into mainstream courses and textbooks.

TPR Plus

Tomlinson (1994) developed Asher's TPR method into a more complete framework, which he calls TPR Plus. Tomlinson claims that TPR Plus is an approach rather than a method as there are no set procedures, unlike Asher's model of TPR. A class using the TPR Plus approach always includes a TPR phase, the objective of which would be to provide a 'relaxed, comprehensible base for other activities in the lesson' (Tomlinson, 1994). In Tomlinson's model, the TPR phase is not restricted to teacher commands directing students to perform actions. It also involves 'dramatisation of stories told by the teacher, playing of games instructed by the teacher, cooking of dishes from recipes given by the teacher, painting of murals instructed by the teacher and searches for hidden bounty directed by the teacher'. The plus phase of the approach typically involves some kind of extension of the TPR-type activity such as 'writing the end of a story partially dramatised; devising, teaching and writing the rules for new games; writing recipes for variations of a typical dish; dramatising the stories depicted in murals; writing clues for treasure hunts'. In TPR Plus it is also common for the teachers to give their script to the students for language awareness work, but only after the TPR and TPR Plus phases. This approach, then, satisfies the learner's need for an analytical experience of the language without disturbing their global experience. The objective of the language awareness work is to facilitate future language acquisition by highlighting features of language with the hope that it will be noticed in future language input.

TPR Plus has the potential of being able to incorporate pragmatic functions of language into its instruction, which is something that could not be done so easily with Asher's original model for TPR, and is something which would be a complete innovation for EFL coursebooks, especially at beginner's level. This is an aspect of language that is fundamental in comprehending communication in language but is nearly always excluded from foreign language teaching. In the language awareness phases of the classes (bearing in mind that language awareness would not start immediately but only after students have reached a certain comprehension threshold; Asher claims twenty hours is enough TPR instruction for students to be able to start talking, although reading and analysis of language may need to be delayed even further, unless it were done in the first language), a part of the focus could be dedicated to analysing pragmatic functions of language. This could be introduced later in the course during TPR phases. Students would have to respond appropriately according to the context in which the utterances are made, i.e., the relationship between speaker and interlocutors, previous events or attitudes of the participants involved in the communication.

An Example of Alternative Materials

Below is the second of a four-unit proposal my colleague, Chris Mares, and I developed for a beginner level course for university or college ESL students in the USA. We believe that these materials offer a real alternative to coursebooks such as *Headstart, Atlas* and *New Interchange* in both thematic content and approach. Although these materials include speaking activities and attention to linguistic and phonological forms at the request of the publisher, the compromise is achieved in a way that still encourages learners to make an affective investment in their learning while catering to the global, right hemisphere of language learners as well as the analytical left hemisphere. The speaking activities do not require learners to produce language orally from an acquired store of language that is not fully developed. Rather, learners read a text they have engaged in creatively and produced in order to provide fellow learners with further input. Most importantly, there is a definite focus on comprehension, meaning and exposure to a wide, varied and engaging input. These materials could potentially be more effective in an EFL environment in which the teacher is competent in both the target language and the learners' L1. After listening to the listening focus stages of each unit, teachers could ask learners to give opinions about the listenings in their L1, and in the creative production phases learners could ask the teacher in their L1 for vocabulary and structures they need in the target language as in Community Language Learning.

Warmer

UNIT 2

Strange Days

Listen to your teacher describe the picture. While you listen, point to the thing your teacher is talking about.

a/w 2.1

Illustration of a college classroom with a teacher sitting on the desk eating a sandwich, two female students dancing, two boys sleeping, a boy combing his hair and a girl reading.

Finish the sentences using words from the list below.

1. In class, I usually ————, ———— and ————.
2. In class, our teacher sometimes ————, ———— and ————.
3. I never ————, ———— or ———— in class.

dance
read
talk
listen
smoke
write
draw
sing

Focus 1

1. Listen and watch your teacher. You don't have to say anything or copy your teacher. Just listen to the tape and watch your teacher act out the instructions.
2. Listen. Number the pictures.

a/w 2.2a	*a/w b*	*a/w c*	*a/w d*
A boy jumping	*A boy and two girls reading*	*A girl and boy clapping*	*A boy dancing*

a/w e *A girl touching a window*	*a/w f* *A girl pointing at a window*	*a/w g* *A boy sleeping*	*a/w h* *Two girls singing*

3. Listen. Draw the instructions.

a/w 2.3 *eight blank squares*			

Focus 2

1. Close your eyes and listen to a description of a classroom.
2. Listen again. Draw what you hear.

a/w 2.4

A classroom window and enough blank space for students to complete the picture.

3. Listen again. Change your drawing if necessary.
4. With a partner check your drawing.

Share

1. With a partner decide who is *student A* and who is *student B.*
Student A complete the park description below with your own ideas.

   The park is really strange today.

   There is a _____ in the park.

   Behind the _____ there are some _____.

   It is 2 o'clock and I am sitting on _____.

   A dog is _____.

   An old man is _____.

   Three birds are _____.

   And some children are throwing a _____.

2. Read your description to student B. Student B will draw your park.
3. **Student B** complete the beach description below with your own ideas.

   The beach is weird today.

   There is a _____ on the beach.

   Next to the _____ there are some _____.

   It's 10 o'clock and I am _____.

A girl is _____ .
Two old women are _____ .
There is a _____ in the sea.
4.   Read your description to student A. Student A will draw your beach.
A/w 2.5
A sun shining high in a sky and enough blank space for students to draw a park or beach scene.

Word Work

1.   Complete the sentences with words from the box.

throwing	reading	raining	cleaning

School is really strange today.
It is 4 o'clock and I am still in class.
Another girl is singing.
A boy is dancing with a mop.
There is a girl next to the window.
It is _____ outside.
A boy is _____ the blackboard.
A boy is _____ a ball.
A girl is _____ .
2.   Listen and check the sentences are completed correctly.
3.   Underline the word that comes directly after **is** in each sentence.
4.   Decide if the word underlined is a noun (n), verb (v), adjective (a) or adverb (adv) and write n, v, a or adv after each sentence.

Useful Information:	
man (noun)	Nouns are things.
play (verb)	Verbs are actions.
slow (adjective)	Adjectives describe things (nouns).
slowly (adverb)	Adverbs describe actions (verbs).

5.   Complete the following generalizations:
The verb 'is' can be followed by *an adverb,* _____ , _____ or _____ .

In question 1 the verb 'is' is followed by _____ the most.
In the other units of this book the verb 'is' is followed by _____ the most.
The verb 'is' _____ .

Sounds

a and *the*

1. With a partner take turns reading this sentence.
   'A boy is throwing a ball.'
2. Listen.

   a.   A boy is throwing *a* ball. /ɛ/
   b.   A boy is throwing *a* ball. /ey/

Which sound did you use to say *a*, /ɛ/ or /ey/?
3. Listen. Circle /ɛ/ or /ey/ after each sentence.

   1.   A girl is smoking a cigarette. /ey/ /ɛ/
   2.   Two girls are singing a song. /ey/ /ɛ/
   3.   A boy and a girl are reading. /ey/ /ɛ/

Listening Scripts

Focus 1

1. Listen to the instructions and watch your teacher follow the instructions.
   Stand up. Sit down.
   Stand up. Sit down.
   Walk. Stop. Turn.
   Walk. Stop. Turn.
   Sit down. Stand up.
   Walk. Stop. Turn.
   Walk. Stop. Turn.
   Point to the window.
   Walk to the window.
   Touch the window.
   Turn.
   Point to the blackboard.
   Walk to the blackboard.
   Touch the blackboard.
   Turn.
   Point to your chair.
   Walk to your chair.
   Touch your chair.
   Turn. Sit down.
   Stand up.
   Dance.
   Smoke a cigarette.

Sing.
Walk. Stop.
Dance.
Smoke a cigarette.
Walk. Stop.
Clap. Sing. Turn. Sit down.

2. Listen and number the pictures.
   Number one. A boy is dancing.
   Number two. A girl is pointing at a window.
   Number three. Two girls are singing.
   Number four. A boy is jumping.
   Number five. A girl and boy are smoking.
   Number six. A girl is touching a window.
   Number seven. A boy and two girls are reading.
   Number eight. A boy is sleeping.

3. Number one. A girl is sleeping. Number one. A girl is sleeping.
   Number two. A boy is singing. Number two. A boy is singing.
   Number three. Two girls are smoking. Number three. Two girls are smoking.
   Number four. Two boys are dancing. Number four. Two boys are dancing.
   Number five. A boy and girl are jumping. Number five. A boy and girl are jumping
   Number six. A boy is touching a window. Number six. A boy is touching a window.
   Number seven. A girl and two boys are reading. Number seven. A girl and two boys are reading.
   Number eight. A girl is pointing at a window. Number eight. A girl is pointing at a window.

Listening scripts

Focus 2

1. Close your eyes and listen to a description of a classroom.
   School is really strange today.
   It is 7 o'clock and I am still in class.
   Some students are sleeping on their desks.
   Four girls are talking and two boys are reading newspapers.
   There is a girl next to the window playing a drum.
   It is raining outside.
   Another girl is singing and a boy is dancing with a mop.
   The teacher is sitting on a table and eating a sandwich.
   Behind the teacher, a boy is cleaning the blackboard.

Another boy is throwing a ball with his left hand and scratching his head with his right hand.

2.   Listen again. Then draw what you hear.
     School is really strange today.
     It is 4 o'clock and I am still in class.
     Some students are sleeping on their desks.
     Four girls are talking and two boys are reading newspapers.
     There is a girl next to the window playing a drum.
     It is raining outside.
     Another girl is singing and a boy is dancing with a mop.
     The teacher is sitting on a table and eating a sandwich.
     Behind the teacher, a boy is cleaning the blackboard.
     Another boy is throwing a ball with his left hand and scratching his head with his right hand.

Word Work

1.   Listen and check the sentences are completed correctly.
     School is really strange today.
     It is 4 o'clock and I am still in class.
     Another girl is singing.
     A boy is dancing with a mop.
     There is a girl next to the window.
     It is raining outside.
     A boy is cleaning the blackboard.
     A boy is throwing a ball.
     A girl is reading.

Listening scripts

Sounds

1.   Listen.

     a.   A boy is throwing **a** ball. /ɛ/
     b.   A boy is throwing **a** ball. /ey/

Which sound did you use to say **a**, /ɛ/ or /ey/?

2.   Listen. Circle /ey/ or /ɛ/ after each sentence.
     1.   A girl is smoking a cigarette. /ey/ /ɛ/
     2.   Two girls are singing a song. /ey/ /ɛ/
     3.   A boy and a girl are reading. /ey/ /ɛ/

References

Allwright, D. (1984) 'Why don't learners learn what teachers teach? The interaction hypotheses', in D. M. Singleton and D. Lettle (eds) *Language Learning in Formal and Informal Contexts*. Dublin: Irish Association for Applied Linguistics, pp. 3–18.

Asher, J. J. (1969) 'The Total Physical Response Approach to second language learning'. *The Modern Language Journal*, **53**, 3–17.

Asher, J. J. (1972) 'Children's first language as a model for second language learning'. *The Modern Language Journal*, **56**, 133–9.

Asher, J. J. (1977) *Learning Another Language through Actions: The Complete Teacher's Guidebook*. Los Gatos, CA: Sky Oaks Productions.

Asher, J. J. (1994) 'The Total Physical Response: a stress-free, brain compatible approach to learning'. *SEAL Journal of the Society for Effective Affective Learning*, Autumn, 22–5.

Beaven, B., Soars, L. and Soars, J. (1995) *Headstart*. Oxford: Oxford University Press.

Colvin-Clark, R. and Taylor, D. (1994) 'The causes and cures of learner overload'. *Training*, July, 40–3.

Dulay, H., Burt, M. and Krashen, S. (1982) *Language Two*. Oxford: Oxford University Press.

Ellis, R. (1989) 'Classroom learning styles and their effect on second language acquisition: a study of two learners'. *System*, **17**, 249–62.

Ellis, R. (1994) *The Study of Second Language Acquisition*. Oxford: Oxford University Press.

Hastings, A. (1995) 'The focal skills approach: an assessment', in F. R. Eckman, D. Highland, P. W. Lee, J. Mileham and R. Rutkowski Weber (eds) *Second Language Acquisition Theory and Pedagogy*. Hillsdale, NJ: Lawrence Erlbaum Associates, Inc., pp. 29–43.

Johnson, J. (1995) 'Who needs another coursebook?' *Folio Journal of the Materials Development Association*, **2** (1), 31–5.

Krashen, S. (1978) 'Individual variation in the use of the Monitor', in W. Ritchie (ed.) *New Second Language Acquisition Research*. New York: Academic Press.

Krashen, S. (1981) *Second Language Acquisition and Second Language Learning*. Oxford: Pergamon Press.

Krashen, S. (1982) *Principles and Practice in Second Language Acquisition*. Oxford: Pergamon Press.

Larsen-Freeman, D. (1986) *Techniques and Principles in Language Teaching*. Oxford: Oxford University Press.

McLaughlin, B. (1987) *Theories of Second Language Learning*. London: Edward Arnold.

McLaughlin, B., Rossman, T. and McLeod, B. (1983) 'Second language learning: an information processing perspective'. *Language Learning*, **33**, 135–58.

Nunan, D. (1995) *Atlas*. Boston: Heinle and Heinle.

Nunan, D. (1999) *Second Language Teaching and Learning*. Boston: Heinle and Heinle.

Nunan, D. (2000) 'Seven hypotheses about language teaching and learning'. *TESOL Matters*, **10** (2).

Oxford, R. L. and Anderson, N. J. (1995) 'A cross-cultural view of learning styles'. *Language Teaching*, **28**, 201–15.

Reid, J. (1987) 'The learning styles and preferences of ESL students'. *TESOL Quarterly*, **21**, 87–111.

Richards, J. C., Hull, J. and Proctor, S. (1999) *New Interchange*. Cambridge: Cambridge University Press.

Sano, M. (1986) 'How to incorporate Total Physical Response into the English programme'. *ELT Journal*, **40** (4).

Stevick, E. (1998) *Success with foreign Languages*. London: Prentice Hall.

Swaffar, J. K. and Woodruff, M. S. (1978) 'Language for comprehension: focus on reading: a report on the University of Texas German program'. *Modern Language Journal*, **62**, 27–32.

Thompson, G. (1996) 'Some misconceptions about communicative language teaching'. *English Language Teaching Journal*, **50** (1), 9–15.

Tomlinson, B. (1994) 'Materials for TPR'. *Folio Journal of the Materials Development Association*, **1** (2), 8–10.

Winitz, H. (1981) *The Comprehension Approach to Foreign Language Instruction*. Cambridge, MA: Newbury House.

CHAPTER

16

Materials for Adult Beginners from an L2 User Perspective

Vivian Cook

This chapter questions some of the underlying ideas represented in a selection of contemporary adult beginners' coursebooks in different languages and suggests some alternatives, building partly on the proposals for linking course materials to SLA research in Cook (1998). Much of the thinking here was shaped in the discussions of the Essex Beginners' Materials Group – a group that meets occasionally at Essex University, made up of modern language teachers, EFL teachers and materials writers.[1]

The starting point is three apparently innocuous assumptions about language teaching materials for adults:

1. *Adult students have adult minds and interests*: The adult coursebook is catering for people who do not think, speak, learn or behave in the same ways as children. Sometimes it may be possible for them to pretend to be children for the purposes of a particular exercise or activity. But this suspension of belief can never be more than temporary; the adult sooner or later reverts to being an adult and will inevitably be treated as an adult second language (L2) user as soon as he/she uses the second language outside the classroom for the everyday purposes of a job, a holiday or indeed academic studies.

2. *Second language users are people in their own right*: L2 users are not just monolingual native speakers with an additional language but people with new strengths and abilities. They not only speak their second language differently from monolinguals but also their first language; they think in different ways from monolinguals; they use the second language for their own purposes – for business, for travelling, for reading poetry, for negotiation, for studying or for many other reasons – negotiating through a second language, translating from one language to another, code-switching from one language to another. The growing evidence for these differences is presented in Cook (ed., forthcoming). Few students need to pass for natives, apart from professional spies; they are instead mediators between two cultures and two languages.

3. *Language teaching has been held back by unquestioning acceptance of traditional nineteenth-century principles*: Twentieth-century language teaching was largely heir to the New Reform method of the 1880s (Howatt, 1984). The principles

of the priority of speech and the avoidance of the first language have been handed down virtually unquestioned through the mainstream teaching trad- ition from situational to audiolingual to communicative to task-based meth- ods. These principles are not particularly justified by current ideas about how people learn second languages; for instance, avoiding the first language assumes the 'coordinate' view of bilingualism that the languages are in separate compartments rather than the 'interconnected' view that sees them as continually linked in many ways which underlies much modern research (Cook, ed., forthcoming). Course-writers should consciously evaluate these principles rather than incorporate them unquestioningly in their coursebooks.

To make the discussions more concrete, we will rely on six representative adult beginner coursebooks of the 1990s, produced by publishers in four different countries: for Italian *Ci Siamo* (Guarnaccio and Guarnaccio, 1997) and *Teach Yourself Italian* (Vellaccio and Elston, 1998), for French *Libre Echange* (Courtillon and de Salins, 1995) and *Panorama* (Girardet and Cridlig, 1996) and for English *Atlas 1* (Nunan, 1995) and *Changes* (Richards, 1998). These are taken as sound examples of modern coursebooks; the criticisms apply just as much to the beginners' coursebook *People and Places* I wrote myself (Cook, 1980), as well as to most modern coursebooks.

At first sight these books look rather similar – bright covers, glossy pages full of colour photos or cartoons, forms and sentences with blanks to fill in, all attract- ively laid out in the manner of a magazine or a colour supplement. Do these apparent similarities extend to their assumptions about the ways in which lan- guage should be taught and about the students themselves and their goals in learning a language? If so, are these assumptions in fact appropriate for the adult language students of the twenty-first century?

Adult Students have Adult Minds and Interests

The adultness of the students has consequences for the coursebook which has to maintain the interest of people who, unlike children, often have particular rea- sons for studying a new language and who have adult interests, social relation- ships and level of intelligence.

The Types of Students Aimed at

To visualize the types of students the coursebooks are intended for one needs to look at the characters they feature and the topics they are about. *Ci Siamo* 'is based on the adventures and travels of a small group of young adults living in a small Italian town', as is *Teach Yourself Italian. Atlas* and *Changes* feature classes of stu- dents of English from different countries, *Libre Echange* and *Panorama* young professionals. The Italian and English courses concentrate on the world of the prospective multilingual student; the message is that, to appeal to students of languages, you write about students of language, not about either native speakers or L2 users. The French coursebooks rely more on young adults in their own social world, most of them native speakers. Out of the 180-odd characters in these books, those with identifiable jobs are students (20), teachers (4), waiters, sailors, doctors, receptionists, civil servants (all with 3), and a cast of one-off lacemakers, entertainers, accountants, ticket-sellers, tramps and others.

The overall impression is of lively young people without cares in the world or plans for the future, except tomorrow's party. They are not people with any particular purpose either in life or in their relationships but are out to have a respectable good time – the population of summer schools in Cambridge or Perugia. Testing the Smile Factor (i.e., the number of smiling faces; Cook, 2001a: 218), the highest concentration is in the first twenty pages of *Atlas* with 54, the minimum in the first twenty of *Libre Echange* with a mere 14 – a concentration otherwise only found in mail-order catalogues and travel brochures. Learning another language is apparently a way of joining this happy group, not of taking an adult L2 user role in the world.

The adoption of student or young people's lives as the model affects the language the students learn. Take for example the question of introductions. The first time that characters introduce themselves in the coursebooks they say:

Changes	Hello. My name is Maria.
Atlas	Hi. I'm Bob.
Ci Siamo	Mi chiamo Lucy, cioè Lucia …
	Lucia Burns.
Teach Yourself	Mi chiamo Marco Russo.
Libre Echange	Je suis François Roux.
Panorama	Je m'appelle Renaud.

The English coursebooks are perfectly appropriate to the language classroom where teachers and young students are on informal terms, removed from the pecking order in the world outside the classroom. Hence first names are the most important terms for immediate use.

But, as we can appreciate from the coursebooks in other languages, introductions are a form of social ceremony, not just a teaching act of identifying people by name. As such, they involve complex assessment of the relationships between the people involved – age, gender, social status, etc. – and a particular formal exchange, with the introducer *inter alia* deciding who to introduce first and whether to provide an appropriate piece of background information about them.

Michel: Entrez Jacky! Je vous presente Pierre.
Jacky: Bonsoir Pierre.
Pierre: Bonsoir Jacky.
Michel: Jacky est une amie de Cecile … (*Libre Echange*, p. 26).

In particular, English first names are still perceived in many places as something to be used only when you know the person well. According to newspaper reports and personal experience, British hospitals, for example, have discovered that many older people feel humiliated by the use of their first names by younger medical staff.

This raises the issue of appropriate titles for people – a big concern outside the classroom wherever different age groups and status relationships are involved. The choice of title is skimped in the English coursebooks. *Changes* demonstrates the use of titles *Mr, Mrs, Miss* (and the rather dated *Ms*). *Atlas* avoids the issue, apart from one-off incidental examples of *Dr Nancy Walters* (p. 18), *Ms Jenny Jordan* (p. 69) and *Mr Michalik* (p. 71); even its enrolment forms do not require 'title' (though the teacher's book compensates by introducing *Mr* and *Ms*, p. 19). The student-in-class-centred approach does not prepare the students for the variety of roles they may have to undertake in the world outside the classroom. Outside the classroom there is a need to be aware of the social roles that people have and to use the correct name and form of address.

The Topics Discussed

The topics that students have to talk about during the course are presumably aimed both at interesting students during the lesson and at enabling them to use the second language for their ultimate goals. A sample of the first ten and last ten pages in each coursebook should represent the range of topics reasonably fairly, in total 156. The most popular are basic functional topics, such as making arrangements or introducing people (48), after which come tourism (20), general information (17) (including statistics and information about the country), identifying and describing yourself and other people (16), making plans and arrangements for activities such as parties (12), discussion (9), tourist attractions (8) and dealing with hotels (4). Culture contributes 6 topics, the Italian and French courses dealing with real films, poems and plays. Finally, a category with 16 examples is topics with no rationale other than teaching, such as identifying countries and nationalities, describing occupations, naming body parts and so on. During these coursebooks the students mostly learn to talk about functional tourist/visitor topics such as buying things and tourist attractions or to discuss each other in general terms ('Are you good at sports?') or to arrange details of their everyday student/tourist lives, such as parties and holidays.

The subject matter is seldom adult, with the exception perhaps of *Libre Echange* or of Carlo admiring Lucia in *Ci Siamo* 'Ha un sorroso carino' – by the last page of the book they have twins. It is a sanitized world of clean-living teenagers untouched by 'sex and drugs and rock 'n' roll'. There is little overlap between what students talk about in language teaching and what adults choose to encounter in magazines, television programmes, newspapers, pop songs, computer games, movies or indeed conversations that go past the preliminary personal information. One simple omission is money; most adults worry about their lack of income and their high level of expenditure, about the price of CDs or the exchange rate against the Euro. Other than the prices in shops, money is never a topic in coursebooks, presumably because students and tourists are not part of the labour force. On a Dublin bus I overheard a group of multilingual EFL students talking. Their topics were either pop or sexual innuendoes, culminating in the memorable remark 'I don't kill women; I only kill mens' (to which the perfectly sensible reply was 'What is mens?').

The blandness of these coursebooks is partly dictated by fears of giving offence on religious or political grounds and of going out of date. But a world in which nobody talks about television, sport, pop music, food, films, gardening, work, current news and so on is a strange place. At the end of these courses the students will be able to discuss a limited range of topics at a general level – 'I think Keiko is interesting. She likes music and art' (*Atlas*, p. 89) – but will be unable to deal with most political, cultural or sporting topics (though the French coursebooks at least mention the Tour de France and dangerous sports and *Changes* has short biographies of Gloria Estafan and Ronaldo). The students are left unprepared for almost any adult topic of conversation in their L2 use. All they can say is 'I can play the piano' (*Changes*, p. 78), 'Do you like swimming? Yes I do' (*Atlas*, p. 44), 'Giochi a tennis? No, mai. Non mi piace' (*Ci Siamo*, p. 80), 'Les jeunes aiment danser sur la musique «techno»' (*Panorama*, p. 27).

Suggestion 1: Materials Aimed at Adults Should be Adult in Theme, Teaching Method and Language

Adultness has then a number of consequences for coursebooks.

Talking about Adult Topics
Rather than just functional exchanges ('Ha un camera singola?') or introductory remarks ('Moi, j'aime le sport'), the teacher could at least be given guidance as to how this could be developed into more adult-like conversation. Previous discussion of topics in language teaching suggested a range including personal information, books and information about language itself (Cook, 1983). Lists of frequent topics for teenagers were compiled in the 1970s (Rutherford *et al.*, 1970) and indeed I based a course, *English Topics*, on them (Cook, 1975); equivalent lists for adults could be devised by checking the topics that adults actually watch on television – soap operas (gossip was top of the teenagers' list), sport (commentaries and gossip), quiz shows, detective 'dramas', news programmes, pop music, films, niche programmes on cookery, gardening and house design, etc. The danger would be choosing the 'high culture' of opera, etc., rather than people's everyday interests such as football. But the topics would have to be explorable to an adult level of conversation, not just 'What is your favourite Olympic sport?'

Using Adult Roles
At one level, students aiming to talk like students is a snake swallowing its own tail; the L2 target needs to escape this vicious circle. At another level, the target is bound to the functional exchanges of short-term visitors to a country, such as

tourists or indeed students; the target needs to incorporate at least people who are living and working in the L2 culture. There needs to be an extension of roles away from the vague world of the current coursebooks, which may perhaps reflect the equally vague aspirations of some teenagers, towards roles in the workplace and social life of adults, as doctors, as travel agents, as social workers, etc., or tennis players, theatregoers, animal rights protesters or whatever. This effect operates on the two levels of the roles intended to attract the students within the actual coursebook and the ways in which the second language will be useful to them in their future lives.

Engaging in Adult Activities

Perhaps in a second language adults can only handle tasks used by seven-year-olds. Perhaps, however, the main virtue of explicit grammar is that it provides a task where the students have to engage their adult level of formal operational thinking in Piagetan terms, i.e., the level of cognitive development at which children can stand outside their own cognitive processes 'to think about thinking'. Course-writers need to think of activities that function at an adult level. The fact that the language and the content have to be readily usable by the beginner does not mean that the tasks have to be puerile.

The communicative teaching method grew in part from the approaches used in English primary schools in the 1970s to rectify language deficiencies in English children; *Talk Reform* (Gahagan and Gahagan, 1970) and *Concept 7–9* (Wight *et al.*, 1972) introduced the role-plays and information gap exercises that have become a staple of modern teaching. Task-based learning has in a sense continued this primary school tradition. Willis (1996) describes six main types of task: *listing, ordering and sorting, comparing, problem solving, sharing personal experience* and *creative*. *Atlas* (teacher's book) lists ten types of task including *classifying* ('putting things that are similar in groups'), *conversational patterns* ('using expressions to start conversations and keep them going') and *cooperating* ('sharing ideas and learning with other students'). None of these would be out of place in the primary school, comparing and classifying being classic primary school activities. The popular matching/mapping exercise, 'Listen again and draw lines to match the words' (*Atlas*, p. 13), the typical tick-the-boxes questionnaire on personal habits (*Ci Siamo*, p. 80), the archetypal giving-directions-from-a-map exercise (*Changes*, pp. 32–3), the universal naming of body parts exercise (*Panorama*, p. 66), comparing individuals' answers in a small group 'Vérifiez en petit groupes si vous avez trouvé les mêmes résultats' (*Libre Echange*, p. 126), none of these activities intrinsically involve adult-level intelligence and skills.

A justification for the use of childlike activities, strongly advocated for example by several members of the Essex Beginner's Materials group, is that second language learning infantilizes people; they *need* to be reduced to the dependent state of little children if they are to succeed, thus justifying, say, extreme forms of audiovisualism. While this may indeed be one basis for successful coursebooks, there is no reason why it should be the only one. To justify infantilization would require a new approach to second language acquisition, say building on the

Vygotskyan theories that are starting to appear (Anton and DiCamilla, 1998), emphasizing the learner's need for appropriate 'scaffolding' from other people. To implement infantilization properly in teaching might require it to incorporate other aspects of infantilization (students asking permission to go to the toilet? A letter from their parents when they're late? Confiscation of objects that the teacher disapproves of, such as mobile phones?). In particular, it would go against the communicative tradition of the teacher as *primus inter pares* and re-establish the teacher as all-powerful controller.

Second Language Users are People in Their Own Right

Adoption of the Native Speaker Goal

In language teaching both language teachers and students have often had a native speaker goal in mind; success is measured by how close the students get to a native speaker norm. Though it is seldom stated explicitly, this probably reflects the everyday feelings of most students and teachers; student progress means getting closer to the native speaker standard. Yet the only language that one speaks as a native is the one you learnt first in early childhood – by definition. The belief in this unattainable goal frustrates teachers and students alike. The alternative is to emulate successful L2 users, not native speakers. With an achievable goal in mind, the atmosphere in teaching can be more positive, always looking to how successful the students are in building up their second language rather than how unsuccessful they are in closing the unbridgeable gap.

The native speaker target implicit in much language teaching reflects, on the one hand, a goal students can never meet, on the other, limits their achievements to what native speakers can do. An L2 user lacks all sorts of abilities and knowledge possessed by a native speaker. But an L2 user can do many things that a monolingual cannot. Oranges are not imitation apples but fruit in their own right.

The native speaker orientation is clearly reflected in the people who are portrayed in the coursebooks. Only 14 out of the 180 characters are marked as L2 users, that is to say 8 per cent; of these 4 are students, 1 a teacher, 1 an entertainer, the rest a chorus of unspecified friends, shoppers and tourists. Clearly L2 users do not concern the course-writers. It is not of course safe to assume from names such as Carlos, Maria, Halil or Tomoko scattered through the English coursebooks that the speakers are non-native speakers, as anti-discrimination decisions in the Scottish educational system have recently shown.

The only proper users of the target language are then overwhelmingly seen as its native speakers; L2 users are shown either as involved in language teaching as students or teachers or as unskilled tourists or visitors. Rarely do the coursebooks present people using the second language as part of their normal social or professional lives; it is a surprise when *Libre Echange* introduces Pierre, the interpreter for the Council of Europe. This cast of characters does not begin to represent the many people successfully using second languages in the world today, probably outnumbering those who use only one language. The celebrities who are introduced in the coursebooks are either native speakers, such as Jacques Cousteau or Whitney Houston, or their bilingualism is not mentioned, such as Martina Hingis and Ronaldo.

Native Speaker Language

The forms and pronunciation that the students are aiming at in these course-books are therefore those of native speakers. But native speakers speak differently when a non-native is around, sometimes descending into foreigner talk; for example, thanking a perceived L2 user is more likely to consist of 'Thank you very much indeed' than the informal 'Thanks' (Cook, 1985). The language of native-to-native situations portrayed in coursebooks is unlikely to be encountered by the students simply because it changes as soon as they become part of the situation. The language of students-to-students might be a different matter, since so much of the coursebooks is about students; however, the L2 user students in the books speak the same native speaker speech as everyone else. Jenkins (2000) has argued in favour of teaching a form of English as an International Language based on the speech of L2 students. This type of syllabus does not, however, encompass the full complexity of L2 use in the world outside the classroom, particularly in the case of international languages such as French and English where the reality is indeed often L2 user speaking to L2 user. The frequency of forms, the gram-matical rules and the types of interaction in native speech are at best a rough guide to what L2 users need.

Suggestion 2: Materials Based on the L2 User Perspective Aimed at Adults should Reflect the Situations, Roles and Language of L2 Users, Not Just Native Speakers

If we accept that the students' manifest destiny is to be L2 users, this needs to be built in to courses, both as the realistic target to aim at and as a motivation for students. The potential for L2 users is to become successful people with two languages, both in the ability to use another language for their own L2 purposes and in the cognitive, cultural and social advantages that knowing another language confers upon them. Cook (forthcoming, a) looks at these in more detail.

L2 User Roles
Existing coursebooks almost fail to mention L2 users, as we have seen. Those that are encountered are students or tourists, who are effectively powerless in the L2 situation. Coursebooks need to present favourable images of L2 users, both the invented characters in their dialogues and the famous characters that are paraded from time to time. Invented characters should be people who are clearly employing second languages in their everyday lives, whether doctors, diplomats, businesspeople, housewives or minority ethnic children, rather than casual users. Famous bilinguals range from Gandhi to Sophia Loren, Einstein to Nabokov, Chopin to Greta Garbo, as seen in the list in Grosjean (1982). Today's

sportspeople, for example, are as multilingual as they come, whether Kournikova or Dettori, Schumacher or Arsène Wenger. Again, the use of famous personalities who have got something out of L2 learning might be a good motivational factor.

L2 User Situations
Similarly, the situations to be presented need to cover the range of L2 uses, not just those of native speakers. What matters is what happens in the doctor's surgery when a native speaker doctor encounters an L2 user patient or an L2 user doctor treats a monolingual native speaker or an L2 doctor sees an L2 patient, not what happens when native doctor meets native patient. While some simple service encounters between tourists and customers and various organizations are found in the coursebooks, few of them depart from the protocols of native speaking to native. The tourist/visitor situations that are taught need then to incorporate the vital L2 use element; changing foreign money or cashing traveller's cheques, going through US immigration as an alien, getting medical help through your insurance cover or reciprocal health arrangements, buying goods for unfamiliar money in unfamiliar quantities with curious taxes added to the price or redeemable on exit from the country. Beyond this, we need to see everyday situations in which L2 users are successfully dealing with each other or with native speakers, say two businessmen with different first languages talking on the phone in English, an Italian estate agent selling a house in Tuscany to a French buyer in French, or simply members of multiethnic communities in Tower Hamlets talking to each other. An example of this in practice can be seen in the Institute of Linguists' examinations for International Communication, which also involve the use of both languages in real-world related tasks.

L2 User Target Language
The consequence of rejecting the native speaker standard is that the appropriate language to model to the students is that of successful L2 users, not native speakers. International Students English (Jenkins, 2000) is one step in the right direction but is limited by being only about pronunciation and only about students. But certainly such a student variety is what the student-oriented English and Italian coursebooks require. On the one hand, we need to know the characteristics of L2 users; Klein and Perdue (1997) have indeed established a basic variety of grammar that learners of several L2s go through which shows what the grammatical target of an L2-user-based beginners' course might look like. But virtually all vocabulary research has looked at frequencies, etc., in native speaker speech, and has seen L2 learners as acquiring these native speaker elements. Perhaps the vocabulary of successful L2 users does indeed mirror native speakers; perhaps it does not. Corpora and descriptions of native speech are secondary information for a L2-user-based approach. The primary information for the coursebook is the language of L2 users, even if for the moment impressionistically.

The Types of Situation Portrayed

Coursebooks inevitably have to present situations in which the second language is used. In the English and Italian student-based courses the situations are primarily the language school, the students' digs and the tourist situations of travelling and shopping: people find their way around town, go to parties, shop in supermarkets and meet each other around college. In the French courses, the situations are more street life, entertainment and sport: people drink in cafés, go to cinemas and discos and date each other. Overall, the situations are student life, visitor/tourist encounters in a country or polite public encounters between people with no specific social roles other than as fellow-students, friends or service roles such as the waiter. These are situations where low-level L2 users encounter native speaker shop assistants, etc., low-level L2 users speak to their fellows or native speakers speak to each other. What is missing are the situations in which high-level L2 users are functioning fully as equals, whether to fellow L2 users or to native speakers.

Language Teaching has been Held Back by Not Questioning Traditional Nineteenth-century Principles

Some of the actual teaching methods follow from the decisions made in the last section. Others rely on deeper, if unacknowledged, principles of language teaching, 'language teaching taboos, such as the mother tongue, grammar, the printed and written word, which have affected our teachers with over-sized guilt complexes, are nothing but superstitions handed down from one innocent victim to the next' (Dodson, 1967: 65).

Reliance on the First Language

The teaching in these coursebooks is almost exclusively through the second language (the exception is *Teach Yourself Italian*). *Ci Siamo* uses English for grammatical explanation and for some instructions for teaching exercises; the other books never mention the first language. As they are produced for use in a variety of countries, this might be seen as a necessity; yet no hints are provided as to how the teacher can make use of the students' first language productively in the classroom. The writers have adopted the nineteenth-century injunction to avoid the first language as far as possible in the classroom rather than seeing it as a resource for teaching (Cook, 2001b). As Howatt (1984: 289) put it, 'the monolingual principle, the unique contribution of the twentieth century to classroom language teaching, remains the bedrock notion from which the others ultimately derive.'

Cook (2001b) found the classic arguments for avoiding the second language based on L1 acquisition and mental compartmentalization of languages were groundless and counter-productive, the argument for maximizing communicative L2 in the classroom was sensible but not the same as L1 avoidance. The point about L2 users is that the two languages are always present in the same mind; one language cannot be totally switched off when the other is being used, whether in terms of vocabulary (Beauvillain and Grainger, 1987), syntax (Cook, 1994), phonology (Obler, 1982) or pragmatics (Locastro, 1987). The absence of a systematic role for the first language from most of these textbooks is throwing away one of the most valuable assets that the L2 learner has.

Emphasis on the Spoken Language

Changes and *Atlas* emphasize 'the four language skills of listening, speaking, reading, and writing', with the order showing the usual precedence of spoken before written; *Ci Siamo* presents dialogues with speech balloons in photo-story style; *Panorama* uses scripts alongside cartoon strips; *Teach Yourself Italian* and *Libre Echange* start each unit with a taped dialogue. Since these courses are primarily books, the spoken basis is less evident than in the audiovisual courses such as *All's Well that Starts Well* (Dickinson *et al.*, 1975). The spoken language is often portrayed through written language. In *Atlas*, written language is mostly used to represent spoken dialogues or to provide cues, lists, etc., for spoken exercises, with rare use of texts longer than a single sentence; in *Libre Echange* it is used for film scripts. *Libre Echange* and *Ci Siamo* provide more use of informative texts, poems, etc. Many of the exercises involve reading aloud, whether of sentences into which the student has inserted words, 'Elise is Martha's . . .', or of substitution tables, 'Sono Carlo/Lucia. Cia, come va/stai?', or turning written into spoken language, 'Domande perché i ragazzi sono andati a Roma di domenica?', or using written information in conjunction with spoken materials, 'Lisez les informations ci-contre et écoutez'.

Again, the overall emphasis on speech follows the nineteenth-century insistence on the priority of the spoken language (Cook, forthcoming, b). Language syllabuses around the world have unquestioningly taken this as axiomatic; the English curriculum in Cuba insists on 'the principle of the primacy of spoken language' (Cuban Ministry of Education, 1999). Howatt claims, 'The spoken language for example is promoted with more determination now than at any time since the Reform Movement' (Howatt, 1984: 289). The arguments for the primacy of speech have not been rehearsed for many years; they include the development of the L1 child, which is beside the point for language teaching that takes on no other feature of first language acquisition, and the historical development of language, which has nothing to do with L2 teaching. Speech and writing have not been looked at in their own right and a rational decision made as to which aspects of each are relevant for the students. The adult literate student thinks and learns in different ways from a non-literate; indeed, modern neurolinguistics research shows that literate people store language in different areas of the brain (Petersson *et al.*, 2000). For the adult literate student, speech is not automatically the primary form of language.'One could nearly say that in a "literate culture" speech is the spelling of writing' (Kress, 2000: 18).

The written language is systematically distorted in these books in the service of the spoken language. Where but in a language teaching book would you find Michelangelo's David with its body parts labelled (*Ci Siamo*, p. 136), a chart to fill in with what you are doing today (*Changes*, p. 72), sentences with fill-in blanks (*Atlas* and *Libre Echange*, almost every page), photos with jumbled poetic captions (*Panorama*, pp. 76–7), lists of words in two columns to be matched (*Atlas*, p. 13)? Spoken language is presented reasonably faithfully through conversations and dialogues; written language is treated as a tool for teaching in any way that suits the course-writer: the message is that only spoken language is real, even if conveyed through writing.

Though one should not understate the value of the spoken language, this attitude does lead to a remarkable neglect of the written language in beginners' language courses. A hurdle for many learners of English is transferring from a writing system that uses meaning-based characters to one that uses sound-based characters; this extends down to the different ways in which the pen is held and to the ways in which letters are formed in writing – English 'os' are made anti-clockwise, Japanese clockwise. Within European languages there are different uses of capital letters; many find the English egocentric for capitalizing only the first person pronoun 'I' rather than the second person 'you', as in German 'Sie' and Italian 'Lei'.

This is before one starts looking at the detailed correspondences between sounds and letters, for example the different spoken correspondences of 'c' and 'g' are briefly mentioned in *Teach Yourself Italian* and *Ci Siamo*, perhaps all that is needed for a language with a comparatively 'shallow' orthography (Katz and Frost, 1992). Learning the letter-names is the extent of the coverage in *Atlas* (p. 25), which calls it 'pronunciation'. *Changes* introduces letter-names in order to spell words aloud (p. 10) and at least explains the different sound correspondences for 's'. Otherwise there is barely a mention of spelling or any other properties of the writing system in the English courses, a strange gap given the well-known problems created by its 'deeper' orthography, which has many aspects other than sound/letter correspondences. Some of the words that L2 students get wrong most often are 'because', 'accommodate', 'beginning', 'their/there/they're', 'different' and 'business' (Cook, 2001a). But these coursebooks provide no help with this whatsoever. Nor do the French courses provide much help, say with the features of the French writing system that differ from other European languages, such as the accents and cedilla, unless concealed in pronunciation practice such as 'Le «e» tombe parfois' (*Libre Echange*, p. 85). Many L2 users vitally need to learn about the properties of the L2 writing system and the idiosyncratic properties of particular words, just as much as they need an adequate pronunciation.

Suggestion 3: Teaching Methods can Go Beyond the Principles of Language Teaching Familiar since the Nineteenth Century

Use of the First Language in the Classroom

Some systematic uses for the first language in language teaching have been described in Cook (2001b); once the use of the first language is countenanced in the classroom, it can be used to give instructions and explanations to increase L2 practice, to link L1 and L2 knowledge firmly together in the students' minds, to help collaborative dialogue with fellow-students and to encourage L2 activities such as code-switching for later real-life use. This could necessarily only be provided in coursebooks for speakers of a particular first language, say French coursebooks for English speakers or English coursebooks for Italian learners.

The first language can be used for a number of different applications with regard to the coursebook.

Conveying Meaning

A key issue in language teaching, relatively undiscussed since the days of audio-lingualism and audiovisualism, is how the teacher presents the meanings of the language to the students, whether of words, functions, grammatical structures or whatever. Most coursebooks provide little help or advice with presentation and acquisition of meaning, which is acquired as if by osmosis from the language input; at most, pictures of concrete objects are provided and some explanation of grammatical meaning. Yet 39 per cent of teachers use the first language for explaining meanings (Franklin, 1990). Conveying meaning through the first language may be as effective as any other means, provided it does not imply that the meanings of the second language are translation equivalents of the first language.

Explaining Grammar

Again 88 per cent of teachers use the first language for explaining grammar (Franklin, 1990). While the technique of FonF – focus on form – has brought grammatical explanation back into the classroom as a follow-on from other activities, the discussion in, say, Doughty and Williams (1998) does not seem to mention which language should be used for the explanation. If the students' conscious understanding of grammatical rules is a crucial element in learning, one needs to ask *which* language acts best as a vehicle for conveying the actual rules. There is no virtue in making the grammatical explanation deliberately difficult by using the students' weakest language. Indeed, explanations may be unwittingly based on the concepts of the second language; it is an interesting question whether, say, a Japanese coursebook for English should use the English categories, say syllables, or the Japanese categories, moras, in its explanations.

A counter-argument is that grammar explanation in the classroom is simply another form of comprehensible input; the students are learning the language by trying to understand some complex topic in the second language; the subject matter is immaterial and might as well be nuclear physics or knitting. If grammar is just another topic to be communicative about, then other topics might well prove more stimulating to students, at least the form of grammar taught in classrooms rather than the more exciting version in say Pinker (1995). Grammatical explanation that is intended to create useful understanding of the target language is, however, something else; it is the message that is important, not the form. If it is understood better through the first language as seems most likely, then it should obviously be conveyed through the first language. While it may be 'educational' to have pre-take-off safety instructions on aircraft in another language, most passengers would probably prefer them to be in a language they have fully mastered.

Giving Instructions and Tests

Rather than having cumbersome simplified instructions for what the students have to do in the second language, these could sometimes be written in the first language. The loss would be a certain amount of genuine communication with the student through the second language; the gain would be not only the students being able follow the instructions more swiftly but also a greater complexity of activities and tests, since the language for setting activities up would no longer get in the way.

Using within Teaching Activities

Without going back to undesirable forms of translation activities, the coursebooks could include activities where the students deliberately have to use both languages, say through code-switching, as in the New Concurrent Method (Jacobson and Faltis, 1990). The activity may get students to explain the task to each other, to negotiate their roles in it and to check their understanding or production of language, all in the first language.

Use of the Written Language in the Coursebook

The general suggestions in Cook (forthcoming, b) can be applied to the design of coursebooks. In addition to the existing provision of written language in the coursebooks for supporting spoken exercises, as scripts of spoken dialogues, as fill-in sentences and forms or as short informative texts, coursebooks need to teach the distinctive features of the written language. The basic elements of the English writing system in terms of spelling, orthography, direction of writing, etc., need to be built in to the beginners' course in one way or another. On the one hand, this may prevent the types of persistent problems one still sees in advanced learners; after many years of French, I still did not have any systematic reason for using an acute or grave accent, because no one taught it to me to the best of my recollection. Written language can be authentic notices, signs, real advertisements, etc.; it can demonstrate proper discourse roles and functions. It can take its place alongside spoken language as a crucial aspect of L2 use, particularly in these days of e-mails, text messages and the web.

Obviously, this analysis has taken an unconventional perspective. There is no intention to imply that these are the only ways of approaching these issues or that they necessarily come as a package. A beginners' course that incorporated any of these ideas would be radically different from materials currently available across languages and across countries. According to the three initial assumptions, the apparent variety of coursebooks on sale is an illusion: none of them bases itself on L2 users, incorporates the first language systematically, uses a range of adult topics and situations or adequately covers writing. The much discussed choices between tasks, functions, lexical syllabuses, etc., are superficial compared to these underlying assumptions, which affect every page of the coursebook. These assumptions may be wrong; the traditional principles may be unchallengeable. But, if they are never brought out into the open, lauded changes in language teaching such as communicative tasks, FonF, lexical syllabuses or whatever, are nothing but the tip of the iceberg, liable to melt in the first rays of the sun, rather than the solid mass hidden beneath the waves.

References

Anton, M. and DiCamilla, F. (1998) 'Socio-cognitive functions of L1 collaborative interaction in the L2 classroom'. *Canadian Modern Language Review*, **54**, 314–42.

Beauvillain, C. and Grainger, J. (1987) 'Accessing interlexical homographs: some limitations of a language-selective access'. *Journal of Memory and Language*, **26**, 658–672.

Cook, V. J. (1975) *English Topics*. Oxford: Oxford University Press.

Cook, V. J. (1980) *People and Places*. Oxford: Pergamon.

Cook, V. J. (1983) 'What should language teaching be about?' *English Language Teaching Journal*, **37** (3).

Cook, V. J. (1985) 'Language functions, social factors, and second language teaching'. *International Review of Applied Linguistics*, **13** (3), 177–96.

Cook, V. J. (1994) 'Timed grammaticality judgements of the head parameter in L2 learning', in G. Bartelt (ed.) *The Dynamics of Language Processes*. Tübingen: Gunter Narr, pp. 15–31.

Cook, V. J. (1998) 'Relating SLA research to language teaching materials'. *Canadian Journal of Applied Linguistics* **1** (1–2), 9–27.

Cook, V. J. (1999) 'Going beyond the native speaker in language teaching'. *TESOL Quarterly*, **33** (2), 185–209.

Cook, V. J. (2001a) *Second Language Learning and Language Teaching*. London: Edward Arnold.

Cook, V. J. (2001b) 'Using the first language in the classroom'. *Canadian Modern Language Review*, **57** (3), 402–23.

Cook, V. J. (ed.) (forthcoming) *The L2 User Perspective*. Clevedon: Multilingual Matters.

Cook, V. J. (forthcoming, a) 'Language teaching methodology and the L2 user perspective', in V. J. Cook (ed.) (forthcoming).

Cook, V. J. (forthcoming b) 'The dogma of the priority of speech in language teaching'.

Courtillon, J. and de Salins, G. D. (1995) *Libre Echange*. Paris: Hatier/Didier.

Cuban Ministry of Education (1999) *Principios que rigen la ensen Í anza del ingles en la escuala media*. Cuba: Ministry of Education.

Dickinson, Leveque and Sagot (1975) *All's Well that Starts Well*. Paris: Didier.

Dodson, C. J. (1967) *Language Teaching and the Bilingual Method*. London: Pitman.

Doughty, C. and Williams, J. (eds) (1998) *Focus on Form in Classroom Second Language Acquisition*. Cambridge: Cambridge University Press.

Franklin, C. E. M. (1990) 'Teaching in the target language'. *Language Learning Journal*, Sept., 20–4.

Gahagan, D. M. and Gahagan, J. (1970) *Talk Reform: Explorations in Language for Infant School Children.* London: Routledge & Kegan Paul.

Girardet, J. and Cridlig, J.-M. (1996) *Panorama.* Paris: European Schoolbooks.

Grosjean, F. (1982) *Life with Two Languages: An Introduction to Bilingualism.* Cambridge, MA: Harvard University Press.

Guarnaccio, C. and Guarnaccio, E. (1997) *Ci Siamo.* Port Melbourne, Victoria: CIS Heinemann.

Howatt, A. (1984) *A History of English Language Teaching.* Oxford: Oxford University Press.

Jacobson, R. and Faltis, C. (eds) (1990) *Language description issues in bilingual schooling.* Clevedon: Multilingual Matters, pp. 3–17.

Jenkins, J. (2000) *The Phonology of English as an International Language.* Oxford: Oxford University Press.

Katz, L. and Frost, R. (1992) 'Reading in different orthographies: the orthographic dept hypothesis', in R. Frost and L. Katz (eds) *Orthography, Phonology, Morphology and Meaning.* Amsterdam: Elsevier, pp. 67–84.

Klein, W. and Perdue, C. (1997) 'The basic variety (or: couldn't natural languages be much simpler?)'. *Second Language Research*, **13** (4), 301–47.

Kress, G. (2000) *Early Spelling.* London: Routledge.

Locastro, V. (1987) 'Aizuchi: a Japanese conversational routine', in L. E. Smith (ed.) *Discourse across Cultures.* New York: Prentice Hall, pp. 101–13.

Obler, L. K. (1982) 'The parsimonious bilingual', in L. Obler and L. Menn (eds) *Exceptional Language and Linguistics.* New York: Academic Press.

Nunan, D. (1995) *Atlas 1.* Boston: Heinle and Heinle.

Petersson, K. M., Reis, A., Askelof, S., Castro-Caldas, A. and Ingvar, M. (2000) 'Language processing modulated by literacy: a network analysis of verbal repetition in literate and illiterate subjects'. *Journal of Cognitive Neuroscience*, **12** (3).

Pinker, S. (1995) *The Language Instinct.* Harmondsworth: Penguin.

Richards, J. (1998) *Changes.* Cambridge: Cambridge University Press.

Rutherford, R. W., Freeth, M. E. A. and Mercer, E. S. (1970) *Topics of Conversation in the Speech of Fifteen-year-old Children.* Nuffield Foreign Languages Teaching Materials Project, Occasional Paper No. 44.

Vellaccio, L. and Elston, M. (1998) *Teach Yourself Italian.* London: Hodder Headline.

Wight, J., Norris, R. A. and Worsley, F. J. (1972) *Concept 7–9.* Leeds: E. J. Arnold and Schools Council.

Willis, J. (1996) *A Framework for Task-Based Learning.* Harlow: Longman.

CHAPTER 17

Talking like Texts and Talking about Texts: How Some Primary School Coursebook Tasks are Realized in the Classroom

Irma K. Ghosn

Introduction

In English language teaching (ELT), the coursebook is a central element and, in the case of English as a Foreign Language (EFL) for the primary school, it is often the only exposure to English, aside from the teacher, that students receive. Although an extensive body of research exists on both how children learn a new language and the effectiveness of different syllabus models on language learning, research into what teachers and students actually do with the coursebook in the classroom is limited. This chapter attempts to shed light onto this rather unexplored area of primary school ELT by discussing classroom episodes which show how different coursebook tasks generate qualitatively very different interactions.

Background

Second language acquisition research of the past two decades points to negotiated interactions as the primary medium through which language learning happens (Hatch, 1978; Long, 1981; Swain and Lapkin, 1995; Gass, 1997). In the classroom, interactions follow a fairly predictable pattern of teacher initiation → student response → teacher feedback (Sinclair and Coulthard, 1975), or evaluation (Cazden, 1988). These IRF sequences are orchestrated by the teacher, primarily through the use of questions and feedback, students having mainly a responding role. The textbook is argued to play a central role in this process (Luke, 1988; Peacock, 1995, cited in Martin, 1999), with Barton suggesting that 'much of schooling can be characterized as talk around texts' (1994: 181). Despite shifting theories and methodological innovations in the field of second language teaching, the coursebook has retained its importance, the more recent courses having evolved into sophisticated materials packages with detailed instructions for application (Littlejohn, 1998).

A wide selection of ELT coursebooks are on the market, attesting to their firm position in the field. In 1988, Sheldon (1988) counted 1623 ELT texts as being available from the US publishers, and UK-produced ELT courses have spread all around the world. Yet, ELT coursebooks have been criticized. Their allegedly limited vocabularies, simple sentence structure and emphasis on form (Fielding *et al.*, 1984) have been argued to offer limited opportunities to deepen learners' awareness of the new language (Hill and Reid Thomas, 1988). Their language is argued not to reflect real-life language (Crystal, 1987; Fox, 1998) while their situations are also claimed to be 'unreal and dull' (Crystal, 1987: 15).

Research of the past decade and a half suggests literature as having a positive influence on children's second language learning (e.g., Aranha, 1985; Tudor and Hafiz, 1989; Elley, 1991; Elley *et al.*, 1996; Elley, 2000), and many primary school ELT courses now also incorporate literary selections, albeit many of them more or less simplified. 'Literature' here refers to non-didactic, ungraded texts of diverse genre, written for children to enjoy. In its broader definition, children's literature includes also informational books. Proponents of literature for language teaching argue that literature enables students to move beyond word and sentence-level awareness of language to a more 'overall awareness' that includes differences in discourse sequence, the ways words link and the understanding of inferences (Lazar, 1994: 116). Being also full of examples of different real-life situations, literature provides language in a variety of registers within a context of discourse, thus promoting awareness of language use, as McKay (1986) suggests. Gregory (1996: 118) proposes that literature is particularly useful for young second language learners, because they can provide scaffolding by developing learners' lexical, semantic, syntactic and orthographic/graphophonic knowledge. Perhaps most importantly, children and literature are a natural match; stories respond to the universal need for narrative (Hardy, 1978) contribute to children's cognitive development (Meek, 1988) and can provide interesting content to talk about.

Much has been written about evaluation of materials (e.g., Sheldon, 1987; McDonough and Shaw, 1993; Cunningsworth, 1995; Tomlinson, 1998; Littlejohn, 1998), and a considerable body of research is available about the effectiveness of different syllabus models (see Ellis, 1994). Yet, despite the recognized importance of interactions on language learning on the one hand, and the centrality of the coursebook on the other, research into what teachers and students actually do with the language teaching coursebook has been scarce at best. Yet, systematic observation of 'tasks-in-process' (Littlejohn, 1998: 191) is necessary if we want to understand how effective the given materials are in creating environments conducive to language learning. This chapter provides a glimpse into actual classrooms to reveal what happens when teachers and students interact around tasks in typical ELT coursebooks and literary texts.

The episodes that will be referred to come from a non-experimental, exploratory study in six primary school classrooms in Lebanon, where a rather curious practice is gaining popularity. Over 200 schools in the country use, for English language teaching, literature-based reading series intended for native English-speaking children. This made it possible to investigate and compare interactions in intact classrooms. The quantitative and qualitative data analyses of twelve hours of videotaped, transcribed observations revealed both qualitatively and statistically significant differences in interactions between the two groups, referred to here as ELT course group (*n* 78) and literature-based (LB) course (*n* 85). (For a full report, see Ghosn, 2001.) All teachers were experienced teachers, and all classes had received formal English language instruction for four years, using the same coursebook series. For discussion here, five episodes were selected as representing typical patterns emerging from the data.

The Textbook 'in Charge'

The study shows that the textbook was, indeed, a key participant in the classroom interactions, with all participating teachers following the coursebook and the accompanying teacher's guide closely. The control and authority delegated to the textbook were further reflected in the teachers' frequent, rather curious, use of the personal pronoun 'they' when initiating activities specified in the textbook:

Teacher 1: Let's see what **they** want us to do here.
Teacher 2: **They** want us to circle the answers here.
Teacher 3: **They** always give us problems to solve.
Teacher 4: **They** want us to practise conversation here.

There is a strong sense that the textbook is firmly in control of what is permissible and what needs to be accomplished. Although the coursebook had considerable authority in terms of set up of tasks, many of the ELT coursebook tasks were realized in unexpected ways.

Talking like Texts

Some of the above cited criticisms of ELT coursebooks can be understood by examining the following examples from fairly recent ELT courses intended for primary schools.

Ben is late. He brushes his teeth and washes his face in a hurry. He dresses quickly ... He dashes to the office, but the office is empty! Oh no! It's Saturday! Poor Ben. He wishes he was back in bed. (Walker, 1996: 74)

Undoubtedly, the text would sound more natural if presented in the narrative, using the simple past tense. The following text offers another example:

I always get up at seven o'clock. I have breakfast in the kitchen with my family ... I always watch TV and play with my toys ... At half past nine I say 'good night' to my mother and father. (Ellis and Bowen, 1998: 10)

This, too, is perhaps 'unreal', 'stiff', and 'dull', and not reflective of real-world language of children. Texts like these typically precede role-play and paired practice of formulaic chunks of language and grammatical forms, which were standard activities in the ELT course classes. Although many other types of activities were found in the coursebooks, this type of accuracy practice formed a core around which much of the interactions were constructed in the classes observed.

In Episode 1, students are expected to ask and answer questions about each other's free-time activities and tell someone else about their partner's activities. They are given a question and answer sample: *What do you do in your free time? I collect coins.* Twelve activity options are also provided, accompanied by illustrations and short captions: *read; listen to music; garden; care for pets; paint; play soccer; play music; cook; bowl; play video games; collect coins; watch TV* (Salazar Herera and Zanatta, 1996: 15). This is how the activity was realized in the classroom (see Appendix 17.1 for transcription conventions):

Episode 1

1	S 1:	*What do you do in your free time?*
2	T:	Now you answer him.
3	S 2:	I *watch TV.*
4	T:	Next. Now you tell us about her activities.
5	S 1:	She watch <
6	T:	She^
7	S 1:	>She watches TV.
8	T:	Now you.
9	S 3:	*What do you do in your free time?*
10	S 4:	I *play video games.*
11	T:	Now you tell us about his activities.
12	S 3:	He play the Nintendo
13	T:	He play^
14	S 3:	He *play video games*
15	T:	He play^, he play^... or he playz^
16	S 3:	He plays
17	T:	OK. Next.

The activity continued until all students had had a turn. Teacher attention appears to be firmly on form (lines 6, 13, 15). Note how student 3 (line 12) uses his own language, but then, misunderstanding the teacher's prompt, corrects his output to conform to the text. The activity, as it played out in this classroom, became more of a drill or a decoding exercise than genuine communication. This is evident in the video, which shows student pairs standing at their desks and bending down to read the phrases in the book. In another course, students are given a dialogue pattern to guide them to talk about their favourite seasons.

What's your favorite season?   *My favorite season is winter.*
Why?   *I like cold, snowy weather.*
What do you do in the winter?   *I go sledding and ice skating.* (Walker, 1986: 113)

They are also given ten further sentences as response models, with colourful illustrations accompanying the text:

My favorite season is summer. I like hot, sunny weather. I go swimming and sailing.
My favorite season is fall. I like cool, windy weather. I go bike riding. I play in the leaves.
My favorite season is spring. I like warm, rainy days. I plant flowers in my yard. (*ibid.*)

This is what happened in the classroom:

Episode 2

1	S 1:	*What do you do in the fall?*
2	S 2:	Fall I go bike
3	T:	Bike riding
4	S 2:	*I play in the leaves.*
5	T:	Okay. Rami and Boutros. Please do the conversation number 4.
6	S 3:	*What is your favorite season?*
7	S 4:	*My favorite<* [pronounced as 'fā'vrit']
8	T:	My, Rami, my fāvo̱rite
9	S 4:	*My favorite season is spring.*
10	S 3:	Why?
11	S 4:	*I like warm, rainy days.*
12	S 5:	*What's your favorite season?*
13	S 6:	(xxx)
14	S 5:	*Why?*
15	S 6:	I want<
16	T:	Hady, when he asks you why, you will answer by 'because, because'
17	S 6:	Because to swimming
18	T:	Because I go
19	S 6:	I go to swim
20	T:	I go swimming
21	S9:	*What's your favorite season?*
22	T:	OK. Now Rania, you answer him.
23	S 10:	*My favorite season is winter.*
24	T:	Why do you like winter?
25	S 10:	Because it's cold.
26	T:	Because it's cold or because you like to play in the snow^
27	S 10:	I like to play in the snow.
28	T:	Now, Hani and Zeina, you do the conversation.

29	S 11:	*What is your favorite season?*
30	T:	[to S 11] And don't say winter!
31	S 12:	[no response]
32	T:	What is your favorite season?

Again, students are producing text and teacher-prompted language rather than communicating with each other, and the teacher seems more concerned about the accuracy of form than the ideas communicated. When students attempt to use their own words (lines 2 and 19), the teacher corrects them. This prompts student 2 to return to the text (l. 5). On line 30, she seems also concerned about students copying previous responses.

The above two episodes were selected for discussion here because they illustrate the typical interactions observed in the ELT course classes. In these tasks, the expected learner output was at word, phrase and sentence level, as opposed to production of extended discourse, and was highly controlled. Being restricted to reading ready answers from texts, it is unlikely to provide the anticipated short cut to communication that Hatch (1978) suggests practice of formulaic language chunks might do. Learners' interactions were limited to the prescribed scenario, as Legutke and Thomas (1991) have speculated. The activities, as they were realized in the classroom, had a distinct drill flavour, with students producing text or teacher-prompted language and being evaluated on their accuracy. As opposed to being unusual, the observations resonate with Nunan's (1987) findings of accuracy of form dominating over fluency in second language classrooms.

The way such activities are structured does not consider the highly teacher-centred classrooms still prevalent around the world (e.g., Sirotnik, 1983; Fuller and Snyder, 1991) and the teacher dominance of language classroom talk (Chaudron, 1988; Lightbown and Spada, 1994; Tsui, 1995). In order for the above described tasks to be realized as intended by the authors, teachers would need to relinquish some of their control of the discourse to allow for more meaningful student–student interaction to take place. That might, however, be difficult, particularly in highly hierarchical cultures. After all, classrooms must be expected to reflect the prevailing values and norms of the cultures within which they are situated.

In addition to the limited and controlled output, the above examples reveal other concerns. First, the role-play and pair practice activities seem to be based on the assumption that the young learners will need the new language for interpersonal communication, to exchange personal information and to talk about their experiences. Yet, this is meaningful only when learners have a genuine need to communicate such information in the new language, not where such communication can happen in one's own language. Moreover, much of the information children are expected to exchange might already be shared among them, such as family members, hobbies, etc. This further contributes to the artificiality of such tasks and language.

A second concern is the cultural context in which these activities are situated. For example, the only activities students picked from the list in Episode 1 were playing video games and watching TV, with one student picking 'play soccer' and one picking 'play music'. This is not surprising, as coin collecting, caring for pets and bowling are not familiar activities among average Lebanese children, and 'soccer' is known as 'football'. Even the seemingly innocent 'garden' can be baffling, first because it is likely to be understood as a noun by children and, second, because gardening, as common as it may be in North American or British contexts, is hardly an activity with which children living in apartment buildings in big cities will identify.

One might also question the seasonal descriptions and the accompanying activities in Episode 2. Although in North America or Europe children will easily identify with the four seasons and the related activities, they are not the same the world over. A colleague from India pointed out how difficult it would be for her students to talk about the four seasons, while playing in the dry fall leaves must be quite unfamiliar for children in tropical or subtropical regions. Unless children have other vocabulary they can substitute to describe their own activities, such exercises are likely to remain personally irrelevant and artificial.

To use Phillipson's term, the situations provided in these coursebooks are reflective of 'educational imperialism' (1992: 61–3). Although having breakfast in the kitchen, watching TV and playing with toys are perhaps experiences shared by children in the Western world, they do not necessarily mirror the daily experiences of children in other parts of the world. Even within Western cultures, children in impoverished and underprivileged areas, or in some ethnic immigrant communities, may not readily relate to this scenario. It is reminiscent of the stereotypical world in the old 'Dick and Jane' (or 'Janet and John') readers where everybody was white, middle class and comfortable, and where all children had two parents, a nice house and time to play with toys. In short, the world of these texts is foreign and very different from the world many of the learners inhabit.

Learning about the target language culture is, of course, an inherent aspect of language learning. However, activities such as those described above are not the best approach to learning about culture. A more interesting approach, and one that also promotes more natural interaction, is to use children's literature, as the episodes below will illustrate.

Talking about Texts

First, compare the earlier cited ELT coursebook texts with an extract from a popular children's story:

So then we went to the shoestore to buy some sneakers. Anthony chose white ones with blue stripes. Nick chose red ones with white stripes. I chose blue ones with red stripes but then the shoe man said, We're all sold out. They made me buy plain white ones, but they can't make me wear them. (Viorst, 1972, unpaginated)

Undoubtedly, more realistic and definitely more interesting than poor Ben's Saturday experience cited above. Children the world over can easily identify with the character's disappointment, and meaningful and personally relevant interactions can be generated when children compare their own similar experiences. Realistic fiction set in the target language culture, but with universal themes, provides an excellent context for developing cultural awareness and affinity with the target language culture.

When teachers and children talked about texts, the discourse was interactive and often carried over several turns, containing both negotiation and scaffolding from the teacher. In Episode 3, from one of the LB course classes, a discussion about rock-climbing was sparked by a short adventure story about mountain climbing:

Episode 3

1	T:	It's exciting. It seems exciting, but it's risky.
2	S 1:	Miss, one day I climbed, one day I climbed in the (xxx). It was fun
3	T:	Yes, so it was fun, but was it scary?
4	S 1:	Yes.
5	T:	Yes^ You were tied to a rope^
6	S 1:	[nods]
7	S 2:	Miss, he was he talking about a parachute⌃ It has a (xx) and he does like
8		this [waves arms indicating a gliding motion]
9	T:	[Nods]
10	Ss:	Yes. I've seen it!
11	S 3:	Near our house there is uh, there is some rocks I climb, climbed, I teach all
12		my friends to climb those rocks.
13	T:	You climb those rocks⌃ Are they very high?
14	S 3:	No, they are like this [moves hand up and down]
15	T:	Small hill or something^
16	S 3:	Yes, Miss.
17	S 4:	[raises her hand]
18	T:	Yes^
19	S 4:	Me and my brother, the little hill was slippy<
20	T:	Slippery^
21	S 4:	>Yes. We climbed it and we went down rolling.
22	T:	Was it fun?
23	S 4:	Yes, Miss.
24	T:	OK. Last one, yes^
25	S 5:	Miss, once I was climbing (xx) with my two best friends to the snow.
26	T:	Was it high the snow?
27	S 5:	Miss till here [motioning]

The episode shows how story content can invite children to share their own experiences. Note how even the brief exchanges can include negotiation and involve the students in elaborating and clarifying their responses.

Here, students are reading about the legend of the mistletoes:

Episode 4

T:	OK. It's Sarah's turn.
S 1:	*The plant to have in your home is mistletoes.*
S 2:	[raises his hand]
T:	Yes. Rami.
S 2:	*New year and Christmas was here.* [stops reading and looks up] Miss, here they wrote 'is mistletoes'. They have to write 'is <u>a</u> mistle<u>toe</u>'.
T:	No, mistletoes can be, is like uncountable, so, mistletoes is OK.
T:	Nehmet.
S 3:	*In the story, a boy was killed by an arrow made from mistletoes.*
T:	Now the mother, her son died, how did the mother feel? He's dead. Her son was killed so how's the mother feel?
S 4:	The goddess was furious
T:	Furious, yes. Because the boy was dead.
S 5:	*The gods talked among themselves and decided* (xxx). *The happy couple agreed that this boy should see a land of peace and* (xx) *and people who meet under it should exchange kisses.*
T:	So I told you the mistletoe is used as a Christmas decoration, and I told you that when two people meet under mistletoe they should kiss each other.
T:	Now they tell us here. Where did they get this habit from?
S 3:	They said here that in Norse legends.
S 7:	Miss
T:	Yes, Maher.
S 7:	Miss, how can they bring him back to life?
T:	This is a legend. I'm telling you that. Now a legend first, a legend is a story that is told from before. And it's not true.
S 7:	like fantasy^
T:	It's like fantasy, yes. They use magic.

There is a sense of continuity and purpose, and the episode shows how intriguing content can generate student initiations, both about language and about the content.

In only one ELT course class, the teacher was observed using the few available simplified reading selections to generate connected discourse. Episode 5 shows students talking about an extract from *Moby-Dick* and comparing their answers about Captain Ahab's mission:

Episode 5

1	T:	Please, the others are going to listen and see now if the answers are similar
2		or not similar. Who can tell what happened? Did the sailors succeed?
3	S 1:	They did not succeed, they did not succeed because the whale didn't give
4		them a chance because shoke, he shake the boat with his mouth
5	T:	So he didn't give them a chance. You mean that he didn't give them
6		a chance [writes on the board]
7	T:	In other words, the whale, or Moby Dick wasˆ
8	Ss:	Surprise!
9	T:	A surprise, excellent. He surprised them
10	T:	Fadia ((go ahead))
11	S 4:	They didn't succeed because the whale surprised them and he he take took
12		and he take the small boat and swam away
13	T:	Aha, he moved the small boat. You mean that he shook the boatˆ
14	S 4:	He pushed the boat
15	T:	OK, thank you. [writes on the board]
16	S 6:	(xxx) Moby Dick is like answer of Ninar but some words were different
17	T:	Were a little different, a little different. OK. She said here that the whale
18		shook the boat.
19		Wait. Do you think they are the same, the same answers?
20	Ss:	No!
21	T:	The first answer was that he surprised them. The second, he
22		shook the boat. Are they the same? Here (xxx) first he
23		surprises them and shakes the
24		boat laterˆ Is there a relationship between these two answers?
25	Ss:	Yes! Yes! [several students eagerly waving their hands]
26	T:	Zeina.
27	S 1:	[Ninar] The whale shake the boat surprise them.
28	S 6:	[Zeina] Ninar said that he shook the boat
29	T:	Ninarˆ
30	S 1:	Because the ship is, the whale is very big and streng<
31	T:	Strong
32	S 1:	>and strong and, and the sailors don't have a a very big idea<

33	T:	idea, yes about the whale
34	S 1:	>about the whale
35	T:	Aha, so^
36	S 1:	So the sailors didn't catch the whale
37	T:	Excellent, Ninar. Very good, so they didn't catch the whale.

Here, the discourse is interactive and connected, and some negotiation is taking place. Students appear to be actively listening to each other's responses, and the high motivation level of students is visible on the video, which shows students eagerly waving their hands, bidding for turns.

The above episodes demonstrate the potential of literature in generating meaningful and connected discourse. When the aim is to get at the meaning, the interactions are genuine as teachers and students exchange ideas, raise questions and negotiate meaning. The exchanges observed around such reading tasks often extended beyond the basic IRF sequence, at times building into 'exchange complexes' (Hoey, 1992: 79, quoted in Jarvis and Robinson, 1997) with negotiation, scaffolding and student questions and initiations.

Discussion

The authors' and teachers' perceptions of how the tasks are to be realized appear to be markedly different. What textbook authors have intended as providing meaningful interaction practice turns out to be something different. When engaged in the role-play and pair practice tasks, students seemed, as Lemke put it (1990: 91) to 'parrot back *words*' (emphasis in the original) without taking ownership of the ideas or the language. In other words, they were talking like text. The central role accorded the textbook is clearly reflected in the classroom episodes. Students look to the text as an authority regarding what they should say and how they should say it, and this is reinforced by the clear teacher expectation of text-perfect language and rejection of any proximations, as shown in Episodes 1 and 2. While this type of practice may provide 'examples to learn' (Cazden, 1988: 108), the examples are limited and, with the focus on accuracy of form, distance the task from the learners and their world and needs.

When interacting around literature, students do not rely on formulaic chunks of language but attempt to express their ideas using their own interlanguage. Both students' and teachers' focus is firmly on the meaning and ideas, rather than accuracy of linguistic forms. Students also ask questions and initiate interactions, unlike during role-play and pair practice. The textbook was also in control in the LB classes in that teachers followed the questioning strategies suggested in the teacher's guide, but, because the aim of these courses is on developing reading comprehension skills, their focus is thus on the meaning as opposed to form. This is reflected in the classroom discourse.

Conclusion

Legutke and Thomas (1991: 7) have asked whether it is 'possible to turn L2 classrooms into whole-person events, where body and soul, intellect and feeling, head, hand and heart converge in action?'. The episodes cited above suggest that, in primary school, it is possible through the use of children's literature. When the research evidence pointing to literature as being associated with significant gains in second language learning is taken together with the above cited examples, there is evidence to suggest that the key to this success may well be found in the interactions that literature generates. Talking about stories provides a meaningful and personally relevant context to interaction in the new language. Carefully selected readings can maintain motivation by maintaining a level of challenge, particularly if the teacher provides appropriate scaffolding feedback and maintains the focus on meaning.

This is not to say that accuracy need not be addressed. The question is more about the approach. While courses for young learners still often begin with accuracy practice and gradually move to reading comprehension, the reverse may, in fact, be more appropriate. In other words, a story provides a beginning point to generate discussion and link the content to learners' experiences. Follow-up activities, such as dialogues, literary journals, letters to the characters and so on, can then be used for accuracy practice. (See, for example, Whiteson, 1996; Ghosn, 1999, for suggestions.) If children are given the opportunity to select such activities, they can also be meaningful and relevant.

Appendix 17.1 Transcription conventions

All names within the transcripts are pseudonyms, and different student speakers are identified as 'S 1', 'S 2', and so on.

The following transcript conventions were used in all the transcripts:

Italics	indicates student or teacher is reading aloud from a given text
(( ))	utterance in L1
(xxx)	unintelligible
[ ]	transcriber's comment
^	indicates a rising intonation (as in a question)
| go went	vertical line indicates overlapping utterance
<	indicates an interruption of utterance
>	indicates continuation of a previously interrupted utterance

References

Aranha, M. (1985) 'Sustained silent reading goes east'. *Reading Teacher*, **39** (2), 214–17.

Barton, D. (1994) *Literacy. An Introduction to the Ecology of Written Language.* Oxford: Blackwell.

Cazden, C. (1988) *Classroom Discourse. The Language of Teaching and Learning.* Portsmouth, NH: Heinemann.

Chaudron, C. (1988) *Second Language Classroom Research on Teaching and Learning.* Cambridge: Cambridge University Press.

Crystal, D. (1987) *Child Language, Learning and Linguistics: An Overview for Teaching and Therapeutic Professions.* London: Edward Arnold.

Cunningsworth, A. (1995) *Choosing Your Coursebook.* Oxford: Heinemann.

Elley, W. B. (1991) 'Acquiring literacy in second language: the effects of book-based programs'. *Language Learning*, **41** (3), 375–411.

Elley, W. B. (2000) 'The potential of book floods for raising literacy levels'. *International Review of Education*, **46** (3/4), 233–55.

Elley, W., Cutting, B., Mangubhai, F. and Hugo, C. (1996) 'Lifting literacy levels with story books: evidence from the South Pacific, Singapore, Sri Lanka and South Africa'. Paper presented at the World Conference on Literacy, Philadelphia, 12–15 March (ERIC Document Reproduction Service No. ED416441).

Ellis, P. and Bowen, M. (1998) *Way Ahead. A Foundation Course in English.* London: Macmillan.

Ellis, R. (1994) *Understanding Second Language Acquisition.* Oxford: Oxford University Press.

Fielding, L., Wilson, P. T. and Anderson, R. (1984) 'A new focus on free reading: the role of trade books in reading instruction', in T. E. Rapahel (ed.) *The Contexts of School Based Literacy.* New York: Random House.

Fox, G. (1998) 'Using corpus data in the classroom', in B. Tomlinson (ed.) *Materials Development in Language Teaching.* Cambridge: Cambridge University Press.

Fuller, B. and Snyder, C. W., Jr. (1991) 'Vocal teachers, silent pupils? Life in Botswana classrooms'. *Comparative Education Review*, **35** (2), 274–94.

Gass, S. (1997) *Input, Interaction, and the Second Language Learner.* Mahwah, NJ: Lawrence Erlbaum Associates.

Ghosn, I. (1999) *Caring Kids: Social Responsibility through Literature.* Beirut: Dar El-Ilm Lilmalayin.

Ghosn, I. (2001) 'Teachers and students interacting around the textbook: an exploratory study of children developing academic second language literacy in primary school English language classes in Lebanon'. Doctoral thesis, University of Leicester.

Gregory, E. (1996) *Making Sense of a New World: Learning to Read in a Second Language.* London: Paul Chapman Ltd.

Hardy, B. (1978) 'Narrative as the primary act of mind', in M. Meek, A. Warlow and G. Barton, (eds) *The Cool Web: The Pattern of Children's Reading.* New York: Atheneum.

Hatch, E. (1978) *Discourse Analysis and Second Language Acquisition.* Cambridge, MA: Newbury House.

Hill, D. R. and Reid Thomas, M. (1988) 'Graded readers: a survey review' (Part I). *ELT Journal*, **42**, 44–52.

Jarvis, J. and Robinson, M. (1997) 'Analysing educational discourse: an exploratory study of teacher response and support to pupils' learning'. *Applied Linguistics*, **18** (2), 212–28.

Lazar, G. (1994) 'Using literature at lower levels'. *ELT Journal*, **48** (2), 115–24.

Legutke, M. and Thomas, H. (1991) *Process and Experience in the Language Classroom*. London: Longman.

Lemke, J. L. (1990) *Talking Science: Language, Learning, and Values*. New York: Ablex.

Lightbown, P. and Spada, N. (1994) *How Languages are Learned*. Oxford: Oxford University Press.

Littlejohn, A. (1998) 'The analysis of language teaching materials: inside the Trojan horse', in B. Tomlinson (ed.) *Materials Development in Language Teaching*. Cambridge: Cambridge University Press, pp. 190–216.

Long, M. (1981) 'Input, interactions and second language acquisition', in H. Winitz (ed.) *Native and Foreign Language Acquisition*. New York: NY Academy of Sciences.

Luke, A. (1988) *Literacy, Textbook and Ideology: Postwar Literacy Instruction and the Mythology of Dick and Jane*. London: Falmer Press.

McDonough, J. and Shaw, C. (1993) *Materials and Methods in ELT*. Oxford: Blackwell.

McKay, S. (1986) 'Literature in the ESL classroom', in C. Brumfit and R. A. Carter (eds) *Literature and Language Teaching*. Oxford: Oxford University Press, pp. 192–8.

Martin, P. W. (1999) 'Bilingual unpacking of monolingual texts in two primary classrooms in Brunei Darussalam'. *Language and Education*, **13** (1), 38–58.

Meek, M. (1988) 'The critical challenge of the world in books for children'. *Children's Literature in Education*, **26** (1), 5–22.

Nunan, D. (1987) 'Communicative language teaching: making it work'. *ELT Journal*, **41** 136–45.

Phillipson, R. H. (1992) *Linguistic Imperialism*. Oxford, Oxford University Press.

Salazer Herrera, M. and Zanatta, T. (1996) *Parade*. Glenview, IL: Scott Foresman and Co.

Sheldon, L. E. (1987) *ELT Textboks and Materials: Problems in Evaluation and Development*. ELT Document 126, Modern English Publications in association with the British Council.

Sheldon, L. E. (1988) 'Evaluating ELT textbooks and materials'. *ELT Journal*, **42** (4), 237–46.

Sinclair, J. McH. and Coulthard, R. M. (1975) *Towards an Analysis of Discourse. The English Used by Teachers and Pupils*. Oxford: Oxford University Press.

Sirotnik, K. A. (1983) 'What you see is what you get – consistency, persistency, and mediocrity in the classroom'. *Harvard Educational Review* **53** (1), 16–31.

Swain, M. and Lapkin, S. (1995) 'Problems in output and the cognitive processes they generate: a step towards second language learning'. *Applied Linguistics,* **16** (3), 371–91.

Tomlinson, B. (ed.) (1998) *Materials Development in Language Teaching.* Cambridge: Cambridge University Press.

Tsui, A. B. M. (1995) *Introducing Classroom Interaction.* London: Penguin.

Tudor, I. and Hafiz, F. (1989) 'Extensive reading as a means of input to L2 learning'. *Journal of Research in Reading,* **12** (2), 164–78.

Viorst, J. (1972) *Alexander and the Terrible, Horrible, No Good, Very Bad Day.* New York: Aladdin Books.

Walker, M. (1986) *Amazing English.* Boston: Addison Wesley Publishing Co.

Whiteson, V. (ed.) (1996) *New Ways of Using Drama and Literature in Language Teaching.* Alexandria, VA: TESOL.

CHAPTER

18

Materials for Specific Purposes

Roger Barnard and Dorothy Zemach

Introduction

As a recognized area of English language teaching, English for Specific Purposes (ESP) is now almost half a century old, but despite this relatively long history there is some disagreement about the exact meaning of the term. It could even be argued that there have been attempts by those directly involved in ESP to claim a separate, and by implication, superior position in the world of EFL/ESL. In our view, these claims are mistaken.

It is important to bear in mind two points at the outset:

a. ESP covers an enormous range of content areas such as business, medicine, the law, engineering, history and art and design; in fact, any area of contemporary academic or professional life in which English is needed.
b. ESP is not an approach, a method or a technique (although simulation and role-play activities are often identified with business ESP courses). The only feature common to all types of ESP course is the selection of the content and teaching approach according to the perceived needs of the learners. Consequently, needs analysis generally plays a more pivotal role in ESP than in EGP (English for General Purposes).

After presenting a working definition of ESP and a brief account of its development, we will present an overview of the present state of the field. We will then discuss the factors involved in preparing various types of materials for ESP courses and make suggestions and recommendations for designing materials. We will then present some recent examples of published materials we have worked on. After considering the question of evaluation, we will discuss possible future developments in ESP.

A Definition

The definition we shall be working with in this chapter states our view of what ESP is at present: English for Specific Purposes (ESP) is an umbrella term that refers to the teaching of English to students who are learning the language for a particular work or study-related reason. The two main areas are:

- English for Occupational Purposes (EOP), concerned with enabling a learner to function in English in a particular job or profession.
- English for Academic Purposes (EAP), which provides learners with the appropriate language skills for pursuing a tertiary-level course taught in English, and/or presenting, researching, and publishing in academic settings.

In fact, the dividing line between ESP and EGP is not always clear; where do we place, for example, a course designed for a Korean businessperson who is to assume a post abroad in the near future? If the learner's proficiency level is very low, a great deal of the course content will probably be of a general English type with emphasis on survival situations. Most would probably agree that the course should be classified as ESP, simply because the aims are clearly defined, and analysis of the learner's needs play an important part in deciding what to include in the course. However, we believe our example demonstrates that ESP should not be regarded as a discrete division of ELT, but simply an area (with blurred boundaries) whose courses are usually more focused in their aims and make use of a narrower range of topics. Most of the points we will address are of equal relevance to the teaching of general English, and we are in agreement with McDonough and Shaw (1993) that both ESP and EGP courses are expected to pay detailed attention to learner needs and expectations, and to respond to them as efficiently and effectively as possible.

Figure 18.1 illustrates two possible branches of the EGP–ESP continuum (in this case EOP), with two highly specialized courses for particular groups of learners on the right. This helps to clarify a number of obvious but extremely important points for designers of ESP materials:

a. Generally speaking, the more focused the course, the greater the knowledge of the specialism required by the course designer and the teacher.

b. The learners will very often know more than the teacher about the topic area of a lesson.

c. The greater the specialization, the more obvious the differences in course content; however, all areas of ESP will share a common basis in general English.

d. In theory, it is easier to predict learners' specific language needs at the ESP end of the continuum.

e. The position of a course on the continuum in no way dictates what approach, method or techniques should be used in class.

f. A course especially developed for a specific context and group of learners will not necessarily be limited to the language used in that context. Depending on the time available, apparently unrelated EGP content can be used to develop fluency and provide variety.

g. The proficiency levels of learners may set limits on the level of specificity of a course. At lower levels, more attention will probably be given to proficiency in general English.

EGP ◄――――――――――――――――――► ESP

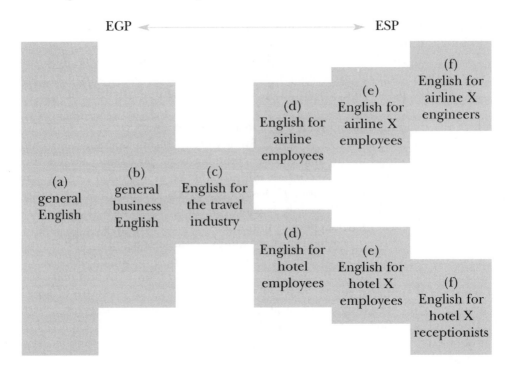

Figure 18.1 Two examples of occupational ESP branches

A Brief History of ESP

We do not have space in this chapter to present a detailed history of ESP, and will briefly mention some of the main developments. For those interested in a more detailed summary, Hutchinson and Waters (1987) and Dudley-Evans and St John (1998) provide excellent accounts.

After World War II, the world came to be dominated by two forces: technology and commerce. For various reasons, most noticeably the power and influence of the United States, the primary language for both fields became English.

Until the 1960s, there had been no concerted effort to design language courses for specific learning objectives; however, in the post-war years, international exchanges in technology and commerce became increasingly important, with English as the lingua franca. Partly due to corporate and governmental pressure, and partly to the wishes of learners who were learning the language for professional or academic purposes, it became clear in the 1960s that there was a need for English courses that were designed to satisfy real-world demands as efficiently as possible. This tendency was accelerated in the 1970s by the considerable investment in English language programmes in the oil-producing countries. Some saw English as a neutral empowering medium (Strevens, 1977), while to others it was (and still is) an agent of international capitalism and 'linguistic imperialism' (Phillipson, 1992; Pennycook, 1994).

In addition, the field of ESP was influenced by developments in linguistics and educational psychology. Although most of these ideas eventually filtered through into mainstream ELT, they made their initial impact in ESP. It is generally agreed that there have been five main currents in ESP which have influenced developments in the field, as follows:

1. *Register analysis.* The first important ESP materials in the 1960s and early 1970s were based on the findings of register analysis, in which the grammatical and lexical features of a topic area were analysed and organized with the aim of making the contents of the course more relevant to learners' needs. Research concentrated mainly on science and medicine-related specialisms. However, register analysis proved to have limited usefulness as far as ESP syllabus design was concerned, partly because grammatical differences from one topic area to another were relatively slight, and analysis was limited to the sentence level.

2. *Discourse and rhetorical analysis.* In the 1970s, attention shifted to understanding how different social contexts influenced the way discourse above the sentence level was used for communication. This included not only grammar and lexis, but levels of formality and management of information, and led to the development of 'functional' syllabuses based on functions as opposed to grammar points. These developments also had a profound effect on EGP materials and courses and the field of genre analysis adopted a similar approach to written texts.

3. *Needs analysis.* The process of collecting, collating and interpreting data on the learner's likely use of the target language has been an indispensable feature of ESP from the beginning, and Munby's highly detailed model (1978) represented the culmination of the 'target situation analysis' approach.

4. *The skills-centred approach.* Skills-centered courses explored the thinking processes that underlie language use, and developments in this area were most noticeable in EAP. Much work was done in South America with courses devoted to reading-skill development. Rather than 'mastering' the language needed for particular contexts within the course period, the objective was to develop skills (e.g., using a dictionary effectively and selecting appropriate reference materials) which could be utilized to increase language ability in the target area after the completion of the course.

5. *The learning-centred approach.* As presented by Hutchinson and Waters (1987), this approach paid greater attention to the affective factors of language learning, and attempted to address learner needs at all stages of course design. One example of this is the observation that, although a typical skills-centered reading course would be devoted almost exclusively to reading activities, a learning-centred reading course would provide practice in other skills, not only in order to complement and reinforce reading activities, but also to make the course more varied and interesting, and thus more motivating.

Present-day ESP

It appears that the dominant areas in ESP are now business English and EAP, and materials range from published courses to situation-specific materials developed by teachers in a company or educational institution. Whereas the emphasis in early ESP was mainly on reading and writing skills, all four language skills are now given equal attention, and emphasis on a skill or skills will depend on the aims of the course.

Dudley-Evans and St John (1998: 30) observe that, in present-day ESP, as in other areas of ELT, 'there is now acceptance of many different approaches and a willingness to mix different types of material and methodologies.' In recent business courses, 'general' English content, e.g., grammar, appears to be more common than before, and more attention is paid to developing effective communication (as opposed to purely linguistic) skills, e.g., making presentations, participating in meetings and, no less importantly, socializing. The blatantly Anglocentric world-view of past materials has generally been replaced by a multicultural approach, discussion activities based on cross-cultural topics being one example. English is presented as an 'international' language, and courses will often feature non-native speakers in recordings.

It may also be true that ESP has become less daunting to EGP teachers as its range of content has broadened; a collection of ESP class activities by Master and Brinton (1998) illustrates this trend with a wide variety of activities that are very similar in form and spirit to those used in EGP classes.

Programmes and Courses

Apart from the degree of specialization mentioned above, there are other variables that an ESP materials designer will need to consider. The most important of these are presented in Figure 18.2.

All these will clearly affect the character of a course, and a few examples should suffice: an in-house language programme will probably be able to draw upon a closely knit group of like-minded full-time colleagues to develop, pilot and revise materials, whereas a teacher in, say, a Japanese university may well be left to his or her own devices. And obviously there is no use devising exercises which rely on the use of video, OHP or computer-aided presentation hardware if these facilities are not available. Finally, if a teacher's knowledge of the specialism is likely to be limited, then support will have to be incorporated into a teacher's handbook or manual.

EAP

English for Academic Purposes can be roughly divided into two camps – English needed to complete academic courses, which might include skills such as writing essays and participating in graduate seminars, and English used in academic

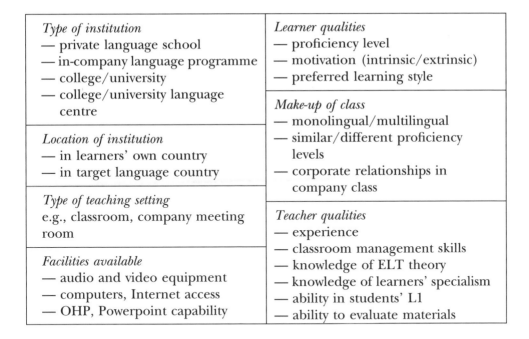

Type of institution — private language school — in-company language programme — college/university — college/university language centre	*Learner qualities* — proficiency level — motivation (intrinsic/extrinsic) — preferred learning style

Location of institution
— in learners' own country
— in target language country
	Make-up of class
	— monolingual/multilingual
	— similar/different proficiency
	  levels
	— corporate relationships in
	  company class

Type of teaching setting e.g., classroom, company meeting room	*Teacher qualities* — experience — classroom management skills
Facilities available — audio and video equipment — computers, Internet access — OHP, Powerpoint capability	— knowledge of ELT theory — knowledge of learners' specialism — ability in students' L1 — ability to evaluate materials

Figure 18.2 ESP course variables

communities, such as reading and writing for journals and giving presentations at conferences.

Into the first camp might fall the sub-specialization of English needed to get accepted to a school. While this is often an area of specialization more popular with learners than teachers, there is undeniably a wealth of materials geared towards helping learners learn language and strategies for taking tests such as the TOEFL (Test of English as a Foreign Language, used for admission to colleges and universities in the United States) and in the UK, IELTS (International English Language Testing System). Grammar and vocabulary might be no different from that presented in standard EGP textbooks, but it is presented in the context of test items. Although some teachers understandably resist the idea of teaching an entire course geared towards passing a certain examination, on the bright side learners enrolled in such courses are usually extremely motivated. The teacher then has the chance to work with this motivation to present English directly geared to academic study. Learners in such courses normally see the value of reading academic texts, writing practice essays, etc., as these formats will also appear in the tests themselves. Whether taking a host of practice tests does anything for a learner's actual language ability, it can familiarize a learner with the test format and thus decrease stress; this is particularly important for learners with minimal computer skills facing the recently computerized TOEFL exam.

EAP courses can include discrete skills such as listening and note-taking for lecture classes, reading strategies to cope with heavy reading assignments in a learner's area of concentration and writing essays and longer papers. Some of these skills, such as writing topic sentences or preparing an annotated bibliography, may not be widely used outside of an academic environment but are crucial to a student's success in a college or university course.

One challenge for the EAP teacher, like the ESP teacher unfamiliar with a learner's field of business, is that different areas of academic study have different styles and requirements. A student taking a humanities seminar will need discussion skills; a student in the sciences may need specialized vocabulary. Learners, too, have different cultural backgrounds: some may be uncomfortable visiting professors during office hours; others may find their style of classroom participation more or less assertive than that of their native speaker classmates. Some textbooks therefore include sections on study skills or coping with the academic environment, and textbooks that present authentic listening or reading passages may draw them from different academic disciplines. It is also important – in fact, crucial – for the ESL teacher to interact with instructors of other courses to find out what is expected of international students in those classes. Will, say, a professor in a business class mark down an international student's paper that contains grammar mistakes which do not obscure meaning? Answers will vary not only from institution to institution but also from professor to professor. This is also an opportunity to obtain examples of readings, vocabulary lists, tests, etc., used in the students' academic classes. Some institutions feature linked classes, where students concurrently take academic classes and ESL classes that share subject matter and, sometimes, materials. Benesch (2001) gives two in-depth examples of linked courses at the City University of New York: EAP/Anthropology and EAP/Psychology, with concrete examples of how the classes negotiated areas such as topic choice and rules and procedures. The EAP classes not only assisted students with language support but also with negotiating skills and a sense of their place (and, Benesch stresses, their rights) at the university.

The field of genre analysis has been crucial in helping researchers, materials developers, and teachers in understanding the varieties of academic English that learners will encounter and hope to master. Swales (1990) offers a thorough yet accessible view of both the approach and results from research into various specific genres. In short, the approach involves analysing typical texts from a given field (for example, dissertations, conference proposals or business faxes), distilling their distinctive features (such as use of the passive voice, reference to previous research or organization of the text), and familiarizing learners with key 'moves' or discourse patterns.

For most, the point of investigating different genres has been to assist learners in joining a given discourse community; without being aware of how to speak and write like a law student, for example, a non-native learner might be shunted aside in spite of high academic ability. Recently, researchers such as Dudley-Evans (1997) and Benesch (2001) have raised concerns about the appropriacy of training learners to dovetail their academic discourse to the Anglo-American model. As increasingly more English language articles are being written and read by non-native English speakers, how should one determine whose genre style is the 'correct' one to serve as the model? Whether teachers are interested in having their students imitate native speaker models or not, however, most would agree on the importance of raising students' awareness that these discourse communities exist and what their salient features are.

Materials to familiarize students with a given genre are necessarily authentic texts. What the teacher can manipulate is the selection of these texts (considering factors such as length and difficulty) and the tasks required of the students. Even low-level learners can study authentic texts critically and note recurring features; carefully graded exercises can lead students through manipulating and then reproducing these same features themselves. More advanced students, of course, can examine more complex texts, and examine them more closely. A student is probably more convinced of the accepted way to write a dissertation abstract after reading several examples than if a teacher or textbook were simply to say 'This is the way you must do it.' See Bhatia (1993) for an example of genre-based ESP materials used in Singapore.

For obvious reasons, much of the work in genre research to date has been done with written texts. An exciting opportunity to study spoken academic English is provided by the Michigan Corpus of Academic Spoken English (MICASE) of the University of Michigan. This databank of transcriptions of spoken English in a university environment (for example, lectures, study groups, office hours) is available – at no cost – on-line at *<http://www.lsa.umich.edu/eli/micase/micase. htm>*. Materials writers wishing to create controlled yet realistic monologues or conversations could search for vocabulary items, collocations or grammatical structures in MICASE and note their frequency and the contexts in which they were most likely to occur.

The Materials Writer

What makes a good materials writer? In our view, he or she must be a good teacher, although not all good teachers will make good materials writers. This is simply because it is possible to be a good teacher and work in virtual isolation from your peers; however, a writer of materials for use by other teachers must be able to present ideas in ways that are clear and unambiguous to different types of teachers. The prospective writer should have (in no particular order):

a.   an acceptable linguistic knowledge of the target language
b.   general teaching experience
c.   teaching experience in the relevant specialism
d.   some degree of knowledge of the relevant specialism
e.   an interest in the relevant specialism
f.   familiarity with learning materials available for the specialism
g.   experience of writing general English materials
h.   an interest in the learning/teaching process
i.   the ability to work with others
j.   the ability to assess the clarity and effectiveness of materials and respond appropriately

Types of Materials

As we have already mentioned, there is a wide variety of subjects covered by the term ESP. Similarly, there is no one type of ESP material. The following are the main types:

a.   Published course materials:

- General business, e.g., *Business Venture* (OUP)
- Specialized business, e.g., *English for International Banking and Finance* (CUP)
- Professional English, e.g., *Oxford English for Electrical and Mechanical Engineering* (OUP)
- Vocational courses, e.g., *Travel File* (Longman)
- Academic English skills, e.g., *Academic Writing for Graduate Students* (University of Michigan Press)
- Content-based or theme-based academic English courses, e.g., *Northstar* (Longman)

It goes without saying that publishers are generally less enthusiastic about publishing materials which have a very limited specialist audience, and when materials are needed for such situations, educational institutions will need to develop their own materials.

b.   Materials prepared by the foreign language section of a corporation for use by its employees.
c.   Materials prepared by a language school or university/college language department for use by its students.
d.   Materials prepared by an individual teacher for use by students in his/her classes.

These types can be further subdivided into materials which:

a.   constitute the main course text;
b.   are used to regularly supplement a published textbook, e.g., to provide a regular listening segment;
c.   are used as occasional supplements to other materials.

We can present this description in table form as seen in Table 18.1. Most teachers will begin their careers as materials writers by writing type 1a, then possibly advance to 1b. Depending on where they teach, they might then collaborate with colleagues formally or informally to produce types 2a or 2b. The organization required to produce a well-designed main text is considerable, and relatively few private language schools are willing to invest the time, effort and money to create ESP course texts from scratch; on the other hand, foreign lan-

Table 18.1 Materials producers and materials types

MATERIALS TYPE	PRODUCED BY individual teacher	private language school/ university language dept./ language section of corporation	publisher
occasional supp.	1a	2a	3a
regular supp.	1b	2b	3b
main text	1c	2c	3c

guage sections in large organizations have been successful, partly because they often employ full-time teachers who can meet regularly to work on projects.

Some teachers who have developed a taste for materials writing will wish to try their hand in the world of publishing, which will bring additional considerations into the equation, such as satisfying market demands identified by the publisher, which the writer may not always agree with. The writer may also have to write the text with one or more co-authors whom he or she will only occasionally (or never) meet. Note that Table 18.1 indicates three uses of published materials; although a published textbook is generally intended to be a main text, it can also function as a regular supplement to a main text, some examples being courses dealing with listening or reading skills, or containing role-play and simulation activities. In practice, of course, textbooks are often used as occasional supplements, although this is rarely the publisher's intention!

First Steps in Preparing ESP Materials

Selection of appropriate language, responding to the needs and wishes of the students, paying attention to effective learning strategies; all these elements are vitally important when preparing ESP materials. However, there are some additional points that we would like to mention:

a. Bear in mind the backgrounds of the teachers who will use the materials. How experienced are they? How much do they know about developments in ELT and ESP? How much do they know about the ESP specialism?
b. There should be a course syllabus which will indicate what kind and what amount of materials are needed. The entire syllabus may be prepared by a department, and may depend solely on materials developed by the staff. At the other extreme, the syllabus may be provided by a published textbook, and supplemented by in-house materials. Whatever the situation, materials should be developed according to guidelines which have been agreed upon by the staff.
c. Allow for personal preference and modification on the part of the teacher.

Materials that can be used in a variety of ways are more likely to have a positive effect on a teacher's performance in class.

d. Ideally, the course syllabus and class materials will be designed not only by a group of teachers who are conversant with the latest developments in ELT and ESP, but who share a similar approach to teaching, who can cooperate on collating and responding to feedback and who are supported by a sympathetic management. As most teachers know, this type of situation is not always the norm.

e. Consider designing guides and templates to aid less experienced teachers to develop materials. For example, if listening material is needed, advice on the selection, editing, recording and re-recording of texts could be presented, together with a brief summary of current thinking in teaching listening skills. This could be supplemented by templates which allow teachers to 'slot in' texts and exercises to produce usable materials.

f. Remember that syllabuses and materials have a limited lifespan. Wherever possible, design a syllabus that allows for partial changes to be made, thus avoiding wholesale changes to a programme that can be disastrous. Design materials that can be revised with a minimum of effort. Do not spend too much time developing materials that have a short shelf-life.

g. Encourage ongoing research into analysis of relevant source texts (written and spoken), and related textbooks. Organize regular meetings/workshops to exchange ideas.

A Recommended Sequence for Preparing Materials

1. Determine the needs and preferences of the students and institution/corporation through questionnaires and/or interviews.
2. Decide what sort of language contexts the course will focus on (e.g., lectures, business meetings).
3. Decide on the categories for presenting the language in the course (e.g., grammar, function, lexis, situation, topic, communicative skill).
5. Decide what language skills and sub-skills the course will focus on (e.g., listening, speaking, reading, writing), taking into account learners' and company's objectives.
6. Design the syllabus; will it be cumulative, or will each unit/lesson be independent?
7. Decide the types of activities that will be used in the course (e.g., individual, pair, group, whole class).
8. Decide on the page layout of worksheets; prepare templates.
9. Prepare the materials.
10. Pilot the materials; collect and collate feedback through questionnaires and interviews.
11. Revise the materials.
12. Use the materials.
13. Get feedback from students, teachers and sponsors during and after the

course through e.g., questionnaires, interviews, classroom observations by peer teachers and managers, videotaping of lessons, lesson comment sheets (see section 12 later).

14. Revise the materials if necessary.
15. Periodically review the course.

This sequence is an ideal, and very often a number of steps will be omitted; however, it does illustrate two important points:

* in the process of materials design, the roles of writers, learners, teachers and sponsors are inextricably interconnected;
* the process is essentially circular; there is no beginning or end – there is never a 'finished product'.

Examples

Owing to space limitations, we will be limiting our examples to a number of activities from a published course in general business English for false beginners (R. Barnard and J. Cady (2000) *Business Venture Book 1* (2nd. edn.), OUP).

This pair work activity from *Business Venture Book 1*, Student Book, p. 14, is based on real-world information taken from the Internet, and illustrates the use of authentic material adapted to provide challenging, motivating practice for high-beginner learners (see Figure 18.3). It involves the exchange of information, with the emphasis on accuracy of content rather than form. The focus on letters and numbers is particularly important at this level. Note the example questions which provide back-up for less able students. Materials designed in-house or by an individual teacher may not achieve the graphic sophistication of this example, but layout should always be carefully considered; an otherwise excellent text and activity can be ruined simply by a badly designed presentation on the page.

A common mistake made by inexperienced materials writers is to cram too much information onto the page; text should always kept to the minimum, and surrounded by liberal amounts of white space. And remember that illustrations are not simply decoration – they can present and clarify information as well as aid retention of the target language.

Example 2 in Figure 18.4 gives another pair work activity, based on material taken from the Internet. Clearly, the Internet is an invaluable source of information for language teachers and materials designers, but it is important to realize that if your materials are to be published in any form, permission must be obtained, wherever your original text comes from. This particular example, which forms part of a unit on company and personal information, originally featured two computer entrepreneurs, and contrasted their (surprisingly similar) careers. Unfortunately, one refused permission for the use of his life history, and the activity had to be modified to feature Ted Waitt alone.

8 **Flight departures**

Student A: Look at the flight departure board below.
Student B: Turn to page 76.

Take turns asking and answering questions to complete the flight
information, e.g.

What's the number of the Seoul flight?
When does the Seoul flight leave?
What's the destination of flight SU 316?

FLIGHT	DESTINATION	DEPARTURE TIME
	Seoul	
JL 005	Tokyo	1:30
SU 316		
DL 072	Istanbul	5:40
AY 004		
SA 202	Johannesburg	6:20
	Paris	
SQ 025	Singapore	9:45
	Rio de Janeiro	
UA 863	Sydney	11:05

Figure 18.3 Example 1 from a student book (*Business Venture*, Book 1, p. 14)

Most would agree that authentic information is desirable in a language course; however, if presented inappropriately, authentic texts can be confusing and demotivating. The materials writer has a number of choices: to use the authentic material in its original form and design tasks that enable lower-level learners to interact actively with the content, or to adapt the text itself, trying to ensure that the original character and discourse features are retained.

Our final example (see Figure 18.5, Example 3) is a workbook reading and writing exercise designed to be completed outside class after related classroom work, and shows that material designed for receptive use away from the pressure

4 A career in computers

Student A: Look at the information below.
Student B: Turn to page 79.

PART 1

1963 Ted Waitt was born.

1983 He enrolled at a college in Ohio.

1985 He dropped out of college.
His grandfather helped him get a bank loan.
He started up his own company by himself.
Gateway began selling computers to stores.

1986 The company earned $1.5 million.

PART 2

1988 Gateway earned $12 million.

1990 It moved its main offices to South Dakota.

1993 It opened its first overseas factory in Ireland.

1994 The company opened showrooms in France and Germany.

1995 It entered the Australian market.

1997 Ted Waitt became a billionaire.

You and your partner have information about Ted Waitt, Chairman and CEO of Gateway. Part 1 of your information contains five mistakes. Student B's information is correct. Ask Student B questions, and correct the mistakes. Ask *yes / no* questions only, e.g.

A: *Was Ted Waitt born in 1963?*
B: *Yes, he was.*
A: *Did he enroll at a college in Ohio in 1983?*
B: *No, he didn't. He …*

When you have finished, answer Student B's questions about Part 2. Your information is correct. Student B's information contains five mistakes.

Figure 18.4 Example 2 from a Student book (*Business Venture*, Book 1, p. 43)

3 Market share

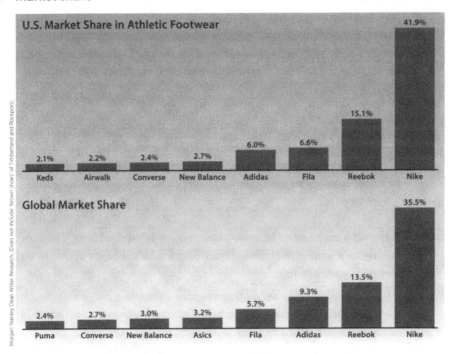

1 Fill in the blanks. Use the information in the charts.

   a Airwalk has a *2.2%* share of the athletic shoe market in the USA.

   b Adidas has a .... share of the athletic shoe market in the USA.

   c 2.4% of the athletic shoes sold in the USA are produced by ....

   d ASICS produces .... of the athletic shoes sold worldwide.

   e The biggest producer of athletic shoes sold worldwide is .... , with 35.5% of the market.

   f The second biggest manufacturer of athletic shoes in the USA is Reebok, which has a .... share of the market.

2 Now write two sentences of your own about the information in the charts.

   a ....

      ....

      ....

   b ....

      ....

      ....

Figure 18.5 Example 3 from a student workbook (*Business Venture*, Book 1, p. 38)

of the classroom can feature a higher level of language. This particular exercise includes four or five ways of describing market share. The related classroom speaking activities feature only one.

An additional point raised by this example is the question of how to deal with potentially controversial topics, in this case business ethics and the pros and cons of globalization. Although the material itself does not refer directly to these issues, the teacher is (one hopes) free to address them in class, either in the form of informal discussion or by developing additional materials.

Evaluation

Because the learning environment is continually changing, even carefully piloted materials need to be evaluated after use in class.

There are two kinds of evaluation, each of equal importance: evaluation by the learners, and evaluation by the teachers. There may also be some kind of evaluation by the sponsor (company or institution).

Although evaluation by teachers and sponsor is relatively simple to organize, evaluation by learners presents a number of problems; for example, should information be gathered in the target language or L1? Should learners be asked to comment on specific activities or the course as a whole? And how much attention should we pay to the information we collect?

Most teachers are familiar with some form of feedback questionnaire. Designing an effective questionnaire is often more difficult than it at first appears, and decisions must be made on such points as whether to use multiple choice or open-ended responses or a combination of the two. We must decide whether to present the questionnaire in the target language or the learner's L1, and also at what point in the course to hand it out; a questionnaire presented halfway through a course, for example, will allow the students to benefit from any modifications that may need to be made to the course as a result of the questionnaire data. If a questionnaire is used in the middle of the course, should we also use a second one at the end of the course? A well-designed questionnaire is time-efficient, and easy to administer and collate. However, there are other ways to obtain feedback, such as interviews and learner diaries, in which a learner can record impressions of a course over a certain period of time, either in the target language or his or her L1.

For the materials developer, a mid-course or end-of-course questionnaire may be useful in terms of obtaining general impressions, but it is sometimes useful to find out how students feel about specific lessons and activities. A particularly effective way of doing this is the lesson comment sheet, which presents questions such as the following (in the target language or in the student's L1) with spaces for responses:

What did you do in today's lesson?
What did you learn in today's lesson?
Which activities did you enjoy? Why?

Which activities didn't you enjoy? Why not?
Did you have any problems? If so, what kind?
Do you have any other comments or suggestions about the lesson?

The comment sheet can be distributed in various ways, but a recommended procedure with, say, a class of fifteen students, would be to divide the class into five groups of three and give the comment sheet to each group in succession as a homework task. The teacher should decide whether responses are to be written in the L1 and/or L2. It would probably be unfair to ask individual students to complete the sheet more than twice in a course.

The Future

The easiest changes to predict in the foreseeable future for ESP materials development involve computers and technology, which will impact at least three main areas:

a. *Subject matter.* In textbooks and teacher-created materials, references to e-mail, the Internet and instant text messaging replace mention of telexes and cables. Computers can even become the focus of study in the classroom: as more information becomes available in English on-line, learners have an increased need to learn typing and web navigation skills; the computer itself thus becomes in a way a 'material'.
b. *Availability of information, authentic texts and opportunities for interaction.* Teachers and learners alike can access documents on-line, perhaps of particular value to those studying or teaching English as a foreign language, who might not have access to an English language library. Learners will therefore have increasing opportunities to find their own materials, and teachers will have greater access to authentic texts. Teachers have increased opportunities for research, whether finding the right textbook by browsing publishers' websites, gathering cultural information for a class reading or accessing corpora to learn more about language as it is being used at the moment.
c. *Ease of creating materials.* As teachers have increased access to computers, they are more easily able to create materials for classroom use. With the addition of graphics, worksheets look better and are more easily understood. When materials can be easily modified, a teacher is more likely to incorporate learners' feedback. If both the teacher and the learners are on-line, materials can be easily sent back and forth at little or no cost.

Although areas such as genre analysis, corpus linguistics, and the use of authentic materials in the classroom are popular as we enter the twenty-first century, no single approach to ESP seems to dominate the immediate horizon. Rather, we feel that increasingly teachers will be able to draw on a wide variety of approaches and methods. The resulting blend may be difficult to label, but should provide exciting possibilities for the ESP teacher and materials developer.

References

Barnard, R. and Cady, J. (2000a) *Business Venture 1 Student Book* (2nd edn.). Oxford: Oxford University Press.

Barnard, R. and Cady, J. (2000b) *Business Venture 1 Workbook.* Oxford: Oxford University Press.

Benesch, S. (2001) *Critical English for Academic Purposes: Theory, Politics, and Practice.* Mahwah, NJ: Lawrence Erlbaum Associates.

Betta, L. and DuPaquier, C. (1998) *Northstar: Focus on Reading and Writing, Intermediate Level.* White Plains, NY: Addison Wesley Longman.

Bhatia, V. K. (1993) *Analysing Genre: Language Use in Professional Settings.* London and New York: Longman.

Corbett, J. (1994) *English for International Banking and Finance.* Cambridge: Cambridge University Press.

Dudley-Evans, T. (1997) 'Genre: how far can we, should we go?' *World Englishes,* **16**, 351–8.

Dudley-Evans, T. and St John, M. J. (1998) *Developments in English for Specific Purposes: A Multidisciplinary Approach.* Cambridge: Cambridge University Press.

Esteras, S. (1999) *Infotech: English for Computer Users.* Cambridge: Cambridge University Press.

Glendinning, E. and Glendinning, N. (1995) *Oxford English for Electrical and Mechanical Engineering.* Oxford: Oxford University Press.

Howatt, A. P. R. (1984) *A History of Language Teaching.* Oxford: Oxford University Press.

Hutchinson, T. and Waters, A. (1987) *English for Specific Purposes: A Learning-centred Approach.* Cambridge: Cambridge University Press.

McDonough, J. and Shaw, C. (1993) *Materials and Methods in ELT: A Teacher's Guide.* Oxford: Blackwell.

Master, P. and Brinton, D. M. (1998) *New Ways in English for Specific Purposes.* Alexandria, VA: TESOL.

Munby, J. (1978) *Communicative Syllabus Design.* Cambridge: Cambridge University Press.

Nunan, D. (1988) *Syllabus Design.* Oxford: Oxford University Press.

Phillipson, R. (1992) *Linguistic Imperialism.* Oxford: Oxford University Press.

Strevens, P. (1977) *New Orientations in the Teaching of English.* Oxford: Oxford University Press.

Swales, J. (1990) *Genre Analysis: English in Academic and Research Settings.* Cambridge: Cambridge University Press.

Swales, J. and Feak, C. (1994) *Academic Writing for Graduate Students: A Course for Non-native speakers of English.* Ann Arbor: University of Michigan Press.

Tomlinson, B. (ed.) (1998) *Materials Development in Language Teaching.* Cambridge: Cambridge University Press.

Widdowson, H. G. (1990) *Aspects of Language Teaching.* Oxford: Oxford University Press.

Comments on Part C

Brian Tomlinson

The most frequent point made in Part C is the obvious but important one that different types of learners need different types of materials. There are some universal principles and criteria for language learning materials, but for materials to be successful in terms of achieving learning objectives materials have to follow principles, criteria and procedures which match the distinctive features of the target learners and the environments they are learning in. An obvious example is the false beginner whose apparent lack of competence belies the time he/she has spent trying to learn the language. Such a learner needs a fresh start with a different approach rather than being asked to do the same thing all over again. Yet most false beginners are asked to work with materials which have been designed mainly for complete beginners (and yet probably sold as catering for the needs of beginners and false beginners – a viable target group in marketing terms). Another example is the university student with many intellectual interests and attributes who is asked to use bland, trivial materials designed for the modern teenager with a short attention span. The problem, of course, is that many distinctive types of learners do not constitute large enough markets to warrant distinctive types of materials. The answer could be global coursebooks with generalizable activities to be used with materials selected by the learners from a diverse bank of texts or from the Internet. Or it could be many more institutions and regions developing their own learner type specific materials.

Another common point in this section is the need for the teacher to help the learners to interact with the materials. No predetermined materials can cater for all their target learners. The learners have to make an effort to interact with the materials so as to connect them to their lives and requirements and the teachers can help them to do this by modifying and supplementing the materials. Of course, this would be easier for the teachers if the materials were designed with this facilitated interaction in mind.

A third point which the chapters in Part C seem to have in common is that it is very important that the coursebook does not become the syllabus. A syllabus should be developed to meet the needs and wants of specific groups of learners and then a coursebook should be selected or developed to achieve a satisfactory match with this syllabus and with the characteristics of specific cohorts of learners.

Of course, a perfect match will never be achieved and the coursebook will need to be modified in the direction of the syllabus and the learners. If the coursebook has actually been designed to cater for this flexibility so much the better. My view on developing materials to match the requirements of specific types of learners is that more use should be made of generalizable activities supported by locally appropriate texts selected from the Internet or from banks of texts developed by the teachers and the learners in relation to their interests, perceived levels and requirements.

I also think that it is time that we accepted the reality that the vast majority of learners of a foreign language (especially learners of English) learn the language in order to communicate with other L2 speakers of that language rather than with native speakers and that this should be reflected in the choice of texts, topics, voices and styles. It also means that the materials should be multicultural rather than being centred on the culture perceived to be the host culture of the language being learned.

Another of my views in relation to specific materials for specific learners is that, although it is important to meet their specific needs and wants, it is also important to remember that they are human beings with broad experience of life, with wide interests and with views, feelings and expertise unrelated to their defining characteristics as learners. In other words, we should meet the requirements of human beings in our materials as well as meet the needs and wants of specific learners. We should narrow the focus without impoverishing the experience.

PART D

Developing Specific Types of Materials

19

Materials for the Teaching of Grammar

Jeff Stranks

It is self-evident that the development of grammatical competence has an important role in second or foreign language learning. However, despite the advent of the so-called Communicative Approach over recent years, and despite the daily evidence offered by learners that the difficulties they encounter in using another language to encode their own meanings are largely to do with lexis and (in the spoken mode) with phonology, the dominance of grammar in teaching materials remains high, to the point of obsession. Furthermore, examination of materials for grammar in coursebooks and supplementary materials reveals that concern with grammatical form continues to take precedence over meaning considerations. As long ago as 1990, Widdowson argued that restricting attention to grammatical form is insufficient:

> Learners need to realize the functions of the device [i.e., grammar] as a way of mediating between words and contexts, as a powerful resource for the purposeful achievement of meaning. A communicative approach, properly conceived, does not involve the rejection of grammar. On the contrary, it involves a recognition of its central mediating role in the use and learning of language. (Widdowson, 1990: 97–8)

If one looks at the majority of practice material offered to learners – single sentence practice, random lexicalization, transformation exercises, wordy and inaccurate 'rules', etc. – it is hard not to conclude that the realizations and recognitions to which Widdowson refers, as to when and where the grammar practised might actually be employed, are mostly left to the learners themselves to come to. Examples of this would be the common practice of teaching and practising 'short forms' such as *Yes I am/No I'm not* as response to open-ended questions – to be discussed in more detail later in this chapter – and that of asking learners to transform sentences in active voice into passive voice (or vice versa). Of the latter, an example is the approach taken by Acevedo and Gower (1996: 23),[1] where learners are told that the passive is used when '*The agent is the new, important information. In English, new information often comes at or towards the end of the sentence*' (a laudable if somewhat limited attempt to refer to the Given-New Principle), information which is then ignored when learners are subsequently asked to identify the subjects and objects in eight sentences, and then to 'rewrite the sentences in the passive voice [including] the agent only where necessary'. When it comes down to it, it is form that matters.

Much of the present position of grammar today with EFL is due to the inherent conservatism of ministries of education and the major publishing houses, but also to the fact that the 'buyer' of materials is not the learners, rather the people who make decisions concerning syllabus and/or book adoptions, where the attitude is essentially one of 'better the devil you know than the devil you don't' – the grammar of many publications is comfortingly familiar and allows teacher-training in particular to prepare teachers for its implementation. The current situation with regard to grammar in the profession is subject, of course, to much criticism, and in particular there is criticism of the way in which the grammar of the language is taught through focusing on a sequence of individual and discrete grammatical items, to which Thornbury (2000) refers as the delivery of 'grammar McNuggets'. Long and Robinson (1998) and others argue that there is too much focus on individual language forms (FonFs) and propose a focus on form (FonF) – in other words, an approach which asks learners to notice language forms as they occur in the data learners are exposed to, and to consider how the form(s) are used to establish particular meanings. This broad approach is also part of Task-Based Learning (TBL) – a book notable for an innovative approach to using texts for examination of language data and focusing on form is Willis (1996).

The endeavour to break up the grammar of a language into discrete chunks for pedagogic purposes brings many difficulties with it, not least among which are decontextualized practice, examples given to and elicited from learners which are randomly lexicalized (as both Widdowson and Lewis have pointed out) and the endeavour to involve learners in production activities which are as controlled as possible to avoid learners attempting to use language which they have not 'learned' yet. Nonetheless, the reality for most writers of grammar materials is exactly that. Classroom teachers producing their own materials for use with their own students perhaps have the greatest chance of innovating, and certainly have the best opportunity to take into account the learners themselves (in particular, the extent to which an aspect of English grammar does or does not pose problems for them given their L1); but once material is for publication (into whatever market), pressures to conform to current norms will frequently require the writer to work within the 'grammar McNugget' framework. This chapter, then, while not condoning this reality, will try to establish some criteria for the creation of grammar materials and suggest some guidelines and thoughts for grammar materials which work within the traditional grammar areas.

The writer of materials for the teaching and learning of grammar has a number of considerations to take into account. These include:

a.   the age and level of the learners who will be using the materials;
b.   the extent to which any adopted methodology meets the expectations of (a) learners, (b) teachers; (c) the educational culture within which the learners and teachers work;

c. the extent to which any contexts and co-texts which are employed in order to present the grammar area(s) will be of interest to learners;
d. the nature of the grammatical areas to be dealt with, in terms of their form, their inherent meaning implications (if any) and how they are used in normally occurring spoken and/or written discourse;
e. the extent to which any language offered to the learners for them to examine the grammar used represents realistic use of the language, and the extent to which activities for learners to produce language containing the target grammar will result in meaningful utterances, and ones which bear at least some resemblance to utterances which the learners would be likely to want to produce in their own, non-classroom discourse;
f. any difficulties that learners can be expected to encounter when learning these areas of grammar, especially with regard to any similarities or differences in form, function, and form/function relationship, between the target language and their mother tongue.

The first three listed here are of course of great importance for anyone working with or designing materials for classroom use. This chapter restricts itself to considering the last three, since the extent to which grammar materials accurately reflect the language and the learners' linguistic needs, and to which they encourage and allow learners to produce language which is of relevance to them, are factors whose absence may result in material which is interesting but of low pedagogic value.

With regard to criteria (d) and (e), one might immediately consider the continuing tendency of materials to avoid normal ellipsis in practice activities which are intended (presumably) to teach language that can be used conversationally, e.g., in Ur and Ribé (2000: 4) learners are presented with exchanges such as: 'What's your name?'/'My name's Debora', 'How old are you?'/'I'm fourteen', 'When's your birthday?'/'My birthday's in September' (etc.). What is clear in such writing is that writers (and/or editors) retain the view that the exemplification of grammatical form(s) is more important than the presentation of naturally occurring language. A further example is an area included in virtually all grammar materials and which is referred to as 'short answers': *Yes I am/No he isn't/No they haven't*, etc. This is normally treated as a stand-alone area – Yes/No questions can simply be answered in this way, and learners are given practice exercises which involve simply question and response. Invariably, no reference is made, or indication given to learners, as to when such responses may or may not be appropriate – the function or pragmatic effect of utterances such as *Yes I do* is ignored. Whitney (1998: 136) includes the following practice of *past* simple: learners are asked to ask and answer with a partner, are given the prompt 'play – football – yesterday' and the example 'Did you play football yesterday?' 'Yes, I did/No I didn't', and then asked to produce further exchanges with prompts such as 'study – a lot – at the weekend' and 'watch – TV – yesterday'. Getting learners to produce only these 'short answers' is presumably based on the belief that they do not have the linguistic armoury to say more; however, their use as encouraged in such exercises could often, in conversational settings, result in learners coming across as brusque, if not downright rude. Such utterances tend not to be used as responses to questions at all, but rather to correct or disagree with another speaker's statement or claim, and would normally be followed up with a correction or further comment. Therefore, these misnamed 'short answers' need to be taught and practised (a) in contexts such as disagreeing or correcting and (b) with appropriate follow-up to the 'short answer', giving exchanges such as: *A: You're late! B: No I'm not. It's only eight-thirty* or *A: Neil Young's American. B: No he isn't, he's Canadian* (etc.). The materials writer wishing to get learners to produce 'short answers' would need to develop possible conversational exchanges which begin with statements that learners can either disagree with (because they know them to be untrue), or else to which they can give a contrary opinion. Exercises might be developed along the following lines:

> A: Mel Gibson's a really good actor. He's British, you know.
> B: _____. He's Australian.

(Learners would be expected to produce *No he isn't* in the gap.)

Practice exercises which develop a theme such as this will, of course, be more complex for the materials writer to produce and for the learner to engage with – however, not to do so easily results in grammar practice which is not *language* practice.

There are many traditional areas of grammar which appear in virtually any grammar syllabus or list of contents and which do not need to be dealt with as separate areas, and certainly not dealt with discretely. One example, to be looked at in some detail here, is 'reported speech'. Willis (1990), among others, has argued that it is unnecessary to treat this as an area of language with its own separate existence and set of rules. (One might also argue that, for conversational language use, it is a relatively unimportant feature of language to teach, since 'Direct speech reporting (where the speaker gives an apparently verbatim report of what someone said) is an important and recurrent feature of conversation' (Biber *at al.*, 1999: 1118)). If we look at what a speaker needs to do in order to produce an utterance in 'reported speech', we will find things such as:

a.   the ability to select a verb which reflects how the 'reporter' views the original speech act (e.g., *say, tell, explain, suggest, admit, ask*, etc.);
b.   knowledge of the implications of the verb selection for the following structure (e.g., *he asked me if . . .* or *he asked me to. . .*);
c.   the ability to refer to periods of time at a deictic distance (e.g., *the day before/ the following day/three weeks later* as opposed to *yesterday/tomorrow/in three weeks' time*, etc.), and also to make other deictic references at a remove (e.g., *the house* as opposed to *this house*, etc.);
d.   when the verb selected for reporting is followed by a 'that . . .' verb phrase, the ability to select an appropriate tense form for the verb in the 'that' clause.

The first three of these need not – and, arguably, should not – be left until the area of reported speech crops up in the syllabus. Learners need to know what the verbs used to refer to different speech acts mean and how to employ them.[2] The verbs have differing grammatical implications: some (*inform/tell/persuade*, etc.) require an indirect personal object; others (*suggest/admit/say*) take either a noun object or a 'that' clause (etc., etc.). But these features are of the verbs themselves, not of reported speech, and need to be taught as the verbs occur during a course. Equally, the time phrases, demonstrative pronouns, etc. have no exclusive linkage with 'reported speech', and can be taught and practised with narratives and so forth.

Many of the so-called features of 'reported speech' can, then, be seen as quite separate and taught as such. Thus an approach can be developed which provides learners with a great deal of the linguistic armoury they need in order to report speech, without teaching them 'reported speech' as such at all.

The fourth point, however – that of selecting the appropriate verb tense form – is perhaps more complex. The verb 'select' is used here consciously – speakers select the tense rather than transform from one to another, and although such selection is not at a very conscious level, native speakers of English will be aware of the effects of differing choices in, for example, *He said he's coming* or *He said he was coming*. In a way very similar to the selection of time phrases (e.g., a reporter of a speech act which referred to 'tomorrow' may employ either the phrase 'the following day', or similar, or else maintain the word 'tomorrow', depending on the circumstances of the time of reporting), the selection of a verb tense form will reflect either the speaker's knowledge of the prevailing time references, or else his/her interpretation of the situation. To illustrate: if someone approaches me as I am writing this and says 'John's arriving tomorrow', and I report this later today, I may report it as 'X said John's arriving tomorrow'. Naturally, if I report this tomorrow, I will no longer refer to 'tomorrow', but to 'today'. However, no matter when the reporting takes place, up to the point of John's arrival or my receipt of other information, I *may* select to use the form 'was arriving' if I so wish. To do so would indicate either (a) 'but I now know that this is no longer the case', or (b) 'it may or may not be the case – I am not willing to vouch for the truthfulness of what I am reporting'. It may be necessary for learners of English to become aware (if they are not already) that these options are open to them.

At this point, what has been said about 'reported speech' is liable to incur the wrath of grammarians such as Swan (2001: 182), who inveighs against what he terms the 'I have seen the light' approach to areas of grammar, and which he describes as follows:

> We normally teach such-and-such a grammatical topic (the present perfect, articles, prepositions, or whatever) by giving a large number of superficial 'rules of thumb'. These don't really get to the heart of the matter, and they give the impression that the relevant grammatical area is bitty and arbitrary. In fact, however, there are deeper underlying patterns which guide native speakers' instinctive choices. If we can tease out these patterns and convey them to our

students, everything will fall into place, and the relevant structures will cease to be problematic.

The preceding argument about 'reported speech' certainly claims that traditional approaches do not get to the heart of the matter, and treat it as 'bitty and arbitrary'. However, this does not necessarily mean, as Swan implies, that no problems will remain. Teaching is required, as suggested above. What is debatable is what the teaching should work on. Speakers of Brazilian Portuguese, for example, if allowed to follow their instincts in tense form selection, will rarely make errors other than of form. (As Swan himself suggests elsewhere (1994: 53), quoting an old American proverb: 'If it ain't broke, don't fix it.') Speakers of other languages, however, may need practice to help them with certain aspects of tense selection. But of what kind?

Much grammar practice in the area of reported speech is of the kind which requires learners to take a given utterance in direct speech and 'transform' it into reported speech, and to do so by 'shifting' the verb tense. It is hard to imagine that this bears any resemblance to what happens in actual language production – and real-time, on-line language production is what learners want and need to be able to work with. Brazil (1995: 239) points out that:

> Sentence grammars, deriving as they do from an abstraction away from potential use, pose questions about the organization of language that seem to have little to do with those engaging the attention of people who are involved in communicating with others.

and one might add that transformation grammar exercises (whether for 'reported speech', 'the passive' or whatever other grammar area) require language learners to make decisions and produce language in a way which is quite divorced from the decisions and production that on-line communication will require.

What alternatives are there to transformation exercises? Lewis (1993: 154) points a possible way forward with a call for an emphasis on grammar as a *receptive* skill:

> 'Awareness raising' is a term which has recently acquired currency in language teaching terminology. The unifying feature behind all these commentators is the assertion that it is the students' ability to **observe accurately**, and **perceive similarity and difference** within target language data which is most likely to aid the acquisition of the grammatical system. Within this theoretical framework, **grammar as a receptive skill** has an important role to play.

This is echoed in many ways by Ellis, who argues for what he terms 'interpretative grammar tasks' which 'focus learners' attention on a targeted structure in the input and ... enable them to identify and comprehend the meaning(s) of this structure. This approach emphasizes input processing for comprehension rather than output processing for production' (Ellis 1995: 88).

The notion of 'grammar as a receptive skill' is not necessarily a new one – exercises have been produced and published over the years which require learners to work with aspects of grammar without actually producing utterances which employ the grammar under consideration. Arguments can and have, however, been made for a conscious adoption of receptive grammar on a theoretical basis, as for example by Batstone (1996: 273) who argues:

> Learners may need time to make sense *of* new language before they are asked to make sense *with* it. [This is an argument] for receptive tasks to be clearly distinct from productive tasks, and for the former to precede the latter.

Following this train of thought, and with the goal of helping learners see what choices are available (or not) with regard to tense selection in reported speech, one might design a receptive grammar activity which encourages learners to look at examples of utterances containing reported speech and to find criteria for categorizing them. Such an exercise could take the following form:

Read the following utterances. They all contain 'reported speech'. Put them into two categories.

Group 1:	*Sentences 1, . . .*
Group 2:	*Sentences 3, . . .*

1. 'I talked to James last week – he said he wasn't going to São Paulo after all. So we went for a beer on Saturday.'
2. 'Alan called – he said he couldn't ring you last week because he had to go to Paris unexpectedly. Can you get in touch with him?'
3. 'I talked to Paul yesterday – he said he isn't working for the bank any more. Did you know?'
4. 'Sara called me this morning – she said she isn't coming to the meeting tomorrow, but she'll e-mail you the information, OK?'
5. 'When I talked to Sara yesterday, she said she was sending the information by e-mail. I don't know why it hasn't arrived yet.'
6. 'There's a Mr Johnson outside who wants to see you. He said it's urgent.'
7. 'I saw Joan this morning – she doesn't look well, she said she hasn't eaten for a week.'
8. 'I phoned the electrician, but he said he couldn't come until the following week. So I fixed it myself. Seems to be working OK!'

Sentences 1, 2, 5 and 8 all illustrate a speaker's use of past forms in reporting speech, whilst 3, 4, 6 and 7 illustrate the use of present tense forms (including, in the case of 7, present perfect). However, unless learners are particularly astute, and/or their first language operates in very similar ways, such an exercise will only alert them to the fact that some reported speech operates with past tense, and others with present. For them to begin to perceive *why* this is so, a further exercise will most likely be required – again, on a receptive level, and possibly along the following lines:

> **Look at the underlined parts of these conversations. Which things do the speakers think are still true? And which things do they think aren't true (any more)?**
> 1. A: 'I asked the new guy, Rolf, where he's from – he said *he's* German.'
>   B: 'German? Alan told me *he was* Swiss.'
> 2. A: 'John's just phoned – he said *he's coming* at 11.00.'
>   B: 'That's strange – when I rang him yesterday he said *he was coming* at 10.00.'
> 3. A: 'Joan said *she's going* to France for her holidays.'
>   B: 'Oh really? She's always changing her mind. Two weeks ago she said *she was going* to Italy.'
> 4. A: 'I can't believe you're ordering sushi! You told me *you didn't like* Japanese food!'
>   B: 'No I didn't – I said *I don't mind* it now and again.'

An exercise such as this, of course, engages learners in a cognitive activity which will not suit all learners. It is certainly not easy. It requires the teacher, as well, to be aware of such things as the use of past tense not only as a device for temporal distancing, but also for psychological distancing (Lewis, 1986) and the use of present tenses for temporal and psychological proximity, in order to help learners perceive this. This may well be unmanageable for many teachers, who perhaps prefer the security of 'rules'; however, 'rules' such as 'put the verb in the direct speech one step back in time' are inaccurate, and the welter of information with which learners are usually bombarded and expected to deal with are arguably more demanding and no less suitable than what the above exercise expects them to do. (Learning the distinctions between aspects of the grammatical system is fundamental to extended grammar learning and control – distinctions between active and passive voice, or the use of 'will' or 'going to', are other examples of this.) To quote Willis (1990: 115), talking about noun phrases but making a comment which is applicable to many other grammar areas:

> most of these exercises are consciousness raising activities. The complexity and unpredictability of [this language] are such that we can offer no prescriptions. All we can do is outline the elements, and encourage learners to examine their experience of the language. It is, however, most important that we do this.

But what about practice which requires learners to produce language? A major difficulty with eliciting reported speech from learners is that of establishing deictic references for the learners, a problem which most transformation exercises solve by ignoring. Rather than asking learners to produce utterances involving reported speech, however, one might well ask them first to make selections, as for example in the following exercise (Stranks, 2001: 28):

Choose the most appropriate verb forms
1. I invited Jim to the party tonight. He said he_____(*wants/wanted*) to come.
2. John's going to live in New York next year. It's odd, because last year he told me he _____(*is going/was going*) to stay in London.
3. Don't worry, Mum. Dad said he_____('*ll/'d*) pick me up from school this afternoon.
4. I don't know why Jim didn't come to the party. Yesterday he said he_____(*wants/wanted*) to come. (etc.)

This exercise poses problems since several examples allow more than one possible choice. Many people involved in ELT – and that includes learners – have considerable difficulty accepting exercises which do not have clearly demarcated right and wrong answers. Unfortunately, however, language – and that includes grammar – is frequently not a matter of correct or incorrect, possible or not possible. The exercise above moves away from the 'right/wrong' syndrome and thus will be unacceptable to many users (especially teachers); however, asking learners to consider which is *more likely* or *appropriate* allows them to perceive that choices are available, and that there are subtle meaning differences between the choices.

Productive exercises, as mentioned before, are often highly controlled. But where choice is possible, such control is very difficult to achieve, and arguably counter-productive anyway. Alternatives in the area of 'reported speech' would include asking learners to think of memorable things that were *actually* said to them at some point in the recent or distant past; asking them to report those speech acts; and doing whatever correction or modification proves necessary. (Doughty and Varela (1998) report on a piece of research which suggests that the correction of grammatical errors performed *during* communication can prove more effective in the acquisition of language forms than controlled practice, although their research did not use the kind of language practice task outlined here.)

Grammar materials sometimes fail learners when they give highly contrived examples of the language point in question. To exemplify aspects of 'reported speech', Jones (1998: 122) has a solitary man reading a book and saying to nobody: '*I don't like this book I'm reading now.*' This is followed by a woman reporting to another: '*He told me he didn't like that book he was reading then.*' It is unclear why the phrases *I'm reading now*, *that* book and *then* would be used by the 'speakers' in these examples, and they do not ring true in the least. However, grammar materials can let learners down in other ways as well. When practice activities or exercises are given to learners to practise a particular aspect of grammar, it would appear to be desirable that the utterances produced in doing the exercise be ones that (a) are feasible language and (b) bear some resemblance to language that the learners themselves might wish to utter. One does not need to look very far to find grammar practice activities in which the learners doing the exercise will produce language which is at best unlikely. A random selection from various published coursebooks follows:

- *Scientists make a lot of clever inventions.* (practising 'a lot of')
- *Athletes must train very hard to be champions.* (practising 'must' as modal for obligation)
- *Has John heard her latest record?* (practising present perfect simple)
- *James and Emma can speak French.* (practising 'can' as modal of ability)

There are also very often instances of utterances which simply state the obvious, sentences of the '*An elephant is bigger than an ant*' variety. The last of the sentences listed above, in particular, illustrates the common tendency not only to lexicalize randomly, but also to encourage learners to use collocations which are in fact rare ('can' is much more frequent for *possibility* than for *ability* and, inconvenient though this may be for materials writers, tends not to be used when talking about things like *speaking a language, driving a car* or *riding horses*). The first of the above actually includes a collocation ('make inventions') which to this native speaker seems to be one which would simply not occur.

It is, admittedly, not necessarily easy to write exercises where the language produced is consistently relevant to the learners (especially when so many learners around the world in fact have little or no desire to use English at all, certainly not in the short term), is within their linguistic capabilities and is faithful to actual language use. However, the professional materials writer in particular is surely bound to attempt to do so, at the very least by maintaining normal features of collocation and lexical aspect. To this end, there is less and less need for the materials writer to rely on intuition (or what has simply been encountered in materials previously published). The existence and availability of language corpora, together with concordancing programmes, make it possible to check out what language users actually *do*, rather than what we think or hope they do. A reference work such as the *Longman Grammar of Spoken and Written Language* (Biber *et al.*, 1999), based on a corpus of over 40 million words, also provides illuminating statistical evidence as to how language is used (showing, for example, that *will* is, somewhat surprisingly, more frequently used than *going to*, and that the modals *will, would, can* and *could* are far more common than other members of that group). There are also commentaries on such things as register, style and collocation, making this kind of work a virtually indispensable tool for writers who wish their grammar materials to reflect actual language use.

Grammar may be necessary – perhaps a necessary evil to some – but let it be seen and acted upon as *part* of language, not a separate feature to be learned for its own sake. The grammar materials writer needs to try to put into the hands of both teachers and learners materials which reflect grammar's 'central mediating role in the use and learning of language'.

References

Acevedo, A. and Gower, M. (1996) *High Flyer Intermediate Students' Book*. Harlow: Addison Wesley Longman.

Batstone, R. (1996) 'Key concepts in ELT – noticing'. *English Language Teaching Journal*, **50** (3).

Biber, D., Johansson, S., Leech G., Conrad, S. and Finegan, E. (1999) *Longman Grammar of Spoken and Written English*. Harlow: Pearson Education.

Brazil, D. (1995) *A Grammar of Speech*. Oxford: Oxford University Press.

Doughty, C. and Varela, E. (1998) 'Communicative focus on form', in C. Doughty and J. Williams (eds) *Focus on Form in Second Language Acquisition*. Cambridge: Cambridge University Press.

Ellis, R. (1995) 'Interpretation tasks for grammar teaching'. *TESOL Quarterly*, **29** (1).

Jones, L. (1998) *New Cambridge Advanced English: Student's Book*. Cambridge: Cambridge University Press.

Lewis, M. (1986) *The English Verb*. Hove: Language Teaching Publications.

Lewis, M. (1993) *The Lexical Approach*. Hove: Language Teaching Publications.

Long, M. H. and Robinson, P. (1998) 'Focus on form: theory, research and practice' in C. Doughty and J. Williams (eds) *Focus on Form in Second Language Acquisition*. Cambridge: Cambridge University Press.

Stranks, J. (2001) *The New You and Me: Grammar Practice 4*. Munich: Langenscheidt Longman.

Swan, M. (1994) 'Design criteria for pedagogic language Rule', in M. Bygate, A. Tonkyn and E. Williams (eds) *Grammar and the Language Teacher*. Hemel Hempstead: Prentice Hall International.

Swan, M. (2001) 'If this is the cure, let's have the disease'. *English Language Teaching Journal*, **55** (2).

Thornbury, S. (2000) 'Deconstructing grammar', in A. Pulverness (ed.) *IATEFL 2000 Dublin Conference Selections*. Whitstable: IATEFL.

Ur, P. and Ribé, R. (2000) *Clearways: Student's Book One*. Cambridge: Cambridge University Press.

Whitney, N. (1998) *Open Doors: Student's Book 1*. Oxford: Oxford University Press/ La Nuova Italia.

Widdowson, H. G. (1990) *Aspects of Language Teaching*. Oxford: Oxford University Press.

Willis, D. (1990) *The Lexical Syllabus*. London: HarperCollins.

Willis, J. (1996) *A Framework for Task-Based Learning*. Harlow: Addison Wesley Longman.

20

Materials for Developing Reading Skills

Hitomi Masuhara

The Reading Behaviour of L2 Learners

Reading the following quotation from Auerbach and Paxton (1997: 238–9), would you be able to guess the ages, levels and nationalities of the L2 learners mentioned?

> many ... learners ... feel they have to know all the words in a text in order to understand it, rely heavily on the dictionary, are unable to transfer positive L1 reading strategies or positive feelings about translation, and attribute their difficulties to a lack of English proficiency.

One of the peculiar phenomena that seem to emerge in L2 reading research from the 1980s to 1990s is the striking resemblance of the reported characteristics of L2 learners' reading behaviour to that depicted in the quotation above. Hosenfeld (1984) provides such examples by describing verbal protocols of unsuccessful readers of foreign languages, in her case studies of 14-year-old Americans learning French and Spanish. Cooper (1984) provides other examples of identical reading behaviours exhibited by his Malaysian university EFL students. Kim and Krashen's (1997) five advanced adult Korean EFL learners also share the same characteristics. Tomlinson (1998b) describes the reading behaviours of Japanese EFL university students in his nineteen experiments as 'consisting mainly of studial decoding of words in order to achieve total comprehension of a text'. Masuhara (1998) confirms such universality in L2 reading behaviour in her research with advanced EFL learners from six European and Asian countries.

All these studies reveal that reading in the L2 seems to mean almost invariably a slow and laborious decoding process, which often results in poor comprehension and in low self-esteem. What is remarkable is the fact that the learners in Kim and Krashen (1997), Tomlinson (1998b) and Masuhara (1998) are proficient L1 readers and yet, even at intermediate and advanced level, they seem to retain many of the typical reading behaviours of unsuccessful readers. As far as language competence is concerned they are classified as far above the threshold level of language competence (Alderson, 1984; Clarke, 1988; Cummins and Swain, 1986) and thus the transfer of L1 reading skills is expected to occur.

What may be causing these persistent L2 reading problems and what can material writers offer as solutions?

An Overview of the Approaches to Teaching L2 Reading from the 1980s to 1990s

Reading Comprehension-based Approaches

Wallace (2001: 26) describes traditional reading pedagogy as an approach which emphasizes 'comprehension in the form of the presentation of text followed by post-reading questions on the text' and Williams and Moran (1989: 225) state that 'Despite the recent emphasis on the reader's personal interpretation, and the attention to tasks designed to develop reading skills, comprehension questions still feature prominently in most published materials.'

Extremely popular series such as *Streamline* and *Headway* could easily be chosen as the classic examples of this approach and our recent review of coursebooks (Tomlinson *et al.*, 2001) confirms Williams and Moran (1989) in that it seems almost impossible to find reading materials which do not contain comprehension questions. Williams (1984) and Nuttall (1982, 1996) list various types and formats of comprehension questions with examples taken from published materials.

Reading comprehension-based approaches take a strong stance in the controversy about whether a text has one meaning or multiple meanings depending on the reader. Williams (1983), for example, suggests that the true meaning is the one that is intended by the writer. He claims that 'the need to preserve communication between the writer and readers requires such an "ideal", even if the reader's comprehension never "matches" in every detail the writer's intention.' Note also that many techniques of assessment and of reading pedagogy seem to depend on the efficacy of this assumption that correct comprehension is achievable and desirable (for discussions of reading assessment see Alderson, 2000). Widdowson (1979), on the other hand, states that texts have potential for meaning, 'which will vary from reader to reader, depending upon a multitudes of factors' but he (1986: v–vi) also adds that 'To say that a text is an *occasion* for interpretation does not mean it is an *excuse* for any interpretation that takes reader's fancy' (italics in original).

Urquhart (1987) maintains that it is impossible even for L1 proficient readers to agree completely on the meaning of a text due to each individual's experiences and he casts a strong doubt on the validity of setting up the writer's intended meaning as the readers' target. According to his view, what readers can achieve is 'interpretation' rather than 'comprehension'. His claim seems to accord with the research findings investigating 'mental representation' in cognitive psychology and neuroscience in recent years (Masuhara, 1998). Mental representation roughly corresponds to the 'meaning of the text' constructed in the reader's mind. The mental representation of a reader depends on connecting the information gained through decoded linguistic data with the knowledge that already exists in the reader's mind. Since each individual's knowledge is the result of constant conceptual reformulation through various experiences, even simple word knowledge like 'a dog' would not mean the same thing to different individuals. For example, when reading about 'a dog' in a text, you might be visualizing a dog that resembles your pet whereas another person may be thinking of a fierce dog next door.

The real issue, it seems to me, is not whether achieving an ideal comprehension of the writer's intended meaning is possible or not but when and why we might need to approximate our meaning closely to that intended by the writer. In L1, we vary the degree of our interpretation according to our reading purpose. Approximating to the reader's intended meaning would be of vital importance when reading legal documents or job specifications because of the potential effect on our lives. However, we might be much more relaxed when reading novels or magazines which allow us to enjoy idiosyncratic interpretations. The problems arise if L2 reading materials are to demand certain reading styles and the attainment of accurate reproduction of the writer's meaning regardless of the genre and the reading purposes (Tomlinson, 2000).

Williams and Moran (1989) point out that many materials do not explicitly state the aims of the comprehension questions. They identify three possible aims:

a.   to check comprehension
b.   to facilitate comprehension
c.   simply to ensure that the learner reads the text

Note that (a) and (c) above seem to contribute mainly to teachers' class management. Teachers may say that they would like (a) 'to check comprehension' so that if there are any misunderstandings, they can help the learners. In this sense, checking comprehension is close to (b) 'to facilitate comprehension', whose focus appears to be on helping learners achieve a higher level of understanding of the texts.

We might like ask ourselves, however, in what way comprehension questions help the learners understand the texts better. The failure to respond appropriately to comprehension questions may tell the teacher and the learner that there might have been some problems during the reading process but the comprehension questions do not give information about the nature of the problems. Furthermore, comprehension questions come after learners have read the text. If there are problems during the comprehension process, then it is before and/or during reading that learners need help, not afterwards. It may even be that the expectation of comprehension checking causes reading problems by encouraging a studial reading habit which in fact inhibits the reading process (Williams and Moran, 1989; Masuhara, 1998, Ch. 5; Tomlinson, 2000). Furthermore, the way comprehension questions immediately follow a text seems to imply to the learners that they should be able to achieve accurate comprehension of all the details straight away. Yet, much L1 reading research, based on proficient readers' verbal protocols, provides ample data that interpretations are gradual and require constant renegotiation with the reader and text (Masuhara, 1998).

The Language-Based Approach

Verbal protocol studies of L2 learners' reading problems give numerous examples of how language processing, especially of vocabulary, gets in the way of achieving comprehension. Paran (1996: 25–34) reminds teachers of the necessity to 'hold in the bottom' in reading pedagogy and emphasizes the importance of nurturing learners' automatic language processing ability in order to facilitate successful reading. Reviewing current coursebooks (Tomlinson *et al.*, 2001) reveals how vocabulary and grammar exercises have a strong presence not only in the general language sections but in the reading sections, too. Many coursebooks have a two-page reading section with a text and activities (e.g., *Lifelines; Headway; Cutting Edge*). Pre-reading vocabulary activities seem popular, reading sections often start with vocabulary activities related to the texts and many reading units feature short texts used mainly for teaching grammar.

The Language-Based Approach to reading seems to have gained support at least twice in ELT: firstly in the 1950s–1960s, then in the 1980s–1990s.

The dominant view around the 1950s and 1960s was that once learners acquired the habit of language use through learning grammar and lexis, they would become able to read fluently (e.g., Fries, 1963). Such behaviourist views led to reading being treated as a means of language practice through the use of simplified texts and graded readers. Readability studies in the 1960s showed that word difficulty and sentence length seem to provide plausible indices for predicting text accessibility (Klare, 1974; Alderson and Urquhart, 1984: xxi–xxv). As Alderson and Urquhart (1984: xxii) point out, readability studies in effect confirmed the layman's view, 'simple English is written in short easy sentences with not too many long words'. It is interesting to note that a recent evaluation of coursebooks (Tomlinson *et al.*, 2001) detected texts with linguistic simplification in many contemporary courses.

The language-based teaching of reading was questioned when it became evident in the 1970s that understanding the linguistic meaning of a text does not equal understanding of the textual meaning (Goodman, 1976; Schank and Abelson, 1977; Smith, 1978; Hymes, 1979) and we became more aware of the active role that the reader plays in the reading process, for example in making use of prior knowledge.

Later on, strong support for the Language-Based Approach to reading came from eye movement studies. Adams (1994: 845) maintains that a text in English seems to be read by fluent readers in 'what is essentially a left-to-right, line-by-line, word-by-word process'. She explains that:

> In general, skilful readers visually process virtually each letter of every word they read, translating print to speech as they go. They do so whether they are reading isolated words or meaningful connected text. They do so regardless of

the ease or difficulty of the text, regardless of its semantic, syntactic, or orthographic predictability. There may be no more broadly or diversely replicated set of findings in modern cognitive psychology than those that show that skilful readers visually process nearly every letter and word of text as they read.

Research also negates the claim that skilful readers use contextual guidance to pre-select the meanings of the words they are going to read. Although it appears as if contexts pre-select the appropriate meanings, research demonstrates that in reality meaning is selected while the language is being processed. The speed of solving the ambiguity of the text gives the impression of the context pre-selecting the meaning. Note, however, the difference between this current understanding and the bottom-up processing view in the 1970s: proponents of bottom-up processing in the 1970s (e.g., Gough, 1972) thought the process was linear and serial from the bottom to the top. The description of bottom-up processing in the late 1980s–1990s, however, hypothesizes parallel occurrence of both bottom-up and top-down operations at the same time (e.g., Rumelhart *et al.*, 1986; Adams, 1994).

The Language-Based Approach to reading appears to have regained support in claiming that in order to read fluently the learners need general language ability and, especially, automatic word recognition. In L2 reading research, there are verbal protocol studies which seem to suggest that vocabulary knowledge is of primary importance in reading and that learners are unable to pay due attention to other linguistic aspects of texts until they have coped with vocabulary (Laufer and Sim, 1985; Davis and Bistodeau, 1993). Vocabulary studies (e.g., Ellis, 1995; Coady and Huckin, 1997; Meara, 1997; Nation, 2001) also seem to indicate that fluent reading requires:

- fast and automatic word identification;
- extensive knowledge of the lexicon;
- the ability to attribute the most appropriate meanings to lexical items in relation to their context and co-text.

Many current coursebooks still seem to use the Presentation, Practice, Production Approach (PPP) to teaching grammar and vocabulary and to make use of reading texts for language teaching (Tomlinson *et al.*, 2001). The current PPP Approach seems to combine the teaching of formal grammar with communication activities (e.g., *Headway, Cutting Edge, Clockwise*). Grammar structures or rules are first presented. Then they are practised in a mechanical or controlled manner. Finally, freer communicative activities (sometimes involving reading) follow.

Finally, it must be noted that recently developments in discourse analysis are being incorporated into language-based reading pedagogy. Carrell (1984, 1985) found that knowledge of textual organization is a significant contributor to reading ability and she advocated the importance in L2 reading pedagogy of including instruction on the macrostructure of texts. And Nuttall (1996) gives more space for discussing discourse than in her previous edition (1982).

The reasons why we learn to read in L1 may mainly be attributed to obtaining non-linguistic outcomes: we read for getting information to suit our different purposes at the time of reading, for gaining pleasure and stimuli, for attaining social advancement, etc. We read for purposes and vary the degree of how carefully we read. L1 adults do not read a text so as to acquire extensive knowledge of, say, hyponyms or synonyms, to practise some syntactical structure such as reduced relative clauses or to analyse the discourse structure of a text. We might start to dread reading if it meant being tested immediately afterwards for instant and perfect comprehension or for displaying newly acquired linguistic knowledge. In L2, however, reading is often taught as a means of learning language. If L2 reading pedagogy is intended to nurture reading ability, I would argue that there should be a clear separation between teaching reading and teaching language using texts. Most of the reading materials try to kill two birds (language and reading) with one stone and seem to fail to hit both targets.

Alderson (1984) summarizes studies which investigate the 'threshold level' in reading below which the reader cannot engage meaningfully with a text, and Tomlinson (2000) recommends delaying reading at the initial stage of language learning because the learners do not yet have enough language to read experientially. This is interesting in that, in L1, there is a fairly clear divide between aural–oral language acquisition and reading acquisition. When formal reading instruction begins at school, L1 children have more or less established:

- Flexible and extensive aural/oral vocabularies
- Intuitive knowledge of English syntax

Furthermore, pre-schoolers may have had considerable opportunities for relaxed, secure proto-reading experiences, such as listening to bedtime stories in which most of the vocabulary in the text is likely to be known and the unknown can be inferred, explained either visually or verbally in interaction with a parent or just be ignored until the pre-schoolers' needs and wants arise. Such an environment resembles what Krashen (1982) advocates as an ideal condition for language acquisition.

Compare this with how L2 learners may learn to read. In L2 reading, instruction begins simultaneously with L2 language learning. Or more accurately, no reading instruction per se is given but the learners are expected to read texts on the assumption that once we learn a language system we should be able to read well.

Obviously the important question to ask is, 'Does pre-teaching of linguistic knowledge help the learners to read better?' 'In general the research leaves us in little doubt about the importance of vocabulary knowledge for reading', note Nation and Coady (1988), after summarizing studies investigating the relationship between vocabulary and reading in both L1 and L2. Note here, though, that the details of the causal link are unclear. We are not sure how the learners acquire automaticity in word recognition, how they build up a large vocabulary and how they cultivate their ability to access flexibly appropriate knowledge of word meanings in relation to context and co-text. It seems the awareness of the importance of automatic accessing of vocabulary has led many coursebooks to present pre-reading vocabulary exercises (e.g., *Lifelines*) so that:

- explicit pre-teaching of vocabulary can help learners acquire or recall language knowledge;
- doing vocabulary work before reading can help learners to comprehend the text better.

But we might like to ask the following questions:

- Can we assume that explicit teaching of vocabulary results in vocabulary being learned?
- Are the pre-selected vocabulary items necessarily the ones that learners will have problems recognizing during the reading of the text?
- Does language work focus the learner's mind on language when reading, thus reinforcing the text-bound L2 learner's typical reading style?
- By being asked to display vocabulary knowledge before reading, are learners with a small vocabulary or made aware of their weaknesses rather than their strengths?
- Does pre-teaching of vocabulary deprive learners of opportunities to guess the meaning of unknown words from the context?

With regard to syntax, Alderson and Urquhart (1984: 157) state that 'the experimental findings suggest that, at least for L1 readers, syntax only becomes a problem when it interacts with other factors.' Such factors could be related, for instance, to vocabulary overload or lack of background knowledge. Davidson and Green (1988) confirmed in their reappraisal of readability studies that sentence structures do not seem to cause major problems in L1 reading comprehension. In L2 reading research, however, the results are more mixed as to the significance of syntax to reading. Alderson and Richards (1977) conducted multicomponential studies investigating the relationship between reading ability and various factors such as vocabulary and syntax. Syntax gave the lowest correlation with reading ability. Berman (1984) maintains, on the other hand, that syntax cannot be ignored as a cause of unsuccessful reading. What seems to be lacking in these studies, however, is understanding of what kinds of syntax the reading process requires. Many of the multicomponential studies investigating the effect of learners' syntactic ability on reading tend to measure general syntactic ability in grammar tests and then correlate the scores with comprehension tests. Can we assume that if a person can successfully transform, for instance, the active to the passive then he/she has the ability to comprehend a passage in which the passive is used? Or that a person, for example, who cannot transform the active to the passive cannot understand the passive when they are reading. I would agree with Adams (1980: 18) in that, in reading, 'Syntax is the primary means by which we can specify the intended relation among words ... not only by disambiguating the referents of words, but also by new relationships among them.' The Language-Based Approach to reading pedagogy seems to hypothesize an equation between the ability to manipulate syntactic operations outside a discourse context (i.e., what grammar tests tend to measure) and the ability to disambiguate syntactical patterns during the reading process. If this often unchallenged equation proves to be invalid, then we might like to reconsider the value of explicit grammar teaching in the reading sections of coursebooks.

The Skill/Strategy-based Approach

Alderson (2000: 110) states, 'the notion of skills and subskills in reading is enormously pervasive and influential, despite the lack of clear empirical justification.' When the term 'skill learning' was used by the proponents of the Communicative Approach in the 1970s, the word was often contrasted with knowledge or conceptual learning. In knowledge learning, for example, learners learn words in the target language consciously and verbally. In skills learning, on the other hand, learners acquire the sensor, motor and cognitive abilities necessary for using a language in an accurate, fluent and appropriate manner. Williams and Moran (1989: 223) note that 'With respect to the terms "skill" and "strategy" ... both research literature and teaching materials display considerable terminological inconsistency.' After listing some varieties and confusions between 'skill' and 'strategy', they summarize that 'In principle, one may distinguish the terms by defining a skill as an acquired ability, which has been automatised and operates largely subconsciously whereas a strategy is a conscious procedure carried out in order to solve a problem (cf. Olshavsky, 1977).'

Researchers have tried to identify the numbers, kinds and nature of 'skills' (e.g., Williams and Moran, 1989; Alderson, 2000) but there are considerable unresolved differences amongst the views. The kinds of skills which seem to attract agreement amongst materials writers include: 'guessing the meaning of unknown words', 'inferring what is not explicitly stated in the text' and 'identifying the main idea'. Williams and Moran (1989: 224) point out a tendency that 'Although no two lists of reading skills are identical, casual inspection suggests that the skills might be grouped roughly into "language related" skills, and "reason related" skills.' 'Guessing the meaning of unknown words' seems to be a typical example of language-related skill (lower-order skills), whereas 'inferencing' or 'identifying the main idea' may be called a more reason-related skill (higher-order skills).

The value of teaching discrete reading skills is controversial but coursebooks continue to provide activities designed to nurture these skills. Nuttall (1985: 199), in her review of reading materials, says 'That it is possible to promote reading skills and strategies ... is still largely a matter of faith, but the number of materials produced show that it is a faith widely held.'

The notion of 'strategy' started to emerge in the materials of the mid-1980s. In these materials readers are considered to be active agents who direct their own cognitive resources in reading. Readers' cognitive resources include knowledge of the reading process and use of a variety of reading strategies (e.g., scanning for specific information).

What skill/strategy-based reading materials seem to share in common are:

- a view that in order to read effectively, readers need a range of skills and strategies
- an awareness that different readers may have different reading problems
- a view that guided practice will help learners learn necessary skills and strategies

The procedures for teaching skills/strategies invariably seems to include a phase in which explicit teaching of a specific skill/strategy takes place followed by some more practice (e.g., Greenall and Swan, 1986; Tomlinson and Ellis, 1987).

Studies analysing successful and unsuccessful readers through verbal protocols added insights to the reading process and the readers' use of effective and ineffective strategies. Just like psychoanalysts trying to gain access to the subconscious level, researchers used introspection of varied immediacy to tap the readers' minds in operation. The research suggests that successful readers are those who are aware of the kinds of texts and the kinds of suitable strategies, and who are able to monitor and control their own strategy use according to the particular purpose of reading (Olshavsky, 1977; Hosenfeld, 1984).

A number of studies have been carried out to explore the usefulness of strategy instruction. The experiments typically involve providing direct explicit instruction of a reading strategy for a certain period of time and its effect is then measured. In L1, consistent positive results have been reported (e.g., Brown *et al.*, 1984; Winograd and Hare, 1988). In L2 reading, however, studies have revealed conflicting results. Some studies reported strategy instruction to have been effective (e.g., Carrell *et al.*, 1989; Kern, 1989). Others reported strategy instruction to have fallen short of the expected results (e.g., Barnett, 1988; Kimura *et al.*, 1993).

Reading is a complex operation which could involve many potential skills/strategies. Each skill or strategy may involve a number of subskills and substrategies. Take an example of the commonly recognized strategy of 'guessing the meaning of an unknown word'. According to Nation and Coady (1988), possible strategic options include: identifying parts of speech of the word, analysing morphological components of the word, making use of any related phrases or relative clauses in the nearby context, analysing the relationships between the surrounding clauses and sentences, etc. The list is far from complete and those listed are strategies related only to vocabulary. In addition, learners might need grammar-related strategies, discourse-related strategies, strategies solving ambiguity by inferencing, etc. The difficulty a learner might face in reading could be any combinations of various skills/strategies. Materials writers have to predict and choose the major ones but there is no guarantee that their selections are the ones each individual needs.

Skills/strategies training seems to be based on an assumption that conscious, explicit and direct teaching of strategies will eventually nurture automatic execution of reading strategies through practice. However, Barnett (1988) points out that being aware of the strategies does not guarantee the readers' ability to use effective skills/strategies at appropriate times.

Masuhara *et al.* (1994) argue that the constant positive results in L1 strategy teaching may be due to the fact that these unsuccessful L1 readers are able to shift their attention to efficient reading strategies because bottom-up processing is automatized. They suspect that strategy training may cause cognitive overload and interfere with the reading process in the case of L2 learners who still require conscious attention to bottom-up processing. They observe that the majority of L2 learners are tackling two things at a time: processing language and constructing meaning of the content. Strategy training imposes a third cognitive load: monitoring the use and control of strategies. The verbal protocol data of L2 learners often reveals that they were paying more attention to metacognitive processing than to the meaning construction which is the whole point of reading.

The Schema-based Approach

From the late 1970s to the early 1980s, researchers of Artificial Intelligence and Cognitive Psychology devoted a large proportion of their attention to the nature and organization of a reader's knowledge (e.g., Minsky, 1975; Rumelhart, 1980; Schank, 1982; see also Bartlett, 1932). Their interest came from their discovery that a computer cannot understand natural language without equipping it with extensive knowledge of the world. There are some varieties in the terms, definitions and functions in the relevant literature but, in sum, schema theory is a theory about knowledge in the mind: it hypothesizes how knowledge is organized in the mind and how it is used in processing new information. Comprehension, according to schematists, happens when a new experience (be it sensory or linguistic) is understood in comparison with a stereotypical version of a similar experience held in memory. Whether we subscribe to schema theory or not (summaries of criticisms of schema theories can be found in Alba and Hashier, 1983; Alderson, 2000), the reading process cannot be explained without acknowledging the vital importance of the knowledge systems in readers' minds.

Williams and Moran (1989) point out the influence of schema theory on the ubiquitous pre-reading activity in EFL materials in the 1980s. Typical pre-reading activities include:

- asking learners to discuss, in pairs or in groups, their personal experience related to the theme or the topic of the lesson;
- asking learners to consider statements, text titles, illustrations, etc.

Some materials tried to provide learners with a series of texts designed to achieve a critical mass (Grabe, 1986) (i.e., sufficient background knowledge about a certain theme to enable readers to achieve successful comprehension). Thus, combined with the emphasis on situations and contexts in the Communicative Approach, teaching materials which group texts by topics seem to have become popular (e.g., Bell *et al.*, 1985).

Some researchers have investigated the significance of schemata in the L2 reading process (Carrell, 1987; Carrell and Eisterhold, 1988). Constant results have confirmed that activating content information plays a major role in learners' comprehension and recall of information of a text. Carrell and Eisterhold (1988), for example, emphasize that the lack of schemata activation is one major source of processing difficulty with L2 learners. Hudson (1982) argues that a high degree of background knowledge can overcome linguistic deficiencies. Carrell *et al.* (1989) showed significant improvement in L2 reading comprehension after schema instruction. Even though there are some studies which alert us to the potentially negative effects of premature commitment to schemata (Steffenson and Joag-Dev, 1984), L2 researchers seem to agree that, if students do not have sufficient prior knowledge, they should be given at least minimal background knowledge from which to interpret a text (Carrell *et al.*, 1989; Dubin and Bycina, 1991).

Comprehension, according to the schematists, happens when a new experience (be it sensory or linguistic) is understood in comparison with a stereotypical version of a similar experience held in memory. For example, a schema of a French restaurant may involve subschemata of a menu, waiter, wines, starters, main course, etc. If a particular group of students is not familiar with a French restaurant schema, should materials writers offer pre-reading activities for all the lacking subschemata? If we take the schematist hypothesis literally, no texts will be comprehended unless the reader has the right and sufficient schemata. The reality is, however, that readers do manage to understand texts even without having corresponding schematic knowledge (Johnson-Laird, 1983).

Cook (1994) argues that authentic texts are too complex to allow readers easily to select and apply appropriate schemata. A schema is a pre-packaged system of stereotypical knowledge and such a fixed structure may not meet the demands imposed by the ever-changing context we find in authentic texts. And Alderson (2000: 17) notes that 'many psychologists and psycholinguists now question the usefulness of schema theory to account for, rather than provide a metaphor of, the comprehension process.' Schema theories do not explain well how the mind creates, destroys and reorganizes schemata or how schemata are retrieved from the memory during the comprehension process. The question remains how can we help the learners to activate the relevant memories to achieve comprehension.

An Alternative Approach to Materials for Teaching Reading

The overview of the approaches used in reading materials in the last two decades seems to leave us with some unanswered questions regarding the universal reading problems of L2 learners which were identified at the beginning of this chapter:

1. How can materials writers help L2 learners to tackle language problems in reading materials?
2. How can materials writers help L2 learners to have higher self-esteem and start enjoying reading fluently?

I would now like to propose an alternative approach to teaching reading which embodies the following principles:

Principle 1: Engaging Affect should be the Prime Concern of Reading Materials

'In the absence of interesting texts, very little is possible,' noted Williams (1986: 42). I would support this view very strongly in that the quality of texts should be given far more weight in reading pedagogy and materials production. In L1 we read because the text is worth reading. We read on because the texts are useful, interesting, engaging, involving, important and relevant to our lives. In materials for teaching L2 reading, however, texts often seem to be selected because they yield to teaching points: vocabulary, syntax, discourse structures, skills/strategies, etc. Sometimes, certain texts are selected because they are easy or they fit the theme of the unit.

A much stronger argument comes from the fact that good texts work on learners' affect, which is vital for deep processing and creates reasons and motivation to read on. Affect is occasionally mentioned in the literature as an additional or peripheral factor, but I would argue that the engagement of affect (e.g., interest, attitude, emotions) should be given prime importance in reading materials production. Mathewson (1994) makes an interesting observation on the sharp contrast between the teachers' positive interests in affect and the seeming lack of interest among researchers. He compared the contents and titles in teachers' journals against those in research publications. Articles that deal with affect proved to be most predominant, for example, in *The Reading Teacher* from 1948 to 1991 (survey results can be found in Dillon *et al.*, 1992). Yet, affective influences on reading do not appear to have stimulated similar interest among researchers.

Neuroscience (i.e., the study of the central nervous systems – the study of the brain) provides evidence, however, that emotion has a longer evolutionary history than human cognition and casts a fundamental and powerful influence on cognition, learning and memory. We learn to repeat behaviours that are accompanied by positive emotional qualities, and we try to avoid discomfort. Emotionally charged memory makes an instant and strong impression and it stays in our memory for a long time. In reading, the same proficient L1 reader may process the same text differently on separate occasions depending on his/her emotional state and the interest and significance he/she gives to the text at the time.

Principle 2: Listening to a Text before Reading it Helps Decrease Linguistic Demands and Encourages Learners to Focus on Meaning

Earlier in this chapter I made a comparison between how L1 pre-schoolers and L2 learners get initiated to reading. In L1 reading, pre-schoolers experience a language acquisition period first through years of aural–oral interaction and then a proto-reading period (e.g., caretakers reading for the children) before they start to read on their own. In L2 reading, language learning and learning how to read start at the same time. One implication might be to apply the L1 sequence to L2 situations (Tomlinson, 2000). The other implication is for the materials to provide proto-reading activities. One simple but uncommon activity is for the teacher to read the text aloud before giving it to the learners. This has the immediate advantage of stopping L2 readers from becoming text-bound. Furthermore, it provides the learners with aural–oral experience that they often lack in a foreign language situation. But there are more fundamental and theoretical reasons. Tunmer and Hoover (1992: 179) claim that 'Reading is now generally viewed as a derived skill that builds on spoken language; the reading process is thought to be grafted onto the listening process.' The hypothesis that the processing of written language is sound-based accords with neuroscientific findings (Bloom and Lazerson, 1988).

A major difficulty for L2 learners beginning to read is the fact that reading requires learners to decode visual stimuli, chunk syntactic and semantic units, extract meaning from the text and integrate it with their relevant memories in order to create the overall meaning of the text. A teacher reading the text to the students can make it accessible to the learners by:

- taking away the cognitive load of processing scripts and sounds at the same time
- chunking a text into meaningful and manageable lengths to help the learners gradually interpret the meaning
- adding prosodic features such as prominence that mark situationally informative pragmatic meaning
- achieving impact through reading a text with suitable affect (e.g., humour, anger)

Principle 3: Reading Comprehension Means Achieving Multidimensional Mental Representation in the Reader's Mind

I would like the readers of this chapter to do three brief experiments:

Experiment 1. Read the following definition of the Japanese word 'sho': 'a wind instrument made of groups of slim and void bamboo stems. Used in traditional Japanese music'.
Reflect upon what effect the definition of the word had on you.
Experiment 2. Read the following definition of a Japanese fruit: 'a round fruit

which grows on a tree and which has a smooth red, yellow or green skin and firm white flesh inside it'.
What can this fruit be?
Experiment 3. Imagine an apple.
What has happened in your minds?

The first and second experiments are what I call unidimensional processing: you extract the meaning from linguistic code. For the first experiment using the word 'sho', not many readers would have previous direct or even indirect experience of the instrument. Lack of relevant knowledge might have left a very unsettling feeling regarding what the instrument may look like or what kind of sounds it may produce.

The second experiment is slightly more tangible if the association is made between the definition and the memory of an apple. Still, linguistic definition might have left some feeling that you may be wrong.

I would predict that the third experiment with a word 'apple' sparked off all sorts of reactions in your minds. Visions of its colour, size and appearance. Texture. Smell. Associated personal memories. Cognitive memory such as 'An apple a day keeps the doctor away'. This experience that the word 'apple' induced in your minds is what I call multidimensional mental representation. Note that your multidimensional experience was non-verbal once you processed the linguistic label 'apple'.

Let us now see what happens when we read a text. Please relax and read the following poem.

> *Refugee Mother and Child*
> No Madonna and Child could touch
> that picture of a mother's tenderness
> for a son she soon will have to forget.
>
> The air was heavy with odours
> of diarrhoea of unwashed children
> with washed-out ribs and dried-up
> bottoms struggling in laboured
> steps behind blown empty bellies. Most
> mothers there had long ceased
> to care but not this one; she held
> a ghost smile between her teeth
> and in her eyes the ghost of a mother's
> pride as she combed the rust-coloured
> hair left on his skull and then –
> singing in her eyes – began carefully
> to part it ... in another life this
> would have been a little daily
> act of no consequence before his

> breakfast and school; now she
> did it like putting flowers
> on a tiny grave.

(Chinua Achebe (1994), 'Refugee Mother and Child')

Reading this poem, what kind of experience did you have?
You might have:

- Experienced images (e.g., the mother, her smile, rust-coloured hair of the child)
- Imagined the environment and had vague sensations (e.g., smell, dust, sound)
- Felt some sort of emotion
- Remembered some personal experience from your past
- Thought about what you have read, heard, seen about refugees in Africa
- Evaluated the skills of the poet

As a whole, readers of this poem might have experienced a series of snapshots or movie-like dynamic images with possibly sounds and smells as well. What you have created in your minds is a 'mental representation' of the poem. What is interesting about this mental representation is that each reader's representation is dynamic and unique, depending on the individual's mental state, mood, experience, etc.

I would argue that meaning construction in a reader's/listener's mind is achieved in a multidimensional way, deriving from the integrated neural interactions of the various parts of the brain (i.e., the sensory, motor, cognitive and emotional systems).

Principle 4: Materials should Help Learners Experience the Text First before they Draw their Attention to its Language

In L1 reading we focus on meaning. I believe that reading materials should offer activities that help the learners focus on the content of the text and achieve personal experience of it through multidimensional representation. By experiencing the text, learners are able to:

- activate the sensory, motor, emotional, cognitive areas of their brain;
- self-project and self-invest in the activities which lead to deeper processing and to fuller engagement;
- have time to make errors and adjustments in connecting verbal codes with non-verbal mental representations;
- have time to talk to themselves in their L1;
- have time to develop inner speech in the L2 before publicly speaking out or writing.

The readers of this chapter might have noticed that many of the conditions listed above accord with what has been suggested as the characteristics of the optimal learning environment in Second Acquisition Theories (Ellis, 1994; Mitchell and Myles, 1998; Tomlinson, 1998a).

The most important principle in providing the experience of the text is to sequence the activities so that the learners can experience the text first before analysing it. Regardless of our developmental stage, we never stop processing the L1 in multidimensional ways, but somehow L2 learners tend to be fed on a diet of unidimensional, linguistic, analytical approaches to language from beginners' level to advanced. No wonder L2 learners are not so successful in achieving multidimensional mental representation when they use the L2.

Conclusion

In the first part of this chapter, it was noted that L2 learners share a very similar text-bound inefficient way of reading. These L2 learners regardless of age, levels or nationality share one common factor: they were taught using the coursebooks that were produced in the last two decades. The learners have received language lessons, skills/strategies lessons, learned the importance of activating the schema and have been tested with comprehension questions. Learners do have language problems, but it is not so much extensive knowledge of the vocabulary or syntax that they need, what they lack is the fun and involving experience of connecting the language with multidimensional mental representation. Below is an example of an approach which can help learners to create multidimensional mental representation in the L2 and thus develop reading confidence and competence.

Little Johnny's Final Letter – An alternative approach

LEVEL		Intermediate onwards
AGE		12 onwards
TIME		60 minutes
LANGUAGE		Four skills
PREPARATION		A poem, 'Little Johnny's Final Letter', by Brian Patten
PROCEDURE	1.	Tell your students that they are going to listen to a poem. Ask them what they think the poem is about by writing parts of the title on the board. Start with 'letter' then add 'final letter' and finally 'Little Johnny's final letter'.
	2.	Tell your students to write answers in groups to the following questions:

i. How old do you think Johnny is?
ii. Where do you think Johnny is?
iii. Who do you think Johnny addressed this letter to?
iv. Why do you think Johnny wrote the letter?

3. Read these extracts from the poem:
    I won't be home this evening, so Don't worry
    Simply gone to get myself classified
    I have taken off my short-trousers and put on long ones
    Heard your plea on the radio this morning, you sounded sad
    and strangely old...
4. Tell your students to go back to their answers in 2 above if they want to.
5. Tell your students to listen to the whole poem. Tell them to see pictures in their mind of what the poem describes.

Little Johnny's Final Letter

> Mother,
>
> *I won't be home this evening, so*
> *Don't worry; don't hurry to report me missing*
> *Don't drain the canals to find me,*
> *I've decided to stay alive, don't*
> *search the wood, I'm not hiding,*
> *Simply gone to get myself classified.*
> *Don't leave my Shreddies out,*
> *I've done with security;*
> *Don't circulate my photograph to society*
> *I have disguised myself as a man*
> *and am giving priority to obscurity,*
> *It suits me fine;*
> *I have taken off my short-trousers*
> *and put on long ones, and*
> *now am going out into the city, so*
> *Don't worry; don't hurry to report me missing.*
>
> *I've rented a room without any curtains*
> *And sit behind the windows growing cold*
> *Heard your plea on the radio this morning*
> *You sounded sad and strangely old...*
>
> Brian Patten

6. Tell your students to go back to their answers in 2 above if they want to.
7. Tell your students to draw in groups one of the following scenes:

      i. Johnny on the day before he wrote the letter to his mother;

      ii. Johnny in his rented room;

      iii. Johnny's mother in the radio studio appealing to Johnny.

8. Read the poem aloud again.
9. Tell your students to add some details to the group picture they produced in 6 above.
10. Distribute the poem and tell your students to read the poem and in groups to add some more details to the picture they produced in 6 above.
11. Tell your students to answer the following questions in groups:

      i. Why do you think Johnny has left home?

      ii. What do you think Shreddies are?

      iii. Why do you think Johnny's mother usually leaves the Shreddies out?

      iv. What does Johnny mean when he talks about taking off his short-trousers and putting on long ones?

12. Explain to your students that, in his letter home, Johnny asks his mother not to do things and gives reasons why she shouldn't. Tell your students to list, in groups, things Johnny doesn't want his mother to do and the reasons he gives under the headings below.

Things Johnny discourages   *The reasons Johnny gives*

13. Explain to your students that this poem is written by one of the Liverpool poets, Brian Patten. Tell your groups to answer the following questions concerning the poet's intentions.

      i. Johnny uses big words and strange expressions. Try to rephrase the following expressions in the poem in a simpler, more straightforward way.
Simply gone to get myself classified.
I've done with security;
Don't circulate my photograph to society
And am giving priority to obscurity,

      ii. Note down possible reasons why the poet used such expressions in Johnny's letter.

14. Tell your students to do one of the activities below. It is important that the students know that they can do the task by themselves, with a partner or in small groups.

   a. Learn to recite the poem as if you are Johnny.
   b. Paint a picture to illustrate the poem.
   c. Write down what you think Johnny's mother said on the radio. When you have finished, practise reading it in the voice of a mother who sounds, 'sad and strangely old'.
   d. Write a dialogue in which Johnny and his mother are talking on the day before he left home.
   e. Imagine that Johnny's mother found him sitting in his rented room. Write a dialogue between Johnny and his mother in his room.
   f. Write either a poem or a short story about a teenager leaving home for the first time.

COMMENTS

Do note that:

- The initial activities all try to stimulate guessing and create mental representation gradually based on their own past experience.
- Students are given repeated opportunities to adjust their answers and drawings. Individual mental representations are gradually modified to get closer to the poet's mental representation reflected in his words. This is also a good chance for learners to connect language with non-verbal mental representation. It is also reassuring to students that they are not being tested.
- Activities and questions up till Activity 10 are meaning focused. Then gradually students' attention is guided to focus on some cultural words (e.g., Shreddies, the significance of long trousers) in relation to the overall meaning. Interesting cultural awareness activities may be employed here.
- Activities 12–13 focus on language but they are there to help deepen the interpretation of the poem.
- Activity 13 also explores the poet's intentions in writing a poem. It provides a good opportunity for students to learn about techniques and effect in literature.
- Activity 14 can be homework but there should be some provision for your students to have an exhibition or display of their hard work.

References

Achebe, C. (1994) 'Refugee Mother and child', in I. Gordon (ed.) *The Earth is Ours: Poems for Secondary Schools*. London and Basingstoke: Macmillan.

Adams, M. J. (1980) 'Failures to comprehend levels of processing', in R. J. Spiro, B. C. Bruce and W. F. Brewer (eds) *Theoretical Issues in Reading Comprehension – Perspectives from Cognitive Psychology, Linguistics, Artificial Intelligence and Education*. Hillsdale, NJ: Lawrence Erlbaum Associates, pp. 11–32.

Adams, M. J. (1994) 'Modeling the connections between word recognition and reading', in R. B. Ruddell, M. R. Ruddell and H. Singer, (eds) *Theoretical Models and Processes of Reading* (4th edn.). New Ark, DE: International Reading Association, pp. 838–63.

Alba, J. W. and Hasher, L. (1983) 'Is memory schematic?' *Psychological Bulletin*, **93**, 203–31.

Alderson, J. C. (1984) 'Reading in a foreign language: a reading problem or a language problem?', in J. C. Alderson and A. H. Urquhart (eds) *Reading in a Foreign Language*. London: Longman, pp. 1–24.

Alderson, J. C. (2000) *Assessing Reading*. Cambridge: Cambridge University Press.

Alderson, J. C. and Richards, S. (1977) 'Difficulties students encounter when reading texts in English'. (Mimeo Research and Development Unit Report No. 8). Mexico City: UNAM.

Alderson, J. C. and Urquhart, A. H. (eds) (1984) *Reading in a foreign Language*. London: Longman.

Auerbach, E. A. and Paxton, D. (1997) ' "It's not the English thing": bringing reading research into the classroom'. *TESOL Quarterly* **31** (2), 237–61.

Barnett, M. A. (1988) 'Reading through context: how real and perceived strategy use affects L2 comprehension'. *Modern Language Journal*, **72**, 150–62.

Bartlett, F. C. (1932) *Remembering*. Cambridge: Cambridge University Press.

Bell, J., Boardman, R. and Buckley, T. (1985) *Variety*. Cambridge: Cambridge University Press.

Berman, R. A. (1984) 'Syntactic components of the foreign language reading process', in J. C. Alderson and A. H. Urquhart (eds) *Reading in a Foreign Language*. Harlow: Longman, pp. 139–56.

Bloom, F. E. and Lazerson, A. (1988) *Brain, Mind and Behaviour* (2nd edn.). New York: W. H. Freeman and Company.

Brown, A. L., Palincsar, A. L. and Armbruster, B. B. (1984) 'Instructing comprehension-fostering activities in interactive learning situations', in H. Mandle, N. L. Stein and T. Trabasso (eds) *Learning and Comprehension of Text*. Hillsdale, NJ: Lawrence Erlbaum.

Carrell, P. L. (1984) 'The effects of rhetorical organisation on ESL readers'. *TESOL Quarterly*, **18**(3), 441–69.

Carrell, P. L. (1985) 'Facilitating ESL reading by teaching text structure'. *TESOL Quarterly*, **18**(3), 727–52.

Carrell, P. L. (1987) 'Content and formal schemata in ESL reading'. *TESOL Quarterly*, **21**(3), 461–81.

Carrell, P. L. and Eisterhold, J. C. (1988) 'Schema theory and ESL reading pedagogy', in P. L. Carrell, J. Devine and D. Eskey (eds) *Interactive Approaches to Second Language Reading*. New York: Cambridge University Press, pp. 73–92.

Carrell, P. L., Pharis, B. G. and Liberto, J. (1989) 'Metacognitive strategy training for ESL reading'. *TESOL Quarterly*, **23**(4), 647–78.

Clarke, M. A. (1988) 'The short circuit hypothesis of ESL reading – or when language competence interfers with reading performance', in P. L. Carrell, J. Devine and D. E. Eskey (eds) *Interactive Approaches to Second Language Reading*. Cambridge: Cambridge University Press.

Coady, J. and Huckin, T. (eds) (1997) *Second Language Vocabulary Acquisition*. Cambridge: Cambridge University Press.

Cook, G. (1994) *Discourse and Literature*. Oxford: Oxford University Press.

Cooper, M. (1984) 'Linguistic competence for practised and unpractised non-native readers of English', in J. C. Alderson and A. H. Urquhart (eds) *Reading in a Foreign Language*. London: Longman, pp. 122–35.

Cummins, J. and Swain, M. (1986) *Bilingualism in Education*. London: Longman.

Cunningham, S. and Moor, P. (1998) *Cutting Edge*. London: Pearson Longman.

Davidson, A. and Green, G. M. (1988) *Linguistic Complexity and Text Comprehension: Readability Issues Reconsidered*. Hillsdale, NJ: Lawrence Erlbaum Associates Publishers.

Davis, F. B. (1968) 'Research in comprehension in reading'. *Reading Research Quarterly*, **3**, 499–545.

Davis, J. N. and Bistodeau, L. (1993) 'How do L1 and L2 reading differ? Evidence from think aloud protocols'. *Modern Language Journal*, **77**(4), 459–72.

Dillon, D. R., O'Brien, D. G., Hopkins, C. J., Baumann, J. F., Humphrey, J. W., Pickle, J. M., Ridgeway, V. R., Wyatt, M., Wilkinson, C., Murray, B. and Pauler, S. M. (1992) 'Article content and authorship trends in *The Reading Teacher* 1948–1991'. *The Reading Teacher*, **45** (5), 362–5.

Dubin, F. and Bycina, D. (1991) 'Academic reading and the ESL/EFL teacher', in M. Celce-Murcia (ed.) *Interactive Approaches to Second Language Reading*. New York: Newbury House, pp. 260–77.

Ellis, N. (1995) 'Vocabulary acquisition: psychological perspectives and pedagogical implications'. *The Language Teacher*, **19** (2), 12–16.

Ellis, R. (1994) *The Study of Second Language Acquisition*. Oxford: Oxford University Press.

Forsyth, W., McGowen, B., Naunton, J. and Richardson, V. (2000) *Clockwise*. Oxford: Oxford University Press.

Fries, C. C. (1963) *Linguistics and Reading*. New York: Holt, Rinehart & Winston. Reprinted 1981: New York: Irvington.

Goodman, K. S. (1976) 'Reading: a psycholinguistic guessing game', in H. Singer and R. Ruddell (eds) *Theoretical Models and Processes of Reading* (2nd edn.). Newark, DE: International Reading Association. Originally published in 1967, *Journal of the Reading Specialist*, **6** (1), 126–35.

Gough, P. B. (1972) 'One second of reading', in J. F. Kavanagh and I. G. Mattingly (eds) *Language by Ear and by Eye*. Cambridge, MA: MIT Press.

Grabe, W. (1986) 'The transition from theory to practice in teaching reading', in F. Dubin, D. E. Eskey and W. Grabe (eds) *Teaching Second Language Reading for Academic Purposes*. Reading, MA: Addison Wesley.

Greenall, S. and Swan, M. (1986) *Effective Reading*. Cambridge: Cambridge University Press.

Hosenfeld, C. (1984) 'Case studies of ninth grade readers', in J. C. Alderson and A. H. Urquhart (eds) *Reading in a Foreign Language*. London: Longman, pp. 231–44.

Hudson, T. (1982) 'The effects of induced schemata on the "short-circuit", in L2 reading: non-decoding factors in L2 reading performance'. *Language Learning*, **32**, 1–31.

Hutchinson, T. (1997) *Lifelines Intermediate*. Oxford: Oxford University Press.

Hymes, D. (1979) 'On communicative competence', in C. J. Brumfit and K. Johnson (eds) *The Communicative Approach to Language Teaching*. Oxford: Oxford University Press, pp. 5–26.

Johnson-Laird, P. N. (1983) *Mental Models: Towards a Cognitive Science of Language, Inference and Consciousness*. Cambridge: Cambridge University Press.

Kern, R. G. (1989) 'Second language reading strategy'. *Modern Language Journal*, **73**, 135–49.

Kim, H. and Krashen, S. (1997) 'Why don't language acquirers take advantage of the power of reading?' *TESOL Journal*, Spring, 26–9.

Kimura, T., Masuhara, H., Fukada, A. and Takeuchi, M. (1993) 'Effectiveness of reading strategy training in the comprehension of Japanese college EFL learners'. *JACET Bulletin*, **24**, 101–20.

Klare, G. R. (1974) 'Assessing readability'. *Reading Research Quarterly*, **10**, 62–102.

Krashen, S. (1982) *Principles and Practice in Second Language Acquisition*. Oxford: Pergamon.

Laufer, B. and Sim, D. D. (1985) 'Measuring and explaining the reading threshold needed for English for academic texts'. *Foreign Language Annals*, **18** (5), 405–11.

Lunzer, E., Waite, M. and Dolan, T. (1979) 'Comprehension and comprehension tests', in E. Lunzer and K. Garner (eds) *The Effective Use of Reading*. London: Heinemann Educational Books.

Masuhara, H. (1998) 'Factors influencing the reading difficulties of advanced learners of English as a foreign language when reading authentic texts'. Unpublished PhD thesis: University of Luton.

Masuhara, H., Kimura, T., Fukada, A. and Takeuchi, M. (1994) 'Strategy training or/and extensive reading?', in T. Hickey and J. Williams (eds) *Language, Education and Society*. Clevedon, Avon: Multilingual Matters.

Mathewson, G. C. (1994) 'Model of attitude influence upon reading and learning to read', in R. B. Ruddell, M. R. Ruddell and H. Singer (eds) *Theoretical Models and Processes of Reading*. Newark, DE: International Reading Association, pp. 1131–61.

Meara, P. (1997) 'Towards a new approach to modelling vocabulary acquisition', in N. Schmitt and M. J. McCarthy (eds) *Vocabulary: Description, Acquisition and Pedagogy.* Cambridge: Cambridge University Press, pp. 109–21.

Minsky, M. L. (1975) 'A framework for representing knowledge', in P. Winston (ed.) *The Psychology of Computer Vision.* New York: McGraw-Hill, pp. 211–27.

Mitchell, R. and Myles, F. (1998) *Second Language Learning Theories.* Oxford: Oxford University Press.

Nation, J. S. P. (2001) *Learning Vocabulary in Another Language.* Cambridge: Cambridge University Press.

Nation, J. S. P. and Coady, J. (1988) 'Vocabulary and reading', in R. Carter and M. McCarthy (eds) *Vocabulary and Language Teaching.* Harlow: Longman, pp. 97–110.

Nuttall, C. (1982) *Teaching Reading Skills in a Foreign Language.* London: Heinemann Educational.

Nuttall, C. (1985) 'Recent materials for the teaching of reading'. *English Language Teaching Journal,* **39** (3).

Nuttall, C. (1996) *Teaching Reading Skills in a Foreign Language* (new edn.). London: Heinemann Educational.

Olshavsky, J. E. (1977) 'Reading as problem solving: an investigation of strategies'. *Reading Research Quarterly,* **12** (4).

Paran, A. (1996) 'Reading in EFL: facts and fictions'. *ELT Journal,* **50** (1), 25–34.

Rumelhart, D. E. (1980) 'Schemata: the building blocks of cognition', in R. J. Spiro, B. C. Bruce and W. E. Brewer (eds) *Theoretical Issues in Reading Comprehension.* Hillsdale, NJ: Erlbaum.

Rumelhart, D. E., McClelland, J. L. and P. D. P. Research Group (eds) (1986) *Parallel Distributed Processing – Explorations in the Microstructure of Cognition.* Cambridge, MA: MIT Press.

Schank, R. C. (1982) *Dynamic Memory.* New York: Cambridge University Press.

Schank, R. C. and Abelson, R. P. (1977) *Scripts, Plans, Goals, and Understanding.* Hillsdale, NJ: Erlbaum.

Smith, F. (1978) *Reading.* Cambridge: Cambridge University Press.

Soars, J. and Soars, L. (1987) *Headway Upper-Intermediate.* Oxford: Oxford University Press.

Steffenson, M. S. and Joag-Dev, C. (1984) 'Cultural knowledge and reading', in J. C. Alderson and A. H. Urquhart (eds) *Reading in a Foreign Language.* Harlow: Longman, pp. 48–64.

Thorndike, R. L. (1974) 'Reading as reasoning'. *Reading Research Quarterly,* **9**, 135–47.

Tomlinson, B. (1998a) 'Introduction', in B. Tomlinson (ed.) *Materials Development in Language Teaching.* Cambridge: Cambridge University Press, pp. 1–24.

Tomlinson, B. (1998b) 'Seeing what they mean: helping L2 readers to visualise', in B. Tomlinson (ed.) *Materials Development in Language Teaching.* Cambridge: Cambridge University Press, pp. 265–78.

Tomlinson, B. (2000) 'Beginning to read forever'. *Reading in a Foreign Language,* **13** (1), 523–38.

Tomlinson, B., Dat, B., Masuhara, H. and Rubdy, R. (2001) 'EFL courses for adults'. *ELT Journal*, **55** (1), 80–101.

Tomlinson, B. and Ellis, R. (1987) *Reading Upper Intermediate*. Oxford: Oxford University Press.

Tunmer, W. E. and Hoover, W. A. (1992) 'Cognitive and linguistic factors in learning to read', in P. B. Gough, L. C. Ehri and R. Treiman (eds) *Reading Acquisition*. Hillsdale, NJ: Lawrence Erlbaum Associates Inc.

Urquhart, A. H. (1987) 'Comprehension and interpretation'. *Reading in a Foreign Language*, **3** (2).

Wallace, C. (2001) 'Reading', in R. Carter and D. Nunan (eds) *The Cambridge Guide to Teaching English to Speakers of Other Languages*. Cambridge: Cambridge University Press.

Widdowson, H. G. (1979) *Exploration in Applied Linguistics*. Oxford: Oxford University Press.

Widdowson, H. G. (1986) 'Foreword', in S. Salimbene *Interactive Reading*. Cambridge, MA: Newbury House.

Williams, E. (1983) 'Communicative reading', in K. Johnson and D. Porter, (eds) *Perspectives in Communicative Language Teaching*. London: Academic Press.

Williams, E. (1984) *Reading in the Language Classroom*. London: Macmillan.

Williams, E. and Moran, C. (1989) 'State of the art: reading in a foreign language'. *Language Teaching*, **22** (4), 217–28.

Williams, R. (1986) ' "Top ten" principles for teaching reading'. *ELT Journal*, **40**, 1.

Winograd, P. and Hare, C. (1988) 'Direct instruction of reading comprehension strategies: the nature of teacher explanation', in C. E. Weinstein, E. T. Goetz and P. A. Alexander (eds) *Learning and Study Strategies: Issues in Assessment, Instruction, and Evaluation*. San Diego: Academic Press, pp. 121–39.

CHAPTER

21

Coursebook Listening Activities

David A. Hill and Brian Tomlinson

Introduction

Despite a variety of publications in the past fifteen years describing and exemplifying systematic approaches to developing listening skills in foreign language learners (e.g., Anderson and Lynch, 1988; Rost, 1990; Rost, 1991; White, 1998; Field, 1998; Buck, 2001), little has changed in that period in the type of listening activity provided in the majority of widely used coursebooks.

According to Field, the typical recent textbook provides the following stages in a listening task:

- pre-listening (for context and motivation);
- extensive listening → questions to establish the situation;
- pre-set questions or pre-set task;
- extensive listening;
- review of questions or task;
- inferring new vocabulary/examination of functional language. (Field, 1998: 110)

Field laments that the model used by textbooks is a product model in which 'success in listening is measured by correct responses to questions or tasks', as opposed to a process model in which teachers would 'follow up incorrect responses in order to determine where understanding broke down and to put things right'. Buck (2001) comments that most classwork done on listening skills is 'bottom-up' rather than 'top-down'. By this he means that there is a concentration on knowledge of the smallest elements of the incoming sound-stream, such as phonemes or individual words, at the expense of wider issues such as general knowledge or experience of the world. Buck concludes that:

> both research and daily experience indicate that the processing of the different types of knowledge (involved in understanding language) does not occur in a fixed sequence, but rather, that different types of processing may occur simultaneously, or in any convenient order. Thus, syntactic knowledge might be used to help identify a word, ideas about the topic of conversation might influence processing of the syntax, or knowledge of the context will help interpret the meaning. (Buck, 2001: 2)

What these two writers suggest, and what Rost (1991) and White (1998) demonstrate in their 'recipe' books of listening activities, is that it *is* possible to be systematic about teaching listening skills, to develop lists of listening subskills which need to be practised and to find appropriate pedagogic vehicles for such practice.

What are Textbooks Providing?

In order to understand more clearly what recent textbooks are providing in the way of listening activities, three Intermediate level students' books were examined: L. Soars and J. Soars (1996), *New Headway English Course* (Oxford University Press); S. Cunningham and P. Moor (1998), *Cutting Edge* (Longman); S. Kay and V. Jones (2000), *Inside Out* (Macmillan Heinemann). The first 50 pages of each book were studied to discover what kind of activities were being offered related to the recorded material presented on the audio cassettes, and printed as tapescripts in the back of the books. In the three books, there were 92 such activities, which can be broken down as follows:

Listening for specific information	39/92
Listen and check	19/92
Pronunciation practice	13/92
Cloze	7/92
Answer questions on the cassette	6/92
Read text and listen to it	3/92
Other	5/92

It can be seen from this that the majority of activities involved the students in the traditional listening comprehension activity of extracting factual information from a spoken text. There is a sense in which the second highest activity type – listen and check – is related to the first, in that the students complete a written task, and then listen for the correct answers on the tape – thereby also listening for specific information, in relation to their answers. The pronunciation activities were varied, working on a range of discrete pronunciation areas such as weak forms, sentence stress and word stress. Cloze activities were largely confined to *Cutting Edge* (6/7), as were the listen and answer activities (4/6) where students wrote a written response to a question asked or statement made on the cassette. On a few occasions, the students were merely asked to listen to a text being read on cassette while they followed it in their books. Probably the most interesting activity types occurred in the 'other' category. *Headway* asked the students to gauge the effect of bald 'Yes/No' answers written in their books, with the question tag 'Yes, I do/No, I don't' answers on tape, working in the area of politeness. The same book also asked students to listen and decide whether the ' 's' ending (e.g., 'it's') was 'it is' or 'it has', which required understanding of the context. *Inside Out* asked students to listen to different pieces of music and relate them to genres of film, thus working on the students' knowledge of the world. The same book also asked the students to write out a nursery rhyme from the words given in jumbled order and then mark the stressed syllables. In one case, in *Headway*, the spoken text appeared to be presenting new language. In almost all cases, the longer taped texts used for listening for specific information were monologues or dialogues, often appearing in the form of an interview.

It is plain that the cassette-related listening activities in any given coursebook only represent a part of the potential listening opportunities in a textbook-based lesson. Other opportunities are provided by simple classroom language such as following the teacher's instructions, or by what are often referred to as 'speaking activities', where the students are involved in an information exchange (which is plainly as much about listening as about speaking, which is either prescribed in the textbook itself, available in supplementary materials or added by the teacher). However, the fact that textbook authors provide such a limited range of listening activities points to a lack of a systematic approach to listening skill work.

What could Textbooks be Providing?

Rost (1991) has used a division of listening activities into four broad types:

Name	Examples of activities
Attentive Listening:	the learners have to give short verbal and non-verbal responses to the speaker in a real-time interaction.
Intensive Listening:	the learners are focused on particular aspects of the language system to raise awareness of how they affect meaning.
Selective Listening:	the learners concentrate on specific pieces of information, learning to attend selectively to what they hear.
Interactive Listening:	learners are helped to become active listeners by working in pairs or small groups with information gap, problem-solving type activities.

White (1998) categorizes listening skills into five broad areas:

Name	Examples of activities
Perception Skills:	skills such as recognizing individual sounds, identifying reduced forms, recognizing intonation patterns.
Language Skills:	skills such as identifying individual words and groups and building up meanings for them.
Using Knowledge of the World:	connecting words to non-linguistic features to get clues to meaning, using knowledge of topic.

| Dealing with Information: | understanding gist meaning, inferring information which is not specifically stated. |
| Interacting with a Speaker: | coping with speaker variations such as speed and accent, recognizing speaker intention, identifying speaker mood. |

Both authors then go on to offer a broad range of recipes for activities which can be adapted to all levels by grading the texts and/or the tasks. Buck (2001) cites a number of taxonomies of listening skills which can also be used, or amalgamated, to provide a principled listening skills syllabus. Were coursebooks to be written using such systematic approaches to listening, they would be doing the language learning and teaching community a great service!

Suggestions for Additional Approaches to Developing Materials for Listening Skills

Sources of Input

In most coursebooks the main source of spoken input is a cassette or a CD-ROM on which fluent native speakers perform scripted dialogues or monologues. Yet in real life the main source of spoken input for most speakers of a foreign language is face-to-face contact with other non-native speakers of the language. Obviously in class learners spend a lot of time interacting face to face with their teacher (although nearly always with the teacher initiating and controlling the exchange) and in some classes the learners spend time interacting face to face with each other. However this face-to-face contact is often incidental to (or even despite) the coursebook and usually takes place during activities in which the main pedagogic goals involve the development of speaking skills. It is rare for coursebooks to include listening activities which feature interaction with the teacher and/or other learners. It is also rare for coursebooks to include listening activities in which the speakers are from outside the cassette and the classroom. And yet it is easy enough in most learning situations for speakers/interactants to be invited into the classroom or for arrangements to be made for learners to participate in listening activities outside the classroom. For example, in one language school in Cambridge teachers from three different classes used to interact live in front of all three classes at the start of a listening lesson and then the learners would go back to their own classroom for the follow-up activities. In a school in Jakarta the students found English-sounding names in the phone book and then rang to invite English speakers to visit their class to give a talk on something they were enthusiastic experts on. And in a school in Japan the students were taken for their listening lessons to the cinema, to the airport, to the theatre and on trains which had announcements in English.

It would not be too difficult for coursebooks to supplement their cassette-based listening activities with activities which make use of the following as sources of input:

- the teacher
- other teachers
- other learners in the class
- learners from other classes (one language school in Cambridge used to encourage learners to give prepared presentations to classes at the level below them)
- invited speakers
- people the learners have phoned
- official speakers in public places
- people interviewed by the learners
- discussion groups outside the school

Types of Input

In 'real life' it is rare that we have to listen to other people's conversations or to strangers on cassettes telling us about their hobbies, plans or ambitions; and I cannot remember ever needing or wanting to do this in a foreign language. Yet, listening to other people's dialogues and listening to short monologues from strangers are the most frequent sources of spoken input in most coursebooks. We would like to see more consideration given in materials development to the sorts of listening events that speakers of a foreign language are likely to need or want to participate in, and much more thought given to the roles that the foreign language speaker might have to play in these events. Only then will we be able to help learners to develop useful listening skills. We would also like to see much more time given in materials to sources of input which have the potential to facilitate language acquisition. This means, for example, making a greater effort to find or develop listening texts which have relevance to the learner, which have affective appeal and which have the potential to engage the learner both cognitively and emotively. It also means involving the learner actively in the listening event either as an interactant or as a listener with a need and purpose.

Additional Types of Relevant Input

Here are some listening events which speakers of a foreign language are likely to need or want to participate in, and which do not often feature in coursebooks (for example, none of the listening events below are included in *Inside Out Upper Intermediate* (2001):

- being taught to do something which they need or want to do
- being taught about something which is useful or interesting
- teaching somebody else to do something and listening to their questions and requests for clarification
- teaching somebody else about something and listening to their questions and requests for clarification
- taking part in discussions with friends about topics of interest and concern

- taking part in phatic communion (i.e., small-talk situations where the main point is to establish social contact rather than communicate information or ideas)
- listening to questions about what they need or want (e.g., in a bank, at a ticket office, in a travel agent)
- listening to announcements (e.g., at airports, at stations, at sports events)
- listening to information (e.g., to train information on the phone, to weather forecasts, to recorded road travel information)
- listening to advertisements (and separating information from persuasion)
- listening to radio programmes for enjoyment and/or information
- listening to music for enjoyment
- watching TV and films for enjoyment

Intake-rich Activities
Listening activities which have potential for achieving rich intake of language could include:

- listening to the teacher reading poems, short stories, extracts from novels, etc.
- listening to a group of teachers acting a scene from a play
- listening to the teacher telling jokes and anecdotes
- listening to other learners reading poems, telling jokes and anecdotes, etc. (but only if they have prepared and practised)
- listening to other learners reading aloud texts which they have enjoyed studying
- listening to other learners doing a prepared presentation on something which really interests them (especially if the listeners have a choice of presenters to listen to)
- watching sports events, news events, documentaries, etc., with commentaries in the target language
- engaging in discussion with their peers on controversial topics

Ways of Facilitating Intake

Just as when we read in our L1, we listen to our L1 in multidimensional ways (Masuhara, this volume; Tomlinson, 2001). That is, we do not only decode the words; we use sensory imaging (especially visual imaging) to represent utterances, we use inner speech to repeat some of the utterances we hear and to talk to ourselves about what we hear, we connect what we hear to our lives and to our knowledge of the world and we respond affectively to what we hear. In other words, we create our own multidimensional mental representation of what we hear, which converges with the representations of other L1 listeners in relation to the literal meaning of the spoken text but diverges in relation to our own needs, wants, experience and attitudes. In this way we maximize the possibilities of rich and relevant intake and of the retention of features of the input which are salient to us. Obviously, it is impossible to achieve equally effective representations in an L2 but helping learners to try to do so can increase their chances both of becoming effective listeners and of maximizing the potential of listening situations for language acquisition.

Ways of helping learners to achieve multidimensional representation of what they listen to include:

- not using listening texts to test understanding of micro-features of the texts (this encourages unidimensional processing of listening texts)
- not concentrating on short, simple listening texts at lower levels (this encourages the habit of micro-processing)
- building up listening confidence by using a Total Physical Response (TPR) approach with beginners (Asher, 1977; Tomlinson, 1994) in which the learners respond physically to instructions spoken by the teacher
- building up listening confidence by not testing learners at lower levels on what they have not understood but giving instead opportunities to make use of what they have understood (e.g., retelling a story to someone who has not heard it)
- getting learners to analyse what they do when listening experientially in the L1 and then encouraging them to try listening in the same ways when experiential listening is appropriate in the L2
- including extensive listening of potentially engaging texts from the earliest levels (and resisting the urge to set tasks to check comprehension)
- facilitating experiential listening by providing whilst-reading tasks which encourage sensory imaging, the use of inner speech, personal connections and affective response (e.g., asking the learners to visualize the main character as they listen to a story, to talk to themselves about how an announcement relates to them, to think of similar situations in their own lives while they listen to an account of the problems of a teenager, to focus on how they feel about a provocative statement, etc.)
- giving instruction on how to listen experientially prior to a listening task (e.g., 'When listening to the description of Betu make sure you try to see pictures and that you think of places that it reminds you of')
- encouraging the teacher and the learners to tell anecdotes about their own experiences in relation to the topic of a lesson
- setting homework tasks which involve learners listening experientially (live or to recordings) to texts which appeal to them (one class in Japan were encouraged to record potentially interesting texts for the class and soon had a thousand cassettes for students to select from for homework listening)

Ways of Developing Listening Skills

Fortunately, the best way of helping learners to develop listening skills is to ensure that the learners are exposed to a wide variety of listening text genres and text types and to provide whilst-listening tasks similar to those suggested above for facilitating intake. In addition, it is useful to make use of a combination of the following approaches:

- Teaching learners about a particular listening subskill (e.g., listening for gist; listening for specific information; listening in order to infer a speaker's attitude) and then providing practice activities.
- Getting learners to do a listening task in which they listen for a specific purpose and then teaching them about the skills they used before providing practice activities.
- Getting learners to do a listening task in which they listen for a specific purpose and then asking them to think and talk about the skills they used before providing further practice activities.
- Giving learners a listening task in which they listen for a specific purpose and getting them to think and talk about what skills and strategies they will use before they begin the activity.
- Giving learners a listening task in which they listen for a specific purpose and getting them to think and talk about what problems they had with the activity before providing guidance and setting them another similar activity.

An Example of Multidimensional Listening Skills Lessons

Lesson 1

1. The teacher tells the class an anecdote about her first day at school.
2. The teacher invites the learners to think about their own first day at school.
3. The teacher reads aloud the poem 'First Day at School' by Roger McGough.
4. An invited speaker (either a teacher from another class or a guest) tells the class about his/her first experience of a particular activity (e.g., mountain climbing, appearing on stage, driving a car).
5. The learners ask the speaker questions about the experience.
6. The teacher tells the class that they are going to visit a country in Africa called Betu. As this will be the first time that any of them have visited Betu, the teacher is going to play them a cassette which gives information about the country. They should listen to the cassette and note down anything which they think is useful or interesting. They are told that they will all travel to Betu together but that after the first day there they will split up into smaller groups who will go off to different parts of the country.
7. The teacher tells the learners to look at the photographs of different parts of Betu in their coursebook (some are of the beaches, some of the mountains and some of the game parks).
8. The teacher plays the cassette.
9. Each learner decides where they want to go in Betu and want they want to do.
10. The learners walk around the classroom telling each other their decisions in 9 above.

11. The learners form groups who want to go to the same place and do similar things.
12. The groups plan their trip to Betu using the headings provided in the coursebook (e.g., Clothes to Take, Other Things to Take, Health Precautions, Other Things to Do before the Trip, Things to Do in Betu, Things to be Careful of in Betu, The Itinerary in Betu).
13. The teacher plays the cassette again.
14. The groups make revisions to their plans in 12.
15. The teacher tells the class that for homework each one of them should imagine their trip to Betu. She warns them that some of the information on the cassette is not completely reliable.
16. The teacher reads the poem 'First Day at School' again and tells the class where they can find it in their coursebook so that they can read it for homework.

Lesson 2

1. The learners sit in their groups from Lesson 1 and tell each other about their imagined trip.
2. Each group decides on a group version of the trip (ideally with lots of interesting and unanticipated events) and prepares a presentation on their trip.
3. Each group gives a presentation on their trip to the rest of the class (or in a very large class to groups who have been to different places).
4. New groups are formed and each group is given the task of writing the script for a more reliable and useful 'Introduction to Betu'.
5. The teacher plays the cassette on Betu once more so that the groups can spot all its deficiencies.
6. The groups write their scripts (and, if possible, record them).
7. Each group reads (or plays) its 'Introduction to Betu' and the other groups are told to listen to it carefully so that they can evaluate it afterwards.
8. After each presentation one group is invited to give a constructive criticism of it and all the groups give it a grade out of 20.
9. After all the presentations, the scores are added up and a winner is declared.
10. Each group is asked to go through the activities in Lessons 1 and 2 above in their minds and to list all the listening skills they needed to use in these activities.
11. The teacher lists listening skills on the board (or OHT) from plenary feed-back from the groups on 10 above.
12. Each group is allocated a different listening skill from the list and is asked to prepare a presentation on that skill for the following week in which they:

   - describe the skill;
   - give examples of when it is useful;
   - give advice on how to develop and use the skill;

- give the other learners a listening task which involves using the skill.

(The teacher could provide the class with a preparation period in which she is available to help the groups in the preparation of their presentations.)

Note

1. The main point of these lessons is that the learners gain a lot of experience of different types of listening from different input sources.
2. The main role of the coursebook in these lessons is to provide:

- relevant and stimulating illustrations;
- cassette input;
- supporting materials (e.g., suggested headings, print versions of texts);
- a lesson plan and advice in the Teacher's Book.

Conclusion

The main point about materials for developing listening skills is that learners can only develop these skills if they do a lot of listening. Therefore, they should spend considerable time in listening lessons actually listening. Teaching and discovery activities can facilitate the development of listening skills too, but spending most of the listening lesson answering comprehension questions after listening to a text (still the norm in many coursebooks) has very little beneficial effect on the development of listening confidence and skills.

Let us spend much less time testing our learners on their recall and comprehension of discrete features of a text (a task beyond many native speakers) and let us spend much more time helping our learners to enjoy listening.

References

Anderson, A. and Lynch, T. (1988) *Listening.* Oxford: Oxford University Press.

Asher, J. (1977) *Learning Another Language through Actions: The Complete Teacher's Guidebook.* Los Gatos, CA: Sky Oak Productions.

Buck, G. (2001) *Assessing Listening.* Cambridge: Cambridge University Press.

Cunningham, S. and Moor, P. (1998) *Cutting Edge.* Harlow: Longman.

Field, J. (1998) 'Skills and strategies: towards a new methodology for listening'. *English Language Teaching Journal,* **52** (2), 110–18.

Kay, S. and Jones, V. (2000) *Inside Out Intermediate.* Oxford: Macmillan Heinemann.

Kay, S. and Jones, V. (2001) *Inside Out Upper Intermediate.* Oxford: Macmillan Heinemann.

Rost, M. (1990) *Listening in Language Learning.* Harlow: Longman.

Rost, M. (1991) *Listening in Action.* Hemel Hempstead: Prentice-Hall International.

Soars, L. and Soars, J. (1996) *New Headway English Course.* Oxford: Oxford University Press.

Tomlinson, B. (1994) 'TPR materials'. *Folio,* **1** (2), 8–10.

Tomlinson, B. (2001). 'Connecting the mind: a multi-dimensional approach to teaching language through literature'. *The English Teacher,* 104–15.

White, G. (1998) *Listening.* Oxford: Oxford University Press.

Materials for Developing Speaking Skills

Bao Dat

Introduction

This chapter first of all highlights some prevalent methodological trends that have strongly influenced and shaped many essential components in the development of material design for spoken language. Secondly, a practical framework will be proposed to serve the designing of materials for speaking skills. Thirdly, I will discuss a rationale for effective instructional materials for the discussed skills and, finally, I would like to open a window for further discussions by throwing light on some methodological aspects that deserve further scholarly attention.

Overview

Setting the Scene: Speaking Skills and the Need for Relevant Materials

One way to understand the notion of speaking skills, as suggested by Bygate (1987: 5–6), is by viewing them in two basic aspects: motor-receptive skills and interaction skills. The former involves a mastering of sounds and structures not necessarily in any particular context. The latter involves making decisions about what and how to say things in specific communicative situations to convey the right intentions or maintain relationships. This perception can be further understood by observing that these two sets of skills must not represent 'clear-cut distinctions' (Littlewood, 1981: 16) or a 'two-stage operation', but from the start structure must be taught in relation to use (Johnson, 1982: 22). Moreover, much research on language awareness also suggests that the teaching sequence does not have to be structured before the communication of meanings, but content-based activities can help learners to experience and respond to meanings first. Arguably, speaking skills are best developed when learners learn eventually to take control of their own performance from an insider perspective (e.g., from that of the learner), rather than being constantly dictated to by outsider manipulation (e.g., by the teacher). Before looking into how materials can be created to meet this need, let me clarify what I mean by developing materials for speaking.

Second language teaching materials, as viewed by Tomlinson (1998: 2), can be created not only by writers, but also by teachers and learners. In other words, the act of developing materials should be understood beyond the act of writing scripts for coursebooks and, in fact, can be a dynamic, creative process which stretches from the writer's desk to the real classroom (e.g., in the form of stories being told or ideas being exchanged).

Tomlinson's perception coincides nicely with Nunan's (1989: 11) vision that communication should be seen as a process rather than a set of products. It is also closely related to what Breen (1984: 47) calls the 'process syllabus'. According to this syllabus, when materials are scripted by a writer, they appear in the form of a predesigned plan, which should not be the final production yet but be open to reinterpretation by the users of that plan (i.e., teachers and learners). Both the designer's original construction and the users' reinterpretation of this plan have the right to join each other in a creative process shaped by participant experiences, attitudes and knowledge. It is through such interaction that predesigned sketches can best be modified to become appropriate materials that promote language learning. In other words, the happening of task implementation in the classroom can serve as a powerful tool for relevant materials to be jointly discovered and created.

This understanding helps explain why many coursebook activities composed according to the writer's own assumptions (while disregarding their users) often do not work well in the real classroom. It also explains why adaptation of coursebooks is constantly called into play, especially when the writer's vision of the classroom process fails to harmonize with the teacher's vision, the learner's needs and the local contexts. Ideally, if materials are constructed for speaking skills, then the interactive process by the designer and the users should take place through speaking, since it would be unrealistic for participants simply to sit there and imagine silently how speech might work from a written script.

Having made my point of departure clear, let me move on to examine the broader context of some major academic trends over the decades that continue to affect the types of materials we are producing at present.

Methodological Trends

Today it has become unrealistic, if not impossible, to discuss materials development for speaking skills without recognizing the dominant impact of communicative language teaching (CLT) on what we do. This acknowledgement comes from two pieces of evidence. First, a look into numerous conversational activities in course materials between the 1970s and the early 2000s consistently and unmistakably reveals the prevailing presence of the communicative approach. Second, it has been widely agreed that CLT has made the teaching of spoken language a good deal more inspiring, effective and meaningful, which is clearly the reason why the approach is still in use and coursebooks using it continue to sell.

Communicative approaches have been evolving through a chain of successive reactions of new versions against previous ones, with new ideas being built on beliefs of how inappropriately languages have been taught. In the mid-1960s, while many theorists still emphasized the learning of the linguistic system as the main method to master a second language (Johnson, 1982: 8–22), criticism aimed at mechanical language practice began to appear, and such expressions as 'communicative, meaningful activities' started to emerge in many academic discussions (Mockridge-Fong, 1979: 91). The 1970s continued to see the most explicit debate with criticism of the structural design, leading to what was regarded by many as the 'communicative revolution' (McDonough and Shaw 1993: 20). However, this change was not viewed by many teachers and learners as a beneficial revolution since it took away all the confidence and security learners used to have, thanks to what they perceived as a systematic and sufficient grammatical input. In view of this, the 1980s began to witness many attempts to make the communicative approach less extreme, that is, by laying emphasis merely on use and ignoring the learners' need for linguistic knowledge (Swan, 1983: 38; 1985: 78; Scott, 1983: 70; Morrow, 1983: 62; Dubin and Olshtain, 1986: 88). Specific points of such reaction were the criticism that the new methodology was attempting to replace the structural approach (Dubin and Olshtain, 1986: 88); the criticism that in fact the new method had not made the learning of grammatical knowledge any easier than before (Swan, 1985: 78); and the appeal not to deny the value of a structural framework in supporting rules for use (Scott, 1983: 70). Alongside these debates, scholarly efforts were invested in how to harmonize the opposing tendencies, by considering the fact that form and use in second language teaching should not be mutually exclusive.

As a result of this compromise view, the early 1990s saw the idea of a multidimensional syllabus becoming more explicitly and systematically addressed, which opened up new possibilities for encompassing a more comprehensive series of teaching dimensions such as functions and notions, roles and skills, themes and situations. The main purpose of this type of syllabus, as pointed out by McDonough and Shaw (1993: 50), is 'to build on a range of communicative criteria at the same time as acknowledging the need to provide systematic practice in the formal proprieties of the language'.

Trends in Materials for Speaking Skills

Arguably, trends in material design tend to progress in parallel with trends in methodology. This should not surprise us, since activities in coursebooks are precisely where principle and practice are brought together. In fact, materials published over the past thirty years have been clear indicators of how the key principles of communicative approaches are incorporated into speaking activities. Although this chapter limits itself to spoken language, it does not seem wise to separate general trends in materials for speaking from those for other basic skills, since these materials are all subject to similar debates and enjoy similar achievements based on the pedagogical philosophy of their time.

Together with changes in pedagogical principles, there have been gradual but constant efforts to improve how materials for speaking skills are designed. A look into how subject matter is treated over the decades might help demonstrate some progress in instructional materials development. For an example of this, let us examine three activity samples that deal with a similar theme, namely describing objects, taken from three English coursebooks published in 1978, 1991 and 1999.

In *Streamline English* (Hartley and Viney, 1978; 1996), Lesson 6: 'A Nice Flat' (see Figure 22.1), the authors ask students to describe a room from a given picture. There is no freedom of choice and hardly any peer interaction involved in this task since all information comes directly from the same visual. Every learner performs the same role.

In *Interchange – English for International Communication*, Book 3, The activity 'Same or Different?', in Unit 12 (Richards, *et al.*, 1991) provides students with several sets of pictures depicting different object items and invites them to discover how these items differ by asking each other questions. This activity utilizes the decoding and encoding of an information gap, which allows students to exchange factual data. There is still no freedom of choice but at least learners are given the opportunity to interact for a purpose. There are two different roles to perform: information seeker and information provider.

In *Language in-Use. Pre-Intermediate* (Doff and Jones, 1999), Activity 1 of Unit 1, 'Description' (see Figure 22.2), invites learners to look at a picture of six different doors and to imagine the rooms behind them. Since there are no right or wrong answers, students are encouraged to process meanings from their own experiences and perspectives. Besides providing freedom of choice, this material takes learners beyond the level of an information gap into two new areas: a reasoning gap, which involves deriving data by inference and perception, and an opinion gap, which encourages personal feelings and attitudes.

Many examples like this one can be found across coursebooks over the years. They demonstrate a shift from the mechanical rehearsal of language structure to a more interactive exchange of factual information, and another shift from the interactive exchange of factual information to a more dynamic processing of personal opinions. It has to be admitted, however, that changes in course materials do not always represent a move from the out of date to the latest, but may happen in reverse. For example, it is observed by Tomlinson (1998: 120) that sometimes a coursebook sells successfully not because it has something new to offer, but because it goes back to what is old.

By and large, many conscious efforts for improvement made by course-writers over the decades have enabled materials design to evolve towards increasingly sophisticated levels. Sometimes such an evolution causes practitioners to feel worried about how to handle all this sophistication effectively in teaching. For example, in the 1980s, some theorists believe that the more sophisticated the syllabus, the more difficult to implement it in the classroom (Eskey, 1984: 79). However, materials development in recent years tends to prove the opposite: as course design becomes more thoughtful, it also tries to make language teaching easier in the classroom by aiming for less teacher preparation (e.g., by improving teachers' manuals).

Examining publishers' claims over several decades is another way to recognize change in materials development. It shows us a gradual transfer from a strictly communicative focus toward a more balanced view in teaching both grammar

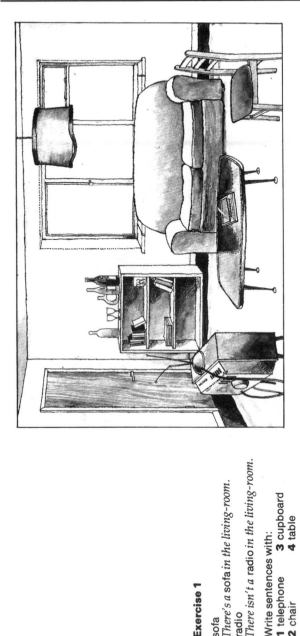

Exercise 1

sofa
There's a sofa in the living-room.
radio
There isn't a radio in the living-room.

Write sentences with:
1 telephone   3 cupboard
2 chair   4 table

Exercise 2

books
There are some books on the shelf.
cups
There aren't any cups on the shelf.

Write sentences with:
1 glasses   3 magazines
2 records   4 bottles

Exercise 3

magazine/table?
Is there a magazine on the table?
books/shelf?
Are there any books on the shelf?

Write questions with:
1 radio/shelf
2 bottles/table
3 records/table

Exercise 4

Where are the bottles? They're on the shelf.
Where's the chair? It's in the living-room.

Answer the questions:
1 Where's the television?
2 Where are the glasses?
3 Where are the books?
4 Where's the sofa?

Figure 22.1 *Activity sample from Streamline English – Departure* (Hartley and Vinery, 1978)

Description

1 Behind the door

There is/are • has got

1 Look at the first door and imagine the room behind it. Examples:

There's a map on the wall.
There are some desks.
It's got a blackboard.
It's got white walls.

2 Write sentences about one of the other rooms. Use words from the box, and add ideas of your own.

bed	table	telephone
chair	magazine	reception desk
lift	shower	television
menu	computer	'no smoking' sign

Show your sentences to another student.

Figure 22.2 Activity sample from *Language in Use. Pre-Intermediate* (Doff and Jones, 1999)

and communication, justified on the grounds that form and use are not necessarily two opposing areas. For example, during the late 1960s and early 1970s, such expressions as 'real-life contexts', 'functionally based', 'meaningful and effective communication' are seen to fill publishers' claims; then, since the early 1990s, the key concepts have become 'systematic development in combination with other three skills practice', 'core grammar structures', 'allowance for different learning styles and teaching situations' – (McDonough and Shaw, 1993: 22, 25, 46).

Despite all this, what remains to be considered further is the issue of how the above balance is treated, and how to avoid teaching form and use as if they are separable items. This concern is based on the reality that some published materials focus primarily on pre-communicative tasks without providing adequate tools for learners to gain communicative skills. As coursebook evaluation sometimes shows, there are still gaps between what some materials publishers assume they do and what they can actually do for learners (see Tomlinson *et al.* 2001: 82).

A Proposed Framework for Developing Materials for Spoken Language

In this framework, we would like to propose and discuss an approach comprising five dimensions for developing materials for speaking skills, namely: (1) conceptualizing learner needs; (2) identifying subject matter and communication situations; (3) identifying verbal communication strategies; (4) utilizing verbal sources from real life, and (5) designing skill-acquiring activities.

Conceptualizing Learner Needs

Materials design should begin from who learners are in order to link language study not only to the learners' future use but also to their present receptivity. As Brindley (1989: 70) indicates, it is important to look at both *subjective needs* and *objective needs* in the learner. The former comprises such areas as the learners' speaking proficiency, the learners' speaking difficulties and real-life conversational situations outside of the classroom, all of which will help the teacher to decide what to teach. The latter includes such aspects as personality, learning styles and preferences, wants and expectations of the course, all of which will help the teacher to decide how to teach.

Some teachers who cannot come into contact with students until the first day of class often find out about learner needs through the first lesson. For example, through a speaking task conducted in pairs or groups, students can be asked to jot down their expectations and pass them to the teacher. This discussion also allows the teacher to listen to samples of students' spoken English to form an impressionistic idea about their linguistic proficiency as well as their ability to handle the given task. However, this practice alone may not be sufficient. Needs assessment, as suggested by Graves (1996: 27), should be viewed as an ongoing process which takes place before, during and after the course. Seeking to know learner needs, after all, does not mean describing learners but, more importantly, it means actually involving learners in the process of developing materials and giving them a voice in their materials.

Translating Needs to Subject Matter and Communication Situations

Knowledge about learner needs will serve as the foundation on which experiential content is selected for instructional materials. As learners reveal what they want to do with the target language, they also directly or indirectly imply the type of environments where the language is exercised. It is now important also to explore the context of such environments and to form some ideas of what skills that society requires of an effective speaker. The more specifically learners state their needs, the more appropriately the subject matter can be established towards appropriate sets of topics, situations, functions, strategies, registers and key structures, as can the sources to build all these components with.

In general, this step is a preliminary effort to outline the instructional content of the target material. Among the more difficult components to search for are perhaps communication strategies, and authentic sources for composing features of natural speech. To support these endeavours, the two sections below will discuss some helpful techniques to make these tasks possible.

Identifying Verbal Communication Strategies

An interesting experiment on spoken English is reported by Tay (1988: 34). In this study, samples of real, spontaneous speech by ten Singaporean university students were played for one hundred British listeners (who were from London and had never been to Singapore before) to listen to and to rate their intelligibility. Five speakers scored more than 80 per cent, two more than 70 per cent; the highest was 89.1 per cent and the lowest 56.4 per cent. As factors that impair intelligibility were sought and analysed, it turned out that the main obstacle was not predominantly pronunciation. Instead, some of the more striking problematic features were identified as interaction strategies, styles and registers, features of spoken proficiency which need to be included in materials design for oral communication.

Conversational strategies must be incorporated in teaching materials because they are essential tools to serve the communication of meanings. One method to do so is by designing tasks for learners to act upon their interlocutor's speech rather than merely concentrating on their own. For example, learners can be helped to practise building talk upon talk, dealing with interaction pressure such as stealing and sustaining turns, handling unrehearsed discourse, controlling their level of diplomacy and courtesy, choosing when to move on to a new topic, winding down a conversation, recognizing signals when their partner wants to leave the conversation and so forth.

Another method is by building into materials many practical devices that can help facilitate oral production and compensate for those communication difficulties arising under time pressure. In this respect, Bygate (1987: 14) suggests five of them: (1) using less complex syntax; (2) making do with short phrases and incomplete sentences; (3) employing fixed conversational phrases; (4) adding filler words to gain time to speak; and (5) correcting or improving what one has already said. These techniques have meaningful implications for instructional materials since they help materials designers become more aware of what is the normal process of speech production. They also help learners realize how temporary and flexible spoken language can be and therefore that imperfection can be tolerated as part of the interactive process.

Utilizing Verbal Sources from Real Life

In many cases, preparing materials might just be one-third of the job, that is, providing opportunities for learning. Implementing and modifying them are what helps bridge the gap between plans and effects. To modify materials, besides what can be used to create a springboard for communication from printed sources such as magazine articles or pictures, we can also utilize many verbal interactions taken from real life and in the classroom.

One method to seek for practical teaching ideas, as suggested by Tay (1988: 36) is by taping learners' peer group interaction in the target language and analysing it. It is through this type of exercise that typical conversational difficulties or obstacles can be identified and translated into problem-based strategies for the teaching of verbal communication. Arguably, this is a realistic way of allowing learners to take part in the materials design process.

Another method is by finding opportunities to compare naturally occurring conversations with designer versions which deal with the same topic. Researchers have provided evidence that many conversations composed by the writer's own assumption of spoken language do not always reflect the actual contexts of use, especially when they skip over many essential strategies required by real-life communication situations (see dialogue scripts discussed by Cunningsworth, 1995: 26; Carter, *et al.*, 1998: 68–9 for examples).

Keeping a diary might also be a realistic way to collect resources for designing speaking activities. Such resources can come from overhearing conversations in public places, from radio or television interviews, from watching dramas or movies or even from our own interaction with native speakers in the target language. Any of such data, provided that it is relevant to our teaching theme, can always be recycled and developed into instructional materials for the classroom.

Designing Skill-acquiring Tasks

Once communication content is outlined and its components are selected, the decisive step is to create relevant tasks that help learners in three essential aspects: to acquire new language, to learn rules of interaction and to experience communication of meanings – though not necessarily in this sequence.

a. To facilitate the acquiring of new language, learners are taught and helped to internalize new language before making it available to discuss topics. Teaching new language can be done by presenting linguistic structures or, more meaningfully, by helping learners to discover for themselves form and function. For internalization to happen, such language can be pushed further into an experiential process, by introducing a series of small orientation tasks that guide learners toward a readiness in both content and language for the communicative topic that will come later. Examples of such tasks can be ranking exercises, brainstorming for key words and expressions, generating ideas around the topic and so on.

b. To learn rules of interaction, learners are provided with conditions to become aware of fundamental skills and capture rules of interaction in the target topic. This can be done in a number of direct or indirect ways, such as allowing learners to read several dialogues within the topic, getting them to listen to conversations read by the teacher or from a tape, drawing learner attention to or encouraging them to discuss some main characteristics of the performance and so on.

c. To experience communication of meanings, learners need conditions for coping with meanings and need purposes for using language. More specifi-cally, they need content-based activities to get them to interact with peers. This can be done by giving learners roles to play, assigning social tasks to be achieved, giving them motivating and attractive reasons to communicate, utilizing gaps in learner knowledge, experiences or attitudes to facilitate sincere exchange, inventing conflicts that lead to personal debates, making up circumstances of misunderstanding to be fixed, creating sticky situations to get out of and so forth.

It is through this classroom process that materials users promote conditions that enable then to be active contributors in task design. It helps the designer see where materials work and fail to work, which will hint at gaps for modification. This process also helps teachers to exploit practical contexts to develop a repertoire of activities that can be adapted every time a course is taught. Such a set of flexible activities might also give individual teachers opportunities gradually to discover their own strength in using certain types of materials.

A Rationale for Effective Materials for Speaking Skills

Drawing from relevant academic discourse and personal experiences in the sec-ond language classroom, I would like to recommend a rationale for materials design for speaking. In this rationale, I lay emphasis on a set of dimensions in learner abilities which, if fully facilitated, will help promote and maximize verbal performance. I argue that effective materials for oral communication should enable learners actively to (1) share and process information; (2) control meanings; (3) choose how to participate; (4) utilize affectivity; (5) utilize individ-ual knowledge; and (6) become aware of ellipsis in spoken language.

Focus on Both Sharing and Processing Information

Speaking tasks should not merely organize for learners, during interaction, to *share* information but should also enable them to *process* it. Sharing information means discovering missing information from one's knowledge gap by learning about it from one or more partners. Processing information means communicating by exchanging what belongs in learners' individuality by allowing learners to use their own backgrounds and personalities.

The latter involves such skills as expressing reactions and preferences, justifying opinions, suggesting solutions, making personal judgements and decisions – as well as extracting personal responses from conversation partners. Only when a task manages to bring out what belongs in learners' individuality will it be able to elicit the most authentic and genuine response from them and thereby makes the interaction most meaningful.

Respect for Learner Control of Meanings

As mentioned earlier in this chapter, communication skills are best developed when learners learn eventually to take control of their own performance from their own perspective, rather than being dictated by the teacher's manipulation. If a task can create this condition, it will succeed in reflecting much real-life communication, where verbal utterances come voluntarily from the speaker's personal decisions.

For this reason, materials should return control to the learner and learners' personal decisions should be respected. This can be done by inviting them to provide a topic from their own interests, raise a question, talk about their own experiences, bring into the classroom stories that they wish to share with others. This can also be done by tasks that leave room for learners' independent thinking and creativity; that stimulate individual attitudes and beliefs; that encourage learners to try their own interactive tactics to achieve communicative purposes. The significance of creating these opportunities for learners means allowing them to be involved in the materials developing process.

Potential for a Range of Learner Choices

Good materials allow for learner choices, which can be provided in a number of different ways. The range of decisions may involve learners choosing their role in a project that involves many partners, choosing a subtask in an activity or choosing a topic from a set of suggested topics.

Where possible, they might give learners a chance to adapt certain aspects of the subject matter. In other words, they should allow learners to assess and decide what they need and do not need from what is provided (Breen and Candlin, 1987: 25). Besides, good materials do not organize interaction by always putting learners together, thus denying their choice, but, to reflect real-life communication, should also encourage learners sometimes to seek their own partners and to decide on the people they want and need to communicate with.

The significance of leaving all of these decisions to the learners is to train learners in developing active participation, responsibility, autonomy and wider personal involvement – all of which represent important features of real-life communication. It is not only what to teach (content) that moves interaction toward the real world, but also how to teach (strategies) which helps learners to develop the active learning attitudes that authentic communication often requires.

Despite all this, it should be noted that giving too much freedom away might risk causing misunderstanding. Learners may start to feel that the teacher is not capable of making decisions and thus may begin to lose confidence in the teacher's leading role. As a solution, Littlewood (1992: 108) suggests organizing for learners to have low-level choices within a structured environment or framework still in teacher control so as to maintain in learners some level of adequacy and security. Over time, the level of learner choices may be increased when learners have become confident enough to survive and support their own framework.

Concern for Learner Affectivity

Learners tend to find it easier to articulate their ideas when they feel emotionally involved and enjoy what is going on. Good materials must therefore be inspiring enough to stir and enhance individual learners' interests, needs and abilities (Brumfit and Robert, 1993: 193) as well as their affective involvement (Breen and Candlin, 1987: 20). 'There is, after all, no better motivation for learning a language than a burning desire to express an opinion in that language or on a subject that one really cares about' (Eskey, 1984: 67). In addition, good materials should be user-friendly by allowing for the learning process to be fun (Tomlinson, 1991: 93; Fontana, 1994: 140) – so long as the kind of humour being employed is not offensive in the learner's culture.

In addition, affectivity can be engaged by building into tasks some degree of controversy or something that provokes learners to exchange different thoughts, share their diverse values and express contrastive attitudes, rather than activities that are likely to indulge similarity and agreement. Good materials should also suggest ways for the teacher to make the process adaptable to a broad spectrum of learners (Hunter and Hofbauer, 1989: ix) to avoid the pitfall of catering to one learner group while frustrating another.

Utilization of Individual Knowledge

If students are given an unfamiliar topic to write about, they can take some time to read or research for that purpose. But if they are given an unfamiliar topic to discuss verbally, they are most likely to give up the attempt to perform, due to the pressure of time inherent in oral communication. For this reason, the content of speaking tasks should not be so uninformed to learners that they do not fully understand the topic (Hutchison and Waters, 1980: 8; Hunter and Hofbauer,

1989: ix) and thus do not know how to discuss it. One example of an unusable activity would be for Thai students to talk about a skiing experience on a mountain when there is in fact no snow in their country. Conversely, good content should not be so familiar to learners that there is nothing left for learners to grapple with, and which, therefore, contains little new information value (Hutchinson and Waters, 1980: 8). One example of this would be for two people of the same country to describe a cultural festival they both know a lot about; or to describe a picture they both see equally clearly.

Utilization of Ellipsis in Spoken Language

Being knowledgeable about colours does not make one a good artist. This is because knowledge has to go through action to be transferred to skills. Materials for speaking skills must therefore encourage and enable learners to process speech by experiencing use, by making quick decisions under the pressure of time and by making do with limited vocabulary. When learners are taking these challenges, they may not be able to compose perfect sentences, but if we look at naturally occurring conversations by native speakers we can see clearly that they do not produce perfect language either (see dialogue scripts by Cunningsworth, 1995: 126; and by Crater *et al.*, 1998: 69). More often than not, during real interaction native speakers do not produce complete sentences as many teachers often demand language students to do.

Furthermore, in the real world, there are instants at which no utterances are made and yet the message can still be transferred from one person to another. For example, when A asks B: 'Did you steal the pen?', B keeps silent. A then understands that the answer is 'yes'. If in actual communication, utterances can be reduced to a zero, then why should teachers demand only complete sentences from learner performance? In fact, speaking materials should encourage learner awareness of the grammar of speech and help them to be conscious of the use of ellipsis in spoken language, which, as Carter *et al.*, (1998: 81) suggest, is an essential grammatical feature of effective interpersonal exchange.

Aspects that Deserve More Attention

In this final discussion, I would like to spotlight two significant areas that seem to be left out of focus in many current materials for speaking skills, namely the issues of catering to learner identity and cultural localization. By bringing them up, I hope to address the often heard complaint by materials users that many course activities tend to rest too much on the writers' own assumptions while ignoring learners' realistic contexts.

The Need for Reflection of Learner Identity

One important ingredient that learners want to see in their course, as Tudor (1996: 158–9) argues, is the opportunity to express their identity in the second language. Yet, many feel that the type of language they learn in many cases does not help them to reflect the kind of persons they are. As learners encounter real-life communication, the overwhelming obstacle is that the ways in which they are taught to perform verbally in the target language has not helped them to represent their level of sophistication and, more importantly, their own individuality. If second language teaching is to be more realistic, this dilemma is worth taking into consideration in materials development.

Classroom reality has revealed concrete cases of how learner identity may be denied. Experienced teachers have seen how adult learners sometimes feel embarrassed by the childish content of many activities that treat them like a group of unintelligent people. For example, instead of being guided to discuss dealing with stress in workplaces or other issues of more personal and mature concern, they are made to talk about the impersonal, 'fictitious Robinson family with a stupid dog and two boring children' (expression from Allwright and Bailey, 1991: 162).

In view of this, materials designers need to make a conscious effort to provide individual learners with the tools to reflect, to a certain extent, the type of people they are. Speaking tasks need to be created in the awareness of learners' level of maturity and education, so that, when verbalizing in the target language, a thirty-year-old intellectual does not have to sound like a three-year-old child and a university student does not have to sound like a primary school pupil (see Tay, 1988: 37–8). Much of this has less to do with linguistic levels than the type of language required to serve the subject matters of individual learners' interests, as well as the kinds of strategies that help train them in discussing those matters.

The Need for Cultural Localization of Materials

Despite all the acknowledged values of communicative language teaching, one should not overgeneralize the power of this approach in materials development on a global basis. In fact, many appeals for focusing on more meaningful use since the 1960s and the shift to a more communicative design since the 1970s have not taken place simultaneously throughout the world, but in many countries such debates are still surprisingly current (McDonough and Shaw, 1993: 22). Take China as one example: the first movement towards CLT only occurred in the early 1990s, the functional syllabus was officially introduced in 1992 and only after long debates for nearly a decade did this approach become popular in the late 1990s (Xiao, 2000). In the meantime, many communicative coursebooks are somehow not warmly received in a number of classrooms in Asia.

It might be interesting to note that one reason for this indifference to CLT may stem from very specific lessons or tasks. Sometimes it is not the approach itself that gets rejected, but rather the exercises being introduced with the approach that bear more responsibility for users' disapproving attitudes. In many cases, activities are not effective simply because their subject matter is not culturally appropriate in the local learning situations. Once local learners and teachers are not interested in the activity and switch off from its content or certain components, there is no ground to convince them to believe in the methods. We bring in a stove to help with the cooking, but supposing the food we offer is not accepted, then no matter how effective the stove is, people might refuse to eat. Likewise, we bring in an approach to help with the teaching, but supposing the content we offer is not accepted, then no matter how effective the approach is, students might refuse to learn.

From a *theorist* viewpoint, it is not unreasonable sometimes to blame the poor instructional effect of the approach on the contextual constraints of many local educational systems, as well as on many local teachers' perceptions and local learners' habits. However, from the perspective of many *coursebook users*, it is sometimes recognized that course materials with little flexibility have ignored the importance of localizing language tasks and have denied learners opportunities for contextual use. In a recent project which systematically evaluated eight current English language courses, we came to realize that very few of them actually provide help in adapting the global course to specific situations. Although at some point cross-cultural awareness activities are provided, 'in most cases they are UK-centred, they describe English people's reactions to exotic places they have visited on holidays, they depict stereotypical and often clichéd behaviour, and they tend to portray non-Western cultures as eccentric, and even bizarre' (Tomlinson, *et al.*, 2001: 86). Now and again complaints can be heard from teachers and learners from many parts of the world when using global coursebooks. One teacher at my institute in Vietnam reveals, 'I hardly know what to do with this lesson that invites my students to talk about how to use parking meters or vending machines which they've never seen, which simply don't exist in our country.' Another teacher from the Ivory Coast admits, 'all the exercises are about unusual things for our country. We are a hot country and also have Muslims. The exercises are about snow, ice, cold mornings, water cisterns; writing and publishing EFL books and making wines. I can tell you I can't do making wine and smoking pot in my country!' (Jolly & Bolitho, 1998: 91). Such comments can run on indefinitely.

Since many courses are written before they actually travel to the real classroom thousands of miles from the authors, local users sometimes realize that their cultures have become marginalized and have little or no room in the materials. As Lin and Warden (1998) imply, although research is being undertaken every day, much of it has been powerfully constrained by certain cultural pre-assumptions and 'little research has been directed to the topic of how the local educational/ teaching environment has influenced students' learning'. Maley (1998: 279) also comments, 'A major dilemma faced by all writers of materials ... is that all learners, all teachers and all teaching situations are uniquely different, yet published materials have to treat them as if they were ... the same.'

There have been occasional insights into how this problem might be addressed. Sridhar (1994: 801) calls for a rethinking of a more culturally authentic theory. Breen and Candlin (1987: 20) recommend that materials should have room for learners to express the values important to them. Langley and Maingay (1984: 97–8) emphasize the need to establish more cross-cultural comparisons in course content. Lin and Warden (1998), discussing ELT in Taiwan and much of Asia, also suggest that cultural differences should contribute considerably to the thrust of the discussion on any issues about language teaching and learning. In a word, what seems to be shared by all these views is that, although profound teaching and learning theories and methodologies seem so well established in certain countries, there must be some facts that require revisiting at a more fundamental level than previously assumed. Material developers need to take into consideration, where possible, the differences of educational systems, learning conditions, teaching and learning styles, the students' cultures of learning and differences in needs for language use in the job market.

At the time of writing, few commercially published and global course materials are able to solve the recurrent problem of suiting the learning needs of local learners. Conditions for localization are often added to many speaking activities as an afterthought rather than being well blended throughout the course as a main ingredient. From a writer perspective, this is a challenging task that requires comprehensive teaching experience with a wide range of learner backgrounds to be able to foresee various possibilities in exploiting the material from different cultural eyes. However, if the course is being developed with a specific audience in mind, this task can become much more manageable. One way to check whether the materials are culturally appropriate and effective is to ask oneself such questions as: Will learners be able to relate the content of the materials to their own situations and experiences in ways that are meaningful and interesting to them? What are the most significant issues in the social discourse of the society where our learners live? What could be some other important values and beliefs embedded within their everyday life?

Conclusion

This chapter has attempted to touch on several major trends in how methodology has been affecting materials design for speaking, as well as where practice in such design has led us. It has suggested and discussed in some detail a framework and a rationale to serve materials development in the discussed skills; and has also recommended further areas that deserve a better place in activities for oral communication, which perhaps should have implications for other skills as well.

Among the main obstacles encountered by material developers in attempting to replicate genuine communication are its intrinsic unpredictability and relative complexity, both of which must be regarded as inherent characteristics of spoken language and must be transferred to instructional materials (Cunningsworth, 1995: 118). The nature of communication reproduced in many current course materials is often far less complex than life, perhaps because simplified language is easy to design into activities that are easy to teach. However, it should be the never-ending responsibility of material writers to form the habit of reconsidering what we have written. Developing materials in a second language is an ongoing, long-term process which involves strategizing in the writer's office, applying to classroom action and modifying on the grounds of real experiences and real contexts of use. No matter how thoughtfully the material may be planned, it should always be open to some degree of writer–user interaction for further revision. This can be done by constantly observing real-life situations, comparing them with our scripted materials to highlight new features and new skills required for learners to operate more effectively in unpredictable communication.

In many cases, using unpublished materials tends to leave us with the inclination and the obligation to revise and modify them all the time, whereas a published version might induce easy trust from users by its final production form and beautiful design. Many years ago, my boss and I received a new teacher who came and joined our institute in Vietnam. When we passed him a set of material handouts developed by a group of local staff over the years, our colleague became silent for a few seconds, looked slightly confused and eventually inquired, 'Don't we have a book?' This spur-of-the-moment reaction partly explains many teachers' lack of confidence and readiness in developing their own materials.

Later on, as our colleague began to teach the course with us, he became more receptive of the materials and together we worked in a team to modify them for our own contexts of use. This exercise reminds us of Alderson's (1980: 134) observation that, as the availability of commercial teaching materials increases, the need for home-made materials becomes more urgent than ever before, as more teachers become aware that 'increased variety is not the solution for their particular situation'. After all, there should be more projects in which teachers are given tools and opportunities to design their own courses. This will enable teachers to produce appropriate materials that harmonize with their students' wants and needs, as well as allowing them to concentrate on their local contexts of use without having to be distracted by attempts to please particular publishers or anonymous markets.

References

Alderson, J. C. (1980) 'A process approach to reading at the University of Mexico', in *Project in Materials Design*. London: The British Council.

Allwright, D. and Bailey, K. M. (1991) *Focus on the Language Classroom: An Introduction to Classroom Research for Language Teachers*. Cambridge: Cambridge University Press.

Breen, M. P. (1984) 'Process syllabuses for the language classroom', in C. J. Brumfit (ed.) *General English Syllabus Design. Curriculum and Syllabus Design for the General English Classroom*. ELT Documents 118. Oxford: Pergamon Press and the British Council.

Breen, M. P. and Candlin, C. N. (1987) 'Which materials?: a consumer's and designer's guide', in L. E. Sheldon (ed.) *ELT Textbooks and Materials: Problems in Evaluation and Development*. ELT Document 126. Oxford: Modern English Publications in Association with the British Council.

Brindley, G. (1989) *Assessing Achievement in the Learner-Centred Curriculum*. Sydney:

Macquarie University, National Centre for English Language Teaching and Research.

Brumfit, C. J. and Robert, J. T. (1993) *A Short Introduction to Language and Language Teaching.* London: Batsford.

Bygate, M. (1987) *Speaking.* Oxford: Oxford University Press.

Carter, R., Hughes, R. and McCarthy, M. (1998) 'Telling tails: grammar, the spoken language and materials development', in B. Tomlinson (ed.) *Materials Development in Language Teaching.* Cambridge: Cambridge University Press.

Cunningsworth, A. (1995) *Choosing Your Coursebook.* Oxford: Heinemann.

Doff, A. and Jones, C. (1999) *Language in Use. Classroom Book. Pre-Intermediate.* Cambridge: Cambridge University Press.

Dubin, F. and Olshtain, E. (1986) *Course Design.* Cambridge: Cambridge University Press.

Ellis, M. and Ellis, P. (1987) 'Learning by design: some design criteria for EFL coursebooks', in L. E. Sheldon (ed.) *ELT Textbooks and Materials: Problems in Evaluation and Development.* ELT Document 126. Oxford: Modern English Publications in association with the British Council.

Eskey, D. E. (1984) 'Content – the missing third dimension in syllabus design', in J. A. S. Read (ed.) *Case Studies in Syllabus and Course Design.* Singapore: SEAMEO Regional Language Centre.

Fontana, D. (1994) *Managing Classroom Behaviour.* Leicester: British Psychological Society.

Graves, K. (1996) *Teachers as Course Developers.* Cambridge: Cambridge University Press.

Hartley, B. and Viney, P. (first published 1978/38th Impression, 1996). *Streamline English – Departure.* Oxford: Oxford University Press.

Hunter, L. and Hofbauer, C. S. (1989) *Adventures in Conversations. Exercises in Achieving Oral Fluency and Developing Vocabulary in English.* New Jersey: Prentice Hall Regents.

Hutchinson, T. and Waters, A. (1980) 'Communication in the technical classroom. You just shove this little chappie in here like that', in *Projects in Materials Design.* London: The British Council.

Johnson, K. (1982) *Communicative Syllabus Design and Methodology.* Oxford: Pergamon Press.

Jolly, D. and Bolitho, R. (1998) 'A framework for materials writing', in B. Tomlinson (ed.) *Materials Development in Language Teaching.* Cambridge: Cambridge University Press.

Langley, G. and Maingay, S. (1984) 'Communicative English for Chinese learners: the implementation of a design', in J. A. S. Read (ed.) *Case Studies in Syllabus and Course Design.* Singapore: SEAMEO Regional Language Centre.

Lin, H. and Warden, C. A. (1998) 'Different attitudes among non-English major EFL students'. *The Internet TESL Journal,* October.

Littlewood, W. (1981) *Communicative Language Teaching. An Introduction.* Cambridge: Cambridge University Press.

Littlewood, W. (1992) *Teaching Oral Communication. A Methodological Framework.* Oxford, UK, and Cambridge, USA: Blackwell.

McDonough, J. and Shaw, C. (1993) *Materials and Methods in ELT.* Oxford: Blackwell.

Maley, A. (1998) 'Squaring the circle – reconciling materials as constraint with materials as empowerment', in B. Tomlinson (ed.) *Materials Development in Language Teaching.* Cambridge: Cambridge University Press.

Mockridge-Fong, S. (1979) 'Teaching the speaking skill', in M. Celce-Murcia and L. McIntosh (eds) *Teaching English as a Second or Foreign Language.* Singapore: Harper & Row.

Morrow, K. (1983) 'Principles of communicative methodology', in K. Johnson and K. Morrow (eds) *Communication in the Classroom.* Harlow: Longman.

Nunan, D. (1988) 'Principles of communicative task design', in B. K. Das (ed.) *Materials for Language Learning and Teaching. Anthology Series,* **22**. Singapore: SEAMEO Regional Language Centre, pp. 16–29.

Nunan, D. (1989) *Syllabus Design.* Oxford: Oxford University Press.

Richards, J. C. (1990) *The Language Teaching Matrix.* Cambridge: Cambridge University Press.

Richards, J. C. with Hull, J. and Proctor, S. (1989) *Interchange – English for International Communication.* Cambridge: Cambridge University Press.

Scott, R. (1983) 'Speaking', in K. Johnson and K. Morrow (eds) *Communication in the Classroom.* Harlow: Longman.

Sridhar, S. N. (1994) 'A reality check for SLA theories'. *TESOL Quarterly,* **28** (4), 800–5.

Swan, M. (1983) 'False beginners', in K. Johnson and K. Morrow (eds) *Communication in the Classroom.* Harlow: Longman.

Swan, M. (1985) 'A critical look at the Communicative Approach', in *ELT Journal,* **39** (2), 76–87.

Tay, M. WJ. (1988) 'Teaching spoken English in the non-native context: considerations for the material writer', in B. K. Das (ed.) *Materials for Language Learning and Teaching. Anthology Series,* **22**. Singapore: SEAMEO Regional Language Centre, pp. 30–40.

Tomlinson, B. (1991) 'English education in Japanese universities'. *Kobe Miscellany,* **17**, 85–99.

Tomlinson, B. (ed.) (1998) *Materials Development in Language Teaching.* Cambridge: Cambridge University Press.

Tomlinson, B., Bao, D., Masuhara, H. and Rubdy, R. (2001) 'EFL courses for adults'. *ELT Journal,* **55** (1), 80–101.

Tudor, I. (1996) *Learner-Centreness as Language Education.* Cambridge: Cambridge University Press.

Xiao Qing Liao (2000) 'How communicative language teaching became acceptable in secondary school in China'. *The Internet TESL Journal,* **6** (10).

CHAPTER
23
Materials for Teaching Vocabulary

Paul Nation

Introduction

Vocabulary teaching has the goal of supporting language use across the skills of listening, speaking, reading and writing, and there has been considerable debate especially in first language teaching as to how this can be done. The core of the debate involves the role played by deliberate, decontextualized vocabulary learning. The arguments against such learning usually include the following points:

1. Deliberate learning can only account for a small proportion of the vocabulary knowledge of learners.
2. Deliberate learning not in a communicative context does not result in much learning.
3. Deliberate learning not in a communicative context does not help later vocabulary use in communicative contexts.

These points are largely wrong and go against the findings of second language vocabulary research. For second or foreign language learners, the deliberate study of vocabulary can account for a large proportion of vocabulary learning. In addition, there is now plenty of evidence to show that deliberate learning can result in large amounts of learning that is retained over substantial periods of time. There may be a small amount of truth in the idea that deliberate learning does not readily transfer to communicative use. Studies of the effect of pre-teaching vocabulary on reading comprehension indicate that such teaching needs to be rich and reasonably intensive if it is to have a positive effect on comprehension. But deliberate learning in conjunction with opportunities for learning through communicative use is far more effective than either of these two types of learning alone. Deliberate learning activities tend to focus on associating a meaning with a foreign language form and, although there is much more to learning a word than making this association, it is a very substantial first step on the way to learning a word.

This chapter describes three ideas that are very important in vocabulary materials development. First, a planned approach to vocabulary development will be much more effective than dealing with vocabulary in ad hoc or opportunistic ways. Second, there are learning conditions that enhance the learning of vocabulary, and a major goal of materials development should be to design materials that are likely to create these conditions. Third, these conditions need to occur in activities that go across the four roughly equal strands of learning from meaning-focused input, learning from meaning-focused output, deliberate language-focused learning and fluency development. A major aim of this chapter is to provide guidelines for vocabulary materials development across the four strands.

Planning Vocabulary Learning

Studies of the statistical distribution of vocabulary confirm what designers of graded readers have put into practice for many years. Namely, there is a relatively small group of words (around 2000) that are much more frequent and useful in a very wide range of language uses than other words in the language. These high frequency words are the essential basis of all language use and deserve a great deal of attention in language teaching materials. Unless learners have very special needs, it makes little sense to focus on other vocabulary before most of these high frequency words have been well learned.

Various lists of these words are available and materials developers need to be familiar with them. Table 23.1 shows four types of vocabulary and their typical coverage of academic texts.

Table 23.1 Vocabulary levels and text coverage

Vocabulary level	Number of word families	Percentage (%) coverage of text	Sources
High frequency words	2000	80	West (1953)
Academic vocabulary	570	10	Coxhead (2000)
Low frequency words	11,000	5	
Proper nouns	–	4.5	

Learners who have control of the high frequency words and who are studying for academic purposes next need quickly to become familiar with general academic vocabulary. This includes words such as *derive, definition, estimate, function*. The best list of these words contains 570 word families and can be found in Coxhead (2000). These words cover between 8.5–10 per cent of academic text and thus make a very important addition to a learner's vocabulary (see Table 23.1). If a similar number of the most common low frequency words were learned, they would only provide around 2.8 per cent coverage of academic text.

When designing vocabulary materials, it is thus very important to take a cost/benefit approach to learning. High frequency words give a much greater return in opportunities for use than low frequency words do.

Conditions for Learning

A substantial and growing amount of research on learning, and vocabulary learning in particular, provides useful guidelines for the psychological conditions that need to occur to enhance vocabulary learning. These conditions include noticing, retrieving and elaborating. Noticing involves paying attention to a word as a language feature. In materials design, noticing is encouraged by using typographical features such as putting the word in italics or bold type, by defining the word orally, or in the text, or in a glossary, by noting the word on the board or in a list at the beginning of the text, by pre-teaching, by getting the learners to note it down or by getting the learners to look it up in a dictionary.

Once a word has been noticed and some memory trace of it remains, it is then possible to use retrieval as a way of strengthening and establishing the learning. Retrieval can be receptive or productive and involves recalling the meaning or part of the meaning of a form when the spoken or written form is met (receptive retrieval), or recalling the spoken or written form in order to express a meaning (productive retrieval). Retrieval does not occur if the form and the meaning are both visible to the learner.

In materials design, retrieval is encouraged through meaning-focused use of the four skills of listening, speaking, reading and writing, through allowing learners time to retrieve and through activities like retelling, role-play or problem-solving where input (often in a written form) is the basis of the production of the output (Joe *et al.*, 1996).

Elaborating is a more effective process than retrieval because it involves retrieval but enriches the memory for an item as well as strengthening it. Examples of elaboration include meeting a known word in listening or reading where it is used in a way that stretches its meaning for the learner (receptive generative use), using a known word in contexts that the learner has not used it in before (productive generative use), using mnemonic tricks like the keyword technique or having rich instruction on the word which involves giving attention to several aspects of what is involved in knowing a word.

Good vocabulary materials design involves designing activities where the conditions for learning just described above have the best chance of occurring with vocabulary at the appropriate level for the learner.

Let us now look at a range of ways in which this can be done across the four strands of meaning-focused input, meaning-focused output, language-focused learning and fluency development.

Designing Input Activities to Encourage Vocabulary Learning

Research on the occurrence of vocabulary in graded readers (Nation and Wang, 1999) indicates that, as long as there is a reasonably high amount of input (about one graded reader per week), there will be plenty of opportunities for spaced receptive retrieval of appropriate vocabulary. That is, because of the vocabulary control used when producing such readers, the new vocabulary gets plenty of repetitions.

Vocabulary learning is greatly helped when listening if the teacher quickly defines unfamiliar words (Elley, 1989) and notes them on the board. In all kinds of activities where input becomes a source of output, such as listening to a text and then having to answer questions, the relationship between the input and the output can have a major effect on vocabulary learning. If the questions following a listening text pick up target vocabulary or the use of target vocabulary from a text and require the learner to adapt it or extend its application in some way, then the condition of elaboration is likely to occur. Here is a brief example from a text about the heavy weight of students' school bags. The text states 'A study has found that school children are carrying very heavy weights every day, and these might be hurting them. These weights are up to twice the level which is allowed for **adults**. Their school bags are filled with heavy books, sports equipment, drinking water, musical equipment and sometimes a computer.' The question after the text is 'How old are you when you are an adult?' Note how this question (a) requires use of the target word *adult*; (b) requires the learner to extend the meaning of the word; and (c) requires the word to be used in a linguistic context different from that in the text. Retrieval and generative use are thus likely to make a strong contribution to the learning of the word. Such questions can also be used where the input occurs through reading.

A reading equivalent of a teacher defining words while the learners listen is the use of a glossary while reading. While glossaries have not always been found to make significant contributions to comprehension, they generally have a positive effect on vocabulary learning. The reading materials designer has the choice of glossing words in the text, at the side of the text, at the bottom of the page or at the end of the text. Glosses within the text require changes to the text and are not always recognized as definitions by readers. Glosses at the bottom of the page or the end of the text make a significant disruption to the reading process. Research suggests that glosses at the side of the text, directly in line with where the glossed word occurs, are the most effective. Long (in Watanabe, 1997) suggests that looking at such a gloss gets considerable attention to a word. The learner sees the word in the text, looks at the gloss and thus sees the word again, and then looks back at the text thus attending to the word for the third time.

Extensive reading programmes involving graded readers can provide ideal conditions for vocabulary learning, but these programmes need to be designed in ways that set up the most favourable conditions for learning. Extensive reading can have the goals of helping learners gain skill and fluency in reading, establish previously learned vocabulary and grammar, learn new vocabulary and grammar, gain pleasure from reading and be encouraged to learn more through success in language use. Learning through extensive reading is largely incidental learning, that is, the learners' attention is focused on the story, not on items to learn. As a result, learning gains tend to be small and thus quantity of input is important.

Graded readers typically cover a range of levels beginning at around 300–500 words and going to around 2000–2500 words. For vocabulary learning, learners should be familiar with 98 per cent of the running words. For fluency development, they need to be familiar with almost 100 per cent of the running words in the texts. Suitable techniques for encouraging extensive reading include explanation of the purpose of extensive reading, book reports, book reviews on a slip in the book, book displays and voracious reader awards. Extensive reading needs to be supported and supplemented with language-focused learning and fluency development. Vocabulary learning from reading can be helped in the following ways. Before each reading, the learners skim to select five or six words to focus on. After reading, they reflect on vocabulary that they met in the text. They collect words while reading for later deliberate word study. The teacher makes activities to see before and do after reading, such as second-hand cloze, information transfer, reporting to the class on words found in the text and answering questions that extend the meaning and use of the words in the text, and the teacher provides the learners with speed reading training. Learners need to move systematically through the graded reader levels choosing enjoyable books, reading at least one graded reader every week and at least five books at a level before moving to the next level. They need to read more books at the later levels and total at least 15–20 readers a year. Both teachers and learners need to make sure that between 95–98 per cent of the running words in a chosen reader are already known.

Material designed for vocabulary learning from input thus needs to provide quantity of input, needs to encourage deliberate attention to vocabulary and needs to have low densities of unknown vocabulary.

Designing Output Activities to Help Vocabulary Learning

Recent work on spoken communicative activities has shown that careful design of the written input for such activities can have a major effect on vocabulary learning. There are some reasonably straightforward design requirements to ensure that the vocabulary will be used in the activities and that it will be used in ways that set up the most favourable conditions for learning. Let us look at an example of a speaking activity called *For and against* to see what the design requirements are and how they can be applied.

The written input: Group A
Around the age of 18, children should be **encouraged** to leave home and take care of themselves.

Your group has to **present** the ideas which **support** this. You do not have to argue in favour of these ideas but you must make sure that the ideas which support it are well understood by everybody before a **decision** is made.

First step: Look at the following ideas, explain them to each other in your group so that everyone understands them. Then put the ideas in order according to their importance with the strongest idea first. Think of one example for each idea to help you explain it to others during the second step.

Children will learn to be **responsible** for their own **decisions**.
Children will learn how to **handle** their **finances**.
Children and parents will have a better **relationship** with each other.
The parents can save for their **retirement**.

Second step: Your group will now split up and you will join with some people from the other group. You must all work together to decide if you all support or do not support the idea about children leaving home.

Group B has similar input except the they have to understand the arguments attacking the idea of children leaving home. They have the following list at the first step.

Children at 18 years old are not **mature** enough to be **responsible** for their own **decisions**.
Children should **support** their parents and help them with the **household** work.
While at home, children can save money to help themselves make a good **financial** start in life.

Let us now look at some design requirements and the features of this activity which make it likely to support vocabulary learning.

1. *The written input to the task contains about 12 target words.* In the example these are in the instructions and in the statements. The vocabulary in the statements is most likely to be used in the discussion, but there may be use of some of the vocabulary in the instructions as learners consider what to do next in each part of the task. Having about 12 words in the task means that around 5–6 may be learned.
2. *The vocabulary is highlighted and repeated in the written input where possible to increase its chances of being noticed and used.* In the example, the target words are in bold and several of them are in the input for both A and B.
3. *The communicative task has a clear outcome which encourages the use of the written input.* The outcome for the *For and against* task is a consensus decision on the proposition. To reach this consensus the arguments in the written input have to be considered and hopefully the vocabulary in them used.
4. *Split information, jobs or roles are used to make sure that all learners are actively involved.* In fact, research shows (Nation, 2001) that learners do not need to participate actively to learn vocabulary from an activity. Involved observers seem to learn just as well as active participators. Nevertheless, it seems wise to increase involvement if that can be done. In the *For and against* activity, the information is split between two groups, A and B, and both sets of information are needed to complete the task.
5. *The task should be broken into a series of steps to give a chance for the words in the written input to be reused at each step.* In the example, the steps are (1) work in

cooperative groups to understand the statements, (2) work in split information groups to reach a consensus, (3) report on the decision and reasons for it
to the rest of the class. If all goes well, much of the target vocabulary will be
used in each of these three steps.

6. *The communication task supports the understanding of the target vocabulary.* This
    can be done through the use of dictionaries, glossaries, pre-teaching or
    negotiation. In the *For and against* task, the work in cooperative groups in
    the first step provides a good opportunity for unknown vocabulary to be
    negotiated.

These same design features can be applied in a very wide variety of tasks (Joe *et al.*,
1996).

There is another type of speaking activity where vocabulary learning is given an
even stronger focus. In this type of activity, the learners read a short text and then
do two or three short speaking tasks each built around a particular word. Here is
an example.

A study has found that school children are carrying very heavy weights every
day, and these might be hurting them. These weights are up to twice the level
which is allowed for **adults**. Their school bags are filled with heavy books, **sports
equipment**, drinking water, musical equipment and sometimes a computer.

1. Which of the following things are sports equipment?

    a sports field; knee guards; a football; the players; sports uniform; goal; a
    bat; scorebook; sports boots

2. At what age does a child become an adult? How important is age in
    deciding when someone is an adult?

Typical task outcomes include choosing, ranking, classifying, analysing and listing
causes. Note how each task explores the meaning and use of a particular word.

There has not been much research on using writing activities as a way of
encouraging vocabulary learning from output, but the design requirements
described above for speaking may be adapted to writing.

Deliberate Language-Focused Learning

There is a wide range of vocabulary learning activities which cover the various
aspects of what is involved in knowing a word. Table 23.2 (Nation, 2001) lists
these aspects along with some of the vocabulary exercises that focus on them.

The design features of these activities will directly affect the conditions for
learning that occur. Let us look at some of the most important features.

Table 23.2 A range of activities for vocabulary learning

form	spoken form	Pronounce the words Read aloud
	written form	Word and sentence dictation Finding spelling rules
	word parts	Filling word part tables Cutting up complex words and labelling their parts Building complex words Choosing a correct form
meaning	form-meaning connection	Matching words and definitions Discussing the meanings of phrases Drawing and labelling pictures Peer teaching Solving riddles Recalling forms or meanings using word cards
	concept and reference	Finding common meanings Choosing the right meaning Semantic feature analysis Answering questions Word detectives (reporting on words found in reading)
	associations	Finding substitutes Explaining connections Making word maps Classifying words Finding opposites Suggesting causes or effects Suggesting associations Finding examples Completing sets
use	grammar	Matching sentence halves Putting words in order to make sentences
	collocates	Matching collocates Classifying items in a concordance Finding collocates
	constraints on use	Identifying constraints Classifying words under style headings

1. *Focus on language items.* Language-focused learning activities are directed towards language features not to the communication of messages. The deliberate attention given to the words speeds up the learning.
2. *Focus on the language system.* Some activities, like filling word part tables, finding spelling rules and reading aloud, draw learners' attention to systematic features of the language. This helps learning by relating new items to particular patterns and encourages thoughtful processing of vocabulary.
3. *Group work.* If the activities are done as group work, there is the opportunity for learners to be sources of new input for each other and there is the opportunity for negotiation, and thus elaborating to occur. For example, if finding collocates is done as a group task, there will be many chances for learners to learn from each other.
4. *Data gathering or gap filling.* If the activities require learners to suggest answers from their previous experience, there is the opportunity for retrieval to occur. When this feature is combined with group work, this could result in elaborating for some learners. For example, if the learners have to suggest collocates for given words, some of those suggested may be from the previous experience of some learners, but some will be new to some of the learners and thus expand the range of associates that they know for a particular word.

Fluency Development

Fluency development activities have the goal of making language items like vocabulary readily available for fluent use. If vocabulary cannot be fluently accessed, then the vocabulary learning has been for little purpose. Activities for developing fluency in vocabulary use do not differ from fluency activities with other fluency goals. This is because fluency development requires meaning-focused language use and thus needs to be done without any particular focus on language features. Fluency development requires different learning conditions from learning from meaning-focused input and output, and language-focused learning.

Fluency is likely to develop if the following conditions are met.

1. *The learners take part in activities where all the language items are within their previous experience.* This means that the learners work with largely familiar topics and types of discourse making use of known vocabulary and structures.
2. *The activity is meaning focused.* The learners' interest is on the communication of a message and is subject to the 'real-time' pressures and demands of normal meaning-focused communication (Brumfit, 1984: 56–7).
3. *There is support and encouragement for the learner to perform at a higher than normal level.* This means that, in an activity with a fluency development goal, learners should be speaking and comprehending faster, hesitating less and using larger planned chunks than they do in their normal use of language.

There need to be substantial opportunities for both receptive and productive language use where the goal is fluency. There must be plenty of sustained opportunity either inside or outside the classroom to take part in familiar meaning-focused tasks.

How can we design fluency activities that make use of the three conditions mentioned above? Fluency activities depend on several design requirements and features to achieve their goal. These can appear in a variety of techniques over the whole range of language skills. By looking at these requirements and features we can judge whether an activity will develop fluency in an efficient way and we can devise other activities that will. Let us look first at a well-researched activity. The **4/3/2** technique was devised by Maurice (1983). In this technique, learners work in pairs with one acting as the speaker and the other as listener. The speaker talks for four minutes on a topic while his/her partner listens. Then the pairs change with each speaker giving the same information to a new partner in three minutes, followed by a further change and a two-minute talk.

From the point of view of fluency, this activity has these important features. First, the user is encouraged to process a large quantity of language. In 4/3/2 this is done by allowing the speaker to perform without interruption and by having the speaker make three deliveries of the talk. Second, the demands of the activity are limited to a much smaller set than would occur in most uncontrolled learning activities. This can be done by control by the teacher, as is the case in most receptive fluency activities such as reading graded readers or listening to stories, or can be done by choice, planning or repetition by the learner. In the 4/3/2 activity, the speaker chooses the ideas and language items, and plans the way of organizing the talk. The 4 and 3-minute deliveries allow the speaker to bring these aspects well under control, so that fluency can become the learning goal of the activity. Note that the repetition of the talk is still with the learner's attention focused on the message because of the changing audience. Third, the learner is helped to reach a high level of performance by having the opportunity to repeat and by the challenge of decreasing time to convey the same message. Other ways of providing help to reach a high level of performance include the chance for planning and preparation before the activity.

We can distinguish three approaches to developing fluency which can all be usefully part of a language course. The first approach relies primarily on repetition and could be called 'the well-beaten path approach' to fluency. This involves gaining repeated practice on the same material so that it can be performed fluently. The second approach to fluency relies on making many connections and associations with a known word. Rather than following one well-beaten path, the learner can choose from many paths. This could be called 'the richness approach' to fluency. This involves using the known word in a wide variety of contexts and situations. The third approach to fluency is the aim and result of the previous two approaches. This could be called 'the well-ordered system approach'. Fluency occurs because the learner is in control of the system of the language and can use a variety of efficient, well-connected and well-practised paths to the wanted word.

Let us now look at a range of activities that put into practice the three conditions of easy demands, meaning focus, and opportunity to perform at a higher than normal level. We will look in detail at two activities and briefly suggest others.

Blown-up books are a useful way of using listening to introduce learners to reading and getting them excited about reading. These very large books have pages which are about eight times the size of ordinary pages and they contain plenty of pictures. Because they are so large, they can be shown to the whole class while the teachers reads them aloud and all the learners can see the words and pictures. These books can be bought or they can be made by using a photocopier that enlarges what it copies.

The teacher reads the story to the learners while they look at the words and pictures. The same story will be read several times over several weeks and the learners will soon be very familiar with the story and be able to say parts of the sentences that they recall from previous readings. To develop fluency, the teacher reads the story a little faster each time.

Listening to stories is particularly suitable for learners who read well but whose listening skills are poor. The teacher chooses an interesting story, possibly a graded reader, and reads aloud a chapter each day to the learners. The learners just listen to the story and enjoy it. While reading the story, the teacher sits next to the blackboard and writes any words that the learners might not recognize in their spoken form. Any words the learners have not met before may also be written, but the story should be chosen so that there are very few of these. During the reading of the first chapters the teacher may go fairly slowly and repeat some sentences. As the learners become more familiar with the story, the speed increases and the repetitions decrease. Learner interest in this activity is very high and the daily story is usually looked forward to with the same excitement people have in television serials. If the pauses are a little bit longer than usual in telling the story, this allows learners to consider what has just been heard and to anticipate what may come next. It allows learners to listen to language at normal speed without becoming lost.

Other fluency activities include a listening corner where learners listen to tape-recorded stories that they and others have written, speed reading training and extensive reading with texts with no unknown vocabulary at all, repeated reading where the same text is reread several times and continuous writing where the focus is on writing a lot on familiar topics.

Becoming fluent requires lots of practice. About 25 per cent of the time in a language course should be given to fluency development activities. The vocabulary requirement of such activities is that there should be no unfamiliar vocabulary in the activities.

This chapter has looked at vocabulary materials development across the four strands of learning from meaning-focused input, learning from meaning-focused output, deliberate language-focused learning and fluency development. It has taken the stance that certain learning conditions need to occur in order to reach learning goals and these conditions can be encouraged by careful materials design. The next step in designing materials is monitoring and evaluating them, and this can be done by looking for signs that the learning conditions are occurring. The careful observation of materials in use is an essential component of good design.

References

Brumfit, C. J. (1984) *Communicative Methodology in Language Teaching: The Roles of Fluency and Accuracy*. Cambridge: Cambridge University Press.

Coxhead, A. (2000) 'A new academic word list'. *TESOL Quarterly*, **34** (2), 213–38.

Elley, W. B. (1989) 'Vocabulary acquisition from listening to stories'. *Reading Research Quarterly*, **24**, (2), 174–87.

Joe, A., Nation, P. and Newton, J. (1996) 'Speaking activities and vocabulary learning'. *English Teaching Forum*, **34** (1), 2–7.

Maurice, K. (1983) 'The fluency workshop'. *TESOL Newsletter*, **17** (4), 29.

Nation, I. S. P. (2001) *Learning Vocabulary in Another Language*. Cambridge: Cambridge University Press.

Nation, P. and Wang, K. (1999) 'Graded readers and vocabulary'. *Reading in a Foreign Language*, **12**, 355–80.

Watanabe, Y. (1997) 'Input, intake and retention: effects of increased processing on incidental learning of foreign vocabulary'. *Studies in Second Language Acquisition*, **19**, 287–307.

West, M. (1953) *A General Service List of English Words*. London: Longman, Green & Co.

CHAPTER

24

Materials for Language through Literature. Rocking the Classroom: Rock Poetry Materials in the EFL Class

Claudia Ferradas Moi

Literature in ELT

What is the role of literature in foreign language education? Is there a place for literary texts in the learner-centred, communicative EFL class? If so, what is meant by *literary texts* and how should they be approached in the classroom? These and other related questions have been the focus of publications and conference presentations in the ELT field in the last few years, as literature, once related to traditional text-centred approaches, started being revisited in the EFL classroom, now within the context of reader-response theory and humanistic approaches.

Literature is well established in the curriculum and its presence is rarely questioned. But why should foreign language teachers be concerned with literature if, as it is often claimed, it has 'little practical application', 'it imposes challenges on the learner', 'it is connected with a specific cultural context' and 'it can be idiosyncratic, even subversive'? In fact, it is my contention that these very qualities of literary discourse can contribute to language acquisition by revealing the creative and expressive potential of language and giving learners access to new sociocultural meanings.

On the grounds that materials should aim at communicative competence, the expressive and poetic functions of language have often been disregarded in ELT, due to the emphasis laid on what is supposedly more practical or useful. Most textbooks aiming at the teaching of English for international communication prioritize *referential language*: 'language which communicates at only one level, usually in terms of information being sought or given, or of a social situation being handled ... it states ... it shows' (McRae, 1991: 3). Learners are taught how to communicate in international contexts through language meant to be as culturally 'neutral' as possible. However, once they have gone beyond that 'survival' level, once they need to express their own meanings and interpret other people's beyond the merely instrumental, *representational language* is needed. By representational language we mean language which, in order that its meaning potential be decoded by a receiver, engages the imagination of that receiver ... Where referential language informs, representational language involves ... Representational materials make an appeal to the learner's imagination: they can be any kind of material with imaginative or fictional content that goes beyond the purely referential, and brings imaginative interaction, reaction and response into play. (McRae, 1991)

It is here that literature has an important role to play. As Henry Widdowson put it in an interview published by the *ELT Journal* in 1983 (quoted in Brumfit and Carter, 1986: 13):

In conventional discourse you can anticipate, you can take shortcuts ... Now you can't do that with literature ... because you've got to find the evidence, as it were, which is representative of some new reality. So with literary discourse the actual procedures for making sense are much more in evidence. You've got to employ interpretation procedures in a way which isn't required of you in the normal (SIC) reading process. If you want to develop these procedural abilities to make sense of discourse, then literature has a place.

Such training in deciphering discourse is a crucial factor in the development of language learning abilities. The use of texts where 'literariness' can be identified and exploited or, to use McRae's distinction, the use of representational language as opposed to a purely referential one, can help EFL students succeed in this respect:

The idea that literature is not 'relevant' to learners is easily quashed. Natural curiosity about the world, and about any text to be read, means that a learner is always willing to make some attempt to bridge the relevance gap which the teacher may fear separates the learner and the text ... The relevance gap is bridged by identification of (if not necessarily with) different ways of seeing the world, and the range of ways of expressing such a vision. (McRae, 1991: 55)

Selecting 'Literary' Materials

While teachers complain that 'students do not read' and that it is hard to get authentic reading materials that are both relevant and motivating for teenage students, a parallel system develops side by side with school literature and its restrictions and prejudices as to what can or should be read. A long-established text-centred canon often dominates the teaching of literature, but this 'parallel system' has its own laws of inclusion and exclusion, its own forms of production, reception and distribution. In it, the concepts of 'text' and 'reading' are stretched to include texts of non-conventional circulation (underground magazines, the production of adolescent writers) as well as graffiti, comics, computer games, video ... thus advocating a strong *synergy between text culture and image culture* (Bombini, 1989). Within it, teenagers enthusiastically read and interpret texts which are relevant to their lives but are usually excluded from the selection of reading materials used at schools: the words of rock songs.

It is my contention that there is room in our language classes for unconventional literary materials, what John McRae has called 'literature with a small l', as well as for Literature traditionally understood as such (McRae, 1991). After all, as Brumfit and Carter (1986: 6 and 10) have stated:

> it is impossible to isolate any single or special property of language which is exclusive to a literary work ... it may be more productive for us to talk about language and literariness rather than 'literary language' ... what is literary is a matter of relative degree, with some textual features of language signalling a greater literariness than others.

Or, as Terry Eagleton (1983) put it: 'Some texts are born literary, some achieve literariness, and some have literariness thrust upon them ... there is no "essence" of literature whatsoever.'

Based on these presuppositions, this chapter explores the advantages of using the words of rock songs as literary texts in the EFL classroom. It presents suggestions for the design of materials to encourage interpretation leading to an awareness of both language and culture.

Rock Poetry in the Classroom

The study of literature based on traditional literary theories has often estranged students from the pleasurable experience of responding to texts, from the challenge of building meaning out of fictional worlds, thus recreating and exploring human experience to deepen their awareness of themselves and of the world. This chapter intends to encourage reflection on the role of rock as a multimedia text within a dialogical approach to reading (Pulverness, 1996): an experience in collective interpretation aiming at the expression of feelings and the exchange of ideas, as well as to imaginative production.

As both a product and producer of media culture, rock lyrics lend themselves easily to the development of multimedia projects in the classroom: audio, video clips and Internet-based materials can not only liven up the EFL class but also help it pass the test of relevance that adolescent students are always submitting it to.

The words of rock songs are short, easy available authentic texts which can be rich in content, culturally loaded and motivating – a springboard to design materials using textual intervention techniques (Pope, 1995), inviting the student to play with the text and meet the challenge of building meaning out of it and to develop content-based projects at different levels.

Exploring Rock Poetry

The word 'rock' is used here in a deliberately broad, even elusive sense. Though a number of labels have sprung up to refer to different popular music genres since the advent of 'rock and roll', the focus of this chapter is on lyrics which can prove useful in the classroom, so, whether pop, hip hop, rap or hard core, all these texts will be referred to as 'rock poems'. But are all rock lyrics to be considered poetry? Indeed, some texts can be said to have a literary texture that invites exploration, while others can be said to be superficial, even silly. Yet, our selection for the classroom will always depend on what we mean by literariness and what the aims of our selection are.

What is the relationship between literature and rock? We can look at this question in at least two ways:

a. Literature in rock.
b. Rock as literature.

Literature in Rock

By this I mean *poems set to music* or lyrics which are *hypertexts* of previous literary works. The term 'hypertexts' is used here as defined by Gerard Genette (1962), who studied the relationships between one text and another, whether explicit or secret. He called this 'transtextuality' (a term abandoned long ago for 'inter-textuality'). Within transtextual relationships, Genette defined hypertextuality as the relationship that links text B (the *hypertext*) to a previous text A (the *hypotext*) in a way which is not a mere commentary. B transforms A without necessarily quoting from A or making explicit allusions to it.

Examples of hypertexts are:

- Alan Parson's Project, 'Extraordinary Narrations', hypertexts of stories by Edgar Allan Poe.
- Iron Maiden, 'The Rime of the Ancient Mariner', based on the poem by Samuel Taylor Coleridge.
- Kate Bush, 'Wuthering Heights', after the homonymous novel by Emily Brontë.
- Rick Wakeman, '1984', after the novel by George Orwell.

Less obvious examples are those songs in which allusions are made to literary works and authors, such as

- The Cranberries, 'Yeats' Grave', in honour of the Irish poet, William Butler Yeats.
- Sting, 'Sister Moon', with its obvious allusion to Shakespeare's sonnet CXXX:

> **My mistress' eyes are nothing like the sun**
> *My hunger for her explains everything I've done.*

- Crash Test Dummies, 'Afternoons and Coffee Spoons', whose title refers to the famous poem by T. S. Eliot, 'The Love Song of J. Alfred Prufrock', an allusion which is confirmed in the lyrics:

Afternoons will be measured out
Measured out, measured with
Coffeespoons and T. S. Eliot.

This is a clear reference to Eliot's line:

I have measured out my life with coffee spoons.

Besides, the song says:

Someday I'll have a disappearing hairline.
Someday I'll wear pyjamas in the daytime

These lines seem to echo others in Eliot's poem:

Time to turn back and descend the stair,
With a bald spot in the middle of my hair –
[They will say: 'How his hair is growing thin!']

and:

I grow old ... I grow old ...
I shall wear the bottoms of my trousers rolled
Shall I part my hair behind? Do I dare to eat a peach?
I shall wear white flannel trousers, and walk upon the beach.

For more on the influence of T. S. Eliot and Jean Paul Sartre's philosophy on this song, visit: *http://www.crashtestdummies.com/albums/god_shuffled_his_feet.html.*

As is the case with any hypertext, these songs are an invitation to build bridges into the literary works referred to or to get to know about the authors mentioned. More important still, they pose an interpretive challenge: can we make sense of the lyrics without being acquainted with the hypotext? And if we can, will our reading be different depending on whether we consider the song on its own or whether we take the hypotext into account?

Rock as Literature
Even when not related to literary works, rock lyrics themselves can be considered poems. Rock lyrics make up an important corpus within the literature of the second half of the twentieth century and our own days, particularly of literature written in English (Ferradas Moi, 1994, 1997). Therefore, they can become a bridge leading to 'canonical' English literature and the culture that produced it or be read as poems in their own right.

Traditionally, the lyrics of popular songs in our century were meant to communicate a verbal message which was easy to understand and in whose decodification music and voice quality were not an obstacle. They respected what Eduardo Romano (1990) calls the 'intelligibility threshold'. In this respect, these songs contrasted sharply with nursery rhymes, ritual songs and folklore in general, where the phonological associations triggered off by the lexical elements have always been more important than the expression of what words mean in everyday language.

But, from the 1950s, rock has radically changed this state of affairs by going back to primitive singing. Now, the singer's voice is but another instrument. People all over the world can recognize the words of songs in English, identify with them and hum or even sing them, no matter how elementary their knowledge of the language, because words are just one more instrument contributing to the whole, regardless of their dictionary meaning. Words have liberated themselves from the duty of meaning something precise and concrete – which has always been the case with poetry.

In the first press report that appeared on the Beatles, Bob Wooler, the disc jockey at the Liverpool Cavern Club, wrote:

> I think the Beatles are No. 1 because they resurrected original style rock'n'roll music ... Here again, in the Beatles, was the stuff that screams are made of. Here was the excitement – both physical and aural – that symbolised the rebellion of youth. (quoted in Wicke, 1990: 64)

This tendency became stronger and stronger. Today, as we all know, it is hardly possible to transcribe the lyrics of the songs our students bring to class in different recording formats. This fact is so widely accepted, even among native speakers of the language in question, that most compact discs are accompanied by a printed transcription of the song lyrics and lyrics web pages are among the most visited sites on the web.

Eduardo Romano (1990) refers to this phenomenon as the 'retribalization of the word', a return to its ritual power: it is the listener who builds up his own 'internal lyrics' by means of the babbling, the humming and the words he hears and their combination with music. And among them there is shouting, the primeval scream, which, as in tribal rites, brings singers and listeners together and allows them to identify as members of a community. What is more, this use of the word as pure sound awakening a plurality of meanings in the mind of the reader, this return to the primitive and the oneiric, inscribes rock lyrics within a literary tradition which goes through Symbolism and nonsense poetry into the avant-garde forms of literary modernism (Cook, 2000: 22–3, 192–3).

Modern literary theory lays emphasis, precisely, upon the active role of the reader rather than on the author's creative genius or on the text as an autonomous entity. Umberto Eco (1979), for example, points out that there are works which challenge the reader to play a central role, to build the work; Roland Barthes (1970) states that the aim of a literary work, rather than to make readers consumers of the text, is to make them producers of it. This seems to be the case with rock readers and listeners. What is more, the primeval scream finds its twentieth-century correlative in the rock recital or live concert, where the participant joins the musicians and singers in a trance-like communion. In this ceremony, the body (movement and clothes worn as a sign of belonging to a certain group) as well as visual elements, such as giant screens, artificial smoke, etc., play an essential part. Without these elements, the 'live' performance and perception of the work are definitely incomplete.

As readers and listeners of rock, we form part of what Stanley Fish (1980) calls an 'interpretive community' capable of applying shared interpretive procedures provided by our context and our culture, but we are, at the same time, free to carry out our own, unique appropriation of the text and its music. Interpreting rock lyrics in class can then become a brilliant opportunity to exchange views, to see how much the members of the community of the classroom have in common and also to learn to see the world from somebody else's perspective.

Rocking the EFL Classroom
Materials based on rock lyrics can focus on a wide range of aspects, from discrete items such as the use of particular grammar points or lexical chains, to thematic and cultural concerns. In all cases, the choice of rock lyrics seems to be justified by the fact that they are authentic and motivating – it is always more fun to study the choice of tenses in a song than in a textbook lesson. Yet, as with all poetry, rock lyrics seem to be particularly useful to

- provide meaningful contexts for the teaching and revision of vocabulary
- encourage discussion on relevant topics
- develop language awareness
- develop cultural awareness

Some extracts from a 'classic' can helps us clarify these points. Take for example, the first stanza in Billy Joel's 'Piano Man', where the man at the piano describes a bar he is playing at:

> *It's nine o'clock on a_____,*
> *the regular crowd_____in,*
> *there's an old man_____next to me*
> *making_____to his tonic and gin.*

Here's a perfectly old-fashioned fill-in-the-gaps exercise. Yet, what would you write in the first blank? Saturday? Friday? If you read on, the song makes it clear that it is a Saturday. Could it be any other day of the week? When do you expect people to crowd into bars in the place you live? The gap becomes much more than good practice for the structure 'on + day of the week': it throws light on cultural habits and encourages meaningful classroom talk.

And what about the second gap? Of course we can write 'walks', 'goes', etc. But how does the text change if we write 'shuffles', which is what the song says? And if we try other 'ways of walking'? The different options help us throw light on 'what language can do' – the lexical choice becomes meaningful, as each change of word builds a different picture of the crowd going into the bar.

And what about the old man? Is he sitting? Standing? Drinking? Of course the third is a useful gap to practise the use of the participle in the structure, but then it also helps us 'visualize' the old man, about whom we will learn more in the next stanza. The characters described by Billy Joel in this song are a sample of the lonely creatures that get together in bars 'to forget about life for a while'. It is interesting to see how lexical choice helps build this picture.

Finally, what is the old man 'making' to his gin and tonic? Students, even advanced ones, usually complain about this gap, as so many words collocate with 'doing' and so few with 'making' in this context. Few of them accept the text's invitation to generate metaphors. But once encouraged, they can come up with beautiful choices such as 'making confessions', 'making questions' and even with the image in the original text 'making love'. In all cases, supporting their choice encourages students to build meaning out of the text and interpret it by appealing to their imaginations.

After the initial gap-filling task and the discussion of the different options, here are some ideas for a series of activities based on the song from which we can select according to students' level, age group and interest – always suiting the task to the learner rather than vice versa.

Understanding and Interpreting

- Once you have completed the gaps, listen to the song and confirm whether what you predicted was similar to the original version or not. If different, do you prefer your version? Why (not)?
- Make a list of the characters presented. What do they all have in common?

Building Texts out of Texts

- Close your eyes and imagine one of the characters. If you feel like it, draw a picture of him. Can you put your picture into words? And what about a day in the life of 'your' character? Can you describe it in detail?
- What would the characters say to each other if they started a conversation? Plan the probable dialogue with a partner. Then dramatize it.
- And what would the characters 'say to themselves'? Write an interior monologue revealing the thoughts and innermost feelings of your character.

Cultural Dialogue

- How similar is the bar described to the ones you go to or others that can be found in your city? Try to describe similarities and differences in detail. Write a list of 'flashes' that describe a typical bar in your city. Put them together to make up a 'poetic enumeration' that can help a foreigner get to know the place where you live and its customs.

- Find other songs that present a similar situation/setting (e.g., Tom Waites' 'The Piano Has Been Drinking'). Compare and contrast the characters, the setting and the atmosphere created. What have you leant about bars in the composer's context? How important are they? How does this compare to your own idea of a bar?

Samples of Students' Work: Upper-intermediate EFL Students from Buenos Aires, Argentina

The texts have gone through a revision process based on peer correction and some suggestions made by the teacher, but accuracy is not the main aim of the tasks described.

Interior Monologues

The Old Man

What am I doing here again?
Okay, I wasted my best years but that doesn't mean that everything is lost; a long time has passed since I worked for the last time.

Look! My cup keeps refilling itself. Nice, a drink for an old man.

I could stop drinking but the feeling of losing my only friend is unbearable.

Martín

Davy

. . . being so lonely here listening to this melancolic melody . . .
What kind of life am I living?
Hate my life . . . If only I could have some friends or a girlfriend to spend my free time with. I don't want to waste my life like this.
Why is life so hard to me?
Saturday night is coming and I don't want to be sitting there drinking my beer and rolling my fags.

Adrián

Bill, the piano man

I can't believe how crowded the bar is today. It looks like a Friday night. There's the old man who asked me to play him a memory. He thinks I'm in the mood for a melody. I really want to return to my youth. I hate my life. I'm not happy being a piano man and supporting myself with the money that people put in my jar.
If only I had the money to become famous. I don't want to be like Paul or Davy. Their life is exactly as mine.

The only person I like is my manager. He really admires me. I'm 40 years old, my ex wife hates me and my life has no sense.

María Eugenia

Cultural Dialogue

The title of the essay below is the name of a tango ('Little Café in Buenos Aires') which depicts the kind of traditional café from the 1940s which is still an icon of urban culture in Argentina.

Cafetín de Buenos Aires

I would like to tell you about a special bar, a bar you won't find anywhere else in the world or in any other city in my country, because it belongs to Buenos Aires, to the inhabitants of Buenos Aires, especially to those who spend their lives in a bar.

Most of the bars are located in the corner of a main avenue and a narrow side street. An atmosphere of sadness and melancholy dresses the walls. In these bars you can smell the aroma of the city mixed with the smoke of cigarettes and hot coffee. No matter what bar you are in, they always have the same characteristics: little square tables, hard chairs, a large bar at the back and some pictures of famous tango singers and some of famous soccer players.

Just sitting at a table you can watch the bar become a real-life play: the waiter, the main actor, always dressed in a white or grey suit, with the large tray held against his body is the person in charge of learning everything as he sees reality through the window of the bar. Then, there are those who go to the bar every day and spend most of the time sitting at the same table and even on the same chair, having coffee, or gin, or 'Legui' and playing cards, particularly a game called 'truco'. These men turn into journalists when, soccer or horse-racing is the subject of conversation, especially on Mondays, and they will suddenly become experienced politicians when they talk politics ... and so on, with every topic they discuss. Finally we find the owner of the bar, generally a Spaniard. He is the butt of everyone's jokes, poor 'gallego'...

I think I have given you a quick glance of a typical café in Buenos Aires. I hope one day you can come over and enjoy the experience yourselves.

Andrés

It can be very useful to put together an 'anthology' of rock lyrics that teachers can resort to in order to design classroom materials based on them. Building this corpus is time-consuming, so it is advisable to keep a file (electronic or on paper) that grows as time goes by. Songs can be grouped thematically or according to any other parameters that teachers can find useful. Saving this corpus on disc or CD allows the user to establish hyperlinks between songs and the activities based on them and between songs linked around a certain topic.

Some useful sites to find lyrics are listed below. Yet, an Internet search can suggest many more up-to-date possibilities (any domain listed here may have changed hands or ceased to exist as I am writing this):

http://www.songfile.com/index_2.html
http://www.lyrics.com/
http://lyrics.astraweb.com/

It is true that students are always interested in top-of-the-chart hits, so that the corpus needs to be constantly updated, but 'classics' like the song discussed above form part of a 'canon' that can prove interesting and relevant over time. For teachers who may be wondering where to start, I can recommend the classics that form part of my list of favourites for the classroom. In most cases, I have found these songs useful because they develop topics that are meaningful, relevant and easy to integrate with usual contents in the syllabus, such as human rights, ecological concerns, homelessness, coping with lack of affection or illness, breaking up, the paranormal, relationships between parents and children, discrimination, etc.

Alanis Morisette, 'Ironic'
Basket Case, 'Under the Bridge'
Blur, 'The Universal'
    'End of a Century'
Bob Dylan, 'All Along the Watchtower'
       'Blowing in the Wind'
       'The Times They are A'changing'
Cat Steven, 'Father and Son'
Elton John, 'The Last Song'
Genesis, 'Land of Confusion'
Kansas, 'Dust in the Wind'
Led Zeppelin, 'Stairway to Heaven'
Mike and the Mechanics, 'Another Cup of Coffee'
Queen, 'Bohemian Rhapsody'
    'The Show Must Go On'
Phil Collins, 'Another Day in Paradise'
Pink Floyd, 'Another Brick in the Wall'
REM, 'Losing My Religion'
Richard Marx, 'Hazard'
Scorpions, 'Winds of Change'
Sting, 'Englishman in New York'
   'Fragile'
   'Moon Over Bourbon Street'
Supertramp, 'The Logical Song'
The Police, 'Russians'

Among recent hits, the following songs have proved highly productive for developing EFL materials:

Orgy, 'Fiction'
Red Hot Chili Peppers, 'Californication'

Robbie Williams, 'Millennium'
Savage Garden, 'Crash and Burn'

Take, for example, 'Californication'. The title itself invites interpretation and discussion. It is interesting to see the word used in EFL journals with reference to cultural and linguistic imperialism:

> The spread of McDonald Duck across the world, with its trivialisation of local cultures, its ravenous appetite for market share at any price, its diffusion of 'American' values, has been widely documented ... In this '*californication*' of the globe, English bears a heavy responsibility. It is English which carries the messages, which serves as the language of the multi-national corporations, which moulds opinion through advertising. (Maley, 2000)

The lyrics make recurrent references to ways in which the American way of life, its myths and stereotypes spread through cultural products such as Hollywood films and popular music. As one of my upper-intermediate students put it: '*Californication means cultural rape*':

> It's the edge of the world
> And all of western civilization
> The sun may rise in the East
> At least it settles in the final location
> It's understood that Hollywood
> sells Californication
>
> . . .
>
> Space may be the final frontier
> But it's made in a Hollywood basement
> Cobain can you hear the spheres
> Singing songs off station to station
> And Alderon's not far away
> It's Californication

The following tasks could lead to discussion of the many references to the topic of cultural imperialism, some of which are highly metaphorical:

Read the lyrics carefully and select elements you identify with California:
....
....
....
....
....
Who is Cobain?
....

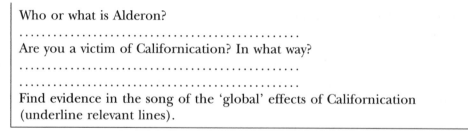

Who or what is Alderon?

· ·

Are you a victim of Californication? In what way?

· ·

· ·

Find evidence in the song of the 'global' effects of Californication (underline relevant lines).

Identifying Kurt Cobain, the late leader of the legendary group Nirvana, and Alderon, Princess Leia's fictional planet in Star Wars, may be a stepping stone to encouraging research on both the group and the film, and perhaps to developing projects on them.

Finally, as mentioned earlier, texts such as 'Californication' are multimedia texts, hubs in a network of formats: text, audio recordings, video clips, Internet sites. All of them can be exploited in the classroom. In this case, the video clip imitates a video game (a reference to yet another cultural product which leads to californication?). Such visual texts do not just 'illustrate' the song: they tell a story or present situations which can be considered independently or which can be read hypertextually, asking ourselves what its relationship with the song is. These kind of video clips, which Thomas Garza (1994: 107) refers to as 'concept videos', can be very useful for developing class materials: 'translating' those images into words, focusing in groups on different aspects of the video, can lead to further interpretations of the song and to new written and oral production tasks.

Take, for example. Michael Jackson's song 'Remember the Times'. The lyrics are repetitive and hardly worth working on – certainly irrelevant from the point of view of their non-existent 'literariness'. However, the funny video clip, which is located in ancient Egypt, is an interesting visual text with a storyline to exploit. It could even be related to a project on ancient cultures if it is not taken as historically true to fact!

Other 'concept videos' are:

Genesis, 'Land of Confusion' (an unsurpassed masterpiece with highly ironic references to the political reality of the 1980s)
Sting, 'All this Time' (a rather funny voyage with little apparent relationship to the highly metaphysical lyrics)
Robbie Williams, 'Supreme' (Jackie Stewart competing on the racing track with singer Robbie Williams himself)

For many of these songs, Internet-based activities are also readily available. They can be simple searches for which URLs are pre-selected, encouraging not only skimming and scanning but also critical consideration of the reliability of the information available on the web. This task on 'Californication' could be used with Intermediate students before dealing with the video clip:

Surf the net and find out:

- when the Red Hot Chili Pepper's album 'Californication' was released

  _____

- how many songs it includes

  _____

- what kind of music genres can be found in it

  _____

About the 'Californication' video:

- What kind of video images have the directors used?

  _____

- Who made the video?

  _____

- What other famous videos have they made?

  _____

Some URLs you can use:

1. Red Hot Chili Peppers On-line
   http://www.redhotchilipeppers.com/
2. Red Hot Chili Peppers/Californication
   http://www.cddb.com/xm/cd/blues/5602ec39a657496ebd03380140732798.html
3. Red Hot Chili Peppers – Californication – Recording details, track-listing, price, ordering
   http://www.netcd.co.nz/Recordings/48787.shtml
4. *http://www.mpmusic.com/Billboard/7854.htm*
5. Red Hot Chili Peppers | Californication. Real Audio Music @ Music Salad.
   http://www.musicsalad.com/html/RedHotChiliPeppers.html
6. Californication – Red Hot Chilli Peppers: reviews *http://www.isr-uk.net/reviews/rhcp_californication.shtml*

Once your search is complete, please answer the following:
How many sites have you visited? . . .
Answer the following questions for all of them:
Did they try to sell you something as you browsed? YES ☐ NO ☐
Who is the author of the page you have read? . . . .
If there is no identifiable author, is there an institution that holds itself responsible for the page's content?
. . . .
In the light of your answers, how reliable is, in your opinion, the information you have found?
. . . .

Conclusion

Rock lyrics and the multimedia texts related to them offer a myriad of creative possibilities for the teacher/materials designer. In our role of teachers, we should never forget that no reading can be considered the definite, final reading and that, as a result, no teacher can provide anything like 'the right interpretation'. As materials designers, we can enjoy creating opportunities for our students to build meaning out of texts which are never obvious, whose indeterminacy and complexity and concern with contemporary issues makes them challenging and motivating.

Rock poetry can open paths into textual and cultural awareness in learner-centred classrooms where the fun of discovering the power of metaphor in culturally loaded texts can be shared by students and teachers alike.

References

Barthes, R. (1970) *S/Z*. Paris: Seouil.

Bombini, G. (1989) *La Trama de los Textos – Problemas de la Enseñanza de la Literatura*. Buenos Aires: El Quirquincho.

Brumfit, C. J. and Carter, R. A. (1986) *Literature and Language Teaching*. Oxford: Oxford University Press.

Cook, G. (2000) *Language Play, Language Learning*. Oxford: Oxford University Press.

Eagleton, T. (1983) *Literary Theory. An Introduction*. Minneapolis: University of Minnesota Press.

Eco, U. (1979) *Obra Abierta*. Barcelona: Ariel.

Ferradas Moi, C. (1994) 'Rock poetry: the literature our students listen to'. *The Journal of the Imagination in Language Learning*, Jersey City State College, **2**, 56–9.

Ferradas Moi, C. (1997) 'Reading rock in the EFL classroom'. *Folio*, 4(1), 28–31.

Fish, S. (1980). *Is There a Text in this Class?* Cambridge, MA: Harvard University Press.

Garza, T. J. (1994) 'Beyond MTV: music videos as foreign language texts'. *The Journal of the Imagination in Language Learning*, Jersey City State College, **2**, 106–10.

Genette, G. (1962). *Palimpsestes*. Paris: Seouil.

McRae, J. (1991) *Literature with a Small 'l'*. London and Basingstoke: Macmillan.

Maley, A. (2000) 'The future of English'. *The English Teacher*, **3**(2).

Pope, R. (1995) *Textual Intervention. Critical and Creative Strategies for Literary Studies*. London: Routledge.

Pulverness, A. (1996) 'Outside looking in – teaching literature as dialogue'. *The Hermetic Garage*, Last Number but Three. La Plata: Argentina, pp. 69–85.

Romano, E. (1990) 'Palabra y Canción', Medios, Comunicación y Cultura 21, Buenos Aires: Argentina.

Wicke, P. (1990) *Rock Music – Culture, Aesthetics and Sociology*. Cambridge: Cambridge University Press.

Discography (songs cited)

Billy Joel (1973) 'Piano man', in *Billy Joel – Greatest Hits – Volume I and II* (1985). Columbia Records.

Brad Roberts (1993, single released 1994) 'Afternoons and coffee spoons', in Crash Test Dummies, *God Shuffled his Feet*. BMG.

Kiedis, Flea, Frusciante, Smith (1999) 'Californication', in Red Hot Chili Peppers, *Californication*. Warner Bros.

Sting (1987) 'Sister Moon', in *Nothing Like the Sun*. A&M Records.

Videos

Genesis (1987) 'Land of confusion', in *Visible Touch*. Atlantic Recording Corporation.

Michael Jackson (1993) 'Remember the times', in *Dangerous – The Short Films*. Epic Music Video.

Robbie Williams (2001) 'Supreme', Vaughan Arnell (dir.).

Sting (1994), 'All this time', in *The Best of Sting – Fields of Gold*. A&M Video.

CHAPTER

25

Materials for Language Awareness

Rod Bolitho

Introduction

Very few modern coursebooks incorporate activities for raising language awareness, despite widespread recognition that awareness-raising tasks encourage
learners to discover and make sense of language for themselves, and that learners,
even at the beginner level, have already acquired a linguistic and conceptual
framework which would allow them to approach a new language from a position
of strength rather than of enforced helplessness and teacher-dependency. The
trend is reinforced by a reluctance by coursebook writers to depart from the
present – practise – produce paradigm for grammar teaching and by the continued insistence in grammar practice materials on using 'cooked' and decontextualized single sentence examples as a basis for their exercise materials (see
Murphy, 1985, and Swan and Walter, 1999, for examples of this). In real communication, however, language hardly ever exists at single sentence level, and
meaning can only be successfully decoded by understanding the complex web of
patterns in written and spoken discourse. This requires work on features such as
lexical and grammatical cohesion, ellipsis and substitution, cultural references,
speaker/writer attitudes and intentions and tense/time relationships, as well as
on the grammatical, lexical and phonological features which are traditionally
emphasized in language systems courses on teacher-training programmes. An
awareness-raising approach can help learners to recognize these features and
discuss their importance in the secure environment of the classroom before
engaging with them in real contexts.

The compromises here are evident. The sentence is a wonderfully convenient
teaching tool. It can be written quickly on a board, used quickly and easily for
turn-taking in class, broken down and analysed into its constituent parts. Authors
and teachers alike are clearly reluctant to abandon it and to enter the minefield
of real texts with all its apparent chaos and hidden traps. Yet, until learners are
given the opportunity to grapple with these complexities, it is unlikely that they
will emerge from their language courses prepared for the encounter with real
language. In this respect, teaching materials continue to lag behind insights from
applied linguistics (see Ellis, 1997, for a discussion of the value of consciousness-
raising tasks in the teaching and learning of grammar) and thinkers about language (see, for example, Lewis, 1993, who offers an observe – hypothesize –
experiment as an alternative to present – practise – produce in approaching the

teaching and learning of new language). Lessons from teachers' handbooks on language, such as those by Bolitho and Tomlinson (1995), which deal with language awareness from a pedagogical perspective, McCarthy (1991), which makes available key insights from discourse analysis, and Arndt *et al.*, (2000), which present a sociolinguistically rooted approach to real language, have yet to filter down in any significant way into teaching materials or classroom practice. Some coursebooks have made attempts to include some language awareness activities (see Tomlinson *et al.*, 2001) but none of them have yet done so in systematic or rigorous ways.

Yet the task for writers of coursebooks and language practice materials is not that difficult. The reader is invited to consider the following activity in the light of the above discussion (see Sample 1).

SAMPLE 1 – for intermediate and/or advanced students

Phrasal verbs.

1. (homework)
    Collect at least five examples each of phrasal verbs in use, either from spoken or written sources. Write each example, in context, on a card or slip of paper.
2. In class, form groups of four. Present your examples briefly to each other, and sort them into categories of your own making. Note down anything interesting that you discover 'along the way'.
3. Each group should present its findings to the rest of the class, using a poster or an overhead transparency.
4. Note down comments and queries from the rest of the class, including the teacher.
5. In your original groups consult grammar books and dictionaries to check out what you have discovered, and revise your categories and conclusions according to what you find out.
6. You now have a way of 'organizing' your knowledge of phrasal verbs. Add new verbs to each category as you meet them.

Commentary

This activity encourages learners to investigate a language point independently and collaboratively. They will discover ways of organizing phrasal verbs according to meaning, form and behaviour, through exploring their lexical and grammatical features for themselves before consulting reference books. Many learners will establish categories that do not seem to be valid at first sight, but it is important that they have done their own research and thinking on the topic, and have learned to use the reference books to check this out. Since grammarians and lexicographers themselves cannot agree on a uniform categorization of phrasal verbs, nor even on what a phrasal verb is or is not, the learners' own categories are likely to be good enough for their own purposes. Typically, in this activity, they will encounter the differences between adverb particles and prepositions, the 'separability' of 'verb + particle' constructions, literal vs. figurative meaning and the frequency of phrasal verbs in informal contexts. The groups I have worked with have found all this out for themselves, and have developed and tested a number of hypotheses about phrasal verbs along the way. The learning experience has depth and lasting value for them.

A Suggested Framework for Language Awareness Activities

It is not feasible within the limited scope of this chapter to illustrate the full range of exercise and activity types for language awareness work. However, it is possible to offer guidance on the key ingredients of a language awareness activity. These are given here to provide readers with a framework for writing their own materials.

- The starting point is usually *language data* of some kind. This may include authentic texts (spoken or written), textbook extracts, extracts from reference books, samples of learner language, learners' beliefs and constructs about language, etc. The data may be used in isolation or comparatively (as in Sample 1, where learners start with extracts from language in use, develop their own constructs and then compare them with 'authorized' versions in reference books).
- The next step is the exploitation of the data through *tasks* which may require learners to explore, to make comparisons, to answer questions, to take notes, to guess or hypothesize, to classify or to categorize. Some of these task types are exemplified in the sample activity above.
- A good task will trigger one or more of the following cognitive *processes*: analysing, analogizing, applying existing knowledge to new contexts, revising existing beliefs and constructs, synthesizing old and new knowledge, evaluating evidence from data, etc. Both higher and lower-order thinking skills (Bloom and Kratwohl, 1965) are involved here, but there is an emphasis on critical and independent thinking rather than on the simple fulfilment of routine tasks such as gap-filling or substitution exercises which many learners can manage blindfold.
- Finally, language awareness activities lend themselves to all the familiar *modes* of work, in and out of class: pair or group work, individual work, whole class work, or self-access work. It is worth noting, however, that many language awareness activities are open-ended in nature, reflecting the ambiguities and complexities which characterize real language in use. This means that there is often no single 'right' answer (see the commentaries in Bolitho and Tomlinson (1995) for an example of this).

This chapter began with an expression of regret that language awareness work has not yet found its way into mainstream published materials. Perhaps that is too much to hope for in the short term, given the conservatism of most publishing houses and the washback effect of public examinations. However, most teachers and authors know, deep down, that there is much more to language than the coursebooks would have us and our learners believe, and that there is a need, at the very least, to supplement existing materials with a more honest and open approach to the intricacies and complexities of real language in use. There is no guarantee that language awareness work will have an immediate impact on learners' ability to use language fluently and accurately, but there is no doubt that it will engage them in thinking critically about how language is used for different purposes, and that it will give a real context to their struggles with language systems.

References

Arndt, V., Harvey, P. and Nuttall, J. (2000) *Alive to Language.* Cambridge: Cambridge University Press.

Bloom, B. S. and Kratwohl, D. R. (1965) *The Taxonomy of Educational Objectives, Handbook 1: Cognitive Domain.* New York: D. McKay.

Bolitho, R. and Tomlinson, B. (1995) *Discover English* (2nd edn.). Oxford: Heinemann.

Ellis, R. (1997) *SLA Research and Language Teaching.* Oxford: Oxford University Press.

Lewis, M. (1993) *The Lexical Approach.* Hove: LTP.

McCarthy, M. (1991) *Discourse Analysis and the Language Teacher.* Cambridge: Cambridge University Press.

Murphy, R. (1985) *English Grammar in Use.* Cambridge: Cambridge University Press.

Swan, M. and Walter, C. (1999) *How English Works.* Cambridge: Cambridge University Press.

Tomlinson, B., Dat, B., Masuhara, H. and Rubdy, R. (2001) 'EFL courses for adults'. *English Language Teaching Journal,* **55** (1).

26

Materials for Cultural Awareness

Alan Pulverness

Introduction

One consequence of the 'communicative turn' taken by ELT since the late 1970s has been the marginalization, and at times the complete exclusion, of culturally specific content in published teaching materials. The shift towards a functional approach to EFL teaching, driven by needs analysis and predictable performance objectives, has coincided with a developing awareness of the growing role of English as an international language. In this climate, it is hardly surprising that cultural specificity is seen at best as a luxury and at worst as an irrelevance. Cunningsworth (1984) stated the case against 'the culture-specific coursebook' in terms which clearly continue to resonate with major ELT publishers:

> A limitation of the culture-specific coursebook is that it will only be of relevance to students who understand the cultural background in which it is set ... Indeed ... a strong portrayal of British life might well prove to be an impediment rather than a help to the learner ... The [learner's] time would be better spent learning the language rather than the structuring of the social world in which the learner is never likely to find himself. (1984: 61–2)

The marketing imperatives of a publishing industry that attempts increasingly to satisfy the perceived needs of a global clientele have been echoed by similar tendencies in an ELT teaching industry reluctant to be stigmatized as neo-imperialist (see Phillipson, 1992; Holliday, 1994; Pennycook, 1994; Canagarajah, 1999). The problematic relationship of culture to language teaching and learning is further complicated by the way in which the concept of culture in language teaching has been freighted with connotations of an outmoded approach to transmitting unmediated facts and information about an implicitly superior 'target' culture. Consequently, the notion of an integrated language-and-culture pedagogy (Byram *et al.*, 1994) that evolved through the 1990s has thus far had relatively little impact on the ELT community.

This chapter proceeds from a strong assumption that language teaching and learning invariably involve issues of sociocultural meaning, and that approaches which disregard the cultural dimension of language are fundamentally flawed. It will question the assumption that in circumstances where English is seen as a lingua franca, it must necessarily be inappropriate to situate the language in a particular cultural context. The argument is based on a model of *inter*cultural foreign language education, in which the process of foreign language learning engages the learner in the role of a comparative ethnographer (Byram, 1989). Entering into a foreign language implies a cognitive modification that has implications for the learner's identity as a social and cultural being, and suggests the need for materials which privilege the identity of the learner as an integral factor in developing the ability to function fully in cultural 'third places' (Kramsch, 1993: 233–59). To develop cultural awareness alongside language awareness, materials need to provide more than a token acknowledgement of cultural identity ('Now write about your country') and address more thoroughly the kind of cultural adjustment that underlies the experience of learning a foreign language. One powerful means of raising this kind of awareness in learners is through literary texts which mimic, or more directly represent, experiences of cultural estrangement.

However, the pedagogical implications extend beyond issues of content: if culture is seen as the expression of beliefs and values, and if language is seen as the embodiment of cultural identity, then the methodology required to teach a language needs to take account of ways in which the language expresses cultural meanings. An integrated approach to teaching language-and-culture, as well as attending to language as system and to cultural information, will focus additionally on culturally significant areas of language and on the skills required by the learner to make sense of cultural difference. An enhanced language syllabus that takes account of cultural specificity would be concerned with aspects of language that are generally neglected, or that at best tend to remain peripheral in course materials: connotation, idiom, the construction of style and tone, rhetorical structure, critical language awareness and translation. The familiar set of language skills would be augmented by ethnographic and research skills designed to develop intercultural awareness.

Objections to a cultural agenda for ELT tend to come from the ethnocentric perspective of the private sector (whether situated in an L2 or an L1 environment), where language teaching is largely constructed as a training enterprise. It is significant that the most innovative materials for teaching language-and-culture have emerged from state sector educational contexts in countries with established and unbroken traditions of teaching culture. The move from *Landeskunde* to 'New Cultural Studies' (Delanoy, 1994) is less problematic for non-native practitioners than what their native counterparts may simply see as an updated version of 'British Life and Institutions'.

There are encouraging signs in some recently published coursebooks of greater cultural relativism and more pluralistic representations of English-speaking cultures. But as long as courses continue to be produced for a global market and construed exclusively in terms of language training, such developments will remain largely cosmetic. This chapter will refer to several recent projects which suggest that the way ahead for integrated language-and-culture materials lies in various kinds of country-specific joint publishing ventures.

The Fifth Skill?

There have been numerous nominations for the coveted title of 'fifth skill', ranging from ICT literacy to self-directed learning, but it may be argued that these are all 'add-ons' to the four basic language skills. Kramsch (1993) claims an altogether higher status for culture:

> Culture in language learning is not an expendable fifth skill tacked on, so to speak, to the teaching of speaking, listening, reading, and writing. It is always in the background, right from day one, ready to unsettle the good language learners when they expect it least, making evident the limitations of their hard won communicative competence, challenging their ability to make sense of the world around them. (1993: 1)

The underlying implication is that language and culture are inextricably intertwined. To treat language, in the manner of most mainstream language courses, as a value-free code is likely to deprive learners of key dimensions of meaning and to fail to equip them with necessary resources to recognize and respond appropriately to the cultural subtext of language in use. Even when neither partner in a spoken or written interaction is a native speaker, the language they are using is the result of social and historical circumstances which give it resonance and meaning. To teach language that is imbued with cultural nuance as though it were purely a means of instrumental transaction is to ignore the shared frame of reference that makes language fully meaningful. In this sense, cultural awareness becomes not the fifth, but the first skill, informing every step of the language learning process, 'right from day one'. Communicative language teaching, in its emphasis on authentic text and genuine interaction, privileges meaning over form, but in excluding cultural meaning, it promotes a model of language that is restricted to transactional functions and referential uses of language. Yet, from moment to moment in any language classroom, whether or not they are aware of the fact, teachers – and teaching materials – are constantly exemplifying the cultural underpinnings of the language.

Culture, as Raymond Williams points out, is 'one of the two or three most complicated words in the English language' (1983: 87). Derived from the concept of cultivation in agriculture, it became synonymous in the eighteenth century with 'civilization'. To be 'cultured' – or, metaphorically, 'cultivated' – was to be civilized, and this notion of culture as 'high culture' survives in the title of Ministry of Culture, in the 'culture' supplements of broadsheet newspapers and in collocations such as 'culture vulture'. Since the late nineteenth century, social anthropology (see Geertz, 1973) has been responsible for a much broader definition of culture as a 'whole way of life', embracing all the behaviours, symbols, beliefs and value systems of a society, and it is this expanded definition that informs much current thinking about the role of culture in ELT (see, for example, Tomalin and Stempleski, 1993). However, resistance to the dominant, monolithic European version of culture suggested by association with 'civilization' can be traced back as far as the late eighteenth century in Germany, when Johann Gottfried Herder (1791) insisted on the need to consider 'cultures' rather than 'culture' in the singular. This alternative, pluralistic strain of thinking about culture has been developed latterly by sociologists identifying subcultures and by social psychologists investigating the behaviour of people functioning in small groups, so-called 'small cultures'.

The 'life and institutions' approach to transmitting cultural knowledge as an adjunct to language teaching draws on the tradition of culture as 'civilization'. A more egalitarian view of culture as a 'whole way of life' has trickled down into some ELT coursebooks, where iconic, tourist brochure images of Britishness have been replaced by material that is more representative of the multicultural diversity of contemporary British life. But, since language training remains the primary agenda, the effect is often unproductive in terms of cultural under-standing, with texts and visuals serving primarily as contextual backdrops to language tasks. Moreover, since the majority of coursebooks are designed to function in as diverse a market as possible, materials design is rarely capable of encompassing the learner's cultural identity as part of the learning process. At most, learners may be called upon to comment on superficial differences at the level of observable behaviours. There is a great deal of incidental cultural infor-mation available in course materials, but it is on the whole an arbitrary selection, and, crucially, it remains just information – learners are not required to respond to it in terms of their own experience or integrate it into new structures of thought and feeling. The subculture of the language learner and the 'small culture' of the classroom tend not to be addressed.

Another Country – They Do Things Differently There

The experience of learning another language is more than simply the acquisition of an alternative means of expression. It involves a process of acculturation, akin to the effort required of the traveller, striving to come to terms with different social structures, different assumptions and different expectations. To pursue the metaphor, when the traveller returns home, his/her view of familiar surround-ings is characteristically modified. The language learner is similarly displaced and 'returns' with a modified sense of what had previously been taken for granted – the language and how it makes meaning.

This sensation of seeing one's own language and culture refracted through the medium of a foreign language and culture reflects what was described by the Russian Formalist critic, Viktor Shklovsky (1917), writing about Tolstoy's literary technique, as 'defamiliarization', or 'making the familiar seem strange':

> After we see an object several times, we begin to recognise it. The object is in front of us and we know about it, but we do not see it – hence we cannot say anything significant about it ... Tolstoy makes the familiar seem strange ... He describes an object as if he were seeing it for the first time, an event as if it were happening for the first time. (Shklovsky, 1917, in Lodge, 1988: 21)

For the majority of learners encountering a foreign language for the first time, their own culture is so familiar, so much a given, that they 'do not see it'. Their culture provides them with one way of looking at the world and their language with one way of doing so. The experience of defamiliarization involved in foreign language learning, described by Byram (1990: 19) as the 'modification of monocultural awareness', suggests that there is largely untapped potential in teaching materials for focusing as much on the source culture as the stimulus culture, and on the effect upon the learner of this modification. I have deliberately avoided using the term 'target culture', which suggests an objective body of knowledge to be assimilated – and probably tested. The term 'stimulus culture' is taken from Lavery (1993) and reinforces the fact that the awareness to be raised is *inter*cultural rather than simply cultural.

One way of sensitizing learners to this process is through a whole range of stimulating literary texts that employ deliberate strategies of defamiliarization, taking readers on voyages of discovery or simply making them look afresh at their everyday surroundings. Genres which typically displace the reader in this way include historical fiction, science fiction and Utopian – or dystopian – fantasies. By electing for a satiric or fantastic mode, writers commit themselves almost inevitably to some kind of defamiliarization. Imagined worlds – Lilliput, Wonderland, Middle Earth – always draw on the existing world; futuristic fictions or texts that construct alternative realities always extrapolate from the present; satire, however wild or grotesque, always arises out of current concerns. Fantasists, science fiction writers and satirists may take us 'out of this world', but they do so only in order to bring us back into it. The value of such writing for learners of language-and-culture is the way in which it may encourage them not simply to observe the *difference* in the Other culture, but to become less ethnocentric and more culturally relativist – to look at their own cultural environment through fresh eyes. Craig Raine's poem 'A Martian sends a postcard home', in which the eponymous visitor from outer space misreads the functions of books, cars, telephones and toilets, is an outstanding example of a writer making use of what Doris Lessing has called 'that other-worldly visitor so useful for enlivening our organs of perception' (in Phillips, 1997: 123). In Peter Ackroyd's novel *The Plato Papers* (Chatto and Windus, 1999), a twenty-third-century historian similarly misinterprets the ancient history of twentieth-century civilization. Once students have got the idea of 'making strange', they can try their hands at writing their own Martian anthropology or futuristic archaeological notes.

Another literary genre that disturbs unquestioned cultural assumptions is the growing body of writing in English that deals directly or indirectly with the immigrant or second generation bicultural experience and the diversity of increasingly multicultural societies. Novels, such as those by the Korean-American Chang-Rae Lee, the Chinese-American Gish Jen, the British Asian Hanif Kureishi, or the British African Diran Adebayo, all reflect what Canadians call the cultural mosaic, and can be read not simply as accounts of culture clash or culture shock, but as documents of a quest for new kinds of cultural identity located in Kramsch's 'third places'. Such intracultural texts can be used in the language classroom to prepare learners for the encounter with the cultural Other and to promote greater intercultural awareness. To build a bridge in the classroom from the literature of cultural third places to the learner's own intercultural experience, students could be asked to experiment with various kinds of textual intervention (Pope, 1995) and imitation. They could be invited to 'recentre' an immigrant narrative from the host community's point of view (Pulverness, 2001), to imagine dialogues, not included in the original text, between representatives of the two cultures, to imagine themselves as immigrants in their own society and so on.

The Culture of Language and the Language of Culture

Course materials are largely governed by a tacit consensus about what should constitute a language syllabus. Apart from a brief pendulum swing in the late 1970s, when the elaborated phrase book of an exclusively functional approach almost entirely displaced grammar, and despite the development of multi-strand syllabuses, the structured, incremental grammatical syllabus remains the principal axis around which the overwhelming majority of coursebooks are organized. The overarching aim of the language syllabus is to develop a command of the language as a systematic set of resources. However, the focus of most teaching materials remains fixed on the content of these resources rather than on the choices that speakers (and writers) make in the course of social interaction. The cultural dimension of language consists of elements that are normally classed as 'native speaker intuition' and which may be achieved by only the most advanced students. As native speakers, we function effectively in our own speech communities not simply by drawing mechanically on an inventory of language items, but by employing the pragmatic awareness which enables us to make appropriate and relevant selections from that inventory. This awareness may not be wholly determined by cultural factors, but it is culturally conditioned. It includes elements such as forms of address, the expression of politeness, discourse conventions and situational constraints on conversational behaviour. Grice's 'cooperative principle' (1975) and Lakoff's 'politeness principle' (1973) have up to now made remarkably little impression on EFL materials. It is lack of awareness of such contextual and pragmatic constraints that is often responsible for pragmatic failure. Although teachers may incidentally address some of these features, there have been few attempts in published materials to deal systematically with the ways in which linguistic choices are constrained by setting, situation, status and purpose. Like many coursebook texts, tasks requiring oral interaction tend to be situated in neutral, culture-free zones, where the learner is only called upon to 'get the message across'.

One recent challenge to the centrality of grammar as an organizing principle for the syllabus is to be found in the 'Lexical Approach' (Lewis, 1993; 1997), with its insistence on language as 'grammaticalized lexis' instead of the customary view of 'lexicalized grammar'. The coursebook inspired by Lewis' work (Dellar and Hocking, *Innovations*, 2000), emphasizes the significance of collocation and lexical phrases, partly subsumed under the category of 'spoken grammar', while key elements of a traditional structure are retained under the less dominant rubric of 'traditional grammar'. This focus on how lexical items cluster together through use and constitute larger units of meaning provides an important design principle for materials that intend to combine cultural learning and language learning. Porto (2001) makes a strong case for taking lexical phrases as a foundation for developing sociocultural awareness from the earliest stages of language learning:

> Given that lexical phrases are context-bound, and granted that contexts are culture-specific, the recurrent association of lexical phrases with certain contexts of use will ensure that the sociolinguistic ability to use the phrases in the appropriate contexts is fostered. (2001: 52–3)

Another lexical area that might profitably be explored by materials writers is suggested by research into cognition and cross-cultural semantics (Wierzbicka, 1991; 1992; 1997). Wierzbicka's research methodology, at word or phrase level, as well as when dealing with broad semantic categories and longer stretches of text and interaction, is one that lends itself to adaptation by EFL materials writers. Her analyses are based on extensive collections of data, exemplifying the use of particular items in multiple contexts, from which she then begins to draw conclusions about the cultural specificity and the semantic limitations of key concepts. On a smaller scale, this rigorously inductive approach might have a particular appeal to learners who are in any case constantly engaged in just this kind of exploration of meaning, albeit in a relatively unstructured fashion. The increasing availability of affordable concordancing software should also make it possible before long for the coursebook treatment of this kind of activity to be open-ended and supplemented by providing learners with the tools to pursue their own further exploration.

One of the most challenging aspects of moving into the culture of another language is the adjustment to different rhetorical structures. Learners have to cope receptively and productively, not just with word-level and sentence-level difference, but with different modes of textual organization. While contrastive studies in rhetoric and text linguistics (e.g., Kaplan, 1966; 1987) have explored the problematic nature of text and discourse across cultures, a great deal of language teaching continues to operate at sentence level. It is generally only on EAP courses in academic writing that text structure receives any substantial attention. Yet sometimes radically different assumptions about the structuring of spoken and written discourse can produce a sense of cultural and linguistic estrangement that all learners have to struggle to come to terms with, often without much help from course materials. A number of recent coursebooks have tentatively included small translation tasks, usually at word or sentence level. More extensive translation activities could raise learners' awareness of how differently ideas may be organized at text level, for example, translating a source text and then comparing its structure with a parallel L1 text on the same topic and in the same genre, or using a 'double translation' procedure, i.e., translation into L1 and then back into L2, comparing the second version with the L2 original.

Limitations of space will normally prohibit extensive treatment of longer texts within the coursebook, but here again the book can serve as a manual, equipping the learner with strategic competence and procedural guidelines as a basis for further work outside the book.

The construction of cultural 'third places' is essentially a critical activity, as it forces learners to become aware of ways in which language is socially and culturally determined. Language awareness has become a rather hollow label, often (e.g., on many pre-service training courses) more or less synonymous with declarative knowledge about how the language works. Van Lier's (1995) definition is more comprehensive and should alert us to the fact that language is always ideologically loaded and texts are always to be 'mistrusted':

> Language awareness can be defined as an understanding of the human faculty of language and its role in thinking, learning and social life. It includes an awareness of power and control through language, and of the intricate relationships between language and culture. (1995: xi)

Critical Language Awareness (CLA) proceeds from the belief that language is always value-laden and that texts are never neutral. Language in the world beyond the coursebook is commonly used to exercise 'power and control', to reinforce dominant ideologies, to evade responsibility, to manufacture consensus. As readers, we should always be 'suspicious' of texts and prepared to challenge or interrogate them. However, in the foreign language classroom, texts are customarily treated as unproblematic, as if their authority need never be questioned. Learners, who may be quite critical readers in their mother tongues, are textually infantilized by the vast majority of course materials and classroom approaches.

A CLA approach implies 'a methodology for interpreting texts which addresses ideological assumptions as well as propositional meaning' (Wallace, 1992), which would require students to develop sociolinguistic and ethnographic research skills in order to become proficient at observing, analysing and evaluating language use in the world around them. It would lead them to ask and answer crucial questions about a text: Who produced it? Who was it produced for? In what context was it published? It would encourage them to notice features such as lexical choice, passivization or foregrounding that reveal both the position of the writer and the way in which the reader is 'positioned' by the text. It would offer them opportunities to intervene creatively in texts, to modify them or to produce their own 'counter-texts' (see Kramsch, 1993; Pope, 1995). It would empower students to become active participants in the negotiation of meaning rather than passive recipients of 'authoritative' texts. In short, it would transform language training into language education.

Small is Beautiful

Up to this point I have been mostly concerned with ways in which the 'international' coursebook might be modified to take in elements of cultural learning in a more integral fashion. The inherent constraints of global publishing will clearly not allow for this to be carried very far. However, in the last few years, there have been a number of country or region-specific joint publishing enterprises, whose point of departure has been the teaching of intercultural awareness in tandem with the foreign language. The British Council has joined forces with local publishers in a number of countries in Central and Eastern Europe (CEE) to produce textbooks (in Romania *Crossing Cultures*, 1998; in the Czech Republic *Lifestyles*, 2000; in Hungary *Zoom In*, 2001), a cultural studies syllabus (in Bulgaria *Branching Out*, 1998),[1] and teachers' resource materials (*British Studies Materials for English Teachers in Poland*, 2000). What has distinguished all of these publications is the fact that they were all initiated through projects responding to teachers' needs and were written collaboratively either by teachers themselves with support and guidance from consultants, or in one case by a consultant with guidance from teachers. Another way of resolving the tension between the economics of large-scale publishing and the real needs of small-scale markets has come from an independent British publisher who commissioned a multilevel language-and-culture coursebook series (*Criss Cross*, 1998–2001) designed specifically for CEE. The series responds both to the practical exigencies of publishing and to the pedagogic needs of teachers and learners through a unique formula: the same core student's books across the market supplemented by locally produced practice books. In this way, markets that are too small to bear the cost of high-quality country-specific materials benefit from a centrally published course, which at the same time is made relevant to particular local needs through targeted practice materials.

Given the major publishers' abiding concentration on marketing 'one size fits all' global coursebooks, local and regional initiatives such as those described above seem to offer the most promising ways of developing and producing materials that fulfil the ideal of teaching language-and-culture. The fact that so many of these publications are the result of cross-cultural writing partnerships also helps to ensure that the process of production is based on a cross-cultural exchange of language and experience of national and classroom cultures, which feeds directly into the materials.

Conclusion

It has to be acknowledged that the innovative projects described in the previous section remain the exception. ELT at large continues to be dominated by the mass market, 'international' coursebook. But here the teacher has a vital role to play in acting as an intercultural mediator and providing some of the cultural coordinates missing from the coursebook.

I have been involved as consultant or writer in several of the CEE projects mentioned above, and in Hungary I was fortunate to observe a wide range of classes in various parts of the country. All the classes I saw were working with coursebooks: *Headway Elementary, Intermediate* and *Advanced; Access to English: Getting On; Blueprint 2; New Blueprint Intermediate; Meanings into Words 2.* The teachers were all sufficiently experienced and confident to take subject matter present in coursebook units as a vehicle for the presentation of language items or the development of language skills and to use it as the basis for exploring cultural dimensions of the topic or theme. Coursebooks provide invaluable resources (topics, texts, visuals, language) and enable teachers and students to structure learning, but they also impose constraints which can be difficult to resist. Teachers who are conscious of this can easily become discouraged by the difficulty of obtaining suitable supplementary resources, but I was impressed by the ways in which all the teachers I observed made use of appropriate extra materials which enabled them to go beyond the coursebook – to use the currently fashionable commercial metaphor, to 'add value' to the coursebook. Examples included: a teacher's own photographs of Hungarian and British houses; text and video extracts from *Trainspotting;* a poem ('Neighbours' by Kit Wright); National Readership Surveys table of socio-economic categories (from Edgington and Montgomery, 1996); students' own family photographs and Christmas cards; jumbled extracts from two contrasting 'background' books; students' posters based on material collected during a study trip to Britain. These materials either compensated for cultural dimensions that were totally absent from the coursebook or took students well beyond the usual end-of-unit gesture of *Now compare this with houses/festivals/occupations, etc., in your country.*

Some of the teachers took topics from coursebook units as springboards for lessons which focused on content rather than concentrating exclusively on language points. This is not to say that language learning was absent, or even incidental, but the primary objectives were clearly to develop critical thinking about cultural issues, resisting the tendency of the materials to use content only to contextualize the presentation and practice of language items. For example, one lesson sprang from a coursebook unit where the topic was homelessness, but the unit was *about* expressions of quantity. The lesson, however, was *about* homelessness, with practice of expressions of quantity arising meaningfully through her use of the material.

There is a crucial distinction between classes that are driven by a language training agenda and those that are informed by cultural learning objectives. There is still a need, of course, for classes where the primary focus is language learning, but here, too, it is important that cultural learning is seen as an integral part of language education and not restricted to the 'cultural studies lesson'. One lesson on writing was an excellent example of this kind of integration. The teacher's primary aim was to raise students' awareness of the conventions and structural norms of writing postcards and informal letters in English, but this was done by getting the learners to carry out a detailed contrastive analysis of a range of authentic texts (received by the teacher) in English and in Hungarian. Thus what could easily have been an exclusively English language lesson achieved its objectives through exposure to and reflection on representative samples of equivalent language behaviour in different cultural contexts.

In any discussion of cultural behaviour, especially in classrooms, where teachers feel the pressure of time and other constraints, it is all too easy to resort to generalizations and to accept particular instances as being 'typical'. One way to avoid this trap is to make use of materials (e.g., first-person narratives) which are self-evidently individual, or even idiosyncratic. Other, more difficult strategies are to remind students at appropriate moments that they should not overgeneralize from particular examples, or to challenge their natural tendency to do so. This happened very interestingly in the lesson on homelessness, when the teacher prompted students to question the generalizations contained in the text, giving rise to the conclusion that 'English people are various'! Another good example in the writing class was the teacher's reminder to her students that they were reading individual examples of informal writing, which they should not necessarily regard as 'typical'.

The lessons I saw in Hungary were neither language lessons illustrating a few bits of cultural information nor lessons on culture with language learning as a kind of by-product. They all succeeded in different ways in combining language learning and cultural learning, so that although at some moments the emphasis may have been in one direction or the other, the overall effect was of lessons in which students were developing both kinds of knowledge as interrelated parts of the same enterprise.

References

Andrews, M. and Colleagues (2001) *Zoom In: Looking into Britain through Hungarian Eyes.* The British Council, Hungary/Callander: Swan Communication.

Bandura, E. and Colleagues (2000) *British Studies Materials for English Teachers in Poland.* The British Council, Poland.

Byram, M. (1989) *Cultural Studies in Foreign Language Education.* Clevedon: Multilingual Matters.

Byram, M. (1990) 'Teaching culture and language towards an integrated model', in D. Buttjes and M. Byram (eds) *Mediating Languages and Cultures.* Clevedon: Multilingual Matters.

Byram, M., Morgan, C. and Colleagues (1994) *Teaching-and-Learning Language-and-Culture.* Clevedon: Multilingual Matters.

Canagarajah, A. S. (1999) *Resisting Linguistic Imperialism in English Teaching.* Oxford: Oxford University Press.

Cichirdan, A. *et al.* (1998) *Crossing Cultures: British Cultural Studies for 12th Grade Romanian Students.* The British Council, Romania/Cavallioti Publishers.

Collie, J. (2000–01) *Lifestyles.* The British Council, Czech Republic/Oxford: Macmillan.

Cunningsworth, A. (1984) *Evaluating and Selecting EFL Materials.* London: Heinemann.

Davecheva, L., Reid-Thomas, H. and Pulverness, A. (1999) 'Cultural studies syllabus and materials: a writing partnership', in C. Kennedy (ed.) *Innovation and Best Practice*. Harlow: Longman, in association with the British Council.

Delanoy, W. (1994) 'Cultural learning in the FL-Classroom: from "Landeskunde" to "New Cultural Studies"'. *ELT News*, **22**. Vienna: The British Council.

Dellar, H. and Hocking, D. (2000) *Innovations*. Hove: Language Teaching Publications.

Edgington, B. and Montgomery, M. (1996) *The Media*. London: The British Council. Ellis, M. and Colleagues (1998–2001) *Criss Cross*. Callander: Swan Communication/ Ismaning: Hueber Verlag.

Geertz, C. (1973) *The Interpretation of Cultures*. New York: Basic Books.

Grice, H. P. (1975) 'Logic and conversation', in P. Cole and J. L. Morgan (eds) *Syntax and Semantics Vol 3: Speech Acts*. New York: Academic Press.

Herder J. G. (1791) *On World History. An Anthology*. Ed. H. Adler and Ernest A. Menze. Armonk, NY: M. E. Sharpe, 1996.

Holliday, A. (1994) *Appropriate Methodology and Social Context*. Cambridge: Cambridge University Press.

Kaplan, R. B. (1966) 'Cultural thought patterns in intercultural education'. *Language Learning*, **16**, 1–20

Kaplan, R. B. (1987) 'Cultural thought patterns revisited', in U. Connor and R. B. Kaplan (eds) *Writing Across Languages: Analysis of L2 Text*. Reading, MA: Addison-Wesley.

Kramsch, C. (1993) *Context and Culture in Language Teaching*. Oxford: Oxford University Press.

Lakoff, R. (1973) 'The logic of politeness: minding your p's and q's', in *Papers from the 9th Regional meeting, Chicago Linguistics Society*, pp. 292–305.

Lavery, C. (1993) *Focus on Britain Today*. Basingstoke: Macmillan.

Lessing, D. (1997) 'In defence of the Underground', in C. Phillips (ed.) *Extravagant Strangers: A Literature of Belonging*. London: Faber and Faber.

Lewis, M. (1993) *The Lexical Approach: The State of ELT and a Way Forward*. Hove: Language Teaching Publications.

Lewis, M. (1997) *Implementing the Lexical Approach: Putting Theory into Practice*. Hove: Language Teaching Publications.

Lier, L. Van (1995) *Introducing Language Awareness*. London: Penguin.

Pennycook, A. (1994) *The Cultural Politics of English as an International Language*. Harlow: Longman.

Phillipson, R. (1992) *Linguistic Imperialism*. Oxford: Oxford University Press.

Pope, R. (1995) *Textual Intervention: Critical and Creative Stategies for Literary Studies*. London: Routledge.

Porto, M. (2001) *The Significance of Identity: An Approach to the Teaching of Language and Culture*. La Plata, Argentina: Ediciones Al Margen/Editorial de la Universidad de La Plata.

Pulverness, A. (2001) *Changing Skies: The European Course for Advanced Level Learners*. Callander: Swan Communication.

Shklovsky, V. (1917) 'Art as technique', in D. Lodge (ed.) (1988) *Modern Criticism and Theory: A Reader*. London: Longman.

Sixty teachers of English in Bulgaria (1988) *Branching Out: A Cultural Studies Syllabus*. The British Council, Bulgaria/Tilia Ltd.

Tomalin, B. and Stempleski, S. (1993) *Cultural Awareness*. Oxford: Oxford University Press.

Wallace, C. (1992) 'Critical literacy awareness in the EFL classroom', in N. Fairclough (ed.) *Critical Language Awareness*. London: Longman.

Wierbicka, A. (1991) *Cross-Cultural Pragmatics: The Semantics of Human Interaction*. New York: Mouton de Gruyer.

Wierbicka, A. (1992) *Semantics, Culture and Cognition: Universal Human Concepts in Culture-Specific Configurations*. Oxford: Oxford University Press.

Wierbicka, A. (1997) *Understanding Cultures through Their Key Words: English, Russian, Polish, German and Japanese*. Oxford: Oxford University Press.

Williams, R. (1983) (revised and expanded). *Keywords: A Vocabulary of Culture and Society*. London: HarperCollins.

Comments on Part D

Brian Tomlinson

Explicit and Experiential Learning

It seems to be agreed by most of the authors in Part D that both explicit and experiential learning are necessary for learners of a foreign language but that neither is sufficient. Explicit learning encourages noticing and highlighting, and facilitates conscious learning and retrieval. Experiential learning facilitates elaborating, relating and valuing, and facilitates subconscious learning and automatic retrieval. The big question is which should come first, explicit or experiential learning. My own view is that it facilitates durable learning if apprehension comes before comprehension, especially if meaning-focused experience of a language feature in context is followed fairly closely by activities requiring the learner to pay attention to characteristics exhibited by that feature in the experienced context and in other contexts of use. This discovery approach to language awareness is equally applicable to grammar learning, to vocabulary learning and to the learning of conventional, stylistic and pragmatic features of discourse (Tomlinson, 1994). It is also applicable to the development of communication skills. The implication for materials development is that learners need motivated and meaningful exposure to language in use both prior to and subsequent to activities inviting the learners to pay conscious attention to features of the language used.

Extensive Listening and Reading

One important point implied by nearly all the chapters in this section is that excellent opportunities for experiential learning can be provided through extensive listening and extensive reading. Language can be acquired and skills developed by listening to or reading at length and leisure texts which are relevant, motivating and engaging (Tomlinson, 2001). To help learners to do this involves providing potentially appealing texts for learners to select from (or helping learners to provide them for themselves). It also means motivating learners to want to listen and read extensively, helping them to develop listening and reading confidence and ensuring that time is made available for them to listen and to read.

Realism

Most of the authors in this section also seem to agree that learning materials should be realistic in the sense that they reflect the reality of language use which learners will encounter outside and after their course. This means exposing learners to authentic materials (i.e., materials written not to teach language but to inform, amuse, provoke, excite, stimulate, entertain, etc.); and it certainly means that a course is inadequate at any level if it consists only of materials in which the language has been so simplified, reduced and focused that it does not resemble 'real' use of language at all. It could also mean that the learners are exposed to some materials which have been written to simulate authenticity and to some materials which resemble 'real' language use except that they have been enriched by an unusual number of examples of a particular language feature or they have had certain language features highlighted (e.g., through the use of bold type, distinctive fonts or underlining). And it could also mean that the learners are asked to participate in some pedagogic tasks which superficially bear no resemblance to 'real-world' tasks but which in fact provide useful opportunities to develop skills which will be important to the learners outside and after their courses. An example of such a task would be a game in which groups compete to assemble a Lego model which replicates a teacher-prepared model which is hidden to everybody except a 'runner' from each group who is permitted to look at the teacher's model and to describe it to his/her group. This is not a task which learners are ever likely to be engaged in in the 'real world' but it can engage them affectively and can help to develop such 'real-world' skills as visualization, giving precise descriptions and seeking clarification. The main point is that materials should provide learners with preparation for real-world language use but that they should do so in ways which recognize the limitations of the learners and the constraints of the classroom and in ways which exploit the resources of the teacher, of the learners themselves and of learning aids.

Affect

Another common theme in Part D, and indeed in the other Parts of the book, is the need for materials, regardless of what they are teaching, to engage learners affectively. Learners are not going to develop listening or reading skills if they are exposed only to bland, neutral or trivial texts which do not stimulate cognitive or emotive responses. They are not going to develop speaking and writing skills if they are not encouraged and stimulated to say what they think is worth saying. And they are not going to learn grammar or vocabulary if they are bored while learning it. Ideally, materials should facilitate learning by helping learners to gain self-esteem, to develop positive attitudes towards the learning experience and to engage themselves both cognitively and emotionally in the learning activities. In other words, learners need to enjoy learning a language if they are ever going to be able to use it successfully.

Multidimensional Learning

In my view, probably the most important point made in Part D is that materials should ensure that language learning is a multidimensional experience. This is a point made explicitly and forcibly by Hitomi Masuhara in Chapter 20 and made implicitly by most of the other authors in Part D. Learners are much more likely to achieve long-term term learning if they learn linguistically and non-linguistically, if they learn visually, aurally, tactilely and kinaesthetically, if they learn consciously and subconsciously, if they learn cognitively and affectively and if they facilitate multidimensional mental representation of the language they present rather than just linguistic processing. More and more research shows the value of rich, varied and multifaceted experiences of language in use. And yet more and more coursebook materials are focusing more and more narrowly on the encoding and decoding of language rather than opening up rich opportunities for experience, engagement and effect.

References

Tomlinson, B. (1994) 'Pragmatic awareness activities'. *Language Awareness*, **3** and **4**, 119–29.

Tomlinson, B. (2001) 'Beginning to read forever'. *Reading in a Foreign Language*, **13** (1), 523–38.

PART E

Training in Materials Development

Materials Development Courses

Brian Tomlinson

Introduction

Before the 1990s, materials development was given little prominence on teacher-training or teacher education courses and there were very few specialist courses training people to develop materials. On initial teacher-training courses it was assumed that the trainees did not have enough experience or expertise to write materials for themselves, on in-service courses materials were often a given which teachers were trained to exploit and on teacher education courses materials development was often considered insufficiently theoretical to deserve its own place on what were often linguistics courses left to the participants to apply. For example, neither my PGCE in ESL course at the Institute of Education, University of London, nor my MA in ESL course at the University of Bangor included components on materials development. Materials development was a practical procedure which was left to specialists to pursue.

Materials development 'was treated as a sub-section of methodology, in which materials were usually introduced as examples of methods in action rather than as a means to explore the principles and procedures of their development' (Tomlinson, 2001a: 66). There were some postgraduate courses which included components called 'Methods and Materials' and some methodology books which included examples of materials in each section or separately at the end of the book (e.g., Dubin and Olshtain, 1986; Richards and Rodgers, 1986; Stevick, 1986, 1989; Nunan, 1988; Richards, 1990). There were also some books and articles which focused on materials evaluation (e.g., Candlin and Breen, 1979; Williams, 1983; Cunningsworth, 1984; Sheldon, 1987, 1988). However, there were very few books or articles published on the principles or the process of materials development and even fewer on its procedures. And without books and articles how could you have courses?

In the 1990s, attitudes began to change. It was realized that not only is materials development an important skill needed by all teachers but also that by engaging in materials development teachers can help themselves both 'to understand and apply theories of language learning' and 'to achieve personal and professional development' (Tomlinson, 2001a: 67). In order to cater for the wants and needs of their particular learners, teachers need to be able to evaluate, select, adapt and supplement materials, and to do this effectively they need to be helped to develop the awareness and skills required for successful materials development. In the process of developing awareness and skills, teachers can also develop the ability to theorize their practice (Schon, 1987), to question their procedures, to check their hypotheses and to find answers to their questions about the processes of language learning and teaching. In response to this realization of the value and power of materials development, a number of books and articles began to appear which focused on the principles and procedures of materials development (e.g., McDonough and Shaw, 1993; Hidalgo *et al.*, 1995; Byrd, 1995; Tomlinson, 1998; Richards, 2001), a number of associations began publishing materials development newsletters (e.g., TESOL, JALT) and in 1993 I founded an association (MATSDA) which organizes materials development conferences and workshops and publishes a journal called *Folio*. At the same time, teacher-training, teacher education and teacher development courses began to include materials development components, teacher-training institutions began to offer short courses in materials development for teachers and institutions and ministries began to organize materials development workshops for their teachers. For example, in the last ten years I have taught MA Materials Development modules at the University of Essex, at Temple University, Tokyo, and at the National University of Singapore, I have run an MA in L2 Materials Development at the University of Luton and I have developed an MA in Materials Development for Language Teaching at Leeds Metropolitan University. I have also taught a materials development component on an RSA/UCLES CELTA course at Language Resources in Kobe, I have run materials development workshops for ministries of education in Botswana, Malaysia, Mauritius, the Seychelles and Vietnam, I have run materials development short courses for teachers at NILE (the Norwich Institute for Language Education) and I have developed a materials development course for teachers at Leeds Metropolitan University. Yet before the 1990s I had rarely worked on a materials development course at all.

The Objectives of Materials Development Courses

In this section I will give my own views as to what the potential objectives of materials development courses should be. Some of my objectives are global and would be aimed at in any course I was involved in. Others are context dependent and would be selected only when they match the local circumstances of the course. In addition, there are obviously other local objectives not included in my lists which would be context unique (e.g., preparing teachers for a new communicative examination for primary school leavers in Vanuatu).

Theoretical

- To provide a concrete experience as a basis for reflective observation and conceptualization (Tomlinson and Masuhara, 2000)
- To raise, investigate and answer questions related to language use
- To raise, investigate and answer questions related to language acquisition
- To raise, investigate and answer questions related to language teaching pedagogy

- To provide opportunities for action research related to language learning and teaching
- To help the participants to become more aware of the needs and wants of the users of language learning materials
- To help the participants to articulate and develop their own tacit theory of language learning and teaching

These are all important objectives of any applied linguistics course and I have found that they are more effectively achieved on a coherent, hands-on materials development course than on a conventional applied linguistics course with its separate components unconnected to any specific practical goal. Wanting to produce effective materials is a powerful incentive to develop knowledge and awareness of language and learning theories which could help the materials developer to produce quality materials.

Developmental

To help the participants to develop greater:

- awareness of the objectives, principles and procedures of language teaching
- awareness of the objectives, principles and procedures of materials development
- awareness of the principled options available to teachers
- awareness of the principled options available to materials developers
- skills as evaluators, adapters, editors and producers of language materials
- sensitivity to the needs and wants of learners and teachers
- ability as language teachers
- confidence and independence as materials developers and teachers
- ability to work in teams and to take initiative
- self-esteem

Obviously the degree of development will depend on such variables as motivation, course duration, course intensity, course follow-up and trainer expertise, but I have found that all the objectives above are achievable on both short courses and one-year MAs, and even on one-day workshops. Perhaps the most effective courses in my experience in achieving these objectives were the in–on service courses which were run in all 27 provinces of Indonesia as part of the PKG English Programme (Tomlinson, 1990). These courses introduced communicative methodology to secondary school teachers by helping them to develop materials during the two in-service phases of the courses, which were then trialled during the two on-service phases of the course. And the trainers were teachers who had developed their own awareness, expertise, confidence and self-esteem at workshops which focused on materials development.

Practical

- To help the participants to develop principled frameworks which will help them to evaluate, adapt and produce materials outside and after the course
- To help the participants to develop a set of principled and localized materials which they can use with their classes
- To help the participants to develop a set of principled and localized materials which can act as models to stimulate and inform subsequent materials development by themselves and their colleagues
- To produce a coherent collection of principled materials which can be used as the basis of a course in a particular institution or region

Although these practical objectives are very important, it is vital that they are not viewed as more important than the theoretical and developmental objectives above. It is too easy to say that a course has failed if the quality of the materials produced during a course is not very high. It is possible that the participants have been stimulated and encouraged and that they will go on to produce high-quality materials after the course. It is also possible that, although the quality of the materials produced is not yet very high, the participants have developed knowledge, awareness, skills and confidence which will help them to become better teachers and teacher trainers. This is what happened on a course I ran once which was monitored by academic experts from teacher-training institutions. The participants thought that the course had been very successful because they had developed a lot of awareness, skills and confidence in a very short time. The academic experts thought the course had been a failure because not all the materials were of a high enough quality for immediate use in the classroom. Guess what I thought.

The Procedures of Materials Development Courses

Study

It is important to read what has been written about materials development, but materials development, either as a practical undertaking or as an academic field, cannot just be read about. There is no received store of wisdom about materials development and certainly no magic procedure which you can read about and then immediately apply in order to produce effective materials. In my experience, the real benefits on materials development courses come not from the greater knowledge gained from study but from the greater awareness and skill which comes from monitored experience of the process of developing materials. However, study does have its place. And that place, in my view, is after experience and reflection and not before it. In that sequence, the study can help to develop the awareness already gained and can contribute to a process of broadening and extending. If the study comes first it can impose an approach which subsequent experience can frustrate and it can determine a process of narrowing and restriction. That is why on my materials development courses I give post-course reading lists but no pre-course reading. Often, though, I also recommend whilst-course reading which might help participants to answer questions they have raised during experiential phases of the course.

Demonstration

I have found that the most valuable way to start any materials development course is to demonstrate materials which are innovative, radical, different and potentially engaging in principled ways. The main objective is not to provide models for emulation but to stimulate curiosity, provide the participants with potentially engaging experience as 'learners' and to provide concrete illustrations of novel principles and procedures for the participants to reflect on and discuss. I have found that this is a non-threatening way to begin a course (the 'trainer' is being evaluated rather than the participants) and that it can be a very effective way of opening up discussion of theories of language learning and of principles of language teaching. It only succeeds if the trainer believes in the approaches demonstrated and if he/she is prepared and able to justify them without imposing them on others.

I have found the following to be the most effective way of starting a course with demonstrations:

1. Outline and explain the process to the participants.
2. Ask the participants to play the role of learners.
3. Teach an extensive part of a unit of materials to the 'learners'.
4. Ask the 'learners' to become course participants again and to recreate the lesson in their heads.
5. Ask the participants in groups to list the main stages of the lesson.
6. Ask the groups to specify the objectives of each stage and to talk about the learning principles which they think underlie it.
7. Hold a plenary discussion in which the groups share their views of the objectives and principles of each stage.
8. Ask each group to profile a group of learners at the language level catered for in the demonstration lesson.
9. Ask each group to evaluate the materials by predicting the effectiveness of each stage for their profiled group of learners.
10. Hold a plenary discussion in which the groups share their evaluations and you contribute any intention or principle of yours which has not been noticed by the groups.

This procedure is repeated with a number of other materials demonstrations (depending on the length of the course) in which the innovative materials demonstrated are different from each other but nevertheless share certain objectives, principles and procedures. The first demonstration usually takes a long time, but subsequent demonstrations usually get shorter as the participants get used to the analysis and evaluation procedures.

Discussion of Statements

The informal and, to some extent, ad hoc reflection and discussion involved in the demonstration phase of the course can be formalized by asking the participants in groups to respond to a list of provocative statements organized into categories. For each statement they are asked to say why they agree or disagree with it, and for any statement they disagree with they are asked to rewrite it so that they agree with it. This is done initially as a group activity and then as a plenary discussion with the main objective not being to reach agreement but to explore the issues. Each participant is then asked to respond individually in writing to each statement and to keep the responses until the end of the course when the participants in groups will discuss any changes of opinion which have occurred.

An example of a statement under the heading 'Teaching Points' would be, 'Learners should never be asked to understand structures which have not yet been taught.' An example of a statement under the heading 'Texts' would be, 'Low-level learners should only be given short texts to read and to listen to.' And an example of a statement under the heading 'Activities' would be, 'Low-level learners should be invited to attempt tasks which are challenging but achievable, and which help them to develop high-level skills.'

Evaluation

I have found it is important to help participants to develop an ability to evaluate other people's published materials in a systematic and principled way before asking them to produce materials of their own. This can not only help them to develop criteria for evaluation which can eventually serve as criteria for developing their own materials; it can also help them to develop confidence as they realize that published materials are not perfect and they become more aware of the qualities required for materials to be effective facilitators of learning.

In this phase of the course, I get the participants to work out the objectives and procedures of pre, whilst and post-use evaluation and to develop, trial and refine banks of evaluation criteria. These sets then form the basis for the development of context specific sets of criteria which are used in Problem-Based Learning activities to evaluate materials in relation to user profiles (Wilkerson and Gijselaers, 1996; Tomlinson and Masuhara, 2000). In my experience, teachers, often used to making quick, impressionistic judgements about materials, find the rigorous process of developing banks and sets of tight evaluation criteria very demanding. But ultimately they find it very rewarding, in that it helps them to evaluate materials more systematically, it empowers them with a greater awareness of the prerequisites for effective materials and it helps them to develop their theories of language learning.

For a full discussion of the objectives and procedures of evaluation, see Chapters 1 and 2 in this volume.

Adaptation

In almost every lesson teachers adapt the materials they are using in order to achieve a closer match with the needs and wants of their learners. Often their adaptations are spontaneous and intuitive and, although they often improve the materials being used, they can create unanticipated problems for the teacher and the learners. On materials development courses I usually spend time helping the participants to develop procedures for systematic adaptation of materials. This initially involves them in following a formal process of:

- profiling a class
- analysing a set of materials
- evaluating the materials
- subtracting sections of the materials
- reducing sections of the materials
- replacing sections of the materials
- expanding sections of the materials
- modifying sections of the materials
- adding sections of materials

After following this process rigorously and formally a couple of times, I find the participants are usually able to make use of that experience to carry out fast adaptations informally and intuitively. I also find that it helps them to develop their own skills in producing effective materials as a preparation for phases of the course when they will be asked to produce complete sets of original materials.

For a full discussion of the principles and procedures of adaptation, see Chapter 3 in this volume.

Critical Modelling

One of the most common procedures on materials development courses (especially those for pre-service teacher trainees) is modelling of exemplar materials. The participants, for example, are provided with a model unit of materials which they then use as a template for producing a similar unit themselves with a different teaching point. My experience of observing this procedure on courses is that it can provide useful practice in materials writing (especially of some of the basic skills, such as writing instructions and questions) but it often leads to unthinking acceptance of a right way of presenting instructional materials. Later on, when the participants are in their classrooms, the restrictive nature of this approach can become evident to frustrated teachers who now realize the limitations of the model but do not have the confidence to change it. This is particularly true of such conventional approaches as PPP (presentation–practice–

production) and of such common techniques as dialogue practice, listen and repeat, substitution drills and role-plays.

Instead of asking participants to imitate a model uncritically, I prefer to present to them a variety of exemplars of material types and frameworks and to help them to evaluate and modify the exemplars before making use of them to develop their own materials. This way the participants develop a critical understanding of the objectives and principles of a variety of approaches and they are able to develop their own flexible models and repertoires before going into (or back to) the classroom. It also means that they become sensitive to the need for variability and can modify their models in response to the requirements of different contexts of learning.

For a full discussion of flexible frameworks for materials development, see Chapter 7 in this volume.

Experience

Ultimately what really counts on a materials development course is the quality of the experience provided of developing materials. The skills required of an effective materials developer cannot be gained from instruction; they can only be developed gradually as a result of quality, hands-on experience. In my experience, that means the skills can only be developed if the experience provided:

- is monitored sensitively and supportively by tutors who have earned credibility as materials developers themselves;
- provides opportunities for reflection and modification;
- is shared with other participants who can pool resources so as to gain from each other;
- encourages experimentation and risk taking while providing safety and security too (see Chapter 28 in this volume for a discussion of how simulations can achieve this effect);
- is staged and sequenced so that awareness and skills gained are immediately made use of to facilitate the gaining of further awareness and skills;
- respects the participants as individuals who bring a lot of relevant knowledge, awareness and skills to the process;
- is stimulating and enjoyable for the participants.

I have found that the most effective way of providing experience in materials development is to move the participants forward gradually through a series of tasks which focus attention and monitoring on discrete skills of materials development while involving them in the production of sections of materials.

An example of such a progression would be:

1. Deciding on a voice (i.e., deciding, for example, whether to talk to the learners in a formal, authoritative voice or an informal, chatty voice)
2. Writing instructions

3. Writing questions
4. Giving explanations
5. Giving examples
6. Selecting texts
7. Writing texts
8. Exploiting tests
9. Using illustrations
10. Layout and design
11. Writing teachers' notes
12. Writing units of materials

Ideally, if time allows, the participants would also be provided with quality experience in producing different types of learning materials, such as:

- integrated skills materials
- listening skills materials
- reading skills materials
- writing skills materials
- speaking skills materials
- extensive reading and listening materials
- grammar materials
- vocabulary materials
- prounciation materials
- communication materials
- coursebook materials
- self-access learning materials
- video materials
- computer-assisted learning materials
- multimedia materials

I have found that it is very important to encourage the participants to work from principled criteria and to progress through a series of drafts which are self-monitored, peer-monitored and tutor-monitored before a 'final' version is produced. It is equally important that this 'final' version is then valued by being, for example, demonstrated to the other participants, made available to the other participants and kept by the producers and the course leader in a quality production.

Reflection

Reflection is the key to development, and participants on my courses/workshops are encouraged to reflect on their views, theories and materials during all phases of the course, outside the course and after the course. For example, they are asked to think about and to articulate their beliefs about language learning and the role that materials should play in it at the beginning of the course when responding to demonstrations on statements given to them, at various stages of the course when they are evaluating, adapting or producing materials, and at the end of the course when they are evaluating their own and other participants' materials. They are also asked each night to reflect on what they have 'learned' during the day about themselves and about materials development (either informally or through keeping journals or diaries). And at the end of the course they are encouraged to keep the reflection process active and informed through reading, through conference attendance, through establishing informal discussion groups and through continuing the process of daily or weekly reflection on their development and use of materials.

Good materials developers are thinking developers who have confidence in their ability and in their materials but who are prepared to rethink and revise their principles and beliefs in response to further stimulus or information. Ideally, the course tutors should fit this definition and it should be the main aim of the course to help the participants to become such materials developers themselves.

Presentation

I have found that four types of participant presentation can be extremely useful in helping the participants to reflect critically on their materials, to elicit useful suggestions for further improvement and to develop confidence.

The first type is informal presentation to another group during the drafting stage of materials production. This can be very useful if the monitoring group is encouraged to ask the presenting group to justify its procedures by reference to its objectives and principles and if the monitoring group can then come up with suggestions for further development of the materials. This procedure works best if it is reciprocal and both groups know they can learn from each other.

Another useful type is the oral presentation to fellow course/workshop participants of the final piece of materials produced on the course/workshop. I now do this on every course/workshop, regardless of its length, and find that it can provide a very positive conclusion as the participants realize how much development has taken place during the course and look forward to making further development after the course (often with the help of informal coffee groups or e-mail groups set up by the participants).

A third type of presentation is conference presentation. This I include on longer courses as part of the programme, but I also encourage and facilitate it for participants on shorter courses. On the MA in L2 Materials Development at the University of Luton, for example, the participants were required to do a joint presentation at an internal conference for teachers and BA students, and an individual presentation at a British Universities Research Student Conference which we organized at the University of Luton. We ran a mini-course in Making Oral Presentations for the participants and we held tutorials to discuss the materials and the participants' plans for presenting them. Many of the participants were apprehensive; but the quality of the materials and the presentations was high, and in the post-course feedback many participants said it was the most useful part of the course. Participants on short courses and workshops I have run throughout the world have also gained expertise and confidence from being encouraged to give presentations at MATSDA (the Materials Development Association) conferences which I organize and at conferences in their local areas.

A fourth type of presentation is article writing. Many of the tasks and assignments on my courses involve writing an article or review for a specific refereed journal. The participants have to find out what the requirements of the journal are and to write their article in such a way that it has a good chance of selection for publication. Detailed feedback is given when the tasks/assignments are returned and participants are encouraged actually to submit revised versions of their articles to the journal. Obviously not every participant does submit and not every submitter is accepted But those who do submit usually get useful feedback from reviewers, and imagine the boost in self-esteem, which, for example, an Indonesian participant on a course at the National University of Singapore received when he had articles accepted by *ELT Journal* and the *RELC Journal*. And imagine the pride I enjoy when I think that seven of the contributors to this book have been students on materials development courses which I have run.

Research

The conventional image of materials development courses is of very practical courses on which the participants are taught to produce materials. In my experience, you cannot develop the ability to become an effective materials developer without thinking about what you are doing. And you cannot think effectively without finding experience, theories and information to stimulate and inform your thinking. One way of doing this is to do applied and action research projects before, during and after a course. Obviously, on a very short course these projects will be mini-projects with very small samples and very limited objectives. But on a long course, such as a Postgraduate Certificate of Education or an MA, extensive research projects can be undertaken which can be of great value to both the participant and their peers. For example, on the MA in L2 Materials Development at the University of Luton, the participants had to conduct three-month research projects which they reported on at a conference, wrote an article on for a journal and applied to their production of a complete course of materials plus a theoretical rationale. And now at Leeds Metropolitan University I am supervising six materials-related PhDs conducted by people who have been participants on materials development courses I have run.

Possible areas for materials development research projects include:

* the materials needs and wants of learners
* the materials needs and wants of teachers (Masuhara, 1998)
* the relative effects of different types of author voice (Beck, *et al.*, 1995)

- the effects on durable learning by adding affect to coursebook materials
- the relative effects of different ways of attempting to achieve the same learning objectives
- ways of producing principled coursebooks which are able to create a market demand and satisfy the requirements of learners, teachers and administrators
- ways of catering for different preferred learning styles in the same unit of materials
- the relative effect of different ways of producing materials (e.g., individual author vs. pair of authors vs. small group of authors vs. large group of authors)
- ways of ensuring systematic and rigorous evaluation of materials
- finding out what teachers actually do with materials in the classroom
- finding out what the particular value is of different types of materials (print vs. audio vs. video vs. multimedia)
- ways of facilitating teacher development through using a textbook
- ways of facilitating teacher development through materials development

Examples of Materials Development Courses

There are many different types of materials development courses, each with its own objectives and constraints. For example, there are:

- short stimulus courses for teachers aiming to develop the awareness, skills and motivation of the participants
- courses for institutions and ministries training teachers to become materials developers for a particular project
- professional training courses aiming to develop the awareness and skills of curriculum developers
- pre-service teacher-training courses with a component on materials development
- in-service teacher development courses with a component on materials development
- teacher education/development courses focused on (or with a component on) materials development

I have been involved in developing all of the above types of courses in the last ten years. What I do for each course is to consider the participant profile, consider the sponsor/participant requirements, consider the constraints (of time, resources, etc.), specify objectives and then apply the appropriate stages of the flexible framework outlined in Table 27.1.

Table 27.1 A flexible framework for materials development courses

Stage	Substages	Objectives
1. *Demonstrations*	i. Demonstration of innovative materials ii. Analysis of material stages iii. Analysis of objectives and principles iv. Evaluation of procedures	i. Impact ii. Exposure to novel approaches iii. Stimulus to think about and discuss issues iv. Articulation and development of individual theories of language learning
2. *Discussion of Provocative Statements*	i. Individual reflection ii. Group discussion iii. Plenary discussion iv. Individual decisions	i. Stimulus to think about and discuss issues ii. Articulation and development of individual theories of language learning iii. Formalization of discussions in 1 and 2
3. *Evaluation of Materials*	i. Development of evaluation criteria ii. Presentation and monitoring of evaluation criteria iii. Application of criteria to the evaluation of sets of materials iv. Revision of criteria	i. Refinement of individual theories of language learning ii. Develop awareness of the objectives, principles and procedures of materials development iii. Develop banks of criteria for future use and development
4. *Adaptation of Materials*	i. Profile of target learners ii. Evaluation of materials in relation to learner profile iii. Adaptation of materials to match wants and needs of learners	i. Develop awareness of the objectives, principles and procedures of materials development ii. Develop awareness of the principles and procedures of matching materials to needs and wants iii. Develop materials development skills

5. *Editing of Materials*	i. Commissioning materials ii. Evaluating commissioned materials iii. Giving written feedback iv. Giving face-to-face feedback	i. Develop awareness and skills of making principled compromise ii. Develop ability to give sensitive and constructive feedback
6. *Materials Writing Practice A*	i. Evaluation of examples of a particular aspect of materials development (e.g., writing instructions) ii. Practice in the particular aspect	i. Develop materials development awareness and skills ii. Develop confidence iii. Develop criteria for use as production criteria
7. *Materials Writing Practice B*	i. Evaluation of examples of a particular type of materials development (e.g., listening materials) ii. Practice in producing the particular type of materials	i. Develop materials development awareness and skills ii. Develop confidence iii. Develop criteria for use as production criteria
8. *Materials Production A*	i. Production of a unit of materials for a specified context of learning ii. Self, peer and tutor-monitoring iii. Revision of materials	i. Develop materials development awareness and skills ii. Develop confidence
9. *Reading and Discussion**	i. Critical reading of articles and books of relevance to materials development ii. Discussion and evaluation of the reading	i. Develop awareness of the objectives, principles and procedures of materials development ii. Articulation and development of individual theories of language learning iii. Find answers to some of the problems encountered during materials development simulations in 8 above

10. *Research***	i. Development of a materials development research project ii. Conducting the research iii. Presenting the findings iv. Applying the findings	i. Articulation and development of individual theories of language learning ii. Find answers to some of the problems encountered during materials development simulations in 8 above iii. Develop research and presentation skills
11. *Presentations*	Presentations relating to the materials produced and/or the research conducted: i. To other groups of participants ii. To internal conferences iii. To external conferences iv. As articles to journals v. As chapters to publishers vi. As book proposals to publishers	i. Clarify thinking ii. Refine materials iii. Develop presentation skills iv. Develop confidence
12. *Discussion of Statements*	i. Group discussion of the same statements as in 2 above ii. Group discussion of further provocative statements iii. Individual decisions	i. Stimulus to think about and discuss issues ii. Articulation and development of individual theories of language learning iii. Revision of the course
13. *Materials Production B*	i. Development of a theoretical rationale for the production of a context-specific course of materials ii. Production of a context-specific course of materials	i. Further develop materials development awareness and skills ii. Further develop confidence iii. Provide evidence of the validity of individual theories and beliefs and the ability to apply them to the production of principled learning materials.

Note:

* Of course, there will also be reading assignments given at the end of each stage to reinforce and develop theories and beliefs.

** Ideally the research project is ongoing and overlaps with other stages rather than being a separate stage in a linear sequence of stages.

I have recently used this framework to help me to develop an eight-day workshop for teachers involved in producing new textbooks at Bilkent University in Turkey, a two-week Materials Development Course for Teachers at Leeds Metropolitan University and a one-year MA in Materials Development for Language Teaching at Leeds Metropolitan University. The workshop included 1, 2, 3, 6, 7, 8 and 11 and concentrated very much on actually producing draft materials for the textbook. The short course for teachers included 1, 2, 3, 4, 6, 7, 8 and 11, and focused on providing monitored practice of producing different types of materials. The MA includes all the stages in the framework as well as modules on Language Acquisition, Language Systems and Language Awareness, and Language Teaching Methodology. The MA is designed to be a coherent preparation for production of a complete course of materials (plus a theoretical rationale) which is presented for examination in lieu of a dissertation and which the participants are encouraged to submit to publishers as a publishing proposal.

Conclusion

After a very busy ten years conducting materials development courses, I am convinced that focusing on materials development is the most effective way of running a course in applied linguistics, as theory can be made relevant and meaningful by reference to practical procedures which are at the heart of the teaching and learning process. It is also the most effective way of helping language education professionals to articulate and develop their own theories of language learning and to develop the skills which they need to apply these theories to practice. I am also convinced that the most effective way to run a materials development course (regardless of its specific objectives) is to provide the participants with concrete experience as a basis for reflective observation and conceptualization.

References

Beck, I. L., McKeown, M. G. and Worthy, J. (1995) 'Giving a text voice can improve students' understanding'. *Research Reading Quarterly*, **30** (2).

Byrd, P. (1995) *Material Writer's Guide*. New York: Heinle and Heinle.

Candlin, C. N. and Breen, M. P. (1979) *Practical Papers in English Language Education, Vol. 2: Evaluating and Designing Language Teaching Materials*. Lancaster: Institute for English Language Education, University of Lancaster.

Cunningsworth, A. (1984) *Evaluating and Selecting EFL Teaching Material*. London: Heinemann.

Dubin, F. and Olshtain, E. (1986) *Course Design.* New York: Cambridge University Press.

Hidalgo, A. C., Hall, D. and Jacobs, G. M. (eds) (1995) *Getting Started: Materials Writers on Materials Writings.* Singapore: RELC.

McDonough, J. and Shaw, C. (1993) *Materials and Methods in ELT: A Teacher's Guide.* London: Blackwell.

Masuhara, H. (1998) 'Factors influencing the reading difficulties of advanced learners of English as a foreign language when reading authentic texts'. Unpublished PhD thesis, University of Luton.

Nunan, D. (1988) *The Learner-Centred Curriculum.* Cambridge: Cambridge University Press.

Richards, J. C. (1990) *The Language Teaching Matrix.* Cambridge: Cambridge University Press.

Richards, J. (2001) *Curriculum Development in Language Education.* Cambridge: Cambridge University Press.

Richards, J. C. and Rodgers, T. (1986) *Approaches and Methods in Language Teaching.* Cambridge: Cambridge University Press.

Schon, D. (1987) *Educating the Reflective Practitioner.* San Francisco: Jossey-Bass.

Sheldon, L. E. (1987) *ELT Textbooks and Materials: Problems in Evaluation and Development.* ELT Documents 126. London: Modern English Publications/The British Council.

Sheldon, L. E. (1988) 'Evaluating ELT textbooks and materials'. *ELT Journal,* **42** (4), 237–46.

Stevick, E. (1986) *Images and Options in the Language Classroom.* Cambridge: Cambridge University Press.

Stevick, E. (1989) *Success with Foreign Languages.* London: Prentice Hall.

Tomlinson, B. (1990) 'Managing change in Indonesian high schools'. *ELT Journal,* **44** (1).

Tomlinson, B. (ed.) (1998) *Materials Development in Language Teaching.* Cambridge: Cambridge University Press.

Tomlinson, B. (2001a) 'Materials development', in R. Carter and D. Nunan *Teaching English to Speakers of Other Languages.* Cambridge: Cambridge University Press.

Tomlinson, B. (2001b) 'Teaching materials evaluation'. *The Information.* BIELT.

Tomlinson, B. and Masuhara, H. (2000) 'Using simulations on materials development courses'. *Simulation and Gaming: An Interdisciplinary Journal of Theory, Practice and Research,* **31** (2), 152–68.

Wilkerson, L. and Gijselaers, W. H. (1996) *Bringing Problem-Based Learning to Higher Education: Theory and Practice.* San Francisco: Jossey-Bass.

Williams, D. (1983) 'Developing criteria for textbooks evaluation'. *ELT Journal,* **37** (3), 251–5.

Simulations in Materials Development

Brian Tomlinson and Hitomi Masuhara

Introduction

Recently, we have been invited to run short materials development courses for teachers of English in Botswana, in Vietnam and at the Norwich Institute for Language Education (NILE), as well as for curriculum developers on national textbook projects in Mauritius and the Seychelles. We also worked together on the MA in L2 Materials Development course at the University of Luton for three years. On these courses we aimed to help the participants to develop both an understanding of the principles of evaluating, adapting and developing teaching materials and also the skills required to apply these principles to the development of effective materials. We did so by using an experiential approach in which learning involves transactions between the person and the environment (Kolb, 1984: 34) and a process 'whereby knowledge is created through the transformation of experience' (Kolb, 1984: 38). Some of these tasks were real-life tasks relating to the participants' working environment (e.g., revising a book they had written) but most of them were simulations, such as adapting a unit of a book for a specified class of learners or selecting and adapting a textbook for use in a particular country.

Advantages of Simulations over Real-life Tasks

We found that simulations had many advantages over real-life tasks. We found like Raser (1969: 15–19) that they were more economical, that they aided 'visibility by making certain kinds of phenomena more accessible for observation and measurement' and that they allowed numerous aspects of a system to be varied 'in ways that yield profitable insights into how the system operates'. They also allowed us to free the participants from the constraints which inhibited their thinking in their usual working environment and to put them in situations which they had never previously encountered. Thus we found that, with a group of curriculum developers in Mauritius, the English specialists were restricted by their normal procedures when asked to develop innovative materials for teaching English but that the other subject specialists (e.g., in biology, home economics and physical education) were far more open-minded and experimental when asked to develop such materials. They were doing what they had never done before and this meant that they had to connect previous experience to new information to help them to solve the novel problems which they were encountering.

Placing the participants of our workshops in novel environments also meant that:

- they were stimulated to use their imagination to visualize the situations they were being asked to put themselves in (e.g., an EFL class in Tokyo for adult Japanese learners of English; a meeting of Advisers in an African Ministry of Education);
- they needed to work out the right questions to ask the informants they were provided with (e.g., about the exposure to English typically available to Japanese learners of English);
- they were in a safe environment in which the 'relatively low cost of an error' (Crookall *et al.*, 1987) encouraged risk-taking and creativity;
- they were encouraged to be open-minded and to consider all potentially relevant suggestions (e.g., using methods such as TPR or Suggestopedia that are not typically used in their own teaching environments);
- they were able to develop repertoires of skills that were potentially transferable to a variety of situations that they might subsequently encounter in 'real-life' (e.g., storywriting skills, editing and advising skills, persuasive skills);
- they developed an understanding of the potential value and the design principles of simulations which allowed them to enrich their own language teaching materials with simulations designed by themselves (Crookall, 1991).

Above all we were able to make abstractions 'from a larger system' in such a way that we were able to select 'elements to emphasise and elements to eliminate' (Greenblat, 1981: 22). We were able to build in factors which we knew would be problematic and which would raise questions and issues for discussion later. We were also able to simplify, reduce and control some of the problematic environments so as to facilitate focus. This control over the environment enabled us to inhibit the tendency of previous experience to bias and affect adversely the process of learning (e.g., Rogers, 1969; Laing, 1995) and the tendency for new experiences to reinforce previous beliefs rather than to bring them into question (e.g., Skinner, 1971). As a result, many participants were able to develop original ideas and materials to match the novel environments, which they would later be able to adapt and develop in relation to their own working environments. Many of them also reported developing confidence and self-esteem and being better equipped and prepared to meet unexpected eventualities in their own jobs than they had been at the beginning of the course. This was true, for example, of two curriculum developers on the MA in L2 Materials Development at the University of Luton who reported not only an increase in confidence, self-esteem, awareness and expertise but also a determination to aid the development of their colleagues by introducing similar experiential approaches to materials development training when they returned home to Ethiopia.

Developing Simulations

As a result of our experience in developing simulations for materials development courses we would recommend the following set of procedures as seen in Figure 28.1. Obviously this is an interactive rather than a strictly sequential process and, in our experience, for example, we often found ourselves going back to revise our objectives in relation to a potentially useful procedure we were developing. The direction of the horizontal arrows in Figure 28.1 indicates the monitoring process which is constantly revising the setting of objectives and the consideration of learning and gaming principles.

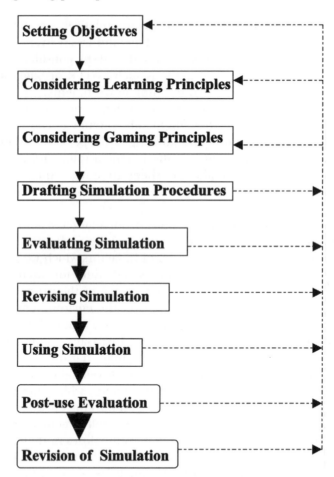

Figure 28.1 Suggested pocedures for developing Simulations

The example (Example 1) below is of a draft simulation which was developed for a group of participants on the MA in L2 Materials Development at the University of Luton. The simulation came very early in their course and was designed to put them in a situation which they had never encountered before in such a way that would help them to develop and use criteria for evaluating materials. The main learning principles behind the simulation were that new awareness and skills can be effectively developed through challenging the learners to collaborate in solving a lifelike and novel problem. The main gaming principles were that the simulation should achieve ecological, psychological and process validity while at the same time achieving the abstraction, reduction and simplification which would enable the learners to benefit from focus and clarity.

Example 1

To Publish or not to Publish?

Imagine that you are a reader for a leading publisher and that you have been sent a proposal for a textbook with a request for you to evaluate it with a view to possible publication.

a. In small groups read the proposal.
b. Establish criteria for evaluating the proposal.
c. Evaluate the proposal against your criteria.
d. Write your reader's report to the commissioning editor who has sent you the proposal.
e. Compare your report with that of another group.
f. Compare your report with the actual report on the materials by a publisher.

After drafting the simulation it became obvious that, if the participants read the proposal before developing their criteria, they would probably allow their initial impressions to dictate the criteria. So a revision was made to the draft which involved the participants reading only the first page of the proposal before starting to develop their criteria. This first page gave them information about the objectives, target audience and content of the textbook but it did not give them any examples of the material.

After doing the simulation with a group of participants we realized that:

• we should have built in a stage in which groups compare and then revise their criteria, a stage in which they revise their criteria after their first experience of applying them and a stage in which they revise their reports after comparing them with another group;
• we should have mentioned that the writer of the proposal would be shown his/her report so that he/she would provide justifications for his/her comments;
• we had omitted a debriefing stage which would have allowed the participants to articulate their thoughts about doing simulations and about what they had learned from doing this particular one;
• we had not indicated that they should make use of the facilitator for feedback and suggestions.

As a result of our post-use evaluation of the simulation we produced a revised version as follows:

To Publish or not to Publish?
Imagine that you are a reader for a leading publisher and that you have been sent a proposal for a textbook with a request for you to evaluate it with a view to possible publication.

- In small groups read the first page of the proposal.
- Establish criteria for evaluating the proposal.
- Read the full proposal and evaluate the proposal against your criteria.
- Revise your criteria.
- Write a draft of your reader's report to the commissioning editor who has sent you the proposal.
- Compare your report with that of another group.
- Revise your report.
- Compare your report with the actual report on the materials by a reader.
- You have just taken part in a simulation. Discuss your views about the value of learning from simulations.
- List what you think you have learned from this simulation.

NB: At any time you can make use of the facilitator for feedback or suggestions.

We developed the suggested procedures above dynamically from our actual experience of developing simulations. Other suggestions for procedures for developing simulations can be found, for example, in Greenblat and Duke (1981), in Herz and Merz (1998) and in Jones (1985, 1995).

Setting of Objectives

Our universal objectives in designing simulations for our materials development courses included:

- To provide experience of selected elements of materials development situations in such a way that the participants could develop new awareness and knowledge, could refine existing skills and could develop new skills.
- To provide opportunities to apply theory to practice and to develop theory from practice, too.
- To help the participants to develop principles, criteria and skills for the evaluation, adaptation and development of teaching materials.
- To help the participants to develop original ideas for new approaches to the development of teaching materials.
- To enhance the self-esteem and confidence of the participants.
- To motivate the participants to become enthusiastic and creative materials developers.

Obviously we also set course specific objectives which took into consideration the interests, needs, abilities and previous experience of the participants and the requirements of the sponsors. Such objectives included 'Improving the ability to write clear instructions', 'Being able to make and to justify decisions for locally appropriate adaptations' and 'Developing language awareness activities for trainee teachers of English'. Examples of very localized, specific objectives would be 'Being able to adapt the ministry textbook so as to cater for learners with kinaesthetic learning style preferences' and 'Being able to develop materials to help local English teachers to make use of other subject textbooks'.

Considering Learning Principles

On our courses we have based our simulations on the following learning principles:

- Learners gain from being mentally active during the learning process and from investing energy and attention in making discoveries for themselves (Tomlinson, 1994). This happened, for example, when a group discovered that a coursebook they had chosen impressionistically for a particular environment was not as suitable as they had thought once they began to apply locally specific evaluation criteria (Tomlinson, 1999).
- Learning from experience is how much of human development occurs (Dewey, 1938; Lewin, 1951; Piaget, 1971; Kolb, 1984). An example of this would be the teachers in Botswana who learned from peer teaching of their materials how complex texts can be made comprehensible through TPR activities.
- Learners need to grasp experience both 'via direct apprehension of immediate concrete experience' and 'through indirect comprehension of symbolic representations of experience' (Kolb, 1984). This was achieved by groups of teachers completing a simulated materials development task in its entirety and then analysing the experience and its products.
- Effective and durable learning involves creating and constantly revising multi-dimensional mental representation of the learning experience (Masuhara, 1998). This can be achieved through visualization and other sensory imaging (Sadoski and Paivio, 1994; Tomlinson, 1996, 1997, 1998d; Arnold, 1998; Masuhara, 1998), through affective involvement (Masuhara, 1998; Schumann, 1998; Tomlinson, 1998d), through the use of inner speech (Sokolov, 1972; Tomlinson, 2000, 2001) and through analytical discussions of problems and issues with fellow participants. It can also be achieved by using such methodologies as Neuro-Linguistic Programming (see, for example, Molden, 1996) and Suggestopedia (see, for example, Lozanov, 1978). To achieve multi-dimensional representation in the workshops we designed the simulations so that, for example, the participants would be given time initially to visualize and to talk in their minds about the situation and the task, so that they would be challenged and involved by the tasks in a relaxed and enjoyable environment,

so that they would work part of the time individually and so that they would spend a lot of the time in group discussion, planning and reflection.

- Collaborative learning not only facilitates the pooling of resources but also stimulates creative and critical thinking and prepares learners for the real-life experience of working and learning together in a team. This was frequently evidenced by participants (such as a young Japanese woman on the MA course at the University of Luton who had been quietly passive in plenary sessions but who suddenly came to life during group simulation tasks).

- Task-based learning not only facilitates learning by doing but it also provides diagnostic evidence of what the participants need to learn and creates for them a readiness to learn it (Tomlinson, 1994, 1998c; Willis, 1997). For example, asking participants to evaluate coursebooks in order to choose one for a specified course often revealed to the participants that they were using impressionistic judgements rather than principled criteria and they were then ready to learn how to develop criteria for evaluation (Tomlinson, 1999).

- Different participants have different preferred learning styles (Kolb, 1984; Kolb *et al.* 1986; Oxford, 1990; Reid, 1997). In any learning experience both analytical and experiential activities need to be provided and visual, auditory and kinaesthetic styles have to be catered for so as to help learners not only to benefit from their preferred style but also to develop their ability to learn through other styles. Thus we designed our simulations so that they involved listening, reading, analysing, acting, problem-solving, creating, visualizing, using inner speech, unplanned and planned speaking, drawing, cutting and pasting and writing.

- It is important not only to help participants to gain new knowledge and develop particular skills but also to help them to develop their multiple intelligences so that they will able to combine them successfully when undertaking future 'real-world' tasks (Gardner, 1993; Christison, 1998). Materials development simulations should therefore help to develop bodily-kinaesthetic, intrapersonal, interpersonal, linguistic, logical-mathematic and spatial intelligences. This we tried to achieve by making sure the participants had to think for themselves, had to interact with others in their group, had to visit other groups, had to do physical things such as making aids and had to design, lay out and illustrate their materials as well as write them.

- Autonomous learning is the main goal of teaching but autonomous learning does not mean learning in isolation. Rather it involves the ability to make independent decisions about what and how to learn and then to make use of all available resources (including peers and teachers). Thus we made sure that self-monitoring, peer monitoring and tutor monitoring were built into the design but that final decisions were made by the participants themselves.

- Most learners learn best when they are stimulated but relaxed, challenged but not threatened and confident but not complacent (Tomlinson, 1998b: 5–22). Such a state plus curiosity and intrinsic motivation can create a positive 'tension-to-learn' (Burns and Gentry, 1998). We tried to achieve such an environment by making sure that a positive, supportive atmosphere was established through pre-simulation activities, by making sure that the 'workrooms' we used were as attractive and comfortable as possible (for example, by getting the participants to arrange the furniture themselves), by setting achievable challenges and by building in off-task relaxation activities. In Botswana we were helped by the teachers bursting into song for five minutes whenever they were beginning to feel a negative tension.

Considering Gaming Principles

A good simulation has psychological reality, structural validity, process validity and predictive validity (Raser, 1969). In other words, in a good simulation the participants view the simulation as realistic because the structure, the processes and the results match those in real-life equivalents. In order to design such a valid simulation we need to achieve consistency and coherence in our specification of the environment. We also need to provide enough descriptive detail and to leave enough inferential gaps to help the participants to achieve constructive visualization of the environment. Above all, we need to inject sufficient vitality into the environment to encourage the participants to suspend disbelief and to achieve engagement with it. It is then important that the reality of the simulation is not broken by the facilitator interrupting the activities or by the participants coming out of role. One way of achieving this is for the facilitator to play and stay within a role throughout the simulation.

As well as simulating reality, we need to help the participants to focus in ways not always possible in real-life situations. To do this we should base the process on the principles of reduction, abstraction and symbolization (Peters *et al.*, 1998: 27). In other words, we should select salient elements from the reference system to focus on, we should simplify these elements and we should mould these elements into 'a new symbolic structure'.

An effective learning simulation contains, in a simplified environment, the learning elements needed to acquire the knowledge and skills required to gain insights into a complex reference system (Peters *et al.*, 1998). In designing learning simulations we need to bear in mind that such simulations should 'provide dynamic problem situations for learners' in such a way that they 'reinforce their theoretical understanding of the interactions in the simulated environment through direct feedback from their actions' (Yeo and Tan, 1999). This can be achieved by building into the design encouragement for the participants to develop and articulate principles in order to guide and evaluate their actions during the simulation. In addition, ongoing and post-simulation feedback opportunities need to be built into the design of simulations. This feedback should include self-feedback, feedback from other participants and feedback from the facilitator(s). In addition to feedback on the performance of the participants, there can be a debriefing stage in which the participants report their reactions to the simulation and discuss what they have learned as a result of doing it. The 'purpose is to examine and analyse the subjective knowledge that has been created during the experience' (Lederman, 1992: 154) and it is in the debriefing stage that 'the meaning of the enactment is clarified; the lessons to be learnt are underlined; and the connections are made to what the students already know and what they need for the future' (Van Ments, 1983: 127). This debriefing stage needs to be separated from the simulation because, 'Role-playing and analysis are incompatible behaviours. One requires total immersion in the problem, the other a deliberate stepping back' (Van Ments, 1983: 130).

Drafting Simulation Procedures

In order to draft simulation procedures, we would recommend the following flexible frameworks which have been found from a process of principled trial and error to facilitate the achievement of the main objectives. On our courses we followed the most situationally appropriate of the types of framework outlined below.

Flexible Framework 1 – Simple Simulations

This type of simulation is simple in the sense that there is a single main task which is a simplification of similar tasks typically undertaken in the reference system.

For simulations which only lasted for one session the following Framework 1 procedure was usually followed or modified:

1. Setting of the environment (concisely on paper and in detail orally by the facilitator).
2. Specification of the problem or task (concisely on paper and in detail orally by the facilitator).
3. Discussion of the task by the participants in groups (and with the participation of the facilitator(s) when invited).
4. Carrying out of the task(s) by the groups (and sometimes by the facilitator(s) too).
5. Comparison of the products with those of other groups and with equivalent products from 'real life'.
6. Group and plenary feedback on the process and the products led by the facilitator(s).
7. Debriefing in which the participants discuss their reactions to the simulation and try to articulate what they have learned from it.

Example 2 below is an example of a Type 1 simulation which was completed during a four-hour workshop session.

Example 2
You are going to teach a multilingual, mixed ability class of young adults in a language school in London. The class is labelled 'Intermediate' but you have been warned by the Principal that the actual level ranges from lower intermediate to upper intermediate. You have been employed because the Intermediate class teacher has suddenly left to take up a post in Taiwan. You have

not yet met the class but you will be teaching them three nights a week from next Monday. The Principal has given you a copy of the book that the students in the class have been asked to buy and has told you to start from Unit 4.

You have not been given a class list but you have managed to find out from the Principal that:

- There are usually about 15 students in the class.

  Most of them work during the day in restaurants, pubs and hotels or as au pair girls.
  You will be teaching the class on Mondays, Wednesdays and Fridays from 7 p.m. to 9 p.m.
  Students often arrive late, tired and hungry.
  The youngest student is 16 and the oldest is 25.
  Most of the students are from Italy and Spain but there are two students from Thailand, three from Korea and one from Taiwan.
  Most of the students want to improve their ability to use English so that they can get good jobs back home.

1. Look at 'Unit 4 Travel' and write an evaluation of it in relation to the class you are going to teach.
2. Describe and justify how you plan to adapt the unit in order to make it maximally useful to your students.
3. Produce an adapted version of the unit.

Flexible Framework 2 – Complex Simulations

Framework 2 simulations are complex in that they involve two or more related tasks and they are located in an environment which, although simplified in relation to its equivalent in the reference system, is specified in more detail than in Framework 1 simulations (the steps in italics indicate additional specifications).

For such lengthy simulations aiming to integrate and develop many skills we have based our procedures on the following flexible framework:

1. Setting of the environment (concisely on paper and in detail orally by the facilitator).
2. Specification of the problem or task (concisely on paper and in detail orally by the facilitator).
3. Discussion of the task by the participants in groups (and with the participation of the facilitator(s) when invited).
4. *Research tasks aiming to find out more information about the environment and to discover resources to help in carrying out the tasks.*
5. Carrying out of the task(s) (by the groups and sometimes by the facilitator(s)

too). This usually involves making choices of existing resources, making decisions about developing resources and determining solutions to 'problems'.

6. *Monitoring of the products of the task(s) by the producing group, by a monitoring group and by the facilitator(s).*
7. *Revision of the task products.*
8. *Presentation of the products.*
9. Comparison of the products with those of other groups and with equivalent products from 'real life'.
10. Group and plenary feedback on the process and the products led by the facilitator(s).
11. Debriefing session in which the participants discuss their reactions to the simulation and articulate what they have learned.

Example 3 is a typical Framework 2 simulation which was carried out over two two-hour workshops on the same day.

Example 3

What Book Shall I Use?

You have just joined the staff of Soho College of Higher Education in London as a part-time teacher of EFL and you have been told that you must decide what textbook(s) to use with the class that has been allocated to you. You have been told that you can use any of the textbooks that are in the Staff Library in Room 201.

a. Go to the pre-term meeting for new EFL staff and talk to the Head of EFL at Soho College (Mr Tomlinson). Try to find out from him all that you need to know about your teaching situation in order to make your decision.
b. Write a profile of your teaching situation.
c. Establish criteria to help you to evaluate the books from which you can choose.
d. From the books available in Room 201 select a short list of books which might meet your criteria.
e. Evaluate your shortlisted books against your criteria and decide which one(s) to use.
f. At a staff meeting tell your Head of Department and the other teachers what book(s) you have chosen and give reasons for your choice(s).

In our experience the simulations which seemed to be most successful in stimulating thought and developing awareness and skills were extended Framework 2 simulations which provided a choice of related tasks and which were designed to continue for up to a week. An example of such a simulation is Example 4, which kept the participants on the MA in L2 Materials Development thinking, questioning and developing for up to eight hours of workshop time. We called this activity a scenario rather than a simulation because it involved the stages of planning, presenting, advising and monitoring which are characteristic of Di Pietro's scenario approach (Di Pietro, 1987).

Example 4

SCENARIO 1 – A BOOK FOR BETU

You have just been appointed as English Language Advisor in the Ministry of Education in Betu, a small country in Central Africa.

A few months before your arrival in Betu, the government decided to change from French medium to English medium in senior secondary schools and at the same time to move to a more communicative approach to the teaching of English as a subject. Last month, the Ministry of Education decided that rather than wait until they can produce a new Betu specific English course they will sign a contract with a British publisher to adapt a successful EFL course to suit the situation in Betu. Last week they signed a contract with Oxford University Press for them to adapt *Headway* for use as the basic course in Betu from the new academic year (in ten months time).

Your first task as Advisor is to advise a Ministry English Textbook Sub-committee which has been set up to liaise with OUP. The Chair of the Sub-committee has asked you to present the following to a meeting of the Subcommittee next week:

1. A recommendation as to which level of *Headway* to start with.
2. General recommendations about adaptations that should be made to the book before it is introduced in Betu schools next year.
3. A sample unit to show what you think the Betu version of *Headway* should look like.

In your group prepare 1, 2 and 3 above and then choose one member of your group to be the Advisor at the meeting of the Subcommittee.

You have been given the following information to help you:

The Students	
Age	15–16
Size of class	40–50
Sex	60% male; 40% female
Hours per week	5
Previous learning of English	4 hours a week for three years from a grammar/translation book written in French
Motivation	high instrumental motivation in the towns, and in the villages for those who want to get jobs in the towns.

| First language | one of fifteen local vernaculars |
| Second language | French |

The Teachers

Level of English	generally good knowledge of English but little experience of using it for communication
Training	theoretical training in education departments at local and French universities plus 'scripted' teaching practice using the 'old' books
Teaching Load	35 hours a week

Betu

Population	1.75 million
Independence	1962 from Belgium
Exports	copra, palm oil, bananas
Industry	light industry; assembly of Toyota cars
Government	democratic but with a Life President

If you feel you need any other information about the situation in Betu ask your predecessor, Brian Tomlinson, who is staying on for a week to help you to settle in.

NB: During the simulation of the meeting you can call a 'time out' at any time to advise your Advisor and/or you can replace your Advisor with a substitute at any time.

4.   Prepare for the role assigned to your group in one of the other scenarios.

Scenario 2 involved being an EFL Textbook Consultant to the Ministry of Education in Tannesia, a large country in South-East Asia, and having to recommend a series of British EFL textbooks which could be adapted for use in Tannesian junior and senior high schools. Scenario 3 involved being a Publishing Editor working for Longman and taking charge of a project which aimed to produce a version of *Intermediate Matters* for first-year university students in Japan. In all three scenarios the participants were given problem-solving, development and presentation roles in one scenario and responding and monitoring roles in another scenario (each group became the receiving group in the simulated meeting in which another group made their presentations). In all three scenarios the facilitators were given roles in which they acted as informants on the simulated environment (for example, in Scenario 2 there was an English Language Advisor called Brian Tomlinson and in Scenario 3 there was a Professor Masuhara from Waseda University, who was visiting Longman for the day to discuss her new book on *Teaching Reading Strategies*). Giving the facilitator roles solves the problem of the facilitator who feels bored and guilty keeping out of the way and prevents the facilitator from breaking the 'reality' of a simulation by frequent intervention.

The initial feedback from this type of extended simulation often included annoyance at having to do a task that was so demanding and yet apparently so unrelated to previous experience and expertise. However, the final feedback was nearly always very positive and stressed the gradual gaining of both awareness and self-esteem as well as the development of transferable skills.

Evaluating the Draft Procedures

Draft procedures should obviously be evaluated against criteria established by reference to the objectives of the simulation and to the learning and gaming principles which were considered prior to the drafting of the procedures. We find that the best way to do this is first of all to answer the question, 'To what extent are these procedures likely to achieve the specified objectives?' When any adjustments have been made to the specified procedures, the next step is to convert the principles into specific and answerable questions and then answer each one with reference to the second draft of the procedures. So, for example, our Learning Principle 1 could be turned into the questions, 'Are the participants required to think for themselves?' and 'Are the participants required to make discoveries for themselves?'. And our Learning Principle 3 could be turned into the questions, 'Does the simulation invite the participants to pool their resources?' and 'Does the simulation require the participants to work in a team?' A similar procedure is followed in relation to the specified gaming principles so that, for example, when evaluating the second draft we might ask the questions, 'Have we extracted the salient elements from the reference system?' and 'Is the simulation likely to achieve psychological validity?'.

Using and Evaluating Simulations

We believe that the facilitators should be intuitively evaluating a simulation while using it but that they should not intervene too much to modify it as doing so breaks the reality and often causes more problems than it solves. The intuitive whilst-use evaluation should then inform a criterion-referenced post-use evaluation which could include feedback from the participants, evaluation of the observed effectiveness of the established environment and the procedures operating on it and evaluation of any resultant products of the simulation.

Conclusion

In a report on controlled experiments that assessed the value of simulations in teaching economics, Herz and Merz (1998) provide empirical results that support Kolb's (1984) model of experiential learning and which indicate that 'the simulation/game seminar outperforms a conventional seminar with respect to all aspects of the learning cycle' (p. 248). We do not yet have the empirical evidence to support our claims, but our conclusion from our considerable experience of using simulations on materials development courses is that, as with most other types of learning situation, the most effective approach for training materials developers seems to be an experiential approach and one of the most effective experiential activities seems to be the simulation. It can be a rich yet economical source of input and it can create the optimum conditions for facilitating the sort of intake which can lead to useful and durable learning. But, of course, this is only true if the simulations are designed in principled and systematic ways and if they are revised after feedback (Peters *et al.*, 1998: 27–9). This is what we are doing on a new MA in Materials Development for Language Teaching at Leeds Metropolitan University and what we hope other facilitators on materials development courses are doing too.

References

Arnold, J. (1998) 'Visualization: language learning with the mind's eye', in J. Arnold (ed.), *Affect in Language Learning*. Cambridge: Cambridge University Press, pp. 260–78.

Burns, A. C. and Gentry, J. W. (1998) 'Motivating students to engage in experiential learning: a tension-to learn-theory'. *Simulation & Gaming*, **29** (2), 133–51.

Christison, M. A. (1998) 'Applying multiple intelligence theory in preservice and inservice TEFL education programs'. *English Teaching Forum*, **36** (2), 2–13.

Crookall, D. (1991) 'Experiential teacher education: a case study in TESOL'. *Simulation/Games for Learning*, **21** (1), 7–30.

Crookall, D., Oxford, R. and Saunders, D. (1987) 'Towards a reconceptualization of simulation: from representation to reality'. *Simulation/Games for Learning*, **17** (4), 147–71.

Dewey, J. (1938) *Experience and Education*. London: Collier Books.

Di Pietro, R. J. (1987) *Strategic Interaction*. Cambridge: Cambridge University Press.

Gardner, H. (1993) *Multiple Intelligence: The Theory and Practice*. New York: Basic Books.

Greenblat, C. T. (1981). 'Basic concepts and linkages', in C. T. Greenblat and R. D. Duke *Principles and Practises of Gaming-Simulation*. Beverley Hills, CA: Sage, pp. 19–24.

Greenblat, C. T. and Duke, R. D. (1981) *Principles and Practises of Gaming-Simulation*. Beverley Hills, CA: Sage.

Herz, B. and Merz, W. (1998) 'Experiential learning and the effectiveness of economic simulation games'. *Simulation & Gaming*, **29** (2), 238–50.

Jones, K. (1985) *Designing Your Own Simulations*. London: Methuen.

Jones, K. (1995) *Simulations: A Handbook for Teachers and Trainers* (3rd edn.). London: Kogan Page.

Kolb, D. (1984) *Experiential Learning: Experience as the Source of Learning and development*. Englewood Cliffs, NJ: Prentice Hall.

Kolb, D., Rubin, I. M. and McIntyre, D. J. (1986) *Organizational Psychology*. Englewood Cliffs, NJ: Prentice Hall.

Laing, R. D. (1995) *The Politics of Experience.* Englewood Cliffs, NJ: Prentice Hall.

Lederman, L. C. (1984) 'Debriefing: a critical examination of the post-experience analytic process with implications for its effective use'. *Simulations and Games,* **15**, 415–31.

Lederman, L. C. (1992) 'Debriefing: towards a systematic assessment of theory and practice'. *Simulation & Gaming,* **23** (2), 145–60.

Lewin, K. (1951) *Field Theory in Social Sciences.* New York: Harper and Row.

Lozanov, G. (1978) *Suggestology and Outlines of Suggestopedy.* London: Gordon and Breach.

Masuhara, H. (1998) 'Factors influencing the reading difficulties of advanced learners of English as a foreign language when reading authentic texts'. Unpublished PhD thesis, University of Luton.

Molden, D. (1996) *Managing with the Power of NLP: Neuro-linguistic Programing for Personal Competitive Advantage.* New York: Prentice Hall.

Oxford, R. L. (1990) *Language Learning Strategies: What Every Teacher Should Know.* New York: Newbury House.

Peters, V., Vissers, G. and Heijne, G. (1998) 'The validity of games'. *Simulation & Gaming,* **29** (1), 20–30.

Piaget, J. (1971) *Psychology and Epistemology.* Middlesex: Penguin.

Raser J. R. (1969) *Simulation and Society: An Exploration of Scientific Gaming.* Boston: Allyn and Bacon.

Reid, J. (1997) *Understanding Learning Styles in the Second Language Classroom.* Englewood Cliffs, NJ: Prentice Hall/Regents.

Rogers, C. R. (1969) *Freedom to Learn.* Columbus, OH: Merrill.

Sadoski, M. and Paivio, A. (1994) 'A dual coding view of imagery and verbal processes in reading comprehension', in R. B. Ruddell, M. R. Ruddell and H. Singer (eds) *Theoretical Models and Processes of Reading* (4th edn.). Newark, DE: International Reading Association, pp. 582–601.

Schumann, J. H. (1998) 'A neurobiological perspective on affect and methodology in second language learning', in J. Arnold (ed.), *Affect in Language Learning.* Cambridge: Cambridge University Press, pp. 260–78.

Skinner, B. F. (1971) *Contingences of Reinforcement.* New York: Appleton-Century-Crofts.

Sokolov, A. N. (1972) *Inner Speech and Thought.* New York: Plenum Press.

Tomlinson, B. (1994) 'Pragmatic awareness activities'. *Language Awareness,* **3** (3 and 4), 119–29.

Tomlinson, B. (1996) 'Helping L2 readers to see', in T. Hickey and J. Williams *Language, Education and Society in a Changing World.* Clevedon, Avon: Multi-lingual Matters, pp. 252–63.

Tomlinson, B. (1997) 'The role of literature in the reading of literature in a foreign language'. Unpublished PhD thesis, University of Nottingham.

Tomlinson, B. (1998a) 'Affect and the coursebook'. *IATEFL Issues,* **145**, 20–1.

Tomlinson, B. (ed.) (1998b) *Materials Development in Language Teaching.* Cambridge: Cambridge University press.

Tomlinson, B. (1998c) 'Review of *A Framework for Task-Based Learning* (Willis, J.)'. *ELT Journal*, **52** (3), 257–59.

Tomlinson, B. (1998d) 'Seeing what they mean: helping L2 learners to visualise', in B. Tomlinson (ed.) *Materials Development in Language Teaching*. Cambridge: Cambridge University Press, pp. 265–78.

Tomlinson, B. (1999) 'Developing criteria for materials evaluation'. *IATEFL Issues*, **147**, 10–13.

Tomlinson, B. (2000) 'Talking to yourself: the role of the inner voice in language learning'. *Applied Language Learning*, **11** (1), 123–54.

Tomlinson, B. (2001) 'Creating meaning with the inner voice'. *Journal of Imagination in Language Learning*, **6**, 26–33.

Van Ments, M. (1983) *The Effective Use of Role Play: A Handbook for Teachers and Trainers*. London: Kogan Page.

Weil, S. W. and McGill, I. (1989) *Making Sense of Experiential Learning. Diversity in Theory and Practice*. Buckingham: Society for Research into Higher Education and Open University Press.

Williams, L. (1984) *Teaching for the Two-Sided Mind*. New York: Touchstone.

Willis, J. (1997) *A Framework for Task-Based Learning*. Harlow: Longman.

Yeo, G. K. and Tan, S. T. (1999) 'Toward a multilingual, experiential environment for learning decision technology'. *Simulation & Gaming*, **30** (1), 70–82.

CHAPTER

29

Materials Development and Teacher Training

Christophe Canniveng and Mertxe Martinez

Introduction

There have been numerous changes in the past two and a half decades in English Language Teaching (ELT). The increasing number of international and national conferences, the formation of Special Interest Groups (SIGs) and the increase of articles published in specialized journals have invited more teachers and researchers than ever to meet and have more to say about what interests them. Thus, this rush of new ideas has brought new thoughts on Second Language Acquisition (SLA) (e.g., Larsen-Freeman and Long, 1991; Ellis, 1994; Nunan, 1999), on language performance (e.g., McNamara, 1996), on methodologies (e.g., Long (in press)), on approaches to syllabus design (e.g., Nunan, 1988b; Willis, 1990), on materials development (e.g., Tomlinson, 1998), on areas of interest such as Languages for Specific Purposes (LSP) (e.g., Robinson, 1991; Dudley-Evans and St John, 1998; Douglas, 2000) and on vocabulary (e.g., Read, 2000; Schmitt, 2000); and such findings have influenced pedagogy.

Published materials seem to reflect this change as their products claim on the one hand to take into consideration learners' needs and to follow closely an approach or method to language teaching on the other. Materials, indeed, as Tomlinson (1998) defines them, refer to anything that is used by teachers or learners to facilitate the learning of a language, whereas materials development refers to anything that is done by writers, teachers or learners to provide sources of language input and to exploit those sources in ways that maximize the likelihood of intake. Teachers, therefore, could appear to act as a 'buffer' between language teaching and learning, and could be expected to adapt flexibly to the roles determined by the objectives of the method and by the learning theory on which the method is based (Masuhara, 1998). Masuhara (*op. cit.*) emphasizes the teachers' central position in language teaching and learning and characterizes them as being the ones who are often in charge of the essential stages of curriculum development by participating in the selection, teaching and sometimes rewriting of the materials. Although materials development and evaluation appear to 'give life' to theory in the language classroom, the literature remains sparse and teacher-training courses give little importance (or even sometimes ignore this area) in their programmes. The assumption seems to be that materials development, selection and evaluation have been taking care of themselves all these years.

In this chapter, we would like to propose new ways of training teachers in pre-service (PRESET) and/or in-service (INSET) courses in materials development and evaluation, not necessarily by inserting materials development components in these courses, but by considering materials development and evaluation as a result of a process that requires an awareness and a deeper understanding of the individual teaching circumstances surrounding theory and practice. Subsequently, materials design will not be seen as the combination between creativity and 'learned' skills made by 'good materials developers', but as a result of a more thorough reflection from the teachers of the situations surrounding the materials used in the classroom and the ability to question and test relevant theory in practice by using gained skills, experience and cognition.

By addressing questions such as 'In which of the teacher's developmental stages should they be introduced to materials development and evaluation? And how?', we are hoping to bring out the real value and the need to include materials development and evaluation in the field of methodology and in teacher-training programmes, and to dissuade those who still believe that, as long as published materials are being provided, materials development and evaluation can be considered as secondary to teaching and learning.

Literature Review

While much has been published on SLA and on a multitude of topics relevant to language teaching and to applied linguistics, there have been fewer books on materials design as, indeed, materials development and evaluation were treated as a subsection of methodology, in which materials were usually introduced as examples of methods in action rather than as a means to explore the principles and procedures of their development (Tomlinson, 2001).

General introductory books on language teaching devote little space to materials development and evaluation (e.g., Haycraft, 1978; Wright, 1987; Harmer, 1991; Rea-Dickins and Germaine, 1992; Ur, 1999). While general and more specific books on syllabus design and curriculum offer at least one unit or chapter with some comments on the subject (e.g., Dubin and Olshtain, 1986; Hutchinson and Waters, 1987), some others devote little if any space to materials (e.g., Nunan, 1988a and b; White, 1988; Johnson, 1989).

In the 1980s, a few publications dealing with some aspects of materials development appeared (e.g., Cunningsworth, 1984; Sheldon, 1987) although, rather than conceptualizing materials evaluation and development, authors particularly focused on their experience of selecting and evaluating as examples of evaluation and exploitation. Other aspects of materials design, such as the use of published materials, the need to adapt and/or supplement materials, and the use of authentic materials, have received some attention (e.g., Candlin and Breen, 1979; Allwright, 1981; O'Neill, 1982; Hutchinson and Torres, 1994; Chambers, 1997; Peacock, 1997; Sheldon, 1988).

It is since the 1990s, however, that materials development has shown its real value, as postgraduate and undergraduate courses started to give more importance to materials design as part of their syllabuses and when materials development became a tool for teachers to help them understand and apply theories of language learning, and therefore to contribute to their professional development. Moreover, the realization that no coursebook can be ideal for any particular class has contributed to materials design research and its conceptualization, as teachers feel more and more the need to be able to evaluate, adapt and produce materials that meet their learners' needs and preferences. Books on principles and procedures of materials development have started to appear on the market (e.g., Skierso, 1991; McDonough and Shaw, 1993; Hidalgo *et al.*, 1995; Tomlinson, 1998). Criteria for evaluation have also been made available even though, while some seemed to be quick and efficient (e.g., Hutchinson, 1987), others were extremely complex (e.g., Breen and Candlin, 1987). And whether simple or complex, such checklists have invariably been intended for the evaluation of published materials only (Block, 1991). Indeed, this type of criteria has been developed having in mind predictive evaluation[1] and, as Ellis (1997) points out, the idea behind these guides is to help teachers carry out an evaluation which aims at determining whether the materials are likely to work in a specific teaching context. He finds, on the other hand, such evaluation to be an enormous undertaking and does not seem to believe in systematically evaluating a complete set of materials. However, a retrospective evaluation[2] could inform the teacher as to whether the learner has learnt as a result of using the materials (Ellis, 1997). Ellis defines retrospective evaluation as being of three different kinds:

- student-based
- response-based (internal)
- learning-based (external)

These interests and realizations have led to an increase in in-service and postgraduate materials development courses and in materials development research for teachers aiming at reflecting and conceptualizing the process of developing materials. Also worldwide organizations connected to materials design are growing (e.g., the Materials Writers Interest Group of TESOL in the USA; JALT in Japan; The Language Teacher in Eastern Europe, MATSDA in UK) and are offering conferences and publications which encourage and enhance research in this field.

The Role of Materials Development and Evaluation in Teacher-training Courses

Why Materials Development is Important in Teacher Training

Materials have always been considered as the only way to supply enriched input in the language classroom, and in this respect have undergone many changes following methodological and other theoretical trends. Whether successful or not, they have been able to provide a natural link between the teachers, the students and the language to be learned.

The selection, evaluation and development of materials, on the other hand, have aroused considerable controversy among professionals. The arguments against using either contrived materials which focus on the features of the language being taught (i.e., short and easy texts helping learners to focus their attention on the target feature) or authentic materials (i.e., ordinary texts not produced for teaching purposes) has made the pendulum swing back and forth. Teachers amidst all this have often been the casualties of this pendulum by suffering the problems imposed by the momentum.

There is no doubt that materials are a central feature for the achievement of successful language learning and they offer structure and consistency in the foreign language classroom. However, teacher-training programmes have not always managed to prepare and equip teachers with the necessary tools to cope with changes in language learning materials.

Overview of the Problems behind Teacher-training Programmes

As mentioned in the introduction, published materials tend to mirror and to follow all the changes that occur in applied linguistics. Materials development can be effectively connected to areas of linguistics such as SLA, sociolinguistics, psycholinguistics, language and discourse analysis and pragmatics; and to teachers' development and their awareness of methodologies while teaching.

The reality shows, however, that textbooks do not conform easily to the developments in notions about teaching and learning that have come out of applied linguistics debates in the last two decades (Hutchinson and Torres, 1994). It also shows that, in pre-service education programmes, textbooks are either criticized and annihilated as failing to meet students' needs and preferences or worshipped as useful references for inexperienced teachers. Moreover, trainees' backgrounds are often neglected (i.e., their previous experience with foreign language learning, their educational background, personality and preferences and, future teaching opportunities are often omitted or not taken into consideration) when approaching materials development.

In-service programmes often do not encourage the teachers to reflect on their particular teaching experiences and to apply their knowledge (i.e., that related to their previous teaching and, in some cases, to their learning of a foreign language) to materials development. Instead, they focus on developing the skills needed for predictive evaluation of materials for general contexts. Although trainees at this stage in their careers believe that 'good teachers' do not systematically follow coursebooks but adapt and sometimes rewrite the materials, they are often not encouraged to go a step forward in their self-development for different reasons:

- The training might not ask the trainees to reflect or take into account their previous teaching experience and background, as materials development and evaluation is presented as a discrete item through theoretical or practical examples which are not related to the relevant teaching contexts of the trainees. For example, in some cases the trainees are presented with new information to replace their old teaching experience, ignoring their personal teaching contexts. Asian countries, such as China, and some African countries do not necessarily have the same teaching framework as European countries have; nevertheless, these trainees (who in some cases are highly successful teachers and curriculum developers in their own countries) get exposed to a very Western-oriented approach to materials development, which does not necessarily fit with their needs and expectations.

- The trainer's lack of motivation (because of the length of the courses being too short to allow the participants to engage fully in exchanging views and experiences and because the trainers themselves do not engage in self-reflection and tend to fossilize their own learning) and lack of understanding (often due to mixed ability groups where there are different cultural and ideological backgrounds between the trainer and the trainees) could cause a lack of drive in the trainees to change their already existing beliefs and practices. For example, trainers work under the very specific constraints of their own curriculums and often present materials development as an isolated component on their courses. General criteria related to materials development, evaluation and adaptation is usually fed to the trainees but there is little time paid to the process of how to develop personal specific criteria to suit the trainees. As a consequence, the trainees do not always engage in self-reflection.

- The pressure to obtain further qualifications prompts teachers to follow short training courses in order to promote their professional careers. For such trainees, knowledge on materials development, teaching commitment, awareness and reflection are not as important as the qualification obtained at the end of the course.

- The new trends which are constantly developed in language teaching and learning might seem irrelevant in the light of the distance between researchers, teachers and materials developers. Indeed, SLA, teachers' cognitions and experience and materials development do not always shed light on each other but often work in isolation.

Therefore, for all the above reasons, we believe that materials development and evaluation as they stand in teacher development need to undergo a radical change if they are to become central in applied linguistics and particularly in teacher-training courses. Teacher-training courses should be more carefully designed as all participants come into the programme with their own theories, experiences and expectations. But as courses are not always able to provide individual assistance, they should aim at the following:

- Helping trainees transfer general knowledge into their particular teaching realities.

- Encouraging an inner exploration of self rather than a search for the outward characteristics of a 'good teacher'.
- Making theory relevant, concrete and applicable at a practical level.

The Role of Materials Development in the Different Stages of Teacher Training

As we have already pointed out, both PRESET and INSET courses aim at different goals when approaching materials development in their courses.

PRESET courses usually take on board inexperienced native speakers (who mainly constitute the bulk of the participants) and some non-native speakers of the language, both wishing to take teaching as a career. The participants' first encounter with materials development comes in the form of being encouraged to develop their creativity and demonstrate their capacity to develop lessons. Cutting and pasting from different resources or following published materials as they are presented become the main ways to solve the lack of teaching experience and knowledge which would need to be developed through reflecting on theory and simple practice. Pre-service courses are primarily concerned with classroom management (e.g., putting students in groups, being friendly and encouraging, giving positive feedback, etc.) and seldom encourage the future teachers to think about the goals, purposes and the learnability behind the materials chosen for their particular lessons. These courses instead use the participants' intuition and creativity as a key to developing materials and teaching lessons.

On the other side, INSET courses prepare their programmes for more experienced teachers who, in most of the cases, have been teaching for several years and arrive with their own experiences, expectations and knowledge.

These courses assume the participants have been developing their primary intuition into theoretical and practical frameworks and that they need to reshape and refresh their knowledge and teaching styles. Therefore, when approaching materials development, the teachers are often offered a set of universal criteria that 'can be used' to develop, select and evaluate any materials in any circumstances. These checklists tend to be either quick and not so efficient or highly complicated and useful only under the supervision of someone more theoretically competent. Teachers are not always encouraged to develop their active thinking and are not always given the opportunities to reflect back on their own teaching successes and failures and create their own particular and appropriate criteria for developing materials.

Furthermore, coursebooks on teacher training and language teaching (e.g., Harmer, 1991; Scrivener, 1994; Gower *et al.*, 1995; Ur, 1999) seem to pay little attention to materials development in their books and often contain only a small isolated section which randomly includes elements of materials development without relating them to relevant theory and teaching practice. Coursebooks, because of their universal nature, cannot fit all circumstances, but teachers should, nevertheless, be helped to develop the reflecting, analysing and evalu-

ating powers to create successful lessons for all the students, needs and personalities there could be in any given situation.

Possible Changes in Teacher Training concerning How and When We Approach Materials Development

As the reader might have already noticed, our approach to materials development
differs from the one which is usually offered when introducing materials development in teacher-training courses. Our belief is that a full understanding of
materials and materials development is essential for successful teaching and
learning, as no teacher can teach without materials. We would like, therefore, to
suggest a different approach to viewing materials development.

Materials development should become an essential component on both PRE-
SET and INSET courses. As is shown in the model (see Figure 29.1), the development of materials which promotes successful language learning comes as a
result of an active, ongoing relationship between SLA theory, teachers' experience and teachers' cognitions.

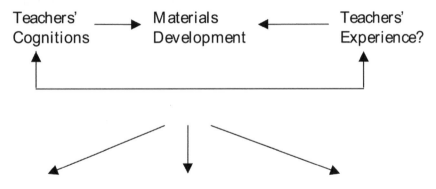

Figure 29.1 Relationship between SLA theory, teachers' experience and teachers' cognition

Materials development, if taken from this different angle, is the product of
theory (SLA), teachers' cognitions (i.e., beliefs, decision-making, attitudes, personality) and teachers' experience (i.e., previous teaching and learning of a
foreign language) informing each other. Materials become usable and teachable
in the language classroom once the teacher has been able to combine these three
elements together and take decisions according to the specific classroom situation. Thus, for example:

- Theoretical understanding of the effectiveness of the different ways of teaching
  grammar will allow the teachers to take the necessary considerations when
  approaching the selection and evaluation of materials.
- Theoretical understanding of the four skills (i.e., speaking, reading, writing
  and listening) will allow the teacher to concentrate on developing these skills
  rather than teaching them.

- The understanding of learners' styles and preferences will also allow the teacher to make certain choices when adapting or selecting materials.
- Teachers' experience with different cultures will also allow for quicker decisions to be taken regarding materials selection.

INSET courses should therefore aim at arriving at Figure 29.1. and trainers should become facilitators of this ongoing process in order to compensate for any lack of theoretical, cognitive or practical experience. Where native and non-native speakers, experienced and/or more theoretically geared teachers join the same course, reflection on past experiences and sharing of relevant theoretical knowledge together with active participation should be promoted in order to pool resources and facilitate individual development.

PRESET courses run with the disadvantage of not being able to draw on the participants' theoretical knowledge and teaching experience, although some trainees might have had experience of foreign language learning. Nevertheless, materials development should still be a central element from which to draw relevant theory, related to what materials to select, use and evaluate and how to use the particular materials according to the specific needs of participants (see Figure 29.2).

Language Teaching Theory

(*the what and how of teaching*)

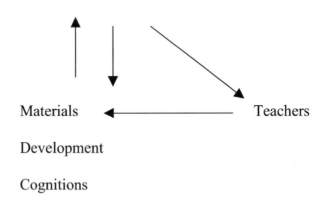

Figure 29.2 Language teaching theory

By analysing and understanding already developed materials, trainees will be able to draw relevant theoretical constructs and those constructs will further inform their theoretical backgrounds.

Professionals involved in teacher training should try to promote more insights as to why and how coursebooks are being created, and more opportunities for the participants to understand the reasons behind the construction of specific teaching materials. As Tomlinson (1998) suggests, if materials are to contribute positively to teacher development, they must not be imposed but they must invite and facilitate reflection, evaluation and adaptation by the teacher and they must involve teachers in their development and trialling.

Conclusion

We began this article by addressing two relevant questions related to materials development and teacher training. Our main concern has been to try and establish a pattern of instruction where materials development becomes more significant in teacher training and teacher development. Our belief has clearly shown the importance of making materials development central in teacher instruction. By considering the central position of materials development, foreign language learning and teaching theory, teachers' cognitions and teachers' experiences have been able to become interrelated and dependent on each other, promoting in this way the individual needs of the teachers and their autonomy.

As Day (1999), states, 'Teachers cannot be developed (passively). They develop (actively). It is vital, therefore, that they are centrally involved in decisions concerning the direction and processes of their own learning.' And in this respect we should add 'the processes of their own teaching'.

References

Allwright, D. (1981) 'What do we need teaching materials for?' *ELT Journal*, **36** (1), 5–18.

Block, D. (1991) 'Some thoughts on DIY materials design'. *ELT Journal*, **43** (3), 211–17.

Breen, M. and Candlin, C. (1987) 'Which materials?: a consumer's and designer's guide', in L. Sheldon (ed.) *ELT Textbooks and Materials: Problems in Evaluation and Development*. ELT Document 126. Oxford: MEP/The British Council.

Candlin, C. N. and Breen, M. P. (1979) 'Evaluating and designing language teaching materials'. *Practical Papers in English Language Education Vol. 2*. Lancaster: Institute for English Language Education, University of Lancaster.

Chambers, F. (1997) 'Seeking consensus in coursebook evaluation'. *ELT Journal*, **51** (1), 29–35.

Cunningsworth, A. (1984) *Evaluating and Selecting EFL Teaching Material*. London: Heinemann.

Day, C. (1999) *Developing Teachers: The Challenges of Lifelong Learning*. London: Falmer Press.

Douglas, D. (2000) *Assessing Languages for Specific Purposes*. Cambridge: Cambridge University Press.

Dubin, F. and Olshtain, E. (1986) *Course Design*. New York: Cambridge University Press.

Dudley-Evans, T. and St John, M. J. (1998) *Development in English for Specific Purposes: A Multidisciplinary Approach.* Cambridge: Cambridge University Press.

Ellis, R. (1994) *The Study of Second Language Acquisition.* Oxford: Oxford University Press.

Ellis, R. (1997) *SLA Research and Language Teaching.* Oxford: Oxford University Press.

Gower, R., Phillips, D. and Walters, S. (1995) *Teaching Practice Handbook.* Hong Kong: Macmillan Heinemann.

Harmer, J. (1991) *The Practice of English Language Teaching.* London: Longman.

Haycraft, J. (1978) *An Introduction to English Language Teaching.* Harlow: Longman.

Hidalgo, A. C., Hall, D. and Jacobs, G. M. (eds) (1995) *Getting started: Materials Writers on Materials Writing.* Singapore: SEAMEO Regional Language Centre.

Hutchinson, T. (1987) 'What's underneath? An interactive view of materials evaluation', in L. Sheldon (ed.) *ELT Textbooks and Materials: Problems in Evaluation and Development.* ELT Document 126. Oxford: MEP/The British Council.

Hutchinson, T. and Torres, E. (1994) 'The textbook as agent of change'. *ELT Journal,* **48** (2), 315–28.

Hutchinson, T. and Waters, A. (1987) *ESP – A Learning-Centred Approach.* Cambridge: Cambridge University Press.

Johnson, R. K. (ed.) (1989) *The Second Language Curriculum.* Cambridge: Cambridge University Press.

Larsen-Freeman, D. and Long, M. H. (1991) *An Introduction to Second Language Acquisition Research.* London: Longman.

Long, M. H. (in press) *Task-based Language Teaching.* Oxford: Blackwell.

McDonough, J. and Shaw, C. (1993) *Materials and Methods in ELT.* Oxford: Blackwell.

McNamara, T. (1996) *Measuring Second Language Performance.* London: Longman.

Masuhara, H. (1998) 'What do teachers really want from coursebooks?', in B. Tomlinson (ed.) *Materials Development in Language Teaching.* Cambridge: Cambridge University Press.

Nunan, D. (1988a) *The Learner-Centred Curriculum.* Cambridge: Cambridge University Press.

Nunan, D. (1988b) *Syllabus Design.* Oxford: Oxford University Press.

Nunan, D. (1999) *Second Language Teaching and Learning.* Boston, MA: Heinle and Heinle.

O'Neill, R. (1982) 'Why use textbooks?' *ELT Journal,* **36** (2), 104–11.

Peacock, M. (1997) 'The effect of authentic materials on the motivation of EFL learners'. *ELT Journal,* **51** (2), 144–54.

Read, J. (2000) *Assessing Vocabulary.* Cambridge: Cambridge University Press.

Rea-Dickins, P. and Germaine, K. (1992) *Evaluation.* Oxford: Oxford University Press.

Robinson, P. (1991) *ESP Today: A Practitioner's Guide.* London: Prentice Hall.

Schmitt, N. (2000) *Vocabulary in Language Teaching.* Cambridge: Cambridge University Press.

Scrivener, J. (1994) *Learning Teaching.* Oxford: Heinemann.

Sheldon, L. (ed.) (1987) *ELT Textbooks and Materials: Problems in Evaluation and Development*. ELT Document 126. Oxford: MEP/The British Council.

Sheldon, L. (1988) 'Evaluating ELT textbooks and materials'. *ELT Journal*, **42** (4), 237–46.

Skierso, A. (1991) 'Textbook selection and evaluation', in M. Celce-Murcia (ed.) *Teaching English as a Second Language*. Rowley, MA: Newbury House.

Tomlinson, B. (ed.) (1998) *Materials Development in Language Teaching*. Cambridge: Cambridge University Press.

Tomlinson, B. (2001) 'Materials development', in R. Carter and D. Nunan (eds) *Teaching English to Speakers of Other Languages*. Cambridge: Cambridge University Press.

Ur, P. (1999) *A Course in Language Teaching, Trainee Book*. Cambridge: Cambridge University Press.

White, R. (1988) *The ELT Curriculum*. Oxford: Basil Blackwell.

Willis, D. (1990) *The Lexical Syllabus: A New Approach to Language Teaching*. London: HarperCollins.

Wright, T. (1987) *Roles of Teachers and Learners*. Oxford: Oxford University Press.

A Practical Experience of Institutional Textbook Writing: Product/Process Implications for Materials Development

Patrick Lyons

Introduction

This chapter presents an overview of the issues involved in institutional textbook writing as reflected in the experiences that Bilkent University School of English Language (BUSEL)[1] has gone through, having produced a suite of textbooks[2] in the period between 1995 and 2000; and having recently undertaken a review and revision of its textbooks, anticipated to cover the period 2001–2005. Specifically, this chapter will look at the nature of the product, and the elements of the process.

Process/product might suggest a linear operation, but the processes BUSEL has undergone have constituted a series of cycles, with its own products, change processes and learning cycles. This notion is supported by the fact that the Textbook Development Project at BUSEL (TBDP) is currently revising its product, and initiating a further process. It is our experience that the writing and publishing of a textbook is only an apparent end point.

What follows is:

1. a definition of the *textbook as product*, and an exploration of this product as part of a delivery system;
2. how the *textbook as process* fits into other institutional processes; this will explore its impact on standards of teaching and learning, as well as the thinking time it offers an institution, and how an in-house textbook might constitute a benchmark or threshold for that institution.

Textbook as Product

To begin at the apparent end point – the product – it must be said at the outset that a textbook is not simply a textbook. A textbook – student's book, teacher's book, workbook, audio cassettes – aims to constitute benefits. A textbook might aim to meet both a higher exit level for learners, and a higher teaching standard for instructors, for example. Defining the textbook in terms of its benefits means BUSEL can keep in mind the multidimensional character of the product.

The Multidimensionality of the Product

As a multidimensional product, the textbook may be regarded as a total product with core and auxiliary dimensions.

To define its core or primary characteristics: an institutional textbook is the provision of *a set of materials for the efficient and effective teaching of a known student body by a known teaching body at a given level to a prescribed standard.* This is what the textbook has to do. However, the core dimensions of the product will be defined according to its user. The core benefit stated above would be likely to be that of the manager. From the student's standpoint the core characteristics will naturally be different. Its core may be defined as *a set of materials for expediting learning at a given level to assure success in institutional assessment.* From the teacher's standpoint the core characteristics will also be different. It may be defined as *a set of flexible materials for expediting teaching at a given level that ensures relevance to the syllabus and adequate opportunities for presentation, practice and production without the aid of extensive supplementary material, as well as adequate opportunities for checking learning and remedial work.*

As with core dimensions, so with the auxiliary dimensions. The textbook's auxiliary dimensions provide supplementary benefits: for example, the book is easy to use, enjoyable, interesting and beneficial. However, easy to use, enjoyable, interesting and beneficial will actually describe auxiliary dimensions that for the manager, teacher and student are quite distinct. What can be said with certainty is that, when the book is considered, what is perceived will depend on who the prospective user is.

It should be clear, then, that in considering the benefits, institutional textbook writing must face the fact that it is dealing with three types of user: managers,[3] teachers and students. For the moment, the chapter will focus on the student and the learner. The managers will be dealt with in more detail in the second part of the chapter in considering institutional textbook writing as process.

The Product from the Viewpoint of Students and Teachers

As we have seen, a textbook can be further defined *as a product* according to its users. Although neither students nor teachers are strictly purchasers in the sense that they have a choice as to whether to buy the book once it is chosen as the coursebook for a given course, nonetheless, clear purchase-behaviour dimensions pertain.

The Students' Viewpoint
Looking at the book from the student perspective first, and at the auxiliary dimensions specifically, the physical nature or tangibility of the book, or books, if

we include the workbook, is significant. For the age group to which our students belong, the majority being in their late teens, their sensitivity to the book's portability is an issue, as they may not wish to use satchels. Again, their age, their interests, what they find interesting and boring have a direct bearing on the manner in which they view the content of the book's themes and topics. Likewise, the appearance of the book is another factor. Does the book look like the textbooks they have experienced before? Many current textbooks show that a great deal of attention has been paid to the appearance of the product. In this area, *Headway* is the genus, with very characteristic care taken in the layout and design of the pages, the use of photographs and illustrations and attractive and agreeable colour schemes, while countless other products comprise the species.

A likeness to textbooks previously used will undoubtedly be of some importance to the student, conferring security and confidence thereby, though students' response is difficult to anticipate. Our unpublished research at BUSEL has shown that the weightiness of our textbooks, with the Student's Books running to over three hundred pages each, is viewed as a positive factor by some students – its weightiness being analogous for them with the book's seriousness – while other students find this aspect of the book intimidating and unwelcoming.

As its aesthetic appearance is part of the overall experience of the textbook, it cannot be ignored. Because of the difficulties in distinguishing between what might normally be considered trite and what serious when looking at the various aspects of the product, it is useful to bear in mind the distinction between core and auxiliary dimensions.

For students, the textbook may be more or less a *convenience product,* and relatively inexpensive, and merely one amongst other textbooks they have bought during their education and, not being self-directed, purchased without a great deal of consideration.

The student perspective might also be looked at in terms of durability. On a mundane level, we may note that the book will be used many times on a course and brought back and forth to school, thus undergoing a lot of wear and tear. It has to survive such treatment; it would be scandalous if the book were to fall apart due to routine usage. However, the durability of the book is related to another issue and design consideration: will the students write in the book or not? If so, what will they write? If not, where will the record of student's participation be located: in the student's notebook, in the student's memory, in teachers' records? If the book is designed so that an essential trace of the learning experience is documented – through study boxes completed by the students themselves and/or vocabulary work for example – it would be expected that the book be used for an extended period after the course for which it was designed had finished.

Again, on a mundane level, if the book is not designed to comprise an essential reference for the student after the course, and if the book bears no mark of students' experience of the course, the financiers of the textbook project may find the book has an energetic second-hand market, and sales after the initial launch will be sluggish. This, too, is an important consideration if the sales of the book are to maintain or justify subsequent technological development.

Durability might also be looked at in terms of the overall product. The textbook does not exist in isolation, but is used as a component of a course. It may even become identified with the whole course as an applied syllabus in some manner. The fusion of the textbook (the goods) and the teaching (the service) or the delivery of the course leads helpfully into consideration of the perspective of the other user: the teacher.

The Teachers' Viewpoint

The teacher's perspective may share certain features with that of the student, but differ in important aspects. For the teacher the textbook has to perform differently. The student's single use of the textbook has to be compared with a teacher's repeated use. The teacher will use the textbook many times during an academic year. In BUSEL this may be as many as four times. No piloting can hope to approximate the level of critical analysis a book will undergo during that period of intensive use, and a textbook in such conditions may become easily jaded for the teacher.

Teachers will expect a benefit from the product, and the textbook will be expected to have identifiable differences/benefits over other textbooks for the same level. These differences and benefits are also expected to be sustained over several applications. However much the writers attempt to anticipate teacher reaction, these differences will be subject to deterioration over time (the same set of materials is going to become dull no matter what), and may also be subject to abrupt change. A textbook that in its approach and methodology reflects say, an acquisition theory of language learning, may be popular at some point in a school's history for any of a variety of reasons, and then suddenly become unpopular or out of step with other developments in the school. This is a risk for the textbook. If the textbook is not flexible enough to adapt to developments in the syllabus, assessment or teaching methodology, the textbook will become irrelevant and no longer valid; it will in effect pass its sell-by date.

Looking at the book from the teacher perspective, the physical nature or tangibility, of the book, or books (if we include the teacher's book and workbook), is likewise significant. Teachers are also sensitive to the book's portability. A teacher will often take the Student's Book and Teacher's Book home for material preparation along with students' homework. The weight may cause consternation and irritation. The Teacher's Book for BUSEL's Pre-Intermediate textbook runs to approximately six hundred pages and is published in two separate though cumbersome volumes. A cautionary tale: after some time, teachers at BUSEL began to undo the ring-binding of the Teacher's Book and take home only those pages relevant to the lessons to be prepared for. As a result, and despite care, the Teacher's Books' physical durability was undermined, as the books fell apart.

Do teachers of the book find the content interesting? And, similarly, the appearance of the book is a further consideration. Does the book look like the textbooks they have experienced before? Can the teachers feel proud of the book? This will certainly be of some importance to the teacher. What if the teacher is embarrassed by the textbook? What if teachers find it looks amateurish and unattractive? They may not like the paper quality. They may not like the book's size.

Maybe the teacher feels no ownership, and *that* is the underlying problem? Perhaps the reason for the book's unpopularity is that it is perceived as not expediting course delivery? Teachers are having to change the way they teach, and they have no faith in this change. Teachers find that they need to prepare many supplementaries if the course is to run satisfactorily. The textbook's approach is so different the students do not know what to do with the book. The teacher feels impotent; it is too difficult to teach; the textbook makes the teachers lose face.

As with negative feedback so with positive. It is not easy to decipher the issues textbooks raise. Some things are easier, some more difficult to monitor. Does the lesson fit the syllabus? Does the lesson match the aim? If not, what is the lesson doing? Does it do what it is doing well or badly? Should we keep it and change its aims? Should we keep it but make radical changes? Should we bin it? Is the book aligned with the level correctly? Has the placement test worked? Maybe the book is OK after all … The questions that will arise are endless.

Durability of the textbook from the teacher's perspective will be related amongst other things to how far it can be relied upon to provide the necessary means to expedite a high level of quality in the delivery of a course of study – qualities that relate to its vitality and adaptability. The book not only guarantees a level of teacher performance, offering support and guidance in delivering the service, but also a level of learning reflected as customer satisfaction. It should be able to do this reliably for different students at different times, without becoming rapidly exhausted.

Equally, this learning should be related to other courses. The students' success at one level should be accompanied with readiness for the next level. If you receive from other teachers, or pass on to other teachers, students who are not equipped for the level of a course of study, previous success can only be seen as specious and will be likely to prejudice any long-term success. In the end, the textbook has to fit into the overall aim of the course of study: in BUSEL's context, admission to faculty, and successful study in an English-medium university.

The Teacher's Book has a great potential for change, and can have major repercussions on the institutional environment. It can change the life of the teacher. By specifying aims in detail – by clarifying aims, by placing lesson aims – in relation to broader institutional aims it can free the teacher from reliance on the Student's Book. It can thus build skills and promote ownership of the course delivery.

The Textbook/Product Experience: Good/Service

The educational experience of the product needs then to be durable; that is, have a long-term effect on teachers' performance in the school, and on students' performance in the school and in the faculty. But are we in danger of asking too much of the textbook? Perhaps the problem is related to the fact that we are looking at the textbook in isolation? Is a textbook not merely an instrument after all? Are we not really talking about courses of study?

To help answer these questions we will look at the textbook and the course of study as two types of product: the *product as good* and the *product as service*, respectively.

We have looked at institutional textbook writing from the product standpoint and how its dimensions may be viewed by the student and the teacher, as well as suggesting a managerial perspective. In the experience of the product by the three sets of users we are looking at the product in terms of the classroom and the service that is provided and consumed: institutional textbook writing from the point of view of the service a school provides.

How does the textbook product fit into BUSEL's overall product – the service it provides its students? It is perilous to isolate the textbook from the overall service of which it is a component. On the continuum between product as good and product as service the school provides both a good (the materials that have been prepared) and a service (the delivery of those materials, as well as the teaching and the other aspects of its total product).

Marketing provides a useful distinction between two types of service: instrumental services and consummatory services. An instrumental service is one where a provider performs a task without the consumer's direct involvement or immediate gratification. Where the consumer is directly involved in immediate gratification the service is called consummatory. Education is a complex service product involving a synthesis of both types: the teacher carries out an educational undertaking for the student, and the student receives instantaneous gratification as the service is consumed.

Dimensions of the Good/Service: Intangibility, Inseparability and Heterogeneity
Marketing also provides a useful delineation of service features. Services are characterized as intangible, inseparable and heterogeneous. Education, or a course of study, is *intangible*. As the service cannot be tried in advance of purchasing, misunderstandings may come about between the consumer and the service provider. In any case, as evaluation and understanding of the intangible is difficult, intangibility has to be made tangible if only symbolically. Certificates for outstanding performance, success in important exams can achieve this. But tangible gratification might be delayed or may ultimately be evasive. In this sense the textbook has a symbolic function as the tangible evidence of an intangible product (the course of study). We need to consider whether this tangible evidence has a positive effect. Does the product inspire confidence? Does it make promises to the consumer? Does it say the right things about the kind of service students will receive?

The members of the textbook project do not necessarily have to come into contact with the textbook's buyers. But the service providers – the teachers – are *inseparable* from the instructional process. The provider and the consumer – at least in language instruction – have to be in the same place for the service transaction to occur.

Unlike the production of the service product, the textbook as a good will be produced, sold and consumed in that order. A course of study, as a service good, reverses that order or nearly so. The lesson is sold first, and then produced and consumed instantaneously in the classroom (so a course of study which uses textbooks makes the classroom the meeting place of two different types of product). Instantaneous consumption is a constraint on the writers of the textbook, and the deliverers of the service. There are only so many lessons that can be performed in a day, and only so much can be consumed over a course. All courses have this constraint, acknowledged or not, witting or not.

In the provision of the product as service produced, it could be argued that there is a distinct temptation for the service provider, the teacher, to become overly production-oriented rather than customer-oriented. This is often characterized as 'teaching the lesson rather than the students'. It indicates an emphasis on technique, methodology, approach – the delivery system – as an end in itself to the detriment of the customer. Teacher training seems sometimes to encourage this perception, and to promote the idea of service provider as artiste – the creative originator of a product (perhaps effectively independent of the customer).

Materials development is subordinate finally to the teacher, and whether or not the service is successfully delivered depends on the consumer's perceptions in the classroom of the teacher. The teacher is therefore the key to success – the most important part of the product. Is the textbook then an immaterial aspect? If not, what is its role in the product experience?

It is recognized that the personal performance of the service provider (teacher) is crucial to the success of the service (the course of study). However, because the teacher is human there will surely be *heterogeneity*. The quality of the learning and the teaching will modulate from classroom to classroom, because of the teacher's knowledge, experience, skill and so forth. There are two strategies calculated to deal with heterogeneity: standardization and customization.

Exacting quality control over learning and teaching can be accomplished through importance given to recruitment standards, teacher training and teacher education, as well as research into customer needs and wants. The strategy of standardization can also take the tactical form of institutional textbook writing – with the aim of providing the necessary information to the teacher in order to expedite delivery of the curriculum by experienced and less experienced teachers. This information can be provided in terms of the materials (an arbitrary – though ideally exemplary – set of materials (Student's Book), with information on this set of materials' function and use (Teacher's Book), with information on how class work can be consolidated and supported outside the class (Workbook)).

By taking into account unique environmental factors (prior language learning, prior education, target language community and so forth on behalf of the students, and likewise consideration of the features of the teaching body), and attempting to design for a level of flexibility, this standardized product may be customized or tailored.

Flexibility in the Delivery of the Product

The question of flexibility is central to textbook design, but difficult to grasp. When a book is described as flexible, what does *flexible* refer to? Does it refer to approach, methodology, technique? We might say that a flexible book helps students at varying levels within a given level reach a certain standard, with no discernible effect exercised by other variables, even experience of the teacher. So does it mean that the book is teacher-proof? Or teaching-proof? Maybe it means that the book does not need a teacher to interpose in the learning process. Does the book merely require an operator someone to keep order, correct obvious errors and mistakes and reel off the key?

Is flexibility a good or bad thing? Many commercially produced textbooks are somewhat bland in content, as is often said, for the apparent reason that they are designed to appeal to as broad a set of users as possible. They are, arguably, and perhaps for the same reason, often bland in approach too; but is this such a bad thing? The book's being amenable to different methods of assessment, methodology and syllabus gives it longevity and dependability and it may be integrated into existing school systems fairly painlessly. The taxon *Headway* can be used as a reference on this point.

Such books are extremely permissive and, as a result, are often perceived as unprincipled and cynical, perhaps even wanton. But what is the obverse? A textbook that wears its pedagogics on its sleeve may not be such an attractive alternative. Highly principled and perhaps in earnest, they may be quite magisterial in tone, methodologically precise, if not actually coercive, and next to impossible to integrate.

Where should an institutional textbook fall on the continuum of flexibility and inflexibility? It would seem that an institutional textbook would be more likely to be in danger of falling into the latter category. The question follows: should an institutional textbook project imitate a commercially produced textbook – to emulate say, its flexibility? Our unpublished research has shown that many teachers found the pre-intermediate book published by BUSEL methodologically aggressive and intolerant of adaptation. At any given level, as all teachers know, there is a great deal of diversity, as indeed there is in each class. The textbook of choice at BUSEL – for all its recognized faults and limitations – is a leading commercially produced textbook.

The Role of the Teacher in the Delivery of the Product

How does an institution – with all its knowledge of its students and teachers, and all its data – design for flexibility? The TBDP (Textbook Development Project) at BUSEL takes the view that flexibility is something initiated by the teacher, and/or the student, and that it is between the students and the teacher the connections are made – the teaching and learning – whereby the textbook is somehow peripheralized or at least decentralized. Nevertheless, the question remains: can flexibility be designed in? Can a book have a flexible quality? A propensity for adaptation?

In the revision of the BUSEL series, stress has been placed on the clarity of lesson aims with an exacting relevance to the syllabus document. Approach, methodology and technique seem less important and much more arbitrary when the focal point is on the aim of a lesson (although the distinction between skills and more overt language-focused lessons is acknowledged). Teachers at BUSEL are encouraged to view materials critically, and teach their own lessons when they wish to, with the proviso that the specified lesson aims are met. If the TBDP insists on a syllabus focus, perhaps the ultimate extreme of such an institutional text-book project would be an anti-textbook project with the provision of no materials at all (except a Teacher's Book and a syllabus). That would give ultimate flex-ibility of approach, methodology and technique. But perhaps flexibility does not refer to approach, methodology or technique at all, or not importantly.

Flexibility of materials is very likely, ultimately, to be a question of teacher training, and that the flexibility of a Student's Book resides – if anywhere – in the teacher. The purpose of the Teacher's Book would then be to augment the teachers' experience with a knowledge of institutional aims, and the purposes and aims of the course they are teaching, along with a knowledge of the means to meet those aims and purposes.

The Teacher's Book and Teacher Training

The question naturally arises as to whether the Teacher's Book can indeed provide the teacher training to help the teacher be flexible in using the coursebook. A fuller discussion of the role and function of the Teacher's Book, and an exploration of its potentials and limitations, is beyond the scope of this chapter, and is planned as a separate article in the near future. However, BUSEL believes the answer to this question is yes. Why yes?

In rewriting the Teacher's Book for the pre-intermediate level we are investi-gating ways of supporting the teaching of the textbook by giving – in addition to the purposes and aims of the each lesson and the overall aims and purposes of the course – information on the use of the various exercises by providing, alongside legitimate teaching notes, a glossary/catalogue of amongst other things the terminology and techniques used by the writers. The assumption here is that the user – the teacher – will have a sound basic knowledge of teaching and learning, and that the Teacher's Book can provide an opportunity for increasing the teacher's *teaching capital* – increasing knowledge, skills and repertoire.

Because this has implications for the size of the Teacher's Book, and because the techniques and terminology of teaching are not restricted to level and will be relevant for other books in the series, the TBDP is currently researching placing the entire Teacher's Book on the Internet. The opportunities provided by hypertext – the highlighted computer-readable text which allows very far-ranging cross-referencing across the net – is one area with enormous potential. To mention briefly further benefits: a digitized, downloadable Teacher's Book, using hypertext, will promote the idea of the Teacher's Book as interactive. It will also allow regular updating. Another benefit, directly for the writers, is that it allows for a certain level of shorthand in the lesson notes.

If the answer is no – to the question of whether the Teacher's Book can provide the teacher training to help the teacher be flexible in using the coursebook – then the Teacher's Book would be basically a manual – an instruction book for the technology (Student's Book) – with the teacher in the role of operative. The extreme alternative would be to go into the minutiae of preparation and delivery. This is a strategy that is likely to tether the teacher to the materials rather than be a support for teacher development. This is contrary to the nature of any rewarding and creative activity such as teaching.

The Textbook as Process

The word *process* is used advisedly. The writing part of institutional textbook writing is only one point in the process. That one point we may see as an end point, or an end process in itself, with its own operations, processes and procedures. It is not anyway *the* end point. Paradoxically, too, it might not be the most important point for the institution. However, it is a determined point where an attempt is made to materialize the best theory and practice as understood and adjudged by the institution at that time.

The Role of Management

The critical acts, or judgements, that the functional and administrative divisions make on the operational, tactical and strategic orientation of the school can constitute influence-relations that will govern decision-making concerning the design of the textbook, as it will the writing. In order for this to happen, the management of BUSEL provides opportunity for institutional thinking to find its way into the design criteria of the textbook. This is not simply a case of having the functional and administrative divisions send a set of guidelines to the directorate or textbook writers and leaving the prioritizing, and elimination, of guidelines, to the addressees.

If we look again at the product we see that the textbook is the context where a number of practical and theoretical considerations meet; one might argue that these considerations could be divided into higher-order and lower-order considerations. However, given the multidimensionality of the product and the role of affect and the distinctness of the product's users, these considerations are not so easily categorized.

It could be argued that the textbook could be written in reference to one particular group's terms. It is obvious that this would privilege any one of the user groups we have mentioned and – given the nature of the relationship between the three different groups of users – be detrimental to the other groups. Accepting that the product has to reflect the needs and wants of each user group, we have arrived at the managerial role in institutional textbook writing, which is to supervise and influence the design process so that a composite of core and auxiliary dimensions important to each group of users is addressed in the product itself. In the previous section, the nature of these needs and wants was outlined.

However, it is essential that the overall aim of the course and the standards set are given primacy and that the textbook *is* – as defined above – a set of materials for the efficient and effective teaching and learning of a known student body by a known teaching body at a given level to a prescribed standard. This principle is the Prime Directive, the principal core dimension.

The Textbook as a Means of Reflection

The decisions that follow upon the initial decision to write a textbook are generated at BUSEL by the interaction of the divisions within the school. This is dialectical in nature. Forums to encourage and allow this to happen are organized regularly with representatives or heads of all or a number of the functional and administrative divisions in the school. This large group is further divided into smaller groups, depending on the purpose of the meetings. Many of these forums may exist prior to the decision to write a textbook and the idea to write a textbook may have come from these forums. The important point is that ideas on the textbook are allowed to be aired and taken into account. Meetings strictly related to the development of the textbook continue pre, while and post-production.

It has been found at BUSEL that, as long as the purpose of the meetings is kept in focus, and as long as consensus sought, they will enrich institutional thinking rather than impoverish it. Discussions and decisions in these meetings constitute the greater part of institutional textbook writing in terms of time, and are arguably the most important part because they allow BUSEL to go back to basics, to first principles if you like, and rethink its most fundamental beliefs and ideas about what it does.

This rethinking will not be limited in its effect to the design of the textbook but will affect to a greater or lesser degree every part of the school. To give an example: in the revision of the first textbook in the BUSEL series we have looked again at how the Student's Book was originally underpinned. This involved looking at the criteria by which lesson aims were chosen. One dimension of this was analysis of the syllabus document itself. Referencing lesson plans to the syllabus was done by comparing all the lesson aims in the textbook with the syllabus objectives for the level. What was found in the analysis referred both to the textbook being analysed and to the criteria we were using. One of the results was a decision to restate and respecify the syllabus objectives more clearly. To exemplify this briefly and simplistically, when tabulating the language objectives we needed to define what the students would be able to understand (receptively) and express (productively) and state each objective functionally with a description of its structure/form, and the contexts in which it would be found by giving examples of use. We also needed to state whether the form and/or meaning had been met before. This led to an experimental revision and respecification of part of the syllabus. The result of this experiment was favourable. Once respecified, it provided more reliable criteria for judging the relevance of a material to a course.

Another example of rethinking came out in a dialogue between curriculum and TBDP (Textbook Development Project) and was again related to the syllabus. It was stated in a meeting with the directorate that the TBDP would aim for 100 per cent coverage of the language items stated in the syllabus. The question that accompanied this decision was how this was to be achieved given the number of language items to be taught? It transpired, however, that dealing with the syllabus in quantitative terms was misleading us. Language items, despite the format of the syllabus, are not stand-alone. The syllabus by its format implied *that* and misled us into thinking language items are so isolated, but this is contrary to what we know to be true. This understanding illuminated a problem in materials production we were having, where materials writers were producing one material to address each language item. This confusing of syllabus format with ontological status – on the surface a purely theoretical issue – was leading to very practical problems in course density. The language item issue was reconceived. Although it would be impossible to use as a syllabus format, it was suggested that, rather than see language items as democratic entities of equal weight, it would be helpful for both curriculum and the TBDP to view language items as imprecise hierarchies in the manner of vocabulary, which might likewise be bundled into broad packages. In thinking of language items in this manner, the gap between syllabus and materials could be bridged. Teaching the present perfect for, say, indefinite time presupposed a level of knowledge and awareness about the use of the simple past related to a recognition of certain time markers and the time or aspect being referred to. In consequence, curriculum and TBDP were able to come up with a schematic representation of materials design which is intended to be published as original research in the near future.

The purpose of these examples is to show how textbook design processes aid reflection and impact on other areas in the school. The opposite is also true. The provisions of the different sets of users will impact on the textbook; the development of a proto-vocabulary syllabus has changed the way in which vocabulary content of the book will be determined, and approached. This is natural given the dialogue that will come about between the textbook group and each functional and administrative division in the school. The example shows this impact may be felt especially by the curriculum, but it is equally true of teacher training, self-access and assessment.

At BUSEL, the TTU (Teacher Training Unit) oversees the production of materials and teacher's notes in the initial stages along with CTU (Curriculum and Testing Unit) and the TBDP (Textbook Development Group). The aim of this liaison is to obtain initial feedback on technical and theoretical issues as well as on the level of teaching expertise required to teach the material. The TTU has the training and expertise plus the extensive experience of the classroom and classroom observation to offer valuable insights into the materials and how they might work and suggestions on how materials might be improved. It also offers its perspective on teaching in the school, which is helpful. In return, the TBDP offers the TTU an experience of textbook writing and the challenges that face the writers and designers of materials outside the training usually provided by the

University of Cambridge Local Examinations Syndicate (UCLES) courses such as the Certificate for Overseas Teachers of English (COTE), an initial in-service training course for practising teachers, and the Cambridge Diploma in English Language Teaching to Adults (DELTA) for more experienced, usually qualified, teachers of adults. It also has the opportunity to view material development from a broader institutional perspective, as the TBDP can share its attempts to balance the demands and pressures exerted on it from the other divisions of the school.

At BUSEL, the gravitational pull between the SAU (Self-Access Unit) and TBDP is great, and has to be prudently addressed. The reason for this is the overlap between homework and self-study, integral parts of any course, and the provision of self-access. How different can they be? How different should they be? To BUSEL this is formulated as a syllabus question. In unpublished research the TBDP has discerned three functions of extra-class activity. Firstly, if we look at a course of study and specify – rigorously and in great detail – what will be taught and what will be assessed we run the risk of curtailing additional effort by the student. Teachers have voiced their concerns about this, calling it 'spoon-feeding'. A student might be able to sail close to the wind and do just enough to pass. How can a school address this? Un-specify the courses?

It is suggested by our research that extra-class activity can be seen as having three relations to the syllabus: it can either be identical (more of the same); ancillary (additional to the course but an extension of course elements); and auxiliary (non-essential extension beyond the course proper). If we take these three classifications of extra-class work, we may divide them between the textbook project (what goes into the workbook) and self-access (what is provided through various media in relation to the course outside the student's book and work-book). Through such a division of self-study provision we are positing a notion that any syllabus can be divided into a great and lesser syllabus, at any given level and/or (they are not exclusive concepts) a real and possible syllabus. If this can be effectively accounted for and executed, the term extra-curricular can be redefined. Through discussion of the boundaries of SAU and the TBDP, the opportunity arises for both to redefine spheres of operation and provision.

On the topic of syllabus design it is often suggested that assessment systems be set up before material development can begin. This is fallacious, or at best a half-truth. It is anyway misleading. At BUSEL the dialectic between assessment systems and materials development is ongoing. It seems fairly banal to state that it is inevitable that developments in one area will create tensions in the other and it is through the resolution of such tensions that the areas of both assessment and materials development can be explored, if not actually refined. In BUSEL, TBDP (Textbook Development Project) work often finds that it requires information from Testing to ensure the relevance of materials. This information may or may not be available, and requires Testing to extend its specification of its tests with reference to the syllabus. It cuts both ways: the TBDP has to make sure it works within the constraints of assessment too. Each division pushes and bears on the other.

A final point on the effect of institutional textbook writing. BUSEL allows its textbooks to compete with other commercially produced textbooks on the market. The decision whether to use the textbook rests after consultation with the heads of teaching units (HTUs). In doing this, BUSEL recognizes that its aim to provide EAP-oriented EFL textbooks to its teachers must be evidenced in substantive product differentiation. This tangible difference aims to provide a functional benefit over the long term. This variation needs firstly to be there in the product, and also be seen to be important. The HTUs constitute the group of operational/middle managers who run courses in the school. In that function they are the final arbiters of what works and what does not work in the classroom. Interaction with the HTUs will be on both a theoretical and practical level, but with a pronounced practical slant. As they represent teachers and are closest to the classroom, their opinion and ideas carry a great deal of weight among the teachers and the other divisions of the school. If the HTUs are unconvinced of the product, the product will simply not be used. The TBDP needs to involve HTUs in aspects of the design and writing of the textbook, and receive their feedback. The HTUs constitute the most influential group in the school.

The purpose of these examples – as stated above – is to show how textbook design processes can impact on each functional and administrative division and how the contrary is also true. Given the dialectical nature of the interaction, this is to be expected. Through this process a better product is aimed for, one where all user expectations are at least addressed, where a sense of ownership is shared and where stakeholder claims are recognized. Ultimately, however, how good the product is depends on the quality of the judgement and execution – an end process in itself, with its own operations, processes and procedures as previously stated.

Conclusion

This chapter has attempted to offer guidance by offering an overview of the issues involved in institutional textbook writing by reflecting on the experiences that Bilkent University School of English Language (BUSEL) has gone through, since the beginning of the textbook projects in 1995, and having produced a suite of textbooks which it is now in the process of revising, looking specifically at the nature of the product, and the elements of the process.

Many of the considerations are set out as questions. Some of these considerations it is argued admit to no solution, only a level of engagement. This is perhaps the most important aspect of institutional textbook writing. In developing textbooks one ought not to expect evolution and progress if by those terms is meant a steady process of improvement. Each textbook writing project will address the same questions, and from the answers it finds most convincing endeavour to materialize the best theory and practice as understood and adjudged by the institution at that time to produce a textbook

Reference

Zikmund, William G. and d'Amico, M. (1996) *Basic Marketing*. Saint Paul, Minneapolis: West Publishing Company.

CHAPTER

31

Personal and Professional Development Through Writing: The Romanian Textbook Project

Ruxandra Popovici and Rod Bolitho

Introduction

In 1990–91, Romanian teachers of English were enjoying their first contacts with colleagues in Western Europe. The British Council in Bucharest commissioned a consultancy visit by Keith Morrow to take stock of the state of ELT in the country and to make recommendations about ways in which the British Council could offer professional assistance. One of his recommendations was the establishment of a textbook writing project. The existing secondary level textbooks were out of date and, from the point of view of teachers, learners and parents, ideologically biased. With the advancement of English to the status of first foreign language in most schools and the tide of change sweeping through the country, the need for new materials was urgent. British publishers were, of course, quick to spot the potential for new markets throughout Central and Eastern Europe, but global coursebooks were never going to meet the specific needs of Romanian learners in the long term. Acting on Morrow's recommendation, the British Council approached the Ministry of Education, a project was formulated and agreed upon, and the College of St Mark and St John was selected as UK partner institution through an open tender. What follows is the story of the eight years of partnership and collaborative effort which ensued, and how the project affected the personal and professional lives of all those who were involved in it.

Who Wants to be a Writer?

In late 1991, the British Council in Bucharest advertised nationally for writers. The applicants were all teachers, mostly from secondary schools. They submitted sample materials on the basis of which a number were selected and called for interview. No one really had a clear idea of what the project would involve and only two or three had ever written for publication before. Finally, a team of fifteen, including a ministry coordinator, was selected for training in the UK. For most of them it was the first visit to the West, and it was a huge incentive. It was a big responsibility for everyone involved, but the sense of excitement and expectancy was palpable.

Building the Team: The Plymouth Experience

So it was that, in April 1992, a group of Romanian would-be writers, fourteen women and a man, arrived in Plymouth for their training course. The period of ten weeks spent living and working together was seminal for the project. They were given an update in methodology, they reviewed and evaluated existing coursebooks, they formulated a working syllabus and divided into writing teams at lower and upper secondary levels. But they did much more. They visited schools, went on trips and to the theatre and made many friends and contacts in the college and the community. They immersed themselves energetically in British culture. One even broke her leg and learned more than she had bargained for about the National Health Service. They shared kitchens and cooked together. They walked and, above all, talked together, often until deep into the night. By the time they left Plymouth, reserve and individualism had begun to give way to a sense of belonging to a team. There was still apprehension, even insecurity, about the magnitude of the task facing them, but everyone was ready to give it a try. As teachers, they wanted to produce something worthwhile for Romanian learners. College tutors were infected by this idealism and fascinated by the challenge. By the end of the course in Plymouth, one of them (Rod) had agreed to take on the role of consultant to the project. Sadly, we lost one member of the team (for personal reasons) at this time, one of only two drop-outs (the other was later, for health reasons) during the seven-year working life of the project. Looking back on it, this was undoubtedly the formative experience that mattered most. It was a time of trust and consensus-building, a time when working partnerships were formed, a chance for each individual to learn how to listen to and value the opinions of their colleagues, but also a time when conflicts were encountered and resolved, and strengths and weaknesses in individuals were revealed.

But could fourteen largely inexperienced writers really author a series of textbooks for the entire eight years of the Romanian secondary cycle? It remained to be seen.

Learning the Hard Way

The Joy and Pain of Writing Together – Learning from Each Other

For the tutors in Plymouth, work with their Romanian colleagues had added a dimension to their thinking about English-language teaching. It had offered them a fascinating glimpse of the realities of life and education in Romania and had begun to overturn some of their own deep-rooted prejudices about life in a one-time Communist country. We were made aware of the strengths and vitality of local language-teaching traditions, of the value accorded to intellectual pursuits, the widespread love of literature and the arts and the strong sense of pride in the regional cultures of Romania. The challenge now was to integrate all of these positive features into textbooks which would retain their Romanian identity but would also display an understanding of the communicative purpose of language teaching and learning which had dominated Western-produced textbooks in the 1980s and early 1990s.

One of the key criteria for the selection of the writers had been geographical. There were good reasons for ensuring that the new textbooks were not written only by writers from the capital city. Romania is a large country with relatively poor transport links, and so the creation of cells of writers in Arad and Timisoara in the west of the country, Sibiu in the Transylvania, Bucharest in the south-east and Lasi in Moldavia was seen as a means of ensuring that no writer would work in isolation.

It was to these regional centres that the writers returned after the course in Plymouth, each mini-group charged with producing the first sample materials for textbooks at Grade 5 level (lower secondary) and Grade 9 (upper secondary). The writers were equipped with home computers (they had received training in word processing during the course in Plymouth) and each had an agreed topic and unit to work on.

When Rod arrived in Bucharest in the late autumn of 1992 for the first in-country workshop, these first draft materials were on the table for discussion. At this first workshop, a working pattern evolved which was to be maintained throughout the project. Drafts were copied and passed to everyone in each sub-team for reading and discussion. At these early meetings, insecurity was still rife and there was a great deal of coded criticism and defensiveness. There was also the occasional conflict or emotional outburst as a unit which one of the writers had laboured over for weeks was criticized or dismantled by others. It became clear that writing these books in a way that would satisfy everyone was going to be no easy task. Sometimes, we struck compromises that not everybody was really satisfied with, just to keep the peace. Often, we worked until late at night to keep up with our own demanding timetable. But we always moved on, fuelled by an endless supply of sweets, chocolates, fruit and other titbits and by a healthy dose of good humour to compensate for the constant drain on our nervous energy.

But this was a learning community, too. Individual qualities and strengths began to emerge within each sub-team: creativity, attention to detail, organizational skills, methodological insight, grammatical knowledge, lateral and critical thinking. People began, gradually, to listen to each other with respect and to see the need to subordinate their own preferences and preoccupations to the wishes of the team as a whole and to the 'grand design' of producing textbooks we could all be proud of.

Ways of giving and receiving feedback was one of the central lessons in team-building strategies during the training course. It took a lot of workshops to practise this and finally defensiveness gave way to open-mindedness, and aggressive criticism to constructive feedback and mutual support. This was a natural process that went along with the development of the team spirit, of the trust among the authors and of the recognition that decisions taken as a team are bound to be better than individual ones. In time, the workshops became a forum for free expression of opinions and the appropriate environment for learning assertiveness and self-esteem.

Phrases such as, 'In my opinion ...', 'Now I can see ...', 'I think you're right', 'X may have a point here' were being heard more and more often to everybody's comfort and relaxation. Gradually 'my unit' was replaced with 'our unit' and this was seen as a gain, not as a loss. We became a strong community sharing the same goals, the same successes and also the same setbacks.

We all went through the experience of the workshops as members of a group and as individuals and ultimately it is this experience which made us aware of our own strengths and weaknesses and helped us act independently during the project and after it.

Discussions ranged over every possible aspect of the books, the treatment of grammar, cultural content, the place of the mother tongue and translation, the appropriacy of illustrations, the teaching load, the learning load, the nature of intensive and extensive reading, the structuring of writing, the pros and cons of authentic and specially written texts and dialogues ... the list could go on.

Workshops were held three, sometimes four, times a year. Between the workshops, the Romanian project coordinators fielded all the problems and concerns of the writers. From her base in the British Council office, the project manager, together with three successive project directors, negotiated her way through the minefields of a changing educational scene and liaised with Romanian and later British publishing houses. There were moments of real crisis in the management of the project and a number of key turning points, such as the decision to change publishers. But a combination of enlightened management, single-minded resolve, good will and happy coincidence kept the project on the rails, if not always on schedule.

We all came to look forward to the workshops. There was a real sense of anticipation at each coming together, as though we all, consultants (Rod was eventually joined by Sue Mohamed who took responsibility for working with the lower secondary team), writers and coordinators, realized that these were special and important milestones in our professional and personal lives.

Lessons from Piloting

The decision to pilot draft materials as they were written was included in the initial project plan. This was a 'first' in the materials production field in Romania, where textbooks had been published for decades without prior consultation with students and teachers. The first sample units in Books 5 and 9 went through large-scale piloting in all the 40 counties of the country. This proved to be a challenge for everybody involved, organizers and writers as well. It took persuading skills to make a local publisher invest time and money into a pilot edition that was not going to bring them any immediate financial gain. Distributing hundreds of booklets into all the regions of the country and then collecting feedback was not an easy job. For the writers, the task of constructing questionnaires for students and teachers was completely new. It required, on the one hand, clarification of the methodological and organizational principles of the textbooks and also the additional skill of writing clear, unambiguous questions, giving an appropriate range of alternative answers, allowing for open comments and striking a balance between the desire to find out as much as possible from the respondents and the awareness that long questionnaires are tiring, burdensome and sometimes demotivating.

Evaluating the feedback from students and teachers was also new and we were all waiting impatiently to see first reactions to our work. These were mostly positive and this was a boost to our work. We were particularly encouraged by the appreciation shown by learners in their responses.

There was also some criticism and we had to cope with it for the first time. The writers' reactions varied from defensiveness to readiness to change parts of the lessons. The evaluation of the answers showed us also that we had to be clearer in passing on our messages to our peers. We realized by the variety of responses from students and teachers that our textbooks were definitely on the cutting edge of innovation in Romanian ELT and were going to challenge some of the educational values of the last decades.

The piloting procedure was repeated in the following years with all the other six textbooks in the series. The size of the sample diminished each time for organizational, financial and competition-related reasons. The reduction in the scale of piloting was compensated for by more targeted questions and the expertise that the team had gained in analysing feedback. Everyone involved got more used to the procedure. Teachers and students became franker and more outspoken and writers more open to feedback.

Lessons from Publishers

The relationship the team had with publishers was one of the most formative in the life of the project. Local expertise in coursebook publishing at the beginning of the 1990s was restricted to typing, to minimum editing and rather unsophisticated design and artwork. The local publisher that produced the first two books in the series acted very much like a printing unit. Consequently, the authors had to take on part of the job of laying out the page, and, together with consultants, that of editing and doing corrections. We tried to work to the best of our abilities and the result was two books that were at the time the first fully coloured and illustrated EFL textbooks for Romania.

With the beginning of the World Bank – Ministry of Education textbook reform in Romania and the setting up of competitions for alternative textbooks for the same level, we saw the possibility of launching an invitation to publishers in Romania and in the UK to tender for the production of the remaining six textbooks in our series. Even when the decision was taken and the announcement went public some of us could not believe that there would be competitors willing to take over the production of our textbooks. To our surprise, the interest was high in both countries and we were able to choose, according to strict criteria, a top UK publisher. For all of us, that was a turning point in the life of our project.

What it meant was, first, the joy of realizing that our materials were interesting for publishers who were used to publishing internationally. Secondly, we learned that professionalism means more work and a lot of training in editorial skills for the authors. Very soon we became one big team, authors, consultants and publishers, and we were all putting our efforts together to produce books to the highest standards. This contributed to the development of the editorial skills and knowledge that professional authors have. The lessons from this four-and-a-half year-long experience were many: working to deadlines, working in partnership with the editors, quick and efficient communication between authors, consultants and editors, the restrictions of a limited number of pages in a book and of a limited number of activities and illustrations in a double-page spread. We learned painfully the meaning of the dreaded word 'overmatter', the difference between 'essential' and 'desirable', the long way from 'hoping to get copyright permission' to 'getting copyright permission', the abrupt realization that artists and actors who record our tapescripts cannot read our minds but only very accurate art briefs and carefully annotated tapescripts. All along, we benefited from the sensitive approach of an editorial team that showed respect for Romanian educational and cultural values and understood well that the training of the authors was one of the aims of the project. The resulting series of six textbooks in complete packages put at a disadvantage the first two books which were published locally, but we take this as an indication of our learning curve from the 'trial and error' stage to professionalism.

These quotations from the publisher and from one of the authors might make the meaning of this working relationship clearer:

> Everyone in our publishing team got caught up and enthused by the momentum of the project. This is a feature of most successful publishing projects but I think it was apparent to an exceptional degree in the *Pathway* project.

> We owe our UK publishers a lot of lessons in professionalism, honesty, support, trust and openness. A bonus we hadn't expected at the beginning of the project.

Choice of Materials – Between Fun and Hard Work

We have always known that one of the keys to the success of our textbooks is to keep up the interest of the students and the teachers. We have constantly tried to find authentic materials, for the right age, with the right content from the methodological point of view, but have always asked ourselves; 'Would they really like it?' 'What modern group would be the best choice?', 'Are these scientific data still new or history already?'. The *what* and the *how* of collecting materials to be included in the textbooks are a permanent preoccupation for a writer and formed part of the experience the authors gathered in the lifetime of the textbook project. We can say 'gathered happily' because fields of activity were Romania, Britain and the USA. The team went back to Britain twice after their initial training, in 1994 and 1997, for top-up programmes which both included time for going to the library and to bookshops, for photocopying, for visiting travel agencies, hunting for leaflets, brochures and also time for interviewing native speakers of English.

In 1995, the efforts of the British Council and the Soros Foundation were supplemented by those of the USIA (United States Information Agency), who understood that, in order to have an 'as-genuine-as-possible' image of America in the textbooks, the authors needed first-hand experience, direct contact with American people, access to authentic materials that the authors could not have found in Romania, in other words, full exposure to the contemporary American way of life.

We owe to these visits the authentic, stereotype-free, vivid approach to British and American life in our textbooks. It is one thing to write about the British or American educational system based on reproducing information from a magazine and a different one to do it after having visited schools in these countries and talked to teachers and students. Meeting Native Americans, African Americans, American and British people of different origins, city folk and country folk, people from Scotland, from Wales, from many other parts of Britain, hearing mid-Atlantic, New Orleans and Arizona accents, Midland or Scottish accents, all this made it a lot more natural and true to life to speak about cultural diversity in these two countries. The careful and informed selection and use of materials and information was another way for the authors to show their sense of responsibility towards the learners. Students' comments on our textbook show their appreciation of the diversity, richness and authenticity of the material that was offered to them.

Presenting Materials to Colleagues – Engaging the ELT Community

The realization that the ideas and principles the textbooks were built around needed to be passed on and made explicit to other teachers came quite early in the project. The link between textbooks and the in-service teacher-training component had been recognized and developed by the British Council in cooperation with the Ministry of Education since the early 1990s and was strengthened with the setting up of a *teacher-training project* that involved teacher training, and trainer training, training inspectors of English and university methodologists throughout the country. The materials written by our team were used in training courses alongside other materials mainly drawn from global coursebooks. The messages that we got were varied. Mostly, interest in our materials was high, and many teachers and students were very enthusiastic. However, particularly at the beginning, there were times when we heard things like: 'textbook *x* is better because it is written by internationally famous textbook writers', 'textbook *y* is glossier and has superb pictures', 'textbook *z* is easier', 'there was more grammar in the *old* textbooks'. It was, of course, tough to cope with even mild criticism, at a time when 'ownership' over the textbooks was developing rapidly among the authors. It was also a time when Romanian professionals were in the course of realizing that divergence of opinions does not have to be taken personally. The lesson we had to learn was that the materials once written belong to a lot more people than the writers. They belong to the whole ELT community, to the students and to their parents. The only way forward was to keep going, stay in touch with our colleagues, be open about our work, listen to opinions, build on good ideas from the field, try and amend those things that were clearly not working and build our case for the things that we believed in and which we felt confident about.

The *Annual General Meetings* organized by the British Council have always been a valuable forum for the exchange of ideas, for updates on all projects and for formal and informal meetings of all key professionals in ELT and wider educational fields in Romania. Gradually everybody at those meetings developed a strong sense of the profession and moreover a sense of their specialism within the profession. We never missed a chance at these meetings and other professional events in the country to speak about the textbooks, to give news about the project and to show our enormous pride in what we were doing.

Our openness, our respect for peers and students, our determination not to stop the piloting of draft materials even in times of tough competition, our decision to revise the first book in the upper secondary cycle as a result of suggestions from teachers and students, all paid off. The books are now more than ever appreciated as a modern series that combines the best of both the Romanian and the UK tradition in EFL and materials writing. What we hear now more and more is 'it's so interesting', 'we learn so many new things in all domains', 'I like the new approach to literature', 'we appreciate this way of developing translation skills', 'this prepares the students better for Baccalaureate', 'I'm sure this prepares me for my future career', 'these textbooks make me progress with my English' and so on.

Once the project was well under way, development of the writers' *presentation skills* was one of the first additional training needs that were identified. This, together with other aspects of textbook writing formed part of a top-up course in the College of St Mark and St John in the summer of 1994. The overall thinking behind the project made it possible to plan and organize in turn the participation of all writers in *professional events in Romania and abroad*: teachers' association conferences, international EFL seminars and workshops, symposiums. For many of the authors it was difficult at the beginning to cope with audiences, large or small, to hear their own voices shaking at times, to feel how nervousness was getting the better of them, to fight insecurity, to try to remember desperately a word that they had carefully thought of before the start, to try to find misplaced transparencies and to realize that time was up before really getting to 'the best' part. But there must have been something about the authors' enthusiasm, their sincerity, the way they articulated ideas and, of course, about the meaning of their presentations and the content of the materials that caught the audiences, because feedback from those conferences was usually very good. There are writers in the team who discovered that the role of speaker or workshop facilitator is second nature to them.

News about the Romanian textbook project started spreading rapidly outside Romania, in the UK and in the region of Central and Eastern Europe and the Caspian Basin. Encouragement and appreciation came from ELT colleagues in different countries, together with requests for the project framework, sample materials, project documents, books or simply 'Please, tell us how it all started', 'How were the writers selected?', 'How do you organize piloting?', 'How do you manage to get the teachers on board?', 'How can you write in such a large team?' and so on. Local textbook projects had hardly been successful in the 1970s and 1980s and people interested in that – teachers, materials writers, publishers, project managers, educationalists – were beginning to realize that the Romanian textbook project had a good chance of being one of the first fully successful ones.

Learning by Reflecting

The times when the authors had the chance to slow down and look back have been rare but the benefits to themselves and to the project have been enormous.

Receiving and interpreting colleagues' and students' feedback on the materials has been a good and healthy way of seeing our work from another perspective. Teaching our own materials and watching colleagues use them helped the authors to become more detached from the writer's perspective and, as a result, more aware of the 'real classroom life' of the books.

In 1995, the British Council commissioned a mid-project evaluation, to be carried out by an external evaluator. In order to put together the evaluation report, Shelagh Rixon, who had been previously acquainted with the project, spent two weeks with the team, attended the writing workshops, talked to teachers, students, officials in the Ministry of Education, editors, consultants, coordinators and of course with the writers themselves. The results of the evaluation, the suggestions and the recommendations were all of great help in our thinking and planning. In addition to that, all project participants involved underwent the process of reflecting on the beginnings of their 'journey', of their initial expectations and further training needs. That was one of the first formal instances when the authors were asked to assess themselves and to put into words their thoughts about the project, its organization, its management and about their own expectations. This required a new understanding of the meaning and role of evaluation, as support for everybody involved, as clarification and possible restructuring, not as a judgemental and threatening inspection procedure.

Four years later, in 1999, we were all trying to face the reality of the end of the project. The last books were out or about to be published, the teachers and students were now well informed about the series and lots of them had taken its methodological principles on board. Our last workshop focused on project members as professionals and project members as persons. We took a broad and, at the same time, deep look at all our work and we did the valuable exercise of articulating once again the tenets that underlie the whole series. We also took a deep breath and looked into ourselves. We talked of the project itself with its highs, lows and turning points, we talked about our personal gains and losses. It was an emotional time. We were all still, without admitting it, very involved in the project, and did not really believe that it was going to end. We talked about a future which was unclear and the danger of a vacuum in our lives.

The sense that this had been a project that went well beyond its initial aims of writing a series of eight textbooks and of training a group of teachers to become materials writers, and that its consequences are far-reaching and worth investigating, led to the decision to carry out a study of the impact of the textbook project. The study, now finished, establishes a methodology for impact studies of materials writing projects. It puts achievements against expectations. It explores the process and the product, the expected and particularly the unexpected, impact. It was carried out within the ELT community in Romania, which emphasizes the participatory nature of the whole project. It also developed research skills within the participants. Writers' involvement in the study varied: some were part of the team that planned and organized it, most of them were part of the data-collecting team, all of them were respondents in the area of the project's impact on the writers. Their answers, which came more than a year after the last workshop, show a sort of 'detached subjectivity' which helped them see deeper and clearer into the whole process and into themselves.

What did it all Mean? The Inner Voice

Development is the key word in this textbook project: development of materials, writers' professional and personal growth, teacher development, change of teaching procedures, change of teaching beliefs, change of roles of teachers and learners, development of learners' independence, all in the context of a fast-changing world.

The quotations below from the authors speak for themselves:

'The project helped me become a better teacher.'
'I feel I would like to take up teacher training now.'
'I now have the courage to try on my own.'
'I have greater confidence, enlarged horizons and I can tell high standards when I see them.'
'I've become a better person.'
'I have the feeling that my whole personality has changed.'
'We started the project as individuals but we finished it as team members.'
'In the course of the project I've become a reflective practitioner.'
'I have learned to work in a team and accept other opinions.'
'I've learned to listen to somebody else's point of view and think twice before jumping to conclusions.'
'I've become more exigent with myself.'
'I've got the feeling of belonging to the ELT family.'
'I've developed a critical eye for my own materials.'
'Decisions about the books and the project were always taken in keeping with the strong sense of accountability.'

'I feel like writing again.'

'The project opened up new professional vistas for me: EFL methodology, tea-cher development, materials writing and evaluation, assessment, presentations at conferences, even consultancy to other ELT projects in the country and abroad.'

It may now be worth looking again at what the authors said and perhaps counting the times the words *change, become* and *develop* occur.

Onwards and Upwards – Life After the Project

One can argue that the quotations above are only words. What are the writers/the project coordinator/the consultants actually doing now? How have they capital-ized on what they learned during the project.

Seven authors continued writing materials: EFL readers, EFL textbooks, text-books in other subjects through the medium of English. Five writers continued and extended their teacher-training and trainer-training activity with groups of teachers inside and outside Romania; two of them are acting as international tutors and consultants for educational projects outside Romania. More than half of the authors are now contributing to other educational and ELT projects organized by the British Council to which they bring their experience and their skills particularly in materials writing. The project coordinator manages another textbook project of a different content and nature, but along the same lines. The two consultants to the textbook project are now fulfilling the same role with textbook projects in Russia, Mongolia and Belarus.

All the participants in the textbook project learned a lot, are willing to learn more. Although we see the textbook project as the most rewarding professional experience we have had, development and learning are a state of the mind that has us in its grip. Our current professional experiences are not, nor would we want them to be, a replica of our project. They are just proof of the commitment to continued professional growth.

From Teaching to Materials Writing Projects – The Round Trip

We have come to see that involvement in materials writing projects is a route to personal and professional development. To illustrate this we offer these con-cluding ideas, which are drawn from the actual experience of the textbook team, on the reflections from participants in the project and on thoughts and feedback from students and other teachers.

What Teachers can Bring to a Materials Writing Project

- A sense of the classroom in which the materials are going to be used, by which we mean: atmosphere, classroom management, types of interaction between students and between the students and the teacher.
- A sense of the students who are going to use the textbook.

- A sense of the teachers who are going to use the textbooks.
- Practical knowledge of how learning takes place: different learning styles, learning strategies, internal processes related to acquisition, selection and retention of new language and new concepts.
- Practical and experiential knowledge of teaching: different teaching styles, different educational contexts, different attitudes to change and innovation.
- Understanding of the students' interests and needs.

What Materials Writing can Bring to Teachers

- Consolidation of their understanding of English Language Teaching methodology.
- Development of syllabus design and materials writing specialist skills.
- Development of systematic and clear thinking through the need to design syllabus, lessons and tasks.
- Articulate expression of thoughts and ideas through the need to present the textbooks to peers.
- Creativity through the need to boost students' interest.
- Selection skills through the need to collect and select materials for the textbook.
- Research skills through the process of piloting sample materials.
- Editorial skills through working with a publisher.
- Enhanced awareness of teacher-training principles.
- Awareness of deadlines and personal time management.
- Increased self-esteem and professional status through the value of a tangible and visible product.
- Increased self-confidence in the classroom through clearer ideas of lesson objectives.

What Projects[1] can Bring to Teachers who Write Materials

- Enhances team spirit and team-work skills which involve: the value of listening actively to others, of sharing ideas, of working together towards a common goal, of reflecting together, positive attitude to feedback to/from the team.
- Enhanced self-awareness through working with others.
- The knowledge and benefit of project management thinking in planning, organization, establishment of working mode, evaluation and redesign.
- Stronger links with teachers and students who are going to use the textbooks.
- New working relationships that may function in other areas.
- More friends.

None of this happens quickly, or automatically. Materials writing in teams requires time, patience, trust and hard work. But in our experience, it's worth it!

Appendix 31.1

The Romanian Textbook Team

Lower Secondary
Alaviana Achim
Liana Capotă (Book 5 only)
Ecaterina Comişel
Felicia Dinu
Alice Mastacan
Ruxandra Popovici
Elena Teodorescu

Upper Secondary
Rada Bălan
Miruna Carianopol
Ştefan Colibaba
Cornelia Coşer
Veronica Focşeneanu
Vanda Stan
Rodica Vulcanescu

Project Manager
Ruxandra Popovici (British Council, Bucharest)

Project Directors
Adrian Odell, Roy Cross, Jeremy Jacobson (British Council, Bucharest)

UK Consultants
Rod Bolitho (College of St Mark and St John, Plymouth), Sue Mohamed (Freelance)

References

Pathway to English, Books 5 and 9 (1994). Bucharest: Editura Didactica si Pedagogica.
Pathway to English, Books 6, 7, 8, 10, 11, 12 (1996–2000). Oxford: Oxford University Press.

Comments on Part E

Brian Tomlinson

Gaining from the Process

The main point that seems to be made by all the chapters in this section is that the process of materials development can be just as valuable as the product. This is not particularly true of a single author mechanically churning out materials to a formula predetermined by somebody else. But it can be very true of a group of people working together to pool their experience and expertise, whether it be to produce a global coursebook, an institutional or national course, an assignment on a course or just some supplementary materials for next week. If the group is given the freedom and resources to determine its own approach and framework (ideally with expert guidance and feedback), the members can gain tremendous awareness of all aspects of the learning and teaching of languages, they can gain skills which will be extremely useful to them afterwards and, above all, they can gain the confidence and self-esteem which all professionals need. In my view, this personal and professional development is best gained if the group is involved in all of the following procedures:

- Needs analysis of the target users
- Determination of pedagogical approach
- Determination of frameworks for developing the materials
- Determination of syllabus
- Drafting sample units
- Trialling the sample units
- Revising the syllabus, approach and frameworks
- Finding and/or developing texts
- Producing the materials
- Monitoring the materials
- Trialling the materials
- Revising the materials
- Editing the materials

And the bonus is that the more the group achieves personal and professional development from the process the greater will be the quality of the product. This important point seems to be recognized by many institutions and projects producing their own dedicated materials but it is a point worth considering by commercial publishers, who could improve the quality of their products by bringing together groups of materials developers and profiting from their combined energy, enthusiasm, confidence and awareness.

Positive Affect Benefits Personal, Professional and Materials Development

From the points made in the chapters in this section and in my comments above, it is apparent that positive affect is not only a prerequisite for successful language learning but it is a prerequisite for successful materials development too. To be successful, a materials development project needs not only to produce a quality product but to provide a quality learning experience for the developers too. In my experience this can only be achieved if the developers are convinced of the value of the project, are stakeholders in the project themselves, are enthusiastic about developing materials, are energetic, creative and imaginative, get on well together, view the project as an achievable challenge, are confident about their ability to contribute to the project and are professional in their approach to the project. Careful selection of the participants can help to achieve this positive affect but the key to success is the credibility, expertise, personality and attitude of the facilitators. If the facilitators are respected, trusted and enthusiastic, and if they provide stimulus, support and feedback in a positive way, there is a good chance that the developers will enjoy the experience and the project will be successful.

Humanistic materials can only be developed by a humanistic process of development.

Materials Development is an Interactive Process

All the chapters in this section emphasize that effective materials cannot be developed in isolation.

For the process and the product to be effective there must be interaction between the materials developers and:

- Their experience of language learning and teaching
- Their experience of prototypical groups of target learners
- Their previous experience of materials and of materials development
- Their theories of language and language learning
- 'Expert' theories of language and language learning
- Other materials developers
- Learners, teachers and administrators

And there must be dynamic interaction too between the materials and:

- The syllabus
- The target examinations
- The discovered needs and wants of the users of the materials
- Corpora of language use
- The real world

Developing Materials is One of the Best Ways to Gain Theoretical and Practical Awareness

Even if the members of the group are never going to become materials developers and even if their products are never going to be used, helping teachers and teacher trainees to cooperate in developing learning materials is one of the most effective ways of getting them to clarify and develop their theoretical knowledge and awareness, and to apply it to the practicalities of helping learners to acquire a language. Even if they are only devising activities to go with a reading text they have to:

- Articulate, develop and apply their theories of the L1 and L2 reading process
- Articulate, develop and apply their theories of learning
- Articulate, develop and apply their theories of language learning
- Consider such learner variables as age, level, motivation, learning styles, needs, wants and objectives
- Consider such teacher variables as age, training, confidence, personality, teaching styles and preparation
- Consider such administrator variables as syllabus requirements, examination requirements, time available, standardization, accountability and costs

And, of course, if they have to develop units for a coursebook they can cover an entire applied linguistics course while doing it.

Expertise in Materials Development can only be Gained through Developing Materials

It is a cliché, but a very important one, that you cannot be instructed to become a good materials developer. You can only be given the experience and helped to gain from it. This is a point which seems to be made emphatically by all the chapters in this section.

In my experience and opinion, this means setting up real (or at least realistic) materials development situations, making clear the objectives and the constraints, being available to provide information, stimulus and support as needed and providing formative and summative feedback designed not to evaluate but to provide opportunities for learning and development.

Conclusion

Brian Tomlinson

Nearly all the chapters in this book express some dissatisfaction with the current state of materials development. There is an awareness of the constraints under which materials developers are operating (especially those working for commercial publishers) but there is also a disappointment that the materials currently being developed do not often match what is needed and wanted by the learners who are going to use them. Particular reservations are expressed by the authors of this book about:

- The focus on learning language items (especially grammar items) in many materials
- The unidimensional nature many of the processes learners are asked to engage in
- The tendency to underestimate the learner both in terms of content and of task
- The triviality and blandness of the content in many commercial materials
- The lack of potential for affective engagement of many of the materials
- The lack of flexibility of many of the materials, both in terms of potential for adaptation, localization and personalization and of the provision of choice for the learner and the teacher
- The mismatch between many of the materials and what second language acquisition research has revealed about the processes of language learning and teaching
- The mismatch between many of the materials and what teachers know can promote language acquisition in the classroom

However, most of the contributors to this volume are fairly optimistic about the future of materials development for language learning and they feel that we can help language learners more by developing materials which:

- Have the potential for affective engagement
- Engage the learners in multidimensional processes which match what we are finding out about mental representation and durable learning

- Relate to the interests and enthusiasms of the learners
- Have been designed to facilitate adaptation, localization and personalization
- Cater for different preferred learning and teaching styles
- Prepare the learners for L1-like processes of language use rather than tie them to L2 models
- Both learners and teachers can enjoy using

Let us hope that more applied and action research will soon be carried out to find out much more about what can make language learning materials effective. And let us hope that publishers and curriculum developers will have the courage and the resources to apply what we find out to what we develop. Maybe then I will manage my lifelong dream of learning and teaching a foreign language successfully.

Notes

Chapter 8

1. Schools in Singapore select textbooks from this list.

Chapter 11

1. At the 2001 IATEFL Conference in York a colloquium was held bringing together aspiring writers, niche publishers, MATSDA and the Society of Authors in an attempt to reactivate more creative publishing.
2. See Brian Tomlinson's 'Publishing Proposal for World-Wide Readers' (August 2001). Two tenets set out there include: no formal linguistic control (authors' intuitive sense of level will be used instead) and no activities or questions.
3. The photocopier has arguably been the most revolutionary piece of technology in its influence on teaching methodology. It is now so taken for granted that we tend to forget what it is like when no handouts are available!

Chapter 12

1. The chapter will focus on reading and writing as, despite remarkable advances in speech processing, voice recognition and artificial intelligence, computers cannot yet simulate the spontaneity and reciprocity of authentic oral interaction.
2. The development of electronic learning materials clearly involves such teamwork, unlike the writer of a textbook who can usually compose relatively independently of others. Each member of the team needs to be well-versed not only in his/her own area of technical expertise but in the theoretical rationale behind the design of the materials. Perhaps the most critical member of such a team is the instructional designer – a role often neglected in the production of such resources.

Chapter 16

1. I am very grateful to the members of the Essex Beginners' Materials Group for their stimulating discussions; the membership has included Suzuku Anai,

Liz Austin, Gladis Garcia, Shigeo Kato, Lou Lessios, Ignazia Posadinu, Peter Treacher and Emi Uchida, all associated with the University of Essex. They may however be startled by the direction in which some of their comments have led me.

Chapter 19

1. References are made in this chapter to various published materials, in order to offer concrete exemplification of points being made. Similar exemplification could have been made choosing examples from other materials. Although certain activities/exercises are criticized, it is not my intention to suggest that the materials cited do not *in toto* have pedagogical value.

2. These verbs are often referred to as 'reporting verbs' and of course are often used to report speech acts. However, they are also used to refer to speech acts in the present and future, in which case they are not 'reporting' anything, and so the label is misleading. There is also the issue of verbs such as 'say', 'tell' and 'ask' being used with continuous aspect on occasions (e.g., *John was saying that the show's been cancelled*) – grammar materials basically ignore this, along with the increasingly frequent use of 'go' as a reporting verb in conversational settings.

Chapter 26

1. For a detailed account of the process involved in producing this syllabus see L. Davcheva, H. Reid-Thomas and A. Pulverness, 1999.

Chapter 29

1. Predictive evaluation: in order to choose what are the best teaching materials available to them and to use in the classroom, teachers are required to carry out a predictive evaluation (Ellis, 1997).

2. Retrospective evaluation: if teachers feel the need to undertake a further evaluation once they have used the materials, then they will have to carry out a retrospective evaluation (Ellis, 1997).

Chapter 30

1. BUSEL is part of Bilkent University, a private English-medium university, the first private institution of its kind in Turkey, which admitted its first students in 1986. There are about 10,000 students at the university, with BUSEL having about 2500 full-time students. Moreover, it provides support English for about 1500 in the university.

2. The suite is called *Bilkent Academic Studies in English* (*BASE*), and comprises four books: *BASE 1* (Pre-Intermediate), *BASE 2* (Intermediate), *BASE 3* (Upper Intermediate) and *BASE 4* (Pre-Faculty). The latter two books cover

BUSEL's exit levels for two and four-year students respectively. Each book is a package containing Student's Book (with audio cassettes), Teacher's Book and variously Workbook, Resource Book and Vocabulary Book.

3. Managers in the BUSEL context are a section of teachers i.e., specialist teachers, who head or constitute administrative and functional divisions within the school. These are the Directorate; the DOS-like managers who head the teaching units (HTUs); Curriculum and Testing (CTU); Teacher Training (TTU); Self-Access (SAU); and the members of the Textbook Project Development Project (TBDP) itself.

Chapter 31

1. Our interpretation of project here is that of processes that involve *team* work in the effort of achieving certain objectives

INDEX

534 *Index*

Tickoo, M. L.   143, 155, 156
TOEFL (Test of English as a For-
    eign Language)   311
Tokyo Shoseki   93
Tomalin, B. and S. Stem-
    pleski   428
Tomlinson, B.   1, 2, 3, 6, 7, 8, 9,
    16, 20, 21, 22, 26, 27, 29, 31,
    43, 72, 74, 107, 109, 110, 112,
    113, 115, 116, 144, 154, 156,
    162, 166, 168, 169, 171, 194,
    263, 264, 292, 340, 341, 342,
    345, 352, 479, 480, 481, 487,
    445, 446, 447, 467, 468, 375,
    378, 386, 369, 370, 355, 439
Tomlinson, B. and A. Maley   7
Tomlinson, B. and H. Masu-
    hara   19, 446, 450
Tomlinson, B. and R. Ellis   348
Tomlinson, B., R. Gower and J.
    Bell   154
Tomlinson, B. *et al.*   4, 7, 8, 23, 26,
    27, 33, 343, 344, 381, 389, 423,
    425
topics in coursebooks, for adult
    beginners   278–9
Total Physical Response   189,
    263–4, 370
TPR Plus   264–5
transferable skills   240
True Colors   132
Tsui, A. B. M.   296
Tucker, C. A.   42
Tudor, I.   387–8
Tudor, I. and F. Hafiz   292
Tunmer, W. E. and W. A.
    Hoover   352
Turner, T. C.   217

unconventional literary materi-
    als   408
underestimation of learners   8
Underhill, A.   194
universal criteria   27–9
Upper Intermediate Matters   174
Ur, P.   480, 484
Ur, P. and R. Ribé   331
Urquhart, A. H.   341

USIA (United States Information
    Agency)   511

van Lier, L.   42
Van Ments, M.   470
Vanuatu   163
Vellaccio, L. and M. Elston   276
verbal communication strate-
    gies   382–3
videos   418
Villamin, A. M.   142, 156
Viorst, J.   297
*The Visual Element in Language
    Teaching*   174
visual elements
    in coursebooks   174–82
        use versus decoration   176–8
    in recent British course-
        books   174–8
visualization   194, 467
vocabulary   344, 479
    conditions for learning   396
    deliberate learning   394
    and fluency development   402–4
    input activities   396–8
    learning conditions   394–5
    materials for teaching   394–405
    output activities   398–402
    planned approach   294
    planning learning   395–6
Vygotskyan theories   281

Wajnryb, R.   6, 171, 192
Walker, M.   293, 295
Wallace, C.   433
Warschauer, M.   216
Warschauer, M. and D.
    Healey   215, 217
Watanabe, Y.   203, 397
Wavelength   4
WebGuide   213
Weir, C. and J. Roberts   41
Wenden, A.   21
Wenden, A. and J. Rubin   21
whilst-use evaluation   24
White, G.   364, 365, 366
White, L.   21
White, R.   480

Whiteson, V.   203
Whitney, N.   331
'Who Needs Another Course-
    book?'   256
Wicke, P.   411
Widdowson, H. G.   ix, 6, 44, 329,
    341, 407
Wierbicka, A.   432
Wight, J. *et al.*   280
Wilkerson, L. and W. H.
    Gijselaers   450
Willams, L.   445
Williams, D.   26, 42
Williams, E.   341
Williams, E. and C. Moran   341,
    347, 349, 3442
Williams, M. and R. L. Burden   19
Williams, R.   351, 428
Williams, Robbie   418
Willis, D.   332, 4479
Willis, J.   7, 280, 330, 468
Windeatt, S. *et al.*   193
Winitiz, H.   262, 263
Winograd, P. and C. Hare   348
word-processing programs   201
World Bank   509
Wright, A.   174
Wright, A. and S. Haleen   174
Wright, J.   193
Wright, T.   480
writers, view of publishers   135–6
writing
    coursebooks   130–61
    creative approaches   183–98
    English for Special Purposes
        (ESP)   313
    in teams   166–7
    textbooks   490–517
written language, use in course-
    books   288–9

Xiao Qing Liao   388

Yalden, J.   141, 142
Yaw, C.   157
Yellowlees Douglas, J.   225
Yeo, G. K. and S. T. Tan   469